Public Law in a Troubled Era

European Monographs Series Set

VOLUME 115

Editor

Prof. Andrea Biondi is Professor of European Law and Director of the Centre of European Law at King's College London

Introduction & Contents/Subjects

As the process of European integration assumes an increasingly complex character, the EU legal system continues to undergo sweeping changes. The European Monographs series offers a voice to thoughtful, knowledgeable, cutting edge legal commentary on the now unlimited field of European law. Its emphasis on focal and topical issues makes the series an invaluable tool for scholars, practitioners, and policymakers specializing or simply interested in EU law.

Objective

The aim is to publish innovative work appealing to academics and practitioners alike. The result is an original and ongoing library of detailed analyses, theories, commentaries, practical guides, and proposals, each of which furthers the cause of meaningful European integration. Cumulatively, the series may be regarded as a 'work in progress' engaged in building a sharply defined representation of law in Europe.

Readership

Academics and practitioners dealing with EU law.

The titles published in this series are listed at the end of this volume.

Public Law in a Troubled Era

A Tribute to Professor Patrick Birkinshaw

Edited by

Katarzyna Gromek-Broc

Wolters Kluwer

Published by:
Kluwer Law International B.V.
PO Box 316
2400 AH Alphen aan den Rijn
The Netherlands
E-mail: lrs-sales@wolterskluwer.com
Website: www.wolterskluwer.com/en/solutions/kluwerlawinternational

Sold and distributed by:
Wolters Kluwer Legal & Regulatory U.S.
920 Links Avenue
Landisville, PA 17538
United States of America
E-mail: customer.service@wolterskluwer.com

ISBN 978-94-035-3576-0

e-Book: ISBN 978-94-035-4106-8
web-PDF: ISBN 978-94-035-4116-7

A volume in honour of Patrick Birkinshaw to mark his contribution to the development of European Public Law and Public Law

Editor

Katarzyna Gromek-Broc, Professor of EU Law, University of Pavia, Vloeberghs Chair in Law, VUB (Vrije Universiteit Brussel), Bruxelles.

Contributors

Gordon Anthony, Professor of Public Law, Queen's University, Belfast; Barrister-at-Law.

Aurélien Antoine, Professor of Public Law, University Jean-Monnet, Saint-Étienne, Director of the Brexit Observatory.

Jean-Bernard Auby, Emeritus Public Law Professor of Sciences Po Paris, France.

John Bell, Emeritus Professor of Law, University of Cambridge.

Andrea Biondi, Professor of EU Law and Director of the Centre of European Law at King's College London.

Mario P. Chiti, Emeritus Full Professor of Administrative Law, Jean Monnet Chair of European Administrative Law at the University of Florence, Italy.

Paul Craig, Emeritus Professor of English Law, St John's College, Oxford.

Anna Facchinetti, Postdoctoral Researcher in International Law, Department of Political and Social Sciences, University of Pavia.

David Feldman, Emeritus Rouse Ball Professor of English Law; Emeritus Fellow of Downing College, University of Cambridge.

Diana-Urania Galetta, Full Professor of Administrative Law and EU Administrative Law, Università degli Studi di Milano.

Fabio Giglioni, Full Professor of Administrative Law, Department of Political Sciences, University of Rome, Sapienza, Italy.

Peter M. Huber, Professor Dr, Justice of the Federal Constitutional Court of Germany, Karlsruhe/Munich.

Sir Jeffrey Jowell KC, Emeritus Professor of Public Law at University College London; Barrister, Blackstone Chambers, London.

Dimitrios Kagiaros, Assistant Professor in Public Law and Human Rights, Durham Law School.

Maria Kendrick, Senior Lecturer in Law in City Law School at City, University of London.

Constantinos Kombos, Minister of Foreign Affairs of the Republic of Cyprus, formerly Associate Professor of Public Law, University of Cyprus.

Massimo La Torre, Professor of Philosophy of Law at the 'Magna Græcia' University of Catanzaro, Italy and Visiting Professor of European Law at the University of Tallinn, Estonia.

Carmen Plaza, Associate Professor of EU and Administrative Law, IDEIR, Complutense University of Madrid.

Yseult Marique, Professor, University of Essex (UK), Research Fellow FöV Speyer (DE) and UC Louvain (BE).

Martina Künnecke McClean, Dr, Lecturer University of Hull, Law School.

Carlo Panara, Professor of Comparative Public Law and Director of the School of Law, Liverpool John Moores University, United Kingdom.

Thomas Perroud, Professor of Public Law at the Panthéon-Assas University, France; Humboldt Fellow, Humboldt University, Berlin.

Stephen I. Pogany, Emeritus Professor, School of Law, University of Warwick.

Tony Prosser, Emeritus Professor of Law, University of Bristol Law School.

Bernard Stirn, Président de section honoraire au Conseil d'Etat, membre de l'Institut de France.

Stephen Tierney, Professor of Constitutional Theory, University of Edinburgh.

Marton Varju, Research Professor, Centre for Social Sciences (ELKH), Institute for Legal Studies, Budapest.

Mike Varney, Associate Professor and Head of Lincoln Law School, the University of Lincoln, UK.

Nikos Vogiatzis, Senior Lecturer, School of Law, University of Essex.

Alison Young, Sir David Williams Professor of Public Law, University of Cambridge and Fellow of Robinson College, Cambridge.

Zheng Zhu, Lecturer, Law School, China University of Political Science and Law, Beijing, People's Republic of China.

Jacques Ziller, Honorary Professor of the Universities of Paris-1 Panthéon Sorbonne and Pavia.

Summary of Contents

Table of Contents

Foreword

I am grateful to Katarzyna Gromek-Broc for her initial suggestion and encouragement to embark on a collection of essays as a dedication to my career in academia. Her enthusiasm in approaching authors and compiling this festschrift was unalloyed, gracious and always in the best of humour. The success of her endeavours is immediately apparent from the renown of the stellar array of authors who responded to her invitation to contribute and who gave so much of their time to make their written contributions. This has been a wonderful testament to record my modest contribution to public law scholarship. I hope that epithet will not be met with the Churchillian put-down when he was informed that Clement Attlee was a very modest personality: 'He has a lot to be modest about!'

The theme of Public Law in a Troubled Era seemed to Katarzyna and me to be an appropriate organising focus to set the context for the essays all of which are written by public lawyers and in some cases jurists. There is always a tension between an executive and an independent judiciary and where the judiciary is not seen as part of the executive as in times of yore, in England at least. While there is a persistence in the tension in relationships in open and relatively open societies adopting a separation of powers and balanced constitution framework of government, recent years have witnessed a world that has been rocked by cataclysmic upheavals starting with the Brexit referendum in 2016, global pandemic, the first war between European nations since 1945, energy crises and international financial turmoil.

The elected autocratic executive has been a worldwide phenomenon under which leaders base their monocratic rule on a direct appeal to popular sovereignty, no matter how slender their majority is. The most dramatic example came from the United States (US) in 2016, but it is not confined to the US – its reach is worldwide. Trump may have departed from the White House, one views developments in the US with keen interest, but his legacy is most pronounced in his appointments to the US Supreme Court, in particular, and other federal courts in the states. Aided by the religious fundamentalism among Trump's appointments a right-wing majority in the US Supreme Court, for that is what they are, has embarked with a messianic zeal to overrule long-standing judgments that gave females a qualified constitutional right to abortion,[1] to remove controls over carrying of guns by private citizens under an originalist interpretation of the second amendment and to remove agency discretion to make rules, here to reduce carbon emissions, that the court considers have not been conferred directly by legislation and the will of the people.[2]

The United Kingdom (UK) has seen egregious features of autocratic rule by the Prime Minister, Boris Johnson. In the UK, the prime minister is prime minister by virtue of his or her control over the House of Commons. With a majority of eighty MPs in that house Johnson's position seemed impregnable in December 2019. He was forced to resign by his Cabinet in July 2022 for repeatedly and persistently failing to uphold high standards of prime ministerial conduct, indeed any standards. Liz Truss, his successor in office as PM, embarked on a major neo-libertarian economic policy with no publicly approved mandate apart from the votes of 81,326 conservative party members representing 57pc of the membership vote for the new party leader and prime minister. The number of eligible UK voters in 2020, the year after the general election, was 47.6 million.[3] The announcement of the new, and in some cases soon-to-be reversed fiscal policies of her Chancellor, led to pandemonium on the world financial markets and the lowest level of sterling against the dollar ever. Massive intervention was needed by the Bank of England to prevent the collapse of pension companies followed by the dismissal of the Chancellor and Truss' resignation.

Turbulent executive behaviour is not confined to common law countries. European Union (EU) Member States have acted contemptuously towards the rule of law under populist national leaders in Hungary and Poland. The greatest excesses in Europe have come from Russia where President Putin has resorted to war-mongering and murder last associated with inter-state relations in the first half of the twentieth century. Regrettably, there are countless other examples of elected autocratic rule in nations around the globe.

Brexit was world-changing and has fomented in the UK a desire for the executive to be free not only of EU legal regulation, which was built on legal order and judicial oversight but also a desire to reduce the role of courts domestically in judicial review and human rights protection. The UK Supreme Court's judgments in the *Miller* litigation[4] provoked Boris Johnson to a manifesto promise to the people to curb the power of unelected judges and to sweep back judicial advances since the 1960s in England, advances which in turn built on judicial precedent from the seventeenth century. The judicial review reforms which emerged in legislation were not as dramatic as the accompanying political rhetoric, and the bill repealing the Human Rights Act (HRA) and replacing it with a Bill of Rights Act was dropped by the incoming Truss as 'politically unworkable'. Hostility to the HRA still resides in many Tory politicians so

1. *Roe v. Wade* 410 US 113 (1973).
2. *Dobbs v. Jackson WHO* USSC No. 19-1392 (24/06/22) on abortion; *New York State Rifle & Pistol Association v. Bruen* USSC No. 20-843 (23/06/22) on right to carry guns; *West Virginia v. Environmental Protection Agency* USSC No. 20-1530 (30/06/22).
3. Electoral statistics, UK – Office for National Statistics (ons.gov.uk).
4. *Miller v. Secretary of State for Exiting the EU* [2017] UKSC 5; *Miller v. Prime Minister* [2019] UKSC 41.

proposals for change are likely to emerge. As I write it is clear that the justice secretary and deputy prime minister did not regard his Bill of Rights Bill as 'going away' so the position is unclear in terms of what will finally emerge. The justice secretary did, however, go away (below).

It seemed that the post-war settlement of liberal democracy and rule-based relationships in national and international affairs, the separation of powers and the rule of law were being put into serious question as judicial independence came under attack when judges took rights against government and governors seriously. If the provenance of judicial decisions was based on 'foreign law', the hostility was expressed even more vehemently by our domestic governors.

The UK government's assault on transnational law and the international legal order has come in two bills. We await to see what emerges in relation to the Bill to repeal the HRA. The Retained EU Law (Revocation and Reform) Bill (September 2022) seeks to bring to an end (to 'sunset') retained EU law's (REUL) existence in the UK, if not by the end of 2023, then by 23 June 2026. All retained EU law will be covered apart from 'primary legislation'. The Bill will significantly amend the EU Withdrawal Act 2018 which maintained EU law on the UK statute book after Brexit as 'retained EU law'. The sovereignty of that retained EU law (REUL) over pre-Brexit domestic law (pre - 31/12/2020) will also cease by the end of 2023, except where it won't. At all times after the end of 2023, REUL that remains in force will be known as 'assimilated law'. New tests will apply to allow the courts to determine whether to depart from retained EU case law or retained domestic case law. The latter refers to decisions of domestic courts interpreting or applying pre-Brexit EU law or EU-derived law. Domestic courts are not bound to depart from such case law but a factor to consider for departure in the case of CJEU case law is that decisions of 'foreign [EU] courts' are not binding on UK courts. A further factor to consider in relation to both sets of retained case law viz., 'the extent to which the retained EU case law otherwise restricts the proper development of domestic law' is asking the domestic court to act as a legislator which the government criticised the courts for doing in the case of judicial review.[5] Relevant provisions of the amendments will remain subject to 'separation agreement law' (section 7C(3) of EU Withdrawal Act 2018) under the 2019 UK/EU withdrawal agreement. Powers to 'restate' REUL including 'assimilated law' may maintain the EU general principles of law, otherwise repealed under the reforms, and the effects of EU legal sovereignty.

5. The Explanatory Notes to the bill state that the tests in clause 7 reflect 'some of the factors' the court of appeal judgment in *TuneIn Inc v. Warner Music UK Ltd & Anor* [2021] EWCA Civ 441 took into consideration. In that case Vos MR stated it was a 'paradigm case' not to depart from the CJEU. The judgment was based on international treaties and courts of states that are parties to such treaties should, 'wherever possible, be striving to achieve harmonious interpretation of them, not individualistic disharmony' [197]. Arnold LJ gave the main judgment and his list of relevant criteria to apply in following the CJEU are at [77]-[83], and on the 'highly persuasive 'character of post Brexit CJEU case law [90]-[91]. 'Philip Moser KC has questioned whether there is a meaningful link between the court of appeal case and the proposed statutory test contained in sub-section 7(3). He pointed out that the relevant statutory words (or similar sentiments) do not appear in the *TuneIn* judgment, and that other important factors mentioned in the judgment (that typically weigh against departing from existing CJEU case law) have been omitted' Monckton Chambers, Webinar on the Retained EU Law (Revocation and Reform) Bill, 28 September 2022 cited by G. Cowie, House of Commons Research Briefing *Retained EU Law (Revocation and Reform) Bill (2022-23)* 37.

Rights, powers, liabilities, obligations and restrictions implemented into UK law by section 2(1) European Communities Act 1972 may be 'reproduced'. All crystal clear! Time to revisit Lon Fuller's *The Morality of Law* and the existence of laws seeking to achieve contradictory objectives. A late government amendment to the bill significantly reduced the number of REUL provisions to be 'sunsetted' by the end of 2023.

The other Bill touching on EU-UK relations is that dealing with the Northern Ireland Protocol (June 2022) which was an integral part of the 2019 withdrawal agreement with the EU. Basically, under the bill, the NIP can be torn up and/or rewritten unilaterally by UK ministers despite its provenance in an EU and international treaty agreed by both the EU and the UK, and therefore binding under EU and international law. The reliance by the UK government on the principle of necessity in international law to justify unilateral repudiation of an international treaty is, quite frankly, risible.[6] Clause 20 of the bill provides that in domestic judicial proceedings relating to the NIP or the withdrawal agreement, a court or tribunal is not bound by any principles laid down, or any decisions made, on or after the day on which this section comes into force by the European Court of Justice. Nor can domestic courts or tribunals refer any matter to the ECJ. But wait! Regulations made by a minister may 'in particular' provide for a procedure to make a reference to the ECJ and where the domestic court or tribunal considers that such a reference is necessary 'for the European Court to deal with that question before the court or tribunal can conclude the proceedings'. You can't, but you can! But what does a domestic court do with the ECJ decision? The explanatory notes glibly state that this 'would then be fed back into the UK court processes'.

I am saddened at how gauche and maladroit these bills make us appear to our colleagues in the EU and elsewhere. They reek of incompetence, confusion and a failure to grasp legal reality. The attempt to justify these ambitions to undermine international law in the NIP bill by invoking Parliamentary sovereignty, as the then attorney general Braverman assayed, is beyond credulity. Parliamentary sovereignty was not meant to set us against the world; it was the means by which the representative chamber took priority over the executive, the Crown, temporal and religious powers. The *Windsor Framework*, agreed between the EU and the UK and which sought to resolve the problems left by the NIP, led Rishi Sunak to halt the NIP bill in the Lords but not 'without prejudice' to future contingencies which presumably could see its revival.[7]

The attempts to try and blow hot and cold simultaneously and to pursue contradictory outcomes in the EU bill will lead to chaos. Truss' dropping of the Bill of Rights Bill was widely regarded as the only sensible thing her government did. In evidence to the Joint Committee on Human Rights, the justice secretary confirmed that the bill will proceed.[8] A bill that has been almost universally condemned in its content

6. House of Lords Library Briefing *Northern Ireland Protocol Bill No 52 (2022-23) N. Newson* 51-53 https://researchbriefings.files.parliament.uk/documents/LLN-2022-0047/LLN-2022-0047.pdf.
7. *HMG Legal Position: The Windsor Framework* p. 2. *See* https://www.gov.uk/government/publications/the-windsor-framework.
8. Joint Committee on Human Rights *Bill of Rights Bill* HC 611 (2022-23) https://committees.parliament.uk/oralevidence/12467/pdf/.

and drafting can expect the stormiest of Parliamentary passages. The resignation of the minister responsible for the bill, Dominic Raab after bullying allegations, led to the end of the bill's Parliamentary progression. When the future of the rights bill was still unclear, Braverman presented the Illegal Migration Bill to the Commons on 7 March 2023. She felt unable to make the statement under section 19(1)(a) of the Human Rights Act 1998 that the bill was compatible with the ECHR. It was widely regarded as breaching the ECHR and the 1951 Refugee Convention. The government's defiance of international human rights law and refugee law seems set to continue with clear implications for the NI Good Friday agreement and the Trade and Cooperation agreement with the EU.

We have come a long way from the hopeful and constructive era in which my work on European Public Law began. We now face contradiction, uncertainty, squabbling and financial insecurity for the foreseeable future.

The essays in this book examine these developments, and developments in this climate, under four headings: Law in a World Turned Upside/Down; Law and Politics: a Shifting Boundary?; Law's Promise; and finally New Bearings. All the authors are committed to a central role for law and the rule of law in governance. Law, that is, that is independent of the executive and political, demagogic, oligarchic and plutocratic powers and which exists to protect the public at large irrespective of privilege, wealth, nationality, creed, sex or colour. Such an ideal is bound to make enemies, upset powerful forces and be accused of crossing ill-defined borders. In our estimation the essays that follow tackle the book's themes from a variety of directions; some directly, others more incidentally and some tangentially. All are concerned with a central role for law in the process of governance. We hope we are not too presumptive when we say that all authors are concerned with what, as lawyers, we can learn from systems apart from our own, and what law can contribute to greater transparency, perspicuity and perspicacity in the exercise of power. This message is conveyed with varying degrees of prominence in the chapters that follow. That message certainly permeates the work of those who have contributed to this *festschrift*. To Katarzyna and all the contributors, thank you again.

Patrick Birkinshaw
6 June 2023

Patrick Birkinshaw: His Work

Patrick Birkinshaw began his academic career in 1976. This was at the University of Hull where he had graduated the year before. After graduation, he qualified as a barrister being called to the bar by the Inner Temple in July 1976. He was initially appointed to teach common law including criminal law, and jurisprudence. His research and teaching interests soon led him into public law. Hull had introduced a new part one integrated syllabus which had combined constitutional law, civil liberties and administrative law over two years. Hull was distinct in giving such emphasis to public law in this integrated module.

In ensuing years his research interests would fall under three main heads: grievance redress, especially through non-judicial informal processes as well as judicial and ombudsman institutions; freedom of information and openness, and then transparency in government and governance and the broader public sector; and from the early 1990s European public law.

Like a large number of law lecturers at that time, he had no experience in doctoral research but immediately on commencing his lecturing duties, he fell under the influence of Norman Douglas Lewis. Douglas, a formidable public lawyer, had received funding support from the SSRC, as it then was, to research procedures in council house allocation. A spin-off from that research involved complaints procedures in local government. It was on this latter topic that Patrick assisted and which led to a chapter with Douglas in Jowell and Partington *Welfare Law and Policy* 'Taking Complaints Seriously' in 1979.

While Douglas moved to a chair in Sheffield in 1978, Patrick remained at Hull for the rest of his career with several spells as a visiting professor at overseas universities including Firenze and Paris II, Pantheon Assas. He carried on working on redress of grievance and in 1985 he published *Grievances, Remedies and the State* in the highly regarded Sweet and Maxwell Modern Legal Studies series. This monograph which looked at grievance redress throughout the public and quasi-public sectors, and which focused on non-judicial dispute processes, was extremely well received. In 1985-86, he was funded by the Northern Ireland Human Rights Advisory Commission to study the role of the ombudsman in investigating claims of religious and political discrimination in Northern Ireland as part of a wide investigation involving various researchers into political and religious discrimination in Northern Ireland. The report to the Secretary of State is at Cm. 237 HMSO (1987).

Researching on grievance redress introduced him to the subject of the lack of openness and closed nature of much of our public life. He had been commissioned by the Town Clerks Education Trust and Local Government Legal Society to conduct a study of the legal duties and powers on local government to provide information and open themselves up to the public and authorities' responses to those duties. In 1985 and 1986 (updated), the Association published *Open Government, Freedom of Information and Local Government*.

This was a precursor on his work *Freedom of Information: The Law, the Practice and the Ideal* (1988 1st ed.) in the much-vaunted Law in Context series then edited by Professors William Twining and Robert Stevens. It went to four editions. Like *Grievances*, it looked at the problem, here a lack of openness and excessive secrecy, throughout the public sector and what freedom of information laws could do to help foster greater openness or transparency as it became. Shortly after the publication of the 1988 work, the Thatcher government 'reformed' secrecy laws and the long process began to get onto the statute book a Freedom of Information Act (FOIA). Local government had already seen the introduction of a FOIA of sorts in the Local Government (Access to Information) Act 1985 and a variety of statutes had introduced highly qualified rights of access to personal information including the Data Protection Act 1984 which only covered digitised data. In 1990, Patrick published *Government and Information: the Law Relating to Access, Disclosure and Regulation* which was aimed at a professional and practising market. This has been published in five editions (most recently in 2019) with a slightly amended title and latterly with the assistance of Dr Mike Varney.

His work on FOI, openness and transparency as desiderata of effective and accountable government led to him being invited in 1997 to act as legal adviser to the Public Administration Committee in its examination of the new Blair government's proposals for a Freedom of Information Act. His colleague as adviser to the committee was Robert Hazel of the Constitution Unit, University College London. The committee examined the white paper on a FOIA and various iterations of the bill that became the Act. Patrick worked with the Committee until the Act was enacted in 2000. It was at the time the most wide-ranging FOIA in the world. He likes to think he made some crucial interventions on the Bill in committee, not least its extension to cover Parliament and MPs who had been left out of original drafts and which led to the investigation of the scandal of MPs' expenses in 2009. On this, he was enthusiastically supported by Richard Shepherd MP, a member of the committee. The main reports from the committee are Third Report of the Select Committee on Public Administration, *Your Right to Know: The Government's Proposals for a Freedom of Information Act* HC (1997-98) 398-I; *Freedom of Information Draft Bill* (1998-99) HC 570 I & II.

He had a further stint as a specialist adviser to the Committee in its investigation into *Whitehall Confidential: The Publication of Political Memoirs* (2005-06). This enquiry was concerned with the disclosure of information obtained on official duties and followed publication of memoirs by senior advisers and diplomats some of the content of which was not deemed to be in the public interest.

Patrick's interest in European public law developed prior to the emergence of the EU in the Maastricht treaty in 1992 and which came into being in 1993. In 1990, he was the UK rapporteur at the Madrid FIDE conference on the topic of public procurement and the implementation of the procurement directives in national law. This was on the recommendation of Lord Slynn of Hadley. He had long been interested in government contracting and how contracts in this field avoided all the conventional accountability devices saving the public accounts committee and press reports. The directives were not well known and in some cases in the UK had been implemented by informal devices such as circulars. This coincided with an increased attention being devoted to the directives which were soon re-cast and which attracted increasing attention from the European Court of Justice. A world of non-legal contamination in UK governance faced the prospect of massive legal regulation to counter discrimination and to enhance transparency in this hitherto, in the UK at least, subterranean world. As a public lawyer who had paid little attention to EEC and EC law, the prospect of the vast influence of what was soon to become EU law on our domestic law was breathtaking. To be ignorant of the impact of EU law would be to remain a child and to be ignorant of the development of our domestic public law; in short to be a poor public lawyer.

In 1992 Patrick inaugurated the Institute of European Public Law at the University of Hull. He was given considerable support in this venture by Professor Ferdinand von Prondzynski who had recently arrived at Hull from Trinity College Dublin and who quickly became Dean of the Law School at Hull. The institute was inaugurated by Sir Leon Brittan, then EC Commissioner for Competition and the detailed arrangements were organised through Sir Leon's assistant, Nick Clegg, subsequently Deputy Prime Minister in the coalition government 2010-2015.

The institute became a workhouse in the research and investigation of European Public Law. This was taken as the influence of EU law and ECHR law on national law, and, crucially, the influence on that European law by national law. The examination also embraced the opportunity for influence of national systems of law on each other, often via the mediation of European laws but sometimes directly.

An international advisory board was established which contained the major figures, academic and practising in this field. These included Sir Leon Brittan (above), Jurgen Schwarze from Freiburg who was a towering figure in European Administrative Law, Lord Slynn, Mario Chiti from Florence, Anthony Lester QC, a paragon among human rights lawyers, Professor Walter van Gerven, advocate general of the ECJ, Roger Errera of the Conseil d'Etat, Jeffrey Jowell, Henri Schermers and John Bell. It was a star-studded cast and it never ceased to amaze Patrick how much time they were prepared to give to assist in the institute's success.

Leading public and European lawyers gave lectures, and research was undertaken for academic bodies, the Commission, the UK government and members engaged in advisory work for governmental and commercial bodies.

Shortly after the inauguration, Patrick embarked on efforts to establish a journal dedicated to EPL. The contract for this was originally signed with Graham and Trotman/Martinus Nijhoff. The party of the other part soon became Kluwer Law

International and then Wolters Kluwer. A team of national and European legal experts was assembled who provided expert commentary from time to time for the journal. The first issue of volume I was published in March 1995. Sir Leon wrote the foreword and let his words take over:

> I am delighted to be given the opportunity to make a few introductory remarks about the journal *European Public Law.* I have been a 'retired' lawyer for some considerable time, but my life in British politics and at the Commission has brought home to me the importance of understanding the legal context in which politics have to operate and the political context in which law has to operate. I consider *European Public Law* to be a bold new venture, exciting in its conception, ambitious in its design and principled in its objectives. It will provide a very useful service for lawyers, administrators, politicians and those whose lives bring them into contact with European law and other European legal systems. When I inaugurated the Institute of European Public Law at Hull University in May 1992, I delivered a lecture on the importance of competition and competition law and I am pleased to say that this is one subject that will be covered by the new journal. I wish the journal, the editor and its distinguished advisory board every success in their well-directed venture.
>
> Sir Leon Brittan QC

Patrick edited the journal from 1994 until 2018 when he retired and handed over the reins to his colleague at Hull and former PhD student Dr Mike Varney.

He had to step down from his directorship of the institute to head the Law School from 1997 to 2002, during which time the school achieved its best-ever research rating under the then HEFC Research Assessment Exercise.

A year's extended leave after these duties allowed him to complete a further monograph for the Law in Context series: *European Public Law* where the ideas developed since 1990 found the light of day although many of the ideas had been delivered embryonically throughout the UK, Ireland and Europe and further afield. The book is now in its third edition published by Wolters Kluwer with a slightly modified title.

The modification was to acknowledge Brexit: *European Public Law: the Achievement and the Brexit Challenge* (2020). His last official engagement before retiring from his university chair in 2017 was to deliver a lecture at the British Academy: 'What Future for Public Law?' which found a home in http://www.ius-publicum.com/repository/uploads/09_12_2017_9_19-IUS_PUB_Birkinshaw_2017.pdf.

Brexit pre-occupied his thoughts from the early stages of Cameron's coalition government and he edited two books with Professor Andrea Biondi from King's College London: *Britain Alone! The Implications and Consequences of UK Withdrawal from the EU* (April 2016) and they were joined by Maria Kendrick for *Brexit: the Legal Implications* (2018) both published by Wolters Kluwer.

Further work with his old friend and colleague Douglas Lewis included *Government by Moonlight: the Hybrid Parts of the State* (1990) Unwin Hyman on the public-private networks at work in the UK constitution, together with Ian Harden, and *When Citizens Complain: Reforming Justice and Administration* (1993) Open University Press. *Reforming the Secret State* (1991) Open University Press was authored by

Patrick alone and published in the series Studies in Law and Politics edited by Douglas Lewis.

As we can see, the theme of law and politics runs through his work and it became a *leitmotif* of this corpus of essays dedicated to his name.

As well as working and advising numerous leading universities on academic matters, he has worked for numerous research bodies including the UK Arts and Humanities Research Council as chair of the post-graduate law, philosophy and theology panel, for the Irish Research Council on numerous panels, for the Finnish Research Council and for French, German and Italian bodies.

The academic world did not absorb all his time and effort. Outside academia from December 2000 to April 2008, he was a member of the Independent Review Panel of Nirex Ltd, the UK adviser on nuclear waste (subsequently the Nuclear Decommissioning Authority) advising on its voluntary code on openness and then its statutory duties to comply with freedom of information laws and making recommendations on related complaints, and on enhanced transparency. He was one of three ombudspersons dealing with complaints about denial of access to information. Nirex was the body responsible for advising the UK nuclear industry in particular on the disposal of nuclear waste. In 2006 it was brought within the Nuclear Decommissioning Authority.

He advised the Capital Markets Authority (Egyptian analogue of the UK Competition and Markets Authority) on adjusting to a freedom of information regime and a climate of openness and transparency.

He acted as senior trainer (with a junior colleague) of judges from the UK Upper Tribunal on laws relating to information rights. This was a jurisdiction they assumed from High Court judges and appellate judges possess the status of High Court judges.

He acted as a consultant and panellist (Belgrade) with OECD on its initiative 'Introducing Freedom of Information laws in South East Europe'.

He was an OECD consultant and rapporteur on the introduction of transparency laws in North Africa.

He was an adviser to the Hong Kong Government on reforming Freedom of Information laws in Hong Kong.

He acted as a consultee on the Ministry of Justice's Review of Freedom of Information legislation through the Independent Commission: https://www.gov.uk/government/uploads/system/uploads/attachment_data/file/504055/Call_for_Evidence_Responses_from_individuals_M_-_P.pdf, pp. 92 et seq.

PUBLICATIONS 2014 to date

This resumé will end by setting out the publications produced by Patrick since 2014. This will give a clear idea of the range of his interests and recent activities.

Journal Editorship

The quarterly journal *European Public Law* is published by Kluwer Law International (1995 to date). I was the editor-in-chief (1994-December 2018).

Recently Published Work

Books

1. *European Public Law – The Achievement and the Challenge* 2nd ed. (new title and complete re-write) (2014) Kluwer Law International, pp. xvii + 693. Last edition 2003.

   New edition contracted for 2020 Wolters Kluwer. New title *European Public Law – The Achievement and the Brexit Challenge*. Now published 2020 xix and 849 pp.
2. *Britain Alone! The Implications and Consequences of UK Withdrawal from the EU* (April 2016) Kluwer Law International; Edited book with Andrea Biondi professor of law at King's College School of Law; pp. xxii + 347. This followed a conference at King's College London in May 2014 with Lord Reed in the Chair.
3. *Brexit: The Legal Implications* (December 2018) Kluwer Law International; Edited book with Andrea Biondi professor of law at King's College School of Law and Dr Maria Kendrick (KCL); pp. xxii + 293. This followed a seminar series at King's College London in 2017-2018.
4. *Government and Information Rights: the Law Relating to Access, Disclosure and their Regulation* (February 2019) with Dr Mike Varney. Bloomsbury Professional, pp. 1010 + intros, indices etc.

Articles and chapters

1. Introduction and Chapter 1 of Britain Alone!
2. 'Regulating Information' in J. Jowell and D. Oliver eds The Changing Constitution 8th ed 2015, Oxford University Press, pp. 378-409 – new addition to the book by OUP, June 2015. This is the leading work within the common law world on the UK constitution.
3. 'Das Verhältnis der Richter und Richterinnen des Vereinigten Königreichs gegenüber Europa und der europäischen Integration. Kompetenzen, Grundrechte und Identität.'

   Volume 3 of EUROPARECHT pp. 267-289 (June 2015) in German.
4. 'United Kingdom Judges and European Integration' Rivista Italiana di Diritto Pubblico Comunitario (2015) pp. 363-386.
5. 'UK National Report' with A. Young (Hertford College, Oxford) and V. Mitsilegas (QMW) in The Role of Constitutions in European and Global Governance. Funded by European Research Council Agreement No. 284316.

   Now in National Constitutions in European and Global Governance: Democracy, Rights and the Rule of Law eds A. Albi & S. Bardutzky 'Europe's Gift to the United Kingdom's Unwritten Constitution – Juridification' pp. 83-139 Springer Open (2019).
6. 'The Spectrum of Administrative Procedures – England and Wales' in Droit comparé de la procédure administrative ed J.B. Auby (2016) Groupe Larcier France pp. 149-177.

7. 'Relations between Parliament, Government and the Courts on Supranational Affairs'. In: A. Antoine (ed), Le Droit public britannique : État des lieux et perspectives, Société de Législation Comparée/Lextenso, 2015, pp. 47-85.
8. 'Valuing Transparency in Government and Media' in Transparency in Politics and the Media – Accountability and Open Government I B Tauris; N Bowles, J T Hamilton & D Levy eds pp. 49-72 (2014). Rothermere Centre for American Studies University of Oxford paper.
9. 'The United Kingdom in Europe and Europe in the United Kingdom – an Indelible Influence' in Verfassung und Verwaltung in Europa eds U Becker, A Hatje, M Potacs, N Wunderlich Nomos Baden-Baden pp. 19-42 (2014).
10. 'Le droit public anglais dans le creuset européen' in Traité de droit administrative européen' 2nd ed. (2014) eds J-B Auby & J Dutheil de la Rochere pp. 761-784, Dalloz.
11. In Greek: 'United Kingdom Judges and European Integration' in (2016) No. 1 To Syntagma 141-170 (Sakkoulas Legal Publishers Greece). An updated version of nos. 3 and 4 above.
12. 'A Perspective on cross-fertilisation between European legal orders and UK Public Law' in B. Bonnet ed, 'Les rapports entre ordres juridiques. Bilan, enjeux, perspectives' LGDJ (Lextenso, France), (2017), pp. 1625-1636.
13. 'National Security and the Limits of Judicial Protection' in an edited volume published by Routledge 2018 New Challenges to Constitutional Adjudication in Europe: A Comparative Perspective, eds Z Szente and F Gardos-Orosz, Ch. 12 pp. 185-213.
14. Ius Publicum Network Review 'What is the Future of Public Law?' (2017) http://www.ius-publicum.com/repository/uploads/09_12_2017_9_19-IUS_PUB_Birkinshaw_2017.pdf.
15. 'Information: Public Access, Protecting Privacy and Surveillance' in J Jowell & Colm O'Cinneide The Changing Constitution 9th ed. OUP (July 2019) pp. 358-390. This is a new chapter.
16. 'General Principles of Law and the United Kingdom' in Goed Bestuur in Perspectif eds A. Buijze, P. Langbroek & R. Widdershoven pp. 67-75 (Wolters Kluwer, 2019).
17. Review article 'Jonathan Sumption Trials of the State: Law and the Decline of Politics' (2020) Amicus Curiae Series 2 Vol. 1 No. 3 459-475.

ISSN 14612097

18. Review article Lions in the Whirligig of Time: Stephen Sedley's Lions under the Throne and Law and the Whirligig of Time (2020) Amicus Curiae Series 2 Vol. 2 No. 121 pp 95-115.
    ISSN above
19. Review Article *The Foundations and Future of Public Law: Essays in Honour of Paul Craig* E. Fisher, J. King and A.L. Young eds (2021) *Amicus Curiae* Series 2 Vol. 2 No. 2.

ISSN 1461-2097

20. 'The Independent Panel's Report on Judicial Review (CP407) and the Government's Consultation Documentation Judicial Review Reform (CP408)' (2021) *Amicus Curiae* Vol. 2(2) 501-520.

ISSN 14612097

21. 'Brexit and the Trade and Cooperation Agreement: Endgame or Prolegomenon' (2021) 27(2) *European Public Law* 229-263.
22. *Chemins Publics* 'UK Government Review of Judicial Review' 23/04/21 https://www.chemins-publics.org/articles/uk-government-review-of-judicial-review.
23. Review Article of: Democracy and Executive Power: Policymaking Accountability in the US, UK, Germany and France Susan Rose-Ackerman (2021). *Amicus Curiae* Series 2 Vol. 3 No. 3 532-540 (2022). https://journals.sas.ac.uk/amicus/article/view/5442/5221.
24. 'The UK's Future Contribution to European Public Law' CERIDAP on the 13.07.2022 https://ceridap.eu/the-uks-future-contribution-to-european-public-law/
25. 'Them's the Breaks' – Boris Johnson's Fall and Exit as Prime Minister of the United Kingdom CERIDAP 4 October 2022.
26. 'Judicial Review and E.U. Law Reviewed' (2022) *Journal of Comparative Law* Vol. 17(2) p. 277.

Katarzyna Gromek-Broc

Introduction

Katarzyna Gromek-Broc

This book is a tribute to Patrick Birkinshaw on the occasion of his retirement from the University of Hull, where he pursued his remarkable career for over 40 years. Patrick Birkinshaw was a Director of the Hull Law School, Research Director, Director of the Institute of European Public Law, established by him and inaugurated by Sir Leon Brittan in 1992. More importantly, he founded in 1994 the *European Public Law* Journal – a leading peer reviewed journal published by Wolters Kluwer – widely recognised for its expertise in European Public Law. He was among the forerunners in this field, he helped to launch the subject as a discipline and define its content. The Journal under his supervision published insightful analyses exploring the dilemmas of the law and politics at the European level, the mutual and reciprocal influence of national systems on European law and vice versa and their interaction, the role of the United Kingdom (UK) in the European Union (EU), and other themes of contemporary constitutionalism. Thanks to him, the journal gained an international recognition. The design of the journal and its evolution are an illustration of his vision and skill in selecting the themes with major relevance for the future of politics and the law in Europe.

With clarity and wit, he has shared his insights with others in the numerous works touching upon different disciplines such as Public Law, Administrative Law, European human rights law and EU Law in which he published widely with special attention to grievance redress, freedom of information and openness and transparency in governance.

Yet, it is not my intention to discuss in detail his vast research scholarship but rather to highlight some landmark publications with which he made a major inroad into the legal field of his interests and to indicate the niche areas in which he was a pioneering explorer.

Since the early years of his career, his work has been infused with the ideal of good governance, transparency, accountability and the observance of the rule of law. This particular attachment to the Government's openness, constitutional guarantees and judicial review engrossed his entire career. His book *Grievances, Remedies and the State* (1985), (second edition published in 1994) dealt with the conflict between the individual and the 'public interest' as laid down by government in which he explored the possibilities for an individual to complain about the operations and policy of governmental institutions and to search for redress. He looked at the possible ways through which grievances could be resolved, considering institutions at central and local level. Some aspects of the book discussing quasi-government, local government, informal remedies and the limitations of the courts in resolving disputes were truly novel. His interests in this area led to another publication: *Open Government, Freedom of Information and Local Government* (1985 and 1986). Soon after, he published 'Government by Moonlight: the Hybrid Parts of the State' (1990) with Ian Harden and Norman (Douglas) Lewis and the compenetration of the public and private in our governance. Several other books dealing with government accountability and good administration should be mentioned here, namely, *Reforming the Secret State* (1991) followed by *When Citizens Complain: Reforming Justice and Administration* (1993) with Lewis. In the first publication, he brought to the reader's attention the problem of an unnecessarily secretive government and a general lack of transparency, whereas in the second, he and Lewis focused on a citizen's right to good administration, a right to complain and to be heard, presenting at the same time some prospects for reform. In grievance redress he followed the lead of Norman Douglas Lewis, his long-term tutor, colleague and close friend. In the 1980s, he was pioneering in the area of what we now refer to as transparency. His book *Freedom of Information: the Law, the Practice and the Ideal* (1988) was a critical step in his career, proving him to be an acknowledged expert on freedom of information, the field that as a young lawyer he had helped to promote and develop. The book, currently in its fourth edition published by Cambridge University Press, has become a leading text on freedom of information in the UK and further afield. The most recent publication in this field co-authored with Mike Varney is *Government and Information Rights: the Law Relating to Access, Disclosure and their Regulation* (5th ed. 2019 Bloomsbury Professional) which focuses on information rights and their enforcement. Furthermore, his textbook on *European Public Law* (2003, Law in Context series) and its subsequent editions used by students, academics and practitioners, was last revised in 2020 when the most recent edition was published. The last edition took account of the events unfolded by the Brexit maelstrom and its continuing challenge.

Brexit is another theme that has particularly preoccupied his attention in recent years and led to several remarkable publications such as *Britain Alone! The Implications and Consequences of UK Withdrawal from the EU* (2016 edited with Andrea Biondi) followed by *Brexit: the Legal Implications* (December 2018) edited with Andrea Biondi and Maria Kendrick. Throughout his published work, he emphasised the importance of responsive government, the importance of access to information and transparency in making government accountable as well as what we have to learn from each other in different traditions of law to frame appropriate principles and systems of public law to meet the myriad challenges of executive power in the modern world.

He also published more than one hundred peer reviewed articles in internationally renowned journals. Mentioning only a few, his article entitled 'Supranationalism, the Rule of Law, and Constitutionalism in the Draft Constitution' (2004) OUP, *Yearbook of European Law*, is one of the most prominent insights into European constitutionalism in light of the proposed, and abandoned, EU Constitution. Another remarkable piece that might seem visionary from a legal if not political perspective was 'The United Kingdom in Europe and Europe in the United Kingdom - An Indelible Influence' (2014). Still in the ambit of EU Law, his article on 'United Kingdom Judges and European Integration' (2015) should be mentioned along with 'Brexit's Challenge to the UK's Unwritten Constitution' (2020) in *European Public Law.*

In addition, publications considering constitutional issues in the domestic, global and comparative perspectives should be cited. In particular, his contribution on 'Regulating Information' in J. Jowell, D. Oliver and C. Cinneide (eds), *The Changing Constitution* (8th ed. OUP 2015), or in the 9th edition of that work (J. Jowell and C. Cinneide (eds)) entitled 'Information: Public Access, Protecting Privacy and Surveillance' (OUP, 2019). Moreover, he participated in the 'UK National Report' with A. Young (Cambridge) and V. Mitsilegas (QMW) on *The* Role of Constitutions in European and Global Governance now published as *National Constitutions in European and Global Governance: Democracy, Rights and the Rule of Law* (A. Albi and S. Bardutzky (eds)) now entitled 'Europe's Gift to the United Kingdom's Unwritten Constitution - Juridification' (2019).

He also widely published outside the UK. For example, he contributed with his piece on 'The Spectrum of Administrative Procedures - England and Wales' in *Droit comparé de la procédure administrative* J.B. Auby (ed.) (2016), and with 'Relations Between Parliament, Government and the Courts on Supranational Affairs' in A. Antoine (ed.), *Le Droit public britannique : État des lieux et perspectives,* Société de Législation Comparée/Lextenso, 2015, and with his article on 'Le droit public anglais dans le creuset européen' in *Traité de droit administrative européen* (2nd ed., 2014).

As previously mentioned Patrick was very absorbed by the Brexit debate and today he offers some sharp reflections on the UK position in the post Brexit scenario, for example in 'Brexit and the Trade and Cooperation Agreement: Endgame or Prolegomenon' (2021) 27(2) *EUP*; 'The UK's Future Contribution to European Public Law' CERIDAP 2022 and most recently 'Them's the Breaks - Boris Johnson's Fall and Exit as Prime Minister of the United Kingdom' CERIDAP 2022 charting Johnson's fall after the Brexit 'triumph'.

Apart from his outstanding research scholarship, he was a successful Director of the Hull Law School. Under his Directorship, the research in the Higher Education Funding Council's Research Assessment Exercise rose from 3aA to 5B, its highest ever rating under the then scoring system, bringing the Law School into the top 20 UK Law Schools for peer reviewed research. Further, under his Research Directorship, 2006-2009, the Hull Law School achieved in the 2008 RAE what proved to be the second highest rating in its history.

His dedication to justice and the value of justice in its service to society emerges at all stages of his career. In addition to his achievements as an author, researcher, educator, editor and professor, he has worked throughout his career as a noteworthy consultant, ombudsman in the nuclear industry and advisor. He advised governments and organisations seeking to reform national legal and judicial institutions to make them more accessible and transparent.

Undoubtedly, Patrick Birkinshaw had a clear vision in everything he embarked upon namely, research, teaching, leadership and administration. His dedication to academic work was exemplary. In his leadership, he was determined to achieve the best possible outcome. He was painstaking in selecting academic staff, supported collaboration and external projects. In his leadership, he promoted the democratic values in which he believed, ensuring transparent processes, for example in recruitment and promotion as well as transparent decision-making. Patrick was also highly appreciated by all students who valued his ideas and teaching skills. He was a great speaker, clear and engaging. Moreover, Patrick was a mentor for young academics, and an inspiring professor and educator, sharp, punctilious and concise he has been an inspiring example. He has also been a great colleague, entertaining, creative and firm in his conclusions.

He gained a truly international reputation, and is well-known and highly regarded on the continent for his insightful and incisive analyses. In some respects, he is 'a European' in the true sense, being at the same time profoundly attached to the best legal traditions of his own nation, and critical of its shortcomings.

In addition to his academic career, he held many leading positions in research and public institutions in the UK. He was a consultant for the Human Rights Commission in Northern Ireland (1985-1986) in its work on religious and political discrimination, a specialist advisor for the House of Commons Public Administration Committee in 1997-2000 on freedom of information legislation, and again with that committee in 2005-2006 on political memoirs, an adviser to HM Treasury and the Cabinet Office on various projects relating to public procurement, freedom of information and redress of grievances, an FOI Ombudsman for Nirex (the Nuclear Industries Regulatory Executive), the UK adviser on nuclear waste and subsequently the Nuclear Decommissioning Authority between 2000 and 2008.

He served as a Member of the Irish Research Council, as a senior panellist for the Schemes Assessment Board, 2002-2008 and more recently a member of the Irish Research Council Postgraduate and Post Doctoral Awards 2010-2018. He sat on the panel of the United Kingdom Arts and Humanities Research Board/Council: Panel Convenor Panel 8 – Law, Philosophy and Religious Studies 2003-2006, and was AHRC Peer Review College Member 2006 to 2008. He was a Visiting Professor at the EUI in Florence in 1997 and at the Université Panthéon-Assas Paris II, autumn term 2003.

Furthermore, he has undertaken numerous consultancies for the UK and overseas governments on freedom of information and transparency. He advised international organisations and governments, for example, in 2008, the Capital Markets Authority (Egyptian analogue of the UK Competition and Markets Authority) on adjusting to a freedom of information regime and a climate of openness and transparency. He was a senior trainer (assisted by a junior colleague) of judges from the UK Upper Tribunal on laws relating to the vast array of information rights. Moreover, he was a consultant and panellist (Belgrade) with the Organisation for Economic Co-operation and Development (OECD) on its initiative 'Introducing Freedom of Information laws in South East Europe', later an OECD consultant and rapporteur on the introduction of transparency laws in North Africa. In 2016, he was an Adviser to the Hong Kong Government on reforming Freedom of Information laws in Hong Kong.

Finally, Patrick was also a great collaborator, precise, thorough, always on time. The publishing editor at Walters Kluwer with whom he had a long-lasting arrangement commented, 'Patrick was one of our best organized editors who always submitted his manuscript one month before the deadline'. The Kluwer editorial team also mentioned how sociable he was, always attending the Christmas lunches at the Piccadilly restaurant in Soho and then, when his favourite haunt closed, at da Mario's restaurant Covent Garden, sometimes with his wife Jane; these lunches were a long tradition at the Kluwer publishing house. Outside his work, he is the life and soul of the party, engaging, funny and entertaining, making people laugh with good wine and blues music. In short, he has been a touching personality and his popularity has been apparent in the process that led to the publication of this book.

This *Liber Amicorum* is an expression of friendship and admiration for a man who has been steadfast and fought for the values in which he believed, inspiring younger colleagues who are ready to take up the baton.

This volume represents the collaboration of 33 authors who enthusiastically accepted taking part in this creative endeavour in honour of Professor Birkinshaw's outstanding academic career and, to whom I am immensely grateful for their time and commitment.

Together, legal scholars, political scientists, practising lawyers, and colleagues considered the pressing themes in contemporary national and European public law, politics, governance, transparency and freedom of information. In their contributions, they also tested and discussed the new boundaries between the law and politics and a juxtaposition between them. Thus, the scope of this book is determined by the spheres of interest of the honouree. It should reflect Professor Birkinshaw's scholarship, his research and his achievements. He has written extensively and knowledgeably about many themes. Somehow, grouping his writings under four headings might seem to be a limitation that is not the purpose of this Festschrift. In contrast, we (the contributors) tried to add something to the repository of scholarship represented by Patrick Birkinshaw's oeuvre. New vistas for study will open up as the autocratic executive seeks to perpetuate itself.

As a final word, we believe that the quality of Patrick Birkinshaw's work is reflected in the outstanding contributions in this volume, and we hope that readers derive not only an appreciation of the authors and the insightful and stimulating analyses they offer, but also an understanding of Professor Birkinshaw's career and his contribution.

PART I Law in a World Turned Upside-Down

CHAPTER 1

Reflections on the Post-Brexit Constitution

Tony Prosser

It gives me enormous pleasure to contribute to this collection in honour of Patrick Birkinshaw and his work. Patrick and I were both appointed to the law school of the University of Hull in 1976 in our first teaching posts. The school provided a wonderful training in law teaching for us, and also in legal research under the tutelage of the late Douglas (then Norman) Lewis. I moved on after a few years, but Patrick stayed and made outstanding contributions to the development both of domestic public law and European public law research, as well as undertaking the burdensome task of running the law school with great distinction.

In this contribution I wish to point to a particular conception of the constitution which was characteristic both of Patrick's work and of my own, and to suggest that this is now under threat post-Brexit by a very different conception which runs directly contrary to it and to other United Kingdom (UK) public law traditions. It is by no means certain which model will triumph, but it is safe to say that the model with which we worked is under greater threat than at any time earlier in our careers.

1 A 'CONTESTATORY' CONCEPTION OF THE CONSTITUTION

Both Patrick and I adopted an approach which saw the UK constitution, and indeed the broader European constitutional arrangements, as essentially concerned with contestation. This is very different from (but not incompatible with) the conventional assertion of Parliamentary sovereignty as the basic principle of the constitution, not least in that the latter is concerned with the legal status of legislation and its application by the courts, whilst our constitutional concerns have been much wider. Nor does it fit neatly in the much-debated contrast between the 'legal' and the 'political' constitutions, combining elements of both.[1] Its origins lie in some forms of republican theory, and it is concerned with the creation and management of institutions, and with procedures and opportunities for scrutiny and deliberation. Its character has been put succinctly by Philip Pettit:

> [t]his points us towards the ideal of a democracy based, not on the alleged consent of the people, but rather on the contestability by the people of everything that government does: the important thing to ensure is that government doings are fit to provide popular contestation, not that they are the product of popular will.[2]

In Maitland's terms, such a 'contestatory' constitution developed, not as an assertion of the divine right of majorities over that of the monarch, but as 'a protest against arbitrary power or, more accurately, against the exercise of power in arbitrary ways'. Its democratic character arose not from any basis in a popular will but in the potential that 'the many minds of many men check each other, one would go this way, another that, so that the steady consistency which is required of those who would exercise power arbitrarily in the face of opposition must be wanting.'[3]

Central to this type of constitution is the establishment of institutional structures which involve scrutiny and deliberative forms of accountability examining the way in which government is run; this includes the roles of the courts and of Parliament but also those of a range of institutions which is far wider. This would include regulatory bodies and the role of European Union (EU) institutions, which have themselves contributed to an opening out and questioning of previously closed areas of government activity in the economic field, such as scrutiny of state aids and public procurement.

Such a 'contestatory' view of the constitution may be seen to underlie both of the celebrated *Miller* cases in which the courts impeded the Government's plans for the implementation of Brexit.[4] The first of the cases protected the deliberative role of Parliament in triggering the withdrawal process, whereas the second, in striking down an unlawful prorogation of Parliament to limit debate, made this explicit; '[t]he Government exists because it has the confidence of the House of Commons. It has no democratic legitimacy other than that. ... The first question, therefore, is whether the Prime Minister's action had the effect of frustrating or preventing the constitutional role of Parliament in holding the Government to account.'[5]

Indeed, the 'contestatory' model provides a basis for what Parliament has done best; the work of select committees and bodies such as the National Audit office, in

1. For these debates *see e.g.* Graham Gee and Gregoire Webber, 'What Is a Political Constitution?', (2010) 30 *Oxford Journal of Legal Studies*, 273-299.
2. Philip Pettit, *Republicanism: A Theory of Freedom and Government* (OUP, 1997) 277; for the importance of these ideas in UK historical experience *see* Adam Tomkins, *Our Republican Constitution* (OUP, 2005) esp. 51-52.
3. Frederick Maitland, 'A Historical Sketch of Liberty and Equality as Ideals of English Political Philosophy from the Time of Hobbes to the Time of Coleridge' in H.A.L. Fisher (ed.) *Collected Papers of Frederic William Maitland, Vol 1* (CUP 1911) 1, 38-9, 79-85.
4. *R (on the application of Miller) v. Secretary of State for Exiting the European Community* [2017] UKSC 5 (*Miller 1*); *R (on the application of Miller) v. the Prime Minister* [2019] UKSC 41 (*Miller 2/Cherry*).
5. Paragraph 55; *see also* paras 46 and 50.

which a degree of independence from direct party control permits fuller deliberation, has been relatively successful compared to very limited scrutiny of legislation by a House of Commons with strong party discipline. In fields outside those covered by Parliament, European experience was fundamental to the development of competition law in the UK.[6] In particular, the EU's state aids regime has also permitted effective outside scrutiny of state interventions in markets and the conduct of industrial policy, without preventing socially necessary support and interventionist environmental policies (which are much more fully developed in other leading EU Member States). European scrutiny of public expenditure through the process of the 'European Semester' has also required fuller examination of public expenditure as a whole than have the weak Parliamentary procedures for authorising public expenditure in advance.[7] In a domestic setting, regulatory institutions themselves, through a process of proceduralisation, have also created spaces for in-depth contestation of policy and its implementation.[8]

Alongside this 'contestatory' conception of the constitution is the growing importance of human rights. This does not, at least in principle, challenge the 'contestatory' model but complements it. In fact, the two are closely connected as contestation requires a strong rights base to function effectively. Rights such as freedom of assembly, personal autonomy and freedom of expression are necessary bases for contestation; moreover, some central elements of a rights-based approach actually extend the scope and depth of contestation, as does, in particular, the employment of the concept of proportionality.[9] Once more, European institutions have been central to this, and the roles of Council of Europe and the European Convention on Human Rights will be crucial elements of such a constitutional conception.

This 'contestatory' approach ties together much of Patrick's work; grievance redress and freedom of information are obviously central concerns of the 'contestatory' conception, whilst the openness to the importance of European jurisdictions emphasises the point that, for contestation to be effective under the conditions of modern regulatory capitalism, it must be transnational. However, due to a number of linked developments, but most importantly through the Brexit process, the 'contestatory' conception is now challenged by a very different rival approach to the constitution and to how it should work.

6. *See* on competition law, Stephen Wilks, 'Agency Escape: Decentralization or Dominance of the European Commission in the Modernization of Competition Policy?' (2005) 18 *Governance*, 431, and on public expenditure Tony Prosser, *The Economic Constitution* (Oxford University Press, 2014), 62-65 and Ch. 5.
7. *See* Prosser, *ibid.*, Ch. 8.
8. *See* Tony Prosser, *The Regulatory Enterprise* (Oxford University Press, 2010).
9. The most profound statement of this necessary link is Jürgen Habermas (translated by William Rehg), *Between Facts and Norms* (Polity Press, 1996).

2 THE CONSTITUTION AND PLEBISCITARY DEMOCRACY

It is common, of course, to point to a surge in populism in many countries throughout the world, and to assess constitutional change in these terms.[10] As I shall explain in a moment, this can usefully illuminate important aspects of constitutional change (including Brexit) but carries with it some dangers. In particular, the concept of populism is an extremely broad one, as the work cited above shows, and indeed there is some controversy about the extent to which it actually represents a form of constitutionalism rather than the latter's nemesis.[11] As a result, populism as a concept could fall into the trap which has been associated with its predecessor, neo-liberalism, in being so broad brush as to provide little useful analytical purchase.

For this reason I prefer to use a different concept which shares some, though not all, of the characteristics of populism; that of plebiscitary democracy. This was characterised by Max Weber as 'a variant of charismatic authority, which hides behind a legitimacy that is *formally* derived from the will of the governed'.[12] As Weber makes clear, this is not incompatible with Parliamentary democracy, but involves a shift in the perception of sources of legitimacy away from debate and deliberation to a popular vote, either in the form of a referendum or a general election.[13] It is hostile to discussion and compromise; 'the plebiscite would also obstruct most seriously the passing of all bills that result from a compromise of conflicting interests, for the most diverse reasons can lead to a "No" if there is no means of accommodating opposed interests through negotiation.'[14]

Boris Johnson, let alone Liz Truss, may seem improbable figureheads for such 'Caesarist' leadership, but other elements of the constitutional vision associated with Brexit fit closely with Weber's model. In particular, there is a strong executive claiming its legitimacy, not from a set of constitutional arrangements which include checks and balances, but from an assumed unitary 'will of the people' expressed through a referendum or a general election. It is the polar opposite to the model set out by Maitland and noted above because it sees legitimacy as a periodic expression of the popular will rather than a continuing process of scrutiny and deliberation. Of course, this model is not limited to the UK, but Brexit has brought it into particular prominence here. It is quite different from the theory of Parliamentary sovereignty (although the latter has been frequently conflated with it in Brexit rhetoric) as it places political sovereignty in an idealised popular will rather than legal sovereignty in the legislature.

10. For examples from a large literature, *see* the contributions in a special issue of the *German Law Journal* in 2019, summarised in Paul Blokker, Bojan Bugaric and Gábor Halmai, 'Introduction: Populist Constitutionalism; Varieties, Complexities, and Contradictions' (2019) 20 *German Law Journal*, 291-295; Jan-Werner Mueller, 'Populism and Constitutionalism' in Cristóbal Rovira Kaltwasser et al. (eds) *The Oxford Handbook of Populism* (Oxford University Press, 2022), 590-603.
11. *See* in particular Mueller, *ibid.*
12. Max Weber, *Economy and Society* (translated and edited by Guenther Roth and Claus Wittich) (University of California Press, 1968), 268 (emphasis retained).
13. *Ibid.*, 1451-1459.
14. *Ibid.*, 1455.

Elements of this conception do link clearly with some broader currents within populism. These include such themes as an inclusionary/exclusionary divide, separating 'true believers' in Brexit, and hence patriots, from a cosmopolitan and metropolitan elite, and a related friend/enemy dualism going back to the work of Carl Schmitt.[15] It is this highly divisive element which distinguishes current debates from the more traditional British concern about executive dominance associated with, for example, 'elective dictatorship'.[16] On the plebiscitary approach, it is not simply a matter of an overmighty executive seeking power but also of a clear distinction in the perceived political legitimacy of different sections of the people and of civil society, masked by a proclaimed unitary popular will.

In the context of Brexit, there is a further, very striking, irony here. The concept of such a popular will is far removed from the traditions of English Conservatism, and indeed of any UK traditional constitutional model. It is in fact closer to that of the French Fifth Republic, with a strong emphasis on the role of the President representing a unitary republican identity. This has been put well by Fintan O'Toole in a penetrating early analysis of Brexit, describing the period of the May Government in which 'the Prime Minister had to embrace a literal but entirely phoney populism in which the narrow and ambiguous majority who voted for Brexit under false pretences must be reimagined as "the people". But this is not English conservatism – it is pure Jean-Jacques Rousseau: the people express the General Will freely in a majority vote but, once they have done so, dissent is treason. The General Will had been established on that sacred referendum day. And it must not be defied or questioned.'[17] Mueller has also noted that '[p]opulists are, after all, often deemed to be heirs of the Jacobins (and, consciously or un-consciously, students of Rousseau).'[18]

Of course, Dicey himself did advocate the use of referendums and toyed with popular sovereignty in his later writings, so there might appear to be a pedigree for a plebiscitary approach in earlier UK constitutional theory.[19] However, his proposed use of a referendum was completely different from that associated with Brexit; it was to be a means of limiting government by providing a popular veto on changes introduced by political parties. It was certainly not a means of enhancing government legitimacy through an appeal to the popular will, this being far closer to Carl Schmitt's advocacy of referendums as 'acclamation' of government.[20] Thus 'the people's veto is at once a democratic institution and, owing to its purely negative character, may be a strictly conservative institution'.[21] Moreover, Dicey's advocacy of referendums was closely

15. *See* Paul Blokker, 'Varieties of Populist Constitutionalism: The Transnational Dimension' (2019) 20 *German Law Journal*, 332-350 and Julian Scholtes, 'The Complacency of Legality: Constitutionalist Vulnerabilities to Populist Constituent Power' (2019) 20 *German Law Journal*, 351-361.
16. *See* Mueller, *supra* n. 10, 595-596. For the concept of 'elective dictatorship' *see* Lord Hailsham, 'Elective Dictatorship', *The Listener*, 21 October 1976.
17. Fintan O'Toole, *Heroic Failure: Brexit and the Politics of Pain* (Apollo, 2019), 147.
18. Mueller, *supra* n. 10, 598.
19. Albert Venn Dicey, Introduction, in Roger E. Michener (ed.) *Introduction to the Study of the Law of the Constitution*, 8th ed. (Liberty Fund Inc., 1982, first published 1915), cviii-cxvii.
20. *See* Matt Qvortrup and Leah Trueblood, 'Schmitt, Dicey and the Power and Limits of Referendums in the United Kingdom, (2022) 42 *Legal Studies*, 396-407.
21. Dicey, *supra* n. 19, cxv.

associated with his extreme hostility to Irish home rule rather than representing a fully-theorised general approach to the constitution.

Such a shift away from a traditional UK (or English) approach towards a more Continental position as part of the Brexit process is astonishing, but it is only one of many unanticipated aspects of that process. How has it changed the actual constitutional arrangements in the UK? Of course, some changes are obvious and stem directly from withdrawal from the EU, though the effects of this have been mitigated both by the role of retained EU law under the European Union (Withdrawal) Act 2018 (though see now the Retained EU Law (Revocation and Reform) Bill) and the major constraints imposed on the UK Government by the Trade and Cooperation Agreement setting our relations with the EU after Brexit.[22] However, the new constitutional approach has already had major implications for less obvious areas of our constitutional arrangements, as I shall set out in the next section.

3 THE ILLEGITIMACY OF INDEPENDENT INSTITUTIONS

Many examples could be used to illustrate this shift to a view of the constitution based on the Government as the instrument of the perceived 'will of the people'. Most celebrated is the hostility to the role of the courts in reviewing governmental actions after its defeats in the two *Miller* cases.[23] This seemed likely to lead to major changes in the availability of judicial review, but in this area the reforms have turned out to be relatively minor, at least for the moment; I shall not discuss them here as they are considered in detail in another contribution to this volume. A similar point could be made about the review of the Human Rights Act. Here the independent reporting panel also recommended only relatively minor reforms, but the Government chose to consult on a much wider and far-reaching range of potential changes.[24] The outcome is uncertain at the time of writing and so will not be dealt with here, except to say that, whilst the assertion of individual rights through the courts is likely to be made more difficult, a major beneficiary of reform is likely to be some sections of the press, due to a proposed upgrading of the role of freedom of expression and a downgrading of privacy rights.[25] It is doubtful that, this reform will prove workable, but it fits nicely into the new constitutional model in which some sections of the press are seen as the mouthpiece of the 'will of the people' and so deserve a constitutionally privileged status.

22. *Trade and Cooperation Agreement Between the European Union and the European Economic Energy Community, of the one part, and the United Kingdom of Great Britain and Northern Ireland, of the other part*, [2021] OJ L149/10.
23. *R (on the application of Miller) v. Secretary of State for Exiting the European Community*; (*Miller 1*); *R (on the application of Miller) v. the Prime Minister* (*Miller 2/Cherry*); *see supra* n. 4.
24. Ministry of Justice, *Human Rights Act Reform: A Modern Bill of Rights. A Consultation to Reform the Human Rights Act*, CP 588 (2021). *See also The Independent Human Rights Act Review 2021*, CP 586 (2021). The bill based on these proposals was withdrawn by the incoming Truss Government, but major change remains likely.
25. Ministry of Justice, *Human Rights Act Reform, supra*, paras 204-217.

A highly revealing shift of emphasis is in attitudes to public bodies which operate at arm's length from central government and have been expected to operate with a degree of independence from it. Such independence does not fit with the new constitutional approach, nor indeed is it compatible with many brands of populism. Thus:

> populists tend to colonize or 'occupy' the state. ... Why, might populists ask indignantly, should the people not take possession of their state through their only rightful representatives? Why should those who obstruct the genuine popular will in the name of civil service neutrality, for instance, not be purged? ... . Second, populists tend to engage in what political scientists call mass clientelism: the exchange of material and immaterial favors by elites for mass political support.[26]

Both of these themes have been evident in a number of areas since 2019. Perhaps the most important, and most dangerous, concerns the Electoral Commission and the Elections Act 2022.[27] The Commission is the independent statutory body which oversees elections and regulates political financing in the UK. The Government introduced the Elections Bill which, as well as introducing highly controversial requirements of photo ID for voting, included provisions for a Strategy and Policy statement setting a strategic direction for the work of the Commission, to be drafted by the relevant minister. This proved highly divisive and was strongly contested during the passage of the Bill. In an unprecedented move, all except one of the members of the Commission wrote to ministers in protest, arguing that the clauses would be 'inconsistent with the role that an independent electoral commission plays in a healthy democracy. This independence is fundamental to maintaining confidence and legitimacy in our electoral system.' Moreover, such provisions had 'no precedent in the accountability arrangements of electoral commissions in other comparable democracies.'[28] Amendments to remove these clauses were passed in the House of Lords by a substantial majority, but they were reintroduced when the Bill returned to the House of Commons.

The Act now provides for the minister to issue a statement setting out the Government's policy and priorities in relation to elections, and the role and responsibilities of the Commission in enabling the Government to meet those priorities. The statement may include guidance relating to particular matters falling within the Commission's functions. The Commission must have regard to the statement and

26. Mueller, *supra* n. 10, 596.
27. For a brief summary of the issues *see* Jacob Eisler, 'The Elections Act in Uncertain Times: Democracy, Partisanship, and the Uncodified Constitution', U.K. Const. L. Blog (16 May 2022), available at https://ukconstitutionallaw.org/2022/05/16/jacob-eisler-the-elections-act-in-uncertain-times-democracy-partisanship-and-the-uncodified-constitution/ (accessed 17 May 2022).
28. Electoral Commission, *Letter from Commissioners: Strategy and Policy Statement Measures in the Elections Bill*, 21 February 2022, available at https://www.electoralcommission.org.uk/who-we-are-and-what-we-do/our-views-and-research/key-correspondence/letter-commissioners-strategy-and-policy-statement-measures-elections-bill (accessed 20 May 2022). The sole member of the Commission not to sign the letter was precluded from doing so by his position in the House of Lords which was considering it.

report annually on what it has done in consequence of it.[29] Although there may be specific motives for restricting the role of the Commission in Governmental anger at actions of the Commission in the Brexit process, the potential restrictions on its independence are far-reaching and troubling for the future. They indicate very clearly the weakness of the largely informal and trust-based norms on which UK government has previously operated; '[t]he party in power has few constraints on its power to modify democratic procedure, other than expression of discontent from the constituency itself – and the manipulation of electoral process by the party in power modulates that very expression of constituent will.'[30]

A further example of attacks on the independence of arm's length institutions can be seen in the case of regulatory bodies, and this offers a revealing contrast with the attitude taken by earlier Conservative Governments. One of the most important effects of the mass privatisation during the Thatcher and Major years during the 1980s and 1990s was the establishment of new regulatory institutions with a degree of independence from government. This was designed to provide a stable environment in which privatised industries could operate free from continual political interference, and so could attract private investors.[31] Such a policy fits neatly with a 'Thatcherite' or 'neo-liberal' approach, encouraging the working of private markets to allocate investment and in which the role of government is to provide a predictable environment within which the markets can operate. Of course, such independence was never total, and it was necessary to coordinate regulation with broader policies through various forms of policy statements and guidance; nor were appointments' processes completely removed from politics (although members of the regulatory bodies have benefited from considerable protection from removal once in office). However, independence has been dependent largely on a culture of respect for the regulators and on non-legally enforceable (but publicly available) governmental rules such as the Governance Code on Public Appointments.[32]

Both a mistrust of independent institutions and clientelism in appointments have been apparent in the treatment of regulatory authorities since 2019. This has been less evident for the major economic regulators than for regulation of the media, a subject of especially great concern to the Government which is highly suspicious of alleged media bias, especially by broadcasters, and which has adopted a 'culture wars' agenda. One example is that of the Online Safety Bill, which will extend the power of the Office of Communications (Ofcom), which regulates broadcast and online media, in relation to online content. If enacted unchanged, it will give the government vastly increased powers over the Office of Communications (Ofcom) which regulates broadcast media, including the ministerial power to direct it to amend its codes relating to online content

29. Elections Act 2022, section 16.
30. Eisler, *supra* n. 27.
31. For the concept of regulatory commitment underlying this *see* B. Levy and P. Spiller, 'A Framework for Resolving the Regulatory Problem' in B. Levy and P. Spiller (eds), *Regulation, Institutions and Commitment* (Cambridge University Press, 1996) 1-35.
32. Cabinet Office, *Governance Code on Public Appointments* (2016) at https://assets.publishing.service.gov.uk/government/uploads/system/uploads/attachment_data/file/578498/governance_code_on_public_appointments_16_12_2016.pdf (accessed 29 September 2022).

in order to reflect government policy. This goes far beyond strategic guidance, covering as it does policy implementation. Despite heavy criticism by the Joint Parliamentary Committee scrutinising the Bill, the Government has refused to remove this clause from the Bill.[33] The parallel with the Elections Act is very clear.

In the same field, there has also been major concern about appointments. The normal approach in the UK previously was that appointments to regulatory boards are for the minister; however, this has been made more transparent through the Governance Code on Public Appointments mentioned above. The Code is not enforceable through the courts but only through the political process; there is review by a Commissioner without direct sanctions. It sets up a semi-independent reviewing process to select names for the minister to approve or select. In the crucially important appointment process for the Chair of Ofcom, the Prime Minister had made it clear that he had a preferred candidate. This candidate had previously been editor of a newspaper strongly supporting the Conservative Government; he was also highly critical of other media organisations, in particular the BBC, which is regulated by Ofcom. The Panel decided that he did not meet the criteria for appointment. The Minister for Digital, Culture, Media and Sport could have overruled the panel, but this would have meant giving reasons in public for doing so. Instead, he rejected all three names put forward by the panel and no appointment was made; instead, the process was started once again with a new panel and revised and more flexible criteria. However, the Prime Minister's preferred candidate then withdrew, claiming that the process had revealed civil service bias against candidates from the private sector.[34] An alternative candidate was eventually appointed; the process attracted a critical report from the House of Commons Digital, Culture, Media and Sport Committee.[35]

This episode was particularly disturbing as it shows a disregard for the political and cultural norms which were previously central to the protection of regulatory independence, especially in the case of appointments. Once more, it reflects a major change since the Brexit referendum in which checks and balances are perceived, not as essential protections for democratic governance, but as standing in the way of government implementation of the 'will of the people' as expressed through a referendum or a general election. Previously, such checks and balances as existed in this area were largely informal with only limited legal governance of appointment processes. As a result, it has proved extremely easy for a determined Government with strong support from key sectors of the press to ignore them and attempt to colonise regulatory bodies with its own supporters.

---

33. House of Lords, House of Commons Joint Committee on the Draft Online Safety Bill, 'Draft Online Safety Bill', HL 129, HC 601 (2021-22), paras 370-378; *Government Response to the Report of the Joint Committee on the Online Safety* Bill, CP 640 (2022), paras 190-192.
34. George Parker and Alistair Gray, 'Dacre Rails at Civil Service as He Pulls out of Ofcom Running', *Financial Times*, 19 November 2021.
35. 'Pre-Appointment Hearing for Chair of Ofcom', HC 48 (2021-2022).

4 THE FUTURE

Was the 'plebiscitary' approach I have outlined limited to the Johnson Government and simply a reflection of his idiosyncratic personality? It is noteworthy that when he defended his premiership he relied on the notion of a direct personal popular mandate rather than Parliamentary legitimacy, something which dramatically misreads existing constitutional norms.[36] However, the approach identified above has continued under his successor. In the selection of the new Prime Minister, the notion of 'the people' was reduced even further to mean only the 81,000 highly unrepresentative members of the Conservative Party who voted for her as party leader.[37] The hostility to contestation is evident in the immediate sacking of the Permanent Secretary to the Treasury by the new Prime Minister, thereby removing a key source of independent advice, and most graphically in the disastrous 'fiscal event' in the first few weeks of the new Government. The Chancellor of the Exchequer deliberately did not frame this as a full budget to avoid the necessity of publishing independent financial projections by the Office for Budgetary Responsibility. The hostile reaction of financial markets and lenders shows clearly how the absence of such an opportunity for contestation destroyed the trust and confidence necessary for the working of the markets.

In the longer term, whether the approach to the constitution after Brexit represents an enduring change to our arrangements remains uncertain. Some of the changes will be difficult to reverse in the foreseeable future; thus there is no likelihood of a reversal of Brexit or even of attempts to shift it to a 'softer' model maintaining at least a customs union. The poisonous domestic atmosphere in which debate is conducted will preclude this for some considerable time; moreover, the UK Government has gone out of its way to squander any goodwill which might have produced a cooperative approach with the EU as the basis for future relations. This suggests that earlier contestatory arrangements derived from EU membership will not be re-instated any time soon, and it is unlikely that new approaches introduced domestically will be as capable of effecting outside scrutiny of government. One example already is that of the new subsidy control regime replacing the EU state aids regime, in which the Competition and Markets Authority will have only an advisory role and in which there will be no independent enforcement authority. Instead, the regime will rely on private enforcement through a form of judicial review before the Competition Appeal Tribunal, though standing for such challenge is limited to those with an economic interest or the Secretary of State and is likely to exclude public interest groups. It is questionable to

36. *See* Chris Smith, 'Boris Johnson's Claim of a "Mandate" from the People Isn't Accurate – Here's How Prime Ministers Really Get Power', *The Conversation*, 8 July 2022 at https://theconversation.com/boris-johnsons-claim-of-a-mandate-from-the-people-isnt-accurate-heres-how-prime-ministers-really-get-power-186615 (accessed 29 September 2022).
37. For a succinct account *see* Rodney Brazier, 'No Way to Pick a PM', U.K. Const. L. Blog (8 September 2022) at https://ukconstitutionallaw.org/2022/09/08/rodney-brazier-no-way-to-pick-a-pm/ (accessed 29 September 2022).

what extent this will provide an adequate means of continuing and consistent scrutiny of subsidies.[38]

On the other hand, it is now patently obvious to all but Brexit true believers that Brexit has not been 'done' and that many loose ends remain. This is most obvious in relation to the Northern Ireland protocol to the Withdrawal Agreement, but also applies in many other fields, such as border checks on goods imported from the EU. It means that there is likely to be a long process of argument and adaptation which may weaken the idea that there is an unproblematic concept of Brexit representing a unitary will of the people; one great success of the Johnson Government has been to disguise the complexities behind precisely this idea. Such a position cannot last forever.

I have emphasised here that the new approach is not, however, related only to matters directly concerning Brexit but extends to many other aspects of relations between government, economy and society. Although I have chosen not to use the concept of populism directly as the basis for my analysis, I have been able to demonstrate that there are strong links between the approach of the Johnson Government and themes characteristic of populism worldwide. This will clearly produce tensions with the development of a calculable and rule-based order which characterised the earlier, market-based or 'neo-liberal' approach to regulation, including at the international level. Much will depend not just on political fortunes within the UK but on the future successes or failures of populist movements in the rest of the world, particularly in the United States. Once more we can see a certain irony here; Brexit has not led to an independent UK free to forge its own way in the world, but to a nation ever more dependent on developments elsewhere whilst being unable to participate in key institutions for managing and contesting change internationally. The spirit of Patrick's work will remain relevant and important, whatever our future relationships with the EU and with other international organisations, and whatever the direction of our domestic constitutional arrangements turn out to be.

38. Subsidy Control Act 2022; for a detailed critique of the provisions when in Bill form *see* George Peretz, 'The Subsidy Control Bill Part I: A New Public Law Regime', U.K. Const. L. Blog (28 October 2021), available at https://ukconstitutionallaw.org/2021/10/28/george-peretz-qc-the-subsidiary-control-bill-part-1-a-new-public-law-regime/ and 'The Subsidy Control Bill Part II: Application to Legislation, Questions & Concerns', U.K. Const. L. Blog (29 October 2021) available at https://ukconstitutionallaw.org/2021/10/29/george-peretz-qc-the-subsidiary-control-bill-part-ii-application-to-legislation-questions-concerns/ (accessed 17 May 2022).

CHAPTER 2

The Rebirth of Parliamentary Sovereignty

Gordon Anthony

1 INTRODUCTION

This chapter picks up on a theme that was central to much of Professor Birkinshaw's work on European public law – the existence of different sites of power above and below the state, and the judicial role in moderating competing claims to legal authority.[1] Its focus is on United Kingdom (UK) law and the rebirth of the doctrine of Parliamentary sovereignty in the years since the Brexit referendum of 23 June 2016. Prior to that event, UK law had been moving towards a more nuanced conception of legal sovereignty, in circumstances where European Union (EU) membership and devolution had led the courts to recognise a category of common law 'constitutional statutes'.[2] In the first edition of his book on European Public Law, Professor Birkinshaw referenced the potential importance of such statutes, albeit he noted that, 'As a matter of law, it is not clear [what they mean beyond being] unsuitable candidates for the doctrine of implied repeal by subsequent legislation.'[3] The post-Brexit case law would suggest that he was right to doubt their ultimate worth: while they have not been expressly disavowed by the courts, they now exist within a constitutional order that has reaffirmed Diceyan orthodoxy as its rule of recognition.[4]

1. *See*, most prominently, *European Public Law: The Achievement and the Brexit Challenge* (Kluwer, 3rd ed., 2020).
2. *Thoburn v. Sunderland CC* [2003] QB 151. Fundamental rights standards – both at common law and under the Human Rights Act 1998 – had also had implications for conceptions of sovereignty. *See, e.g.*, *R v. Secretary of State for the Home Department, ex p Simms* [2000] 2 AC 115 and M. Elliott, 'Beyond the European Convention: Human Rights and the Common Law' (2015) 68 *Current Legal Problems* 85.
3. *European Public Law* (Butterworths, Lexis Nexis, 2003), p. 157.
4. For example, *R (Miller) v. Secretary of State for Exiting the European Union* [2017] UKSC 5, [2018] AC 61, 143, para. 60, Lord Neuberger. For a pre-Brexit statement, see *Pham v. Secretary of State for Home Department* [2015] UKSC 19, [2015] 1 WLR 1591, 1617, para. 80, Lord Mance.

In tracing this rebirth of sovereignty, this chapter considers three cases on devolution and Brexit. The cases – *Miller I; Scottish Continuity Bill*; and *Re Allister*[5] – raised novel questions about the devolution settlement, which the courts were to answer in an avowedly orthodox manner. In terms, this meant that the courts gave only a limited weight to devolution legislation that had previously been described as constitutional in form and, moreover, as a harbinger of a 'divided sovereignty'.[6] Indeed, while each of the devolution statutes for Scotland, Northern Ireland and Wales contain express provisions on the legal sovereignty of the Westminster Parliament,[7] the rulings in *Miller I, Scottish Continuity Bill* and *Allister* made it clear that that version of sovereignty remained unabridged by the experience of devolution (and that of EU membership before it). In *Miller I*, it was thus held that the sovereign powers of the Westminster Parliament are unconstrained by the Sewel convention on legislative consent and the powers of the devolved institutions; in Scottish Continuity, it was noted that devolution is not akin to federalism and that the powers of the Scottish Parliament are to be read on that basis; and, in Allister, the Court of Appeal in Northern Ireland held that the Westminster Parliament had intended to override aspects of the Act of Union between Ireland and Great Britain – a constitutional statute – when legislating to give effect to the Ireland-Northern Ireland Protocol in the EU-UK Withdrawal Agreement of 2019.

The chapter begins with a short section that outlines how conceptions of sovereignty had become more nuanced prior to Brexit, including through the courts' recognition of common law constitutional statutes. It then examines *Miller I, Scottish Continuity Bill*, and *Allister*, noting how the courts moved to limit the potential that had been associated with the common law. While this perhaps begs the anterior question of how far the courts ought to use the common law to refashion the constitution, the reality is that they had been doing so in evermore creative ways prior to Brexit.[8] The chapter concludes with some more general comments about the current institutional balance within the constitution and whether that merely reflects, what Professor Birkinshaw has described as, a 'constitutional heritage' in which 'Parliamentary Sovereignty is the lynchpin'.[9]

2 SOVEREIGNTY'S REVISION

The story of how orthodox conceptions of sovereignty came under strain in UK law is one that is well-known – EU membership laid bare the challenge of competing claims

5. *R (Miller) v. Secretary of State for Exiting the European Union* [2017] UKSC 5, [2018] AC 61; *Re UK Withdrawal from the European Union (Legal Continuity) (Scotland) Bill* [2018] UKSC 64, [2019] AC 1022; and *Re Allister's Application* [2022] NICA 15, [2022] 3 CMLR 8.
6. The phrase is most famously associated with Lord Steyn's *dictum* in *Jackson*: *see Jackson v. Attorney-General* [2005] UKHL 56, [2006] 1 AC 262, 302, para. 102.
7. Scotland Act 1998, section 28(7); Northern Ireland Act 1998, section 5(6); Government of Wales Act, section 107(5).
8. *See* Sir John Laws, *The Common Law Constitution* (Cambridge University Press, 2015) and *The Constitutional Balance* (Hart Publishing, 2021).
9. *Supra* n. 1, p. 209.

to legal authority, whilst devolution (as linked to sub-national identities and institutions) gave further form to the idea of a divided sovereignty.[10] The corresponding concept of 'constitutional statutes' was first referenced in the celebrated Thoburn case on the primacy of EU law, where Laws LJ explained why, in Factortame, the European Communities Act 1972 had prevailed over the Merchant Shipping Act 1988.[11] In his judgment, Laws LJ explained that EU law enjoyed primacy because the European Communities Act 1972 was not subject to implied repeal and could instead be overridden only where the Westminster Parliament used 'express words in [a] later statute, or ... words so specific that the inference of an actual determination to effect the result contended for [is] irresistible'.[12] His approach was one that took UK courts closer to that which had long been adopted by the courts of other Member States, as it emphasised that 'The fundamental legal basis of the [UK's] relationship with the EU rests with the domestic, not the European, legal powers.'[13] The Supreme Court later said that his ruling had provided 'important insights' into how the challenge of EU membership might be met, in that instance in a case which raised oblique questions about domestic constitutional fundamentals and the obligations of membership.[14]

Thoburn's significance for the devolution settlement lay in the fact that Laws LJ also described the Scotland Act 1998 and (what is now) the Government of Wales Act 2006 as constitutional statutes (the Northern Ireland Act 1998 was likewise described as a 'constitution' by the House of Lords in the case of Robinson).[15] This was to prove to be a foundational statement that resulted in a large body of case law that, at its height, hinted at a nascent federalism in the UK. Although there were a number of Supreme Court rulings that held that an expansive interpretation of the various devolution Acts would not always be merited,[16] there were other cases that made it clear that devolution represented a level of governance with an enhanced democratic legitimacy. For instance, in the Axa case, the Supreme Court considered the question of how closely the courts should scrutinise the choices of the devolved legislatures, and ruled that restraint would often be merited.[17] While Lords Hope and Reed stated that the Scottish Parliament is not legally sovereign, they emphasised that it is a 'self-standing democratically elected legislature'[18] and that, '(w)ithin the limits set by the

10. *See* R. Rawlings, P. Leyland and A. Young (eds), *Sovereignty and the Law: Domestic, European and International Perspectives* (Oxford University Press, 2013).
11. *Thoburn v. Sunderland CC* [2003] QB 151; and *R v. Secretary of State for Transport, ex p Factortame (No 2)* [1991] 1 AC 603.
12. [2003] QB 151, 187.
13. *Ibid.*, 189.
14. *R (Buckinghamshire CC) v. Secretary of State for Transport* [2014] UKSC 3, [2014] 1 WLR 324, 382-383, para. 208, Lords Mance and Neuberger. *See also* the discussion of the constitutional relationship with EU law in *Pham v. Secretary of State for Home Department* [2015] UKSC 19, [2015] 1 WLR 1591.
15. [2003] QB 151, 186; and *Robinson v. Secretary of State for Northern Ireland* [2002] UKHL 32, [2002] NI 390, 398, para. 11, Lord Bingham.
16. *Attorney General v. National Assembly for Wales Commission* [2012] UKSC 53, [2013] 1 AC 792 and *Imperial Tobacco Ltd v. Lord Advocate* [2012] UKSC 61, (2013) SC (UKSC) 153. *See too, e.g., Re Agriculture Sector (Wales) Bill* [2014] UKSC 43, [2014] 1 WLR 2622.
17. *Axa General Insurance v. HM Advocate* [2011] UKSC 46, [2012] 1 AC 868.
18. [2012] 1 AC 868, 911, para. 46, Lord Hope.

[Scotland Act] ... its power to legislate is as ample as it could possibly be'.[19] Moreover, in Re Recovery of Medical Costs for Asbestos Diseases (Wales) Bill,[20] Lord Thomas came close to giving legal effect to a concept of divided sovereignty in the UK. This case arose when the Counsel General referred to the Supreme Court the legality of a Bill that would have allowed the Welsh Ministers to recover from employers and insurers some of the costs of treating persons for work-related illnesses on the National Health Service. Lord Thomas, for the minority, again considered the question of how closely the courts should scrutinise devolved democratic choices, before indicating that 'great weight' should be given to the public interest choice of the Welsh Assembly. Stating that he 'would find it difficult to make any logical distinction in the context of the United Kingdom's devolved constitutional structure between [the devolved] legislatures and the United Kingdom Parliament in according weight to the evaluation of the different choices and interests in respect of matters which are within the primary competence of the legislatures',[21] his Lordship concluded that he could not 'see why in principle the United Kingdom Parliament in making legislative choices in relation to England (in relation to matters such as the funding of the NHS in England) is to be accorded a status which commands greater weight than would be accorded to the Scottish Parliament and the Northern Ireland and Welsh Assemblies in relation respectively to Scotland, Northern Ireland and Wales'.[22] It was an approach that had already been envisaged by other judges speaking in an extra-curial capacity.[23]

Such statements did not (of course) amount to a final departure from an orthodox view of sovereignty, although they did make it clear that devolution had an element of embeddedness within the UK constitution. That impression was to be added to by political developments in relation to the Sewel convention that was mentioned in the introduction, above. That convention governs the circumstances under which the Westminster Parliament can legislate for devolved matters, where it seeks to respect devolved legislative competence by providing that: 'the UK Parliament [will] not normally legislate with regard to devolved matters except with the agreement of the devolved legislature'.[24] While the convention originally existed only as a form of 'soft law' – and was thereby one of the so-called 'conventions of the constitution' – it was later to be codified in the devolution legislation that applies in Scotland and Wales (but not in Northern Ireland).[25] This was in direct response to the Scottish independence referendum of 2014, where the growth of nationalism (query: popular sovereignty) had created very real pressures for realignment within the UK constitution. Section 28(8) of the Scotland Act 1998 thus placed the Sewel convention on a statutory footing, whilst

19. [2012] 1 AC 868, 944, para. 146, Lord Reed.
20. [2015] UKSC 3, [2015] AC 1016.
21. [2015] UKSC 3, [2015] AC 1016, 1059-1060, paras 118-119.
22. [2015] UKSC 3, [2015] AC 1016, 1060, para. 122.
23. *See, e.g.*, Lady Hale, 'The UK Supreme Court in the UK Constitution', 12 October 2012, p. 23, at https://www.supremecourt.uk/docs/speech-121012.pdf.
24. *See* para. 14 of an intergovernmental Memorandum of Understanding at https://www.gov.uk/government/publications/devolution-memorandum-of-understanding-and-supplementary-agreement, last accessed 9 October 2022.
25. On conventions of the constitution *see* P. Leyland, *The Constitution of the United Kingdom: A Contextual Analysis* (4th ed., Hart Publishing, 2021), Ch. 2.

section 63A provided that: 'The Scottish Parliament and the Scottish Government are a permanent part of the United Kingdom's constitutional arrangements.' Sections A1 and 107(6) of the Government of Wales Act 2006 were to like effect as regards the governance of Wales.

3 SOVEREIGNTY'S REBIRTH

The three cases that illustrate how the courts have returned to a Diceyan view of the constitution start with the split UK-wide vote during the Brexit referendum. As is well-known, voters in England and Wales voted to leave the EU, whilst those in Northern Ireland and in Scotland voted to remain (and by some margin). This served to deepen existing fissures within the UK's constitutional system and highlighted very different political preferences within its constituent parts. Indeed, the challenge was to be particularly pressing as regards Northern Ireland, where historical political tensions complicated negotiations about the terms under which the UK might withdraw from the EU under Article 50 of the Treaty on European Union (TEU). The result was the (still contested) Ireland-Northern Ireland Protocol that sought to avoid a 'hard border' on the island of Ireland but which created an economic border in the Irish sea.[26]

3.1 *Miller I*

The Sewel convention was to be central to the *Miller* case, or certainly that part of it which concerned devolved powers. The central question in the case was, of course, whether the UK government could rely upon the Royal prerogative/executive treaty-making powers to provide notification of withdrawal under Article 50 TEU, or whether it could do so only on the basis of an Act of the Westminster Parliament. In a detailed and novel judgment, the Supreme Court famously held that an Act of Parliament was required to effect notification because, among other things, the prerogative powers cannot generally be used to change statute law or the common law, or to remove rights from individuals.[27] In terms of devolution, this gave rise to the question of whether the Sewel convention should apply given that an Act of Parliament authorising notification would have implications for devolved competences.[28] The Supreme Court started its analysis on this point by noting that the Sewel convention means that the UK Parliament will not normally legislate with regard to devolved matters without agreement and that there had been previous instances in which the devolved institutions had passed Sewel motions in relation to Acts of the Westminster Parliament that

26. *See* C. McCrudden (ed.), *The Law and Practice of the Ireland-Northern Ireland Protocol* (Cambridge University Press, 2022). Note that, at the time of copy-editing, the so-called "Windsor Framework" has been agreed between the UK and EU and that this will modify significant elements of the original Protocol.
27. For commentary *see* M. Elliott, J. Williams and A. Young (eds), *The UK Constitution after Miller: Brexit and Beyond* (Hart Publishing, 2018).
28. *See* C. McCrudden and D. Halberstam, 'Miller and Northern Ireland: A Critical Constitutional Response' (2017) 8 *UK Supreme Court Yearbook* 1.

had specifically addressed their devolved powers.[29] However, this was essentially an exercise in context-setting, as the remainder of the ruling focused on the political nature of the Sewel convention and its resultant non-enforceability in law. In adopting that position, the Court acknowledged that judges could 'recognise the operation of a political convention in the context of deciding a legal question' and that the Sewel convention 'has an important role in facilitating harmonious relations between the UK Parliament and the devolved legislatures'.[30] Nevertheless, the Court was ultimately of the view that, 'Judges ... are neither the parents nor the guardians of political conventions' and they 'cannot give legal rulings on [their] operation or scope, because those matters are determined within the political world'.[31] This was so notwithstanding that the Sewel convention had been written into legislation – that legislation was said simply to recognise 'the convention for what it is, namely a political convention ... the purpose of the legislative recognition of the convention was to entrench it as a convention.'[32]

Two related points can be made about *Miller I*. The first concerns the sequencing in the Supreme Court's ruling, which served to position devolution as a secondary concern. While the Court made mention of the importance of the devolution settlement in Northern Ireland in particular, it proceeded on the understanding that the fundamental question before it was whether the Royal prerogative could be used to trigger notification under Article 50 TEU. By focusing first on this question, the Court inevitably took itself towards an initial finding about the powers of the sovereign Parliament, where the majority emphasised that it 'would not accept that the so-called fundamental rule of recognition (ie the fundamental rule by reference to which all other rules are validated) underlying UK laws has been varied by [membership] or would be varied by [withdrawal]'.[33] The second point concerns the implications of this finding. In short, by holding that the doctrine of Parliamentary sovereignty remained unabridged by the fact of EU membership, the Court would have had to reason against itself to find that the Sewel convention could act as a brake on the exercise of powers by the sovereign Parliament. *Miller I* thereby directly contradicted the idea that sovereignty had been divided in the context of EU membership or, more importantly, that it could be in the context of devolution. The fact that Sewel had been written into a 'constitutional statute' thus did not alter that position and the European Union (Notification of Withdrawal) Act 2017 came to be enacted without devolved consent.

3.2 Scottish Continuity Bill

The issue of consent also provided the backdrop to the Scottish Continuity Bill.[34] At source, this was a dispute about the power to legislate for the domestic law effects of

29. [2018] AC 61 164, para. 140, referencing, among others, the European Communities (Amendment) Act 2008, Wales Act 2014, the Scotland Act 2016.
30. [2018] AC 61, 165-166, paras 146 & 151.
31. *Ibid.*, para. 146.
32. [2018] AC 61, 166, paras 148-149.
33. [2018] AC 61, 143, para. 60.
34. *The UK Withdrawal from the European Union (Legal Continuity) (Scotland) Bill – A Reference by the Attorney General and the Advocate General for Scotland* [2018] UKSC 64, [2019] AC 1022.

Brexit, where legal certainty was taken to require that much of EU law should remain in force pending possible future amendment (at either the central and/or the devolved levels). The UK government had here introduced a Bill that later became the European Union (Withdrawal) Act 2018, which repealed the European Communities Act 1972 but kept much of EU law in place as 'retained EU law' and included rules about when UK Ministers and those in the devolved territories could amend such law. However, the Scottish government was of the view that these rules amounted to a 'power-grab' as UK Ministers could make some decisions in respect of Scotland, and this led it to refuse to recommend a Sewel motion in favour of the UK government's Bill and to introduce its own withdrawal Bill in the Scottish Parliament. That Bill – the UK Withdrawal from the European Union (Legal Continuity) (Scotland) Bill – sought to protect the role of the devolved institutions by, among other things, limiting the powers of UK Ministers to amend the law of Scotland. By section 17 of the Bill, UK ministers could do so only when they had first obtained the consent of the Scottish Ministers for any proposed change.

The legality of the Bill was referred to the Supreme Court by the UK government's law officers where, as has already been noted above, the Court ruled that the Scottish Parliament's powers were constrained by the terms of the Scotland Act 1998. While the Court's ruling was prefaced by a statement about the constitutional importance of the devolved institutions, it equally emphasised that those institutions are not legally sovereign and that this reflected 'the essence of devolution: in contrast to a federal model, a devolved system preserves the powers of the central legislature of the state in relation to all matters'.[35] The Court on this basis noted that the Scottish institutions' refusal to provide consent for the UK government's Bill did not affect the legal validity of the UK Withdrawal Act, and it proceeded to place questions about the lawfulness of the Scottish Bill within a traditional, sovereigntist paradigm. This was most pronounced in relation to section 17, where the Court read that section as in conflict with section 28(7) of the Scotland Act 1998, which provides that devolution to Scotland 'does not affect the power of the Parliament of the United Kingdom to make laws for Scotland'. The Supreme Court here held that, were section 17 to enter into law, that would set at nought those provisions of the European Union (Withdrawal) Act 2018 that allow UK ministers to make subordinate legislation for Scotland. For the Court, this was not legally possible, as 'the UK Parliament remains sovereign, and its legislative power in relation to Scotland is undiminished'.[36] The Court expressed the point as follows:

> [T]he power of the UK Parliament to make laws for Scotland includes the power to make laws authorising the making of subordinate legislation by Ministers and other persons. An enactment of the Scottish Parliament which prevented such subordinate legislation from having legal effect, unless the Scottish Ministers gave their consent, would render the effect of laws made by the UK Parliament conditional on the consent of the Scottish Ministers. It would therefore limit the power of the UK Parliament to make laws for Scotland, since Parliament cannot

35. [2019] AC 1022, 1048, para. 41.
36. *Ibid.*

> meaningfully be said to 'make laws' if the laws which it makes are of no effect. The imposition of such a condition on the UK Parliament's law-making power would be inconsistent with the continued recognition, by section 28(7) of the Scotland Act, of its unqualified legislative power.[37]

This ruling makes it clear that the devolution case law has settled upon a resolutely non-federal model of sovereignty. While there were certainly aspects of the ruling that drew upon the Court's earlier reasoning in Axa and so on – the Court emphasised again that the Scottish Parliament has full plenary powers within the limits of the Scotland Act 1998[38] – the judgment ultimately rested upon the same, Diceyan model of legal sovereignty that had informed *Miller*. This could be seen not just in the Court's approach to the effects of the absence of a Sewel motion, but also in its various references to the sovereignty of the UK Parliament, as is codified in section 28(7) of the Scotland Act 1998. Given the point, it might well be doubted whether Lord Thomas' earlier comments in Welsh Asbestos Diseases will ever amount to anything more than a statement of ambition rather than constitutional principle.

3.3 *Re Allister*

The remaining case to be considered is *Re Allister*, which concerned the legality of the Ireland-Northern Ireland Protocol that forms part of the EU-UK Withdrawal Agreement of 2019. As is well-known, the Protocol is intended to avoid a 'hard border' on the island of Ireland as one aspect of a wider attempt to protect the Belfast Agreement of 1998 'in all its dimensions'.[39] In broad terms, it does so by keeping Northern Ireland within the EU's customs union and single market in goods, where 'legal hybridity' means that EU law applies under the Protocol and UK law outside it.[40] Of course, the converse of this is that there is an economic sea border between Great Britain and Northern Ireland, and Allister came to query whether this could be compatible with Northern Ireland's constitutional arrangements. This was notably so given the 'consent' principle that underlies the Belfast Agreement and the Northern Ireland Act 1998 – the foundational idea that Northern Ireland is a part of the UK and will remain so while that it is the wish of a majority of its electorate.[41]

The key issue in Allister was what the courts should do in the event of a conflict between two constitutional statutes. At its height, this was a point about the relationship between section 7A of the European Union (Withdrawal) Act 2018 and Article 6 of the Act of Union (Ireland) Act 1800 (which essentially guarantees the free movement of goods within the UK's own internal market). Section 7A of the Act of 2018 is a 'catch-all' provision that gives domestic legal effect to the Withdrawal Agreement

37. [2019] AC 1022, 1050-1051, para. 52.
38. *See, e.g.*, [2019] AC 1022, 1039-1040, paras 12-13.
39. Protocol, at Article 1(3). See note 26 above regarding the significance of the so-called 'Windsor Framework'.
40. *See further* G. Anthony, 'The Protocol in Northern Ireland Law', in McCrudden (ed.), *supra* n. 26, p. 118.
41. *See* R. MacGinty et al., 'Consenting Adults: The Principle of Consent and Northern Ireland's Constitutional Futures' (2001) 36 *Government and Opposition* 472.

including the Protocol 'without further enactment' and requires that all other Acts of Parliament are 'to be read and [have] effect' subject to (in this context) the Protocol. The argument that was advanced in Allister was that, while Thoburn had addressed the relationship between a constitutional statute and an ordinary statute, its reasoning ought to apply equally to the relationship between two constitutional statutes. This was said to mean that section 7A (as found in the constitutional statute that had replaced the European Communities Act 1972) could not impliedly repeal Article 6 of the Act of Union (found in another constitutional statute), but rather that section 7A could override Article 6 only through express words to that effect. It was also argued that, insofar as the Protocol is incorporated under section 7A, this is inconsistent with the 'consent' principle in the Belfast Agreement and section 1 of the Northern Ireland Act 1998.

Judgment at first instance was given by Colton J who held: (i) that section 7A overrode Article 6 because Parliament had deliberated at length about giving effect to the Withdrawal Agreement and had been 'fully sighted of the terms of and consequences' of doing so;[42] and (ii) that section 7A did not offend the consent principle because, whatever changes had been effected by the Protocol, they did not ultimately affect Northern Ireland's status as a part of the UK. His reasoning in this regard was upheld, on appeal, by the Court of Appeal. Keegan LCJ (with whom Treacy LJ agreed) surveyed case law on, among other things, the enduring relevance of the doctrine of the legal sovereignty of the Westminster Parliament and said: 'Cognisant of these principles the court must examine the core legislative provisions and conduct an exercise in statutory interpretation in this case'.[43] Having considered the legal framework in detail, she accepted that there was an inconsistency between the Protocol and Article 6 of the Act of Union but that it was clear from the wording of section 7A that it was to take priority over Article 6 and that it did so by requiring that Article 6 be read 'subject to' the terms of the Protocol. For Keegan LCJ, this meant that the case was not about implied repeal and that there thus was 'no conflict with the principles enunciated by Laws LJ in Thoburn ... even if there is a doubt they [the words in section 7A] are "so specific that the inference of an actual determination to effect the result contended for [is] irresistible" ... there can be no doubt in relation to Parliamentary intention'.[44] McCloskey LJ, concurring, concluded that: 'the Act of Union, notwithstanding its constitutional stature, is not immune from modification by primary legislation ... there has been no implied repeal of [Article 6] ... it has been lawfully modified by primary legislation'.[45] Keegan LCJ and McCloskey LJ were also of the view that the consent principle had not been offended – as McCloskey LJ put it: 'The fundamental thrust of the Act of Union remains unchanged. [Northern Ireland], constitutionally, remains part of the UK. The statutory EU withdrawal arrangements have not altered this any more than [the fact of EU membership] did.'[46]

42. [2021] NIQB 64, paras 82-114 (the quoted words are at para. 111).
43. [2022] NICA 15, paras 94-135 (the quoted words are at para. 135).
44. [2022] NICA 15, para. 195.
45. *Ibid.*, para. 403.
46. [2022] NICA 15, 412.

Allister is on appeal to the Supreme Court at the time of writing, and it remains to be seen how (if?) the apex court will approach the conflict between two constitutional statutes. Certainly, if the reasoning of the Court of Appeal is adopted, this will perhaps further diminish the potential that originally lay within Thoburn. While that judgment had placed formal limitations on the Westminster Parliament's powers – where parallel developments in relation to common law fundamental rights standards had suggested that there might even be substantive limits to Parliament's powers[47] – the prevailing impression after the Court of Appeal's ruling in Allister is of a narrowing role for the 'common law constitution'.[48] In the event that the Supreme Court's ruling continues with that approach, the rebirth of sovereignty may be complete.[49]

4 CONCLUSION

This chapter began by referencing Professor Birkinshaw's 2003 note of caution about the effects of common law constitutional statutes and whether they would have implications beyond the doctrine of implied repeal. In what followed, it used *Miller I*, Scottish Continuity, and Allister to highlight how traditional conceptions of sovereignty have since limited the reach of 'devolution statutes' as 'constitutional statutes'. While the broader point about the rebirth of sovereignty might equally have been made with reference to other case law (whether concerned with devolution, or not[50]), the post-Brexit case law on devolution has revealed in particularly sharp form what that rebirth means for contemporary understandings of the UK's constitution. In short, it is now clear that constitutive power in the UK is (again) to be understood as a centralising concept and that the courts will not readily unsettle a perceived 'constitutional heritage'.[51] This is so notwithstanding an older – and famous – judicial dictum: '[T]he principle of the unlimited sovereignty of Parliament is a distinctively English principle which has no counterpart in Scottish constitutional law.'[52]

How, then, to conclude? Certainly, it might be said that the change in *Miller I*, Scottish Continuity, and Allister should not be overstated, as the pre-Brexit case law had never actually rejected Diceyan sovereignty but rather had noted the challenges it faced and how those might be met. However, it is undeniable that the courts have since also sought to distance themselves from difficult post-Brexit constitutional questions either by noting them as political (*Miller I*) or relying upon old orthodoxy (Scottish Continuity, Allister). While this may well be the type of approach that courts in other systems would adopt at a time of fundamental legal and political change, it cannot be

47. *See, e.g.*, *Re Moohan* [2014] UKSC 67, [2015] AC 901, 925, para. 35, Lord Hodge.
48. On which *see* Laws, *supra* n. 8.
49. Judgment was delivered by the Supreme Court on 8 February 2023 at [2023] UKSC 5, [2023] 2 WLR 457. The Court, in dismissing the appeal, did not elaborate upon the nature and role of constitutional statutes.
50. For example, *R (Miller) v. Prime Minister* [2019] UKSC 41, [2020] AC 373 and *Reference by the Lord Advocate of devolution issues under paragraph 34 of Schedule 6 to the Scotland Act 1998* [2022] UKSC 31, [2022] 1 WLR 5435 (on the question of whether the Scottish Parliament has the power to legislate for a referendum on Scottish independence).
51. Birkinshaw, *supra* n. 1.
52. *MacCormick v. Lord Advocate* 1953 SC 396, 411, Lord Cooper.

doubted that the common law has at least partly withdrawn into itself in the recent case law. It is an approach to constitutive power that may well have come full circle across the timeline of Professor Birkinshaw's distinguished career – from the original challenge of EU membership in 1973 to the even greater challenge of Brexit.

CHAPTER 3

Through the Looking Glass: The Subversion of Democracy, Human Rights and the Rule of Law in Hungary

Stephen I. Pogany

1 INTRODUCTION

In trying to make sense of developments in constitutional law and politics in Hungary - which has been governed by Prime Minister Viktor Orbán and his Fidesz party since 2010 - Lewis Carroll's *Through the Looking-Glass* offers a surprisingly reliable guide. In Hungary, as in the realm in which Alice found herself, an apparently familiar world reveals itself to be bizarre, confounding and disturbing. Believing impossible things and accepting that words have new and improbable meanings are essential skills for anyone wishing to thrive in Orbán's Hungary - as in the world through Alice's looking glass.

With appropriate references to Lewis Carroll's invaluable book, this chapter examines some of the most important developments in Hungarian public law and politics since 2010. In the view of the overwhelming majority of legal experts, political scientists and others, legislation and other measures introduced by Fidesz have had a wholly negative impact on democracy, the rule of law and human rights in Hungary.[1]

1. *See*, in particular, János Kornai, *Hungary's U-Turn: Retreating from Democracy*, 26:3 Journal of Democracy 32-48 (2015); Gábor Halmai, *Illiberal Constitutionalism? The Hungarian Constitution in a European Perspective*, in Stefan Kadelbach (ed.), *Constitutional Crises in the European Union* 84-103 (Nomos 2018). *See also*, various other book chapters, journal articles and working papers by Gábor Halmai listed at: https://me.eui.eu/gabor-halmai/publications-other/; Kim Lane Scheppele, *Understanding Hungary's Constitutional Revolution*, in Armin von Bogdandy & Pál Sonnevend (eds), *Constitutional Crisis in the European Constitutional Area* 111-124 (Hart/Beck 2015); András L. Pap, *Democratic Decline in Hungary* (Routledge 2018); András Bozóki & Daniel Hegedüs, *The Rise of Authoritarianism in the European Union: A Hybrid Regime in Hungary*, in

The respected American NGO, Freedom House, considers Hungary to be no more than 'partly free',[2] a damning indictment of the Orbán regime's record in office over the past 12 years. By contrast, when Fidesz returned to power in 2010, after a period in opposition, Hungary was widely regarded as a functioning liberal democracy. Gábor Halmai, chief counsellor to the first president of Hungary's Constitutional Court and now Professor of Comparative Constitutional Law at the European University Institute in Florence, has emphasised that, 'Hungary was one of the first and most thorough political transitions, which provided all the institutional elements of constitutionalism: checks and balances and guaranteed fundamental rights'.[3] In addition to regular free elections and constitutional guarantees concerning a broad range of civil and political rights, Hungary possessed a cadre of experienced, independent-minded judges. In marked contrast to the situation today,[4] a broad range of print and electronic media reflected the diversity of political opinion in Hungary. Investigative journalists and political commentators from both the Left and the Right were able to find outlets for their work.

Over the past 12 years, Orbán and Fidesz have transformed Hungary's political and constitutional landscape. As Halmai notes, Hungary 'represents the first, and probably model case, of constitutional backsliding from a full-fledged liberal democratic system to an illiberal one with strong authoritarian elements'.[5] For the sociologist and former government minister, Bálint Magyar, Hungary has degenerated under Fidesz into a post-communist mafia state whose essential features replicate those of Putin's Russia.[6] While Fidesz has been careful to preserve the outward forms of democracy, its substance has been systematically dismantled.[7]

2 HUNGARY: THE SURPRISINGLY SHORT ROAD FROM POST-COMMUNISM TO POST-DEMOCRACY

Hungary's political transition in 1989-1990, from Soviet-style communism to a functioning multi-party democracy, occurred without major incident, in marked contrast to

Jürgen Mackert, Hannah Wolf & Bryan S. Turner (eds), *The Condition of Democracy* vol. 2 Ch. 8 (Routledge 2021); Anna Donáth, *Absolutely Corrupted: The Rise of an Illiberal System and the Future of Hungarian Democracy*, 27:2 Brown Journal of World Affairs 1-22 (2021); Zoltán Fleck, Nóra Chronowski & Petra Bárd, *The Crisis of the Rule of Law, Democracy and Fundamental Rights in Hungary*, MTA Law Working Papers (2022/4), https://jog.tk.hu/mtalwp/the-crisis-of-the-rule-of-law-democracy-and-fundamental-rights-in-hungary; Zsuzsanna Szelényi, *Tainted Democracy: Viktor Orbán and the Subversion of Hungary* (Hurst & Co. 2022).

2. Freedom House, *Freedom in the World 2022*, https://freedomhouse.org/country/hungary/freedom-world/2022.
3. Halmai, *Illiberal Constitutionalism?*, *supra* n. 1, at 86.
4. *See, e.g.*, the highly critical report by the Council of Europe Commissioner for Human Rights, *Memorandum on freedom of expression and media freedom in Hungary*, Strasbourg, 30 March 2021 (CommDH(2021)10).
5. Halmai, *Illiberal Constitutionalism?*, *supra* n. 1, at 86.
6. Bálint Magyar, *Post-Communist Mafia State: The Case of Hungary* (CEU Press 2016).
7. Joseph Weiler, *Orbán and the Self-Asphyxiation of Democracy*, 31:1 The European Journal of International Law 3 (2020).

countries including the former Czechoslovakia and Romania.[8] Czechoslovakia's ageing communist leaders reluctantly ceded power in mid-December 1989 after a series of massive demonstrations, in Prague and other cities, that were initially met with violent repression.[9] In Romania, popular protests in Timişoara, Bucharest and other cities, triggered a power struggle within the ruling communist party that culminated in the hasty trial and execution of the country's president, Nicolae Ceauşescu, in late December 1989, together with his wife. Romania's subsequent transition to a genuine, multi-party democracy occurred fitfully and over a period of years.[10]

By contrast, political transition in Poland and Hungary was accomplished in a comparatively peaceful and orderly fashion following 'round table' talks. In Hungary, communist authorities sat down with leaders of fledgling opposition parties and the heads of civil society organisations and trade unions, in the summer and autumn of 1989, to negotiate the transition to democracy and the rule of law.[11] After almost half a century in which the power and authority of Hungary's Soviet-backed communist regime could not be challenged without risk of incurring significant penalties, free, multi-party elections were held in March 1990. These resulted in the formation of a conservative, centre-right government headed by an historian, József Antall. Although Hungary's communist-era constitution was not repealed outright by the new administration, the text had been very heavily amended some months earlier to bring it into line with western democratic norms.[12] In another important break with the communist era – during which law and legal institutions were subordinated to the dictates of the Communist party – Hungary's parliament enacted legislation, in October 1989, establishing a constitutional court with far-reaching powers. The court, particularly under its first president, László Sólyom, went on to play a decisive role in shaping Hungary's transition to democracy and the rule of law.[13]

The main elements of an unprecedented ideological consensus – spanning the two, formerly divided halves of Europe – were set out in November 1990 in the Charter of Paris for a New Europe. Concluded under the auspices of the Conference on Security and Co-operation in Europe (now the Organization for Security and Co-operation in Europe (OSCE)), the participating states – including Hungary and the other post-communist countries of the Central and Eastern Europe (CEE) region – declared that 'Europe is liberating itself from the legacy of the past' and undertook to 'build,

8. *See, generally,* Timothy Garton Ash, *We the People* (Granta Books 1990). *See also,* Victor Sebestyen, *Revolution 1989,* Part 3 (Phoenix 2010).
9. Sebestyen, *supra* n. 8, 368-379.
10. Tom Gallagher, *Theft of a Nation,* esp. Chs 3-4 (Hurst & Company 2005).
11. Garton Ash, *supra* n. 8, 55-60.
12. Istvan Pogany, *Constitutional Reform in Central and Eastern Europe: Hungary's Transition to Democracy,* 42:2 International & Comparative Law Quarterly 332, at 338-339 (1993).
13. *See, e.g.,* Ethan Klingsberg, *Judicial Review and Hungary's Transition from Communism to Democracy: The Constitutional Court, the Continuity of Law, and the Redefinition of Property Rights,* 1992:1 Brigham Young University Law Review 41-144 (1992); Kim Lane Scheppele, *The New Hungarian Constitutional Court,* 8:4 East European Constitutional Review 81-87 (1999); László Sólyom & Georg Brunner, *Constitutional Judiciary in a New Democracy* (University of Michigan Press 2000); Catherine Dupré, *Importing the Law in Post-Communist Transitions* (Hart Publishing 2003).

consolidate and strengthen democracy as the only system of government'.[14] The participating states also affirmed that, '[h]uman rights and fundamental freedoms are the birthright of all human beings, are inalienable and are guaranteed by law ...'.

Yet, just a few years after Orbán and Fidesz returned to power in 2010, constitutional law experts and others began to issue dire warnings that human rights, democracy and the rule of law were under threat in Hungary. Princeton University's Kim Lane Scheppele stated bluntly that the enactment of a new Hungarian constitution or Fundamental Law, in 2011, had 'felled the tree of democratic constitutionalism that Hungary planted in 1989'.[15] The eminent Hungarian economic historian, János Kornai, was no less critical of the measures introduced by Fidesz. In a lengthy article published in the Journal of Democracy, in 2015, Kornai emphasised that, 'the executive and legislative branches [in Hungary] are no longer separate; both are controlled by Prime Minister Orbán, who has positioned himself at the very pinnacle of power'.[16] Kornai, an emeritus professor at Harvard University, argued that, 'the basic institutions of the rule of law have been abolished or weakened' by the Orbán regime, and that the country's new constitution or 'Fundamental Law',[17] lacked democratic legitimacy. As Kornai explained, the new constitution had been 'drafted by a small group within Fidesz without any wide public discussion', while 'the document was pushed through' the Hungarian parliament 'in short order'.[18]

Since returning to office in 2010, Orbán and Fidesz have succeeded in hollowing out Hungarian democracy, undermining constitutionally protected rights and subverting the separation of powers. In addition to achieving dominance of the legislative branch of government, they have appointed a succession of Fidesz loyalists to the office of head of state and have introduced measures to restrict the independence of the judiciary.[19] In addition to these ominous developments, the bulk of important print and electronic media organs in Hungary are now in the hands of Fidesz appointees, loyal party allies and pro-government foundations.[20] As a consequence, there are few significant media outlets willing to host opposition politicians or publish criticism of government policies. However, to fully grasp the insidious nature and effects of

14. For the text of the Charter of Paris for a New Europe *see* https://www.osce.org/mc/39516.
15. Scheppele, *supra* n. 1, at 111.
16. Kornai, *supra* n. 1, at 35.
17. *Ibid.*
18. *Ibid.*
19. *See, e.g.*, Viktor Z. Kazai & Ágnes Kovács, *The Last Days of the Independent Supreme Court of Hungary?*, VerfBlog (13 October 2020), https://verfassungsblog.de/the-last-days-of-the-independent-supreme-court-of-hungary/. *See also*, *Hungarian lawmakers appoint new top court president despite judges' rejection*, Reuters (19 October 2020), https://www.reuters.com/article/hungary-court-idINL8N2HA2VU.
20. Tamás Fábián, *Orbán's influence on the media is without rival in Hungary*, Euraktiv (30 March 2021), https://www.euractiv.com/section/media/news/orbans-influence-on-the-media-is-without-rival-in-hungary/; Patrick Kingsley, *Orbán and His Allies Cement Control of Hungary's News Media*, The New York Times (29 November 2018), https://www.nytimes.com/2018/11/29/world/europe/hungary-orban-media.html.

Fidesz's ambitious and authoritarian political project we must return to Alice and her adventures through the looking glass.[21]

3 THE LANGUAGE OF CONSTITUTIONALISM IN ORBÁN'S HUNGARY

> 'When I use a word', Humpty Dumpty said in a rather scornful tone, 'it means just what I choose it to mean – neither more nor less'.
>
> Lewis Carroll, *Through the Looking-Glass*

Just as Alice was baffled by Humpty Dumpty's habit of ascribing new meanings to certain words, anyone studying Hungary's constitution, particularly as it operates in practice – or the utterances of the prime minister and his political associates – may experience a similar sense of confusion. Like Humpty Dumpty, the Orbán régime has endowed certain words and phrases, including 'democracy' and 'Christian culture', with definitions that cannot be found in any dictionary or encyclopaedia.

3.1 Democracy

Although scholars, lawyers, and political activists have understood democracy in various ways,[22] there is broad agreement that democracy is not simply a synonym for majoritarianism. An authentically democratic society must, at a minimum, accommodate basic individual freedoms, respect the rights of minorities and possess judicial or other mechanisms that seek to prevent governments from exceeding their powers. For example, the preamble of the treaty establishing the Council of Europe refers to 'individual freedom, political liberty and the rule of law, principles which form the basis of all *genuine democracy*' (my emphasis).[23] The 1990 Charter of Paris for a New

21. András Sajó has cautioned against labelling illiberal democracies in Hungary and elsewhere as 'authoritarian':

> Of course, illiberal democracies may drift toward despotism, and as they do so, their authoritarian (illiberal) elements become increasingly obvious. But to call them authoritarian does not render justice to the brutality of the oppression that characterizes authoritarian regimes. (András Sajó, *Ruling by Cheating* 20 (Cambridge University Press 2021)).

However, in the view of the present author, brutality is merely *one* of various means by which authoritarian regimes may impose their will; it is not a defining feature of authoritarianism. As Orbán and Fidesz have triumphantly demonstrated, alternative voices can be muted or even silenced – in the academy, in the cultural sphere and in the media – without recourse to brute force. While preserving the outward trappings of democracy, Orbán has succeeded in fashioning an authoritarian and rigidly hierarchical governing system in which power and authority are ultimately concentrated in his hands.

22. *See, e.g.*, Ludwig Beckman, *Democracy*, Oxford Research Encyclopaedia of Politics (29 November 2021), https://oxfordre.com/politics/view/10.1093/acrefore/9780190228637.001.0001/acrefore-9780190228637-e-2001.

23. For the text of the Statute of the Council of Europe *see* https://rm.coe.int/1680306052.

Europe, mentioned above, adopts a broadly similar definition, emphasising that '[d]emocracy has as its foundation respect for the human person and the rule of law' and that democracy has a 'representative and pluralist character'. The eminent sociologist, Ralf Dahrendorf, argued that democracy means giving the people '*a voice* in the exercise of power' (my emphasis).[24] Dahrendorf dismissed the notion that virtually *any* decision taken by a majority of citizens must be implemented by a democratic polity as a matter of course. Dahrendorf also emphasised the importance of a credible 'system of checks and balances' to prevent governments, even democratic governments, from abusing their power.

Since 2010, 'democracy' has acquired a completely different meaning in Hungary under successive Fidesz administrations. Systems of checks and balances that could prevent the Fidesz government from implementing its policies have no place in Orbán's populist and fundamentally regressive conception of democracy. Nor do freedoms, notably lesbian, gay, bisexual, and transgender (LGBT+) rights, that conflict with traditional 'Christian' values. The Fundamental Law, introduced by Fidesz, defines marriage as 'the union of one man and one woman' (Foundation, Article L(1)), while same-sex couples are effectively precluded from adopting children. As far back as July 2014, Orbán boasted that, 'the new state that we are constructing in Hungary is an illiberal state, a non-liberal state,' in which liberalism has been replaced with 'a different, special, national approach'.[25]

In this corrupted vision of 'democracy', human rights – far from constituting an essential attribute of democracy – are viewed with suspicion as a potential threat to the unity and integrity of the nation and to the preservation of traditional values. Drawing on the radical nationalist thinking that dominated political discourse in Hungary and in much of East Central Europe during the inter-war era, Orbán has contended that: 'the Hungarian nation is not simply a group of individuals but a community that must be organised, reinforced and … constructed'.[26] Although he has declined to say so explicitly, Orbán evidently sees himself as uniquely qualified to assume the task of organising, reinforcing and constructing the Hungarian nation.

For the Princeton political scientist, Jan-Werner Müller, Orbán's notion of 'illiberal democracy' represents 'an attack on democracy's very foundations'.[27] Müller also rejects subsequent efforts by Orbán to characterise his ideology as 'Christian

24. Ralf Dahrendorf, *A Definition of Democracy*, 14:4 Journal of Democracy 101 at 103 (October 2003).
25. *See* Prime Minister Viktor Orbán's Speech on 26 July 2014 at the 25th Bálványos Summer Free University and Student Camp held at Băile Tuşnad, Romania, https://2015-2019.kormany.hu/en/the-prime-minister/the-prime-minister-s-speeches/prime-minister-viktor-orban-s-speech-at-the-25th-balvanyos-summer-free-university-and-student-camp.
26. *Ibid.*
27. Jan-Werner Müller, *The Problem with Illiberal Democracy*, Social Europe (27 January 2016), https://socialeurope.eu/the-problem-with-illiberal-democracy. *See also*, Pap, *supra* n. 1; Donáth, *supra* n. 1.

democracy'.[28] Yet, despite repeated denunciations by scholars and the human rights community – as well as sustained criticism by western governments and opposition politicians in Hungary – Orbán and Fidesz continue to emulate Humpty Dumpty by insisting that democracy means just what they choose it to mean, neither more nor less.

3.2 Christian Culture

Despite growing up in a family in which religion played little or no part, Prime Minister Orbán has become a passionate, self-proclaimed champion of 'Christian culture'.[29] In opposing large-scale immigration to Europe from other continents, Orbán has warned that 'Europe's Christian culture is already barely able to maintain its own set of Christian values',[30] and has insisted that 'Christian culture … is the cornerstone that holds the architecture of European civilisation in place'.[31] Orbán has called for the formation of 'a strong, Christian civic Hungary in a strong and Christian Europe'.[32]

Yet there is little evidence to suggest that Orbán's conception of 'Christian culture' or of 'Christian values' – which he rarely chooses to elaborate – is informed by conventional Christian teachings. Pastor Gábor Iványi of the Hungarian Evangelical Fellowship has stated bluntly that the Orbán regime, 'has nothing in common with Christianity'.[33] In an interview following the introduction of exceptionally harsh measures to deal with asylum seekers entering Hungary, Pastor Iványi commented:[34]

> Unfortunately, the steps taken by the prime minister to protect Christianity cannot really be taken seriously … as a believer I do not think that there is divine inspiration behind the zeal. Moreover, I believe that…the steps and statements made in the case of refugees are fundamentally contrary to the biblical principles and the expectations of Jesus Christ. Refusal, starvation, creating bureaucratic and legal hurdles, and spreading false news about asylum seekers is particularly anti-Christian behaviour. This is a shock to Bible-believing Christians, and it could also be a disgrace in the eyes of non-religious people.

---

28. Jan-Werner Mueller, *Christian Democracy or Illiberal Democracy?*, Project Syndicate (29 January 2020), https://www.project-syndicate.org/commentary/christian-democracy-or-viktor-orban-illiberalism-by-jan-werner-mueller-2020-01?barrier=accesspaylog.
29. On the absence of religion from Orbán's upbringing *see, e.g.*, Christopher Adam, *Hungary's Orbán Family and Religion* (Hungarian Free Press, 15 April 2016), available at: https://hungarianfreepress.com/2016/04/15/hungarys-orban-family-and-religion/.
30. Quoted in Matthew Karnitschnig, *Orbán says migrants threaten 'Christian' Europe*, Politico (3 September 2015), https://www.politico.eu/article/orban-migrants-threaten-christian-europe-identity-refugees-asylum-crisis/.
31. *PM Orbán at Church Consecretation: 'No Freedom and No European Life Without Christian Culture'*, Hungary Today (8 April 2019), https://hungarytoday.hu/pm-orban-at-church-consecration-no-freedom-and-no-european-life-without-christian-culture/.
32. Viktor Orbán's address at the presentation of the discussion document 'Signs of the Times' (30 October 2015), https://2015-2019.kormany.hu/en/the-prime-minister/the-prime-minister-s-speeches/viktor-orban-s-address-at-the-presentation-of-the-discussion-document-signs-of-the-times.
33. Patrick Kingsley, *He Used to Call Viktor Orban an Ally. Now He Calls Him a Symbol of Fascism*, New York Times (15 March 2019), https://www.nytimes.com/2019/03/15/world/europ, e/viktor-orban-hungary-ivanyi.html.
34. *Ibid.*

Far from seeking inspiration in the scriptures, Orbán has weaponised Christianity in order to 'attack domestic and foreign opponents' and 'to weaken democratic checks and balances'.[35] In the view of critics, 'Orbán's Hungary provides a clear warning of how easily Christianity can be distorted and used to erode democracy.'[36]

Orbán uses terms such as 'Christianity' and 'Christian culture' in a tribal sense, rather than as moral or spiritual categories. For Orbán, 'Christianity' and 'Christian culture' are convenient labels to distinguish Hungarians and other 'right thinking' – and invariably white – Europeans from ethnic, religious, political and other groups that Orbán's propaganda has portrayed as alien and threatening. At various times, such groups have comprised Muslims, Africans, Asians, Roma, Jews, liberals, leftists, sexual minorities, international financiers and feminists. However, in appropriating 'Christianity' and 'Christian culture' for unashamedly political purposes, Orbán and Fidesz have stripped these terms of their essential ethical underpinnings.

In weaponising 'Christianity' and 'Christian culture' – and in emptying these terms of moral or spiritual content – Orbán and Fidesz are, prima facie, in breach of their obligations under Hungary's Fundamental Law.[37] This stipulates that, '[t]he protection of the constitutional identity and Christian culture of Hungary shall be an obligation of every organ of the State' (Foundation, Article R(4)). Arguably, Orbán and Fidesz have also flouted the requirement laid down in the Fundamental Law to, "ensure an upbringing for children" in accordance with the values based on the constitutional identity and Christian culture of our country' (Freedom and Responsibility, Article XVI(1)). As emphasised by Pastor Iványi et al., 'Christian culture', as properly understood, is incompatible with the crude, unreflective nationalism, rampant xenophobia, thinly veiled antisemitism,[38] and inhumane treatment of asylum seekers that have characterised successive Fidesz governments.

4 BELIEVING IMPOSSIBLE THINGS

> Alice laughed. 'There's no use trying,' she said: 'one can't believe impossible things.'
> 'I daresay you haven't had much practice,' said the Queen. 'When I was your age, I always did it for half-an-hour a day. Why, sometimes I've believed as many as six impossible things before breakfast.'
>
> Lewis Carroll, *Through the Looking-Glass*

35. Garret Martin & Carolyn Gallaher, *Viktor Orbán's use and misuse of religion serves as a warning to Western democracies*, *The Conversation* (27 October 2020), https://theconversation.com/viktor-orbans-use-and-misuse-of-religion-serves-as-a-warning-to-western-democracies-146277.
36. *Ibid.*
37. For the text of the Fundamental Law of Hungary, as amended through to 23 December 2020, *see, e.g.*, https://www.parlament.hu/documents/125505/138409/Fundamental+law/73811993-c377-428d-9808-ee03d6fb8178.
38. On antisemitism in Hungary *see, generally*, Stephen Pogany, *Reinventing the Protocols of the Elders of Zion: Anti-Semitism in Orbán's Hungary*, in Alfredo Alietti & Dario Padovan (eds), *Clockwork Enemy: Xenophobia and Racism in the Era of Neo-populism* 97-136 (Mimesis International 2020).

As in the world through Alice's looking glass, a sizeable proportion of Hungary's voters have learnt to believe impossible things – a trait that Fidesz has both encouraged and exploited. In recent years, Fidesz has persuaded a large tranche of the Hungarian electorate that homosexuals are incipient paedophiles,[39] that Muslim asylum seekers – very few of whom actually wish to settle in Hungary – pose a mortal threat to the country's traditions and Christian culture, and that a nonagenarian Hungarian-Jewish philanthropist and financier, George Soros, is plotting to destroy Europe. However bizarre and outlandish such claims may appear to outsiders, they are treated as irrefutable facts by Fidesz's core supporters, and by others on the far right of Hungary's political spectrum.

4.1 Believing Impossible Things: The Demonisation of George Soros

According to the *Protocols of the Elders of Zion* – a fabrication compiled by Tsarist secret service agents in the final decade of the nineteenth century – a cabal of powerful Jews is plotting to take over the world by encouraging strife and dissension amongst nations and weakening them by all other possible means.[40] In a speech in Budapest, on 27 June 2017, Prime Minister drew on the *Protocols* and on a slew of classic antisemitic tropes in accusing the Hungarian-Jewish financier and philanthropist, George Soros, of endangering Europe's peace and stability with an elaborate money-making scheme:[41]

> In the background now there is ... one ... determined and successful money man, who regards himself as a superior being. Unfortunately for us he happens to be Hungarian, and his name is George Soros ... He has a plan, and he doesn't even bother to hide it: he has made it public. He wants to see one million migrants coming from a different cultural background settled in Europe every year: by force, if needs be, and even against the express wishes of the European people. We must not be naive, and when it comes to such a financial speculator we should just ignore the humanitarian blather. If he really wanted to help, he would take his money to where it is needed, rather than increasing and importing the trouble to Europe. He works in the financial sector – in speculation – where money can only be made by ruining millions of people, by short-changing them. So of course there is no question of his being motivated by good intentions. Those in Budapest who seek to whitewash him deserve better and present a sorry sight. The truth is that George Soros is a speculator who operates an extensive mafia network, and who is threatening Europe's peace and future. For him migration is good business ... .

Hungary's Prime Minister knew that his remarks about Soros were both unfounded and inflammatory. Far from encouraging increased flows of migrants to

39. *Orban's dirty little trick: Conflating pedophilia with homosexuality*, Kafkadesk Budapest Office (13 June 2021), https://kafkadesk.org/2021/06/13/orbans-dirty-little-trick-conflating-pedophilia-with-homosexuality/.
40. Walter Laqueur, *The Many Lives of 'The Protocols of the Elders of Zion'*, Mosaic (4 December 2017), https://mosaicmagazine. com/essay/history-ideas/2017/12/the-many-lives-of-the-protocols-of-the-elders-of-zion.
41. *Prime Minister Viktor Orbán's speech at the closing event for the National Consultation* (27 June 2017), https://miniszterelnok.hu/prime-minister-viktor-orbans-speech-at-the-closing-event-for -the-national-consultation/.

Europe or personally profiting from migration, as Orbán alleged, Soros had called for the development of a coherent, pragmatic and ethical European asylum policy, following a massive increase in the number of applicants seeking asylum in Europe.[42]

However, Orbán made his remarks in the knowledge that many right-wing Hungarians would find them perfectly plausible – particularly if the allegations were repeated regularly in the Fidesz-controlled media. With parliamentary elections scheduled for April 2018, Orbán's election strategy was based on highlighting the supposed dangers Hungary faced from Muslim 'migrants', Jewish financiers,[43] and other 'foreign' elements. Orbán and his advisers understood that, with sufficient help from a compliant media sector, Soros could be readily cast as a bogeyman or hate figure in a country where believing impossible things, especially about Jews, has a long and ignoble history.[44]

Fidesz's sweeping election victory, in April 2018, was due, in the main, to the scale of the resources available to the governing party and its allies, to the credulity, xenophobia and ingrained antisemitism of a substantial segment of Hungarian society, and to the impact of Hungary's strikingly partisan media. Unlike the Queen in *Through the Looking-Glass*, who had to practise for half an hour a day in order to master the art of believing impossible things, setting aside time for daily practice is unnecessary in Orbán's Hungary. Switching on the television or radio, reading almost any national or local newspaper, or scrolling through most Hungarian internet news sites is sufficient – provided it's done with sufficient regularity. Poorly educated voters living in small towns and villages – the core of Fidesz's electoral base – can be persuaded to believe impossible things, whether about Muslim asylum seekers or an elderly Jewish financier, through prolonged exposure to Hungary's heavily partisan media.[45]

---

42. George Soros, *Rebuilding the Asylum System*, Project Syndicate (26 September 2015), https://www.georgesoros.com/2015/09/26/ rebuilding-the-asylum-system/.
43. In a subsequent speech, delivered just weeks before the general election, Orbán went even further in invoking the spectre of an invisible – but all too clearly Jewish – adversary:

    > We must fight against an opponent which is different from us. Their faces are not visible, but are hidden from view; they do not fight directly, but by stealth; they are not honourable, but unprincipled; they are not national, but international; they do not believe in work, but speculate with money; they have no homeland, but feel that the whole world is theirs. They are not generous, but vengeful.

    Orbán Viktor's ceremonial speech on the 170th anniversary of the Hungarian Revolution of 1848 (15 March 2018), https://www.miniszterelnok.hu/orban-viktors-ceremonial-speech-on-the-170th-anniversary-of-the-hungarian-revolution-of-1848/.
44. *See, generally*, Raphael Patai, *The Jews of Hungary* esp. Chs 5, 6, 9, 31 (Wayne State University Press 1996). The enthusiastic reception of a 'diary' written by a virulently antisemitic author, Cécile Tormay, which was originally published in Budapest in 1920, is revealing. In her 'diary', which is largely a work of fiction, Tormay attributes the 'dissolution of Rome', the 'fate of Egypt', the 'decline of Spain' and many other historical calamities to Jewish power and malevolence – a thesis that would surprise most conventional historians. Cécile Tormay, *An Outlaw's Diary: The Commune* 38 (Philip Allan & Co. 1923). Tormay and her 'diary' continue to be held in great esteem by many conservative Hungarians, including senior figures in Fidesz.
45. On the composition of Fidesz's electoral base *see* Máté Pálos & Miklós Hajdu, *Fidesz-tarolással jár együtt az iskolázatlanok magas aránya*, G7 (7 April 2022), https://g7.hu/kozelet/20220407/fidesz-tarolassal-jar-egyutt-az-iskolazatlanok-magas-aranya/. On the dominance of Hungary's media sector by Fidesz-aligned elements *see supra* n. 20, and the accompanying text.

Fidesz's 'capture' of most of the influential media platforms in Hungary has been identified as a threat to democracy by the Council of Europe Commissioner on Human Rights.[46] However, it also constitutes a flagrant breach of Hungary's Fundamental Law, which stipulates that: 'Hungary shall recognise and protect the freedom and diversity of the press, and shall ensure the conditions for free dissemination of information necessary for the formation of democratic public opinion' (Freedom and Responsibility, Article IX(2)). In reality, Fidesz has done everything in its power to reduce the diversity and freedom of the press in Hungary, and has treated the free dissemination of objective, verifiable information as a potential threat to its political ascendancy.

5 CONCLUSIONS

> 'Well, in our country,' said Alice, still panting a little,
> 'you'd generally get to somewhere else – if you ran very fast
> for a long time, as we've been doing.'
> 'A slow sort of country!' said the Queen.
> 'Now, here, you see, it takes all the running you can do,
> to keep in the same place.'
>
> Lewis Carroll, *Through the Looking-Glass*

The dwindling numbers of journalists, scholars and writers in Hungary who remain determined to expose the corruption, nepotism and authoritarianism of the Orbán government are having to run faster and faster just to stay in the same place. As the fate of the Central European University (CEU) and of a succession of independent media platforms illustrates – Népszabadság, Klub Rádió, Index, etc. – it is becoming increasingly difficult for independent voices and institutions to operate in Hungary. They have been variously forced to close (e.g., Népszabadság),[47] compelled to relocate most of their activities abroad (e.g., the CEU),[48] deprived of their editorial independence (e.g., Index), or arbitrarily denied a licence to broadcast (e.g., Klub Rádió).[49] Many of the remaining independent media platforms are in a state of almost constant financial crisis due to government policies and the well-founded fears of potential advertisers and subscribers that they will be subject to retaliation by the authorities if they are known to support 'dissident' media outlets. As the Council of Europe Commissioner on Human Rights noted in a recent memorandum on freedom of expression and media freedom in Hungary:[50]

46. Memorandum on freedom of expression and media freedom in Hungary, *supra* n. 4, paras. 27, 28, 40.
47. Krisztina Than & Marton Dunai, *Thousands rally after Hungary's leading leftist newspaper unexpectedly shuts*, Reuters (8 October 2016), https://www.reuters.com/article/us-hungary-newspaper-idUSKCN1280NU.
48. Stephen Pogany, *CEU and Hungary's War Against the Enlightenment*, Social Europe (15 November 2018), https://socialeurope.eu/ceu-and-hungarys-war-against-the-enlightenment.
49. *MFRR calls for EU action as Hungary's last independent radio is silenced*, Media Freedom Rapid Response (4 February 2021), https://www.ecpmf.eu/mfrr-calls-for-eu-action-as-hungarys-last-independent-radio-is-silenced/.
50. *Memorandum on freedom of expression and media freedom in Hungary, supra* n. 4, para. 40.

> The combined effects of a politically controlled media regulatory authority and sustained and distorting state intervention in the media market have eroded the conditions for media pluralism and the freedom of expression in Hungary. While independent voices can still be heard ... such voices have been systematically crowded out. Free political debate and the free exchange of diverse opinions, which are the prerequisites for democratic societies to thrive, have been severely curtailed, particularly outside the capital. The situation is exacerbated by sustained smear campaigns against human rights defenders and independent voices, which are designed to stifle civil society and send a clear and chilling message that there will be prompt retaliation against any form of criticism against the government.

As in the perplexing world that Alice discovered through the looking-glass, visitors to Hungary, particularly if they are alert and politically literate, will encounter a strange and disconcerting environment. Familiar words and phrases - democracy, Christian culture, human rights, constitutionalism, the rule of law - no longer mean what they do in most other European countries or in constitutional democracies in other continents. The Orbán regime has appropriated these terms and, Humpty Dumpty-like, it has given them new definitions of its choosing.

Attentive visitors to Hungary will also discover that, like the Queen in *Through the Looking-Glass*, many Hungarians have learnt to believe impossible things. Exposed to relentless disinformation by the Fidesz-dominated media, a sizeable proportion of Hungarians - particularly those unable to access news or other information from foreign sources - genuinely believe that a Jewish nonagenarian living in New York state is plotting to undermine Hungary's political independence and cultural integrity, that liberals and human rights activists are facilitating the destruction of Europe by promoting the interests of refugees and sexual minorities, that Vladimir Putin is fully justified in waging a bloody and destructive war against Ukraine, and that only Viktor Orbán and Fidesz can be trusted to govern Hungary and to safeguard its vital interests. Together with efforts by the government in Warsaw to drastically undermine judicial independence in Poland,[51] Orbán's determination to dismantle the remnants of liberal constitutionalism in Hungary is a salutary reminder of the need to defend the values proclaimed over 30 years ago in the Charter of Paris for a New Europe.

51. On the background to successive infringement proceedings launched by the EU Commission against Poland arising, in part, from the latter's failure to safeguard judicial independence *see, e.g.*, *Rule of Law: Commission launches infringement procedure against Poland for violations of EU law by its Constitutional Tribunal* (22 December 2021), https://ec.europa.eu/commission/presscorner/detail/en/ip_21_7070. On 15 July 2021, the Grand Chamber of the Court of Justice of the European Union ruled, *inter alia*, that the disciplinary regime introduced for judges in Poland is incompatible with Article 19(1) of the Treaty on European Union. Case C-791/19, *European Commission v. Republic of Poland* (15 July 2021). In separate proceedings concerning the Disciplinary Chamber of the Polish Supreme Court the Court of Justice imposed interim measures on Poland. Case C-204/21 R., *European Commission v. Republic of Poland* (14 July 2021).

CHAPTER 4

Is There a Concept of Law of Exception in France? Some Reflections on the Legal Issues Raised by the COVID-19 Pandemic

Jacques Ziller

This contribution is based on the main part of the introduction to a study in the French language on the law applied in France since the outbreak of the COVID-19 virus. It was carried out in May 2021 at the request of the European Parliament's research services.[1] Like other authors of national studies I was asked to present the concept of 'droit d'exception' in scholarship, its historical evolution, and the main mechanisms that were in force in French law to deal with 'abnormal situations'. These questions have led me to a new reflection, which I believe could be of interest to Patrick Birkinshaw a distinguished European scholar who has always been deeply interested in comparative law.

The French legal system has long developed mechanisms to deal with emergencies, exceptional circumstances and crisis situations, giving the executive branch of government specific means that go beyond those applicable in normal times. The terms 'droit d'exception' has a pejorative connotation in France.[2] Nevertheless, we had to use

1. *Droit d'exception, une perspective de droit comparé – France : lois d'urgence pour faire face à l'épidémie de Covid-19*, EPRS | Service de recherche du Parlement européen, PE 690.624 – Mai 2021. If no other mentions the translations from French are mine.
2. V. SECRÉTARIAT GÉNÉRAL DE LA DÉFENSE NATIONALE: *La France face au terrorisme – Livre blanc du Gouvernement sur la sécurité intérieure face au terrorisme*, La Documentation française, 2006, available at https://www.vie-publique.fr/rapport/28148-france-face-au-terrorisme-livre-blanc-sur-la-securite-interieure p. 53: 'In terms of principles, our country has chosen to build an original penal system to prevent and repress terrorism. The central element is the law of 9 September 1986, adopted after the wave of attacks perpetrated in 1985 and 1986. It is not a law of exception. It is a specialised criminal regime adapted to the particular nature of terrorism. The fight against terrorism is not the only one to be covered by a specialised law. This is also the case for organised crime.'

these terms for comparison purposes, in the sense of the law of exceptional situations 'in a democratic society based on the rule of law' – to use the terminology of the European Convention for the Protection of Human Rights and Fundamental Freedoms (ECHR).

In France health and economic crisis caused by the COVID-19 epidemic led to the adoption of the law of 23 March 2020, which introduced the concept of a 'state of health emergency' (état d'urgence sanitaire). It was useful to see how the 'law of exception' has been analysed by French scholarship and to trace its evolution in the French legal order in order to allow comparison with the legal orders of other European Union states without risking too much misunderstanding, before presenting and analysing the law in force in 2020-2021, and more specifically that resulting from the COVID-19 epidemic.

1 'LAW OF EXCEPTION': THE CONCEPT IN FRENCH SCHOLARSHIP

Montesquieu wrote in L'Esprit des lois, published in 1748: 'I confess, however, that the practice of the freest peoples that have ever been on earth makes me believe that there are cases where it is necessary to put, for a moment, a veil over liberty, as one hides the statues of the gods'.[3] This reflection was refuted by Mirabeau, one of the most important politicians of the Revolution of 1789, who wrote L'Essai sur le despotisme[4] while he was imprisoned in Vincennes from 1777 to 1780: 'This deserves to be examined without doubt; for the testimony of this illustrious and respectable philosopher against the liberty that he has sometimes defended so well, although one has never dared to say it all, is truly frightening. [...] Let us dare to say that this great man has embellished a very false maxim with an imposing image'.[5]

To put these quotations in context, François Saint-Bonnet's summary is worth quoting: 'When the triumphant discourse of absolute monarchy prevailed in the 17th century, the monarch was not denied any power. The question of the state of emergency becomes almost irrelevant, at least in legal terms, because the king never has to break the law to safeguard his state. On the contrary, preservation from ruin is the very foundation of absolute monarchy. The question became topical again when, from the 17th century onwards in political and legal philosophy, and from 1789 in fact, it was intended to limit once more the power of rulers by law'.[6]

The two quotations from Montesquieu and Mirabeau sum up the French debate on the law of exception; but it was not until the First World War that reflections on necessity, urgency or exception really developed in legal scholarship, in particular with

3. Montesquieu: *De L'Esprit des lois*, Book XII, Chapter XIX *Comment on suspend l'usage de la liberté dans la République.*
4. Mirabeau: *Essai Sur Le Despotisme*, 1776, reprint, London, Gale, 2011.
5. Mirabeau: *Des Lettres De Cachet Et Des Prisons D'Etat : Ouvrage Posthume, Composé En 1778* (1782), Chapter IX.
6. Saint-Bonnet, F.: 'L'État d'exception. Présentation de l'ouvrage l'État d'exception, Paris, PUF (Léviathan), 2001', in *Revue juridique de l'Ouest*, 2004-2, pp. 233-247; available at https://www.persee.fr/doc/juro_0990-1027_2004_num_17_2_2772.

the two great masters of public law of the time, Hauriou and Duguit[7] and their contemporary Carré de Malberg.[8]

In my opinion there is no general concept of 'droit d'exception' or 'état d'exception' in French legal scholarship. Although the fashion of citing Carl Schmitt's writings while neglecting to take into account his role as a leading Nazi jurist has also become widespread in France over the last few decades, it would be a misunderstanding to attribute to him an influence on French public law scholarship with regard to the subject studied here. At most, it can be said that Schmitt found in Hauriou some of his ideas on exception, which he then took to extreme consequences that Hauriou, a liberal conservative, would certainly not have adopted. On the contrary, if there was an influence of German legal scholarship on French legal scholarship of public law, it was through the notion of the rule of law (Etat de droit - Rechtstaat), developed in particular in France by Carré de Malberg with a view to overcoming the limits of the classic principle of legality that were due to the traditional conception of public law since the French Revolution, based on the notion taken from Jean-Jacques Rousseau of 'law as an expression to the general will'. One of the fundamental reasons for the late development of legal thinking on exception in French public law is undoubtedly due to constitutional instability: no less than 15 constitutional texts succeeded one another in less than a century, from the Revolution of 1789 to the constitutional laws of the Third Republic of 1875, which were de facto suspended by the constitutional law of 10 July 1940 that conferred full powers on the Government under the authority and signature of Marshal Pétain to take any measure necessary to promulgate a new Constitution of the 'Etat français' (as opposed to the 'République française'). Following the two referendums of 1946, the constitutional laws of 1875 were replaced by a new constitution, known as that of the Fourth Republic, and then by the constitution of 4 October 1958, known as the Fifth Republic, which is currently in force.

The First World War led the Government to adopt a number of measures,[9] sometimes challenged by appeals for annulment ('recours pour excès de pouvoir') before the Conseil d'État (C.E.); publicist scholarship did not fail to comment on the case law, in particular the Heyriès judgment of 28 June 1918, which admitted the possibility of suspending the application of an act of Parliament by government decree. This was the beginning of the doctrinal debate on the law of exceptional circumstances.

---

7. V. EISENMANN, CH.: 'Deux théoriciens du droit : Duguit et Hauriou', in *Revue philosophique* 1930, p. 231 f.
8. *See* in particular CARRÉ DE MALBERG, R.: *La loi, expression de la volonté générale*, Paris, Economica, reprinted 1984 and CARRÉ de MALBERG, R.: *Contribution à la théorie générale de l'État*, Paris, Sirey, 1920 (CNRS, reprinted 1962). Carré de Malberg is considered to be the major scholarly source of the introduction in France of judicial review of acts of Parliament. This review, which began with the 1946 Constitution, was consolidated with the 1958 Constitution and considerably developed thanks to the 2008 constitutional revision, which introduced the procedure of 'priority question of constitutionality'.
9. *See* in particular SAINT-BONNET, F.: 'L'abnégation des hommes, le sacrifice de la légalité. La Grande Guerre et l'impossible naissance d'un droit administratif d'exception', in *Jus Politicum - Revue de Droit Politique*, n° 15, 2016, available at http://juspoliticum.com/article/L-abnegation-des-hommes-le-sacrifice-de-la-legalite-La-Grande-Guerre-et-l-impossible-naissance-d-un-droit-administratif-d-exception-1064.html.

Maurice Hauriou (1856-1929) applauded the C.E.'s jurisprudence in Heyriès, with the oft-quoted consideration that 'It must be recognised that laws of individual guarantees are made for normal times, and that for a long time the need to suspend them, at least in part, in abnormal times, when the salvation of the State takes precedence over individual convenience, has been noted'.[10] The rest of his reasoning, which is less often quoted, must be taken into consideration in order to understand it: 'The executive power does not acquire the right to suspend all kinds of laws; it acquires the right to suspend those that would halt the progress of the State, even the laws of individual guarantees, because abnormal times bring to the forefront what, in normal times, is in the background; in normal times, individual liberty is in the forefront; in times of war, it is the legitimate defence of the State. The constitutional interpretation provided here by the administrative judge is slightly constructive, as the Americans say [...]'.[11] Hauriou 'considers that the rule according to which the executive must carry out its mission of Government is constitutional in nature and prevails over the others: the safeguarding of the fatherland must not be sacrificed to legality'.[12] Hauriou used the term necessities in wartime and peacetime.

Léon Duguit (1859-1928) - a great opponent of Hauriou, who rejected in favour of the theory of public service the latter's theory of public authority as a basis for administrative law - considered the Heyriès judgment to be 'incoherent' and 'dangerous'.[13] He considered that government could adopt regulations 'outside the cases where the law expressly gives them the power to do so' but that it was necessary 'to avoid at all costs ending up with the German theory of Nothrecht'.[14] To do this, such 'regulations of necessity' could only be adopted under three cumulative conditions: '1° There must be a foreign war, an armed insurrection or a general strike of civil servants; (2) It must be materially impossible to convene Parliament, or at least Parliament must not have been convened, and there must be such urgency that the minimum time necessary to convene and convene Parliament cannot be postponed; (3) The legislative regulation must be made with the intention, expressed or not, but real, that it should be submitted to Parliament for ratification as soon as it is possible to convene it at its first meeting'.

In contrast to these two authors, Raymond Carré de Malberg (1861-1935) - author of A History of Exception in Roman Law and in Ancient French Procedure[15] - absolutely rejected 'any law of necessity, even if it were only a conditional right to issue regulations of necessity subject to subsequent validation'. As the philosopher Marie Goupy excellently summarises: 'Such a law of necessity, whatever its forms or modes

---

10. Hauriou, M.: 'Pleins pouvoirs du gouvernement pendant la guerre et droit à la communication du dossier', Note under C.E., 28 June 1918, *Heyriès*, Sirey 1922.3.49. Available under *Revue générale du droit on line*, 2015, number 15499 (www.revuegeneraledudroit.eu/?p = 15499).
11. *Ibid.*
12. According to the very good synthesis of Cassella, S., in his thesis *La Nécessité en Droit International: de l'état de nécessité aux situations de nécessité*, The Hague, Martinus Nijhoff, 2011, p. 106.
13. Duguit, L.: *Traité de droit constitutionnel, Tome Troisième La Théorie générale de l'État*, 3rd ed., 1938, pp. 178 and 756.
14. *Ibid.*
15. Carré de Malberg, R.: *Histoire De L'exception En Droit Romain Et Dans L'ancienne Procédure Française*, Paris, Rousseau, 1887, reprinted in Nabu Press, 2010.

of application, is radically contrary to the positivist theses defended by Carré de Malberg, for whom there is no other law than positive law. But, in addition, the jurist makes a severe criticism of the thesis according to which circumstances could authorise the Government, from a legal point of view, to issue decrees outside its legal powers, albeit under the condition of subsequent validation'.[16] As the same author points out, Carré de Malberg, on the other hand, admitted 'a political theory of the state of necessity: his argument here therefore concerns only the legal character of such regulations of necessity'.[17]

In fact, rather than a scholarly debate on the 'law of exception', it was part of a wider debate concerning three distinct, albeit related, issues: separation of powers - between Parliament and Government - the definition of statutes - in the material or formal sense - and the legitimate limitations of rights and freedoms, which have been reserved to the legislator since the Revolution of 1789. In the background to this debate, it should be remembered firstly that since the Revolution the principle of equality admits no exceptions (the Civil Code of 1804 was maintained in force during the restoration of the Monarchy in 1815); secondly, that legislative power is normally exercised by a parliament elected by direct universal suffrage (male at that time) - already applied in 1791-1792, then from 1799 to 1815 and finally from 1848 onwards (despite restrictions for French nationals living abroad, the clergy, the military and prisoners) - and thirdly, that the unitary nature of the French Republic implies a united and centralised legislative power - which does not, however, prevent a progressive decentralisation of executive functions.

In order to avoid misunderstandings, it is also necessary to clarify the constitutional context in which these three authors were operating. The three constitutional laws of 1875 were far from being a coherent whole and did not include a declaration of rights. The law of 25 February 1875 on the organisation of public powers contained only nine articles with a total of 566 words, and provided that 'Legislative power is exercised by two assemblies: the Chamber of Deputies and the Senate' (Article 1) and that 'The President of the Republic [...] promulgates the laws when they have been voted by the two Chambers; he supervises and ensures their execution [...] each of the acts of the President of the Republic must be countersigned by a minister' (Article 3). Parliamentary practice had attributed the exercise of executive power to the Government headed by a President of the Council (a body not provided for in the constitutional laws). Following the wartime precedent, from 1924 onwards, the Governments got into the habit of adopting 'decree-laws' (décrets-lois), for which they requested prior authorisation from the Chambers. The discussion on the exception was focused on the question of the constitutionality of the decree-laws, which could not be decided by the supreme courts (C.E. and Cour de Cassation). It was the C.E. which, developing general principles of law, tried as far as possible to fill the gaps in these texts by

16. Goupy, M.: *L'essor de la théorie juridico-politique sur l'état d'exception dans l'entre-deux guerres en France et en Allemagne: une genèse de l'état d'exception comme enjeu pour la démocratie*, Thèse de doctorat de philosophie, École normale supérieure de Lyon, 2011, p. 83. *See* by the same author: *L'état d'exception ou l'impuissance autoritaire de l'État à l'époque du libéralisme*, Paris, CNRS, 2016.
17. *Ibid.*, p. 81, note 202.

referring to the content of the Declaration of the Rights of Man and of the Citizen of 1789 on the one hand, and by developing the theory of exceptional circumstances on the other. To this must be added the judge made theory of government acts (actes de gouvernement), the scope of which had been reduced since its invention in the 1830s, and which allowed the C.E., in a context of growing governmental instability, not to interfere in the relationship between Parliament and Government by reviewing acts concerning this relationship. The Constitutions of 1946 and 1958 attempted to remedy these shortcomings by setting up numerous instruments for rationalised parliamentarism, which only really made their effects felt with the 1958 Constitution.

In addition to Hauriou, Duguit and Carré de Malberg, Joseph Barthélémy (1874-1945), who strongly criticised the measures adopted during the First World War on the basis of the 1849 State of Siege Act, should be mentioned;[18] liberal at the time, Barthélémy later became increasingly reactionary and was Minister of Justice from 1941 to 1943 under the regime of Marshal Pétain.

According to my opinion, after the Second World War, the more recent French scholarship was essentially limited to commenting on the positive law established since 1946, with only in some cases more extensive references to the theses developed in France and Germany between the two world wars.[19] The scholarship has had little influence on the development of positive law regarding exception; the case law of the supreme courts and the Conseil constitutionnel, as well as the opinions of the C.E. on draft legislation, have had a decisive role in the evolution of the law. Since the ratification of the ECHR in 1974, the case law of the European Court of Human Rights has played a growing role and has also led to the development of the doctrine on Article 15 of the ECHR – Derogation in case of urgency.[20]

2 LAW OF EXCEPTION AND FRENCH LAW: HISTORICAL EVOLUTION

It was with the Revolution of 1789 that France adopted for the first time a written constitutional text, which enshrined the separation of powers: the 'Articles of Constitution' voted between 3 September and 1 October and promulgated on 3 November 1789 by King Louis XVI at the same time as the Declaration of the Rights of Man and the Citizen of 26 August. The terms 'exception', 'emergency', or 'derogation' do not appear in them. The general rule does not suffer any exception since the abolition of privileges during the night of 4 August, as specified in Article 1 of the Declaration of Rights: 'Men

18. Barthélémy, J.: 'Le droit public en temps de guerre', in *Revue du Droit Public*, 1915 (pp. 134-162, pp. 310-359 and pp. 545-575), 1916 (pp. 73-119 and pp. 552-586) and 1917 (pp. 146-151). Saint-Bonnet, cited *supra* n. 6.
19. *See* in particular Goupy, M. cited above, as well as de Beaud, O. and Guérin-Bargues, C.: *L'état d'urgence: une étude constitutionnelle, historique et critique*, Paris, LGDJ, 2nd ed. 2018.
20. *See, e.g.*, Tavernier, P.: 'Commentaire de l'article 15', in Pettiti, L.-E., Decaux, E. and Imbert, P.-H. (eds): *La Convention européenne des droits de l'Homme. Commentaire article par article, Paris, Economica*, 2nd ed. 1999, p. 489 f., and Coussirat-Coustère, V.: 'La réserve française à l'article 15 de la Convention européenne des droits de l'homme', *Journal du Droit International*, 1975, pp. 269-293.

are born and remain free and equal in rights. Social distinctions can only be based on the common good'. It is therefore established in French public law that there can be no derogation from the principle of equality before the law. The principle of equality was taken up again two years later in the Preamble to the Constitution of 1791: 'There is no longer, for any part of the Nation, nor for any individual, any privilege or exception to the common law of all French people'.

It is essential to recall a series of details concerning the following constitutions in order to understand the evolution of the 'law of exception' up to the adoption of the first law on the state of siege in 1849 and since then, because France has a long experience of exceptional circumstances, which explain the content of the positive law in force in 2020 when the epidemic developed, and then during the epidemic of COVID-19.

3 FROM THE CONSTITUTION OF 1791 TO THE SECOND REPUBLIC

In the Constitution of 1791, only the application of exceptional rules of procedure was provided for in cases of emergency for the adoption of decrees by the legislature, with only one reading instead of three. Emergency decrees (at the time the term decree was synonymous with law) were provisional in nature and were in any case adopted by the ordinary legislature. The question of a law of exception arose when France went to war in 1792, because Louis XVI vetoed acts deemed necessary by the National Assembly. It was then that Condorcet (1743-1794, mathematician, economist, philosopher and important politician of the Revolution) theorised for the first time what would later be taken up by Hauriou in particular: 'an irrevocable [constitutional] law which would prevent action when action is obviously necessary, and which would leave the national will no means of manifesting itself when public salvation demands that it pronounce itself; such a law would be an absurdity and a veritable tyranny'. During the same debate, the deputy Torné quoted Cicero: 'it matters little [....] that [extreme measures] were not in conformity with the Constitution; the true Constitution is all in these words: the salvation of the fatherland is the supreme law'[21] [salus populi suprema lex esto].[22] The King was suspended from his powers against the text of the Constitution, following the episode of the flight to Varenne (20-21 June 1792).

After the beheading of Louis XVI and the abolition of royalty by the Decree of 21-22 September 1792, the National Convention declared on 25 September 1792 that 'the French Republic is one and indivisible' and set about formulating a new Constitution, which was approved by a referendum (the first held in France), the results of which were proclaimed on 4 August 1793. The Constitution of 1793, or Constitution of Year I, contained no provision for a state of exception or emergency, even though France was at war and the Convention – elected by universal suffrage – introduced the Terror. A decree of 19 Vendémiaire Year II (10 October 1793) proclaimed the Government 'revolutionary until peace' and formally suspended the application of the

21. Quoted by Saint-Bonnet, *supra* n. 6, p. 241.
22. Cicero: *De legibus*, III, 3, 8, https://www.thelatinlibrary.com/cicero/leg3.shtml.

Constitution. All powers were concentrated by the Convention, including part of the criminal justice, in the hands of the Comité de Salut Public, a parliamentary standing committee chaired by Robespierre (1758-1794).

After the fall of Robespierre on 27 July 1794, the Constitution remained suspended. A new text was drawn up and approved by referendum: the Constitution of Year III, of 22 August 1795. This text established a very strict separation of powers between the bicameral Legislative Body elected by censual vote and the five-member Directory elected by the Legislative Body, a separation designed to guarantee against dictatorship. As in the Constitution of 1791, exceptions were only made to the ordinary legislative procedure in cases of emergency, with a reduction in the number of readings. Revision of the Constitution was particularly difficult, which was one of the reasons – from a formal point of view – for Napoleon Bonaparte's coup d'Etat on 9 November 1799 (18 Brumaire). The Directory was replaced by a three-member Consulate which had a new text drafted in 11 days, adopted on 13 December, the Constitution of 22 Frimaire An VIII, promulgated on 25 December 1799 and subsequently ratified by plebiscite on 7 February 1800. The Constitution did not contain a declaration of rights and established a very limited and unbalanced separation of executive and legislative powers between, on the one hand, three Chambers exercising legislative power on the proposal of the C.E., and, on the other, an executive power of three members (Consuls) dominated by the first of them, Napoleon Bonaparte, the other two having only an advisory function. This text was amended by the organic senatus-consult of 28 Floréal Year XII (18 May 1804), known as the Constitution of the Year XII, which replaced the Consulate with a hereditary Empire and further reduced the little separation of powers that existed between the executive and the legislature. Neither the text of 1799 nor that of 1804 contained provisions for exception or emergency: such provisions were not necessary because of the concentration of powers. The Acte additionnel aux Constitutions de l'Empire of 22 April 1815, drafted by the liberal opposition leader Benjamin Constant (1767-1830), transformed the Empire into a parliamentary monarchy; the text, which only applied until the following July, did not contain any provisions for exception or emergency either, even though France was still at war.

A year earlier, following the abdication of Napoleon Bonaparte, the heir to the Bourbon royal family, Louis XVIII, restored the Monarchy by a Declaration of 2 May 1814 and on 4 June 'granted' the Constitutional Charter which became the constitution of France until 1830 – with the parenthesis of the 'Hundred Days' of Napoleon's return between 20 March and 8 July 1815. The Charter established a parliamentary monarchy on the model of the Kingdom of England before the political role of the Sovereign was erased in 1685. There was thus a double responsibility of the Government, before the King who appointed the ministers and to whom belonged 'the executive power', and if necessary before the Parliament, because the Chamber of Deputies could impeach them and the Chamber of Peers judge them 'for high treason'. In practice, the Charter allowed for a full bicameralism; legislation had to be passed by a majority of both Houses and the King 'made the regulations and orders necessary for the execution of the laws and the security of the State'. Louis XVIII's successor in 1824, his brother Charles X, faced with a liberal majority in the Chamber following the 1830 elections, passed ordinances suspending the freedom of the press and amended the Charter without the agreement of the Chambers, which led to the revolution of 27, 28 and 29 July. The Chamber of Deputies called his distant cousin the Duke of Orleans to the throne and both Chambers amended the Charter extensively, published as the Constitutional Charter of 14 August 1830. The new Charter reinforced the separation of powers and the parliamentary character of the regime. The Constitutional Charter did not contain any specific provision for emergency or emergency law in either the 1814 or the 1830 version. The use of ordinances - in principle an act of the executive function - by Charles X in practice established a regime of exception and was considered unconstitutional by the opposition. From the outset, the 'July Monarchy' was marked by insurrectionary movements that were aggravated by the economic situation, the emergence of an exploited working class, and the conservatism of the Guizot government.

After less than 18 years, this led to the revolution of 22-25 February 1848 in Paris, which opened the cycle of liberal revolutions in Europe. A Provisional Government was established, to prepare for the election of a Constituent Assembly in April, which drafted the Constitution of 1848, known as the Second Republic, of 25 November. The Constitution established a very strict separation of powers between the President of the Republic, who held executive power and was elected by universal suffrage for four years without the possibility of re-election, and the National Assembly, which held legislative power and was elected for three years. Article 68 provided that in the event of an attempt by the President to dissolve the National Assembly, prorogue it or obstruct the exercise of his mandate, he was automatically deposed, and executive power passed to the Assembly. As with the previous texts, the only provisions concerning urgency concerned the reduction of the number of readings necessary for the adoption of a law.

It was under the ordinary procedure that the National Assembly drew up and adopted the law of 9 August 1849 on the state of siege - still in force in an amended version - which was applied during the Paris Commune, from 1871 to 1874, and then during the two world wars, from 2 August 1914 to 12 October 1919 and from 1er September 1929 to 12 October 1945.

4 FROM THE SECOND EMPIRE TO THE FOURTH REPUBLIC

The rigidity of the 1848 Constitution led Louis-Napoleon Bonaparte, elected President of the Republic in 1848, to the coup d'Etat of 2 December 1851. On 14 January he promulgated the new Constitution of 1852, which was modified by Imperial Decree of 2 December 1852, transforming the Republic into an Empire. The Constitution of 1852 established a regime quite similar to that of the First Empire, although simpler and with a slightly more pronounced separation of powers. Apart from the usual provision for the reduction of the number of readings in case of emergency for the adoption of the law, the Constitution of 1852 contained for the first time particular provisions, allowing the Senate on the proposal of the President of the Republic [Emperor], to provide 'by emergency measures, for all that is necessary for the running of the Government' in case of dissolution of the Corps Législatif by the latter. Unlike the Corps Législatif, which was elected by direct universal suffrage for six years, the Senate was composed of members almost all of whom were appointed by the President of the Republic [Emperor]. The Constitution was amended in 1870 – approved by plebiscite on 8 May and entered into force on 21 May – with the establishment of a system of parliamentary monarchy, including the abolition of the Senate's emergency powers in the event of dissolution. On 19 July of the same year France declared war on Prussia; the Emperor capitulated on 2 September and on 4 September the Republic was proclaimed. A provisional government had a new electoral law passed by the National Assembly, and the elections of 8 February 1871 set up a new Assembly which had great difficulty in adopting a new constitution, because of its division between two opposing monarchist currents and the Republicans.

The National Assembly adopted three constitutional laws, conceived as provisional texts, but which endured: the Constitution of 1875, of the IIIrd Republic, paradoxically guaranteed the longest period of constitutional stability that France had known so far: 65 years (the same as for the current constitution of 1958). These constitutional laws had established a parliamentary regime characterised by full bicameralism, with a Government appointed by the President of the Republic (elected by the Chambers together) and accountable to both the Chamber of Deputies and the Senate, which had equal powers to pass laws. The Chamber of Deputies could be dissolved by the President of the Republic only after the Senate had given its assent – which never happened. The Chamber was elected by direct universal suffrage and the Senate by indirect suffrage – 225 elected by the departments and colonies, and 75 by the National Assembly. The provisional nature of these texts and the fact that the law on the state of siege had been in existence since 1849 explain why they contained no provisions relating to exception or emergency, apart from the obligation for the President of the Republic to promulgate within three days the laws declared urgent by the two Chambers.

On 10 July 1940, when France was invaded by German troops and the Government was withdrawn to Vichy, the two Chambers of Parliament, meeting as the National Assembly, voted full powers to Marshal Pétain to head the Government and prepare a 'new constitution for the French State'. This constitution was never promulgated and Marshal Pétain's regime therefore remained a regime of exception in every sense of the word, based on a series of provisional texts until the establishment of a Provisional Government presided over by General de Gaulle on 3 June 1944, installed in Paris after the Liberation on 31 August. The constitutional law of 2 November 1945 organised the provisional regime which allowed the adoption, after two referendums, of the Constitution of the Fourth Republic.

In all, in less than two centuries, since the 'Articles of Constitution' of November 1789, France had thus experienced provisional or exceptional regimes for a total of more than 12 years, and was at war in Europe for 26 years, with the occupation by enemy troops of part of its territory in 1792-1793, 1815, 1870-1873, 1914-1918 and 1940-1942, as well as its entire territory in Europe in 1942-1944, i.e., a total of more than 12 years; to this must be added three revolutions and two coups d'état.

In 1946, two constitutional texts were drafted. A first draft of the Constitution of 19 April 1946 was rejected by referendum on 5 May; it established a regime of strong concentration of powers by the National Assembly. It also contained a declaration of rights, completer and more updated than that of 1789, which took over from the Constitution of the year III the principle of resistance to oppression in its Article 21: 'When the Government violates the freedoms and rights guaranteed by the Constitution, resistance in all its forms is the most sacred of rights and the most imperious of duties'. As usual, the text contained provisions on emergency legislative procedure, as well as on the extension of the mandate of deputies in case of emergency. The text drew the lesson of the events of June-July 1940 with a Title IX Exceptional Provisions, which allowed the adoption by the National Assembly of a 'law proclaiming the Republic in danger', and to extend the mandate of deputies, and which prohibited the dissolution of the Assembly during its application. This was the first time in France that a constitution contained such provisions for exceptional circumstances. No reference was made to Articles 1-21 relating to freedoms. To this must be added Article 124, according to which 'In the event of occupation of all or part of the metropolitan territory by foreign troops, no revision procedure may be initiated or continued', and Article 125 prohibiting any revision that would undermine 'the republican form of government' – in reference to the 1940 law instructing Marshal Pétain to prepare a 'new constitution for the *French state*' (emphasis added).

After the rejection of the April draft, a new text was elaborated by a new Constituent Assembly, and adopted by referendum on 13 October 1946: the Constitution of the Fourth Republic, which established a stronger separation of powers with a rationalised parliamentary system. The 1946 Constitution established a rationalised parliamentary system with a bicameral parliament: the Government, headed by the President of the Council of Ministers, was accountable only to the National Assembly, which could override amendments adopted by the Council of the Republic (upper house of Parliament). The Constitution did not contain a Declaration of Rights, but a Preamble, still in force, which completed the Declaration of 1789. As usual, and as in the previous text, there were provisions for the emergency legislative procedure. Similarly, the text of Articles 124 and 125 of the April draft was included in Articles 94 and 95. However, the provisions relating to exceptional circumstances were not included. The Constitution of 1946 was subsequently revised by a constitutional law of 7 December 1954, which, among other things, created a legal basis for the adoption of a state of siege regulation by law by supplementing Article 7 of the Constitution.

The Constitution did not, however, provide for a state of emergency, which was regulated by a law of 3 April 1955 on the state of emergency, which is still applicable more than 60 years later and has since been amended. This law was adopted following the insurrection in Algeria – which was not considered a colony but an integral part of the Republic – on 1st November 1954 by the Front de libération nationale, which led to 414 attacks between November 1954 and April 1955, killing 104 people and wounding 86. The law of 3 April 1955 immediately instituted the application of the state of emergency on the territory of Algeria for a period of six months, which was extended for six months on 7 August 1955, and which ended on 16 December 1955.

On 13 May 1958, a military coup was attempted in Algiers with the aim of preventing the installation of the Pflimlin government and imposing a change of policy in favour of keeping Algeria within the Republic. On 17 May, the National Assembly voted for the application of a state of emergency throughout the country, which remained in force until 1er June. From 24 May, a military operation by the putschists was carried out in Corsica, which threatened to be extended to Paris. In response to this danger, following the resignation of the Pflimlin Government, President René Coty appointed General de Gaulle as President of the Council on 1er June, who formed a Government of National Unity with most of the parties represented in the Assembly, except the Communist Party. On 3 June, the National Assembly passed Law No. 58-520 of 3 June 1958 on the full powers granted to the Government of General de Gaulle and a constitutional law. The former gave the Government the power to adopt decrees 'necessary for the recovery of the nation' for a period of six months, which could, in particular, adopt, modify or replace legislative provisions in force, and which had to be ratified by the National Assembly at the end of this period. Although entitled 'with full powers', the law placed limits on these decrees in accordance with the needs of a state governed by the rule of law. The constitutional law instructed the government to draw up a constitutional bill respecting a series of principles relating to democracy, the separation of powers and the protection of freedoms, according to a precise procedure requiring a referendum for its adoption.

5 THE FIFTH REPUBLIC

The new constitutional text thus prepared was submitted to a referendum on 28 September 1958 and approved by 82.60% of voters with a turnout of 80.63% of the electorate. The Constitution of the Fifth Republic came into force on 4 October 1958.

The new Constitution was prepared with the participation of the main leaders of the political parties supporting the government – almost all political parties except the Communist party – as well as members of the C.E. and professors of law. This explains why the main feature of the 1958 Constitution is a highly rationalised parliamentarism, which draws the lessons from the governmental instability of the Third Republic after the First World War, and from the inadequacy of the provisions of the 1946 Constitution to remedy it.

The Government is accountable only to the National Assembly, which has the last word in legislative matters as under the Fourth Republic. The Government has a number of means at its disposal to cope with the absence of a stable majority and to speed up debates when necessary; the Constitution establishes a precise division of regulatory areas between the bicameral Parliament, which votes on the law, and the Government, which adopts decrees, which should also strengthen the efficiency of the legislative and executive work, under the control of an independent Constitutional Council.

Moreover, General de Gaulle wanted to learn the lessons of the disastrous end of the Third Republic in 1940, by giving the President of the Republic a status and appropriate means in the event of serious danger to the territory as in 1940 and to ensure the functioning of the institutions of the French Community – which replaced the French Union of 1946, itself replacing the French colonial Empire – in a context marked by the first decolonisation. He was elected by a college of some 80,000 electors, parliamentarians and elected representatives of the departments and communes; since the revision adopted by referendum on 28 October 1962, the President has been elected by direct universal suffrage, without any change in the powers conferred on him by the Constitution. The text of 4 October 1958 does not include a Declaration of Rights, but is formally linked to the Declaration of 1789 and the Preamble of the Constitution of 1946, which form an integral part of the 'bloc de constitutionnalité' which includes the constitutional texts in force as well as the 'Fundamental principles recognised by the laws of the Republic'[23] identified by the jurisprudence of the Conseil constitutionnel and the C.E.

With regard to the subject matter of this chapter, the relevance of the provisions relating to the emergency legislative procedure and ordinances, which perfect similar mechanisms established by previous constitutions, should be highlighted in particular. More precisely than the Constitutional Act of 7 December 1954, the 1958 Constitution provides that a state of siege is decreed in the Council of Ministers and that its extension beyond 12 days can only be authorised by Parliament (Article 36). However, the Constitution does not mention a state of emergency. An important innovation is Article 16 which contains provisions similar in part to those of Title IX of the draft constitution of April 1946, which allow the President of the Republic to act, after review by the Conseil constitutionnel

Without going into the merits of the texts and jurisprudence relating to exceptional circumstances, it can be stressed that the 'law of exception' existing in 2020 is the fruit of a very long experience of wars, coups d'Etat and violent disturbances, which the institutions of the Republic have tried to deal with by preserving human rights and fundamental freedoms and democracy, and by adapting the separation of the executive/legislative powers to the necessity of emergency measures. This is why the constitutional revision of 23 July 2008 on the modernisation of the institutions of the Fifth Republic introduced into the constitutional text the notion of 'state of crisis' (Articles 42(4) and 48(3), a concept which is not defined by the constitutional text, but which one can think of as referring in particular to the state of siege and the state of emergency. The rules and principles of the Constitution and the laws in force were in principle also adapted to deal with natural disasters, in particular earthquakes, storms, cyclones and tidal waves, which are frequent in tropical overseas territories. The constitutional rules were also adapted to complement the existing rules to deal more specifically with a disaster such as the COVID-19 epidemic.

23. These are essentially fundamental laws of the IIIème Republic (18975-1940) relating in particular to freedom of association, freedom of the press and trade union freedom, secularism and the regime of public schools, as well as, where appropriate, certain laws of the Ière Republic (1793-1804) and the IIème Republic (1848-1851).

6 THE POSITIVE LAW ON EXCEPTIONAL CIRCUMSTANCES OR CRISES AT THE TIME OF THE COVID-19 PANDEMIC

Apart from the law of 23 March 2020, a series of earlier legislative provisions still in force are intended to enable the public authorities to deal with exceptional circumstances or crises. A distinction must be made between, on the one hand, the law of 3 April 1955 on the state of emergency and, on the other, numerous provisions scattered throughout the legislation, particularly concerning natural disasters, which could be described as the ordinary law of exceptional circumstances. It should be emphasised that Law No. 2020-290 of 23 March 2020 on the emergency response to the COVID-19 epidemic does not in any way derogate from the rules and principles established by the 1958 Constitution; its rapid adoption is due to the application of these rules in a context where the President of the Republic and the Government could count on a solid majority in the National Assembly.

The President of the Republic and the Government did not wish to apply the law on the state of emergency, and although the law of 23 March 2020 contains a Title I entitled 'The state of health emergency', it is a very different regime from that of the law of 1955.

7 THE ORDINARY LAW OF EXCEPTIONAL CIRCUMSTANCES

In budgetary matters, the Organic Law n° 2001-692 of 1 August 2001 relating to the finance laws contains two fundamental provisions allowing for unforeseen calamities or expenses to be met by an allocation for accidental expenses established in advance (Article 7), as well as by additional credits opened by decree, then ratified by Parliament (Article 13).

In economic matters, Article L.410-2 of the Commercial Code also allows the Government to take temporary measures to combat excessive price increases or decreases in the event of a crisis situation.

In terms of insurance, there has been legislation on the state of natural disasters for four decades. There is also important legislation on agricultural disasters. In terms of health, even before it was reinforced in March 2020 by the law on a state of health emergency, Article L.3131-1 of the Public Health Code allowed the Minister of Health to prescribe the necessary measures in the event of a 'serious health threat' and to empower prefects to take measures to implement his decisions, including individual measures, for example confining people or imposing compulsory vaccinations or prescribing medicines.

The exercise of these powers is of course subject to judicial review by the administrative courts, as well as by the criminal courts in the event of punishment of the offence. The Code of Administrative Justice contains a series of provisions relating to urgency which are particularly relevant to the subject here examined. It is possible before the administrative courts to ask the interim relief judge – a single judge e to order provisional measures.

The référé-liberté, to which Article L.521-2 of the Code applies, allows the interim relief judge, who decides in principle within 48 hours, to decide 'all necessary measures' to safeguard a fundamental freedom, which may include an injunction against the administration: 'When a request to this effect is made and justified by the urgency of the matter, the interim relief judge may order all measures necessary to safeguard a fundamental freedom which a legal person governed by public law or a body governed by private law entrusted with the management of a public service has seriously and manifestly illegally infringed in the exercise of one of its powers. The interim relief judge shall give a ruling within forty-eight hours'. The référé-liberté has developed remarkably since the beginning of the COVID-19 epidemic.

The summary procedure, to which Article L.521-1 of the Code applies, allows the suspension of the execution of administrative decisions that do not seriously and manifestly infringe a fundamental freedom (e.g., a refusal of a residence permit). The interim relief judge decides within a period of time varying from 48 hours to one month or more depending on the urgency.

It is also useful to mention Article L.211-6 of the Code of relations between the public and the administration, according to which 'When absolute urgency has prevented a decision from being motivated, the lack of motivation does not taint this decision with illegality. However, if the interested party so requests, within the time limits of the contentious appeal, the authority that took the decision must, within a period of one month, communicate the reasons to him or her'.

The Penal Code contains a chapter (Articles 699-700) dedicated to the jurisdiction in case of war, mobilisation, state of siege or state of emergency, which is not relevant to the present study.

8 THE LAW OF 3 APRIL 1955 ON THE STATE OF EMERGENCY

The term 'law of exception' can be applied to both state of emergency and state of siege legislation, since they derogate from the ordinary law of exceptional circumstances outlined above. During the outbreak of the COVID-19 epidemic there was obviously no question of declaring a state of siege, and even if the President of the Republic Emmanuel Macron had a martial tone in his address to the French on 16 March 2020, it was obvious that he had not envisaged it. Similarly, it was clear that the state of emergency legislation would not be applied, even though it is applicable 'in case of events which, by their nature and gravity, have the character of a public calamity', but that legislation specific to the current epidemic would be proposed to Parliament. It is important to highlight the main features of the 'state of emergency' legislation, which is clearly distinct from the 'health emergency'. Article 1 of the Law of 3 April 1955 determines the possible territorial scope as well as the situations in which a state of emergency may be declared: 'in case of imminent danger resulting from serious harm to public order', or 'in the event of events which, by their nature and gravity, are of the nature of a public disaster'.

A state of emergency is declared by decree in the Council of Ministers (Article 2) and, beyond 12 days, can only be extended by act of Parliament (Article 2) which sets the definitive duration (Article 3). It ceases at the end of the period provided for, or by a decree, or 15 days after the resignation of the Government or the dissolution of the National Assembly (Article 4).

Once a state of emergency has been declared, the Government, the Minister of the Interior or the prefects, as the case may be, may adopt various measures restricting the exercise of public freedoms. The Minister of the Interior and the prefects may, in areas where the state of emergency is in force, prohibit the movement of persons or vehicles in places and at times fixed by decree (Article 5(1)); order the temporary closure of theatres, public houses and places of assembly and prohibit meetings, processions, parades and gatherings (Article 8).

Other provisions of the law on the state of emergency concern the maintenance of public security through the adoption of repressive measures such as residence bans (Article 5(4)), the dissolution of associations (Article 6(1)), the handing over of weapons (Article 9), house arrest (Article 6), house searches with the possible detention of individuals on the premises, or the blocking of Internet sites (Article 11).

Judicial review of these measures is carried out under ordinary law by the administrative and criminal courts.

It is clear that most of these measures are not relevant in a situation like the COVID-19 epidemic, which is why their application was not considered. The fact that the law of 23 March 2020 creates a 'state of health emergency' does not mean that it is based on the law on the state of emergency; neither its purpose nor its effects are the same, apart from the limitations on the movement of people or vehicles or the temporary closure of theatres, pubs and places of assembly.

9 CASE LAW: THE THEORY OF EXCEPTIONAL CIRCUMSTANCES

In the absence of a constitutional review of laws prior to the 1958 Constitution, the Cour de cassation and the C.E., as well as the Tribunal des Conflits (composed equally of members of the two supreme courts) have developed particularly relevant jurisprudence regarding the protection of public freedoms and fundamental rights in exceptional circumstances.

In the nineteenth century, the C.E. developed the theory of the cases in which the action of annulment (recours pour excès de pouvoir) may be brought – in other words, the grounds for the action for annulment, which were by the way taken up in the Treaty establishing the European Economic Community of 1957 (EC Treaty) in what is now Article 263 Treaty on the Functioning of the European Union: lack of competence, violation of essential procedural requirements, violation of the law (including the Constitution), and misuse of power (use of a power for a purpose other than that provided for by the law). It then limited the application of the theory of government acts to international relations and relations between government and parliament and considered decrees and regulatory acts in general as administrative acts liable to annulment. It also developed the use of general principles of law to circumvent the absence of legal value – until 1946 – of the Declaration of 1789. Finally, it has developed the review of decisions of administrative police authorities with the prohibition of general and absolute measures, a proportionality review technique less systematic in its method than that of the Court of Justice of the European Union or German law, but with a similar result

As far as the judicial courts (civil, criminal, commercial and labour) are concerned, the theory of assault and battery (voie de fait), according to which an action of the administration that is particularly serious in terms of infringing a public freedom, lacking a legal basis or grossly violating the rules of procedure, fell outside the jurisdiction of the administrative court. This theory has lost much of its relevance since the administrative courts were given injunctive powers in 1995.[24] On the other hand, the judicial courts, headed by the Cour de Cassation, remain in the front line in the case of criminal sanctions, which apply in particular to the refusal to apply administrative police decisions.

As far as administrative courts are concerned, the theory of exceptional circumstances is particularly relevant for this study, on the one hand because it inspires most of the constitutional and legislative regimes analysed above, and on the other hand because it remains applicable despite the considerable evolution of French constitutional law since the judgement of the C.E. of 28 June 1918, Heyriès which first established it. According to the C.E.'s own summary, 'The theory of exceptional circumstances authorises the administrative authority to disregard the usual rules of competence and form, but also the respect of substantive principles [for example, freedom of movement]. The administrative judge controls the measures taken under this theory. It assesses the very existence of exceptional circumstances, ensures that the administration was actually unable to take the measure in question in a regular manner and verifies that the acts were taken in the general interest, in particular to ensure the continuity of the State, and were made necessary by the particular circumstances of the moment'.[25]

More than Heyriès, a C.E. judgement of 18 May 1983, Rodes illustrates this theory and why it could apply in the circumstances of the COVID-19 epidemic. In Rodes, in order to deal with a period of eruption of the La Soufrière volcano in the summer of 1976, the Prefect of Guadeloupe had issued a series of orders which went beyond the ordinary police powers of the Prefect, notably by delimiting a so-called dangerous zone subject to a total evacuation order, and by making access to this zone subject to a pass issued by the Prefecture's services, and to the obligation to comply with the instructions of the civil and military authorities. In an atmosphere of controversy fuelled by dissension among vulcanologists as to the risks presented by this eruption, appeals were lodged with the competent administrative court, which rejected them; on appeal, the C.E. noted the elements that made it an exceptional circumstance and confirmed the judgment with a reasoning that is useful for understanding how the theory of exceptional circumstances works:

24. V. Éveil-Lard, G., (ed.): *La guerre des juges aura-t-elle lieu? – Analyse comparée des offices du juge administratif et du juge judiciaire dans la protection des libertés fondamentales*, 2016, online at www.revuegeneraledudroit.eu; in particular the article by T. Augustin: 'La victoire du juge administratif: le nouvel équilibre de l'emprise et de la voie de fait'.

25. https://www.conseil-État.fr/ressources/decisions-contentieuses/les-grandes-decisions-du-conseil-d-État/conseil-d-État-28-juin-1918-heyries.

> Considering that, from the documents in the file, it appears that from the beginning of July 1976, the 'La Soufrière' volcano experienced an unusually high level of activity consisting of eruptions, earthquakes, clouds of ash and mud spills; that these phenomena increased during the month of August, and in particular on 9, 12 and 13 August, and caused panic among the population, which was evacuated from the area threatened by the volcano; that, while the report submitted on 23 July 1976 by the mission of the Institut de Physique du Globe was moderately optimistic, the subsequent conclusions of other specialists were, on the other hand, alarming and announced a major eruption of the volcano on 15 August; that, consequently, in view of these exceptional circumstances of time and place, the prefect was allowed, in the interest of public order, and taking into account the urgency and the limited nature of the geographical area concerned, to issue the above-mentioned orders of 13, 15 and 19 August 1976; that, in view of the new eruptions which occurred in September and, to a lesser extent, in October, he was allowed, for the same reasons, by his order of 15 September 1976, to maintain in force some of the provisions of the order of 15 August, while attenuating their scope, and, by his order of 1 October, to prescribe measures suitable for ensuring the gradual return to normal life in the dangerous zone.

While it was possible for the Government to hope that in the event of a challenge before the administrative courts to the measures taken to deal with the COVID-19 epidemic, the concern for transparency and legal certainty led it to draw up two specific bills, which became the law of 23 March 2020 (No. 2020-290) and the organic law of 30 March 2020 (No. 2020-365) – an organic law was necessary for a particular aspect concerning the time limits for justice. In its opinion on the draft law in question, the C.E. stressed that 'if the jurisprudential theory of exceptional circumstances was able to provide a basis for Decree No. 2020-260 of 16 March 2020 regulating travel in the context of the fight against the spread of the COVID-19 virus, which was issued by the Prime Minister on the basis of his general police powers, and if Article L.3131-1 of the Code of Public Health gave their legal basis to the measures taken by the Minister of Health, such as his order of 14 March 2020 on various measures relating to the fight against the spread of the virus, the existence of a health disaster makes it useful to have a special state of emergency regime in order to have an organised and clear framework for intervention in such a case'.[26]

The purpose of the new legislation was therefore not to introduce exceptions to the ordinary law of exceptional circumstances but to clarify the conditions of application to the COVID-19 epidemic.

10 THE LAW OF 23 MARCH 2020 URGENTLY TO ADDRESS THE COVID-19 EPIDEMIC

Both the adoption and the successive revisions of the Emergency Act of 23 March 2020 to deal with the COVID-19 epidemic and the Organic Act No. 2020-365 of 30 March 2020 to deal with the COVID-19 epidemic, which took place with particular speed, were

26. https://www.conseil-etat.fr/avis-consultatifs/derniers-avis-rendus/au-gouvernement/avis-sur-deux-projets-de-loi-d-urgence-pour-faire-face-a-l-epidemie-de-covid-19.

based on the ordinary law established in the 1958 Constitution. Similarly, the delegation to the Government to take measures by ordinance does not derogate from Article 38 of the Constitution. In substance, the law provides, as has been done in other European countries, for exceptional and provisional measures, but from the point of view of the legal basis and the procedure, it would be wrong to describe it without further clarification as a 'law of exception'.

The legal regime specific to the COVID-19 epidemic is often referred to simply as a 'state of health emergency', but the law of 23 March contains provisions other than those necessary to contain the contagion and to equip the health services urgently; it also concerns economic emergency measures and specific electoral provisions, since municipal elections were scheduled for all the communes of France in March; in addition, the organic law of 30 March contains provisions relating to time limits for justice.

A very clear summary of the law of 23 March is given in the Minutes of the Council of Ministers of 18 March 2020, which explains the purpose of its provisions.[27] The law has four titles.

Title I on the state of health emergency. In the words of the Report: 'Our law currently has two bases for taking health measures: the general police power of the Prime Minister and Article L.3131-1 of the Code of Public Health, which allows the Minister of Health to take, in the event of an epidemic "threat", "any measure to protect the health of the population". For very serious health disasters, such as that of COVID-19, a state of health emergency regime is created, which makes it possible to base any regulatory or individual measure limiting certain freedoms in order to combat the epidemic'.

Title II is devoted to economic emergency measures and adaptation to the fight against the COVID-19 epidemic, and includes powers to take measures by ordinance. According to the Report:

> Firstly, economic and social measures are concerned: support for the cash flow of companies, direct or indirect aid to companies, limiting the termination of employment contracts, use of paid leave, simplification of the law on collective procedures, deferment of water and electricity bills for very small companies, etc. Secondly, this title contains various administrative or jurisdictional measures to adapt legal deadlines, the rules of criminal procedure on pain of nullity, the convening of general meetings of companies or co-ownership managers. Thirdly, the law includes authorisations to facilitate childcare in the context of the closure of childcare facilities. Particular attention is paid to the most vulnerable people with, for example, the extension of the winter truce to suspend rental evictions. Similarly, the law includes measures for people with disabilities, making it possible to adapt the conditions for organising medical and social services and to avoid a breakdown in rights. Finally, provisions are included to ensure the continuity of the functioning of local government bodies.

Title III is devoted to the postponement of the second round of municipal elections. According to the Report: 'On the one hand, the municipal councillors elected

27. https://www.gouvernement.fr/conseil-des-ministres/compte-rendu-du-conseil-des-ministres-du-18-03-2020.

on 15 March in the first round remain in office. On the other hand, in about 5,000 communes, the second round is postponed. The bill specifies the rules applicable to the municipalities and inter-municipalities concerned during the intermediate period between the two rounds [...]'.

Title IV, which was not mentioned in the minutes of the Council of Ministers, concerns parliamentary oversight: in order for them to carry out their mission, the deadline for the report of committees of enquiry set up before the publication of the law and whose report has not yet been tabled will be extended to eight months; their mission may not continue beyond 30 September 2020.

The (ordinary) law of 23 March is accompanied by an organic law of 30 March. The minutes of the Council of Ministers state in this regard that 'Ordinance No. 58-1067 of 7 November 1958 on the organic law on the Conseil constitutionnel provides that the priority question of constitutionality procedure is governed by time limits both before the administrative and judicial courts and before the Conseil constitutionnel. Failure to examine priority questions raised in the context of a dispute before the Conseil d'Etat and the Cour de Cassation within a period of three months leads to setting aside these courts, the matter being referred to the Conseil constitutionnel ex officio. The COVID-19 epidemic prevents these courts from convening as a panel and, consequently, from meeting the time limits for judgment. Therefore, the draft organic law provides that the three-month time limit for the transmission of priority questions of constitutionality by the C.E. and the Cass. Court as well as the three-month time limit within which the Conseil constitutionnel must rule on a transmitted question be suspended until 30 June 2020'.

The provisions of the Code of Public Health introduced by the law of 23 March were supplemented and amended by Law no. 2020-546 of 11 May 2020 extending the state of health emergency and supplementing its provisions, which adds a new Article L.3136-1 to the Code of Public Health, by Law No. 2020-856 of 9 July 2020 organising the end of the state of health emergency, which maintains in application some of the provisions relating to the health emergency for an additional period, then by Law No. 2020-1379 of 14 November 2020 authorising the extension of the state of health emergency and carrying various measures for managing the health crisis and finally by Law No. 2021-160 of 15 February 2021 extending the state of health emergency.

Title III of the Act of 23 March has since been amended by Act No. 2020-760 of 22 June 2020 to secure the organisation of the second round of municipal and community elections in June 2020 and to postpone consular elections and completed by Act No. 2021-191 of 22 February 2021 postponing the general renewal of departmental councils, regional councils and the assemblies of Corsica, French Guiana and Martinique from March to June 2021.

The provisions of Titles III and IV, as well as the declaration of a two-month state of health emergency by Article 4 of the law, and the organic law, are in themselves measures to deal with the COVID-19 epidemic. The other measures are not contained in the law itself, but in its implementing decrees and in the ministerial and prefectorial orders adopted on the basis of the new provisions of the law, as well as in the ordinances and implementing decrees.

The Act of 23 March was subsequently amended by Act No. 2020-760 of 22 June 2020 to secure the organisation of the second round of municipal and community elections in June 2020 and to postpone consular elections, presented to the Council of Ministers on 27 May, adopted on second reading by the National Assembly on 16 June and by the Senate on 17 June; by Ordinance n° 2020-390 of 1 April 2020 relating to the postponement of the second round of the general renewal of municipal and community councillors, Paris councillors and councillors of the Lyon metropolis in 2020 and the establishment of public aid for 2021, and by Ordinance n° 2020-562 of 13 May 2020 aimed at adapting the functioning of local institutions and the exercise of competences of local authorities and local public establishments to the extension of the state of health emergency within the framework of the epidemic of COVID-19 Law No. 2021-689 of 31 May 2021 on the management of the end of the health crisis was published in the Official Journal on 1 June 2021. It establishes a transitional regime from 2 June to 30 September 2021, during which time the Prime Minister may restrict travel and the use of public transport, the opening of establishments open to the public, gatherings, meetings and events. The law gives a legal basis to the health pass, which is part of the European initiative of the digital green certificate. The Constitutional Council, seized by 70 deputies, ruled in Decision No. 2021-819 DC of 31 May 2021 that the text was in conformity with the Constitution, with one reservation of interpretation, namely that the national health data system, which does not contain the surnames and forenames of individuals, nor their registration number in the national register of identification of natural persons, nor their address, must not contain their telephone or electronic contact details either.

With the further waves of the pandemic, there have been subsequent laws to adapt to the evolution of the health situation. At the time of writing, the pandemic has not ceased, and although most limitations have been reduced, some of them are still in place. I do not think however that those limitations justify the use of the term 'law of exception' which remains quite pejorative as demonstrated by their indiscriminate use in the electoral campaigns.

CHAPTER 5

Climate Change: Turning the World (and Public Law) Upside-Down

Carmen Plaza[*]

1 INTRODUCTION

Climate change is undoubtedly turning the world upside-down and, hence, deeply impacting Public Law.

Over the last three decades, a growing scientific certainty about the causes and effects of global warming, followed by an increasing social concern, have characterized one of the greatest challenges facing global governance: Climate change, a phenomenon that has been described as the 'defining issue of our age'.[1] More recently, just after the second part of the Sixth Assessment Report of the Intergovernmental Panel on Climate Change was released in March 2022,[2] UN Secretary-General Antonio Guterres warned that 'We are sleepwalking to climate catastrophe'.[3] This apocalyptic statement was made in the disruptive international context marked by the sequelae of a two-year-long global pandemic and the outbreak of the Ukrainian War in the heart of Europe.

* To Prof. Patrick Birkinshaw, for his invaluable contribution to the theory and practice of European Public Law over more than four decades, and for his kindness and generosity always.

1. UN Secretary-General Ban Ki-moon, *Opening Remarks at 2014 Climate Summit* (23 September 2014), https://media.un.org/en/asset/k1x/k1xlehldqj. Among other academics that had made this same statement *see* William Nordhaus, *The Climate Casino: Risk, Uncertainty, and Economics for a Warming World* 4 (Yale University Press, 2013).
2. IPCC, *Climate Change 2022 Impacts, Adaptation and Vulnerability Working Group II Contribution to the Sixth Assessment Report. Summary for Policymakers* [hereinafter, IPCC WGII (2022) AR6 Synthesis Report].
3. A. Gutierres, *Speech of the Secretary General of United Nations*, The Economist's Sustainability Summit, 19 March, https://media.un.org/en/asset/k1c/k1caka4eie.

As a matter of fact, natural disasters related to climate change and the social protests demanding more ambitious policies to address this phenomenon, have compelled more than twenty States and 2000 regional and local authorities to declare a 'climate emergency',[4] along with the European Parliament.[5] In early 2020 the climate emergency was relegated to the background by the global emergency triggered by COVID-19. This health emergency led to the adoption of public measures to control the pandemic of an intensity hitherto unknown: from population lockdowns to strong restrictions on different economic activities. However, in December 2020 the UN Secretary-General again urged the world leaders to declare a climate emergency in their countries,[6] and climate change regained momentum in the international agenda in the run-up to the UN Climate Change Conference (COP26) held in Glasgow last November 2021.

Yet, the complex legal regimen built up over three decades is still unable to give an effective answer to this 'existential threat', as has been depicted in the new 'European Climate Law'.[7] In this scenario, climate change poses extraordinary challenges to Global Governance and Public Law: it is crucial that all the spheres of public and private power cooperate and act in the pursuit of common and ambitious objectives in a context of uncertainty, in light of the best available scientific knowledge, and taking due account of the role played by different actors – public and private – that have an impact on the environment and can contribute to combating this phenomenon.[8]

This short essay in honour of Professor Birkinshaw will focus on the role played by two different non-governmental actors of climate change governance and their impact on Public (Climate) Law: scientists through expert panels and committees, and citizens through emerging channels of public participation, in particular citizen's assemblies.

To this end, it gives first a brief overview of the development of Global Climate Governance. Next, it examines the role of expert knowledge in the climate law regime and the proliferation of public scientific organs. It follows an account of some 'new' trends in public participation in the field of climate change, with the rise of deliberative instruments such as climate change citizens' assemblies. Finally, this chapter ends with some final considerations that wrap up how these two actors interact to influence climate decision-making and its implementation by public authorities, which intensify

4. The first climate emergency declarations took place at the local level in December 2016. States began to join in 2019 (the first being the UK on 1 May 2019). *See* https://climateemergencydeclaration.org.
5. European Parliament resolution of 28 November 2019 on the climate and environment emergency (2019/2930(RSP), P9TA(2019)0078.
6. https://www.reuters.com/article/uk-climate-change-un-summit-idUSKBN28M0IR.
7. Regulation (EU) 2021/1119 of the European Parliament and of the Council of 30 June 2021, establishing the framework for achieving climate neutrality and amending Regulations (EC) No 401/2009 and (EU) 2018/1999.
8. Elinor Ostrom, *A Polycentric Approach for Coping with Climate Change Policy*, World Bank Research Working Paper 5095, 2009; Andrew Jordan et al., *Governing Climate Change Polycentrically: Setting the Scene*, Chapter I, in Governing Climate Changes: Polycentricity in Action? (Jordan et al. eds, Cambridge University Press, 2018).

– or even mutate – their role in the realm of Public Law. It assesses critically how these non-governmental actors take on a new protagonism in the face of the challenges posed by climate change.

2 CLIMATE CHANGE GOVERNANCE AND LAW AT A GLANCE

In the last three decades, a complex and multilevel regimen on climate change has been built up. However, its complexity has not been paired with effective answers to the challenges posed by global warming. As examined below, there have been two different types of non-governmental actors that have constantly warned about and demanded more ambitious measures: a vast majority of scientists, who have consistently signalled the risks of delaying more effective measures, and grassroots movements and non-governmental organizations (NGOs) which request urgent actions to combat climate change and ensure sustainable development.

As is widely known, the bases of the current climate regime were set in 1992, with the signature of the United Nations Framework Convention on Climate Change (UNFCCC). The Convention laid the foundations for international cooperation in the fight against climate change among 197 countries (including the European Unión and its Member States). Five years later, the Kyoto Protocol imposed legally binding CO_2-reduction targets on developed-country Parties (a commitment that lasted from 2008 to 2020). Currently, the 2015 Paris Agreement establishes the goal of 'Holding the increase in the global average temperature to well below 2°C above pre-industrial levels and pursuing efforts to limit the temperature increase to 1.5°C above pre-industrial levels'.[9] All the UNFCCC Parties have committed to prepare, communicate, and maintain successive 'Intended Nationally Determined Contributions' (INDCs) to combat climate change in accordance with the principle of 'common but differentiated responsibilities' (CBDR) and respective capabilities to achieve this target.[10]

At the European Union (EU) level, the Lisbon Treaty (1997) added to the objectives of the EU Environmental Policy the promotion of measures at the international level to 'combating climate change' (Article 191 of the Treaty on the Functioning of the European Union). The EU has also developed a wide panoply of secondary EU legislation and legal instruments on climate change: it has established a European carbon market (the first international emissions trading system in the world);[11] it has enacted binding national emission targets for each Member State;[12] and it has adopted

9. Article 2.1.
10. Articles 2.2. and 4. Further, *see* Daniel Bodansky, *The History of the Global Regimen* in *International Relations and Global Climate Change* 23-40 (MIT Press, 2001); Daniel Bodansky, Jutta Brunnée & Lawanya Rajamani, *International Climate Change Law* (Oxford University Press, 2017); Geert Van Calster & Leonie Reins (eds), *The Paris Agreement on Climate Change: A Commentary* (Elgar Commentaries series, 2021).
11. Directive 2003/87/EC of the European Parliament and of the Council of 13 October 2003 establishing a system for greenhouse gas emission allowance trading within the Union and amending Council Directive 96/61/EC, OJ L 275, 25.10.2003, pp. 32-46.
12. Currently *see* Regulation (EU) 2018/842 of the European Parliament and of the Council of 30 May 2018 on binding annual greenhouse gas emission reductions by the Member States from

directives harmonizing the national legal orders on issues such as energy efficiency,[13] renewable energy,[14] and geological storage of carbon dioxide.[15] Furthermore, it has designed different tools to structure the EU climate change governance.[16] Finally, within the framework of the European Green Deal,[17] the EU has approved a new 'European Climate Law' that establishes the legal framework for enhancing climate ambition and increasing EU and Member States' actions to achieve climate neutrality by 2050.[18]

In this global and regional framework, the States (and the regional and local entities within) have adopted a cascade of strategies, plans, and legal instruments intending to fulfil their international and EU commitments to fight against climate change.[19] In several EU Member States, climate change regulations have evolved from fragmented and scattered pieces of legislation, initially adopted to comply with the Framework Convention on Climate Change (FCCC) and EU Law, to the enactment of comprehensive laws on climate change. Thus, in 2008 the United Kingdom (UK) passed its pioneer first Climate Change Act; in 2019 Germany adopted its Klimaschutzgesetz, and in 2021 France enacted the Loi Climat et Résilence, and Spain its first Ley de Cambio Climático y Transición Energética. The 'European Climate Law' also reflects this trend toward a more systematic and holistic legislative approach to combating climate change and adapting to its effects.

However, in spite of this complex and 'polycentric' regimen, facts are stubborn things, and the results are so far insufficient: according to the FCCC Secretariat and Intergovernmental Panel on Climate Change (IPCC) reports, the emissions trends and the level of ambition shown by the National Determined Contributions (NDC) under the Paris Agreement 'depart from a trajectory consistent with limiting global warming to below 2°C'.[20] As the Intergovernmental Panel on Climate Change forecasts, if the international community and the States do not take more effective actions to mitigate

---

2021 to 2030 contributing to climate action to meet commitments under the Paris Agreement and amending Regulation (EU) No 525/2013, OJ L 156, 19.6.2018, pp. 26-42.

13. Directive (EU) 2018/2002 of the European Parliament and of the Council of 11 December 2018 amending Directive 2012/27/EU on energy efficiency, OJ L 328, 21.12.2018, pp. 210-230.
14. Directive (EU) 2018/2001 of the European Parliament and of the Council of 11 December 2018 on the promotion of the use of energy from renewable sources, OJ L 328, 21.12.2018, pp. 82-209.
15. Directive 2009/31/EC of the European Parliament and of the Council of 23 April 2009 on the geological storage of carbon dioxide, OJ L 140, 5.6.2009, pp. 114-135.
16. Regulation (EU) 2018/1999 of the European Parliament and of the Council of 11 December 2018 on the Governance of the Energy Union and Climate Action (OJ L 328, 21.12.2018, pp. 1-77).
17. European Commission, The European Green Deal, COM(2019)640 final.
18. Regulation (EU) 2021/1119 of the European Parliament and of the Council of 30 June 2021, establishing the framework for achieving climate neutrality and amending Regulations (EC) No 401/2009 and (EU) 2018/1999.
19. *See* Edwin Woerdman, Martha Roggenkamp & Marijn Holwerda, *Essential EU Climate Law* (Edward Elgar, 2022).
20. IPCC (2019) *Special Report on Global Warming of 1.5. Summary for Policymakers*, p. 7. *See also* FCCC Secretariat report, *National Determined Contributions under the Paris Agreement. Revised synthesis report by the Secretariat to the Conference of the Parties*, 25 October 2021, FCCC/PA/CMA/2021/8/Rev.1, pp. 5-6, https://unfccc.int/sites/default/files/resource/cma2021_08r01_E.pdf. For an academic critical assessment *see* David G. Victor, *Global Warming Gridlock: Creating More Effective Strategies for Protecting the Planet* (Cambridge University Press, 2011); of the same author *Prove Paris was More That Paper Promises*, 548 Nature 25 (2017).

and adapt to this phenomenon, climate change could eventually result in an environmental, social, and economic crisis with more severe effects than those caused by the COVID-19 pandemic, or even in a global collapse in the long term.[21] Such a global crisis could eventually bring governing systems and democratic frameworks under severe stress.[22]

Thus, climate change involves unprecedented challenges. In this scenario, it is worthwhile to note the different roles played in global climate governance by the two types of non-governmental actors demanding more ambitious and urgent measures to combat climate change: scientists and social movements. Though their roles are very different and might be even antagonists in some respects,[23] there are important interactions and synergies between them as regards production and access to information, participation in decision-making, and finally even in the judicial enforcement of climate change law.

3 UNCERTAINTY, PRECAUTION, AND THE ROLE OF SCIENCE IN THE CLIMATE CHANGE REGIME

The best available scientific knowledge, paired with objective and transparent information, is fundamental for the enactment of any environmental policy and law, as both are essential to ensure wide political and social support, and the effectiveness of any environmental rule.[24]

Science has played a particularly crucial role in the realm of climate governance, where there has always been an important degree of scientific uncertainty paired with a high political and social controversy. The articulation of epistemic communities,[25] and expert committees to produce, collect, assess, and transmit scientific information to public authorities and society has been fundamental in the negotiation and enactment of the international Climate Change regime, and its implementation at the EU and national levels.[26] As a matter of fact, the implementation of the Paris Agreement requires important economic and social transformations that should be based on the best available science.

21. *See* IPCC (2019) Special Report on Global Warming of 1.5. Summary for Policymakers; IPCC (2022), *Climate Change 2022 Impacts, Adaptation and Vulnerability Working Group II Contribution to the Sixth Assessment Report. Summary for Policymakers*, p. 15 (hereinafter, IPCC WGII (2022)).
22. Daniel Lindvall, *Democracy and the Challenge of Climate Change*, International IDEA Discussion Paper 3/2021, p. 8. On the similarities and differences between these two global emergencies, *see* Candice Howarth et al., *Building a Social Mandate for Climate Action: Lessons from COVID-19*, 76 Environmental Resource Economy 1107-1115 (2020).
23. Frank Fischer, *Democratic Prospects in the Age of Expertise*, 5 (Duke University Press, 2003).
24. In 1972, the Stockholm Declaration already included a principle devoted to the role of science in environmental protection (Principle 18).
25. For a concept and role of epistemic communities, *see* Peter Haas, *Epistemic Communities*, 698-715, in Oxford Handbook of International Environmental Law (Lavanya Rajamani & Jacqueline Peel eds, 2nd ed. Oxford University Press, 2021).
26. Sam Jonhston, *The Role of Science*, 255-256, in Oxford Handbook of International Environmental Law (Lavanya Rajamani & Jacqueline Peel eds, 2nd ed. Oxford University Press, 2021).

The IPCC has led this task from the run-up to the 1992 UNFCCC and has also deeply influenced EU and national Climate Law enactment and implementation. Furthermore, we have also witnessed in recent years the proliferation of climate expert committees at the national and EU levels. The key role that the IPCC plays, and the recent emergence of climate expert committees at all the policy levels (EU, national and regional) make evident the difficulties of balancing the role of science in the design of climate policy and law.

3.1 The Principle of Precaution and the Role of the IPCC

In the late eighties, when the causes and consequences of global warming were immersed in scientific uncertainties and controversy, the IPCC was founded under the auspices of the United Nations Environment Programme and the World Meteorological Organisation 'to provide internationally co-ordinated scientific assessments of the magnitude, timing and potential environmental and socio-economic impact of climate change and realistic response strategies'.[27] Ever since the IPCC has supplied scientific information on climate change to the international community and national governments for the development of climate policies.

The IPCC is an international body, with 195 member-representatives of Governments, which publishes periodical reports on climate change based on a worldwide assessment of published research work in this field. The reports are written by hundreds of leading scientists, undergo review by thousands of experts to ensure that the reports reflect the full range of views of the scientific community, and are finally approved by the IPCC.[28]

The First Assessment Report of the IPCC, published in 1990, acknowledged as 'certain' that emissions resulting from human activities were substantially increasing the atmospheric concentrations of greenhouse gases, enhancing the greenhouse effect, and resulting on average in an additional warming of the Earth's surface. It also stated that there were many uncertainties in its predictions, particularly regarding the timing, magnitude, and regional patterns of climate change.[29]

Two years later, in 1992, the Rio Declaration enshrined at the global level the 'precautionary principle' in the following terms: 'Where there are threats of serious or irreversible damage, lack of full scientific certainty shall not be used as a reason for postponing cost-effective measures to prevent environmental degradation' (Principle

27. UN General Assembly Resolution 43/53, *Protection of global climate for present and future generation* (43rd sess. 1988-1989), 6 December 1988.
28. Https://www.ipcc.ch. For an in-depth analysis *see* André Will, *Epistemic Communities and the Creation of the Intergovernmental Panel on Climate Change* (GRIN Verlag, 2020).
29. *See* IPCC First Assessment Report Overview and Policymaker Summaries and 1992 IPCC Supplement (1990 and 1992), https://www.ipcc.ch/report/climate-change-the-ipcc-1990-and-1992-assessments/.

15).[30] This principle made the signature of the UNFCCC possible since the First IPCC Report had already stated that climate change was perceived as 'a threat of serious or irreversible damage'. The UNFCCC Preamble also echoed this first IPCC Report[31] and the precautionary principle is also enshrined in its Article 3.3. Furthermore, according to Article 21.2 UNFCCC, the Secretariat of the UNFCCC shall 'cooperate closely with the IPCC to ensure that the Panel can respond to the need for objective scientific and technical advice'.[32] Following this mandate, the subsidiary bodies of the UNFCCC, such as the Subsidiary Body for Scientific and Technological Advice (SBSTA) and the Subsidiary Body for Implementation, have developed channels of cooperation with the IPCC.[33]

The following IPCC reports likewise triggered new developments in the climate change regime. The Second Assessment Report (1995), for example, preceded the negotiation for the Kyoto Protocol (1997); and the Fifth Assessment Report (2014), informed the negotiations and policy formulation toward the 2015 Paris Agreement.[34] Furthermore, the Paris Agreement has emphasized the role of science in climate policies: its Preamble recognizes 'the need for an effective and progressive response to the urgent threat of climate change on the basis of the best available scientific knowledge'; according to Article 4.1 the Parties 'aim' to undertake rapid reductions of greenhouse gas emissions 'in accordance with best available science'; and, according to Article 7.4, they also acknowledge that adaptation action 'should be based on and guided by the best available science' currently collected by the successive reports of the IPCC.

In its latest reports, the IPCC has stressed the urgency of enhancing ambition to fulfil the objectives of the Paris Agreement.[35] Last November 2021, at the UN Climate Change Conference, the COP26 adopted the Glasgow Climate Pact which 'resolves to pursue efforts to limit the temperature increase to 1.5°C', and recognizes that achieving this target requires 'rapid, deep, and sustained reductions in global greenhouse gas emissions, including reducing global carbon dioxide emissions by 45°C by 2030 relative to the 2010 level and net-zero around mid-century, as well as deep reductions in other greenhouse gases.'[36]

30. For a detailed analysis, *see* Jacqueline Peel, *Precaution*, Ch. 18, pp. 303-318, in Oxford Handbook of International Environmental Law (Lavanya Rajamany & Jacqueline Peel eds, 2nd ed. Oxford University Press, 2021); Nicolas de Sadeleer, *Implementing the Precautionary Principle* (Earthscan, 2007).
31. Paragraph 4.
32. Further, *see* Jonathan Wiener, *Precaution and Climate Change*, in The Oxford Handbook of International Climate Change Law (Cinnamon Carlane, Kevin R. Gray & Richard Tarasofsky eds, Oxford University Press, 2016).
33. SBSTA, Cooperation with the Intergovernmental Panel on Climate Change, Progress Report, FCCC/SBSTA/1996/18, 4 December 1996, available at https://unfccc.int/sites/default/files/resource/docs/1996/sbsta/18.pdf.
34. UNFCCC, Cooperation with the IPCC, available to https://unfccc.int/topics/science/workstreams/cooperation-with-the-ipcc/background-cooperation-with-the-ipcc.
35. *See* IPCC Special Report on Global Warming of 1.5°C. Summary for Policymakers (2019), and IPCC WGII (2022) AR6 Synthesis Report.
36. Advance unedited version available at https://unfccc.int/sites/default/files/resource/cma3_auv_2_cover%20decision.pdf.

In addition, the IPCC has developed guidance to help Parties deal with data uncertainties and manage emission inventories: the IPCC 2019 Refinement to the 2006 IPCC Guidelines for National Greenhouse Gas Inventories,[37] used by all Parties to prepare their annual emission inventories.

In short, the IPCC follows a scientific deliberative process, and it plays a key role in the international and national decision-making processes as well as in the enactment and implementation of the Climate Change Law at all levels.

3.2 The Proliferation of Expert Committees on Climate Change

At the national level, the 2008 UK Climate Change Act established an independent expert committee – the Committee on Climate Change – as a body corporate with the task of (i) giving advice to the UK and devolved governments on climate policy issues such as level of 2050 targets or carbon budgets; (ii) reporting annually to Parliament on progress made in reducing its emissions and preparing measures to adapt to the impact of climate change; (iii) submitting each five years reports on the progress made in achieving the gas reduction targets; (iv) and to providing advice or other assistance on request.[38] This Committee, novel in its conception, has become a model for the creation of advisory bodies specialized in climate change in other states such as France, Spain, and Germany.[39]

Also the 'EU Climate Legislation' has recently underscored the importance of scientific expertise and the best available evidence to the EU's achievement of climate neutrality by 2050 and to the creation of a favourable regulatory environment to adapt to climate change.[40] Thus, it establishes a 'European Scientific Advisory Board on Climate Change' (Article 3) to serve as a scientific and technical reference on climate change in the EU, complementing in this area the work of the European Environment Agency (EEA).[41] This committee shall act independently and avoid any overlap with the mission of the IPCC at the international level.[42] Among its tasks are considering the latest scientific findings of the IPCC reports, providing scientific advice and publishing reports on existing and proposed EU objectives and measures, raising awareness of climate change and its effects, and stimulating dialogue and cooperation between scientific bodies within the EU (paragraph 2). The EU Climate Legislation underlines as well the role that national climate advisory bodies – such as the ones already established in the several Member States and now in Spain – can play in providing expert scientific advice on climate policy to the relevant national authorities, inviting

37. Available at https://www.ipcc.ch/report/2019-refinement-to-the-2006-ipcc-guidelines-for-national-greenhouse-gas-inventories/.
38. Part 2 of the 2008 Climate Change Act.
39. For a general overview of the emergence and role of these committees in different European countries, *see* Nick Evans & Matthias Duwe, *Climate Governance Systems in Europe: The Role of National Advisory Bodies* (Ecologic Institute; IDDRI, 2021).
40. Recitals 24, 31, 34, 37.
41. Article 10bis of Regulation (CE) n° 401/2009.
42. Recital 24.

each Member State to establish a national advisory body and to inform the EEA of its establishment (Article 3.4).

This constellation of scientific panels and bodies has formed a network that throws light on the causes and consequences of global warming, constantly updating the knowledge that is essential to orient and assess the policy measures to mitigate or adapt to this phenomenon. Science is, however, necessary but not sufficient to define the public interests as regards the degree of risk – or threats of harm – that society is willing to accept, nor does it help to define the rules for allocating the costs of action or damages for inaction.[43] These decisions are in the remit of policymakers and legislators that, in a democratic society, should be based on the will of the people.

4 PUBLIC PARTICIPATION: THE RISE OF CITIZENS' ASSEMBLIES ON CLIMATE CHANGE

4.1 Climate Change and Public Participation in a Global Context

Public participation is hence another essential instrument of climate governance. According to Principle 10 of the Rio Declaration on Environment and Development, 'Environmental issues are best addressed with the participation of all concerned citizens, at the relevant level'. Effective participation of the various stakeholders and the public is considered a key factor in the improvement of the quality and implementation of measures taken by public authorities, the strengthening of the transparency and control of decision-making processes, the rule of law, and democracy, and the reinforcement of the legitimacy and social acceptance of decisions for the protection of the environment.[44]

Principle 10 of the Río Declaration has been the catalyst that triggered the inclusion of provisions for public participation in major environmental treaties, such as the UNFCCC in 1992, where the Parties committed to promoting and facilitating at the national, subregional, and regional levels public participation in addressing climate change and its effects and subsequently developing adequate responses (Article 4(a)(iii)). And later, new provisions on public participation were also included in the Paris Agreement (Articles 6 and 12).

Furthermore, Principle 10 of the Rio Declaration also crystallized in 1998 in the form of a binding treaty with the adoption of the United Nations Economic Commission for Europe (UNECE) Convention on Access to Information, Public Participation in

---

43. Jane Ellis, *Perspectives on Discourse in International Environmental Law: Expert Knowledge and Challenges to Deliberative Democracy*, Ch. 5, 124, in Environmental Discourses in Public and International Law (Bradd Jessup & Kim Rubenstein eds, Cambridge University Press, 2012).
44. *See* Gerd Winter, *Theoretical Foundations of Public Participation in Administrative Decision-Making*, 31, in 2 Environmental Democracy and Law (Gyula Bándi ed., Europa Law Publishing, 2014); Goda Perlaviciuta & Lorenzo Squintani, *Public Participation in climate Policy Making: Toward Reconciling Public Preferences and Legal Frameworks*, One Earth, April 2020, at pp. 341-347; Carmen Plaza, *La aplicación de las disposiciones del segundo pilar del Convenio de Aarhus en España. Los avances y los viejos retos*, 9 Revista Catalana de Dret Ambiental, pp. 3-4 (2018).

Decision Making, and Access to Justice in Environmental Matters (the Aarhus Convention). This regional agreement – ratified by 46 Eurasian countries and the EU – was then described as 'the most ambitious venture in the field of environmental democracy under the auspices of the United Nations.'[45] It is based on the premise that sustainable development can be achieved only through the involvement of all stakeholders. This Convention is the first environmental legally binding instrument to link the protection of the environment with human rights already enshrined in the Universal Declaration of Human Rights and every international and regional treaty for the protection of fundamental rights hereinafter: the right to receive information, the right to participate in public decision-making processes and the right to effective judicial protection.[46] As regards the right to public participation in decision-making, the Aarhus Convention requires ratifying Parties (EU and States) to ensure effective public participation at all levels of decision-making. However, while Article 6 of the Aarhus Convention lays down particularly precise obligations in relation to the authorization of specific activities or projects, it regulates with a decreasing degree of intensity the participation in the elaboration of plans, programmes, and policies relating to the environment (Article 7) and in the elaboration of general provisions (Article 8), which play a major role in climate change mitigation and adaptation.

The Aarhus Convention was followed, two decades afterwards, by the Agreement on Access to Information, Public Participation and Access to Justice in Environmental Matters in Latin America and the Caribbean, signed in Escazú on 4 March 2018. These two regional treaties expand the scope of these procedural rights as essential instruments for the protection of the environment in any democratic society. Furthermore, they guarantee their enjoyment not only to individuals but also to environmental NGOs, acknowledging and strengthening the vital role that they play in the preservation of our common environmental heritage.

At the EU level, new directives on access to environmental information and public participation in environmental matters were adopted to harmonize national legislation accordingly,[47] and the Aarhus Regulation applies the provisions of this Convention to the EU institutions and bodies.[48] In the particular field of climate change, the EU Regulation 2018/1999 on the Governance of the Energy Union and Climate Action also imposes an obligation on the Member States to establish a multi-level climate and energy dialogue. In this framework, essential instruments for climate and energy governance, such as integrated national energy and climate plans,

45. Ban Ki-Moon, *The Aarhus Convention: And Implementation Guide*, 2nd ed., Foreword, p. 3 (UNECE 2014); Michel Prieur, *La participation d'Aarhus, instrument universel de la démocratie environnementale, Revue Juridique de l'Environnement n. spécial*, pp. 9-29 (1999).
46. Michel Prieur, *ibid.*, p. 17. Luc Lavrysen, *The Aarhus Convention: Between Environmental Protection and Human Rights*, 647-671 (Parcours des droits de l'homme 2010).
47. Directive 2003/35/EC of the European Parliament and of the Council of 26 May 2003 providing for public participation in respect of the drawing up of certain plans and programmes relating to the environment OJ L 156, 25.6.2003.
48. Regulation (EC) No 1367/2006 of the European Parliament and of the Council of 6 September 2006 on the application of the provisions of the Aarhus Convention on Access to Information, Public Participation in Decision-making and Access to Justice in Environmental Matters to Community institutions and bodies (amended by Regulation 2021/1767), OJ L 264, 25.9.2006.

can be discussed. The EU Climate Legislation adds a channel for active participation and discussion of the achievement of the EU's climate neutrality objective and the different scenarios envisaged for energy and climate policies, including in the long term, and to review progress. The EU Climate Legislation further stresses the importance of active participation of all economic and social actors in the attempt to achieve the climate neutrality objectives, requesting the Commission to engage with all sectors of society, as well as using all appropriate instruments, including the European Climate Pact, to involve citizens, social partners, and stakeholders, and to promote dialogue and the dissemination of science-based information on climate change and its societal aspects (Article 9).

Despite the important progress in public participation fostered by the Aarhus Convention, public participation has still got a long way to go to effectively contribute to the delimitation of the general interest in environmental protection.[49] Overall, participation remains asymmetric: the public is more likely to participate in the adoption of specific decisions or projects closer to their personal interests, than in the adoption of plans, programs, and provisions of a general nature.[50] Furthermore, the greater the number of people involved in a decision-making process, the more difficult it will be to ensure 'effective participation' of those who have an interest in having their position considered. Participatory processes involving a wide range of stakeholders in decision-making present fundamental challenges and have even been regarded by some authors as 'inherently problematic'.[51] The same might be said of the case of public participation in matters related to climate change, where a great deal of the decisions are taken at the International, European, and national levels.[52]

On the other hand, the increasing public concern about global warming, and the complex policy options and trade-offs that must be considered seem to require additional channels of public participation. Therefore, some European States – and even the EU – have resorted lately to other (and more deliberative) forms of public participation, such as climate assemblies.

4.2 The Rise and Proliferation of Citizens' Climate Change Assemblies or Conventions

Public concern about climate change has increased in parallel with IPCC reports ascertaining the man-made causes of global warming and forecasting the risks that it entails. In 2021 most EU citizens identified climate change as the most serious problem

49. Carmen Plaza, *supra* n. 44, p. 64.
50. The Aarhus Convention requires States Parties to ensure effective public participation at all levels of decision-making. However, while Article 6 of the Aarhus Convention lays down particularly precise obligations in relation to the authorization of specific activities or projects, it regulates with a decreasing degree of intensity the participation in the elaboration of plans, programmes, and policies relating to the environment (Article 7) and in the elaboration of general provisions (Article 8).
51. Roger Few, Katrina Brown & Emma Tompkins, *Public Participation and Climate Change Adaptation: Avoiding the Illusion of Inclusion*, 7(1) Climate Policy 46-59, 48 (2007), DOI: 10.1080/14693062.2007.9685637.
52. *Ibid.*

facing the world, despite the persistence of the COVID-19 pandemic.[53] Further, a survey conducted by United Nations, with 1.2 million respondents in 50 countries, found that 64% of people said that climate change was an emergency, and younger people (under 18) were more likely to agree with this statement.[54] The tip of this 'iceberg' is the proliferation of new citizen protests such as the massive climate marches, student climate strikes, or the various campaigns promoted by global organizations and movements such as 'Fridays for Future', 'Campaign against Climate Change', or 'Extinction Rebellion',[55] movements that give shape to new youth activism that demands urgent and more ambitious measures in the fight against climate change.[56] However, recent social research has also concluded that 'there is little public consensus on climate policy, and that whatever consensus in favour of a proactive climate policy exists, it is fragile', since 'when it comes to solutions, most publics are also a bundle of contradictions: most want the government (and, for Europeans, the EU) to drive environmental policy, and a vast majority don't think governments are doing enough – but support for measures plummets the minute these are likely to have an impact on everyday life (taxes on flights, gasoline, congestion charges, for instance)'.[57] Furthermore, it seems that not only climate is not creating consense, but it also has the capacity to fragment the political landscapes further.[58] Consequently, these social movements coexist with politicians' perception of a lack of sufficient public support for the adoption of more ambitious measures to combat climate change as they could have an important economic and social impact and entail a considerable change in citizens' lifestyles.[59]

To fill these gaps between politicians and citizens, and to channel public discontent with climate change policies and laws, some states (such as Ireland, the UK, France, and Spain, among others) have promoted new deliberative formulas featuring the constitution of ad hoc citizens' assemblies to debate and propose new climate change mitigation and adaptation measures to the public authorities.

A citizens' assembly is a group of citizens with a public mandate for deliberating on a particular issue, where members are selected by lot from the entire population through a process that takes into account demographic criteria to ensure that the group is close to a 'miniature reflection' of the society (mini-publics) and represents its

53. European Commission, *Climate Change*, Special Eurobarometer 513, March-April 2021, Luxembourg, p. 4.
54. UNDP & University of Oxford, *The Peoples' Climate Vote* (2021), https://www.undp.org/publications/peoples-climate-vote.
55. Neil Cunningham, *Averting Climate Catastrophe: Environmental Activism, Extinction Rebellion and Coalitions of Influence*, 30 King's Law Journal 194 (2019).
56. For an analysis of these movements *see* Karen O'Brien et al. *Exploring Youth Activism on Climate Change: Dutiful, Disruptive, and Dangerous Dissent*, 23(3) Ecology and Society 42 (2018).
57. *See* Counterpoint, *Green Wedge? Mapping dissent against climate policy in Europe*, Open Society Europan Policy Institute, pp. 4, 6-8 (2021).
58. *Ibid.*, p. 4.
59. Stefan Drews & Jeroen Van den Bergh, *What Explains Public Support for Climate Policies? A Review of Empirical and Experimental Studies*, 16 Climate Policy 855-876 (2016).

diversity (according to parameters such as gender, age, socio-cultural level, etc.).[60] In order to ensure knowledgeable deliberation, the members of the assembly are informed and learn about the selected topic assisted by experts (in this case on the causes and consequences of climate change, as well as on possible measures to mitigate or adapt to this phenomenon). Through informed deliberation they agree on policy recommendations or proposals for actions that are transmitted to the commissioning public authority that has committed to responding to or acting on participants' recommendations in a timely manner.

A relatively new formula of public participation, it tries to compensate for the limitations ascribed to both representative democracy and the traditional organic and procedural participation mechanisms.[61] In the realm of climate change, these assemblies have been presented as instruments that can help to improve legal responses to the climate emergency by overcoming barriers such as short political mandates, citizen involvement in the adoption of decisions that will affect their future, and increasing legitimacy and acceptance of new decisions.[62]

As briefly examined below, in some cases the proposals resulting from these assemblies have in fact been reflected in the drafting of the second generation of laws against climate change.

These instruments of public participation drew on the notion of deliberative democracy and particularly on Habermas' discourse theory of law and politics, which promotes citizens' meaningful participation in the public sphere, contributing to collective decisions through reasoned consensus based on sound argument and reliable evidence. Thus, this instrument of participation allows citizens affected by a norm to be informed and are encouraged to think critically about competing alternatives and to discuss different reasons underlying political choices to reach agreements around the best arguments to influence formal decision-making in legislative bodies.[63] Habermas argues that this discursive procedure contributes to the rational character of collective decisions.[64] Along this line authors such as Ackerman and Fishkin also propose the use of instruments such as deliberative polling to overcome the deficiencies of representative democracy.[65]

60. Graham Smith & Maija Setälä, *Mini-publics and Deliberative Democracy*, 300, in The Oxford Handbook of Deliberative Democracy (Andre Bächtiger et al., eds, Oxford University Press, 2018).
61. For an overview of how public authorities from all levels of government has increasingly turned to these deliberative mechanisms to tackle complex policy problems, *see* OCDE, *Innovative Citizen Participation and New Democratic Institutions Catching the Deliberative Wave* (OCDE 2020).
62. *Ibid. See* Leslie-Anne Duvic-Paoli, *Re-imagining the making of Climate Law and Policy in Citizens' Assemblies*, 11 Transnational Environmental Law 2, p. 6, n. 30 (2022).
63. In particular, *see* Jurgen Habermas, *Between Facts and Norms: Contributions to a Discourse Theory of Law and Democracy* (The MIT Press, 1998).
64. *Ibid. See further* Walter F. Baber & Robert V. Bartlett, *Deliberative Environmental Politics*, 23-26 (MIT, 2005).
65. Bruce Ackerman & James S. Fishkin, *Deliberation Day*, 26, in Debatin Deliberative Democracy (James S. Fishkin & P. Laslett eds, Blackwell Publishing, 2003). *See also* What is Deliberative Polling?, Center on Democracy, Development and the Rule of Law, Standford, https://cdd.stanford.edu/what-is-deliberative-polling/.

The result of the deliberation of these mini-publics is often a survey or a report that reflects what those citizens prefer once they are informed and have discussed different options to deal with a public issue. They might also contain recommendations for the Legislator or the Government. As regards the relationship between the classical instruments of representative democracy (popular vote in free and fair elections) and deliberative democracy (mini-publics, citizens' assemblies, or deliberative polls), it has been argued that 'If we can have both deliberation and mass participation, we can infuse the political process, periodically, with what might be called collective informed consent'.[66]

Along these lines, the OECD Council adopted on 14 December 2017 a Recommendation on Open Government that promotes initiatives of deliberative democracy,[67] according to which Adherents should '8. Grant all stakeholders equal and fair opportunities to be informed and consulted and actively engage them in all phases of the policy-cycle ...'; and '9. Promote innovative ways to effectively engage with stakeholders to source ideas and co-create solutions ...'.[68] The Organisation for Economic Co-operation and Development (OECD) has also drawn a set of 'Good Practice Principles for Deliberative Processes for Public Decision Making' to provide policymakers with 'useful guidance' as to the establishment of deliberative processes and the implementation of provisions 8 and 9 of this Recommendation.[69] Among them, highlights principles such as 'purpose'; 'representativeness' (the participants should be a 'microcosm' of the general public, selected by random sampling); 'privacy' (respect for participants' privacy to preserve their independence; thus, their identity may be publicized only once the process has ended, at the participants' consent); 'inclusiveness' (considering how to involve under-presented groups); 'integrity' (requiring that the process should be run by an arm's length co-ordinating team different from the commissioning public authority); 'accountability' (as the commissioning public authority should publicly commit to responding to or acting on participants' recommendations, and monitor the implementation of all accepted recommendations); and 'evaluation' (anonymous evaluation by the participants to assess the process based on objective criteria).[70] Furthermore, the principle of 'transparency' plays a particularly essential role: the deliberative process should be announced publicly before it begins; the process design and all materials 'should be available to the public in a timely manner', and funding source should be disclosed, and the commissioning public authority's response to the recommendations and the evaluation should be publicized. It goes without saying that without real transparency, there is no guarantee whatsoever of compliance with any of those other principles, and the whole process might be distorted to tilt the balance towards the commissioning authorities' political interests.

66. Bruce Ackerman & James S. Fishkin, *ibid.*, p. 26.
67. OCDE/Legal/0438 available at https://legalinstruments.oecd.org/en/instruments/OECD-LEGAL-0438.
68. *Ibid.*
69. OCDE, *Good Practice Principles for Deliberative Processes for Public Decision Making.* https://www.oecd-ilibrary.org//sites/b40aab2a-en/index.html?itemId=/content/component/b40aab2a-en#.
70. *Ibid.*

In short, these citizens' assemblies are presented as new instruments to improve democracy and climate governance and complement both the existing channels of public participation and representative democracy. However, as pointed out below, they can also give rise to new overlapping and legitimacy problems.

4.3 An Overview of Some Pioneer Experiences of Climate Change Assemblies in Europe

Among all the EU countries that have made use of this form of participation, Ireland stands out first.

The Irish State has recurred to citizen assemblies for more than a decade to promote debates and public participation on particularly complex or socially controversial issues.[71] In July 2016, the Irish Parliament mandated an Assembly of 99 citizens randomly selected but taking into account criteria aimed at ensuring representation of various sectors of Irish society (gender, age, social status, geographical distribution) to make recommendations on measures to advance the fight against climate change and to reform its Climate Change Act of 2015.[72] The Assembly finally submitted thirteen policy recommendations to Parliament,[73] which have been taken into consideration for the amendment of its Climate Change Act and the promotion of new measures to address the climate emergency.[74]

In the cases of France and the UK, citizens' assemblies were convened in 2019, in the context of various citizen protests directly or indirectly related to the problem of climate change.

As a reaction to the 'yellow waistcoats' protest, the President of the French Republic convened the Convention Citoyenne pour le Climat (composed of 150 citizens randomly selected to ensure their representativeness according to criteria of gender, age, education, and geographical area), with the mandate to define new measures and proposals aimed at reducing greenhouse gas emissions to below 40% of 1990 levels by 2030. The French government committed itself to take on board and submit to Parliament the measures recommended by the Assembly with a view to the elaboration and adoption of new rules against climate change.[75] Its deliberations were scheduled in six sessions from October 2019 to February 2020, and the result was a document with 149 proposals on the basis of which a new Bill to combat climate change was drafted,

71. *See* Silvia Sutue, *Constitutional Conventions in the Digital Era: Lessons from Iceland and Ireland,* 38:2 Boston College International and Comparative Review 260-264 (2015).
72. https://www.gov.ie/en/publication/984d2-climate-action-and-low-carbon-development-amendment-bill-2020/.
73. Recommendations of the Citizens' Assembly, *How the State can make Ireland a leader in tackling climate change,* https://2016-2018.citizensassembly.ie/en/How-the-State-can-make-Ireland-a-leader-in-tackling-climate-change/Final-Report-on-how-the-State-can-make-Ireland-a-leader-in-tackling-climate-change.
74. Climate Action and Low Carbon Development (Amendment) Bill 2021 (Bill 39 of 2021). *See* Lala Muradova, Hayley Walker & Francesca Colli, *Climate Change Communication and Public Engagement in Interpersonal Deliberative Settings: Evidence from the Irish Citizens' Assembly,* 20:10 Climate Policy 1322-1335 (2020).
75. https://www.conventioncitoyennepourleclimat.fr/.

and submitted to the French Assembly and the Senate.[76] Finally, the new *Loi n° 2021-1104 portant lutte contre le dérèglement climatique et renforcement de la résilience face à ses effets* was adopted the 22 August 2021.[77]

In the UK, at the height of the Extinction Rebellion movement, the Climate Assembly was the result of the commitment of Parliament and the Government to achieve carbon neutrality by 2050. The Climate Assembly UK was convened by six House of Commons Committees with the mandate of making recommendations to the Government and Parliament on how to reach this target.[78] Composed of 108 randomly selected members, its sessions – which took place between late June 2019 and mid-May 2020 – culminated in a report containing detailed recommendations on ten priority areas for action, which was debated in the House of Commons, and which will be used by the six committees of Parliament to inform future parliamentary work on climate change.[79]

These three assemblies have had an uneven but unquestionable influence on climate law-making in their respective States.[80] Furthermore, following their experience, this deliberative instrument has proliferated in other European states such as Germany,[81] Denmark,[82] and Finland,[83] as well as in regions, and municipalities within the EU States, such as Scotland,[84] or Budapest,[85] among others.

Spain is one of the States that has followed these precedents but with some substantial differences. The creation of a Citizens' Assembly did not precede the adoption of a new law on climate change, or the amendments to former legislation. On the contrary, it was created following the mandate of the first Spanish Act on Climate Change, adopted in 2021 which Article 39.1 requests the Spanish government to strengthen the already existing public participation mechanisms 'through the establishment of a Citizen's Climate Change Assembly at the national level'. This provision also 'recommends' that regional and municipal governments convoke citizens' assemblies at their levels. As regards its composition, Article 39.1 only requires that the Assembly 'will take into account the principle of balanced representation between women and men and will include the participation of young people'. The detailed regulation was completed by an Order adopted by the Ministry of Ecological Transition

76. *Rapport de la Convention citoyenne pour le climat à l'issue de son adoption formelle dimanche, 21 juin 2020. Résultat du vote sur le rapport global*, https://propositions.conventioncitoyennepourleclimat.fr/pdf/ccc-rapport-final.pdf.
77. *Loi n° 2021-1104 du 22 août 2021 portant lutte contre le dérèglement climatique et renforcement de la résilience face à ses effets. See* Nora Stirn, *Le nouvel élan paticipatif de la Convention citoyenne pour le climat et ses répercurssions sur la procédure de revisión de la Constitution*, 127(3) Revue Française de Droit Constitutionnel 147-173 (2021). Fernando López Ramón, *Cambio climático y participación a la francesa*, 57 Rev. aragon. adm. pública, 119-147 (2021).
78. *See* for a full account https://www.climateassembly.uk.
79. Climate Assembly UK, *The Path to Net Zero* (2020), https://www.climateassembly.uk/report/.
80. For an in-depth comparative analysis *see* Lesslie-Anne Duvic-Paoli, *supra* n. 62 at 15-22.
81. https://buergerrat-klima.de.
82. https://kefm.dk/klima-og-vejr/borgertinget- and Assemblée citoyenne sur le climat – Le Conseil danois de la technologie (tekno.dk).
83. https://sites.utu.fi/kansalaisraati/.
84. https://www.demsoc.org/projects/scotland-climate-assembly.
85. Daniel Oross, Esxter Mátyás & Sergiu Gherghina, *Sustainability and Politics: Explaining the Emergence of the 2020 Budapest Climate Assembly*, 13(6100) Sustainability 1-13 (2021).

in September 2021.[86] With regard to its composition, according to Article 2.2 of the Ministerial Order the selection should be made by 'an independent technical team' and should follow a methodology 'that ensures randomness, preserves the quality and representativeness of the sample, and is based on criteria such as age, gender, educational level, geographical origin and the attitude towards climate change typical of Spanish society.' It also excluded from the Assembly any person 'holding an elected office or political representation, or employees of political parties or their foundations, are excluded from the Assembly' (Article 2.3).

The Citizens' Climate Assembly, which took place in six sessions from December 2021 to May 2022, finally approved and voted on a set of 172 recommendations that were included in a final report presented to the Council of Ministers on 11 July 2022.[87] The transposition of these recommendations into new measures to combat climate change will depend on the political will to introduce more ambitious measures to move as fast as possible to the carbon neutrality target.[88]

Finally, the EU has also used deliberative participation in the context of the recent Conference on the Future of Europe, held between March 2021 and May 2022. The Conference, convened by the Joint Declaration of the President of the Council, the President of the European Parliament, and the President of the European Commission on 10 March 2021 was held to 'give citizens a voice on what matters to them', and included the fight against climate change as one of its key themes.[89] Citizens' participation was articulated essentially through three modalities, which included formulas of direct participation, representative participation, and deliberative participation. As instruments of deliberative participation, the European institutions undertook to organize European Citizens' Panels, whether at European, national, regional, or local levels. Four Citizens' panels at the European level were designed, gathering a total of 400 people that should be 'representative in terms of citizens' geographical origin, gender, age, socio-economic background and level of education.'[90] Panel 3 was devoted to 'Climate Chante, environment, health' and formulated a series of recommendations that were presented to the plenary session of the Conference. As to the procedure for selecting the panel members, the Commission signed specific contracts with a private organization that was in charge of designing the methodology for the recruitment of randomly selected participants.[91] Finally, the Plenary put forward its

86. *Orden TED/1089/2021, de 29 de septiembre, por la que se establece la composición, organización y funcionamiento de la Asamblea Nacional para el clima.*
87. Asamblea Ciudadana para el Clima. *Una España más segura y justa ante el cambio climático ¿Cómo lo hacemos?. Informe Final de Recomendaciones* (2022). https://asambleaciudadanadelcambioclimatico.es/recomendaciones/.
88. Carmen Plaza, *La emergencia de asambleas ciudadanas de cambio climático en la Unión Europea. El caso de España*, 124 Revista Brasileira de Estudios Políticos 45-76 (2022).
89. Joint Declaration of the European Parliament, the Council and the European Commission on the Conference on the Future of Europe Engaging with citizens for democracy – Building a more resilient Europe 2021/C 91 I/01.
90. https://futureu.europa.eu/assemblies/citizens-panels.
91. https://futureu.europa.eu/uploads/decidim/attachment/file/20890/Specific_Contract_1_-_selection_citizens_panels.pdf.

proposals to an Executive Board of the Convention, that drew up a report on the outcome.[92]

The proliferation of this new instrument of deliberative participation has been explained not only in terms of better decision-making and of reinforcing democratic legitimacy in decision-making, but also as a way of facilitating the adoption of more ambitious measures by endorsing those that, in principle, politicians might discard due to a possible electoral cost.[93] However, for the assemblies to serve to this end, it is essential they have a clear and fully transparent regulation of their constitution, task, and decision-making process to reduce the risk of bias or undue influences on the outcomes. Otherwise, such deliberative fora would run the risk of becoming irrelevant as a mere 'political performance' or, even worse, it would eventually lead to both mistrust in public authorities and a negative perception of the outcome.[94]

5 SOME FINAL CONSIDERATIONS ON THE INTERPLAY BETWEEN EXPERT KNOWLEDGE AND PUBLIC CONCERN: BEYOND BETTER 'DECISION-MAKING'

The impact of the IPCC and expert committees goes beyond gathering and assessing the best available knowledge to be considered in the policy and rulemaking process. Their reports, indeed, lay the scientific bases for the adoption of political decisions and legal instruments which entail deep changes in the models of production and consumption. And, as the 1972 Stockholm Declaration already stated, the achievement of any environmental goal 'will demand the acceptance of responsibility by citizens and communities and by enterprises and institutions at every level, all sharing equitably in common efforts' (paragraph 7).

Expert bodies, and the IPCC in particular, also play an essential role in shaping public opinion. Thus, the IPCC Reports are widely publicized by conventional and social media and, as social studies have suggested, trust in scientists' statements about the environment has been consequential in the process of opinion formation on climate change.[95] Further, the best available knowledge is also essential for the functioning of the instruments of deliberative participation. This communication between experts and citizens has a high potential to improve both, decision-making procedures and their results for better policies and laws.[96] Reliable and transparent knowledge help to

92. Conference on the Future of Europe, Report on the final outcome (2022).
93. *See* Lala Muradova et al., *supra* n. 73, pp. 1322-1323; Stuart Capstick et al., *Climate Change Citizens' Assemblies*. CAST Briefing Paper 03, p. 3 (2020).
94. *See* Claire Miller & Rich Wilson, *Getting Climate Citizens' Assemblies Right*, Carnegy Europe, 5 November 2020, https://carnegieeurope.eu/2020/11/05/getting-climate-citizens-assemblies-right/ka9g; *see* Lesslie-Anne Duvic-Paoli, *supra* n. 62, p. 7, Rebecca Wells, *Citizens' Assemblies and Juries on Climate Change: Lessons from Their Use in Practice*, in *Addressing the Climate Crisis Local Action in Theory and Practice*, Ch. 11, pp. 123-124 (Candice Howarth et al. eds, Palgrave Macmillan, 2022).
95. *See* Bo Maclnnis & Jon A. Krosnick, *Trust in Scientists' Statements about the Environment and American Public Opinion on Global Warming*, Political Psychology: New Explorations, 487-526, at 505 (2016).
96. Jane Ellis, *supra* n. 43, 141.

widen social support for the enactment and implementation of new measures. Therefore, it is essential to avoid failures, biases, and bad practices in the process of supporting and gathering scientific knowledge. Research scandals such as the so-called 'Climategate' in 2009,[97] undermine both public and private trust in scientists' information. Such failures might, in short, weaken the scientific or technical bases of legal instruments and their reliability for public opinion.

Furthermore, as expert bodies increase knowledge on climate change, the uncertainty regarding the causes and effects of global warming narrows, helping to ascertain the adaptation and mitigation measures to achieve the goals of the Paris Agreement and to finetune how each State should contribute to the achievement of the Paris Agreement goals.[98]

This trend of increasing scientific certainty and social concern has, likewise, legal consequences for the implementation and judicial enforcement of new legal instruments. As a matter of fact, the exponential rise of climate litigation can be seen as a consequence of the interaction among the following factors:

- an ever-improving knowledge of the phenomenon of climate change;
- the access of citizens and NGOs to such information which nurtures their discontent with the national measures adopted by National Legislators and/or Executives to comply with their commitments under the Paris Agreement;
- a wider locus standi for citizens and NGOs promoted by the Aarhus Convention and Escazú Agreement, and the increasing exercise of the rights of access to justice to enforce the Paris Agreement;
- the strategic litigation carried out by foundations, NGOs, and climate change movements, and the spillover effects that the successful cases are provoking in other countries and jurisdictions.[99]

Citizens and NGOs have open access to the best available scientific data and knowledge that has been increasingly used to support their legal arguments on substantive legal issues, such to assess the fulfilments by the State of the commitments assumed under the Paris Agreement, to estimate how climate change increases the risk of a given harmful event putting in peril individuals' rights – or even fundamental

97. The international scandal revealing 'research corruption' and censorship of scientists' voices of researchers who were sceptical about whether global warming was happening. *See* Bo Maclnnis & Jon A. Krosnick, *ibid.*, pp. 489-496; Anthony Leiserowitz et al., *Climategate, Public Opinion, and the Loss of Trust*, 57(6) American Behavioral Scientist, 818-837 (2012).
98. Violetta Ritz, *Towards a Methodology for Specifying States' Mitigation Obligations in Line with the Equity Principle and Best Available Science*, 12(1) Transnational Environmental Law 95-104 (2023). Roberto Buizza et al., *The Role of Science in Climate Change Litigation*, BIICL Blog, https://www.biicl.org/blog/29/the-role-of-science-in-climate-change-litigation.
99. As the cases on climate change litigation have multiplied exponentially in the last years, the legal literature on this topic has equally proliferated. *See, e.g.*, Wolfgang Kahl & Marc-Philippe Weller (eds), *Climate Change Litigation: A Handbook* (Beck, HartKahl & Nomos, 2021); Francesco Sindico & Makane Moïse Mbengue (eds), *Comparative Climate Change Litigation: Beyond the Usual Suspects* (Springer, 2021).

rights –, to establish a causal link between emissions and (human) rights violations and, therefore, to determine the attribution of responsibilities and remedies.[100]

Equally, national judges and courts are increasingly considering climate scientific data when adjudicating in favour of these litigators.

In short scientific knowledge and the public are closely interacting in their response to the climate emergency, and their influence is jointly increasing, not only as instruments for better law-making in the field of climate change, but also in the processes of climate law implementation and judicial enforcement.

Both science and public participation might be of course misused. Science (in the form of the proliferation of expert committees that we are witnessing) might be used as an excuse for magnifying technocracy and to avoid political responsibility. Equally, citizens' assemblies and other deliberative forms of public participation are not free from the risk of manipulation and used by policymakers in self-interested ways. For example, they could be used as a democratic pantomime designed to justify new measures or to deceivingly strengthen their 'legitimation'; they could also use as an excuse to 'socialize' and 'blur' their political responsibility, or even they could be used to promote populist answers to the complex issues of climate change. In these cases, these instruments will indeed contribute to the weakening of Public Law and to the deterioration of democracy itself.

The proper functioning of both, expert bodies and citizens' assemblies, requires clear mandates and strict public procedures for the designation of their members and to guarantee their independence and transparent working methods. In the case of citizens' assemblies, their role and the nature of the outcomes of the deliberative process should also be made crystal clear to avoid any confusion or overlapping with the essential 'deliberative' decision making-processes of constitutional representative organs of the State, such as the Executive or even the Parliament. Likewise, the scope of 'accountability' to the citizens' assembly assumed by the commissioning public authority should also be previously determined. Nevertheless, only an appropriate legal framework can guarantee the fulfilment of these requirements to ensure a legitimate, independent, and transparent functioning of these deliberative processes. The degree to which society identifies with the citizens' assemblies will depend on this legal framework. Only if the citizens' assemblies are well regulated it is possible to guarantee that their recommendations are truly representative.

In the end, when science and public participation are used in a healthy democracy their joint efforts through different instruments of Public Law (such as decision-making processes and judicial review) should strengthen environmental democracy. The big question is whether their positive interactions will be intense enough and quick enough to contribute to an effective response to the climate emergency in time.

100. Roberto Buizza et al., *supra* n. 98.

CHAPTER 6

EU Constitutional Principles Revisited in the Polish Crisis of the Judiciary

Katarzyna Gromek-Broc

1 INTRODUCTION

The Polish judicial crisis has dominated the European debate for seven years. It is at the origin of an unprecedented number of judicial decisions and it has tested the effectiveness of the procedures never activated before. More importantly, the judiciary crisis brought to the fore questions of constitutional importance for the European Union (EU). It refreshed a discussion on the EU Membership and the duties incumbent on the Member States under the Treaties. The Polish crisis has become an EU crisis bringing to the fore the core EU values and fundamental principles that we thought were well-established and for granted. While Polish democratic backsliding undermines the EU democratic foundations, and is a threat to the EU legal order,[1] the EU strategies, the Court of Justice of the European Union (CJEU) decisions and legislation generated on this occasion tend to boost the existing constitutional foundation of the EU. First, the principle of supremacy under scrutiny in the 'Polish' case law triggered the CJEU response that supplemented the concept with some precisions. Secondly, the Rule of Law,[2] a core value of the EU enshrined in Article 2 TEU acquired a new substance. In its context, the notion of 'effective judicial protection' was clarified and gained a new

1. Laurent Pech, Patryk Wachowiec & Dariusz Mazur, Poland's Rule of Law Breakdown: A Five-Year Assessment of EU's (In)Action, *Hague Journal on the Rule of Law*, 13(1), 2021, 4343 at https://doi.org/10.1007/s40803-021-00151-9.
2. Patrick Birkinshaw, Supranationalism, The Rule of Law, and Constitutionalism in the Draft Constitution, *Yearbook of European Law*, 23(1) 2004, 199-223, https://doi.org/10.1093/yel/23.1.199, Patrick Birkinshaw, Book Review: *Strengthening the Rule of Law in Europe: From a Common Concept to Mechanisms of Implementation*, edited by Werner Schroeder (Oxford: Hart Publishing, 2016), *European Public Law*, 23(3) (2017), 643-647, https://doi.org/10.54648/euro2017035.

definition in EU Law.[3] Furthermore, the crisis motivated a number of strategies aiming at ensuring compliance with the EU core values. It started with a dialogue, followed by the activation of the Commission's Rule of Law Framework, followed by the procedure under Article 7(1) TEU. In case of persistent violations of the Rule of Law, the Commission according to Article 7 TEU could take gradual steps against the Member State including sanctions.[4] The Commission adopted a number of recommendations in the case of Poland.[5]

Subsequently, the procedure under Article 260 TFEU was triggered for failure to comply with the CJEU judgments,[6] imposing penalties for ignoring the CJEU order. Lastly, the Conditionality Regulation was adopted in 2020, providing more stringent rules in case of violation of the EU Law.

This contribution will first revisit the core constitutional principles such as supremacy and the Rule of Law in light of the Polish crisis (section 2). It reiterates the discussion on constitutional pluralism and the debate on parallel sources of norms well-present in Polish jurisprudence right from the beginning of the Polish membership in the EU. It briefly discusses Articles 4(2) and 4(3) TEU often relied on by the Polish Constitutional Tribunal. In particular, it looks at the new wave of the CJEU case law on Supremacy revisiting the 'Simmental Formula'. It also discusses the concept of the Rule of Law, its content and the criteria for assessment, finishing with its recent codification in the Conditionality Regulation. Subsequently, the contribution explores how the principle of supremacy was accommodated in earlier jurisprudence of the Polish Constitutional Tribunal (section 3). It also considers the Polish judicial reforms 2017-2019 leading to democratic backsliding (section 4), the CJEU standpoint (section 5), the Polish Constitutional Ruling defying EU Supremacy (section 6) and the recent amendments to the 2017-2019 reforms designed to unlock the EU funds (section 7). It argues that despite the infringement procedures, the CJEU Orders, CJEU landmark decisions, penalties and the EU frozen Funds, the observance of the Rule of Law in Poland does seem to improve. Meanwhile, the CJEU clarified many ambiguities surrounding the concept of the Rule of Law, Supremacy and effective judicial protection.

---

3. Aurélien Raccah, EU vs. Poland: Preventing Political Control over Judiciary, in Diane Fromage (ed.), *Jacques Ziller: A European Scholar* (European University Institute, 2022), 162 http://hdl.handle.net/1814/74983.
4. European Commission, Rule of law framework, https://ec.europa.eu/info/policies/justice-and-fundamental-rights/upholding-rule-law/rule-law/rule-law-framework_en, accessed 10 August 2022.
5. Commission Recommendation (EU) 2018/103 of 20 December 2017 regarding the rule of law in Poland complementary to Recommendations (EU) 2016/1374, (EU) 2017/146 and (EU) 2017/1520 at https://eur-lex.europa.eu/legal-content/EN/TXT/?qid=1555061792039&uri=CELEX%3A32018H0103, Commission Recommendation (EU) 2017/1520 of 26 July 2017 regarding the rule of law in Poland complementary to Recommendations (EU) 2016/1374 and (EU) 2017/146 at https://eur-lex.europa.eu/legal-content/EN/TXT/?qid=1555064402661&uri=CELEX%3A32017H1520; Commission Recommendation (EU) 2017/146 of 21 December 2016 regarding the rule of law in Poland complementary to Recommendation (EU) 2016/1374 at https://eur-lex.europa.eu/legal-content/EN/TXT/?qid=1555064086018&uri=CELEX%3A32017H0146.
6. Case C-441/17, *Commission v. Poland*, EU: C:2018:255.

2 TESTING THE LIMITS OF THE EU CONSTITUTIONAL PRINCIPLES

Polish Reforms of the Judiciary undertaken since 2015, have challenged the very foundation of the EU Law violating the EU constitutional principles such as the Rule of Law and Supremacy. Both principles have been a cornerstone of the EU integration process allowing for its success, rapid development and territorial expansion. The respect for the Rule of Law that in essence entails ensuring effective judicial protection, is inserted in Article 2 TEU and considered one of the common values on which the EU is based. It is a prerequisite for the protection of all EU values and democracy.[7] It is often acknowledged that 'the values of Article 2 TEU are 'untouchable core' of the EU legal order.[8] There is a strong relationship between the Rule of Law and Supremacy of EU Law. Any dispute involving the Rule of Law would inevitably raise the supremacy issue. The principle of Supremacy has been a tool in hands of the Court to maintain the EU democratic standards and also to prevent any backsliding in respect of the Rule of Law. Another way of the interaction of these two principles is explored by Kochenov. He argues that the CJEU uses the Rule of Law instrumentally to 'reinforce EU law's supremacy claim'.[9] Unlike the Rule of Law, embedded in the Treaty, the principle of Supremacy is of jurisprudential origin[10] and its development is probably the most apparent evidence of the European Court of Justice's activism. The Court, through its authoritative judgments shaped its contours, for example ruled that the EU law Supremacy[11] applies to all national law, adopted before or after the EU Act and that national law conflicting with the EU law should be set aside and more recently, even considered as void.[12] In the recent 'Polish Saga', the CJEU went to rule that in exceptional circumstances supremacy of EU does not only require disapplication of

7. EU Commission, Upholding the Rule of Law at https://ec.europa.eu/info/policies/justice-and-fundamental-rights/upholding-rule-law_en, accessed 10 August 2022; *see* Patrick Birkinshaw, *European Public Law: The Achievement and the Brexit Challenge* (3rd ed., Kluwer, 2020), *see* Laurent Pech & Petra Bárd, The Commission's Rule of Law Report and the EU Monitoring and Enforcement of Article 2 TEU Values, 2022 at https://www.europarl.europa.eu/RegData/etudes/STUD/2022/727551/IPOL_STU(2022)727551_EN.pdf.
8. Nikos Lavranos, 'Revisiting Article 307 EC: The Untouchable Core of Fundamental European Constitutional Law Values and Principles', in F. Fontanelli, G. Martinico & P. Carrozza (eds), *Shaping Rule of Law Through Dialogue: International and Supranational Experiences* (Europa Law Publishing 2009); in Dimitry Kochenov, Rule of Law as a Tool to Claim Supremacy, Reconnect Working Paper No. 9 – September 2020, at https://reconnect-europe.eu/wp-content/uploads/2020/09/RECONNECT_WP9_Kochenov.pdf; 5 Jacques Ziller, La primauté du droit de l'Union européenne, Département thématique des droits des citoyens et des affaires constitutionnelles, Direction générale des politiques internes de l'Union PE 732.474 – Mai 2022, http://www.europarl.europa.eu/supporting-analyse.
9. Dimitry Kochenov, Rule of Law as a Tool to Claim Supremacy, Reconnect Working Paper No. 9 – September 2020, at https://reconnect-europe.eu/wp-content/uploads/2020/09/RECONNECT_WP9_Kochenov.pdf; *see also* for the general discussion, Patrick Birkinshaw, United Kingdom Judges and European Integration, *Rivista italiana di diritto pubblico comunitario*, 25(2) 2015, 363-386.
10. Case *Flaminio 6/64 Costa v. E.N.E.L.* [1964] ECLI:EU:C:1964:66.
11. Case 106/77 *Amministrazione delle Finanze dello Stato v. Simmenthal SpA*. [1978] ECLI:EU:C:1978:49.
12. C-487/19 *W. Ż. and des affaires publiques de la Cour suprême* [2021] ECLI:EU:C:2021:798.

national law incompatible with EU Law but forces national courts to consider incompatible national law as null and void.[13] In brief, supremacy has unrivalled merits, allowed for the effective enforcement of EU Law making it unparalleled and unique to date.[14] On one hand, the recognition of EU Supremacy by the national courts has never been straightforward and the latter used various strategies to obviate it or to narrow its application either by declaring a part of EU law *ultra vires*, raising fundamental rights or evoking constitutional identity under Article 4(2) TEU.[15] In particular, Article 4(2) allowing for some scrutiny of the EU acts in favour of the protection of national constitutional identity, has been a source of confusion in the recent years. Dimitrakopoulos observes that from the CJEU perspective,[16] 'it is clear that Article 4(2) does not grant Member States a carte blanche to deviate from EU law on the basis of the respect of their national identity'.[17] He points out that the Court sees this provision limited in scope allowing a Member State to invoke the national identity as a legitimate public interest as a justification for a national measure, that breaches the EU fundamental freedoms.[18]

On the other hand, however, a degree of compromise was reached. The founding Member States unequivocally agreed that the arising new legal order necessitated a strong commitment to this principle. The national constitutional courts surrendered to the idea, that as a result of a transfer of competences to the EU, Member States' constitutions are not the unique source of constitutional authority in these States.[19] This implies a coexistence of constitutional norms coined by Walker as 'constitutional pluralism'.[20] Such a coexistence requires considerable efforts from the national constitutional courts and also CJEU to avoid conflicts. Part of the problem is a lack of

13. Case C-573/17, *Popławski*, EU:C:2019:530; Case C-219/17, *Berlusconi*, EU:C:2018:1023; Joined Cases C-202 & 238/18, Rimševics *v. Latvia*, EU:C:2019:139, Case C-487/19, *C-487/19 – W. Ż. and des affaires publiques de la Cour suprême*, 2021, ECLI:EU:C:2021:798 https://curia.europa.eu/juris/liste.jsf?num = C-487/19; Michael Dougan, The Primacy of Union Law over Incompatible National Measures: Beyond Disapplication and Towards a Remedy, *Common Market Law Review*, 59, 2022, 1301-1332.
14. *Ibid.*; Jacques Ziller 2022, La primauté du droit de l'Union européenne, Département thématique des droits des citoyens et des affaires constitutionnelles Direction générale des politiques internes de l'Union PE 732.474 – Mai 2022, http://www.europarl.europa.eu/supporting-analyse.
15. Gabor Halmai, Absolute Primacy of EU Law vs Pluralism: The Role of Courts, *EUI*, 2018 at https://me.eui.eu/wp-content/uploads/sites/385/2018/05/IJPL_Special_Issue_Concluding_remarks_Halmai_final.pdf.
16. Case C-208/09 *Sayn-Wittgenstein* [2010] ECLI:EU:C:2010:806.
17. Ioannis Dimitrakopoulos, Conflicts Between EU Law and National Constitutional Law in the Field of Fundamental Rights, 2018 https://www.ejtn.eu/PageFiles/17318/DIMITRAKOPOULOS%20Conflicts%20between%20EU%20law%20and%20National%20Constitutional%20Law.pdf.
18. *Ibid.*, Dimitrakopoulos I, 4, Case C-208/09 *Sayn-Wittgenstein*; C-58/13 *Torresi* [2014] CLI-:EU:C:2014:2088.
19. Krystyna Kowalik-Bańczyk, Should We Polish It Up? The Polish Constitutional Tribunal and the Idea of Supremacy of EU Law, *German Law Journal*, 6(10), 2005, 1355 https://doi.org/10.1017/S207183220001436X published online by Cambridge University Press.
20. Neil Walker, The Idea of Constitutional Pluralism, *Modern Law Review*, 65(3) 2002, 317-359. Neil Walker, Constitutional Pluralism Revisited, *European Law Journal* 22 (2016), also Edinburgh School of Law Research Paper No. 2016/12, Europa Working Paper No 2016/05, available at SSRN: https://ssrn.com/abstract=2775820 or http://dx.doi.org/10.2139/ssrn.2775820, Neil

delineating competences and relying instead on a goodwill and mutual accommodation.[21] Nonetheless, even in the most respectful relationship, clashes are sometimes inevitable. Maduro sees in constitutional pluralism a solution for a mutual respect believing that the margin for dissent left to national courts will promote a healthy dialogue between the CJEU and the national courts.[22] In contrast, Kelemen argues the concept of constitutional pluralism is dangerous and undermines the constitutional foundations of the EU.[23] Yet, Maduro observes that any support for constitutional pluralism is only possible within the 'general agreement on a common set of principles to guide it [while reminding] "constitutional courts that they are part of a system" [...] and must try to accommodate these needs and interpret their national constitutions in that light.'[24] Yet, the reading of Article 4(2) TEU on the respect for national identities should be placed within the ambit of Article 4(3) TEU imposing the obligation of sincere cooperation and mutual respect.

Almost 60 years after the decision in *Costa*,[25] supremacy divides the politicians and fuels the academic debate. Ziller observes that despite its unquestionable importance, the concept of supremacy of EU law remains fragile.[26] Possibly, its jurisprudential origin and development have contributed to this fragility but at the same time it allowed for some flexibility, adaptability and promoted its dynamic evolution. As mentioned, the recent case law is strengthening this principle by going beyond mere

---

Walker, 'Late Sovereignty in the European Union, 2000-2001 European Forum', paper S. Bartolini, T. Risse & B. Strath (eds), (1999) *Between Europe and the National State: The Reshaping of Interests, Identities and Political Representation, RSCAS-EUI, EUR 82, 1* inn Kowalik-Banczyk & Neil Walker (eds), *Sovereignty in Transition*, Hart, 2003, 3-32, *see also* N. MacCormick, 'The Maastricht Urteil: Sovereignty Now', *European Law Journal*, 1, 1995, 259; Neil Walker, 'The Idea of Constitutional Pluralism', *Modern Law Review*, 2002, 317; Miguel Maduro, 'Contrapunctual Law: Europe's Constitutional Pluralism in Action', in N. Walker (ed.), *Sovereignty in Transition* (Hart, 2003), 501; also *see* Matej Avbelj & Jan Komárek (eds), *Constitutional Pluralism* (Hart, 2012).

21. Gabor Hamail, quoting Miguel Maduro, 'Contrapunctual Law: Europe's Constitutional Pluralism in Action', in Neil Walker (ed.), *Sovereignty in Transition* (Hart, 2003).
22. Miguel Maduro, Some Preliminary Remarks on the PSPP Decision of the German Constitutional Court, *VerfBlog*, 2020/5/06, https://verfassungsblog.de/some-preliminary-remarks-on-the-pspp-decision-of-the-german-constitutional-court/, DOI: 10.17176/20200506-133802-0.
23. R. Daniel Kelemen, Is Differentiation Possible in Rule of Law? *Comparative European Politics*, 17, 019, 246-260 https://doi.org/10.1057/s41295-019-00162-9.
24. Miguel Maduro, Some Preliminary Remarks on the PSPP Decision of the German Constitutional Court, *VerfBlog*, 2020/5/06, https://verfassungsblog.de/some-preliminary-remarks-on-the-pspp-decision-of-the-german-constitutional-court/, DOI: 10.17176/20200506-133802-0.
25. *Ibid.*, Case 6/64, *Flaminio Costa v. E.N.E.L.* https://eur-lex.europa.eu/legal-content/EN/TXT/?uri=celex%3A61964CJ0006, *ibid.*, Case 6/64 *Flaminio Costa v. ENEL* [1964] ECR 614, para. 3. *Ibid.*, Case 106/77 *Amministrazione delle Finanze dello Stato v. Simmenthal SpA* [1978] ECR 629. Case 11/70 *Internationale Handelsgesellchaft mbH v. Einfuhr* [1970] (Solange I). Case 69-85 Re *Wunsche Handelsgesellschaft* (22 October [1986] (Solange II)) *see* Jan Komárek, Playing with Matches: The Czech Constitutional Court's Ultra Vires Revolution, *VerfBlog*, 2012/2/22, https://verfassungsblog.de/playing-matches-czech-constitutional-courts-ultra-vires-revolution/, DOI: 10.17176/20170505-090350. Case C-399/09 *Marie Landtovd v. Ceskd sprdva socialniho zabezpeceni* [2011] ECR I-5596.
26. *Ibid.*, Ziller Jacques, look Komarek, Jan Komarek, so Ziller must be Jacques Ziller The Primacy of European Union Law, European Parliament Policy Department for Citizens' Rights and Constitutional Affairs Directorate-General for Internal Policies of the Union, 2022, PE 732.474, July 2022.

disapplication of incompatible national law claiming that such law should be declared void.[27] Yet, the attempt to insert it in the Treaty never materialised what was interpreted by the opponents as a deliberate choice not to recognise its absolute nature, and might constitute an interpretative argument for the national courts to argue that the Member States did not want to commit to it otherwise they would have included it in the Treaty.[28] The opposite argument could also be sustained. The Declaration 17 annexed to the Lisbon Treaty (of the same value) explicitly acknowledges its existence and the jurisprudential acquis: 'The fact that the primacy principle is not included in the future Treaty will in no way modify the existence of this principle or the case law of the Court of Justice'.[29] Although, placing primacy in the Declaration and not in the Title 1 TEU on Common Provisions, could also support the opposite view that Member States did not want to commit fully to it. In sum, the principle of supremacy is still surrounded by a considerable degree of ambiguity[30] and incertitude and that fact was smartly manipulated by national Constitutional Courts in particular the Polish Constitutional Tribunal in their justifications to depart from it. Avbej argues that even the term supremacy or primacy (used here interchangeably) inhabits a different meaning and its denomination is not accidental but points towards one of the following models: the hierarchical, the conditionally hierarchical or the heterarchical model.[31] Whereas the hierarchical one would imply an absolute supremacy, the conditionally hierarchical model would allow for some degree of autonomy of the Member States considering supremacy not as absolute principle, but 'one according to which law, EU and national, is supreme within its own sphere'.[32] He argues that this model allows for a misunderstanding of EU law since the national judges' views would be grounded in their own supremacy perspective ignoring 'the whole', they are a part.[33] Leaving a leeway for interpretation opened the door for the constitutional courts to deviate from its strict application as the courts did in Germany, Italy, the Czech Republic, Denmark, Romania and Poland. The Polish Constitutional Tribunal in its audacious judgment of 7 October 2021, ruled that Articles 1 & 19(1) TEU were incompatible with the Polish Constitution, therefore inapplicable.[34] It seems that more frequent non-compliance of national courts

---

27. Michael Dougan, The Primacy of Union Law over Incompatible National Measures: Beyond Disapplication and Towards a Remedy: The Primacy of Union Law over Incompatible National Measures: Beyond Disapplication and Towards a Remedy of Nullity?, *Common Markter Law Review* 59 2022, 1301-1332
28. *Ibid.*; Jacques Ziller Jacques, The Primacy of European Union Law, European Parliament Policy Department for Citizens' Rights and Constitutional Affairs Directorate-General for Internal Policies of the Union, 2022, PE 732.474, July 2022, 14.
29. *Ibid.*, 14.
30. Avbeil Matej, Supremacy or Primacy of EU Law – (Why) Does It Matter?, *European Law Journal*, 17(6) 2011, pp. 744-763.
31. *Ibid.*, 744.
32. Joseph H.H. Weiler, *Constitution for Europe* (OUP, 1999), 20, in Matej Avbeil *ibid.*, 747.
33. Matej, *ibid.*, at 755.
34. Polish Constitutional Tribunal, judgment Ref. No. K 3/21, 7 October 2021 at https://trybunal.gov.pl/en/hearings/judgments/art/11662-ocena-zgodnosci-z-konstytucja-rp-wybranych-przepisow-traktatu-o-unii-europejskiej Koen Lenaerts, 'Our Judicial Independence and the Quest for National, Supranational and Transnational Justice', in G. Sevik, M.-J. Clifton, T. Haas, L. Lourenço & K. Schwiesow (eds), *The Art of Judicial Reasoning: Festschrift in Honour of Carl Baudenbacher* (Springer 2019), 155-174.

prompted the CJEU to reinforce its hierarchical nature. In its judgment *W. Ż.*, the CJEU strengthened the remedy for incompatibility of a national act with the principle of Supremacy from disapplication to the declaration of nullity.[35] The CJEU ruled that in light of the principle of supremacy the Member States are under an obligation to give full effect to EU law and a national measure even of a Constitutional authority cannot 'undermine the unity and effectiveness of EU law'.[36] Thus, the Polish dispute over the judiciary adds a new content to this principle.

The most contested issue has always been an absolute nature of the principle of supremacy, that comes to fore when the EU law clashes with the Member States' Constitutions. The problem only apparently was resolved in the early supremacy case in which the ECJ clarified that supremacy of EC Law applies to all national norms, including constitutional norms.[37] But, the Lisbon Treaty acknowledges in its Article 6 TEU that general principles arising from the Member States Constitutions are equally important.[38] Article 6(3) TEU reads: 'Fundamental rights, as guaranteed by the European Convention for the Protection of Human Rights and Fundamental Freedoms and as they result from the constitutional traditions common to the Member States, shall constitute general principles of the Union's law.'[39] Thereby, this Article needs to be read in conjunction with Article 4(3) TEU on sincere cooperation and mutual respect allowing mutual accommodation that efficient dialogue between the CJEU and national courts should foster. In short, the delineation of what comes with the constitutional traditions or national identity under Article 4(2) TEU is somehow obscure leaving the national Courts with insufficient guidance. But, Avbelj argues that the 'unconditional supremacy of EU law is not indispensable for efficient and uniform application of EU Law' but rather is a source of tension.[40] Similarly, the conditionally hierarchical model leads to the situation where the judicial actors argue their own rightness that turns to pursue their own interests that are detrimental to the process of EU integration.[41]

Conversely, the observance of the Rule of Law acquired a general consensus considered as 'the backbone of modern constitutional democracies'[42] and, 'benchmark of political legitimacy'[43] recognised in Article 2 TEU as a fundamental principle and a value of the EU. Previously broadly defined, it entails a transparent, accountable and

35. C-487/19 *W. Ż. () and des affaires publiques de la Cour suprême* – nomination 2021, https://curia.europa.eu/juris/liste.jsf?num=C-487/19.
36. *Ibid.*; M. Dougan, The Primacy, 2022 at 1319
37. Case 11/70 *Internazionale Handelsgesellschaft*, [1970] ECR 1125; Krystyna Kowalik-Bańczyk, *supra*, 1356.
38. *Ibid.*, Krystyna Kowalik-Bańczyk 1356.
39. *Ibid.*, Ioannis Dimitrakopoulos, Conflicts Between EU Law and National Constitutional Law in the Field of Fundamental Rights, https://www.ejtn.eu/PageFiles/17318/DIMITRAKOPOULOS%20Conflicts%20between%20EU%20law%20and%20National%20Constitutional%20Law.pdf.
40. *Ibid.*, Avbeij, 756.
41. *Ibid.*, Avbelj.
42. Commission, 'Communication to the European Parliament and Council, A New Framework to strengthen the Rule of Law' (Communication) COM(2014) 158 in Laurent Pech et al., Meaning and Scope of the EU Rule of Law, Work Package 7, 2020 at https://reconnect-europe.eu/wp-content/uploads/2020/05/D7.2-1.pdf.
43. Jeremy Waldron, 'The Concept and the Rule of Law' (2008) *Georgia Law Review* 1 in Laurent Pech et al. Meaning and Scope of the EU Rule of Law, Work Package 7, 2020 at https://reconnect-europe.eu/wp-content/uploads/2020/05/D7.2-1.pdf.

democratic EU that guarantees effective judicial protection by impartial courts.[44] Yet, the Commission outlined its basic components such as legality, legal certainty, prohibition of arbitrariness and respect for human rights.[45]

Nonetheless, in the recent years, its meaning and its scope have been increasingly challenged by Hungary, Poland and Romania. Hungary and Poland, for example, argued that the EU Treaty lacked a definition of the Rule of Law. In addition, Hungary and Poland in their Action for Annulment of the Regulation 2020/2092 argued that the Rule of Law 'cannot be the subject of a uniform definition in EU law and must be specifically defined by the legal systems of each Member State'.[46] Subsequently, the Conditionality Regulation 2020/2092[47] provided an insight into its content and codifies the existing definition.[48] Article 2 (also acknowledged in recital 3) of the Regulation defines the Rule of Law in a way in which it 'includes the principles of legality implying a transparent, accountable, democratic and pluralistic law-making process; legal certainty; prohibition of arbitrariness of the executive powers; effective judicial protection, including access to justice, by independent and impartial courts, also as regards fundamental rights; separation of powers; and non-discrimination and equality before the law'.[49] Whereas, Article 3 clarifies what should be understood by the breach of the Rule of law.[50] In addition, Recital 6 states that 'while there is no hierarchy among Union values, respect for the rule of law is essential for the protection of the other fundamental values [...] on which the Union is founded, such as freedom, democracy, equality and respect. There can be no democracy and respect for fundamental rights without respect for the rule of law and vice versa.'[51] Hence, the new definition clearly rejects the Polish Government's argument that the judicial system is an internal matter of each Member State. The elements of the definition unequivocally legitimise the EU intervention in administration of justice in Poland.[52] The independence of Polish

44. Mattias Kumm, 'The Idea of Socratic Contestation and the Right to Justification', *Law and Ethics of Human Rights* 4 (2010), 142-175 in *ibid.*, Kochenov D. Reconnect.
45. Commission, Communication, from the Commission to the European Parliament and the Council. A new EU Framework to strengthen the Rule of Law,/COM/2014/0158 final/ in Matteo Mastracci, Judiciary Saga in Poland: An Affair Torn Between European Standards and ECtHR Criteria (30 December 2020), 9 *Polish Review International & European Law* 39 (2020), Available at SSRN: https://ssrn.com/abstract=3757494.
46. Opinions of Advocate General Campos Sánchez-Bordona, 2 December 2021 in Cases C-156/21, *Hungary v. European Parliament and Council*, EU:C:2021:974, para. 267 and Case C- in Case C-156/21, *Hungary v. European Parliament and Council*, EU:C:2021:974, para. 267 and Case C-157/21, *Poland v. European Parliament and Council*, EU:C:2021:978, in Laurant Pech *supra*.
47. Conditionality Regulation (EU, Euratom) 2020/2092 of the European Parliament and of the Council of 16 December 2020 on a general regime of conditionality for the protection of the Union budget, at ELI: http://data.europa.eu/eli/reg/2020/2092/oj.
48. Laurant Pech, The Rule of Law as a Well-Established and Well-Defined Principle of EU Law, *Hague Journal on the Rule of Law*, https://doi.org/10.1007/s40803-022-00176-8, *see also* Conditionality Regulation (EU, Euratom) 2020/2092.
49. *Ibid.*, Conditionality Regulation (EU, Euratom) 2020/2092 of the European Parliament and of the Council of 16 December 2020 on a general regime of conditionality for the protection of the Union budget, at ELI: http://data.europa.eu/eli/reg/2020/2092/oj.
50. *Ibid.*
51. *Ibid.*
52. Laurant Pech, The Rule of Law as a Well-Established and Well-Defined Principle of EU Law, Hague Journal on the Rule of Law, https://doi.org/10.1007/s40803-022-00176-8.

judiciary has been intensively debated and generated an extensive CJEU and European Court of Human Rights (ECtHR) case law.[53] The latter, while interpreting Article 6 of European Convention on Human Rights (ECHR), provided helpful insights into the content of judicial independence and impartiality through the elaboration of the assessment criteria such as the way judges are appointed, the duration of the term of the appointment, the guarantees against outside pressures or whether the body presents an appearance of independence.[54] The CJEU relied on these criteria in its 'Polish jurisprudence' on judicial independence. Kochenov observes that the Rule of Law is acquiring a new substantive meaning 'via the articulation of EU law's understanding of independence of the judiciary and the principle of judges' irremovability'.[55] In fact, the CJEU case law never delivered that many decisions,[56] concentrated, in such a short period of time.[57] The Regulation itself gave rise to an action for annulment brought by Poland and Hungary, rejected by the CJEU in February 2022.[58] The Court acknowledged that the Rule of Law as a core value represents the identity of the EU and the Regulation does not infringe the principle of legal certainty. It also found that the legal basis for the Regulation, Article 322(1)(a) TFEU was adequate and that the Regulation does not bypass the procedure under Article 7 TEU.[59] Subsequently, the Commission triggered the Conditionality Mechanism under the Regulation against Hungary.[60]

53. Recently cases ECtHR: *Dolińska-Ficek and Ozimek v. Poland*, App. Nos 49868/19 and 57511/19, 2022, *Advance Pharma sp. z o.o v. Poland*, App. No. 1469/20, 2022, *Stępka v. Poland* App. No. 18001/22; case *Żurek v. Poland*, 2022, interim measure in the case *Raczkowski v. Poland* App. No. 33082/22, *Włodzimierz Wróbel and Andrzej Stępka*, granted interim measures on 8 February 2022.
54. Matteo Mastracci, Judicial Independence: European Standards, ECtHR Criteria and the Reshuffling Plan of the Judiciary Bodies in Poland, *Athens Journal of Law*, 5(3) 2019, 323-350 at 332, https://doi.org/10.30958/ajl.5-3-6 doi = 10.30958/ajl.5-3-6; cases *Brudnicka and Others v. Poland*, App. no. 54723/00, 2005; *Kyprianou v. Cyprus*, App. no. 73797/01, 2005; *Henryk Urban and Ryszard Urban v. Poland* App. no. 3614/08, 2010.
55. Dimitry Kochenov & Petra Bárd, 'The Last Soldier Standing? Courts Versus Politicians and the Rule of Law Crisis in the New Member States of the EU', *European Yearbook of Constitutional Law*, 1 (2019), 243-288.
56. Luke Dimitrios Spieker, The Conflict over the Polish Disciplinary Regime for Judges – An Acid Test for Judicial Independence, Union Values and the Primacy of EU Law, *Common Market Law Review* 59, 2022, 777-812. Case C-791/19, *Commission v. Poland* (Régime disciplinaire des juges), (Grand Chamber) of 15 July 2021, EU:C:2021:596; Case C-204/21 R, *Commission v. Poland*, Order of the Vice-President of the Court of 14 July 2021, EU:C:2021:593; Case C-204/21; R, *Commission v. Poland*, Order of the Vice-President of the Court of 27 October 2021, EU:C:2021:878.
57. Marek Safjan, 'Prawo do skutecznej ochrony sadowej', (2020/5) *Palestra*, 5, 25.
58. Cases 156/21 and C-157/21 *Action for Annulment of the Regulation 2020/2092*, 16 February 2022, ECLI:EU:C:2022:98.
59. Matteo Bonelli, Constitutional Language and Constitutional Limits: The Court of Justice Dismisses the Challenges to the Budgetary Conditionality Regulation, *European Papers*, 7(2), 2022, European Forum, Insight of 25 July 2022, pp. 507-525 ISSN 2499-8249 – doi: 10.15166/2499-8249/574, also J Morijn, 'A Closing of Ranks: 5 Key Moments in the Hearing in Cases C-156/21 and C-157/21',14 October 2021, Verfassungsblog verfassungsblog.de.
60. Andrzej Sadecki, Conditionality Mechanism: Hungary Facing the Threat of Withheld EU Funds at https://www.osw.waw.pl/en/publikacje/analyses/2022-09-20/conditionality-mechanism-hungary-facing-threat-withheld-eu-funds.

3 SUPREMACY IN THE EARLY POLISH CONSTITUTIONAL TRIBUNAL'S CASE LAW

Since Poland joined the EU, the Polish attitude towards the EU was accurately framed by Cichocki as 'the Polish Euro-indifference'.[61] Poland was not participating in efforts to strengthen the EU or finding the solutions to the numerous crises but has concentrated on the gains the EU membership brings. Some scholars comment that Poland has demonstrated a 'complete lack of involvement in European matters'.[62]

From the start, the principle of supremacy of EU law did not follow a congruent line of interpretation in Polish jurisprudence. The Polish Constitutional Tribunal considered supremacy in a number of cases regarding the accession procedure K11/03,[63] bio-components in gasoline and diesel K 33/03[64] in which it looked at the compatibility of EU Law with Article 31(3) of the Polish Constitution,[65] or participation of foreigners in European Parliamentary elections K 15/04,[66] in which it decided that Article 174 of the law concerning elections to the European Parliament conforms with Article 4.1 of the Constitution.[67] Compatibility with the Constitution was also raised in the case K 24/04 on inequality in competences of Sejm and Senate committees in respect of EU legislative proposals.[68] The case concerned Article 9 of the Polish Law of 11 March 2004[69] on the cooperation of the Council of Ministers with the Sejm and the Senate in matters related to the EU membership. It excluded the obligation imposed on the Council of Ministers to seek the opinion of the competent authority on the draft legal act of the EU prior to its examination in the Council of the EU, pursuant to Article 10(2) and Article 95(1) of the Constitution.[70] The Constitutional Tribunal held that Article 9 of the above law is inconsistent with Article 10(2) and Article 95(1) of the

61. Piotr Cichocki, 3 *Przeglad Zachodni*, Polish Attitudes Towards the European Union, 2011. Available at: https://www.researchgate.net/publication/277262049_Polish_Attitudes_Towards_the_European_Union [accessed Oct 23 2021].
62. *Ibid.*
63. Polish Constitutional Tribunal, Judgment K11/03 at https://sip.lex.pl/akty-prawne/dzu-dziennik-ustaw/wyrok-trybunalu-konstytucyjnego-sygn-akt-k-11-03-17031042: also https://sip.lex.pl/akty-prawne/dzu-dziennik-ustaw/wyrok-trybunalu-konstytucyjnego-sygn-akt-k-11-03-17031042.
64. Polish Constitutional Tribunal, Judgment of 21 April 2004, K 33/03 Bio-Components in Gasoline and Diesel at https://trybunal.gov.pl/.
65. https://trybunal.gov.pl/fileadmin/content/omowienia/K_33_03_GB.pdf.
66. Polish Constitutional Tribunal at https://isap.sejm.gov.pl/isap.nsf/download.xsp/WDU20041301400/T/D20041400TK.pdf.
67. https://isap.sejm.gov.pl/isap.nsf/download.xsp/WDU20041301400/T/D20041400TK.pdf, p. 15.
68. Decision of Polish Constitutional Tribunal, K 24/04 https://www.saos.org.pl/judgments/107175 K24/04; Krystyna Kowalik-Bańczyk, Should We Polish It Up? The Polish Constitutional Tribunal and the Idea of Supremacy of EU Law, *German Law Journal*, 2005, 1355-1366.
69. Article 9 ustawy z dnia 11 marca 2004 r. o współpracy Rady Ministrów z Sejmem i Senatem w sprawach związanych z członkostwem Rzeczypospolitej Polskiej w Unii Europejskiej (Dz. U. Nr 52, poz. 515), https://www.saos.org.pl/judgments/107175 K24/04.
70. https://www.saos.org.pl/judgments/107175 K24/04.

Constitution to the extent that it omits the obligation to consult the competent authority under the Senate's bylaws.[71]

Further, the Constitutional Tribunal in the *European Arrest Warrant* case[72] demonstrated some respect for the principle of supremacy,[73] denying it straight after in the *Validity of Accession Treaty* case.[74] In this judgment, the Constitutional Tribunal rejects the absolute nature of the principle of supremacy.[75] The claim was brought by the deputies who were against the decision of Poland joining the EU and the general acceptance of the *acquis communautaire*. The deputies opposed the accession agreement and in particular, the system of Central Banks seen as threatening Polish sovereignty and the superiority of the Polish Constitution.[76] The Constitutional Tribunal referring to Article 8 of the Polish Constitution rules that the Constitution is the highest source of law in Poland; the international obligations also need to be respected implying therefore that there will be a set of parallel rules that would coincide in Poland.[77] In its decision hostile to EU supremacy, the Tribunal declared that 'it is to the Member States and not the ECJ to appraise whether the EU Institutions acted within the limit of their competences and if they did not, supremacy does not apply at all'.[78] Kowalik-Bańczyk warned in 2005 that the decision was worrying since it could force Polish judges to disregard EU measures because they conflict (in their opinion) with the Polish Constitution.[79] The subsequent Polish Constitutional Tribunal's decision in 2010 (K32/09) on the conformity of the Lisbon Treaty with the Constitution ruled that there are constitutional limits of the conferral of the competences to an international organisation where such a conferral could endanger the constitutional foundations of

71. /1/A/2005 Wyrok z dnia 12 stycznia 2005 r.Sygn. akt K 24/04, Sentencja została ogłoszona dnia 18 stycznia 2005 r. w Dz. U. Nr 11, poz. 89.
72. Polish Constitutional Tribunal, Judgment of 27 April 2005, P 1/05 at https://trybunal.gov.pl/fileadmin/content/omowienia/P_1_05_full_GB.pdf.
73. Polish Constitutional Tribunal, Judgment of 27th of April 2005, European Arrest Warrant.
74. Judgment of 11 May 2005, K 18/04, English and German Summary available at: www.trybunal.gov.pl, commentary in *ibid.*, Krystyna Kowalik-Bańczyk, Should We Polish It Up? The Polish Constitutional Tribunal and the Idea of Supremacy of EU.
75. K 18/04, Konstytucyjność przekazania kompetencji organizacji międzynarodowej (astrid-online.it) https://www.astrid-online.it/static/upload/protected/K_18/K_18_04_GB.pdf accessed 10 August 2022.
76. K 18/04, Wyrok Trybunału Konstytucyjnego Opublikowano: OTK-A 2005/5/49, Dz.U.2005/86/744, LEX nr 155502 at https://konstytucyjne.home.amu.edu.pl/wp-content/uploads/2018/12/Wyrok_TK_K-18-04.pdf.
77. Constitutional Tribunal, Judgment of the Polish Constitutional Tribunal concerning the constitutionality of Poland's accession to the European Union (release of 11th May 2005) at http://www.proyectos.cchs.csic.es/euroconstitution/library/documents/Polish%20Constitutional%20Tribunal_Judgment%20Polands%20accession%20to%20the%20EU.pdf.
78. *Ibid.*, Krystyna Kowalik-Bańczyk; Poland's accession to the European Union (release of 11 May 2005) at http://www.proyectos.cchs.csic.es/euroconstitution/library/documents/Polish%20Constitutional%20Tribunal_Judgment%20Polands%20accession%20to%20the%20EU.pdf: Constitutional Tribunal Decision, Judgment of the Polish Constitutional Tribunal concerning the constitutionality of Poland's accession to the European Union (release of 11th May 2005) at http://www.proyectos.cchs.csic.es/euroconstitution/library/documents/Polish%20Constitutional%20Tribunal_Judgment%20Polands%20accession%20to%20the%20EU.pdf.
79. P. Kubicki and M. Margoński, Prymat bezwzględny czy względny, *Rzeczpospolita*, 25.07.2005, C3 in *ibid.*, Krystyna Kowalik-Bańczyk.

Poland.[80] Also in case SK 45/09 Polish Constitutional Tribunal ruled on the compatibility of EU secondary legislation with the Polish Constitution departing from CJEU's well-established jurisprudence.[81]

In any event, these decisions embrace the thesis of the Polish resistance to the absolute nature of the principle of supremacy opting for a coexistence of two superior sources of law, well embedded in the concepts such as constitutional pluralism, composite constitutionalism,[82] or multilevel constitutionalism.[83] Nonetheless, Poland was not the only one questioning the absolute nature of the principle of supremacy in the recent years, just to mention the Danish case *Ajos*,[84] or a widely discussed decision in *Weiss II* of the German Federal Constitutional Court in Karlsruhe on 5 May 2020.[85] Kozlowski warned in 2021 that the decision in *Weiss II*, might have set a dangerous precedent for other Member States to challenge or even to defy compliance with this principle.[86]

4 DEMOCRATIC BACKSLIDING: THE LAW & JUSTICE PARTY (PIS) REFORMS OF THE JUDICIAL SYSTEM IN POLAND

The battle for the independence of Polish Courts started in 2015 when a combined presidential and parliamentary victory of the populist Law and Justice Party (PiS)[87] sharply ended the process of democratisation, and rebuilding of the democratic institutions started more than two decades before. The Law and Justice Party (PiS)

80. Polish Constitutional Tribunal, Judgment of 24 November 2010 at https://trybunal.gov.pl/fileadmin/content/omowienia/K_32_09_EN.pdf, also Peter Cleppe, An Overview of National Top Courts Challenging the Supremacy of EU Law, 12 October 2012 at https://www.brusselsreport.eu/2021/10/12/an-overview-of-national-top-courts-challenging-the-supremacy-of-eu-law/.
81. Polish Constitutional Tribunal, Judgment SK 45/09 https://trybunal.gov.pl/fileadmin/content/omowienia/SK_45_09_EN.pdf.
82. Ingolf Pernice, 'Theorie und Praxis des Europäischen Verfassungsbundes', in Callies (ed.), *Verfassungswandel im europäischen Staaten- und Verfassungsverbund* (Mohr Siebeck, 2007) in Gabor Halmai, Absolute Primacy of EU Law vs. Pluralism: the Role of Courts – Concluding Remarks, at https://me.eui.eu/wp-content/uploads/sites/385/2018/05/IJPL_Special_Issue_Concluding_remarks_Halmai_final.pdf.
83. I. Pernice, 'Multilevel Constitutionalism in the European Union', 5 *European Law Review*, 2002, 511 in *ibid.*, Halmai.
84. Case C-441/14 *Dansk Industri (DI), acting on behalf of Ajos A/S v. Estate of Karsten Eigil Rasmussen* [2016] ECLI:EU:C:2016:278.
85. German Federal Constitutional Court, judgment of the Second Senate of 5 May 2020, 2 BvR 859/15, 2 BvR 1651/15, 2 BvR 2006/15, 2 BvR 980/16 (PSPP judgment); BVerfG, Judgment of the Second Senate of 05 May 2020 – 2 BvR 859/15 *(Weiss II);* at https://www.bundesverfassungsgericht.de/SharedDocs/Entscheidungen/DE/2020/05/rs20200505_2bvr085915.html.
86. J. Kozlowski, A Game of Thrones: The Battle for the Supremacy of EU Law Following Weiss II, 2 *York Law Review* 191 (2021).
87. Wojciech Sadurski, How Democracy Dies (in Poland): A Case Study of Anti-Constitutional Populist Backsliding (17 January 2018). Sydney Law School Research Paper No. 18/01, Available at SSRN: https://ssrn.com/abstract=3103491 or http://dx.doi.org/10.2139/ssrn.3103491 Kochenov D. & Bárd P., 'The last soldier standing? Courts versus politicians and the Rule of Law crisis in the new Member States of the EU', *European Yearbook of Constitutional Law* 1 (2019), 243-288.

came to power with its legal and political reform that undermined the fundamentals of democratic institutions.[88] Straightaway in 2015, the winning party presented its reform of the Constitutional Tribunal that distorted the principle of separation of power set up in the Polish Constitution.[89] Sadurski comments that PiS went so far as 'to dismantle institutional checks on the government (including paralysis of the Constitutional Tribunal, and then conversion of it into an active supporter of the government) and to erode a number of individual and political rights, such as the right to assembly and privacy.'[90] This happened through a combination of different measures and a smart manipulation of the composition of the judges sitting on the Constitutional Tribunal. Apart from 'taking over' of the Constitutional Tribunal' the Government quickly dissolved the National Council of the Judiciary and created a new one, (neo) National Council of Judiciary elected by the politicians and not the judges.[91] Further attacks on the judiciary consisted in lowering the retirement age for the judges in the Supreme Court that resulted in the compulsory retirement for some. In addition, the subsequent reforms created two new Chambers in the Supreme Court, the Disciplinary Chamber and the Extraordinary Control and Public Affairs Chamber both controlled by the ruling party. Further, disciplinary proceedings against the judges were introduced in the hands of the Minister of Justice.[92] The latter merged with the prosecutor's office and as a head of the ruling party controlled the system of public prosecution.[93]

The PiS party radical reforms of the judiciary brought in 2017-2019 violated the most important constitutional guarantees such as the principle of separation of power enshrined in Article 10 of the Polish Constitution.[94] Further, the reforms disregarded a key article 173 on judicial independence stipulating that courts and tribunals constitute

88. Wojciech Sadurski, *ibid.*
89. Ustawa z dnia 19 listopada 2015 r. o zmianie ustawy o Trybunale Konstytucyjnym (Dz. U. poz. 1928); Ustawa z dnia 22 grudnia 2015 r. o zmianie ustawy o Trybunale Konstytucyjnym (Dz. U. poz. 2217);Ustawa z dnia 22 lipca 2016 r. o Trybunale Konstytucyjnym (Dz. U. poz. 1157); Ustawa z dnia 30 listopada 2016 r. o statusie sędziów Trybunału Konstytucyjnego (Dz. U. poz. 2073); Ustawa z dnia 30 listopada 2016 r. o organizacji i trybie postępowania przed Trybunałem Konstytucyjnym (Dz. U. poz. 2072); Ustawa z dnia 13 grudnia 2016 r. Przepisy wprowadzające ustawę o organizacji i trybie postępowania przed Trybunałem Konstytucyjnym oraz ustawę o statusie sędziów Trybunału Konstytucyjnego (Dz. U. poz. 2074). Helsinska fundacja praw Czlowieka i Obywatela, 2019, Rządy Prawem zamiast Rządów Praw – Zagrozenia dla Ochrony Praw Człowieka w Polsce w latach 2015-2019 (2019) at https://www.hfhr.pl/wp-content/uploads/2019/09/Rz%C4%85dy-prawem-FIN-web.pdf.
90. *Ibid.*, Wojciech Sadurski, How Democracy Dies (in Poland): A Case Study of Anti-Constitutional Populist Backsliding, 17 January 2018 Law, Political Science, DOI:10.2139/SSRN.3103491 Corpus ID: 158304600, Sydney Law School Legal Studies Research Paper No. 18/01.
91. Draginji Nadaždin, Jak Władza Wykonawcza Przejęła Władzę Sądowniczą https://amnesty.org.pl/kampanie/wolne-sady-wolni-ludzie/.
92. *Ibid.*
93. Wojciech Sadurski, The European Commission Cedes Its Crucial Leverage Vis-à-Vis the Rule of Law in Poland, *VerfBlog*, 2022/6/06, https://verfassungsblog.de/the-european-commission-cedes-its-crucial-leverage-vis-a-vis-the-rule-of-law-in-poland/, DOI: 10.17176/20220606-182327-0.
94. Polish Constitution, OJ Dz.U.1997.78.483 Akt obowiązujący Wersja od: 21 października 2009 r. Art. 10. [The Principle of Separation of Powers] 1. The Constitution of the Republic of Poland is based on the division and balance between the legislative, executive and judiciary powers.

a separate branch of government and are independent of the other branches.[95] They also contravene Article 179, providing that the President appoints judges for an indefinite period as well as Article 186 stating that the National Council of Judiciary shall be the guardian of the independence of the judicial system in Poland. In addition to the above, the PiS reforms were also incompatible with Article 187.1 on the composition of the National Council of the Judiciary.[96] Finally, some other principles that will not be discussed here such as the principle of social pluralism, the principle of religious, philosophical and philosophical impartiality of public authorities, a pillar of the Polish Constitution were also infringed. In December 2015, the Constitutional Tribunal ruled on the first wave of the PiS Reforms adjudicating constitutionality of the 2015 Act,[97] concerning the nomination of the new judges and maintaining in office the previous ones.[98] The Tribunal, although substantially impaired by the 2015 reform, stood up for the Constitution.[99] Nonetheless, the Constitutional Tribunal was increasingly subjected to political pressure. Sadurski commented that the Constitutional Tribunal was disabled 'through legislative bombardment, involving the enactment of numerous laws meant to paralyse its operation, and through court packing, including openly unconstitutional means'.[100]

In 2016, the European Commission started a dialogue with the Polish government activating for the first time the Rule of Law Framework, followed by the Rule of Law Recommendations over 2016 and 2017.[101] None of these steps was able to stop Polish Government from pursuing its radical plans to subject the judicial system to political control. In December 2017, the Commission initiated the procedure under Article 7(1), used for the first time, for the violation of the Rule of Law.[102] In fact, neither the

95. Case K 34/15, 2015 at https://trybunal.gov.pl/en/hearings/judgments/art/8866-ustawa-o-trybunale-konstytucyjnym.
96. Constitution of the Republic of Poland, Articles 186.1. and 187.1.
97. Marcin Wiącek Constitutional Crisis in Poland 2015-2016 in the Light of the Rule of Law Principle. In A. von Bogdandy, P. Bogdanowicz, I. Canor, C. Grabenwarter, M. Taborowski and, M. Schmidt (eds), *Defending Checks and Balances in EU Member States*. Beiträge zum ausländischen öffentlichen Recht und Völkerrecht, vol 298 (Springer, 2021), https://doi.org/10.1007/978-3-662-62317-6_2.
98. Polish Constitutional Tribunal, case 185/11/A/2015 https://trybunal.gov.pl/en/hearings/judgments/art/8866-ustawa-o-trybunale-konstytucyjnym.
99. Tomasz Tadeusz Koncewicz, Of Institutions, Democracy, Constitutional Self-Defence and the Rule of Law: The Judgments of the Polish Constitutional Tribunal in Cases K 34/15, K 35/15 and beyond, *Common Market Law Review*, 53(6) 2016, 1753-1792, at https://doi.org/10.54648/cola2016149; Tomasz Tadeusz Koncewicz, Bruised, but Not Dead (Yet): The Polish Constitutional Court Has Spoken, *VerfBlog*, 2015/12/10, https://verfassungsblog.de/bruised-but-not-dead-yet-the-polish-constitutional-court-has-spoken-2/, DOI: 10.17176/20170529-162502.
100. Wojciech Sadurski, *Poland's Constitutional Breakdown* (OUP, 2019).
101. *Ibid.*; Commission Recommendation (EU) 2017/146 of 21 December 2016 regarding the rule of law in Poland, complementary to Recommendation (EU) 2016/1374 C/2016/8950 ELI: http://data.europa.eu/eli/reco/2017/146/oj; Official Journal of the European Union, L 228, 2 September 2017 Commission Recommendation (EU) 2018/103 of 20 December 2017 regarding the rule of law in Poland complementary to Commission Recommendation (EU) 2017/1520 of 26 July 2017 regarding the rule of law in Poland complementary to Recommendations (EU) 2016/1374 and (EU) 2017/146,
102. *Ibid.*, *see also* 2021 Rule of Law Report (2021/2180(INI)) at https://ec.europa.eu/info/policies/justice-and-fundamental-rights/upholding-rule-law/rule-law/rule-law-mechanism/2021-rule-law-report_en.

Commission nor the Council were sufficiently firm and decisive to put Poland to the wall. Pech et al. observe that during the COVID-19 pandemic, the Council did not organise a single Article 7 hearing.[103] The Commission was slow to react, waited almost two years before activating Article 7(1) TEU despite evidence of persistent violation of the EU principles.[104] Further, it has continued its minimalistic approach till most recently, first while setting milestones and second while assessing the Polish government's amendments in June 2022. Yet, it was manifest that the situation was only getting worse and the Commission should have used all possible tools to prevent the consistent degradation of the democratic guarantees.

Between 2015-2019, the Sejm adopted over 20 laws on the administration of justice, independent institutions and the protection of fundamental rights and freedoms. The law passed so far has been used instrumentally, primarily as a tool for realising the particular interests of the ruling coalition.[105] Polish democratic backsliding reached its apogee with the so-called 'Muzzle law' subjecting judges to disciplinary investigations, hearings and sanctions for the content of their decisions.[106] The PiS ruling party has progressively but consistently taken control over authorities that it did not control itself. Since 2015 the situation deteriorated further worsening the relationship with the EU. The Polish Government ignored the Commission's Recommendations and all the efforts to establish a dialogue and to address the problem before any escalation. Subsequently, Polish democratic backsliding[107] has been at the origin of many CJEU decisions and the latter took the opportunity to refine the definitions of the EU fundamental principles such as supremacy and the rule of law.[108]

In 2018 the Commission initiated another infringement procedure, this time, questioning the new rules on retirement of judges, in particular their application to the first president of the Supreme Court that shortened the President's mandate.[109] The

103. *Ibid.*, Pech et al. 20.
104. *Ibid.*, 21.
105. Helsinska fundacja praw Czlowieka i Obywatela, 2019, Rządy Prawem zamiast Rządów Praw – Zagrozenia dla Ochrony Praw Człowieka W Polsce, 2019 w latach 2015-2019 https://www.hfhr.pl/wp-content/uploads/2019/09/Rz%C4%85dy-prawem-FIN-web.pdf 256.
106. Law 20 December 2019, The Muzzle Act, Ustawa z dnia 20 grudnia 2019 r. o zmianie ustawy – Prawo o ustroju sądów powszechnych, ustawy o Sądzie Najwyzszym oraz niektórych innych ustaw at https://sip.lex.pl/akty-prawne/dzu-dziennik-ustaw/zmiana-ustawy-prawo-o-ustroju-sadow-powszechnych-ustawy-o-sadzie-18954631?_ga=2.152251642.2121715069.1667065926-1231126736.1666477938#xd_co_f=NDdhODYwMTAtMzYzMi00ODc5LWEyZDYtNjdiNTkxZWQ1NDg1~.
107. Wojchiech Sadurski, On the Relative Irrelevance of Constitutional Design: Lessons from Poland (13 June 2019). Sydney Law School Research Paper No. #19/34, Available at SSRN: https://ssrn.com/abstract=3403327; *see also* D. Kochenov and L. Pech, Respect for the Rule of Law in the Case Law of the European Court of Justice (SIEPS, 2021). *See also* Laurent Pech and Sébastien Platon, 'Judicial Independence under Threat: The Court of Justice to the Rescue in the ASJP Case', *Common Market Law Review*, 55(6), 2018, 1827-1854 at DOI: 10.54648/COLA2018146.
108. Judgment of 22 February 2022 (Case C-430/21), https://eucrim.eu/news/cjeu-again-finds-romanian-judicial-system-flawed/ on Romanian justice system.
109. European Commission, Commission Staff Working Document, 2022 Rule of Law Report Country Chapter on the rule of law situation in Poland, Accompanying the document, Communication from the Commission, 2022 Rule of Law Report – The rule of law situation in the European Union, COM(2022) 500 final, Brussels; Rule of Law: Commission launches

president of the Republic of Poland could prolong the judges' mandate for three years renewable once.[110] However, the use of this power is at the discretion of the president of the Republic of Poland, in the absence of any criteria that would justify the president's decision and more importantly, no judicial review is available from the president's decision.[111] The retirement provisions introduced by the reform were manifestly an attack on the judges' independence and impartiality of the Supreme Court, and the full renewal of the panel ensured almost undisturbed government influence. Following the Commission's action for failure to fulfil the obligations under the Treaty, the CJEU imposed an interim relief on Poland and ordered reinstatement of the judges who were forced to retire.[112] Despite the CJEU Order, the Polish government did not reinstate the judges: quite the opposite, it continued introducing new laws in a total disrespect of the EU values.

The Polish Supreme Court seized the CJEU with a preliminary ruling regarding the compatibility with Directive 2000/78/EC (Articles 2 and 9), compatibility with Article 47 of the Charter of Fundamental Rights, right to a remedy and effective judicial protection and judicial independence of the Disciplinary Chamber of the Supreme Court.[113] More importantly, the Supreme Court raised a crucial point on EU Law regarding the power to disapply legislation clashing with the EU Law.[114]

The saga continued in 2019 when the Commission initiated another infringement procedure concerning the newly introduced disciplinary regime against judges.[115] The new law subjected the ordinary court judges to 'disciplinary investigations, procedures and ultimately sanctions, on account of the content of their judicial decisions'.[116] In the meantime, the Polish government through the Law of 21 November 2018,[117] removed the controversial provision on compulsory retirement at the age of 65. In exchange for

infringement procedure to protect the independence of the Polish Supreme Court, 2 July 2018 https://ec.europa.eu/commission/presscorner/detail/en/IP_18_4341.

110. Rule of Law: Commission launches infringement procedure to protect the independence of the Polish Supreme Court, 2 July 2018 https://ec.europa.eu/commission/presscorner/detail/en/IP_18_4341.
111. *Ibid.*
112. Case C-619/18 R *Commission v. Poland*, EU:C:2018:852 and EU:C:2018:910. Also https://ec.europa.eu/commission/presscorner/detail/en/ip_21_1524.
113. https://curia.europa.eu/juris/liste.jsf?num = C-585/18, Case, C-585/18 *A. K. and Others v. Sąd Najwyzszy (Independence of the Disciplinary Chamber of the Supreme Court)* https://curia.europa.eu/juris/liste.jsf?num = C-585/18.
114. C-585/18, *A.K. (Independence of the Disciplinary Chamber of the Supreme Court)* at https://curia.europa.eu/juris/liste.jsf?num = C-585/18.
115. Rule of Law: European Commission launches infringement procedure to protect judges in Poland from political control, 3 April 2019 at https://ec.europa.eu/commission/presscorner/detail/es/IP_19_1957.
116. *Ibid.*, also Wojchiech Sadurski, How Democracy Dies (in Poland): A Case Study of Anti-Constitutional Populist Backsliding (17 January 2018). Sydney Law School Research Paper No. 18/01, Available at SSRN: https://ssrn.com/abstract = 3103491 or http://dx.doi.org/10.2139/ssrn.3103491.
117. Law of the 21 November 2018, Ustawa z dnia 21 listopada 2018 r.o zmianie ustawy o Sądzie Najwyzszym http://orka.sejm.gov.pl/proc8.nsf/ustawy/3013_u.htm.

this concession, the government claimed that there is no need for a preliminary ruling and since then openly dissuaded the courts to make a reference to the CJEU.[118]

5 THE CJEU STANDPOINT AND THE FIGHT FOR JUDICIAL INDEPENDENCE IN POLAND

One of the earlier CJEU decisions in the Polish democratic backsliding saga considered the Minister of Justice's discretionary power to prolong the mandate of judges who have reached retirement age, as well as a power to appoint or dismiss the Court Presidents, undermining the independence of Polish courts and the conformity of the reforms with Articles 2 TEU, 19(1) TEU in combination with Article 47 of the EU Charter of Fundamental Rights.[119] In particular, the new rules for the prolongation of the judges' mandates allow the Minister of Justice to exert influence on individual ordinary judges through the vague criteria undermining the principle of irremovability of judges.[120] The Court decided that the Polish Law introducing the above rules is contrary to EU law.[121] Soon after, the CJEU was seized to consider the independence and impartiality of two judicial bodies: the (neo) National Council of the Judiciary, created in 2017, whose members' appointment depended on Sejm,[122] and the newly created Disciplinary Chamber of the Polish Supreme Court designed to hear cases against the judges, that due to its composition, the appointment procedure and its operation raised serious questions on the extent to which it was independent from the legislative and executive power.[123]

The CJEU in its landmark decision[124] made three important points. First, it provided a definition of 'an independent and impartial Tribunal' by reference to the criteria stemming from the ECtHR case law, second, decided that it was up to the referring court to determine according to the relevant factors whether it applies to [the Court in question], and third, building on its own earlier judgment in *Simmenthal* declaring that the national court must set aside any provision of national law which

118. Michał Ziółkowski, Two Faces of the Polish Supreme Court after 'Reforms' of the Judiciary System in Poland: The Question of Judicial Independence and Appointments, *Journal on Law and Integration*, 5(1), 2020, 347-362.
119. Case C-192/18 *Commission* v. *Poland*, (Grand Chamber), 5 November 2019 at ECLI-:EU:C:2019:924, https://curia.europa.eu/juris/document/document.jsf;jsessionid = D6BFAD4 CFFD094567EF89DA7F745B0A6?text = &docid = 219742&pageIndex = 0&doclang = EN&mode = req&dir = &occ = first&part = 1&cid = 7814358.
120. *Ibid.*, Case C-192/18, *Commission v. Poland*, ECLI:EU:C:2019:924, 5 November 2019, commentary at https://www.europeansources.info/record/case-c-192-18-commission-v-poland/.
121. *Ibid.*
122. *Ibid.*; Michał Ziółkowski, Two Faces of the Polish Supreme Court After 'Reforms' of the Judiciary System in Poland: The Question of Judicial Independence and Appointments, *Journal on Law and Integration*, 5(1), 2020, 347-362, at 349.
123. Common Position on the Judgment in Joined Cases *A.K. and Others* (C-585/18, C-624/18 and C-625/18) https://ruleoflaw.pl/common-position-on-the-judgment-in-joined-cases-a-k-and-others-c-585-18-c-624-18-and-c-625-18/.
124. Joined Cases *A.K. and Others* C-585/18, C-624/18 and C-625/18 ECLI:EU:C:2019:982.

may conflict with EC Law,[125] the Court ruled that national courts are under the duty to disapply acts breaching EU Law.[126] This is an important standpoint on EU supremacy confirming its predominant place in EU integration.

Moreover, the CJEU provided criteria for assessment of an impartial tribunal by stating 'a national court is not an independent and impartial tribunal within the meaning of the EU law where the objective circumstances in which that court was formed, its characteristics, and the means by which its members have been appointed are capable of giving rise to legitimate doubts, in the minds of subjects of the law, as to the imperviousness of that court to external interference'.[127] The CJEU warned that 'the independence of the judiciary must be ensured in relation to the legislature and the executive'.[128] 'In that regard, it is necessary that judges are protected from external intervention or pressure liable to jeopardise their independence.'[129] The Court pointed out that 'the substantive conditions and detailed procedural rules governing the adoption of appointment decisions are such 'that they cannot give rise to reasonable doubts, in the minds of individuals, as to the imperviousness of the judges concerned to external factors and as to their neutrality with respect to the interests before them, once appointed as judges'.[130] The CJEU when defining an independent court made a reference to Article 6(1) of the ECHR, invoking the concept of an appearance of independence while assessing if the body is independent or not.[131] The third point raised by the Court brought a new element to the concept of supremacy of EU law strengthening the *Simmenthal* formula: 'the principle of the primacy of EU law must be interpreted as requiring the referring court to disapply the provision of national law [that is contrary to EU Law]'.[132] The CJEU reminded us that in light of the principle of the primacy of EU law the referring court is under the duty to disapply any provision of national law whose jurisdiction to hear and rule on the cases does not meet the requirements for independence and impartiality.[133] Further, it clarified the meaning of judicial impartiality and independence in EU Law, adding some discernible content to Article 2 TEU. Despite its non-negligible merits, the judgment was a disappointment for some who expected a direct condemnation of the reforms in Poland.[134]

Ziółkowski explored three hypotheses that the CJEU could have followed in this case: either, to establish a minimum standard of judicial independence as suggested by

125. Case 106/77 *Amministrazione delle Finanze dello Stato v. Simmenthal SpA*. [1978] ECLI identifier: ECLI:EU:C:1978:49.
126. ECLI:EU:C:2019:982.
127. Piotr Uhma, Joined Cases C-585/18, C-624/18, C-625/18, *American Journal of International Law*, V. 114, (4), October 2020, pp. 743-749 DOI: https://doi.org/10.1017/ajil.2020.80.
128. Joined Cases C-585/18, C-624/18 and C-625/18 ECLI:EU:C:2019:982 para. 124.
129. *Ibid*., para. 125.
130. *Ibid*., para. 134.
131. *Ibid*.; Piotr Uhma, Joined Cases C-585/18, C-624/18, C-625/18, *American Journal of International Law*, 114(4), October 2020, 743-749 DOI: https://doi.org/10.1017/ajil.2020.80.
132. Cases C-624/18 and C-625/18, ECLI:EU:C:2019:982.
133. *Ibid*.; Joined Cases C-585/18, C-624/18 and C-625/18 ECLI:EU:C:2019:982.
134. Laurant Pech, Patryk Wachowiec & Dariusz Mazur, Poland's Rule of Law Breakdown: A Five-Year Assessment of EU's (In)Action, Hague *Journal on the Rule of Law*, 13, 2021, 1-43.

AG Tanchev,[135] or to condemn openly the judicial reforms in Poland or to set up the test of the appearance of independence according to which national judicial authorities could assess the impartiality of the court.[136] The CJEU chose the third solution, a diplomatic and prudent move, recalling the purpose of the preliminary ruling and its significance for all EU Member States.[137]

The Polish response to the CJEU judgment amounted to a number of conflicting decisions, the fight between the Chambers of the Supreme Courts, ending with a judgment of the Constitutional Tribunal ostensibly departing from the CJEU ruling.

Two decisions of the Chambers of the Supreme Court merit attention. The first one, the Labour Law and Social Security Chamber of the Supreme Court followed the CJEU Judgment, reiterating the formula that the national court is under the duty to follow the CJEU judgment and should disapply any conflicting provision.[138] It ruled first that 'procedural rules of the appointment of the judges to the Disciplinary Chamber do not lead to belief that they are clear of any doubts as to the independence of these persons from external factors and their neutrality [is not in question]'.[139] The Labour and Security Chamber noted that 'Disciplinary Chamber is 'depriving judges of the Supreme Court of the right to two-instance proceedings since an appeal can only be lodged with a different panel of the Disciplinary Chamber'.[140] This type of competence indicates *a priori* violation of the constitutional guarantees of a two-instance proceedings'.[141] It also ruled that neither the Disciplinary Chamber or the Council of the Judiciary are independent courts within the meaning of EU Law.[142] Consequently, the Supreme Court revoked the resolution of the Council of the Judiciary and granted the appeal to the claimant.[143]

Unfortunately the December judgment of the Labour Law and Social Security Chamber enjoyed its full authority for a short time and must be contrasted with the Extraordinary Control and Public Affairs Chamber's Resolution adopted just weeks later.[144] The latter embraced the government's line of argumentation. It stated for example, that appointments of judges cannot be questioned before any court and there is no appeal procedure to challenge this appointment. As a result, the test of

135. Opinion of Advocate General Tanchev delivered on 27 June 2019 (1) Joined Cases C-585/18, C-624/18 and C-625/18, *A.K.* (C-585/18) ECLI:EU:C:2019:551.
136. *Ibid.*, Michał Ziółkowski, Two Faces of the Polish Supreme Court after 'Reforms' of the Judiciary System in Poland: The Question of Judicial Independence and Appointments, *European Papers*, 5(1), 2020, European Forum, Insight of 2 June 2020, 347-362 doi: 10.15166/2499-8249/362. Michał Krajewski & Michał ZiółkowskI, A. Court of Justice: EU Judicial Independence Decentralized: *A.K.*, *Common Market Law Review*, 57(4), 2020, 1107-1138, https://hdl.handle.net/1814/67954.
137. *Ibid.*, M. Krajewski & Michał Ziółkowski, EU Judicial Independence Decentralised.
138. Sygn. akt III PO 7/18 *On the appeal of A. K.* 5 December 2019, para. 83. http://www.sn.pl/sites/orzecznictwo/orzeczenia3/iii%20po%207-18-2.pdf.
139. *Ibid.*, para. 63. According to para. 134 of the CJEU decision.
140. *Ibid.* (not a proper appeal).
141. *Ibid.*, para. 64.
142. Sygn. akt III PO 7/18, para. 88. http://www.sn.pl/sites/orzecznictwo/orzeczenia3/iii%20po%207-18-2.pdf.
143. *Ibid.*, para. 88, also Ziółkowski 353.
144. I NOZP 3/19 para. 32.

appearance cannot be applied to any facts before the appointment.[145] The Supreme Court, the Chambers united, tried to settle the dispute with a new judgment that followed the content of the December Resolution of the Labour Law and Social Security Chamber and implemented the CJEU ruling.[146] The further events resemble a political intrigue. The Supreme Court ruling was disregarded by the Disciplinary Chamber and the Council of the Judiciary.[147] Further, the Constitutional Tribunal, openly supporting the Government's position ruled that the Supreme Court decision following the Judgment of the CJEU was in violation of the Polish Constitution in particular the Parliament's power to adopt laws.[148] It ruled that the Supreme Court's Resolution[149] of 23 January was unconstitutional and null and dissuaded the judges from the implementation of the CJEU judgment.[150] In February 2020 the 'Muzzle Law' came into force, preventing among other things Polish courts from making reference to the CJEU.[151] Stinicka observes that the aim of this Act was to prevent Polish courts from scrutinising the appointment procedure and questioning the independence of the neo Council of the Judiciary.[152]

The CJEU in its Order of 14 July 2021[153] ordered the Polish government to suspend the activities of the Disciplinary Chamber as well as to amend the provisions of the 'Muzzle Law' that do not comply with the EU standard judicial independence.[154] Still, the Polish Constitutional Tribunal refused to apply the CJEU's interim measures.[155] Notwithstanding, the Commission infringement procedures and the CJEU Orders the Polish government does not seem to surrender and comply with EU Law.

145. INOZP 3/19.
146. Resolution 23 January 2020, Case No. BSA I-4110-1/20 at Case BSA I-4110-1/20, Resolution of the Formation of the Combined Civil Chamber, Criminal Chamber, and Labour Law and Social Security Chamber (Sup. Ct. Pol. 23 January 2020) (Pol.), available at http://www.sn.pl/aktualnosci/SiteAssets/Lists/Wydarzenia/AllItems/BSA%20I-4110-1_20_English.pdf, also Michał Krajewski, Michał Ziółkowski, EU Judicial Independence Decentralised.
147. *Ibid.*, Michał Ziółkowski 361.
148. Constitutional Tribunal case Kpt 1/20; *see also* Resolution of 23 January 2020, case No. BSA I-4110-1/20. Constitutional Tribunal, judgement of 20 April 2020, case U 2/20. Act of 8 December 2017 Amending the Act on the National Judiciary Council and Others Acts, (Polish) Official Journal, 2018, No. 3.
149. Resolution of 23 January 2020, case No. BSA I-4110-1/20.
150. Kpt 1/20, U 20/20, Kpt 1/20 decision of 28 January 2020.
151. *Ibid.*, Piotr Uhma, Joined Cases C-585/18, C-624/18, C-625/18, *American Journal of International Law*, 114 (4), October 2020, 743-749 DOI: https://doi.org/10.1017/ajil.2020.80.
152. Dominika Sitnicka, Extraordinary Control and Public Affairs Chamber to Euthanise the Supreme Court's Own Resolution https://ruleoflaw.pl/extraordinary-control-and-public-affairs-chamber-to-euthanise-the-supreme-courts-own-resolution/12, February 2020.
153. Case C-204/21 R, *Commission v. Poland*, Order of the Vice-President of the Court, 14 July 2021, EU:C:2021:593.
154. Luke Dimitrios Spieker, Case Law: The Conflict over the Polish Disciplinary Regime for Judges – An Acid Test for Judicial Independence, Union Values and the Primacy of EU Law: *Commission v. Poland, Common Market Law Review* 59, 2022, 777-812.
155. Polish Constitutional Tribunal, Decision on 14 July 2021, P 7/20 | 14 VII 2021.

6 DEFYING EU SUPREMACY: POLISH CONSTITUTIONAL TRIBUNAL JUDGMENT OF 7 OCTOBER 2021

The decision of Polish Constitutional Tribunal on 7 October 2021 is the most articulated example of the Member State's defiance of the principle of supremacy of EU Law. This judgment comes a year after the German Constitutional Court questioned supremacy in the *Weiss II* case.[156] However, the Polish Constitutional Tribunal was twice as arrogant as the German Constitutional Court declaring a whole set of the provisions of the EU Treaty incompatible with the Polish Constitution and therefore invalid. The decision was a response to Prime Minister Mateusz Morawiecki's application to settle the issue of primacy of national law, in particular the Polish Constitution over EU law. He questioned whether the principle of supremacy of EU law was consistent with the Polish Constitution. His application was a reaction to the CJEU judgment[157] and regarded a referral from the Polish Supreme Administrative Court regarding the appointment of judges to the neo National Council of the Judiciary. The CJEU ruled that the amendments made to the Act on the National Council of the Judiciary, which led to the abolition of effective judicial control of the Council's decisions on submitting motions to the President, violate EU law.[158] The CJEU reiterated its supremacy formula on disapplication of the conflicting national law: 'where it is proved that the second subparagraph of Article 19(1) TEU has been infringed, the principle of primacy of EU law must be interpreted as requiring the referring court to disapply those provisions and to apply instead the national provisions previously in force while itself exercising the judicial review envisaged by those latter provisions.'[159] This was clearly the judgment that Prime Minister Mateusz Morawiecki and his ruling party (PiS) did not like and did not accept. He questioned the EU's interference into the Polish judicial reforms claiming that the EU exceeds the limits of its competences. The Constitutional Tribunal decided in line with Morawiecki's expectations and ruled that the CJEU's interference into Polish judicial reforms 'violates the principle of the Rule of Law, supremacy of the Constitution and the principle of preserving sovereignty in the process of European integration'.[160] In short, the Constitutional Tribunal manifestly disregarded the core values of the EU and the EU acquis declaring that CJEU jurisprudence empowering national courts to abrogate national laws conflicting with the EU Law is inconsistent with the Polish Constitution.[161]

156. Case C-493/17 *Weiss and others v. Bundesregierung*, EU:C:2018:1000 – 'Weiss I' followed by Bundesverfassungsgericht (BVerfG) of 5 May 2020.
157. Case C-824/18 *A.B. and Others (Nomination des juges à la Cour suprême – Recours)* [2021], ECLI:EU:C:2021:153.
158. *Ibid.*
159. *Ibid.* (last paragraph of the decision).
160. Zosia Wanat, Court Ruling Puts Poland on a Collision Course with the EU's Legal Order, 7 October 2021, at https://www.politico.eu/article/poland-european-union-constitution-justice-treaties/.
161. Trybunał Konstytucyjny uznał wyzszość prawa polskiego nad prawem unijnym, 7 October 2021 https://www.onet.pl/informacje/onetwiadomosci/tk-uznal-wyzszosc-prawa-polskiego-nad-prawem-unijnym/nfywm7v,79cfc278.

The Tribunal found that the provisions of the EU Treaty are unconstitutional to the extent that the EU Institutions operate outside the limits of powers conferred by Poland in the Treaties, and according to which 'the Constitution is not the highest law in the Republic of Poland' (that otherwise should be evident).[162] While assessing Article 1, first and second paragraphs, in conjunction with Article 4(3) TEU the Constitutional Tribunal ruled that 'a) the European Union authorities act outside the scope of the competences conferred upon them by the Republic of Poland in the Treaties; b)[according to these provisions] the Constitution is not the supreme law of the Republic of Poland [...] [all the above is] inconsistent with Article 2, Article 8 and Article 90(1) of the Constitution of the Republic of Poland.'[163] Similarly, the Constitutional Tribunal decided in point 2 that 'Article 19(1) TEU, second subparagraph allowing tribunals to 'bypass the provisions of the Constitution in the course of adjudication – is inconsistent with Article 2, Article 7, Article 8(1), Article 90(1) and Article 178(1) of the Constitution'.[164] More importantly, in point 3, Constitutional Tribunal states 'Article 19(1), second subparagraph, and Article 2 TEU– insofar as, for the purpose of ensuring effective legal protection in the areas covered by EU law and ensuring the independence of judges – they grant domestic courts (common courts, administrative courts, military courts, and the Supreme Court) the competence to: a) review the legality of the procedure for appointing a judge, including the review of the legality of the act in which the President of the Republic appoints a judge – are inconsistent with Article 2, Article 8(1), Article 90(1) and Article 179 in conjunction with Article 144(3)(17) of the Constitution.'[165] It is also incompatible with the Polish Constitution to 'b) review the legality of the National Council of the Judiciary's resolutions [...], c) determine the defectiveness of the process of appointing a judge.'[166]

The Constitutional Tribunal took the stand that it was up to the Republic of Poland to shape the system of justice in its own country; the matter which belongs to the Polish constitutional identity. Therefore, any power in this regard has never been transferred to the EU and remains an exclusive competence of the Polish legislator. Moreover, according to the provisions of the Constitution, such a transfer could never take place.[167] Thus, the CJEU jurisprudence which interferes with the Polish system of administration of justice falls within the sphere of Polish constitutional identity, which

162. *Ibid.*
163. Constitutional Tribunal, Judgment K 3/21 of 7 October 2021 at https://trybunal.gov.pl/en/hearings/judgments/art/11662-ocena-zgodnosci-z-konstytucja-rp-wybranych-przepisow-traktatu-o-unii-europejskiej *see also* Fryderyk Zoll, Katarzyna Południak-Gierz and Wojciech Bańczyk, Primacy of EU Law and Jurisprudence of Polish Constitutional Tribunal Recent Developments in the Light of the Polish Constitutional Tribunal's Case Law, June 2022, EU Parliament https://www.europarl.europa.eu/RegData/etudes/STUD/2022/732475/IPOL_STU(2022)732475_EN.pdf.
164. *Ibid.*, K 3/21.
165. *Ibid.*
166. Constitutional Tribunal, Judgment K 3/21 of 7 October 2021 at https://trybunal.gov.pl/en/hearings/judgments/art/11662-ocena-zgodnosci-z-konstytucja-rp-wybranych-przepisow-traktatu-o-unii-europejskiej.
167. Trybunał Konstytucyjny uznał wyzszość prawa polskiego nad prawem unijnym, 7 October 2021 https://www.onet.pl/informacje/onetwiadomosci/tk-uznal-wyzszosc-prawa-polskiego-nad-prawem-unijnym/nfywm7v,79cfc278.

is beyond the competences of the EU. Nonetheless, the Constitutional Tribunal acknowledged supremacy of EU Law if the EU is not acting *ultra vires*.[168] Having said that the decision of the Constitutional Tribunal is clearly an attack on the EU supremacy.[169] For example, the judge-rapporteur declared that 'Tribunal does not rule out that in the future it will directly review the constitutionality of the CJEU rulings, including removing them from the Polish legal system'.[170] Such a declaration was also included in the communication published by the Constitutional Tribunal after the judgment K 3/21.[171]

One of two dissenting judges in this case, Piotr Pszczółkowski was of the view that this case should have been discontinued since the application was not suitable for substantive examination by the Constitutional Tribunal.[172] The second dissenting judge, Jarosław Wyrembak emphasised that Prime Minister Mateusz Morawiecki did not define the constitutional problem requiring the decision of the Constitutional Tribunal.[173] Scholars expressed a similar view, arguing that the first part of the judgment deals with assumptions, there is no conflict between Polish and EU Legal order and it is impossible to discern a clear obligation from it for example, how Poland could align with EU standards.[174] Biernat & Łętowska argue that collision of norms was artificially created and the real aim of the proceedings was 'to provide cover for ordinary national legislation to lower the standard of judicial independence below the level required by both the Polish Constitution and EU law'.[175] Pszczółkowski believed that the Prime Minister's application only apparently concerned the control of the indicated norms, and the head of government actually aimed to undermine the legal effects of specific judgments of the CJEU in the Polish legal system.[176] He argued that

168. https://www.europarl.europa.eu/RegData/etudes/STUD/2022/732475/IPOL_STU(2022)732475_EN.pdf.
169. Nina Półtorak, Kilka uwag o skutkach wyroku Trybunału Konstytucyjnego w sprawie K 3/21 dla stosowania prawa unijnego przez polskie sądy, *Europejski Przegląd Sądowy* (2021), No. 12, p. 13.
170. Stanisław Biernat & Ewa Łętowska: This Was Not Just Another Ultra Vires Judgment!: Commentary to the Statement of Retired Judges of the Constitutional Tribunal, *VerfBlog*, 2021/10/27, https://verfassungsblog.de/this-was-not-just-another-ultra-vires-judgment/, DOI : 10.17176/20211027-182911-0.
171. *Ibid.*
172. Trybunał Konstytucyjny uznał wyzszość prawa polskiego nad prawem unijnym, https://www.onet.pl/informacje/onetwiadomosci/tk-uznal-wyzszosc-prawa-polskiego-nad-prawem-unijnym/nfywm7v,79cfc278.
173. *Ibid.*, https://sip.lex.pl/akty-prawne/dzu-dziennik-ustaw/wyrok-trybunalu-konstytucyjnego-sygn-akt-k-3-21-19154129, also dissenting opinions https://archiwumosiatynskiego.pl/archiwum/sentencja-decyzji-tk-z-7-pazdziernika-2021-roku-w-sprawie-k-3-21/.
174. https://www.europarl.europa.eu/RegData/etudes/STUD/2022/732475/IPOL_STU(2022)732475_EN.pdf, 24.
175. *Ibid.*, Stanisław Biernat & Ewa Łętowska, This Was Not Just Another Ultra Vires Judgment!: Commentary to the statement of retired judges of the Constitutional Tribunal, *VerfBlog*, 2021/10/27, https://verfassungsblog.de/this-was-not-just-another-ultra-vires-judgment/, DOI: 10.17176/20211027-182911-0.
176. The application, due to its appearance, was not suitable for substantive examination by the Constitutional Tribunal.

the Prime Minister sought to undermine the effectiveness of specific judgments of the CJEU that in the end would legitimise the actions of the Parliament and the Government to continue the judicial reforms.[177] Florczak-Wątor observes that in fact the judgment does not produce any legal effect and argues that certain statements such as 'the process of European integration as depriving Poland of its sovereignty' cannot be taken seriously otherwise Poland would have to leave the EU.[178] Judge Pszczółkowski did not see any other effects of this judgment either, rather than deepening of the legal chaos.[179] In addition, the Constitutional Tribunal is not in a position to derogate from the rules of international law.[180] He points out that the ruling of the Constitutional Tribunal undermines the effectiveness of EU Law questioning not only the EU's competence, but also the competences of Polish courts to decide on the compliance of national laws with EU law.[181] The judgment only demonstrates Polish Government's unwillingness to engage in any dialogue in this matter. Rather, it was a government's attempt to undermine the EU fundamental principles, the authority of the CJEU landmark decisions on supremacy, going against EU primary law enshrined in Article 19 TEU and Article 267 TFEU. La Pace rightly observes 'the Treaty excludes the possibility for States to interpret the EU Law in a manner which is a distinct from the interpretation of the CJEU'.[182]

7 THE POLISH GOVERNMENT'S AMENDMENTS: ILLUSORY COMPLIANCE WITH THE EU LAW

In the end, the Polish Government was pressurised to make some amendments to its equivocal 2017-2019 judiciary reform in a tentative to unlock EUR 35.4 billion recovery and resilient plan. This money should allow Poland to quickly recover after the COVID-19 pandemic and to facilitate a green and digital transition.[183] From the Polish

177. *Ibid.*
178. Monika Florczak-Wątor, (Nie)skuteczność wyroku Trybunału Konstytucyjnego z 7.10.2021 r., K 3/21. 'Ocena znaczenia orzeczenia z perspektywy prawa konstytucyjnego', *Europejski Przegląd Sądowy* (2021), No. 12, p. 11.
179. Trybunał Konstytucyjny uznał wyzszość prawa polskiego nad prawem unijnym, 7 October 2021 https://www.onet.pl/informacje/onetwiadomosci/tk-uznal-wyzszosc-prawa-polskiego-nad-prawem-unijnym/nfywm7v,79cfc278.
180. Fryderyk Zoll, Katarzyna Południak-Gierz & Wojciech Bańczyk, *Primacy of EU Law and Jurisprudence of Polish Constitutional Tribunal Recent Developments in the Light of the Polish Constitutional Tribunal's Case Law*, June 2022, EU Parliament https://www.europarl.europa.eu/RegData/etudes/STUD/2022/732475/IPOL_STU(2022)732475_EN.pdf
181. Trybunał Konstytucyjny uznał wyzszość prawa polskiego nad prawem unijnym, 7 october 2021, https://www.onet.pl/informacje/onetwiadomosci/tk-uznal-wyzszosc-prawa-polskiego-nad-prawem-unijnym/nfywm7v,79cfc278.
182. F. Lorenzo, Pace at Di pace Pace-BlogDUE-1.pdf: Lorenzo F. Pace, Il principio del primato è 'sotto attacco'? Brevi note su (presunti) limiti scaturenti dalle Costituzioni nazionali e dal sindacato delle Corti costituzionali, ottobre 2022 also Stefan Auer & Nicole Scicluna, Poland Has a Point about the EU's Legal Supremacy, *Politico* at https://www.politico.eu/article/poland-court-eu-legal-supremacy/.
183. *Ibid.*, European Commission, Press Release, NextGeneration EU: European Commission endorses Poland's E35.4 billion recovery and resilience plan, 1 June 2022 at https://ec.europa.eu/commission/presscorner/detail/en/ip_22_3375.

government's perspective, the efforts have been made to comply with the Court of Justice's ruling of 15 July 2021.[184] The Commission conditioned disbursement of the EU funds upon a number of changes to the law on the judiciary introduced between 2017 and 2019. The requirements are set up in four milestones (substantially three) addressed to Poland.[185] In the first place, the word 'milestones' usually associated with finance and investment, sounds bizarre in this context. It is not about 'a bet on the future',[186] but about the democratic values, which constitute a precondition for the further progress of EU Integration. Secondly, their content is also summary leaving Poland with the door open to maintain a number of anomalies of the judicial system that distorts the balance of power. One could expect that the Commission's position would give considerable weight to the importance of the subject matter namely the Rule of Law and Supremacy, the very foundation of the EU. The Commission's message was central to defend the values of the EU, protect the Supremacy of EU law, to serve as a lesson and guidance to other Member States. Unfortunately, this message does not come across from the Commission's milestones. On the contrary, its light approach undermines the values of the EU and the authority of the CJEU judgements. In essence, milestones are minimalistic and even their successful and full implementation would not restore the Rule of Law in Poland.[187] Sadurski points out that the profound dismantlement of the democratic judicial institutions is not captured by the Commission's milestones.[188]

In a nutshell, the Commission requests in its milestones to liquidate the Disciplinary Chamber and to replace it with a new judicial body that complies with EU Law (milestone 1). Judges should be exempted from any disciplinary liability for the content of their judicial decisions, for referring a question to CJEU and for any checks of impartiality of another Court (milestone 2).[189] Poland should also strengthen the procedural rights of the parties in disciplinary hearings (milestone 3)[190] and the judges

184. https://curia.europa.eu/juris/document/document.jsf?text=&docid=244185&pageIndex=0&doclang=en&mode=req&dir=&occ=first&part=1&cid=4403797.
185. European Commission, Press Release, NextGeneration EU: European Commission endorses Poland's E35.4 billion recovery and resilience plan, 1 June 2022 at https://ec.europa.eu/commission/presscorner/detail/en/ip_22_3375, my analysis follows 4 points identified by the Commission, the commentators refer often to 3 in the following order (Abolition of the Disciplinary Chamber Reinstatement of the judges unlawfully suspended; Removal from the disciplinary system of judges' liability for their judicial decisions)): *Ibid.*, Wojciech Sadurski, The European Commission Cedes Its Crucial Leverage Vis-à-Vis the Rule of Law in Poland, *VerfBlog*, 2022/6/06, https://verfassungsblog.de/the-european-commission-cedes-its-crucial-leverage-vis-a-vis-the-rule-of-law-in-poland/, DOI: 10.17176/20220606-182327-0.
186. Maximilian Steinbeis, Millstones, *VerfBlog*, 2022/6/03, https://verfassungsblog.de/millstones/, DOI: 10.17176/20220604-062241-0.
187. *Ibid.*, Wojciech Sadurski & Laurent Pech, Covering Up and Rewarding the Destruction of the Rule of Law One Milestone at a Time, *VerfBlog*, 2022/6/21, https://verfassungsblog.de/covering-up-and-rewarding-the-destruction-of-the-rule-of-law-one-milestone-at-a-time/, DOI: 10.17176/20220621-153415-0.
188. *Ibid.*, Wojciech Sadurski.
189. European Commission, Press Release, NextGeneration EU: European Commission endorses Poland's E35.4 billion recovery and resilience plan, 1 June 2022 at https://ec.europa.eu/commission/presscorner/detail/en/ip_22_3375.
190. *Ibid.*

whose rights were compromised by the Disciplinary Chamber should have a right to have their cases reviewed by an impartial Tribunal (milestone 4).[191]

In line with these requirements the Polish Parliament passed the Law on 9 June 2022 introducing a number of amendments regarding the points raised by the Commission.[192] Regarding the point 1, the new Act in its Article 8, states that the Disciplinary Chamber of the Supreme Court is liquidated and replaced by a new body the Chamber of Professional Responsibility – Article 1, point 17 of the Act.[193] The new Chamber is composed of 11 judges appointed from all the judges of the Supreme Court for a five-year term of office 'in the secret draw procedure after that time they return to their regular duties in the Supreme Court'.[194] The judges are elected by the President of the Republic of Poland.[195]

The Act in Article 1 point 34, Article 2 point 2, Article 4 point 4, Article 5 point 3, also addresses the second milestone raised by the Commission, explicitly excluding any liability for submitting a request for a preliminary ruling, for the content of their judicial decisions, or for verifying whether another court is independent, impartial, and established by law.[196] These activities cannot be a disciplinary offence.[197] Nonetheless, at the same time Article 2 §3 adds that 'the circumstances surrounding the appointment of a judge may not constitute the sole basis for challenging a judgment issued with the judge or challenging their independence and impartiality'.[198] Therefore, there could not be any question regarding irregularities of the judges appointed during the 2017-2019 reform.

Milestone 3 required by the Commission appears to be accommodated in Article 1. 17, of the Act.[199] Nevertheless, the request is formulated in broad terms making it difficult, at least according to Polish commentators, to assess the extent to which the Act fulfilled its role to strengthen the procedural rights of the parties in disciplinary proceedings. What is meant by effective judicial protection should not call for any explanation. But a better formulated, more prescriptive and further detailed milestone would leave Polish Government with less room to obviate it.

191. *Ibid.*
192. Law of the 9 June 2019, O.J. Poz. 1259, Ustawa o zmianie ustawy o Sądzie Najwyzszym oraz niektórych innych ustaw, https://isap.sejm.gov.pl/isap.nsf/download.xsp/WDU20220001259/O/D20221259.pdf.
193. *Ibid.*, Article 1 point 17 of the Act (Article 22a-22e of the Act on the Supreme Court), Law of the 9 June 2019, O.J. Poz. 1259, https://isap.sejm.gov.pl/isap.nsf/download.xsp/WDU20220001259/O/D20221259.pdf.
194. *Ibid.*, Law of the 9 June 2019, O.J. Poz.1259 https://isap.sejm.gov.pl/isap.nsf/download.xsp/WDU20220001259/O/D20221259.pdf.
195. *Ibid.*, Article 1.17 *see also* Krzysztof Grajewski, Nowelizacja ustawy o Sądzie Najwyzszym z 9 czerwca 2022 r. – zmiana prawdziwa czy pozorna? *Przegląd Prawa Konstytucyjnego*, 2022/5, 30.
196. *Ibid.*, Law of the 9 June 2019, O.J. Poz. 1259 https://isap.sejm.gov.pl/isap.nsf/download.xsp/WDU20220001259/O/D20221259.pdf.
197. *Ibid.*
198. *Ibid.*, Article 2§3 *see also* Krzysztof Grajewski, Nowelizacja ustawy o Sądzie Najwyzszym z 9 czerwca 2022 r. – zmiana prawdziwa czy pozorna? *Przegląd Prawa Konstytucyjnego*, 2022/5, 30.
199. *Ibid.*; Article 1 point 17 of the Act (Articles 22a-22e of the Act on the Supreme Court).

Milestone 4 is addressed in Article 9 of the Act.[200] The new Chamber of Professional Responsibility is to 're-examine on the first session of the Chamber all the cases in which the Disciplinary Chamber suspended any judge or allowed any judge to be prosecuted in disciplinary proceedings and remuneration of a judge was reduced as long as the disciplinary proceedings are pending'.[201]

Arguably, the conditions set up in milestones were satisfied to some extent. It is clear, however, that milestones do not settle the dispute on the observance of the Rule of Law. In addition, the new law legalises some irregularities that previously have manifestly undermined the independence of the judiciary. Still, before the Act was passed, there were some options for amendments providing better guarantees for the judges.

Sadurski notes that the Commission approved the Polish amendments before the final version of the draft on 1 June, depriving itself of any bargaining power in negotiations with the Polish government and removing 'any incentive to take on board seriously the Commission's misgivings as to the regulations of courts and judges'.[202] The rejected amendments concerned the annulment of rulings of the Disciplinary Chamber and the requirement of 'at least seven years in the Supreme Court for the judges to sit on the Chamber of Professional Responsibility'.[203] They were included in the Senate Bill with some other smart solutions such as the ineligibility of the judges of the liquidated Disciplinary Chamber for any Chamber of the Supreme Court.[204] Alas, these proposals did not stand a chance due to the Commission's haste to approve the Polish Government's reform.[205] This is regrettable because the Senate Bill by imposing the condition of at least seven years of service in the Supreme Court to sit on the new Chamber of Disciplinary Responsibility, excluded eligibility of the neo-judges controlled by the ruling party PiS.[206]

Upon the Commission's recommendations the Council approved the Polish Plan, deeming the amendments sufficient on 17 June 2022.[207] It is disappointing, the least we

200. *Ibid.*, Law of the 9th of June 2019, O.J. Poz. 1259 https://isap.sejm.gov.pl/isap.nsf/download.xsp/WDU20220001259/O/D20221259.pdf.
201. *Ibid.*
202. *Ibid.*
203. Leszek Szymanski, President Signs Bill Scrapping Disputed Disciplinary Chamber for Judges PAP 13 June 2022 at https://www.thefirstnews.com/article/president-signs-bill-scrapping-disputed-disciplinary-chamber-for-judges-31038.
204. Wojciech Sadurski, The European Commission Cedes Its Crucial Leverage Vis-à-Vis the Rule of Law in Poland, *VerfBlog*, 2022/6/06, https://verfassungsblog.de/the-european-commission-cedes-its-crucial-leverage-vis-a-vis-the-rule-of-law-in-poland/, DOI: 10.17176/20220606-182327-0; *see also* Roman K. Adamczewski, Rażące naruszenie prawa w orzecznictwie sądów administracyjnych, *Rzeczpospolita*, 2018, 13.03: 3.
205. Senat zdecydował o wniesieniu do Sejmu projektu ustawy o zmianie ustawy o Krajowej Radzie Sądownictwa, ustawy o Sądzie Najwyzszym oraz niektórych innych ustaw (komunikat) 8.06, 2022, *Polityka i społeczeństwo CIS*: at https://pap-mediaroom.pl/polityka-i-spoleczenstwo/cis-senat-zdecydowal-o-wniesieniu-do-sejmu-projektu-ustawy-o-zmianie.
206. Wojciech Sadurski, The European Commission Cedes its Crucial Leverage Vis-à-Vis the Rule of Law in Poland, *VerfBlog*, 2022/6/06, https://verfassungsblog.de/the-european-commission-cedes-its-crucial-leverage-vis-a-vis-the-rule-of-law-in-poland/, DOI: 10.17176/20220606-182327-0.
207. https://www.consilium.europa.eu/en/press/press-releases/2022/06/17/recovery-fund-ministers-welcome-assessment-of-poland-s-national-plan/.

can say, to see the Institutions compromising the Rule of Law. Pech argues that the Commission decided to sacrifice the Rule of Law allowing the Polish government to continue [its unfair play].[208] Since Russia's aggression on Ukraine, Poland has become increasingly strategically important for the security of the EU, to support the EU anti-Putin agenda and to host the Ukrainian population fleeing the war. Nevertheless, it seems that the Institutions traded off the Rule of Law and the EU values have become some sort of exchange token. The EU Parliament expressed some deep concerns, pointing out that the EU values are not negotiable and 'cannot be treated as a bargaining chip'.[209] It stressed that the Commission, 'as the guardian of the Treaties, should use all tools at its disposal to ensure compliance with the values enshrined in Article 2 TEU and the primacy of EU law'[210] and not blindly accept the Warsaw solution and to adjust 'variables for reasons of political convenience.'[211] Even though, the Commission itself was divided over this decision. Vice-President of the Commission, Timmermans, was against such an approval, believing that the Polish cosmetic changes would not restore the Rule of Law in Poland.[212]

The most important issue in the Commission's milestones refers to the full and unconditional acceptance of the judgments of the CJEU. It was rightly noted that this requirement should not be set up in a milestone given that compliance with EU Law is a general obligation of the Member States without financial reward attached to it. Thus, any prospect of financial gain for compliance 'produces the perverse effect of providing financial incentives to comply [with EU Law]'.[213] Yet, the Polish recent legislative steps do not provide evidence of unconditional acceptance of the CJEU judgments or the recognition of supremacy of EU Law; they rather confirm the opposite.

The Polish government's amendments adopted in June came into force on 15 July 2022.[214] As mentioned, the changes are cosmetic and unable to address the long lasting problems of the distorted separation of powers and the undue influence of the executive on the judiciary. Nonetheless, restoring the Rule of Law was not the intention of the Polish Government, anyway. The new body, the Chamber of Professional Responsibility (milestone 1) seems to change only its name. The problem with its composition and the nomination of judges persists and the reform clearly does not show any signs of discontinuity with its predecessor the Disciplinary Chamber. The association of judges (KOS), in their Open Letter to Ursula von der Leyen requested the

208. *Ibid.*, brackets added.
209. https://www.europarl.europa.eu/doceo/document/TA-9-2022-0240_EN.html.
210. *Ibid.*
211. Lili Bayer, European Judges Sue Council over Polish Recovery Plan, 28 August 2022, https://www.politico.eu/article/european-judges-sue-council-over-polish-recovery-plan/.
212. Jennifer Rankin, Senior Official Criticises EU Handling of Poland's Covid Recovery Plan, Guardian, 3 July 2022 at https://www.theguardian.com/world/2022/jul/03/senior-official-criticises-eu-handling-of-poland-covid-recovery-plan.
213. Alberto Alemanno, Censuring von der Leyen's Capitulation on the Rule of Law, *VerfBlog*, 2022/6/08, https://verfassungsblog.de/censuring-von-der-leyens-capitulation-on-the-rule-of-law/, DOI: 10.17176/20220609-032746-0. in Laurent Pech, *ibid.*, *see also* Mirosław Wyrzykowski, Michał Ziółkowski, Illiberal Constitutionalism and the Judiciary in *Routledge Handbook of Illiberalism* (Routledge, 2021).
214. The Law OJ of 9 June 2022 https://isap.sejm.gov.pl/isap.nsf/download.xsp/WDU20220001259/O/D20221259.pdf.

removal of all neo-judges from the Supreme Court, i.e. the judges whose nomination procedure was politically influenced and violated the rule of law.[215] They claimed that the liquidation of the Disciplinary Chamber aimed at removing the neo-judges from the Supreme Court.[216] Instead, almost all of them remain in the Supreme Court, following a mere reshuffle. The judges previously nominated by the National Council of the Judiciary, as well as the judges composing National Council of the Judiciary are eligible for the office. The First President of the Supreme Court should address to the judges of the liquidated Disciplinary Chamber written proposals offering further service in one of the chambers of the Supreme Court.[217] A refusal or a lack of declaration on the part of these judges will result in retirement.[218] The selection of judges for the new Chamber of Professional Responsibility lies with the President of the Republic of Poland's competence. In fact, among the 11 judges chosen by the President of Poland out of 33 judges of the Supreme Court, 6, thus more than a half in the Chamber are neo-judges,[219] nominated by the neo National Council of Judiciary.[220] Immediately after the Supreme Court's judges formulated a written reservation to the procedure under Article 12 of the Act of 9 June 2022 amending the Act on the Supreme Court.[221] They claimed that the procedure contravenes Article 6.1 of the ECHR stipulating that the court is to be 'legally constituted, impartial and independent'. The procedure for selecting judges to the new Chamber of Professional Responsibility does not meet the requirement that the court must be established by law. The law establishing the procedure for the selection of judges must derive from the legislative rather than the executive power. Appointing a court by a discretionary decision is excluded since no

215. Committee to Defend Justice KOS urges President of the European Commission not to give up on implementation of CJEU judgments on judicial independence in Poland, 30 May 2022, at https://ruleoflaw.pl/committee-to-defend-justice-kos-urges-president-of-the-european-commission-not-to-give-up-on-implementation-of-cjeu-judgments-on-judicial-independence-in-poland/.
216. *Ibid.*, Committee to Defend Justice KOS urges President of the European Commission not to give up on implementation of CJEU judgments on judicial independence in Poland, 30 May 2022, at https://ruleoflaw.pl/committee-to-defend-justice-kos-urges-president-of-the-european-commission-not-to-give-up-on-implementation-of-cjeu-judgments-on-judicial-independence-in-poland/.
217. Article 10 of the Law of the 9 June 2022, *see also* Mateusz Mikowski, Marcin Jabłoński, Izba Dyscyplinarna SN przestała istnieć. Co to oznacza? https://serwisy.gazetaprawna.pl/orzeczenia/artykuly/8492461,izba-dyscyplinarna-sn-nowelizacja-ustawy-o-sadzie-najwyzszym.html#co-z-sedziami-orzekajacymi-w-id.
218. *Ibid.*, Mateusz Mikowski, Marcin Jabłoński, Izba Dyscyplinarna SN przestała istnieć. Co to oznacza? https://serwisy.gazetaprawna.pl/orzeczenia/artykuly/8492461,izba-dyscyplinarna-sn-nowelizacja-ustawy-o-sadzie-najwyzszym.html#co-z-sedziami-orzekajacymi-w-id.
219. Jakub Jaraszewski, 17 September 2022, https://twitter.com/J_Jaraczewski/status/1571211030511996935?s=20&t=tzYAc62eS0WdcRv4LXMHfg.
220. Sześciu neo-sędziów wyznaczonych do nowej izby Sądu Najwyzszego. Sędzia Gąciarek: to nie jest sąd legalnie powołany, 18 September 2022 at https://tvn24.pl/polska/szesciu-sedziow-neo-krs-wyznaczonych-do-izby-odpowiedzialnosci-zawodowej-sadu-najwyzszego-sedzia-piotr-gaciarek-komentuje-6118425.
221. Zastrzezenia niektórych sędziów Sądu Najwyzszego do przeprowadzenia losowania do Izby Odpowiedzialności Zawodowej SN. *Monitor Konstytucyjny*, 10.08.2022 https://monitorkonstytucyjny.eu/archiwa/22668.

discretion is allowed in the selection of court's members.[222] The old judges are those who previously did not object to collaborate with the neo-judges.[223] In light of the long lasting row for the independence of the Polish judiciary in which the neo National Council of Judiciary was found by the CJEU not to be an independent and impartial Tribunal, the Law of 9 June 2022 does nothing to address this. Hence, it appears clear that the Polish Government is continuing to exercise political control over judges. The judges of the liquidated Chamber, who decide to remain in the Supreme Court, can take part in the draw for the new chamber. Thus, nothing prevents the judges from the dissolved Disciplinary Chamber from becoming members of the new Chamber of Professional Liability.[224]

As mentioned, milestone 2 was addressed by the 9 June 2022 Law and concentrated mainly on the removal of any liabilities for making a reference to the CJEU. However, it did not repeal the 'Muzzle Act', which explicitly forbids judges from examining the appointments of other judges or for refusing to form a judiciary panel with a neo-judge.[225] This means that they will still be able to be disciplined and prosecuted.[226] Another shortcoming of the 9 June 2022 Act consists of a peculiar Independence test according to which 'the circumstances surrounding the appointment of a judge may not constitute the sole basis for challenging the judgment delivered by that judge or challenging his independence and impartiality'.[227] In other words, the circumstances of appointment of judges cannot be questioned.[228] In fact, it legalises the appointment of judges according to the procedure that both the CJEU and the ECtHR found in violation of the Rule of Law and Article 6 of the ECHR. Nonetheless, the new procedure testing impartiality and independence of a judge gives each defendant or plaintiff the right to have his case heard by a court.[229] Confirmation of the charges against a judge would exclude them from this particular case, but in no way would it formally undermine the judge's status. This test applies to pending or initiated cases but not to the cases already adjudicated although the draft bill of this law (not

222. ECtHR, Case *Gumundur Andri Ástrásson v. Iceland,* App no. 26374/18, 2019 https://hudoc.echr.coe.int/fre#{%22itemid%22:[%22001-191701%22]}; Case *Xero Flor W Polsce Sp. Z O.O. v. Poland* App. no. 4907/18, 2021 https://hudoc.echr.coe.int/fre#{%22itemid%22:[%22001-210065%22]} Case *Sokurenko And Strygun v. Ukraine,* App. nos. 29458/04 and 29465/04), 2006, https://www.menschenrechte.ac.at/orig/06_4/Sokurenko.pdf.
223. Prezydent wybrał członków nowej izby w Sądzie Najwyzszym. Wśród nich jest sześciu neo-sedziów, 18 September 2022 at https://wiadomosci.onet.pl/kraj/prezydent-wybral-czlonkow-nowej-izby-sn-wsrod-nich-jest-szesciu-neo-sedziow/1m6gvlf.
224. https://serwisy.gazetaprawna.pl/orzeczenia/artykuly/8492461,izba-dyscyplinarna-sn-nowelizacja-ustawy-o-sadzie-najwyzszym.html#co-z-sedziami-orzekajacymi-w-id.
225. Marek Domagalski, Agata Łukaszewicz, 26.05.2022, Uchwalona w czwartek nowela ustawy o Sądzie Najwyzszym umozliwia wznowienie postępowań sędziom, którym likwidowana teraz Izba Dyscyplinarna uchyliła immunitet. https://www.rp.pl/sady-i-trybunaly/art36379761-dyscyplinarki-i-testowanie-sedziow.
226. *Ibid.*
227. *Ibid.*
228. Kristie Bluett, Jasmine Cameron and Scott Cullinane, Poland's Judicial Reform Falls Short of EU Expectations, Complicating Cooperation Against Russia, 3 October 2022 at https://www.justsecurity.org/83324/polands-judicial-reform-falls-short-of-eu-expectations-complicating-cooperation-against-russia/.
229. *Ibid.*

retained), included its application to the already decided decisions.[230] The Justice Defence Committee (KOS) association of judges also insisted on the removal of the provisions of the 'Muzzle Law' that constituted an object of the CJEU infringement procedure in case C-204/21 *Commission v. Poland*,[231] making it possible to prosecute a judge only because he/she questions the status of another judge or raises the legality of the appointment procedure.[232] As mentioned, the amendments of 9 June 2022 did not remove the most contested provision of the Muzzle Act, Article 107 §1, item 3. Instead, the new law introduces a new disciplinary offence called 'denial of administering justice' that intends to punish those judges who refuse to form a judicial panel with a neo-judge.[233]

Regarding milestone 4, the new law in force since 15 July 2022 provides that a judge against whom a final disciplinary judgment was issued by the Disciplinary Chamber or a resolution was passed, legally authorising prosecution, has the right to file a motion to reopen the proceedings until 16 January 2023.[234] Such applications will be examined by the new Chamber of Professional Responsibility.[235] Thus, there is no immediate reinstatement or the right to full automatic compensation as requested by the association of judges in their Open letter to the President of the EU Commission.[236]

The new Professional Responsibility Chamber will examine the justifications behind the disciplinary proceedings inquiring why the disciplinary measures were taken, why the immunity of certain judges was revoked, why they were suspended or/and their remuneration was reduced.[237] Nonetheless, the examination of the past decisions does not necessarily mean that the judges in question will be reinstated. The EU Parliament found it regrettable that there is no possibility for 'the immediate reinstatement of all the unlawfully suspended judges to their former positions'.[238] Instead, the procedure for reinstatement allows for a delay of more than a year with an uncertain outcome.[239] In addition, the decision concerning the reinstatement remains at the discretion of the Chamber of Professional Responsibility whose impartiality is questionable.

Polish judges pointed out that the Act of 9 June 2022 should have included the reform of the disciplinary chambers operating in Appeal Courts. Those chambers (courts) whose members were appointed by the Minister of Justice are not independent

230. *Ibid.*
231. CJEU case C-204/21, *Commission v. Poland*, at https://curia.europa.eu/juris/liste.jsf?lgrec=fr&td=%3BALL&language=en&num=C-204/21&jur=C.
232. KOS' open letter. https://ruleoflaw.pl/committee-to-defend-justice-kos-urges-president-of-the-european-commission-not-to-give-up-on-implementation-of-cjeu-judgments-on-judicial-independence-in-poland/.
233. *Ibid.*
234. Krzysztof Sobczak, Nowelizacja ustawy o Sądzie Najwyzszym wchodzi w zycie, 15 July 2022, https://www.prawo.pl/prawnicy-sady/likwidacja-izby-dyscyplinarnej-ustawa,515236.html.
235. *Ibid.*
236. *Ibid.*
237. *Ibid.*
238. https://www.europarl.europa.eu/doceo/document/TA-9-2022-0240_EN.html.
239. Andrzej Marian Swiątkowski, *Reforma wymiaru sprawiedliwości* (Justice reform), Kraków 2022; Lily Bayer, European judges sue Council over Polish Recovery Plan, https://www.politico.eu/article/european-judges-sue-council-over-polish-recovery-plan/.

and their existence is contrary to the Polish Constitution[240] and Article 2 TEU. Yet, the current amendments suffer the same failure in relation to the ordinary courts in which the previous irregularities might continue. This issue is not negligible given that the Disciplinary Chamber during its existence considered 474 lawyers' cases, 259 of which concerned prosecutors and judges in ordinary courts.[241]

Ultimately, the Polish judicial saga is not about to end anytime soon. It looks like the Act passed in June 2022 amending the 2017-19 judiciary reforms is more a political calculation in the hope to unblock the EU money from the Resilience and Reconstruction Funds, rather than a real commitment to restore the Rule of Law in Poland.[242]

8 CONCLUSION

On the positive side, the Polish judicial crisis was the opportunity for the CJEU to re-examine the fundamental concepts of the EU Law. The Court does not seem to accept the arguments allowing a national tribunal to scrutinise the concept of supremacy; on the contrary, it strengthened it in the 'Polish Saga' cases. In addition, it seems that reliance on Article 4(2) is limited in scope. Further, the earlier Polish jurisprudence embraced the idea of constitutional pluralism while adhering to the EU acquis. Moreover, the concept of the Rule of Law was filled with substance, developed by the CJEU and the ECtHR decisions[243] that mutually explored their respective case law. Finally, a well-articulated definition of the Rule of Law provided in the Conditionality Regulation is able to oppose the Polish Government's argument that the Justice System is an internal matter of the State and the EU measures unduly interfere in Polish internal affairs.

Furthermore, many procedures dealing with the violation of the constitutional principles were tested in the crisis for the first time. Some proved to be very weak. The Rule of Law Framework, promoting a dialogue had mainly a dissuasive function. Similarly, the procedure under Article 7.1 TEU manifestly lacked efficacy. However, the Conditionality Regulation is promising and hopefully will bring more compelling rules.

The conclusion to be drawn from the Polish case is that democratic backsliding is not over yet. On the contrary, the recent amendments only confirm the Polish government's resistance to secure independence of the judiciary. After all, the political party in power (PiS) has systematically eroded democratic guarantees subjecting the judiciary to political influence and did so consistently over seven years throughout the subsequent law reforms. Pech et al, define it as a 'Soviet-style justice system'

240. *Ibid.*, Marek Domagalski, Agata Łukaszewicz Dyscyplinarki i testowanie sędziów, 26, 5, 2022 at https://www.rp.pl/sady-i-trybunaly/art36379761-dyscyplinarki-i-testowanie-sedziow.
241. *Ibid.*
242. Jakub Jaraczewski, Just a Feint?: President Duda's Bill on the Polish Supreme Court and the Brussels-Warsaw deal on the rule of law, *VerfBlog*, 2022/6/01, https://verfassungsblog.de/just-a-feint/, DOI: 10.17176/20220602-062115-0.
243. *Ibid.*; Matteo Mastracci, Judiciary Saga in Poland: An Affair Torn Between European Standards and ECtHR Criteria (30 December 2020). 9 *Polish Review International & European Law* 39 (2020), Available at SSRN: https://ssrn.com/abstract=3757494.

reminiscence from the past,[244] in terms of its arbitrariness, discretion and disrespect for the international obligations. The situation of the judiciary has worsened regardless of the numerous EU infringement procedures and abundant CJEU and ECtHR case law. One thing is certain that there is no political will to engage with any serious reforms. The legislative amendments adopted in June 2022 had only one goal to unlock the EU funds. Polish 'adequateness' to the conditions set up in milestones is only apparent. The efforts to address milestones requested by the Commission were minimal, in practice simply confirming the previous status quo. The new Professional Responsibility Chamber replacing the liquidated Disciplinary Chamber is in prevalence composed of the neo-judges, nominated by non-independent and non-impartial tribunal according to the CJEU ruling,[245] the latter, neo-NCJ is still in operation, recommending new judges to the President who happily appoints them.[246] The President of the Republic enjoys full power to appoint the judges of the Supreme Court whereas unlawfully disciplined judges will not be immediately restated or compensated but only their cases will be reviewed in a year's time with an uncertain outcome. Even worse, the 'Muzzle law' allowing unfounded disciplinary hearings against judges remains in place. Polish case was also a test for the EU Institutions. Alas, the EU Institutions approached the problem of repetitive violations of the Rule of law and Supremacy of EU law with almost unhealthy levity.[247] First, milestones do not seem to be an appropriate mechanism to address persistent violations of the constitutional principles of the EU Law, a very foundation of the EU on which the EU is based. They cannot capture the profound and systematic degradation of the Polish justice system and a deep reconstruction of its institutions.[248] Secondly, the Commission seems to do 'too little and too late'[249] and was accused by the EU Parliament to prioritise 'political convenience' over the Rule of Law.[250] This was an attitude that could be explained but not justified.[251] In fact, Poland's strategic position at the external border of the EU has become increasingly important for the EU since Russia's invasion of Ukraine. But,

244. *Ibid.*, Laurent Pech, P Wachowiec & D. Mazur, Poland's Rule of Law Breakdown: A Five-Year Assessment of EU's (In)Action. *Hague Journal Rule Law 13*, 1-43 (2021), https://doi.org/10.1007/s40803-021-00151-9.
245. CJEU, Case C-791/19 [2021] at https://curia.europa.eu/juris/document/document.jsf?text=&docid=244185&pageIndex=0&doclang=en&mode=req&dir=&occ=first&part=1&cid=4403797.
246. Wojciech Sadurski, The European Commission Cedes Its Crucial Leverage Vis-à-Vis the Rule of Law in Poland, *VerfBlog*, 2022/6/06, https://verfassungsblog.de/the-european-commission-cedes-its-crucial-leverage-vis-a-vis-the-rule-of-law-in-poland/, DOI: 10.17176/20220606-182327-0.
247. For further discussion *see ibid.*, L. Pech, P. Wachowiec & D. Mazur, Poland's Rule of Law Breakdown: A Five-Year Assessment of EU's (In)Action. *Hague Journal Rule Law* 13, 1-43 (2021), https://doi.org/10.1007/s40803-021-00151-9.
248. *Ibid.*, Sadurski.
249. *Ibid.*, Pech and *ibid.*, Sadurski.
250. https://www.europarl.europa.eu/doceo/document/TA-9-2022-0240_EN.html.
251. *Ibid.*, Wojciech Sadurski.

could the Polish generous immigration policy toward Ukrainians 'outweigh its systemic departure from the Rule of Law'?[252]

252. *Ibid.*, Alberto Alemanno, Censuring von der Leyen's Capitulation on the Rule of Law, *VerfBlog*, 2022/6/08, https://verfassungsblog.de/censuring-von-der-leyens-capitulation-on-the-rule-of-law/, DOI: 10.17176/20220609-032746-0.

CHAPTER 7

Reflections on the *Francovich* Remedy

Martina Künnecke McClean

1 INTRODUCTION

In his monograph European Public Law, the Achievement and the Brexit Challenge, Patrick Birkinshaw concludes that in the field of public liability, an 'area of traditional concern, we have seen the most striking of dialogues and developments between our domestic system and European systems influencing the way in which our law progresses. As pointed out, the development is not all one way. The result should not be exaggerated; but the influence should not be denied'.[1] Unfortunately the 'wind of change'[2] is now going in a different direction.

Paragraph 4 of Schedule 1 of the European Union (Withdrawal) Act 2018 provides: 'There is no right in domestic law on or after IP completion day to damages in accordance with the rule in Francovich.'

This contribution aims to reflect on the famous remedy of Member State liability in the United Kingdom (UK) legal system.

2 OF RIGHTS AND REMEDIES

'Francovich' type claims have been a well-known route for redress for UK-based applicants who pursued compensation for breaches of Community law. The Francovich rule was later revisited and extended by the Court of Justice of the European Union (CJEU). They have provided a route for compensation where businesses or individuals have suffered damage due to non-compliance with European Union (EU) law or incorrect transposition of EU law.

1. P. Birkinshaw, *European Public Law: The Achievement and the Brexit Challenge*, Wolters Kluwer 3rd ed., 2020, p. 630.
2. *Ibid.*, §10.02, p. 575.

When Mr Francovich filed his claim he did not realise that one of the most discussed cases in EU law would carry his name and would be the object of much academic and political debate to come.[3]

The remedy of Member State liability for breaches of Community law, and a right to monetary compensation, was established in the cases of Francovich[4] and Brasserie du Pêcheur and Factortame.[5] In European Member States it is now accepted and forms part of a national framework of liability provisions. However, as is well known, the new remedy received some early criticism. Harlow called the decision by the European Court of Justice 'reckless' and said it represented an 'act of defiance by the ECJ ...'.[6] Others went as far and accused the Court of 'judicial law-making and the undermining of the rule of law'.[7] This argument was used by the German government which had argued in the case of Brasserie du Pêcheur and Factortame that legislation was required when creating a right to damages. The Court's view on this is well known. It referred to Article 215 [now 288 Treaty on the Functioning of the European Union] which refers to the general principles of state liability known in the Member States. The reference to the legal systems of the Member States could be understood as an opportunity for research into comparative legal analysis of existing frameworks of state liability in the various Member States. However, disappointingly in reality it appears as if this is not the case and Article 215 contains a legitimisation for the Court of Justice to develop judge made law whilst considering the opinions of the Advocate Generals and the judges' own research into academic literature.[8]

With similar scepticism Horsley states more recently that '[t]he Court's reasoning in Francovich directly challenged the nature of the EU legal order as a system of limited attributed competences and, in particular, the position of Member States within that system as constituent authorities'.[9] He further states that the additional remedy was a 'truly remarkable move' for a Court as it only ever had the role of discharging an 'agency function within a system of limited attributed competences'.[10] The Court of Justice had made it clear in its Francovich decision that 'A further basis for the obligation of Member States to make good such loss and damage is to be found in Article 5 [now 10] of the Treaty, under which the Member States are required to take all appropriate measures, whether general or particular, to ensure fulfilment of their obligations under Community law.'[11] Unlike many of the critics of the decision, Arnull argued that 'at the very least we may therefore conclude that there is an adequate legal basis in the Treaty and the legal systems of the Member States to justify the introduction of the principle of State liability. The case law on the subject does not, it

3. F. Nicola & B. Davis, *EU Law Stories*, Cambridge University Press (2017), 339.
4. Cases C-6/90 and C-9/90 *Francovich* [1991] ECR I-5357, 428.
5. (C-46/93) EU:C:1996:79 (5 March 1996).
6. C. Harlow, Francovich and the Problem of the Disobedient State, *European Law Journal* 2, 1996, 199, 222.
7. S. Douglas-Scott, *Constitutional Law of the European Union*, Pearson, 2002, p. 322.
8. F. Ossenbühl, *Staatshaftungsrecht*, 5th ed., C.H.Beck, 1998, 579, 580.
9. T. Horsley, The Court of Justice of the European Union as an Institutional Actor: Judicial Law-Making and Its Limits, Cambridge University Press, 2018, 140-141.
10. *Ibid.*, 22.
11. Cases C-6/90 and C-9/90 *Francovich* [1991] ECR I-5357, 428.

is submitted, represent an example of contra legem behaviour on the part of the Court'.[12]

It was emphasised that the remedy of Member State liability cannot be viewed in isolation from the Member States' obligations under Community law more broadly. As Arnull points out: 'The Treaties are silent on the matter, although it might be thought that such liability is a corollary of primacy and direct effect, in that the payment of damages may in some circumstances be the only way of upholding an individual's rights under Community law.'[13] The main actors are national judges in giving life to the remedy of Member State liability when interpreting European and national law provisions. Following from this the authority of the Court's judgments on Member State liability and national judgments providing the remedy within the national judicial system is to be viewed emphatically in connection with the principle of supremacy of Community law.[14]

Craig's view is that 'the ECJ has been at its most creative in this area'. In his view 'the need for effective remedies to safeguard EU rights is reflective of the principle ubi ius, ibi remedium, which is found in many national legal systems. The duty incumbent on Member States to take all appropriate measures to ensure fulfilment of their Union obligations is especially salient in a polity such as the EU, but resonates with analogous obligations in federal or confederal systems'.[15] Conceptual differences between English and continental legal systems could therefore act as one of the reasons why abandoning the Francovich remedy can be disaggregated from the existence of any rights under EU law. Many continental legal systems are centred on rights (Rechtsansprüche) and causes of action. Comparatists have noted that the English legal system has never provided a clear distinction between substantive and procedural administrative law.[16] English law is concerned with remedies rather than rights: 'Ubi remedium, ibi ius'. Austin conceived of law in a typically English way by focusing on the remedy rather than a body of law as, for instance, that developed in France in the 19th century. In Germany, the individual right against a public authority to an act or omission of that authority is always accompanied by a procedural means to effectuate this act or omission directly: 'Ubi ius ibi remedium'. Further, in German Law some topics dealt with by the English Courts under the heading of 'remedies' would not be considered as procedural topics. The liability of public officials, for instance is covered in 'substantive' rather than 'procedural' provisions in the German Civil Code.[17] It has been argued, however that the continental view on rights and remedies has also echoed in early

12. A. Arnull, European Union Law and the Contra Legem Principle, *European Law Review* 47(3), 2022, 291, 306.
13. A. Arnull, *The European Union and Its Court of Justice*, Oxford EC Law Library, 1999, 149.
14. P.-C. Müller-Graf, 'Die Verantwortung mitgliedstaatlicher Gerichte für die Autorität des Unionsrechts'. In G. Barrett, J.-P. Rageade, D. Wallis & H. Weil (eds), *The Future of Legal Europe: Will We Trust in It? Liber Amicorum in Honour of Wolfgang Heusel*, Springer, 2021, 584.
15. P. Craig, The EU, the Member States and Damages Liability (July 5, 2021). In M. Heidemann (ed.), *The Transformation of Private Law – Principles of Contract and Tort as European and International Law*, Springer (2023), available at SSRN: https://ssrn.com/abstract=3880596, p. 32.
16. J. Schwarze, *European Administrative Law*, Sweet & Maxwell, 1992, 148.
17. *See* Article 34 Basic Law in connection with Article 839 Civil Code.

common law case law.[18] Beal refers to the case of *Ashby v. White*[19] which contains the premise that the existence of a right requires a remedy. Lord Holt CJ said that 'if the plaintiff has a right, he must of necessity have a means to vindicate and maintain it, and a remedy if he is injured in the exercise or enjoyment of it; and indeed it is a vain thing to imagine a right without a remedy; for want of right and want of remedy are reciprocal'.[20] However, other comment suggests that the *Ashby v. White* principle is a myth and largely misunderstood because the final decision in the House of Lords never adopted Lord Holt's reasoning in his dissenting speech delivered in the Queen's Bench division.[21] To conclude it is at least clear that the application of the ubi ius principle did not find the same application it finds in continental legal systems and is subject to some debate in the common law. The loss of the Francovich remedy does not necessarily mean that there is no remedy for breaches of Community law in English law. There may well be statutory claims for compensation should retained EU law rights be infringed. However, Francovich as a judge made remedy has been abandoned.

3 REMOVAL OF *FRANCOVICH*

Paragraph 4 of Schedule 1 of the European Union (Withdrawal) Act 2018 stipulates in quite an authoritarian style that there is generally 'no right in domestic law on or after [the end of the transition period] to damages in accordance with the rule in Francovich'. This means that this 'key remedy' has now been 'turned off' as Barnard[22] expressed it where a breach occurred on or after Exit Day.

Paragraph 4 of Schedule 1 is then subject to the transitional provisions stipulated under paragraph 39 of Schedule 8. 39 (3): Section 5(4) and paragraphs 3 and 4 of Schedule 1 do not apply in relation to any proceedings begun, but not finally decided, before a court or tribunal in the UK before exit day. In particular, sub-paragraph (7) delays the prohibition in the Act on seeking Francovich damages in domestic law for two years after exit day. This ensures that the Act does not prevent individuals from continuing to claim such damages in domestic law where a breach of EU law occurred before exit day. In other words, it provides for a two-year window for accrued claims to be brought by the end of 2022.[23]

When reflecting on the arguments for excluding the Francovich remedy in English law the lack of connection with the EU legal order stands out as the main reason. The UK government's view was that 'The UK government responded to the EU

18. K. Beal QC, *Ubi Ius, Ibi Remedium*: Do the Union Courts have the 'Latin for Judging', *Judicial Review*, 20(3), 2015, 115.
19. (1703) 92 ER 126.
20. *Ibid.*
21. T. Sampsell-Jones, The Myth of *Ashby v. White*, 8 *University of St. Thomas Law Journal* 40, 2010, 49.
22. C. Barnard, Retained EU Law in the UK Legal Orders: Continuity Between the Old and the New. In A. Lazowski & A. Cygan (eds), *Research Handbook on Legal Aspects of Brexit*, Legal Studies Research Paper Series, Edward Elgar, 2022. University of Cambridge Faculty of Law Research Paper No. 27/2021 p. 10, available at https://papers.ssrn.com/sol3/papers.cfm?abstract_id=3947215.
23. https://www.legislation.gov.uk/ukpga/2018/16/schedule/1; last accessed 13 October 2022.

law framework by rolling back existing judicial remedies. The Francovich remedy is linked to EU membership' and 'will no longer be relevant after we leave'.[24] In the same vein Lord Keen of Elie stated: 'The UK will no longer be under an obligation to implement directives after exit, so the ability to claim Francovich damages would not be possible as a post-exit cause of action.'[25] The UK government's rationale for the removal of the remedy might therefore be seen in the link between supremacy of EU law and the obligation under EU law but somewhat limited to the implementation of directives. The UK government can find partial support in some commentators who see in the Francovich principle 'an extension of supremacy of EU law, ensuring its full effectiveness'.[26]

Others refer to the 'federalist aspirations' of the damages action under EU law: 'In EU Law, a liability action (especially if successful) is tangible evidence of a loss of sovereignty as the individual, by appealing directly to the supranational authority, "reduced" the Member State to just another tortfeasor.'[27] The nature of retained EU law, however, which has been given superior status to earlier domestic law is however, somewhat nebulous in this context. If the Francovich principle was 'an extension of supremacy of EU law', then surely supreme retained EU law should be treated similarly to maintain consistency. Section 5(2) of the European (Withdrawal) Act 2018 provides that 'Accordingly, the principle of supremacy of EU law continues to apply on or after IP completion day so far as relevant to the interpretation, disapplication or quashing of any enactment or rule of law passed or made before IP completion day.' This section has not been without controversy as is evidenced here: 'We consider that the notion of maintaining the "supremacy principle" following exit amounts to a fundamental flaw at the heart of the Bill. We do not consider that clause 5 clearly operates to bestow "supremacy" on retained EU law once exit day arrives. The "supremacy" on retained EU law once exit day arrives.' Against the recommendations of the Select Committee, the drafters of the EU (Withdrawal) Act 2018 maintained the terminology but not the theoretical consequences. In other words, the term 'supremacy' in the EU (Withdrawal) Act 2018 has therefore adopted a different meaning; it is no longer to be understood as an EU term but a culturally specific UK term in the Withdrawal legislation. Whilst 'supremacy' of retained EU law was to continue, the remedy for breaches was to be removed. At the time of writing the UK government has introduced a new Bill which is seeking to repeal the principle of retained EU law supremacy by the end of 2023.[28] In reversal of the order under the EU (Withdrawal) Act 2018 the Bill then

24. A. Lang, V. Miller & J.S. Caird, Commons Library Briefing, Number 8140, EU (Withdrawal) Bill: The Charter, General Principles of EU Law, and 'Francovich' Damages, 17 November 2017, 31.
25. European Union (Withdrawal) Bill, Volume 791: debated on Tuesday 8 May 2018, 117: Schedule 8, p. 64.
26. S. Douglas-Scott, The Constitutional Implications of the EU (Withdrawal) Act 2018: A Critical Appraisal, Queen Mary University of London, School of Law, Legal Studies Research Paper, No. 299/2019, 7.
27. A. Biondi & M. Farley, Damages and Liability Actions in EU Law. In R. Schütze & T. Tridimas (eds), *Oxford Principles of European Law* (Vol. 1). Oxford University Press, 2018, 1040-1063, 1045.
28. Subsection A1 in The Retained EU Law (Revocation and Reform) Bill 2022; https://bills.parliament.uk/bills/3340 last accessed 13 October 2022.

also seeks to allow for the principle of supremacy to be re-instated by way of the introduction of secondary legislation in individual areas of retained EU law.[29]

Before the coming into force of the EU (Withdrawal) Act 2018 there was support for the continued application and even the extension of the Francovich principle in the House of Lords: Lord Davis of Stamford, for instance commented: 'I dare say it will be said by the Government on this subject that Francovich will not be appropriate after we have left the Union because we will not be part of it anymore and the whole purpose of Francovich is to provide a remedy to those who are disadvantaged by the non-observance of Union law in the EU. My view is that we should make sure that those people who currently enjoy those rights and remedies – which is all our citizens – should continue to enjoy them in respect of the same laws as they do at present, in other words in respect of retained law. There could be a very reasonable and attractive agenda that would say that we should extend the Francovich principle from a Union law or a retained law to the generality of law in this country – British law, English law, Scots law et cetera.'[30] Lord Davis refers to the remedial relief individuals can seek in the courts around the country and pays respect for the rule of law. His speech also conveys the appreciation of the unifying effects of a ius commune.

The Francovich remedy is as discussed earlier very much about the rule of law and the creation of an effective remedy for the infringement of rights. There is little mention in the Explanatory notes on the Withdrawal of the need for protecting citizens' rights other than the view that there would be other remedies available for the protection of individuals. This raises some interesting questions with regard to the scope of protection of the Francovich remedy. The Court of Justice made it clear that 'The full effectiveness of Community rules would be impaired and the protection of the rights which they grant would be weakened if individuals were unable to obtain redress when their rights are infringed by a breach of Community law for which a Member State can be held responsible.'[31] Dougan emphasises that the scope of the Francovich remedy is primarily concerned with providing individuals with a remedy for breaches of Community law. In his view less importance is attached to the idea of punishing national governments for failing to comply with their obligations under EU Law.[32] Fears of floodgates of Francovich-type state liability cases were never confirmed. Empirical research showed that the remedy remained 'residual and exceptional' in Member States.[33] Lock's research in 2012 concludes that Member State

29. Subsection A3 in The Retained EU Law (Revocation and Reform) Bill 2022; https://bills.parliament.uk/bills/3340 last accessed 13/10/2022. *Explanatory notes Retained EU Law (Revocation and Reform) Bill Explanatory Notes*, p. 13; https://publications.parliament.uk/pa/bills/cbill/58-03/0156/en/220156en.pdf; last accessed 13 October 2022.
30. European Union Withdrawal Bill, Volume 789 debated on 5 March 2018, Lord Davis of Stamford, 43: Schedule 1, p. 16, line 27.
31. Cases C-6/90 and C-9/90 *Francovich* [1991] ECR I-5357 para. 33.
32. M. Dougan, Addressing Issues of Protective Scope within the Francovich Right to Reparation, *European Constitutional Law Review* 13(1), March 2017, 124.
33. Marie-Pierre F. Granger, Francovich Liability Before National Courts: 25 Years On – Has Anything Changed?. In Paula Gilliker (ed.), *Research Handbook on EU Tort Law*, Elgar, 2017, 95; T. Lock, Is Private Enforcement Through State Liability a Myth? – An Assessment 20 Years after Francovich, *Common Market Law Review* 49(5), 2012, 1675-1702.

liability is not an effective private enforcement mechanism. Only 22% of the then 37 cases in Germany succeeded and 28% of the 25 cases in the UK were successful at the time of his research.[34] More recently it has been noted that more research into the monetary success of the damages claims is needed to be able to analyse the claims made in Member States under this head of tort.[35] It is also worth noting that the Francovich remedy was enforced by national courts and is largely reliant on the application of domestic law due to its hybrid nature. Empirical evidence shows little reason to suggest that the Francovich remedy caused extensive budgetary concerns. Further, the remedy was largely implemented through national law provisions and often failed due to the high threshold of the 'sufficiently serious' test. Whilst it protected the rights of individuals and the rule of law, in political debates Francovich became symbolic of the perceived loss of sovereignty during EU membership. As discussed the preservation of the term 'supremacy' in the European Union (Withdrawal) Act 2018 EUWA is not entirely coherent with this sentiment and illustrates the conceptual difficulties the drafters of the EUWA faced. To conclude it appears that the end of Francovich is simply designed to prevent legal challenges to Government action. With the disappearance of the Francovich remedy from the toolkit of UK lawyers, it is therefore worth examining whether other remedies for breaches of Community law might be available in English law.

4 THE REAPPEARANCE OF THE *FRANCOVICH* REMEDY

Whilst the remedy is gone after the two-year window closes by the end of the year, retained rights in EU law will remain for some time. It follows that in important areas of law such as Environmental law it will be harder to bring an action against the government for breaches of obligations under retained EU law.[36]

As discussed earlier Francovich stands for the protection of the individual against the state. Judge Giuseppe Frederico Mancini, the Italian lawyer who drove the protection of workers' rights and who was instructive in the formulation of the Francovich principle believed in the protection of the individual.[37]

A recent and one of the last cases using the Francovich remedy illustrates the importance of this remedy. *QH (Afghanistan) v. Secretary of State for the Home Department*[38] concerned a claim for damages by a young Afghan who was born in Afghanistan and later joined his British uncle in the UK at the age of 16. His application for asylum was refused wrongfully and he was removed to Germany where he spent three years fighting the deportation and then seeking compensation. The Court of

34. T. Lock, Is Private Enforcement Through State Liability a Myth? – An Assessment 20 Years after Francovich, *Common Market Law Review* 49(5), 2012, 1675-1702, 1685.
35. A. Biondi & M. Farley, Damages and Liability Actions in EU Law. In Robert Schütze & Takis Tridimas (eds), *Oxford Principles of European Law* (Vol. 1, pp. 1040-1063), Oxford University Press, 2018, 1063.
36. https://www.politicshome.com/news/article/government-accused-of-chilling-bid-to-block-compensation-claims-after-brexit; last accessed 1 September 2022.
37. F. Nicola & B. Davis, *EU Law Stories*, Cambridge, 2017, 345.
38. [2022] EWCA Civ 421 (01 April 2022).

Appeal held that amongst other breaches this constituted a breach of Article 27 of the Dublin III Regulation. It was decided that this breach had been sufficiently serious and that he was entitled to Francovich damages.

The question remains as to what is going to happen if applicants will not be able to claim Francovich compensation in cases like this. The Francovich remedy was previously embedded in English private law. Liability for breach of Community law was comparable to a breach of statutory duty.[39] This had been considered in the Factortame V decision.[40] Lord Hobhouse relied on previous case law, i.e., *Garden Cottage Foods*[41] and *Bourgoin v. MAFF*[42] and held that the duty was imposed by way of the European Communities Act 1972. The decision in *Phonographic Performance Limited v. Department of Trade and Industry and Another*[43] which was concerned with the alleged incorrect transposition of the Rental Rights and Related Copyrights and Related Rights in the Information Society Directive (2001/29) confirmed this. The court made important statements as to the nature of the claim. It held that a claim in damages for breach of Community law 'gives rise to a correlative right in one who has suffered such damages' and that such a 'right is not discretionary'.[44] The Crown had argued that the cause of action is 'sui generis' resulting in a public law claim which 'ought to be pursued in a public law claim' in proceedings for judicial review. Such a procedure 'will enable the court to exercise control over the claims and the periods for which they may be pursued'. The Crown argued that in this case the court should strike out the claim as an abuse of process. It was held that this interpretation of the nature of the claim would be 'to subject the rights of an individual to a discretion and a time limit much more restrictive than those normally appropriate to a private law claim for breach of statutory duty and would itself constitute a breach of Community Law'.[45] Despite the fact that the courts ruled that the European remedy should be considered as a breach of statutory duty it is still not clear whether the term is used in a wide non-technical sense or whether the traditional tort was referred to. It has been argued that 'the Eurotort is simply to be classified as a tort in domestic proceedings and the repeated references to breach of statutory duty are a redundancy'.[46] The creation of torts such as the Euro tort as a breach of statutory duty has even been described as 'obscure'.[47] It is, however an important point for two reasons. With a view to the discovery of pure economic loss the distinction is crucial: the traditional breach of statutory duty allows such a recovery more liberally, the tort of negligence does not.[48]

39. T. Cornford, *Towards a Public Law of Tort*, Ashgate, 2008, 2230; Jack Williams, Francovich Claims Are Dead, EU Relations Law https://eurelationslaw.com/blog/francovich-claims-are-dead-long-live-francovich-claims; last accessed 9 August 2022.
40. [1998] 1 CMLR 1353.
41. [1984] AC 130.
42. [1986] QB 716.
43. [2004] 3 CMLR. 31.
44. *Ibid.*; para. 47.
45. *Ibid.*, para. 50.
46. K.M. Stanton, 'New Forms of the Tort of Breach of Statutory Duty', *Law Quarterly Review* 120, 2004, 324 [329].
47. *Ibid.*, at 340.
48. *Ibid.*, at 341.

A separation of domestic law and a free-standing cause of action in Community law as seen in German cases does not feature in the English decisions. Secondly, this approach might allow for a reassessment of Francovich in English courts.[49] The flexible common law approach may have been more prepared to accommodate the European remedy in its domestic system of torts and provide an effective protection of Community law rights. It is, of course now well established that the Francovich remedy is a breach of statutory duty.[50] As a private law cause of action in tort, breach of statutory duty is subject to procedural provisions provided for in other pieces of legislation.

In a recent blog Williams assesses whether there might be a reappearance of Francovich claims in the courts.[51] He states that 'a claim for Francovich damages is a private law cause of action in tort (breach of statutory duty) and is subject to the six-year limitation period in section 2 of the Limitation Act 1980. This means that the EU (Withdrawal) Act 2018 reduces the limitation period for such claims'.[52] He considers whether there might be a way to challenge the provisions in the EUWA. He suggests that it might be possible to argue that the provisions in the EU (Withdrawal) Act 2018 should be 'read down' in accordance with section 3 Human Rights Act 1998. Article 1, Protocol No. 1, European Convention on Human Rights (ECHR A1P1) provides as follows:

> Every natural or legal person is entitled to the peaceful enjoyment of his possessions. No one shall be deprived of his possessions except in the public interest and subject to the conditions provided for by law and by the general principles of international law.

The preceding provisions shall not, however, in any way impair the right of a state to enforce such laws as it deems necessary to control the use of property in accordance with the general interest or to secure the payment of taxes or other contributions or penalties.

In the recent case of *R v. The Proprietor of H Schools, ex parte AA*[53] it was confirmed that the Strasbourg Court has interpreted the concept of 'possessions' broadly. The claimants had sought damages for discrimination at school under Part 6 of the Equality Act 2010 and argued that there was a breach of their rights in ECHR A1P1. As well as tangible property, the term possessions has been held to include various intangible rights and legitimate expectations to payments or assets of various kinds.[54] The concept of 'possessions' has an autonomous meaning which is independent of the formal[55] classification in domestic law and is not limited to the ownership of physical goods: certain other rights and interests constituting assets can also be

49. J. Williams, Francovich Claims Are Dead, EU Relations Law https://eurelationslaw.com/blog/francovich-claims-are-dead-long-live-francovich-claims; last accessed 1 September 2022.
50. *Arriva v. Department for Transport* [2019] EWCA Civ 2259.
51. J. Williams, Francovich Claims Are Dead, EU Relations Law https://eurelationslaw.com/blog/francovich-claims-are-dead-long-live-francovich-claims; last accessed 1 September 2022.
52. *Ibid.*
53. [2022] EWHC 1613 (Admin).
54. *Ibid.*, 47.
55. https://www.echr.coe.int/Documents/Guide_Art_1_Protocol_1_ENG.pdf; p. 7, last accessed 8 September 2022.

regarded as 'property rights', and thus as 'possessions' for the purposes of this provision. The High Court confirmed that a claim for damages in this case was a 'possession' within the meaning of A1P1.[56] More problematic is the requirement that the claimant can show that there was a legitimate expectation to the possession.[57] These are complex questions and the success of challenges to the shorter limitation period contained in the EU (Withdrawal) Act 2018 is uncertain. Time will tell whether the courts will be seized with this issue. There is some hope now as it appears that plans to repeal the Human Rights Act 1998 have been dropped.[58] Only time will tell whether a challenge to the EU (Withdrawal) Act 2018 might be brought in the UK or even Strasbourg and provide applicants with more time to seek justice. The Human Rights Act 1998 could perhaps still come to the rescue should an applicant want to argue that the shorter limitation period is in breach of Human Rights.

5 CONCLUSION

Much has been said about the Francovich remedy which has become synonymous with the body of case law that was established by the Court of Justice of the EU over a span of nearly 30 years. It is not only famous case names that will no longer play a role in British courts. Despite the relatively small number of successful claims in the UK, Francovich had found its prominent place within a myriad of complex domestic principles on public liability and inspired judges and academics. It provided an avenue for redress and stood for the protection of rights and the rule of law and it opened avenues for cross-fertilisation. Rights without remedies are not much use. Let us hope for the wind to change again. In Judge Frederico Giuseppe Mancini's words: 'In any event, aren't professors even if they are judges, entitled to a bit of daydreaming?'[59]

56. [2022] EWHC 1613 (Admin) 55.
57. *Ibid.*, with reference to *Draon v. France* (2005) 43 EHRR 40.
58. https://www.theguardian.com/law/2022/sep/07/liz-truss-halts-dominic-raab-bill-of-rights-plan; last accessed 8 September 2022.
59. G. Frederico Mancini, The Italians in Europe, *Foreign Affairs*, 79(2), March-April, 2000, 122-134, at 134.

PART II Law and Politics: A Shifting Boundary?

CHAPTER 8

Law and Politics: Standing on Shifting Sand

Alison L. Young[*]

The line between law and politics has always been difficult to draw. In the United Kingdom (UK), however, it appears to have become increasingly controversial following the Brexit referendum. Were the two *Miller* decisions the culmination of a judicial takeover, with law intruding too far into politics? Are current post-Brexit reforms a means of redressing this imbalance, or an exemplification of populism, the judiciary being another elite institution that should be made inferior to the will of the people, as expressed through politics?

As Patrick Birkinshaw's work recognises, there are no easy answers to these questions. Discussions of this boundary, particularly by members of the government who feel that the judiciary are going too far, wrongly assume that there are easily defined lists of legal and political powers. However, as Birkinshaw correctly argues:

> [t]here are not ideal separate worlds of politics, law, and government. We know that there are adjudicative functions, legislative functions and executive or governmental functions. Initially, distinctions are easy to draw. However, these functions seep into each other.[1]

It is unsurprising, therefore, that, whilst commentators agree that the line between law and politics has shifted through Brexit and into the post-Brexit constitution, there are strong disagreements as to whether this change is a move in the right direction.

Noting a change in the balance between law and politics, therefore, should not be a cause for concern. Even if we are not happy with the direction of travel, this may be the price we pay in a constitutional system that does not rely on a codified constitution;

* The author would like to thank Hayley J Hooper for her comments on an earlier draft.

1. P. Birkinshaw, 'Jonathan Sumption: *Trials of the State: Law and the Decline of Politics*' (2020) 2 Amicus Curiae 459, at 470.

which neither provides a clear justification for, and delineation of, the role of the courts, nor which clearly defines and limits executive powers.

However, as Birkinshaw also astutely notes, tensions between the legislature, the executive, and the judiciary in the UK constitution are 'normal and constructive where there is mutual respect between the branches of the state'.[2] Indeed, for Birkinshaw, 'our constitution works best when the three branches work constructively together'.[3] The purpose of this chapter is to ask whether recent events show the three branches of government working together to achieve a good balance between law and politics, or whether they exemplify a loss of mutual trust which may threaten the delicate balance between law and politics on which the UK constitution rests. It will argue that most of the recent fluctuations in the divide between law and politics can be explained in terms of the usual tensions. However, there is also evidence of a weakening in mutual trust, particularly as regards actions of the executive. This is a worrying tendency which, if left unchecked, may threaten the separation of powers, and ultimately the rule of law, in the UK constitution.

1 A DELICATE BALANCE

It is no secret that the current Conservative government is concerned that the divide between law and politics has been tipped too far in favour of legal controls, intruding into the political sphere.[4] This was illustrated, perhaps most forcefully, by the Prime Minister's response to the *Miller; Cherry* decision[5] – the prorogation case – where he stated in Parliament that 'I think that the judiciary were wrong to pronounce on what is essentially a political question'.[6] The Conservative Party Manifesto also promised to examine broader aspects of the constitution, including ensuring that 'judicial review is available to protect the rights of the individuals against an overbearing state, while ensuring that it is not abused to conduct politics by another means'.[7] This promise has materialised, albeit in a more attenuated manner than was anticipated.[8]

The above statements illustrate two ways of analysing the distinction between law and politics; motive and subject matter. Are applicants motivated by politics, using the law to win political battles they lost in the political arena and thereby blurring the

2. P. Birkinshaw, 'The Independent Panel's Report on Judicial Review (CP 407) and the Government's Consultation Document on Judicial Reform (CP 408)' (2021) 2 Amicus Curiae 501, at 501.
3. *Ibid.*, at 511.
4. *See, e.g.*, the following editorial by Chris Grayling: https://www.dailymail.co.uk/news/article-2413135/CHRIS-GRAYLING-Judicial-review-promotional-tool-Left-wing-campaigners.html.
5. *R (Miller) v. Prime Minister; Cherry v. Advocate General for Scotland* [2019] UKSC 41, [2020] AC 373.
6. HC Deb vol. 664, Col 775 (25 September 2019).
7. Conservative Party Manifesto 2019, p. 48.
8. Judicial Review and Courts Act 2022, Part 1. These provisions provide for greater remedial flexibility, establishing prospective only and suspended quashing orders, as well as removing judicial review over decisions of the Upper Tribunal to refuse to hear an appeal from a decision of the First-tier Tribunal. The Government's response to the Independent Review of Administrative Law (IRAL) appeared to promise more stringent reforms that would have placed greater restrictions on judicial review. (https://www.gov.uk/government/consultations/judicial-review-reform).

divide between law and politics? There are problems with this approach. Judicial review is designed to facilitate individuals to bring challenges to decisions of public bodies that harm their individual rights, alongside challenges that ensure the rule of law is upheld and the government does not commit 'public wrongs' by acting outside the sphere of their legal powers. Both of these purposes could also have political motivations. Individuals will bring a legal challenge because they think a decision of a public body is wrong. Does it matter if this is motivated by politics, or a deep sense of injustice, if, in both cases, the court is looking at whether the public body in question broached the legal limits on its power? It may also be difficult to discover, and easy to disguise, one's motivation for bringing an action for judicial review.

There also exist sufficient mechanisms for filtering out problematic actions for judicial review that really are 'politics in disguise'. Individual applicants have to demonstrate that they have 'sufficient interest' to bring an action for judicial review.[9] Courts have also refused to grant permission to bring actions for judicial review that appear to have little, if any legal argument,[10] or which appear to raise moot issues,[11] as well as refusing to provide standing to prevent politically motivated challenges.[12] It is difficult to conclude, therefore, that politically motivated challenges pose a fundamental problem for the division between law and politics. This may explain why measures to tackle this perceived problem were not included in recent reforms to judicial review. Although the Bill of Rights Bill 2022 proposed that only victims of human rights restrictions would have sufficient interest to bring a legal challenge, the Bill has failed to progress through Parliament and its future hangs in doubt following the resignation of Dominic Raab as Lord Chancellor.

Distinguishing between law and politics on the basis of subject matter, separating legal from political questions, is more promising, though ultimately equally problematic. This relies on the assumption that there are spheres of power that are legal and others that are political. Political issues should be non-justiciable, as unsuited for the courts. The most recent account of non-justiciable issues can be found in the Supreme Court's decision in *Shergill v. Khaira*,[13] which concerned, *inter alia*, whether the court could determine religious issues for the purposes of applying a trust. The Supreme

9. Senior Courts Act 1981, section 31(3).
10. *See, e.g.*, *Wightman v. Advocate General* [2018] CSIH 18. Permission was originally refused for a petition seeking judicial review to request a reference to the Court of Justice of the European Communities to determine whether the UK had the power to unilaterally withdraw from the European Union (EU) Treaties. The applicant was granted permission on appeal, only after the legal arguments were refined and given the important constitutional nature of the challenge. The court was acutely aware of the need to avoid courts being used to bring purely political challenges.
11. *R (Counsel General for Wales) v. Secretary of State for Business, Energy and Industrial Strategy* [2022] EWCA Civ 118, which rejected a general challenge to the impact of the UK Internal Markets Act 2020 on the Government of Wales Act 2006. Challenges to lawmaking capacity of the Senedd Cymru could not be made in the abstract and needed to be framed in response to specific legislation.
12. *DSD (Worboys) v. Parole Board* [2018] EWHC 694 (Admin), [2019] QB 285, which refused to grant permission to the Lord Mayor of London to challenge the parole decision of John Worboys on the basis of this being of general interest to the safety of Londoners.
13. [2014] UKSC 33, [2015] AC 359.

Court noted that there were two types of non-justiciable issues. First, an issue is non-justiciable if it is 'beyond the constitutional competence assigned to the courts under our conception of the separation of powers'.[14] This would include, for example, executive matters which directly affect the UK's relations with a foreign state[15] and the constitutional limits of the competence of the court vis-à-vis Parliament.[16] Second, issues are non-justiciable when they are 'claims or defences which are based neither in private law rights or obligations, nor on reviewable matters of public law'.[17] This would include, for example, domestic disputes where there was no intention to enter into legal relations, or non-justiciable prerogative powers.[18]

Case law surrounding the list of justiciable – and non-justiciable – prerogative powers illustrate the problems of adopting an approach to the divide between law and politics that is based on subject matter. Lord Roskill's list of 'no go' areas for the courts included 'the making of treaties, the defence of the realm, the prerogative of mercy, the grant of honours, the dissolution of Parliament and the appointment of Ministers'.[19] However, the courts have nevertheless reviewed the use of prerogative powers in these areas. First, all prerogative powers are subject to judicial review as regards their existence and extent, even those that appear on Lord Roskill's list of non-justiciable prerogative powers.[20] Second, courts have reduced the list of non-justiciable prerogative powers, particularly as regards review of the prerogative power of mercy.[21] It is also possible to think of situations in which prerogative powers which appear to be purely political – e.g., the giving of honours or the appointment of Ministers – may nevertheless raise legal issues that would require court intervention. Would this be the case, for example, if there was evidence of fraud, or of threats of violence to the Prime Minister or his family in order to compel the appointment of a particular Minister? Whilst the English High Court, at least, has not abandoned the idea that there are some

14. *Ibid.*, at [42].
15. *See, e.g.*, *Buttes Gas v. Hammer and Occidental Oil (Nos 2 and 3)* [1982] AC 888, where the courts will check to determine if there is a domestic issue that will nevertheless trigger the competence of the UK Courts. See also *R (Al Haq) v. Secretary of State for Foreign and Commonwealth Affairs* [2009] EWHC 1910 (Admin) and *R (Khan) v. Secretary of State for Foreign and Commonwealth Affairs* [2014] EWCA Civ 24, [2014] 1 WLR 872, and, reaching the opposite conclusion, *R (Abassi) v. Secretary of State for Foreign and Commonwealth Affairs* [2002] EWCA Civ 1598 and *R (Youssef) v. Secretary of State for Foreign and Commonwealth Affairs* [2016] UKSC 3, [2016] AC 1457.
16. *See, e.g.*, parliamentary privilege of freedom of expression, found in the Bill of Rights 1689, Article 9.
17. *Shergill v. Khaira* [2014] UKSC 33, [2015] AC 359, at [43].
18. *See, e.g.*, those listed by Lord Roskill in *Council of Civil Service Unions v. Minister for the Civil Service* [1985] AC 374.
19. *Ibid.*, at 418.
20. *See R (Miller) v. Secretary of State for Exiting the European Union* [2017] UKSC 5, [2018] AC 61 and *R (Miller) v. Prime Minister; Cherry v. Advocate General for Scotland* [2019] UKSC 41, [2020] AC 373. *See also* J. Williams, 'Prerogative Powers after *Miller*: An Analysis in Four Es' in M. Elliott, J. Williams and A.L. Young (eds) *The UK Constitution after Miller: Brexit and Beyond* (Hart, 2018), 39.
21. *See R v. Secretary of State, ex parte Bentley* [1994] QB 349 and *Lewis v. Attorney General of Jamaica* [2001] 1 AC 50, *Pitman v. The State* [2017] UKPC 6, [2017] 3 WLR 790, *Pratt v. Attorney General of Jamaica* [1993] UKPC 1, [1994] 2 AC 1 and *Lendore v. Attorney General of Trinidad and Tobago* [2017] UKPC 25, [2017] 1 WLR 3369.

prerogative powers that are purely political and immune from judicial review,[22] it may be that this is because the legal issues raised by our imaginary examples would trigger legal control through the use of the criminal law, rather than through judicial review.

The slippery nature of the subject-matter approach to the division between law and politics is understandable when we place this approach in its context. After providing his list of non-justiciable prerogative powers in *Council of Civil Service Unions v. Minister for the Civil Service*, Lord Roskill concluded that '[t]he courts are not the place wherein to determine whether a treaty should be concluded or the armed forces disposed in a particular manner or Parliament dissolved on one date rather than the other'[23] His justification focuses less on the subject matter of the prerogative per se and more on the nature of the question a court may be asked to determine within that subject matter. Legal questions concern the law. Political questions are concerned with merits. Courts should not determine the merits of entering into a Treaty, or of choosing to dissolve Parliament on one date as opposed to a different date. Their concern is with legal issues - whether it would be lawful to enter into a Treaty or to dissolve Parliament.

This distinction too, however, may be difficult to determine with precision. There are those who criticise, for example, both the standard of *Wednesbury* unreasonableness[24] and the emerging standard of proportionality as failing to provide a standard of review that ensures courts are confined to an assessment of the legality of the way in which a public body has exercised its power, these standards of review demonstrating, instead, how courts are really assessing the merits of a decision.[25] In a similar manner, constitutional conventions and the Ministerial Code, both of which have been deemed to be 'extra-legal' have nevertheless been capable of being taken into account by courts when they raise, or are relevant to, legal issues. Whilst courts have not enforced either conventions or the Ministerial Code per se,[26] nevertheless courts have determined the scope of conventions when relevant to determining a legal issue,[27] in addition to interpreting provisions of the Ministerial Code when this aided the determination of matters that were suitable for the courts.[28]

Given these difficulties, how are we to assess whether changes in the distinction between law and politics undermine the constitution, or help to ensure a more effective set of checks and balances? In previous work I have argued that to approach the distinction between law and politics as depending upon subject matter, or upon legal and political issues, or legality and the merits, effectively put the cart before the

22. *R (Miller) v. Prime Minister* [2019] EWHC 2381 (QB).
23. [1985] AC 374, at 418.
24. *Associated Provincial Picture Houses Ltd v. Wednesbury Corporation* [1948] 1 KB 223.
25. *See, e.g.*, J. Goodwin, 'The Last Defence of *Wednesbury*' (2012) PL 445, T.A.O. Endicott, 'Proportionality and Incommensurability' in G. Huscroft, B. Miller and G. Webber, *Proportionality and the Rule of Law* (CUP, 2014), at 311 and P. Sales, 'Rationality, Proportionality and the Development of the Law' (2013) 129 Law Quarterly Review 223.
26. *See R (Miller) v. Secretary of State for Exiting the European Union* [2017] UKSC 5, [2018] AC 61.
27. *Attorney General v. Jonathan Cape* [1975] 3 WLR 606 and *Evans v. Information Commissioner* [2012] UKUT 313 (AAC).
28. *R (Gulf Centre for Human Rights) v. The Prime Minister* [2016] EWHC 1323 (Admin) and *R (FDA) v. Prime Minister and Minister for the Civil Service* [2021] EWHC 3279 (Admin).

horse.[29] These approaches use the distinction between law and politics in order to define the separation of powers between Parliament, the government, and the courts. However, a preferable approach is to focus first on the separation of powers, doing so by examining the distinct institutional features of these three instruments of government, examining in particular the way in which they reason. In addition, we need to investigate the way in which these institutions interact. These interactions can serve two purposes: they can help institutions to work together to make better decisions, and they can be means through which to refine the separation of powers itself, determining which institution is more constitutionally suited to taking particular governmental decisions or actions.

This approach to the separation of powers is mostly applied in the field of human rights protections, focusing in particular on the allocation of roles between Parliament and the courts. Parliament is better suited to balancing interests than the courts, given that it provides a forum in which wider points of view can be heard and evaluated. Courts are dependent on parties to bring issues before them and only consider the issues they raise. In addition, when it can be reasonable to disagree about how to balance these competing interests, Parliament's democratic status provides a good constitutional reason for the authority of Parliament to make this choice. Its choice should be representative and, should it fail to be so, it is possible for the electorate to choose different Members of Parliament who they believe are more capable of making representative choices. Courts, on the other hand, are better able to protect rights. The UK upholds the principle of judicial independence, meaning that courts do not need to ensure their choices are representative. They may be better able to recognise when minority rights have been infringed through the democratic process which tends to favour a solution that is in line with the wishes of the majority.

Moreover, Parliament makes general decisions. Courts focus on the specific issue before them. This means that the judiciary can recognise situations in which a general measure, which may provide a good protection of rights, nevertheless fails to protect rights when applied to a specific individual. Parliament is also forward-looking. Legislation is designed to change the law. Courts are backward looking and conservative – in the sense of conserving legal principles. Courts reason by looking at previous case law, discerning similarities and differences between those cases and the specific case before the court. To the extent that courts change the common law, they do so incrementally, building on past precedents. This makes courts more suited to recognising and preserving long-standing principles of the common law, drawing it to the attention of Parliament when legislation may undermine these long-standing principles. In addition, it influences the remedies that each can provide. Courts may point out when a right has been breached, overturning decisions and awarding damages for this breach. Parliament is more able to provide future remedies by modifying the law, or by providing a structure through which rights can be provided or protected.[30]

29. A.L. Young, 'The Relationship Between Parliament, the Executive and the Judiciary' in J. Jowell and C. O'Cinnéide (eds) *The Changing Constitution* (OUP, 2019), 325.
30. A.L. Young *Democratic Dialogue and the Constitution* (OUP, 2017).

Similar conclusions underpin the distinction between the judiciary and the executive when applied to the division between law and politics applied through the provisions of judicial review. The fusion between the legislature and the executive means that some of the differences between the legislature and the judiciary and between the judiciary and the executive remain the same. The executive initiates most legislation. The executive implements policy decisions. It is also indirectly elected, making it more democratically accountable than the judiciary.

There are also important differences. Parliament is sovereign. The executive is not. This means that it is possible for courts to strike down unlawful executive measures. Also, the extent to which courts should recognise the democratic credentials of the executive depends on the identity of the person taking the decision, and the extent to which this measure has received democratic scrutiny. An individual decision of an immigration official refusing a visa is different from the decision of a Secretary of State determining general visa requirements. Scrutiny of delegated legislation that has been subject to the affirmative or super-affirmative resolution procedure is, in turn, distinct from an exercise of a discretionary power.

However, merely recognising the need to focus on these institutional distinctions is not sufficient to provide a clear delineation to the distinction between law and politics. It may provide some further guidance, as well as recognise that the distinction between law and politics is context-dependent. It cannot provide complete clarity as the distinction between law and politics is contestable. It can be reasonable to disagree about the relative constitutional role of the legislature, executive, and the courts. These relative roles also fluctuate over time. This explains the importance of focusing on inter-institutional interactions. Interactions may help to refine the distinction between law and politics as each institution collaborates to refine this distinction when applied to novel situations. It may also provide a mechanism through which each institution can challenge a situation when it thinks that the distinction between law and politics has been drawn in the wrong place.

This is best explained through examples. I discussed above the way in which the case law has evolved concerning the list of prerogative powers that are non-justiciable as regards judicial review over the exercise of that power. In the *Miller v. Prime Minister* decision at first instance, for example, the High Court first noted the extent to which the list of non-justiciable prerogative powers had been eroded.[31] Lord Pannick, representing Gina Miller, argued that the law had evolved to such an extent that the court no longer focused first on whether the subject of the prerogative power was suited for the court, but rather focused instead on whether the specific issue raised with regard to that prerogative power was a legal issue. The High Court was unwilling to accept this argument. However, it did recognise a pattern to the case law where the courts had apparently eroded Lord Roskill's lists. All of the cases concerned a use of prerogative powers where there had been an impact on particular individuals. This was not the case as regards the use of the prerogative power of prorogation.[32] The High Court also

31. [2019] EWHC 2381 (QB), at [36].
32. *Ibid.*, at [37]-[40].

recognised that political prerogatives are non-justiciable, defining the 'essential characteristic' of a political issue as 'the absence of judicial or legal standards by which to assess the legality of the Executive's decision or action'.[33] The decision as to when Parliament should be prorogued, and for how long, was essentially political in nature and therefore non-justiciable.[34]

The first instance judgment in *Miller v. Prime Minister* is an example of an incremental development of the common law, the courts slowly moving the distinction between law and politics. Whilst it did not remove the need to consider subject matter, it places this firmly in the context of situations in which there are no legal, justiciable controls over that subject matter, tempered by a consideration of an issue that has an impact on a particular individual. These developments match institutional distinctions between the executive and the courts. The executive is politically accountable – albeit as regards the prorogation of Parliament, these mechanisms are indirect and stem more from the ability of the electorate to take these decisions into account at a general election, given that the only real means of Parliament being able to hold the executive to account for a prorogation decision is through the use of a vote of no confidence. Despite these concerns, the executive is still more politically accountable than the courts. Also, it shows that courts are more willing to consider an issue as legal, as opposed to political, when it affects individuals. This, again, recognises the relatively better ability of courts to protect individual rights as opposed to balancing general interests. There was no specific reaction of the executive to this decision, understandably given the High Court agreed with the Government's legal argument. Any input could only be through the legal argument made by the Government's counsel.

A different form of interaction took place in the Supreme Court's decision in *Miller*; *Cherry*. The Supreme Court did not question the conclusions as to the justiciability of the prerogative power of prorogation as regards controls over the exercise of that power. Instead, it concluded that its legal control was over the extent of a prerogative power. In addition, as I have argued elsewhere, this is best understood as giving rise to a different form of interaction.[35] The courts were concerned to intervene to protect Parliament from an action of the executive which significantly eroded the ability of Parliament to perform its constitutional function. In doing so, the court was challenging an implied distinction drawn by the executive – that prorogation was purely political and that there were no limits on the scope of the prerogative power. Courts were challenging more directly the distinction between law and politics. This challenge did prompt a reaction from the executive – albeit indirectly. First, as noted above, the Prime Minister stated in Parliament that, whilst he respected the decision of the judiciary, he did not agree with its conclusion and was convinced that prorogation was purely political. Second, the Dissolution and Calling of Parliament Act 2022 includes a specific non-justiciability clause, ensuring that courts cannot question

33. *Ibid.*, at [47].
34. *Ibid.*, at [51].
35. A.L. Young, 'The Prorogation Case: Re-inventing the Constitution or Re-imagining Constitutional Scholarship' in D. Clarry (ed.) *The UK Supreme Court Yearbook: Volume 10, 2018-19 Year* (Appellate Press, 2021) 357.

the exercise, the existence, or extent of the prerogative power of the dissolution of Parliament.[36]

When assessing changes to the distinction between law and politics, therefore, we need to distinguish between incremental changes which reflect a refinement of the distinction, based on a focus on the relative institutional and constitutional features of the Government and the courts and situations in which changes have been made to push back against a perceived intrusion by another institution of government, crossing the line between law and politics rather than incrementally refining the distinction. Institutions of the constitution should work together to refine the distinction between law and politics, based on their distinct institutional and constitutional characteristics. However, we need to be wary of changes that occur without this cooperation, where one institution pushes back against a perceived illegitimate change to the distinction between law and politics. These changes undermine, as opposed to reinforce, the necessary mutual trust between the legislature, the executive, and the courts which is central to the UK's predominantly political, uncodified constitution.

2 MUTUAL LACK OF RESPECT?

The *Miller*; *Cherry* case indicated areas in which there was evidence of a perception by the current Government that the balance between law and politics had been drawn in the wrong place, with courts deciding issues that were political as opposed to legal. Evidence of this perception can also be found in recent, and ongoing, areas of constitutional reform. Following its manifesto promise, the Government initiated an Independent Review on Administrative Law (IRAL) in July 2020. The review's report, alongside the government's response and a further consultation on judicial review reform, was published in March 2021. The foreword to the Government's response, written by the then Lord Chancellor, Robert Buckland KC, noted that the 'Panel's analysis identified a growing tendency for the courts in Judicial Review cases to edge away from a strictly supervisory jurisdiction, becoming more willing to review the merits of the decisions for themselves, instead of the way in which those decisions were made'.[37] The Lord Chancellor also set out the intention of his reforms to affirm 'the role of the courts as 'servants of Parliament',[38] suggesting that courts had transgressed the boundary between law and politics, performing functions that belonged to Parliament.

These statements are insufficient to demonstrate a lack of mutual respect between the Government and the courts. Nevertheless, there is a suspicion of a growing mistrust given that the Lord Chancellor's remarks gave an accurate assessment of the content of the IRAL report. The government's response to IRAL, and its further consultation exercise, also suggested broader changes than those that had been

36. Dissolution and Calling of Parliament Act 2022, section 3.
37. Ministry of Justice, 'Judicial Review Reform: The Government Response to the Independent Review of Administrative Law' CP 408, March 2021, Foreword, para. 2.
38. Ministry of Justice, 'Judicial Review Reform: The Government Response to the Independent Review of Administrative Law', para. 4.

recommended by IRAL and which were supported by a minority, as opposed to a majority, of those who had submitted evidence to IRAL. The Judicial Review and Courts Bill 2021 was not as radical as the government's response might have suggested, bringing in reforms that were broadly in line with those suggested by IRAL. Moreover, following a successful amendment in the House of Lords, the Act removed one provision which incentivised courts to grant suspended and prospective only quashing orders on a wider basis; the clause stated that courts 'must' grant a suspended or prospective only quashing order if to do so 'would, as a matter of substance, offer adequate redress ... unless it sees good reason not to do so'.[39] Does this willingness to weaken proposed reforms to judicial review show an underlying respect for the judiciary, recognising that courts can be trusted to exercise a discretionary power over remedies? Or can it also be read as a willingness to use rhetoric when describing the role of courts, indicative of an underlying mistrust, coupled with an inability to legislate in a manner that undermines the distinction between law and politics given the opposition of the House of Lords?

A similar duality arises with regard to the Government's proposed reforms of the Human Rights Act 1998. The Government first established a panel to carry out an Independent Human Rights Act Review (IHRAR). The Government then published the report, alongside its response and a further consultation exercise on human rights reform. The then Lord Chancellor, Dominic Raab, stated that the Government's intention was to provide a 'clearer demarcation of the separation of powers between the courts and Parliament'.[40] The Government's case for reform focused on the extent to which courts had expanded human rights, particularly through the use by the European Court of Human Rights of the 'living tree' approach to the content of Convention rights. Second, courts had used the powers under the Human Rights Act to read legislation in a manner compatible with Convention rights too extensively, intruding into politics by changing as opposed to interpreting the wording of legislation.[41] Courts were also accused of interpreting Convention rights as requiring extensive positive obligations to protect rights, meaning that they were straying into politics by becoming involved in policy choices that were affecting public expenditure.[42] These reform suggestions went beyond those provided by the IHRAR. Is this indicative of a lack of trust in the judiciary, or a desire to work with the courts to correct an imbalance in the distinction between law and politics?

The suspicion that the Government is motivated by a lack of trust in the judiciary, as opposed to a desire to collaborate to refine the distinction between law and politics, is reinforced by the way in which the human rights reform proposals were based on assessments that had not taken account of more recent judicial decisions or focused on specific examples rather than general trends. This is particularly notable with regard to the reform proposals regarding the extent to which courts should follow decisions of

39. Judicial Review and Courts Bill 2021, clause 1(9).
40. Ministry of Justice, 'Human Rights Act Reform: A Modern Bill of Rights. A Consultation to reform the Human Rights Act 1998' CP 588, December 2021, p. 3.
41. Human Rights Act 1998, section 3.
42. Ministry of Justice, 'Human Rights Act Reform: A Modern Bill of Rights. A Consultation to reform the Human Rights Act 1998' CP 588, December 2021, Chapter 3.

the European Court of Human Rights, which failed to take account of more recent case law demonstrating how and when UK courts did not follow decisions which they felt failed to take account of English law, or where there were mistakes in how the European Court of Human Rights had reasoned about rights.[43]

Further evidence of a growing potential mistrust stems from how recent case law has refined the distinction between law and politics, but that this has either gone unnoticed by the Government or has not influenced the Government's position on judicial review or human rights reform. The UK Supreme Court is arguably adopting a more cautious approach which reflects a possible refinement of the distinction between law and politics. This can be seen, for example, in the way in which the Court is reasoning, focusing more on a legalistic as opposed to a principled approach, focusing more on legal minutiae, including the interpretation of statutory provisions or precedent, rather than looking at over-arching legal principles.[44] Second, courts are continuing to show deference to Parliament when applying proportionality in human rights cases. Third, there is evidence of the Supreme Court being aware of situations in which the divide between law and politics may be undermined when applicants may use judicial review for political purposes.

This 'legalistic' turn has been recognised by Conor Gearty.[45] In *Begum*, for example, Lord Reed's judgment unpacked a complex series of appeals, focusing on the extent to which the Court of Appeal had applied the correct legal test, as opposed to looking at general principles, applying these to reach a specific outcome of how these principles should apply to the facts, particularly in terms of the impact on Begum.[46] Similarly, in the *UNCRC Reference*, Lord Reed's judgment, again, focused on the wording of legislation, as interpreted in the *Legal Continuity Reference* case, rather than looking at broader principles underpinning the devolution settlement.[47] This careful analysis has been criticised for providing a broad reading of parliamentary sovereignty.[48] The Supreme Court was also reluctant to interpret the Scotland Act 1998 differently, as a constitutional statute. This legalistic approach is also illustrated in a series of judgments looking at statutory interpretation, where the Supreme Court is adopting an approach that focuses on the words of statutory provisions, interpreted

43. *See, e.g.*, *R v. Horncastle* [2009] UKSC 14, [2010]2 AC 375, *Attorney General's Reference (No 60 of 2013)*, *R v. McLoughlin; R v. Newell* [2014] EWCA Crim 188; [2014] 3 All ER 73, *Hicks*, [2014] EWCA Civ 3, [2014] 1 WLR 2152, *R (Hallam) v. Secretary of State for Justice* [2019] UKSC 2, [2019] 2 WLR 440, *Hafeez* [2020] EWHC 155 (Admin), [2020] 1 WLR 1296 and *Sanchez v. Government of the United States of America* [2020] EWHC 508 (Admin).
44. *See* A.L. Young, 'Public Law Cases and the Common Law: A Unique Relationship?' in E. Fisher, J. King and A.L. Young (eds) *Foundations and Future of Public Law* (OUP, 2020) and '*Miller* and the Future of Constitutional Adjudication' in M. Elliott, J. Williams and A.L. Young (eds) *The UK Constitution After Miller: Brexit and Beyond* (Hart, 2018).
45. C. Gearty, 'In the Shallow End' (2022) 44(2) London Review of Books, 27 January 2022, available at https://www.lrb.co.uk/the-paper/v44/n02/conor-gearty/in-the-shallow-end.
46. *Begum v. Secretary of State for the Home Department* [2021] UKSC 7, [2021] 2 WLR 556.
47. *Reference by the Attorney General and the Advocate General for Scotland - United Nations Convention on the Rights of the Child (Incorporation) (Scotland) Bill* [2021] UKSC 42, [2021] 1 WLR 5106.
48. M. Elliott and N. Kilford, 'Devolution in the Supreme Court: Legislative Supremacy, Parliament's "Unqualified" Power, and "Modifying" the Scotland Act', U.K. Const. L. Blog (15 October 2021) (available at https://ukconstitutionallaw.org/).

against their context and purpose. In *Fylde Coast Farms*, for example, the Supreme Court applied this approach to statutory interpretation, upholding a short six-week time period in planning decisions and preventing the bringing of challenges at a later stage that were effectively challenging a decision made earlier in the planning process.[49]

An awareness of the need for a deferential approach in order to maintain the divide between law and politics is illustrated most prominently in human rights cases. In *Elan-Cane*, for example, the Supreme Court concluded that the lack of provision for a neutral gender on UK passports did not contravene Convention rights. The Supreme Court was very reluctant to develop UK law beyond the current scope of Convention rights as set out in decisions of the European Court of Human Rights.[50] This awareness of the need for deference is also seen in the case law not involving Convention rights. In *The Project for the Registration of Children as British Citizens*, the Supreme Court clarified the scope of the principle of legality, which only applies when legislation potentially restricts a fundamental common law right.[51] This did not include access to UK citizenship; unlike access to the courts, this was not a fundamental common law right. Courts have also continued to be deferential in cases involving socioeconomic rights. This can be seen, in particular, in a recent Supreme Court case, which challenged the legality of the two-child cap for working tax credits.[52] The Supreme Court also recognised the importance of giving greater weight to the reasoning of Parliament in these cases, where courts usually apply a 'manifestly without reasonable foundation' test when applying proportionality. The Supreme Court did recognise that this may not be suited to cases where welfare benefits or tax credits discriminated against other, protected, characteristics – e.g., race or gender.

This Supreme Court case also illustrates the third potential refinement of the divide between law and politics. The court recognised that many of the public interest groups bringing the case had also campaigned to Parliament, with some of them providing evidence to parliamentary committees. Whilst explaining the extent to which courts can rely on this evidence, giving more deference to Parliament when there is evidence of political debate, it is important to recognise that courts and Parliament reason differently. In particular, it is not the job of the court to critically evaluate parliamentary debate.[53]

There is ample evidence, therefore, that the Supreme Court is aware of and constantly refining the distinction between law and politics in a manner that aims to uphold mutual trust and respect between Parliament, the government, and the courts – even if not all may agree with the court's approach to this distinction. This can be contrasted not only with the Government's statements in Parliament and responses to consultation exercises, but also with evidence of governmental behaviour which hints

49. *R (Fylde Coast Farm) v. Fylde Borough Council* [2021] UKSC 18, [2021] 1 WLR 2794.
50. *R (Elan-Cane) v. Secretary of State for the Home Department* [2021] UKSC 56, [2023] AC 559.
51. *R (The Project for the Registration of Children as British Citizens) v. Secretary of State for the Home Department* [2022] UKSC 3, [2022] 2 WLR 343.
52. *R (SC, CB and 8 children) v. Secretary of State for Work and Pensions* [2021] UKSC 26, [2022] AC 223.
53. *Ibid.*, at [180]-[184].

at a further potential lack of respect for courts. In *Majera*, it became clear that a Minister, who thought a court bail order was unlawful, decided to treat this order as a 'nullity' and, instead, impose alternative bail conditions rather than bring an action for judicial review to challenge the court order.[54] The Supreme Court reinforced that Ministers are legally obliged to follow court orders – something which one would suggest would hardly need to be said in a legal system in which there is mutual trust between Parliament, the government, and the courts. In *Craig*, the government ignored a declaratory order, for two years, thereby undermining 'the mutual trust which underpins the relationship between the Government and the courts'.[55] This mutual trust motivates courts to refrain from issuing coercive orders, relying instead on declaratory orders which it expects the government will follow out of respect for courts and for the rule of law. Declaratory orders only work effectively because the UK 'is a society governed by the rule of law, where the Government can be trusted to comply with court orders without having to be coerced'.[56]

Craig and *Majera* may be examples of rare mistakes. However, *R (HM) v. Secretary of State for the Home Department* may suggest otherwise.[57] The first paragraph of the judgment contained an admission by the Secretary of State that she was operating an unlawful policy, seizing mobile phones, and copying data from immigrants who arrived in the UK from France after crossing the channel in small boats.[58] The Minister also had to apologise to the court for a failure to comply with the duty of candour when responding to the claim for judicial review.[59]

Even if this is not evidence of a general trend of mistrust and a failure on the part of government departments to respect the rule of law and court judgments, these specific examples are concerning in and of themselves. A lack of mutual trust and respect for the law undermines the ability of the institutions of the constitution to work together to continually refine the distinction between law and politics to reflect changing circumstances. Instead, it pushes institutions to focus more on protecting their constitutional rights, further undermining trust as it pushes each possible refinement to a potential constitutional crisis.

3 CONCLUSION

The distinction between law and politics is elusive. I have argued above that it is too simplistic to regard the distinction in terms of distinct spheres, or subject matter. It is also difficult to distinguish between law and the merits. Instead, I have argued that the precise nature of divide between law and politics varies over time. It reflects the different institutional and constitutional powers of Parliament, the Government, and the courts, focusing in particular on how these institutions take decisions. We rely on

54. *R (Majera) v. Secretary of State for the Home Department* [2021] UKSC 46, [2022] AC 461.
55. *Craig v. Her Majesty's Advocate* [2022] UKSC 6, [2022] 1 WLR 1270, at [46].
56. *Ibid.*
57. [2022] EWHC 695 (Admin).
58. *Ibid.*, at [1].
59. *Ibid.*

the institutions of government working together to refine the distinction, making incremental changes that aim to reinforce mutual trust and respect. This system of refinement is fragile. It is open to abuse if institutions look more to reinforcing their own powers, undermining mutual trust and respect, rather than working together to uphold the delicate separation of powers in the UK constitution.

Whilst there is possible evidence of a lack of trust, and even a potential willingness to abuse the trust placed in the government by other institutions, this evidence is inconclusive. Rhetoric may suggest the government strongly believes that the courts have strayed too far into the realms of politics and that their wings need to be clipped. However, this is not supported by the evidence, particularly as regards recent Supreme Court decisions. The government's rhetoric may also fail to materialise in legal reform designed to change the balance between law and politics. The evidence of a lack of respect for court decisions in *Craig* and *Majera*, however, is worrying. It is to be hoped that these are exceptional cases, in a manner similar to the *Miller* decisions. If the delicate balance between law and politics in the UK constitution is to be maintained, then there is a need for trust to be restored, in particular, between the government and the courts.

CHAPTER 9

Ethical Standards Between Politics and Law*

Yseult Marique

In *Government by Moonlight*, Professor Birkinshaw wrote: 'the foundation of the British constitution will be taken to be the aspiration that public actors and their agents should be accountable for their decisions and non-decisions, which in turn requires a high degree of public visibility of the working of government. This is the logic which underpins claims about the virtues of an autonomous courtroom and the recallability of representatives elected to a legislature whose confidence the executive branch of government must retain'.[1] How crucial this 'public visibility in the working of government' is has come to the fore in particular in a series of recent scandals, instances of conflicts of interest and inappropriate behaviours. Examples can be found at the European level with Jose Barroso, the former President of the European Commission turned advisor to Goldman Sachs,[2] and with Neelie Kroes advising Uber lobbies during her cooling-off period after leaving her position as European Union (EU)

---

* This contribution is a modest way to thank Professor Birkinshaw for his enthusiastic support and constructive discussions in matters pertaining to Brexit over a number of years, and in particular a very warm welcome in Hull just a week before the Brexit referendum. This contribution offers an outsider's perspective on a specific series of events pertaining to the UK politics and constitutional life. From the author's Belgian perspective, 'crises' are a normal part of the political, legal, and constitutional process. What matters is what is done to overcome them and how they are given meaning for the next stages of the political, legal, and constitutional process. Professor Birkinshaw provides his take on this same set of events in 'Them's the Break - Boris Johnsons' Fall and Exit as Prime Minister of the United Kingdom' available at https://ceridap.eu/thems-the-breaks-boris-johnsons-fall-and-exit-as-prime-minister-of-the-united-kingdom/?lng=en .

1. P. Birkinshaw, I. Harden and N. Lewis, *Government by Moonlight – The Hybrid Parts of the State* (London Unwin Hyman 1990) 185.
2. L. de Sousa, 'Barroso and Goldman Sachs: Has the EU Regulatory State Yielded to Big Business Interests?' *LSE European Politics and Policy (EUROPP) Blog*, 22 July 2016.

commissioner in charge of competition.[3] In Germany, Gerard Schröder's position in Gazprom,[4] whilst benefitting from an office in the Bundestag, was eventually denounced – but this had to wait until the strategic time when Russia had invaded Ukraine and the gas supply from Russia to Germany had become toxic.[5]

This chapter focuses on the role of ethical standards in United Kingdom (UK) politics over the pandemic period between 2020 and 2022, a snapshot in the long history of the development of ethical standards and a nugget that is illustrative of the strategic instrumental use that politicians can make of integrity in public life. Although ethical standards are no wonder solution and can even be seen as a 'soft' tool to discipline politicians, it does contribute to call them to account, and they were proven to play a distinctive role in the interstice between the UK political constitution and the UK legal constitution during the pandemic crisis between 2020 and 2022.

The emergence of the ethical standards is first briefly recapped, then a snapshot of the ethical crises during the period 2020-2022 is provided, before suggesting one possible interpretation of ethical standards between law and politics in the contemporary UK constitution.

1 THE PERIOD 2020-2022 IN CONTEXT:[6] THE EMERGENCE OF ETHICAL STANDARDS

In November 2021, former Prime Minister John Major eloquently contrasted his role with that of the then Prime Minister Johnson in the face of mounting scandals of various natures:

> When [the cash for questions scandal] happened I set up the Nolan committee on standards in public life to stop it, which has been a huge success. The striking difference is this: in the 1990s I set up a committee to tackle this sort of behaviour.
>
> Over the last few days we have seen today's government trying to defend this sort of behaviour. Sleaze is unacceptable, was unacceptable when I was there, and I suffered a great deal of pain and anguish over it ... It needs to be stopped.[7]

Both Prime Ministers were losing their grip on their ministers, but one set in motion a process for adopting and monitoring ethical standards, which ended up trapping the other one.

3. https://euobserver.com/eu-political/155496.
4. S. Wood, 'Understanding' for Russia in Germany: International Triangle Meets Domestic Politics' (2021) (34:6) *Cambridge Review of International Affairs* 771-794.
5. K. Connolly, 'Ex-German Chancellor Gerhard Schröder under Fire for Meeting Putin', *The Guardian*, 3 August 2022 available at https://www.theguardian.com/world/2022/aug/03/ex-german-chancellor-gerhard-schroder-under-fire-for-meeting-putin.
6. This section builds on Y. Marique and S. Boyron, 'La responsabilité financière des décideurs publics anglais – Vers une nouvelle culture administrative répressive?' in S. Damarey (ed.) *Responsabilité financière des gestionnaires publics* (Mare et Martin 2022) 275-295.
7. N. Slawson, '"Shameful": John Major Hits Out at Handling of Owen Paterson Scandal', *The Guardian*, 6 November 2021 available at https://www.theguardian.com/politics/2021/nov/06/shameful-john-major-hits-out-at-handling-of-owen-paterson-scandal.

2 NOLAN PRINCIPLES

After *The Guardian* broke the story of the 'cash-for-questions' scandal in 1994,[8] the then Prime Minister Sir John Major invited Lord Nolan to examine the standards of propriety in public life. This led to the establishment of the Committee on Standards in Public Life chaired by Lord Nolan and the adoption of a list of seven principles of public life for a deontological and ethical framework for the action of public decision-makers: selflessness, integrity, objectivity, accountability, openness, honesty and leadership.[9] Thus, every public decision-maker is responsible for his/her decisions and must submit to control mechanisms. Moreover, s/he must act with integrity and avoid being influenced (for example, by compromising situations or by the acquisition of any gains). Likewise, s/he should act and express him/herself with honesty in the performance of his/her duties. All of these principles tend to create a political culture where ethical standards should be respected. These principles have trickled into a number of codes and institutions that are in charge of monitoring and enforcing standards. The Committee on Standards in Public Life itself remains active by regularly advising and reporting on standards of public life in the UK.

3 MINISTERIAL CODE

Another code of ethics adopted to regulate officials' behaviour applies to the government and ministers: the Ministerial Code.[10] It was first published in 1992 under Major and built on internal guidance that had regulated similar matters until then. It is re-adopted under each new Prime Minister. The objective of the Ministerial Code is to set out the standards of conduct expected of ministers and how they have to discharge their duties. Ministers are also 'expected to maintain high standards of behaviour and to behave in a way that upholds the highest standards of propriety' (paragraph 1.1). The Code 'should be read against the background of the overarching duty on Ministers to comply with the law and to protect the integrity of public law' including observing the Seven Principles of Public Life (paragraph 1.3) mentioned above.[11] Among other things, ministers must inform Parliament accurately and precisely.[12] The Ministerial Code reads as follows: 'Ministers who knowingly mislead Parliament will be expected to offer their resignation to the Prime Minister'.

Under the Ministerial Code, the Prime Minister is the person in charge of judging the respect of those standards and deciding on the appropriate consequences for their breach (paragraph 1.6). If a breach is alleged, the Prime Minister decides whether an

8. D. Hencke, 'Tory MPs Were Paid to Plant Questions Says Harrods Chief', *The Guardian*, 20 October 1994 available at https://www.theguardian.com/politics/1994/oct/20/conservatives.uk.
9. P. Bew, 'The Committee on Standards in Public Life: Twenty Years of the Nolan Principles 1995-2015' (2015) (86:3) *Political Quarterly* 411-418.
10. Cabinet Office, Ministerial Code, available at https://www.gov.uk/government/publications/ministerial-code.
11. The principles are included in Annex A of the Code.
12. Paragraph 1.3.c.

investigation either by the Cabinet Office or the Independent Advisor on Ministers' interests is to be initiated (paragraph 1.4). The Independent Adviser on Ministerial Interests[13] is independent of government and expected to provide impartial advice to the Prime Minister. S/he may recommend in confidence to the Prime Minister what sanction should be considered as a result (paragraph 2.4) and may require that any advice provided to the Prime Minister on the outcome of such an investigation is published in a timely manner (paragraph 2.5).[14] This process was followed in the investigation of the conduct of Priti Patel, after accusations of bullying led to the resignation of her Permanent Secretary. Prime Minister Johnson's rejection of the findings of the investigation led to the resignation of the Independent Adviser on Ministerial Interests, Sir Alex Alan.[15] The Ministerial Code does not provide any specific mechanism for monitoring how the Prime Minister respects the standards of public life, meaning that s/he is the judge of his/her own behaviour.

In short, the Ministerial Code sets out the rules that in some form organise how the principle of political accountability is supposed to work within the political and constitutional system. It leaves room for political considerations in the way in which its respect is monitored and enforced.[16] It is not legally binding as such; however, the way in which the Prime Minister exercises his/her power under the Code can be judicially reviewed.[17] Furthermore, it provides a framework that makes these political decisions more public, such that they are no longer taken behind closed doors.[18]

4 STANDARDS FOR THE PARLIAMENT, THE CIVIL SERVICE, AND SPECIAL ADVISERS

While there is no statutory basis for the Ministerial Code, the situation is different for the standards applicable to the Parliament, the civil service and special advisers (spads) for which the overall system is broadly similar to the ministerial code, with the most noticeable exception being that their standard systems are partly put on a statutory footing.

13. The website of the Independent Adviser on Ministers' Interests is available at https://www.gov.uk/government/organisations/independent-adviser-on-ministers-interests/about.
14. HM Government, *Independent Adviser on Ministers' Interests – Terms of Reference*, available at https://www.gov.uk/government/publications/terms-of-reference-for-the-independent-adviser-on-ministers-interests--2.
15. M. Reid, 'The UK and the Scottish Ministerial Codes: Nemo Judex in Causa Sua?' (2021) (3/4) *Judicial Review* 178-186. The resignation statement is available at https://www.gov.uk/government/news/lord-evans-statement-on-the-resignation-of-sir-alex-allan-kcb.
16. *Ibid.*, 182.
17. *R. (on the application of the FDA) v. Prime Minister and Minister of the Civil Service* [2021] EWHC 3279 (Admin). H. Hooper, 'The Ultimate Arbiter of the Code' (2022) (26:2) *Edinburgh Law Review* 239-244.
18. C. Haddon, 'The Handling of the Priti Patel Bullying Inquiry Has Fatally Undermined the Ministerial Code', Institute for Government, 2020 available at https://www.instituteforgovernment.org.uk/blog/priti-patel-bullying-inquiry-undermined-ministerial-code.

In 2009, a parliamentary expenses scandal exposed by the *Daily Telegraph* broke out, leading to seven parliamentarians being jailed.[19] This led to the introduction of a system of parliamentary ethics and conduct,[20] in the hope of rebuilding trust between the electorate and Parliament and strengthening the integrity, probity, and impartiality of Members of Parliament. The Parliamentary Standards Act 2009 was adopted, which entrusted the oversight of parliamentary expenses to an independent authority: the Independent Parliamentary Standards Authority (IPSA).[21] This complements the Code of Conduct for Members of Parliament[22] adopted in the wake of the Nolan Committee's recommendation in 1995.[23]

In the last weeks of his government, Prime Minister Gordon Brown pushed through the Constitutional Reform and Governance Act 2010 to put the civil service and special advisers[24] and their respective codes of conduct on a statutory footing. The code for civil servants sets out four key ethical principles: integrity, honesty, impartiality, and objectivity.[25] For each principle, the code provides clearly written practical explanations. The Civil Service Commission is tasked with ensuring compliance with the code of conduct.[26]

5 WHY DOES THIS MATTER?

The overall picture is one of many shades: standards of public life have been enunciated in formal documentation since 1995 and their importance is reiterated

19. J. van Heerde-Hudson (ed.), *The Political Costs of the 2009 British MPs' Expenses Scandal* (Basingstoke Palgrave Macmillan 2014).
20. A. Kelso, 'Parliament on Its Knees: MPs' Expenses and the Crisis of Transparency at Westminster' (2009) (80:3) *Political Quarterly* 329; N. Allington and G. Peele, 'Moats, Duck Houses and Bath Plugs: Members of Parliament, the Expenses Scandal and the Use of Web Sites' (2010) (63:3) *Parliamentary Affairs* 385-406.
21. The website of the Independent Parliamentary Standards Authority is available at https://www.theipsa.org.uk/.
22. House of Commons, *Code of Conduct and Guide to Rules*, available at https://www.parliament.uk/business/publications/commons/hoc-code-of-conduct/.
23. IfG, 'MPs' Code of Conduct', 9 November 2021, available at https://www.instituteforgovernment.org.uk/explainers/mps-code-conduct.
24. Section 15(1) defines them as follows: 'a person ("P") who holds a position in the civil service serving an administration mentioned below and whose appointment to that position meets the applicable requirements set out below. ...

    The requirements are –

    (a) P is appointed to assist a Minister of the Crown after being selected for the appointment by that Minister personally;
    (b) the appointment is approved by the Prime Minister;
    (c) the terms and conditions of the appointment (apart from those by virtue of section 8(11)) are approved by the Minister for the Civil Service;
    (d) those terms and conditions provide for the appointment to end not later than –
        (i) when the person who selected P ceases to hold the ministerial office in relation to which P was appointed to assist that person, or
        (ii) if earlier, the end of the day after the day of the poll at the first parliamentary general election following the appointment'.
25. Section 7(4) of the *Constitutional Reform and Governance Act* 2010.
26. Section 9 of the *Constitutional Reform and Governance Act 2010.*

through the adoption of specific codes for ministers, members of Parliament, civil servants and spads. Bodies and processes monitor their respect. The room for political decisions when it comes to finding a breach and deciding on the relevant sanction remains, however. Calls for strengthening the powers of the ethical bodies or for ensuring better identification of breaches have been made. Courts have been asked to review the powers exercised under these codes. The whole system does not seem totally satisfactory. In 2020, the Chair of the Nolan Committee expressed his belief in the importance of standards, however:

> [P]ower is lent to us to be used for the good of the public.
>
> This is where the principles take effect. It is a norm in UK democracy that, for example, we expect office-holders to use public funds for the common good, and not to enrich themselves or their families. We expect elected representatives to work for their vision of the common good, rather than acting for their own personal advantage. And we take for granted, that there should be fairness in the decision-making processes – in areas such as policy, planning, and procurement – that will shape our future.[27]

6 THE PERIOD 2020-2022: AN EPIDEMIC OF CRISES[28]

The period 2020-2022 will be remembered as the pandemic time, when the UK government had to make emergency decisions to fight the COVID-19 virus. The overall emergency, the uncertainty linked to the virus at first, the lack of masks and of personal protective equipment, as well as the need to limit freedom of movement created a political context where power, opportunities, boundaries, and risks were blurred. Transparency and accountability of executive action were limited and parliamentary control weakened, especially in the first year of the pandemic.[29] A former Conservative Prime Minister lobbied a Department that subsequently demonstrated 'unusual interest' in the accreditation of a failing business to obtain financial support during the pandemic.[30] VIP procedures were set up to procure the much needed material,[31] although some of this material ended up not being used.[32] Money was lavished to help the economy survive, especially in the summer of 2020: speed was prioritised over

27. Lord Evans, *The Hugh Kay Lecture: Are We in a Post-Nolan Age?*, speech delivered on 11 November 2021 available at https://www.gov.uk/government/speeches/the-hugh-kay-lecture-are-we-in-a-post-nolan-age.
28. Small sections of this part draw on L. Marsons and Y. Marique, 'The Politization of the Civil Service' (2022) *Revista Catalana de Dret Públic – Catalan Journal of Public Law* 93-111.
29. R. Cormacain et al., *The Marginalisation of the House of Commons under Covid Has Been Shocking: A Year on, Parliament's Role Must Urgently Be Restored* (London Hansard Society, 2021).
30. NAO, *Investigation into the British Business Bank's Accreditation of Greensill Capital* (2021-22 HC 301) para. 12.
31. D. Conn, 'Emails Emerge of "VIP Route" for UK Covid Test Contracts', *The Guardian*, 23 September 2021 available at https://www.theguardian.com/world/2021/sep/23/emails-emerge-of-vip-route-for-uk-covid-test-contracts.
32. D. Conn, 'Half of PPE Procured by UK Using "VIP" Companies Has Not Been Used', *The Guardian*, 11 February 2021 available at https://www.theguardian.com/world/2022/feb/11/half-of-ppe-procured-by-uk-using-vip-companies-has-not-been-used.

value for money.[33] All of this led to abuses of the system in all quarters: fraud was so pervasive that the governmental anti-fraud team soared to more than 16,000 staff,[34] with Lord Agnew, a senior government member and Peer, resigning due to the government failing in handling fraudulent COVID-19 business loans.[35] Local councillors misused the system to their benefit.[36] Questions were raised as to how major procurements were awarded - although the courts dismissed the case, the usual rules were not followed.[37] If we zoom in on the executive and people in a significant position of adopting key decisions or influencing them, a litany of problems comes to mind from all corners. These examples can be divided into two distinct categories: the personal crises - cases where a specific person became caught up in a scandal for having broken behavioural expectations placed on them; and the structural crises - cases that affected large parts of the UK society.

First, in Spring 2020, a crisis emerged with Dominic Cummings, a special advisor to the then Prime Minister who was mostly known for being the architect of the Leave campaign and for having been found in contempt of Parliament.[38] He strongly defended his position that he had not broken the lockdown rules whilst driving far away from his home to 'test his eyesight'.[39] He finally went in the autumn of 2020, after falling out with the Prime Minister - and also his wife. Cummings' departure led to a reorganisation in Downing Street, geared especially at mending the troubled relationships with backbenchers.[40]

Secondly, the lead expert scientist during the pandemic, Professor Neil Fergusson, was forced to resign in May 2020, as he had not respected the rules in place and had met with his lover during a lockdown period.[41] He apologised for undermining the governmental message about lockdown. This outcome is strikingly different from the one reserved for Dominic Cummings around the same time. The Prime Minister did not offer his confidence in the same manner to both of his advisors.

---

33. NAO, *The Bounce Back Loan Scheme: An Update* (2021-22 HC 861).
34. Gov.UK, *Government Counter Fraud Function and Profession,* available at https://www.gov.uk/government/groups/counter-fraud-standards-and-profession; https://www.gov.uk/government/news/joint-taskforce-relaunched-to-protect-against-rise-in-fraud-crime; Cabinet Office, *Guidance: Fraud Control in Emergency Management* (gov.uk 26 March 2020).
35. 'Conservative Minister Resigns in Anger over Covid Fraud', *BBC,* 24 January 2021 available at https://www.bbc.co.uk/news/uk-politics-60117513.
36. 'Wolverhampton Councillor Claimed Covid Grant for Shut Takeaway', *BBC,* 17 December 2021 available at https://www.bbc.com/news/uk-england-birmingham-59701935; CPS, 'Ex Councillor and Wife Convicted for Trying to Exploit Covid-19 Bounce Back Loans', 17 December 2021 available at https://www.cps.gov.uk/cps/news/ex-councillor-and-wife-convicted-trying-exploit-covid-19-bounce-back-loans.
37. *R (on the application of Good Law Project Ltd and another) v. Secretary of State for Health and Social Care* [2022] EWHC 46 (TCC).
38. Committee of Privileges, *Conduct of Mr Dominic Cummings* (1490 HC 2017-19).
39. 'Barnard Castle: Cummings Challenged over Lockdown Trip to Durham', *BBC,* 19 July 2021 available at https://www.bbc.co.uk/news/av/uk-politics-57894747.
40. P. Walker, D. Sabbagh and R. Syal, 'Boris Johnson Boots out Top Adviser Dominic Cummings', *The Guardian,* 13 November 2020 available at https://www.theguardian.com/politics/2020/nov/13/dominic-cummings-has-already-left-job-at-no-10-reports.
41. 'Coronavirus: Prof Neil Ferguson Quits Government Role after "Undermining" Lockdown', *BBC,* 6 May 2020 available at https://www.bbc.co.uk/news/uk-politics-52553229.

Thirdly, Brexit caught up with the UK and brought to light doubts that were plaguing the senior civil service. In September 2020, Sir Jonathan Jones resigned as Treasury Solicitor following a suggestion from the government that it would be prepared to breach the Ireland/Northern Ireland Protocol, which forms part of the UK/EU Withdrawal Agreement, in a 'specific and limited' way through the United Kingdom Internal Market Bill.[42] Rowena Collins Rice, Director General of the Attorney General's Office, followed Sir Jonathan in resigning on the same ground.[43] Later on, Attorney General Suella Braverman would be strongly criticised by Sir Jonathan Jones when she advised the government in favour of the Northern Ireland Protocol Bill, which was also intended to reverse part of the UK/EU Withdrawal Agreement.[44] These cases illustrate Endicott's claim that the rule of law depends strongly on individual commitment by government officials[45] and that senior UK civil servants are ready to resign for it.

Fourthly, Parliament stumbled on a crisis of its own when the Prime Minister tried to save one of his colleagues, Owen Paterson MP, a former cabinet minister, from being suspended for 30 days, a sanction that the IPSA had recommended for his use of his position in favour of two firms in breach of the code of conduct.[46] The Government initiated a revision of the standards system, whose adoption by the parliamentary majority meant that Owen Paterson would not have to be suspended. However, this led to mayhem – with the suspicion that the Prime Minister might have been seeking to protect himself even more than his colleague.[47] The reform was dropped[48] – one of the many U-turns by the government. In the meantime, Parliament had been perceived as seeking to protect one of its members.[49]

Finally, a series of questions that had dogged the government and the Prime Minister, such as questions about holiday accommodation provided to the Prime

42. R. Johnstone, 'Government Legal Chief Jonathan Jones Resigns in Row over Brexit Deal Changes' *Civil Service World*, 8 September 2020 available at https://www.civilserviceworld.com/news/article/government-legal-department-head-jonathan-jones-resigns-in-row-over-brexit-deal.
43. 'Senior Government Lawyer Quits over Brexit Plans' *BBC*, 8 September 2020 available at https://www.bbc.co.uk/news/uk-politics-54072347.
44. For a criticism by Sir Jonathan: https://www.instituteforgovernment.org.uk/blog/northern-ireland-protocol-bill; https://ukconstitutionallaw.org/2022/05/30/sir-jonathan-jones-qc-hon-the-northern-ireland-protocol-international-law-and-the-attorney-general/.
45. T. Endicott, 'The Impossibility of the Rule of Law' (1999) *Oxford Journal of Legal Studies* 1-18.
46. Committee on Standards, *Mr Owen Paterson* (797 HC 2021-22).
47. T. Helm et al., 'Return of the Sleazy Party: The Conservatives and the Owen Paterson Affair', *The Guardian*, 7 November 2021 available at https://www.theguardian.com/politics/2021/nov/07/return-of-the-sleazy-party-the-conservatives-and-the-owen-paterson-affair.
48. A. Allegretti, 'Tory U-Turn Complete as MPs Approve Owen Paterson Report', *The Guardian*, 16 November 2021 available at https://www.theguardian.com/politics/2021/nov/16/jacob-rees-mogg-owen-paterson-mistake-lobbying-report.
49. P. Rogerson, 'Sleaze Row: Paterson Vote "Completely Undermines Trust", Says Ex-government Legal Chief', *The Law Society Gazette*, 4 November 2021 available at https://www.lawgazette.co.uk/news/sleaze-row-paterson-vote-completely-undermines-trust-says-ex-government-legal-chief/5110406.article.

Minister by a Conservative Party donor in Mustique,[50] the 'unwise'[51] but not illegal refurbishment of the Prime Minister's apartment (that is until fresh information surfaced making the Independent Adviser on Ministerial Interests express doubt about his initial findings[52]). Partygate - i.e., the gatherings by officials in official buildings during lockdown times to celebrate Fridays, birthdays, staff departures, etc., at all hours of the day and night - caught up with the civil service, the government and finally the Prime Minister himself. Lord Hennessy, a leading historian and Peer, considered the fines issued by the London Metropolitan Police (MET) to senior ministers, including the Prime Minister and the Chancellor, to be a 'most severe constitutional crisis'.[53] However, these fines did not lead in and on themselves to the Prime Minister's resignation, but the overall handling of Partygate associated with a pattern of behavioural lapses,[54] including repeated denials that rules had been broken by officials, did contribute to the Prime Minister's ultimate demise.

Obviously, the pandemic period between 2020 and 2022 was exceptional - boundaries on power were especially loosely defined and controlled by the usual political and judicial means. Criticisms are easy to make with the benefit of insight. The rules during lockdown were changing fast because the situation was changing in a context of uncertainty. If some political decisions might have been different - especially at the outset of the health crisis - the major problem that this litany of crises and scandals highlights is not merely that rules were broken by different officials over a number of months but an insufferable reality: at a time when most of the UK population were struggling with health issues, economic uncertainty, sick and dying relatives, the people in government were dancing to the tune of Abba's songs. The disconnect between reality and power was for all to see.

Furthermore, what these personal crises epitomise is a triple reality of a much deeper crisis. First, if there had been no pandemic, the major political issue would have been the social, economic, and political consequences of Brexit and the inability of the government to deliver the huge opportunities that Brexit was supposed to unleash for 'Global Britain'.[55] Secondly, if Brexit was built on the idea of 'taking back control', it seemed that those now back in control were not able to respond to the 'cost of living crisis' and the frightening statistics accompanying it for the winter of 2022.[56] Humans do not live on bread alone, but bread matters. The historian side of the UK Prime

50. Committee on Standards, *Boris Johnson* (549 HC 2021-22).
51. 'Downing Street Flat: PM Cleared of Misconduct but Acted Unwisely, Says Watchdog', *BBC*, 28 May 2021 available at https://www.bbc.co.uk/news/uk-politics-57280418.
52. 'Downing Street Refurbishment: What Is the Row About?', *BBC*, 7 January 2022 available at https://www.bbc.co.uk/news/uk-politics-56878663.
53. I. Wells, 'No 10 Parties: PM's Lockdown Fine Constitutional Crisis, Says Historian', *BBC*, 17 April 2022 available at https://www.bbc.co.uk/news/uk-politics-61134002.
54. O. Amos, 'Boris Johnson Resigns: Five Things That Led to the PM's Downfall', *BBC*, 7 July 2022, available at https://www.bbc.co.uk/news/uk-politics-62070422.
55. *See* the creation of a Brexit Opportunities Unit in the Cabinet in June 2021 and the limited outcome of its work: https://www.instituteforgovernment.org.uk/explainers/benefits-brexit.
56. A. Shipman et al., 'How to Tackle the UK Cost of Living Crisis - Four Economists Have Their Say', *The Conversation*, 15 August 2022 available at https://theconversation.com/how-to-tackle-the-uk-cost-of-living-crisis-four-economists-have-their-say-188625.

Minister, who likes to have his cake and eat it,[57] might have recalled Marie-Antoine's major mistake when she answered the hungry crowd and gave them cake. Thirdly, the UK territorial constitution is under more pressure than ever, with Northern Ireland turning increasingly resolutely towards reunification with the Republic of Ireland,[58] Scotland calling for a new independence referendum,[59] Wales detaching its legal and judicial system from England,[60] and England not having any dedicated institutional structure apart from Westminster and the UK government itself.

These three structural crises reinforce each other at the political, socioeconomic, and institutional levels. Tackling them face on should have been a priority for a government that was in the extremely rare position – in the UK and in many Western democracies – of enjoying a majority of 80 in Parliament. But it failed miserably even to attempt to start sorting things out. However, there is a hinge between the personal and the structural crises: the personal crises highlight the widening disconnect between the population and its representatives in parliament and government. As the Prime Minister resigned in July 2022, he resigned because his behaviour – and that of those in his close circle – showed that there was 'a rule for us and a rule for them' – a claim first expressed by an advisor to the Leader of the Opposition in May 2020,[61] hammered home by a Prime Ministers' Questions (PMQ) from the Leader of the Opposition[62] and a tweet on 30 June 2021,[63] and profusely reiterated in the media.[64] In

57. Literally as the MET fined him for his birthday cake party (A. Cowburn, 'Boris Johnson's Partygate Fine Is for "Ambushed with Cake" Birthday Event, No 10 Confirms', *The Independent*, 12 April 2022 available at https://www.independent.co.uk/news/uk/politics/boris-johnson-fine-birthday-party-b2056485.html) and figuratively (R. Behr, 'The Tories Said We Could Have Our Cake and Eat It – Now They Are Stuffed and Voters Are Hungry', *The Guardian*, 22 December 2021 available at https://www.theguardian.com/commentisfree/2021/dec/22/tories-cake-stuffed-boris-johnson-covid-restrictions-freedom).
58. W. Ellis, 'The Inevitability of a United Ireland', *Politico* available 18 May 2022 available at https://www.politico.eu/article/the-inevitability-of-a-united-ireland/; 'Polling Shows "Increasing Trajectory in Support for Reunification" says Sinn Féin's Declan Kearney', *The Irish News*, 28 July 2022 available at https://www.irishnews.com/news/northernirelandnews/2022/07/28/news/polling_shows_increasing_trajectory_in_support_for_reunification_says_sinn_fe_in_s_declan_kearney-2783559/.
59. N. Sturgeon, *Statement to Parliament*, 28 June 2022, available at https://www.gov.scot/publications/ministerial-statement-independence-referendum/.
60. R. Rawlings, 'Wales and the United Kingdom: A Territorial Constitutional Policy Drive' (2022) (10:5) *Territory, Politics, Governance* 714-732.
61. B. Nunn, '"One Rule for Them": How a Simple Slogan Helped Change the Political Landscape', *The Guardian*, 26 December 2021 available at https://www.theguardian.com/commentisfree/2021/dec/26/one-rule-for-them-how-a-simple-slogan-helped-change-the-political-landscape.
62. 'There is a pattern here. When Dominic Cummings broke the rules by driving to Barnard Castle, the Prime Minister backed him; when the Housing Secretary unlawfully approved a £1 billion property deal for a Tory donor, the Prime Minister backed him; when the Home Secretary broke the ministerial code, the Prime Minister backed her; and when the Health Secretary broke covid rules, the Prime Minister tried and wanted to back him too. Every time it is the same old story. Is it not the case that while the British people are doing everything asked of them, it is one rule for them and another rule for everybody else?' (https://hansard.parliament.uk//commons/2021-06-30/debates/EFB3D0E1-5D11-4BB3-A899-253CAED3B75D/Engagements#contribution-90A0395A-D123-40F4-B041-78783D54C660). HC PMQ 30 Jun 2021.
63. https://twitter.com/Keir_Starmer/status/1410260085008265216.
64. For example Nunn, *supra* n. 61; P. Toynbee, 'One Rule for Us, Another for the Tories: At Last a Labour Truth Cuts Through', *The Guardian*, 9 December 2021 available at https://www.

the Diceyan constitution, equality before the law, and equal treatment for citizens and for powerholders remains as paramount in 2022 as it was in 1889. This remains the ethical, political, and legal crux of the UK constitution.

7 A BRIGHT LIGHT SHINING AMID THE GLOOM? WHEN THE RULES HAVE A SIGNALLING FUNCTION

Once this bleak picture has been acknowledged, one can identify glimpses of optimism: rules – legal and ethical – matter, even under the UK political constitution. While it is said that the success of political constitutionalism depends on the individual self-restraint of powerholders, the pandemic crises drive a different truth home. Anybody holding a position of power may be tempted to abuse it;[65] believing otherwise is naïve. But political constitutionalism is not primarily about self-restraint and personal integrity, any more or less than legal constitutionalism would be. Political constitutionalism is primarily about the primacy of political judgement over the way in which power is exercised, over the criteria against which it is assessed, curbed, and even terminated. The Ministerial Code for instance includes what might be called 'top-down' conventions.[66] It formalises and fleshes out in prescriptive non-legal rules the political convention of ministerial accountability and of the Commons' confidence in the government. It formalises, expresses, and provides a blueprint against which behaviours can be judged, individual (Prime) ministers have to provide an account for their decisions and choices, and outsiders can make up their minds. The overall system relies on political judgement and games of leveraging ethical standards and their implementation, much more than a legal, judicial, and technocratic application of the ethical standards, although political games can call upon such technocratic interpretation if/when it suits them.

theguardian.com/commentisfree/2021/dec/09/one-rule-for-us-another-for-the-tories-labour-truth-cuts-through-boris-johnson-keir-starmer; R. Syal, '"One Rule for Them": Who Else Has Fallen Foul of Covid Rules?', *The Guardian*, 18 July 2021 available at https://www.theguardian.com/politics/2021/jul/18/who-else-has-fallen-foul-of-covid-rules-boris-johnson-rishi-sunak; O. Jones, 'Dominic Cummings Has Shown It's One Rule for the Establishment, Another for Everyone Else', *The Guardian*, 25 May 2020 available at https://www.theguardian.com/commentisfree/2020/may/25/dominic-cummings-one-rule-establishment-sacrifices; V. Harrison and M. Farrer, '"One Rule for Them": Newspapers Savage Boris Johnson over Party Scandal', *The Guardian*, 9 December 2021 available at https://www.theguardian.com/politics/2021/dec/09/one-rule-for-them-newspapers-savage-boris-johnson-over-party-scandal; C. Riddell, 'Coronavirus Lockdowns: It's One Rule for Them – Cartoon', *The Guardian*, 10 October 2020 available at https://www.theguardian.com/commentisfree/picture/2020/oct/10/coronavirus-lockdowns-its-one-rule-for-them-cartoon.

65. Montesquieu, *Esprit des Lois*, 1748, T1 Chapter 4 ('*c'est une expérience éternelle, que tout homme qui a du pouvoir est porté à en abuser ; il va jusqu'à ce qu'il trouve des limites*'). Similarly in J. Griffith, 'The Political Constitution' (1979) (42:1) *Modern Law Review* 1-21, 3: 'Societies are by nature authoritarian. Government even more so'.
66. A. Perry and A. Tucker, 'Top-Down Constitutional Conventions' (2018) (81:5) *Modern Law Review* 765-789, 774-777.

Among the many current crises in the world, the rule of law is often identified as undergoing particular challenges. In the UK as well, the media,[67] politicians[68] and scholars[69] have hinted at the challenges arising from the various crises mentioned above – in particular with regard to the Northern Ireland Protocol, and more generally the cavalier use by the government of its powers, whereby they are trying to use it to strengthen the powers of the police, restrain protest,[70] curb the BBC's independence[71] or design processes to outsource immigration to Rwanda,[72] while an 'ethical model for decision making' has been introduced in immigration matters.[73] However, the picture seems to be more nuanced when we zoom in on the specific crises mentioned above. First, the controversial part of the Internal Market Bill was removed in the final Act.[74] The legality of the Rwanda scheme is subject to judicial review and has been put on hold.[75] When it comes to ethical standards, the law and ethical guidance remain relevant and have a signalling function when it is broken or amended for expediency purposes.

The first example of this assertion is that the reforms to the IPSA – which would have seen the Authority replaced by a parliamentary committee chaired by an MP from the majority – were voted by the parliamentary majority with strong involvement of the whips. Yet, the media and political backlash were instantaneous and the government's U-turn immediate.[76] The problem was that the amendment introduced by the Government to suspend the vote on Alan Paterson was a breach of a convention that the government does not interfere with Parliament's discipline. According to the Chair of the Nolan Committee, it was 'an extraordinary proposal ... deeply at odds with the best traditions of British democracy'.[77] The opposition refused to sit on the proposed

67. J. Freedland, 'Britain Has a Decision to Make: The Rule of Boris Johnson – Or the Rule of Law?', *The Guardian*, 17 June 2022 available at https://www.theguardian.com/commentisfree/2022/jun/17/britain-has-a-decision-to-make-the-rule-of-boris-johnson-or-the-rule-of-law.
68. For instance, former Prime Minister Major in his speech at the Institute of Government in February 2022 (https://www.theguardian.com/commentisfree/2022/feb/10/democracy-governments-failings-trust-john-major-boris-johnson).
69. *See* for instance the constitutional tracker – https://ukconstitutionalreformtracker.org/.
70. *Police, Crime, Sentencing and Courts Act* 2022.
71. J. Waterson, 'Emily Maitlis Says "Active Tory Party Agent" Shaping BBC News Output', *The Guardian*, 24 August 2022 available at https://www.theguardian.com/media/2022/aug/24/emily-maitlis-says-active-tory-party-agent-shaping-bbc-news-output.
72. 'What Is the UK's Plan to Send Asylum Seekers to Rwanda and How Many Could Go?' *BBC*, 7 September 2022 available at https://www.bbc.co.uk/news/explainers-61782866.
73. UK Visa and Immigration, 'The Ethical Decision-Making Model', 11 November 2021 available at https://www.gov.uk/government/publications/the-ethical-decision-making-model.
74. K.A. Armstrong, 'Governing With or Without Consent – The United Kingdom Internal Market Act 2020', *U.K. Const. L. Blog* (18 December 2020) (available at https://ukconstitutionallaw.org/2020/12/18/kenneth-armstrong-governing-with-or-without-consent-the-united-kingdom-internal-market-act-2020/).
75. *N.S.K. v. the United Kingdom (application no. 28774/22, formerly K.N. v. the United Kingdom).*
76. https://www.theguardian.com/politics/2021/nov/04/boris-johnson-makes-u-turn-over-anti-sleaze-regime-for-mps-owen-paterson.
77. Quoted by E. Dávid-Barrett, 'Shirking Self-Regulation? Parliamentary Standards in the UK' (2022) *Public Integrity* DOI: 10.1080/10999922.2022.2075632.

committee, challenging its legitimacy and the media started querying parliamentarians' conduct.[78] The standards committee has since proposed a new code of conduct for MPs.[79]

The second example is the investigation by Sue Gray into Partygate and the breaches of lockdown and the social distancing regulations on government premises. The whole Ministerial Code appears at first to be weak: the Prime Minister is the ultimate arbiter of potential breaches and their sanctions, even when he himself might be the offender; he is also the person authoring the code and in a position to amend it as indeed he did on 27 May 2022,[80] two days after the release of the Gray report.[81] The Committee on Standards of Public Life commented in a reserved manner on the amendments.[82] In short, this is a prototype of possible window-dressing and a system lacking teeth. It could have been a total paper tiger. Yet, at the moment it mattered, Sue Gray's investigation was played out largely in the media. The total sum of ways in which the Prime Minister behaved – amending the Ministerial Code, foundering during a liaison committee meeting,[83] and apologising for his behaviour for no longer than 10 minutes – led to his resignation – an admission that he did not have the confidence of Parliament despite having survived a leadership challenge from within his Party a few days before.[84] Among the concurring factors, the main stumbling block ended up being that the Prime Minister did not respect the expectation to tell the truth to Parliament. The Ministerial Code requires ministers 'who knowingly mislead Parliament' to resign.

78. E. Dávid-Barrett, 'Shirking Self-Regulation? Parliamentary Standards in the UK' (2022) *Public Integrity*, DOI: 10.1080/10999922.2022.2075632.
79. 'Committee announce proposed package of reforms to tighten lobbying rules', 29 November 2021 available at https://committees.parliament.uk/work/596/code-of-conduct/news/159262/committee-announce-proposed-package-of-reforms-to-tighten-lobbying-rules/; 'Standards Committee proposes new Code of Conduct for MPs', 24 May 2022 available at https://committees.parliament.uk/committee/290/committee-on-standards/news/171033/standards-committee-proposes-new-code-of-conduct-for-mps/.
80. Cabinet Office, *Revisions to the Ministerial Code and the Role of the Independent Adviser on Ministers' Interests*, 27 May 2022 available at https://www.gov.uk/government/publications/revisions-to-the-ministerial-code-and-the-role-of-the-independent-adviser-on-ministers-interests.
81. Cabinet Office, *Findings of Second Permanent Secretary's Investigation into Alleged Gatherings on Government Premises during Covid Restrictions*, 25 May 2022, available at https://assets.publishing.service.gov.uk/government/uploads/system/uploads/attachment_data/file/1078404/2022-05-25_FINAL_FINDINGS_OF_SECOND_PERMANENT_SECRETARY_INTO_ALLEGED_GATHERINGS.pdf; Cabinet Office, *Investigation into Alleged Gatherings on Government Premises during Covid Restrictions – Update*, 31 January 2022 available at https://assets.publishing.service.gov.uk/government/uploads/system/uploads/attachment_data/file/1051374/Investigation_into_alleged_gatherings_on_government_premises_during_Covid_restrictions_-_Update.pdf.
82. CSPL, 'Lord Evans Correspondence with Lord True on the Ministerial Code' 30 May 2022 available at https://www.gov.uk/government/publications/lord-evans-correspondence-with-lord-true-on-the-ministerial-code.
83. F. Heyward, 'Boris Johnson's Liaison Committee Appearance Was a Fittingly Humiliating Finale', *The New Statesman*, 6 July 2022 available at https://www.newstatesman.com/politics/conservatives/2022/07/boris-johnsons-liaison-committee-appearance-fittingly-humiliating-finale.
84. 'Prime Minister Boris Johnson wins Tory confidence vote', *BBC*, 6 June 2022 available at https://www.bbc.co.uk/news/av/uk-politics-61713912.

Intricate questions of interpretation about the meaning of this expression arose.[85] The House of Commons ordered an investigation into the Prime Minister's statements to Parliament[86] about the non-occurrence of parties in Downing Street to ascertain whether the Prime Minister has misled the House.[87] A positive finding would have led former Prime Minister Johnson to be found in contempt of parliament. The privilege committee however flags that the threshold for this differs from the one set in the Ministerial Code.[88] In a way, this is effective political constitutionalism, if the standards used by Professor Alison Young are relied upon:[89] 'Political constitutionalism requires effective political controls, mutual institutional respect, and institutional self-restraint.'[90] The political controls worked and when institutional respect (and personal self-respect) broke down, when a government did not practise institutional self-restraint, the political consequences had to be drawn by the Prime Minister.

Overall, these examples suggest that the UK Constitution remains tipped in favour of a political constitution above a legal constitution, with the major sanction being confidence in the Prime Minister by the House of Commons more than any legal sanctions. The legal rules are weak. No court or judge was called upon to adjudicate these various crises, and the ethical processes are even weaker, yet they seem to exhibit an unexpected resilience when tested. It is not that the ethical norms can be said to be especially robust, but they are now embedded in institutional processes and documents that allow for tracking their respect, changes and possible violations and fiddling with them. This allows the opposition to denounce them, the media to comment on them, and the public to express its disappointment or anger, and to set in motion a gradual weakening of the powerholders. In this way, the Ministerial Code illustrates how ethical standards are part of interlocking mechanisms, reinforcing each other and ultimately leading to reciprocal and systematic resilience, in a way predicted by Perry

85. M. Gordon, 'The Prime Minister, the Parties, and the Ministerial Code', *U.K. Const. L. Blog* (27 April 2022) (available at https://ukconstitutionallaw.org/2022/04/27/mike-gordon-the-prime-minister-the-parties-and-the-ministerial-code/).
86. Committee of Privileges' resolutions available at https://committees.parliament.uk/committee/289/committee-of-privileges/; 'Privileges Committee publish report setting out processes and procedures for inquiry on Rt Hon Boris Johnson MP', 21 July 2022 available at https://committees.parliament.uk/committee/289/committee-of-privileges/news/172278/privileges-committee-publish-report-setting-out-processes-and-procedures-for-inquiry-on-rt-hon-boris-johnson-mp/.
87. 'Boris Johnson to Face Probe over Claims He Misled Parliament about Lockdown Parties', *BBC*, 21 April 2022 available at https://www.bbc.co.uk/news/uk-politics-61177313.
88. Sir Ernest Ryder, 'The Privileges Committee Is the Servant of the House of Commons, and Will Conduct Its Inquiry with a Commitment to Fairness and Transparency Throughout', 24 August 2022 available at https://committees.parliament.uk/committee/289/committee-of-privileges/news/172837/sir-ernest-ryder-the-privileges-committee-is-the-servant-of-the-house-of-commons-and-will-conduct-its-inquiry-with-a-commitment-to-fairness-and-transparency-throughout/. For criticism of the procedure, *see* V. Bogdanor, 'This Inquiry into the PM Is Not Consistent with Natural Justice', *Telegraph*, 11 August 2022 available at https://www.telegraph.co.uk/news/2022/08/11/inquiry-pm-not-consistent-natural-justice/.
89. A. Young, 'Why "Partygate" May Be the Beginning of the End', *VerfBlog*, 23 April 2022, https://verfassungsblog.de/why-partygate-may-be-the-beginning-of-the-end/.
90. *Ibid.*

and Tucker.[91] In the Partygate crises, these very features and dynamics did not seem to lead to the illegitimacy cause of concern identified by Perry and Tucker in consolidating power in the Prime Minister however,[92] but to its very opposite: the ultimate overwinning of a concern for truth and integrity at least towards Parliament, as the political representative of the UK citizens.

Overall, three things are striking, however. First, many distinct problems need to accumulate to lead to this political sanction. Secondly, the overall period of time and energy wasted dealing with these scandals was overwhelming and they could have been better used to address UK structural crises. That there were no easy solutions for these crises left room for a rotting climate to settle and persist. Thirdly, the Opposition was not immune to complaints about its own Beergate.[93] Yet, it managed to deliver a focused attack on the well-known weaknesses of the Prime Minister – in particular his loose relationship with the truth – and to expose the dual standards for the powerholders and the rest of the population, hence reversing the Prime Minister's populistic tendencies and undercutting his credibility among his own MPs.

8 CONCLUSIONS

The interlocking system of ethical standards – and especially these aspects of the operation of the ethical standards that shed light on the workings of the system, such as the publication of Sue Gray's report, the resignations of the Independent Adviser on Ministerial Interests, the formal change of the Ministerial Code in the midst of the crisis, and the start of an inquiry by the privilege committee against the Prime Minister – allowed the Opposition, the media, and the public to call the ultimate powerholder to account. The pandemic period in post-Brexit times was unusual in its challenges. The limelight caught up with the Prime Minister. Partygate made public private events at the core of government – the boundaries faded in the face of the lockdown regulations when the private and the public, the family and the professional[94] collapsed altogether for most of the UK population. In a different context, Professor Birkinshaw noted: 'If public and private are thought of as separate territories, then they can be identified by drawing lines in advance of particular decisions, policies and controversies. Government can then be bound by rules, announced in advance, which decide the area of public accountability. In this way constitutional legitimacy might be combined with

91. A. Perry and A. Tucker, 'Top-Down Constitutional Conventions' (2018) (81:5) *Modern Law Review* 765-789, 787.
92. *Ibid.*, 788.
93. A. Sparrow, 'What Is Beergate and Why Does It Matter?', *The Guardian*, 8 May 2022 available at https://www.theguardian.com/politics/2022/may/08/what-is-beergate-and-why-does-it-matter.
94. To the credit of the former Prime Minister, that his official home is located in the same building as his office may not have made it easy to separate family and work (*see* the birthday celebration and the garden social event – R. Mason, H. Stewart and P. Walker, 'Boris Johnson and Staff Pictured with Wine in Downing Street Garden in May 2020', *The Guardian*, 19 December 2029 available at https://www.theguardian.com/politics/2021/dec/19/boris-johnson-and-staff-pictured-with-wine-in-downing-street-garden-in-may-2020).

pure political choice over the extent of the public sphere.'[95] The exceptional time of crises during the period 2020-2022 leads us to tentatively suggest that what matters is the pre-existence of public - legal or non-legal - rules and of an institutional and political framework that allows for tracing and debating their existence and respect.

95. Birkinshaw, Harden and Lewis, *supra* n. 1, 280-281 (underlining included in the original).

CHAPTER 10

How European Is French Public Law?

John Bell

Patrick has many achievements, but one of his most significant scholarly contributions has been to open our eyes to the presence of European public law.[1] European public law is not primarily the law which governs the administration of the European institutions. For countries which give direct effect to European Union (EU) law and the European Convention, the main issue is how to integrate the different sources of national law, domestic and supranational, into a harmonious system. Rejecting Teubner's metaphor of European law as an 'irritant',[2] the function of the national judge is both to be the first line in applying supranational European laws and to be the person who integrates domestic law and European laws in a way that is seamless for the citizen and the administration. Path dependence shapes the distinctive character of the public law of each Member State, but the States work together on a common European enterprise. So their laws get adjusted to achieve this purpose.

In this chapter, I want to explore this question in relation to the French public law, primarily in its top courts, the Conseil d'Etat and the Conseil constitutionnel. In broad terms, the first deals with administrative law and the second deals with constitutional law. The legal basis for their relationships with supranational law is different, but they have to operate effectively together.

In formal terms, the French Constitution is superior to EU law because it provides the authority to EU law in domestic law under Articles 88-1 to 88-4 of the Constitution. Under Article 88-1, EU law has primacy over incompatible domestic legislation. The supremacy of the Constitution is even more clear in relation to the European Convention because Article 55 of the Constitution confers a status higher than domestic legislation on reciprocal treaties that have been duly ratified. Consequently, ordinary

1. Not least through P. Birkinshaw, *European Public Law: The Achievement and the Brexit Challenge*, 3rd ed., Kluwer, Alphen aan den Rijn, 2020.
2. G. Teubner, 'Legal Irritants: Good Faith in British Law' (1998) 61 *Modern Law Review* 11.

French courts can give effect to provisions of EU law and ratified treaties even when they conflict with domestic legislation. They are the primary bodies for integrating European law. Formally, it is not unconstitutional for the French legislator to legislate contrary to EU or European Convention law. So the Conseil constitutionnel does not rule on such questions. Its function is to rule on constitutional rights and freedoms. All the same and as a matter of practice, it tries to avoid incompatibilities with supranational law and its approach influences the other courts. This is especially true when cases are submitted by the Cour de cassation (in private and criminal law) and the Conseil d'Etat (in public law) to the Conseil constitutionnel for a preliminary ruling on the constitutionality of legislation involved in litigation.

1 NEGOTIATING LUXEMBOURG

Although the French Constitution is formally superior to European law, contemporary French law has sought to soften the challenge that this obviously poses to the claim of the Court of Justice of the European Union (CJEU) since *Costa v. ENEL*[3] in 1964 that EU law is superior to (all) national law. Since 1989, the administrative courts have recognized the superiority of EU law over national law, a reversal of an earlier reluctance largely brought about by a change of generation at the top of the Conseil d'Etat.[4] These decisions were also stimulated by a decision of the Conseil constitutionnel in an electoral case (which is equivalent to an administrative court function) in which it recognized that the election rules could be judged by reference to the European Convention on Human Rights (ECHR).[5]

In 2004, the Conseil constitutionnel upheld as compatible with the French Constitution the provision in the (abortive) European Constitution which expressly stated that Union law prevailed over national laws of Member States, since this did not add to status of Union law that was recognized by Article 88-1 of the Constitution.[6] In addition, decisions of 2004 and 2006 explicitly held that Article 88-1 had as a consequence that the transposition of a directive was 'a constitutional requirement' which the Conseil constitutionnel would enforce. The only exception was where the directive breached a rule or principle 'inherent in the constitutional identity of France to which the constituent authority has not consented'.[7]

3. ECJ 15 July 1964, Case 6/64, ECLI:EU:C:1964:66.
4. J. Bell and F. Lichère, *Contemporary French Administrative Law* (Cambridge: Cambridge University Press 2022) (hereafter 'Bell and Lichère'), pp. 11-13. *See* CE Ass. 3 February 1989, *Compagnie Alitalia*, no. 70452, Leb. 44 and CE Ass. 20 October 1989, *Nicolo*, no. 108243, Leb. 190 concl. Frydman; RFDA 1989, 824 note Genevois, 993 note Favoreu. The present author was told by a senior member of the Conseil d'Etat already in June 1986 that this change would happen once certain leading members retired.
5. CC 21 October 1988, *5e circonscription du Val d'Oise*, AJDA 1989, 128 note Wachsmann.
6. CC decision no. 2004-505 DC of 19 November 2004, *European Constitution*; J. Bell, 'French Constitutional Council and European Law' (2005) 54 *International and Comparative Law Quarterly* 735.
7. CC decision no. 2004-496 DC of 10 June 2004, *Digital Economy*, Rec. 101, para. 7; CC decision no. 2006-540 DC of 27 July 2006, *Authorship Rights*, Rec. 88, para. 19.

The Conseil d'Etat developed this idea of a constitutional obligation to transpose EU directives in 2007. In *Arcelor*,[8] the Conseil d'Etat was faced with a claim that the transposition of a directive breached the French constitutional principles of equality and freedom of commerce in that greenhouse gas quotas applied to steelmaking, but not to the manufacture of plastics. The court decided that, where the constitutional principle had an equivalent in EU law, it should decide on that basis and not simply on the basis of the national constitutional principle. It then sent a preliminary reference to Luxembourg on the question of whether the directive breached the principle of equality as a matter of EU law. In other words, the Conseil d'Etat chose to operate as an EU court, rather than simply as a national court in the way the claimant wished.

In *Perreux*,[9] directive no. 2000/78/CE which required Member States to secure a reverse burden of proof in cases of direct or indirect discrimination, had not been transposed at the time of the litigation. All the same and reversing the decision in *Cohn-Bendit*,[10] the Conseil d'Etat gave effect to the directive in relation to a civil service appointment. More recently, when faced with a French Government claim that the CJEU had interpreted EU law in a way which was contrary to the French Constitution, the Conseil d'Etat refused to find a conflict between national security concerns on anti-terrorism measures and EU concerns on data protection. In *La Quadrature du Net*,[11] on a reference from the French courts, the CJEU decided that general and indiscriminate requirements that data holders retain and hand over information to the state on grounds of national security could only be allowed in limited circumstances. The Conseil d'Etat applied this by interpreting the national legislation so as to make lawful most of what the Government wished to ensure for its anti-terrorism policy but it required the retention to be reviewed more frequently than the Government planned in order to meet EU data protection concerns. These cases illustrate the desire of the Conseil d'Etat these days to conciliate commitments to the theoretical priority of the national constitution and the practical necessity to ensure that France's commitment to the (normal) priority of EU law prevails.

The Conseil constitutionnel, guardian of the Constitution, is now adopting a similar position. Its decision in Air France[12] concerned the constitutionality of a provision of the immigration code which required a transporter to return a non-EU citizen entering France without a visa to the point at which the immigrant had started the transport, if French authorities so requested. This simply implemented an EU directive. Air France complained that it was contrary to the French Constitution (Article 12 of the Declaration of the Rights of Man) for the state to delegate the exercise of public force to a private individual. The Conseil constitutionnel simply repeated the formula cited above that, unless the directive introduced a breach of the constitutional identity of France in a way that had not been approved by the constituent body, it had no

8. CE Ass. 8 February 2007, *Société Arcelor Atlantique et Lorraine*, no. 287110, Leb. 55 concl. Guyomar.
9. CE Ass. 30 October 2009, *Perreux*, no. 298348.
10. *Infra* note 36.
11. CJEU Grand Chamber, 6 October 2020, Cases C-511/18 and 512/18, *La Quadrature du Net*, ECLI:EU:C:2020:791; CE Ass. 21 April 2021, *La Quadrature du Net*, no. 393099.
12. CC decision no. 2021-940 QPC.

jurisdiction to intervene where the national legislation simply implemented necessary and unconditional provisions of a directive. It added the rider that it would only intervene where the rule or principle of essential French constitutional law did not have an equivalent in EU law. The Conseil was stressing that its role in reviewing the transposition of EU directives should be considered as very limited. If the legality of a directive and its national implementing legislation is questioned, then this is a matter for the Luxembourg Court consistent with its case law in *Foto-Frost.*[13]

2 NEGOTIATING STRASBOURG

The very long saga of the role of the commissaire du gouvernement has been documented elsewhere.[14] In brief, French administrative court procedure since 1830 had a member of the judiciary who spoke independently and in the public interest on the legal issues in litigation. He was an amicus curiae much like the Advocate General in the Luxembourg CJEU, which was modelled on the commissaire. But the major difference was that the commissaire retired with the judges and sat in a non-voting capacity during the deliberations (and he frequently spoke in those debates). In addition and unlike the parties to the case, he saw the draft judgment in advance of the hearing and so his remarks could be targeted to it. The Strasbourg Court held that to allow one party to attend the deliberation and see the draft judgment breached the appearance of impartiality of the court and this rule was declared contrary to the Convention first in relation to the Luxembourg Conseil d'Etat and then in relation to the French Cour de Cassation.[15] The message was clear. The Conseil d'Etat reacted by attempts to persuade Strasbourg that this long-standing practice was no threat to a fair trial. It even amended parts of its procedure to allow the parties to see the commissaire's arguments in advance, but to no avail. The Strasbourg court repeated its position in relation to the Cour des Comptes in 2006. Despite protests from some of the most senior French judges (including a member of the Strasbourg court), the ruling prevailed and the commissaire was renamed 'public reporter' (rapporteur public) and given a more restricted role which was more compatible with the Strasbourg rulings.[16]

By contrast, the French took the initiative in relation to Strasbourg on the question of laïcité (secularism).[17] The Conseil d'Etat in 1989 had advised the Government on the compatibility of Moslem girls wearing headscarves in schools. The Stasi

13. ECJ 22 October 1987, Case 314/85, *Foto-Frost v. Hauptzollamt-Lübeck* [1987] ECR 4199.
14. *See* J. Bell, 'The Role of the Commissaire du Gouvernement and the European Convention on Human Rights' (2003) 9 *European Public Law* 309; J. Bell, 'Interpretative Resistance Faced with the Case-Law of the Strasbourg Court' (2008) 14 *European Public Law* 137; J. Bell, 'From "Government Commissioner" to "Public Reporter": A Transformation in French Administrative Court Procedure?' (2010) 16 *European Public Law* 533. Bell and Lichère, pp. 17-18.
15. ECHR 28 September 1995, *Procola v. Luxembourg*, Appl. no. 14570/89, (1995) 22 EHRR 193; ECHR 7 June 2001, *Kress v. France*, Appl. no. 39594/98, AJDA 2001, 675 note Rolin.
16. B. Genevois, 'Conserver l'apport du *commissaire du gouvernement* tout en prenant compte de la jurisprudence européenne' AJDA 2006, 900 ; ECHR Grand Chamber 12 April 2006, *Martinie v. France*, Appl. no. 58675/00, AJDA 2006, 986, (2007) 45 EHRR 15.
17. *See generally* J. Bell, 'Secularism French Style' (2017) 23 *European Public Law* 237.

Report of 2003[18] reviewed this issue and this led to a Law in 2004 banning the wearing of ostentatious religious symbols in schools. During the parliamentary deliberations, Jean-Paul Costa, then a judge of the European Court of Human Rights, gave evidence. He was a senior member of the Conseil d'Etat at the time of its advice in 1989, so, unsurprisingly, he suggested that the ban on religious signs did not violate fundamental freedoms. He also expressed the view that the ban on religious signs would be upheld, should it come to his Court. Soon after the French Law was passed, a Section of the European Court of Human Rights in Strasbourg heard *Leyla Sahin*,[19] a case involving a ban on the wearing of Moslem dress in a Turkish university. The Court drew on the Stasi report and the French Law as indicating a diversity of opinion in Europe and favoured a wide margin of appreciation for national legislators. This view was then upheld in 2005 by the Grand Chamber, in which Costa sat as a Judge. The Strasbourg Court's ruling was then drawn on with approval by the French Conseil constitutionnel in a decision of November 2004.[20] It concluded that the interpretation given by the Strasbourg Court did not create any incompatibility between the EU Charter and French constitutional principles of secularism. That view was confirmed in *SAS v. France*,[21] when the 2010 loi banning the wearing of the full-face veil in public was upheld by the Strasbourg Court.[22] The French managed to get their distinctive view before the Strasbourg Court and to influence its views in a way which did not conflict with fundamental French values.

These cases illustrate the way in which French legislators and judges may seek to influence the supranational rulings which affect them. But it also illustrates that, ultimately, the French tend to give way to the European direction.

3 ADMINISTRATIVE PROCEDURE

Until 2015, France did not have a comprehensive code of administrative procedure equivalent to the American Administrative Procedure Act 1946 or the German Verwaltungsverfahrensgesetz 1969. It had a number of specific rules relating to specific bodies or matters and general principles developed by the Conseil d'Etat. Some of these had been enshrined in legislation. Some rules were developed domestically, but some measures in 1978 and 1979 owed their inspiration to the Council of Europe's recommendation of 1977.[23] The work of the Commission on Codification which produced the text in 2014 and 2015 was authorized by a law in 2013 which explicitly referred to a recommendation by the Council of Europe in 2007 that countries consider enacting a

18. Commission de réflexion sur l'application du principe de laïcité dans la République, *Rapport au Président de la République* (Paris 2003).
19. ECHR Grand Chamber 10 November 2005, *Leyla Sahin v. Turkey*, Appl. no. 4774/98; earlier hearing of 29 June 2004.
20. CC decision no. 2004-505 DC of 19 November 2004, *Constitution for Europe*, para. 18.
21. [2014] ECHR 695, Appl. no. 43835/11. M. Hunter-Hénin, 'Living Together in an Age of Religious Diversity: Lessons from Baby Loup and SAS' (2015) *Oxford Journal of Law and Religion* 1.
22. For criticism, *see* Ilias Trispiotis, 'Two Interpretations of "Living Together"' (2016) *Cambridge Law Journal* 580.
23. *See* Emilie Chevalier in U. Stelkens and A. Andrijauskaite, *Good Administration and the Council of Europe: Law, Principles and Effectiveness* (Oxford University Press, 2020), para. 5.41.

code of administrative procedure to promote good administration in the interests of all.[24] This project may have received an impetus from the French signature of the Council of Europe recommendation, but the Council had been considering the issue with limited success. The French code did not adopt the structure of the Council of Europe model (general principles, rules and remedies), but followed a more traditional French pattern: (i) correspondence between the public and the administration; (ii) decisions taken by the administration; (iii) access to administrative documents; and (iv) remedies. Its focus was on hard rules, rather than ethical principles. Indeed, the major influence on the content of the Code was the EU's adoption of the principles of good administrative behaviour developed by the European Ombudsman and approved by the European Parliament in 2001, implementing the right to good administration in Article 41 of the Charter of Fundamental Rights.[25] But that code drew on good practice from across the Union, not least from France which was early in developing rules on matters such as access to public documents (Article 23). Supranational bodies need the experience and examples from nation states to provide the basis for selecting good practice. Involvement in European-level processes provides the context for developing national rules, since this contributes to the benchmarks for effective policies. But national rules also provide the basis for the development of European-level standards. So there is a virtuous circle of expectations and standards.

4 THE INTERACTION OF EUROPEAN AND NATIONAL COURTS

We can take the problem of overcrowding in prisons as an illustration of the interaction between different French national courts and the Strasbourg Court. Since *Kudla v. Poland*[26] European Court of Human Rights has built up a body of case law protecting prisoners against detention in conditions in which human dignity is not respected. Included within this has been prison overcrowding. In France, the prison population grew from 47,837 in 2001 to 70,818 in 2019, a rate of over-population of 138%.[27] France had successfully defended one 2015 case on Article 13 ECHR by showing that the interlocutory procedure in the administrative courts could give rise not only to damages, but also to preventive remedies such as injunctions against prison authorities.[28] In that case brought by a prisoner support group, the Conseil d'Etat upheld injunctions against prison authorities to undertake works.[29] But in a later 2020 case, JMB,[30] 40 prisoners challenged the effectiveness of remedies against prison conditions where prison governors were obliged to take in all prisoners sent to them. As a result, the recommended space of 3 square metres per prisoner could not be respected and

24. *See* Rapport by H. Portelli, Sénat session extraordinaire 2012-13, no. 742, p. 28.
25. *See* European Ombudsman, *The European Code of Good Administrative Behaviour* (2013); Bell and Lichère, p. 222; Chevalier, para. 5.48.
26. ECHR, 26 October 2000, *Kudla v. Poland*, Appl. no. 30210/96, [2000] ECHR 512.
27. AJDA 2020, 1068 note Avvenire.
28. *See* ECHR 21 May 2015, *Yengo v. France*, Appl. no. 50494/12, AJDA 2015, 1289.
29. CE ord 22 December 2012, *Société française de l'Observatoire internationale des prisons*, no. 364584, AJDA 2013, 12.
30. ECHR 30 January 2020, *JMB v. France*, Appl. no. 9671/15, AJDA 2020, 1064 note Avvenire.

privacy in toilets was not possible. In this case, the Strasbourg Court found France violated Article 3 of the Convention in not respecting human dignity and Article 13 in not providing effective preventive remedies for individual grievances through the administrative courts. The Cour de cassation responded promptly by interpreting the remand in custody provisions of the Code of Criminal Procedure (Code de procédure pénale (CPP)) to include respect for human dignity. Although not expressed in Article 144 CPP as a ground for refusing to continue remand in custody, the court interpreted Article 144-1 CPP as impliedly requiring respect for this right.[31] That decision, like the earlier decisions of the administrative courts, illustrates the way in which French courts have been imaginative in taking their lead from the Strasbourg Court and developing preventive remedies in the face of apparent powerlessness in the administration to do anything to improve the situation.

The Cour de cassation case involved a request to submit a preliminary question of constitutionality (QPC) to the Conseil constitutionnel. In ruling on this QPC, the Conseil constitutionnel reprimanded the Cour de cassation.[32] It stated that the judge required to rule on the seriousness of the claim to a QPC 'cannot base his decision on the interpretation of the contested legislative provision which conformity to France's international agreements requires. Neither is it for the Conseil constitutionnel seised of such a QPC to take account of the interpretation in order to decide on its conformity to the rights and liberties which the Constitution guarantees'. In other words, the issue of constitutionality should not be muddled with the issue of how a domestic law can be interpreted consistently with international treaty obligations. This is because the constitution is superior to any treaty. That said, the Conseil constitutionnel proceeded to hold the relevant provisions of Article 144-1 CPP to be unconstitutional because they failed to permit the judge to refuse to continue a remand in custody on the basis that human dignity was not respected. Although the Conseil based the constitutional value of human dignity on the Preamble to the 1946 Constitution, it was clearly finding a way of aligning French law on fundamental rights with the approach of the Strasbourg Court.

In a decision 17 days later than the Conseil constitutionnel, the Conseil d'Etat[33] decided that the administration had to give effect to the principles recognized by the European Court of Human Rights in relation to degrading and inhuman treatment. It did issue injunctions requiring the prison authorities to provide covers for the exercise yards, privacy for toilets in cells with multiple occupants, repair windows and improve lighting. But it did not immediately enjoin the use of containers to hold prisoners or require the provision of toilets in all exercise yards. Rather it asked for further information on the ability of the administration to carry out such improvements, leading to further orders.[34] It took the view that the necessity for such improvements depended on the means available to the administration. When the prison authorities

31. Crim. 8 July 2020, no. 20-81739; AJDA 2020, 1383.
32. CC 2 October 2020 no. 2020-858/859 QPC, AJDA 2020, 2158 note Bonnet and Gahdoun.
33. CE 19 October 2020, *Garde des sceaux c Section française de l'Observatoire internationale des prisons*, no. 439372, AJDA 2021, 694 with critical note by J. Schmitz.
34. CE 18 November 2020, *Section française de l'Observatoire internationale des prisons*, no. 439444.

had not carried out its injunctions after two years, the Conseil did impose an astreinte, a daily penalty to enforce compliance.[35] But it accepted that some work in relation to replacing containers might take until 2025, five years from the original decision.

So we see here on the one hand the desire to balance the distinct character of the French Constitution and to be aware of the practical limitations on the administration and its priority in relation to European legal provisions. But, on the other hand, there is a very clear influence from Strasbourg shaping the direction of the case law of all three supreme courts.

5 DIALOGUE

It is now over 40 years since a leading French judge coined the phrase 'le dialogue des juges' to describe the relationship between French and European supranational judges. Commissaire du gouvernement Bruno Genevois in *Cohn-Bendit* argued that 'At the European community level, there should be neither a judges' government nor a judges' war, there must be room for a dialogue between judges'.[36] In the intervening time that relationship has persisted and deepened. French public law judges have always had an international outlook and that has extended to Francophonie and connected countries (such as Lebanon and Egypt).[37] These are countries of traditional French influence and where training and cooperation have persisted beyond national independence. Europe was less prominent in the collection of volumes on the Bicentenary of the Conseil d'Etat in 1999, but it has increased in prominence in the succeeding 20 and more years. The dialogue takes place in formal and informal ways, though the latter are the most important.

Formally, there are references from national courts to the CJEU and attention is paid to the decisions of that Court in general. With Protocol 16, that opportunity for dialogue has opened up with the European Court of Human Rights. But Claes and de Visser are right that this is more an opportunity for the supranational court to state positions which national courts are meant to follow.[38]

More generally, the French public law courts monitor the Luxembourg and Strasbourg case law for issues that affect them. Within the Section du Rapport et des Etudes, there is a special unit dealing with European law. The task of the European unit is to ensure that the Conseil is briefed on norms which are developed inside the institutions of the EU. The Conseil constitutionnel secretariat also monitors what is happening in Strasbourg. Specific decisions that follow or mirror a supranational court are not just the product of special research, but reflect a long-standing engagement with that court's work as an integral part of a common project.

35. CE 11 February 2022, *Section française de l'Observatoire internationale des prisons*, no. 452354.
36. Genevois in his conclusions to CE Ass. 22 December 1978, *Ministre de l'Intérieur c Cohn-Bendit*, no. 11604, Leb 524; D 1979, 155. *See generally*, Bell and Lichère p. 11.
37. *See* the various sections of *La Revue Administrative, numéro spécial: Les juridictions administratives dans le monde* (Paris, 1999).
38. M. Claes and M. de Visser, 'Are you Networked Yet? On Dialogues in European Judicial Networks' (2012) 8 *Utrecht Law Review* 100, 104.

Informally, there are a number of channels of communication. For many years, the Luxembourg Court has invited visits by delegations of national judges. In such meetings, that Court can brief the visitors on its perspectives on issues and the visitors have the opportunity to present some of their concerns. This is, of course, in addition to the opportunity to contact the national judge in each of the Strasbourg and Luxembourg courts or their cabinets for insights into current developments. Such contacts may well be informal. Many of the French national judges at both courts have been drawn from the French Conseil d'Etat which facilitates dialogue with the national courts. Apart from visits, there are many conferences in which judges from European courts and other national courts meet and contribute, both in public and in private.[39]

The concept of 'dialogue' is difficult.[40] In brief, a dialogue involves a reasoned engagement with the other party. It involves listening, reflecting and responding in a context in which the parties are on some form of equality. It thus differs from hierarchical orders given to inferiors. The evidence that this takes place is often difficult to pin down. The easiest evidence is the formal responses contained in judgments or annual reports. The least clear evidence is the product of informal encounters between significant figures in each court which then find their way into the thinking of the different courts in their subsequent work. Claes and de Visser[41] point to the importance of judicial networks, both physical and virtual in which exchanges and dialogues can happen. These include associations, conferences and professional virtual media groups. Regular gatherings of supreme courts, especially constitutional and administrative courts supplement the direct relationships between supranational courts and national courts. The existence of such networks provides a context of community within which judicial dialogue can take place. In many ways, the existence of contact points between judges, both horizontally and vertically, within the two supranational legal orders is much easier to map than the dialogues which may result from those interactions. All the same, there is a danger that the vertical element dominates.

If we understand the interpersonal element, then it is easier to see how the vertical element does not dominate. One dimension is to look at the particularly close relationship of the Conseil d'Etat with both supranational courts. At the time of writing, the French judge in both courts is a member of the Conseil d'Etat. Members of the Conseil have formed parts of the cabinet of the judges. A previous member of the Strasbourg Court, Costa was a member of the Conseil d'Etat and ensured that there were discussions of a formal kind with members of the French Parliament. The French have appointed established judicial figures to both courts. By contrast the British have never appointed a serving judge to the Strasbourg Court.

---

39. *See* C. Soulard, 'Cour de cassation et dialogue des juges' in F. Lichère, L. Potvin-Solis and A. Raynouard (eds), *Le dialogue entre les juges européens et nationaux : incantation ou réalité ?* (Brussels: Bruylant, 2004), 95 at p. 98.
40. *See* M. Amos, 'The Dialogue Between UK Courts and the European Court of Human Rights' (2012) 61 ICLQ 557 at pp. 558-559; Claes and de Visser, *supra* n. 38, pp. 102-105.
41. *Supra* n. 37, pp. 109-110. The pattern of networks is more fully presented in M. Claes and M. de Visser, 'Courts United? On European Judicial Networks' in A. Vauchez and B. de Witte (eds), *Lawyering Europe: Europe as a Transnational Field* (Hart, 2013), 75.

6 CONCLUSION

Each institution, national or supranational, has its own autonomous sphere of work. But as Poitevin-Solis suggests,[42] dialogue is part of the duty of cooperation between judges in their shared activity of advancing European case law in achieving the common projects of the EU or the European Convention. She takes her lead from Vedel in noting that the unity and coherence of the French legal system are not compromised by the existence of different legal systems within the same legal order. Similarly, different national legal systems can co-exist within a coherent European legal order.[43] In her view, legal orders are not closed off, but mutually benefit and influence each other.[44] It is not simply a negative approach of self-limitation.

The various examples given in this chapter show that French judges and lawmakers take seriously their role as European judges whilst asserting their distinctive role as guardians of national sources of law. European public law, though important, does not efface the huge body of national public law, but there is mutual influence.

42. L. Poitevin-Solis, 'Concept de dialogue entre les juges en Europe' in Lichère, *Le dialogue, supra* n. 39, 19 at pp. 25 and 58.
43. *Ibid.*, pp. 37-38.
44. *Ibid.*, p. 55.

CHAPTER 11

The Boundaries Between Law and Politics in French Administrative Law: The Case of the 'Actes de Gouvernement'

Aurélien Antoine

Patrick Birkinshaw was often involved in French academic projects. Some pages of his major opus European Public Law reveal his profound interest in the evolution of French public law, particularly the progress of constitutionalism and judicial review in France (or recours pour excès de pouvoir). The role of the judge has been entrenched with the development of the Etat de droit (which is partially synonymous with the British 'rule of law'[1]) since the Second World War. Far from a 'mouth of the law', the judge is now the cornerstone of a democratic society which aims to protect the citizens' rights and liberties. The European Court of Human Rights defines 'the ideals and values of a democratic society' not only by the sole respect of free elections, but by a wider set of principles and rules which include the independence of the judge from the other powers and the judicial control of public authorities' decisions.[2] In his book The Rule of Law,[3] Lord Bingham explains the latter dimension by two principles: 'exercise of

1. For a comparison between the rule of law and the Etat de droit, *see Report on the Rule of Law*, CDL-AD (2011) 003, Adopted by the Venice Commission at its 86th plenary session (Venice, 25-26 March 2011); D. Fairgrieve, '*Etat de Droit* and Rule of Law: Comparing Concepts: A Tribute to Roger Errera', *Public Law* 2015/1, p. 40; A. Antoine, 'Rule of Law and "*Etat de Droit*": Comparing British and French Conceptions of Law', in G. Gadbin-George & E. Gibson-Morgan, *United Kingdom and France: Friends and/or Foes? (Trans)cultural and Legal Unions and Disunions*, Éd. Le Manuscrit, coll. Auctoritas, 2019, p. 77.
2. *See* ECHR, *Kjeldsen, Busk Madsen and Pedersen v. Denmark*, 7 December 1976, nos 5095/71; 5920/72; 5926/72, § 53; and 7 July 1989, *Soering v. The United Kingdom*, no. 14038/88, § 87.
3. T. Bingham, *The Rule of Law*, Penguin, 2011, p. 224.

public powers in good faith and without exceeding the limits of such powers and not unreasonably' and 'law, not discretion'.[4]

Despite their differences, the rule of law and the Etat de droit have the mutual purpose of confining discretionary power by the citizens' capacity to challenge public authorities' decisions before the courts. In French administrative law, the retraction of discretionary power leads to the extension of the principle of legality. Over the last decades, the administrative judge has extended his control on public authorities' decisions and actions. This evolution can be perceived through four major developments. The first is an in-depth judicial review by a more detailed legal qualification of facts and by the control of proportionality.[5] The second is the development of new or more powerful remedies to enforce judgments (such as ordering injunctions or monetary penalties against a public authority[6]). The third important evolution is the creation in 2000 of an emergency interim application which aims to strengthen the protection of rights and liberties (référé-liberté).[7] The fourth main tendency is the progress of justiciability. There are increasingly fewer public authorities' acts which cannot be challenged before the courts. For a long time, in the category of regulatory decisions, only general measures like secondary legislation, decrees or by-laws could be subject to review. The Conseil d'Etat (the Supreme Court of the administrative order of jurisdiction in France) has extended the scope of the judicial review to some acts which were previously considered as non-justiciable because they didn't modify or affect the legal order (contrary to a decision administrative which has a direct normative effect).[8] Since 1970,[9] the Conseil d'Etat has ruled that more administrative regulatory acts (for instance, internal measures taken by ministers to explain how the administration has to apply the law, specify details and technical recommendations to administrative services to ensure uniformity of the application of a superior legal text, explain an official position on a legal matter, or regulate the internal organisation of a public service like a prison or a hospital) can be subjected to a judicial review in certain legal circumstances when they affect the situation of a citizen or a company due to their consequences on their rights or liberties. These acts potentially cover circulars,[10]

4. *See* J.N. Shklar, 'Political Theory and the Rule of Law', in A. Hutchinson & P. Monahan (eds), *The Rule of Law: Ideal or Ideology*, Carswell, 1987, p. 1; T. Carothers, 'Promoting the Rule of Law Abroad', *Carnegie Endowment for International Peace, Rule of Law Series*, n° 34, 2003, p. 3.
5. CE, 19 May 1933, *Benjamin*, no. 17413 and 17520, Rec. p. 541. For a very strong control upon administrative decision called 'the balancing test' developed by administrative courts on a matter of expropriation of private property for public utility, *see also* the leading case CE, 28 May 1971, *Ville Nouvelle Est*, no. 78825, Rec. p. 409.
6. *Loi no. 80-539 du 16 juillet 1980 relative aux astreintes prononcées en matière administrative et à l'exécution des jugements par les personnes morales de droit public*; *Loi no. 95-125 du 8 février 1995 relative à l'organisation des juridictions et à la procédure civile, pénale et administrative.*
7. *Loi no 2000-597 du 30 juin 2000 relative au référé devant les juridictions administratives.*
8. CE, 29 January 1954, *Institution Notre-Dame du Kreisker*, Rec. p. 64.
9. CE, 11 December 1970, *Crédit Foncier de France*, Rec. p. 750.
10. CE, 18 December 2002, *Mme Duvignères*, Rec. p. 463; 8 June 2016, *Association française des entreprises privées*, no. 383259, Rec. p. 230.

guidelines (lignes directrices),[11] instructions, memoranda, informative updates, internal administrative measures (mesures d'ordre intérieur)[12] or any other act of soft law.[13]

The progress of legality principle is not only circumscribed to technical administrative regulatory acts or due to a wider conception of the decision administrative. Its deeper influence can be illustrated by another legal phenomenon: the extension of the Conseil d'Etat's jurisdiction to challenge decisions taken by the Executive which are traditionally considered as sovereign political acts which cannot be controlled by Parliament or reviewed by the courts. The core justification for the non-interference of the other constitutional powers is the principle of separation of powers. This category in French administrative law is well known as 'actes de gouvernement' despite the fact that this expression has not been formerly quoted by the Conseil d'Etat since the Second World War, apart from two leading cases.[14] It is a doctrinal qualification based on case law.

The concept of actes de gouvernement is not easy to understand because they have all the appearances of administrative decisions, but cannot strictly be defined as such. From an institutional point of view, an acte de gouvernement is decreed by the Executive Branch of the Government. Moreover, they often have the form of a decree. In addition, there is no precise definition of an acte de gouvernement and it is impossible to find a limited list set out in a legal text. The only way to concretely understand what an acte de gouvernement is to refer to the Conseil d'Etat's case law which, as previously underlined, often does not refer to this expression. Moreover, the laconism of its judgments on this matter precludes every attempt to identify criteria. As Benoît Plessix explains, 'it is rather by its evolution and its aims that acte de gouvernement can properly be defined legally'.[15] We should add 'and by taking into account the constraint of the Etat de droit'.

The legal framework of the actes de gouvernement could be compared in British public law to some residual powers linked to the royal prerogative which cannot be challenged in courts (e.g., in foreign affairs the 'Crown acts of State'[16] or treaty-making power[17]). There are many similarities between them and the actes de gouvernement. First of all, the legal categories of the royal prerogative and the actes de gouvernement

11. *Crédit Foncier de France.*
12. CE, 17 February 1995, *Hardouin and Marie*, Rec. pp. 82 and 85.
13. CE, 21 March 2016, *Fairvesta* and *Numericable*, Rec. pp. 76 and 89; 19 July 2019, *Mme Le Pen*, no. 426389, Rec. p. 326; 12 June 2020, *GISTI*, Rec. p. 192.
14. CE, 2 March 1962, *Rubin de Servens et autres*, Rec. p. 143. Before 1945, the expression 'actes de gouvernement' is quoted in more cases (*see* CE, 5 December 1838, *Duchesse de Saint-Leu, Princesse Camerata et consorts, Joseph Napoléon, Prince de Canino, Dame Laetitia, Comtesse de Montfort, Prince Jérôme Napoléon*, Rec. p. 641).
15. *Droit administratif général*, LexisNexis, 3rd ed., 2020, § 299.
16. *See Rahmatullah (no 2) v. Ministry of Defence*; *Mohammed v. Ministry of Defence*, [2017] AC 649, [2017] UKSC 1, Lady Hale § 7. *See also Buttes Gas & Oil Co v. Hammer (No. 3)* [1982] A.C. 888; [1981] 10 WLUK 333 (HL); *Belhaj v. Straw* [2017] UKSC 3; [2017] A.C. 964; *R v. Bow Street Metropolitan Stipendiary Magistrates ex p Pinochet Ugarte (No 3)* (*Pinochet (No 3)*) [2000] 1 AC 147 (HL).
17. *See Miller 1*, §§ 55 and 92.

are subject to high controversy and characterized by 'ambiguities'.[18] For instance, in France, very famous lawyers sustained that actes de gouvernement should not exist or have no legal existence.[19]

Secondly, the most important dimension the actes de gouvernement and a few royal prerogatives share is undoubtedly the fact 'that courts could determine whether a prerogative claimed by the Crown actually existed'.[20] As a result, we can apply these conclusions of the Review of the Executive Royal Prerogative Powers published by the UK Ministry of Justice in 2009: similar to the royal prerogative power, the scope of the actes de gouvernement 'is notoriously difficult to determine. It is clear that the existence and extent of the power is a matter of common law, making the courts the final arbiter of whether a particular type of prerogative power exists. The difficulty is that there are many prerogative powers for which there is no recent judicial authority and sometimes no judicial authority at all'.[21] Another analysis applied to the royal prerogative is suitable for the actes de gouvernement. As Jack Williams writes about the prerogative, 'there is no such thing as a non-justiciable prerogative power per se. Instead the standard of this review is likely to depend upon the subject matter and issues raised …'.[22] In *Miller 2*, the Supreme Court shares a similar point of view: the justiciability of the prerogative 'would depend on the nature and subject matter of the particular prerogative power being exercised'.[23] The same conclusion is expressed by French scholars about actes de gouvernement.[24]

Thirdly, the British courts' reluctance to review some prerogative powers is based on justifications also admitted for the actes de gouvernement: the separation of powers; and the reference to their nature and subject matter[25] which implies a distinction between legal matters which are reviewable, on the one hand; and high-policy or international subject matters, on the other hand, which are not amenable to judicial review. In United Kingdom (UK) public law, these motives can be partially identified in leading cases *General Communications HQ (GCHQ)* and *Shergill v. Khaira.*[26]

The judicial consequence is also the same for actes de gouvernement and for some royal prerogatives: the non-justiciability of these executive acts. The meaning of

18. P. Craig, *Brexit and the UK Constitution*, in J. Jowell & C. O'Cinneide (eds), *The Changing Constitution*, OUP, 9th ed., 2019, p. 97.
19. L. Michoud, *Des actes de gouvernement: Annales de l'enseignement supérieur de Grenoble*, Imprimerie et lithographie F. Allier, 1889, 71 p.; M. Virally, 'L'introuvable acte de Gouvernement', *RDP* 1952, p. 31. For a complete view of the most important academic researches dealing with the *actes de gouvernement*, *see* B. Plessix, *supra*, § 305.
20. M. Elliott, *Public Law*, OUP, 4th ed., 2020, p. 569.
21. *Review of the Executive Royal Prerogative Powers: Final Report*, 2009, § 27.
22. 'Prerogative Powers after *Miller: An Analysis in Four E's*', in M. Elliott, J. Williams & A. Young (eds), *The UK Constitution after* Miller, Hart Publishing, 2018, p. 51.
23. § 35. *See Council of Civil Service Unions v. Minister for the Civil Service* [1985] AC 374.
24. *See* B. Plessix, *supra:* 'c'est plutôt par son évolution et par ses objets que l'acte de gouvernement peut être juridiquement cerné'. *See also* S. Roussel & C. Nicolas, 'De l'injusticiabilité des actes de gouvernement', *AJDA* 2018, p. 491.
25. *Council of Civil Service Unions v. Minister for the Civil Service*, [1985] AC 374 (GCHQ case), Lord Roskill, § 418.
26. [2014] UKSC 33, [2015] AC 359, §§ 42 et seq. *See also R v. Secretary of State for Foreign Affairs, ex parte Everett* [1989] QB 811. Lord Mance, 'Justiciability', *ICLQ* 2018, 67(4), p. 739. *See also Miller 2*, § 36.

non-justiciability is clear in its consequences in French administrative law. It means a court refuses categorically to adjudicate the case: it is simply out of its constitutional function. The Conseil d'Etat ruled that it lacked jurisdiction to hear the case as far as an acte de gouvernement is concerned ('incompetent to adjudicate').

So, a French administrative law academic who studies the non-justiciability of actes de gouvernement could accept Lord Sumption's opinion in *Rahmatullah (no 2)*: '"Non-justiciability" is a treacherous word, partly because of its lack of definition, and partly because it is commonly used as a portmanteau term encompassing a number of different legal principles with different incidents'. He adds that non-justiciability 'should be reserved for cases where an issue is said to be inherently unsuitable for judicial determination by reason only of its subject matter. This may result in a court declining to determine an issue notwithstanding its relevance to the dispute between the parties ... or because its determination is not within the constitutional competence of the courts'.[27]

Non-justiciable prerogative powers and actes de gouvernement entail the same crucial questions for a lawyer: what are the boundaries between law and politics? Is there a clear limit to judges' competence? Is the progress of the rule of law and the Etat de droit so irresistible that, in the future, no more acts decreed by the Executive will benefit from a judicial immunity? Is the survival of non-justiciable administrative acts a kind of a residual miscarriage of justice?[28] Does the doctrine of 'political questions' have a future?

These questions are central in UK public law studies and have seen new dramatic doctrinal developments since the *Miller* cases[29] (and in the 2000s with *Bancoult*[30]). However, British scholars seem to pay little consideration to how courts in the French semi-parliamentarian democracy deal with this basic issue of public law identified in all legal systems governed by the rule of law or Etat de droit.[31] However, there is a real interest to confront points of view on this matter to ensure that it is better understood on both sides of the Channel.

This chapter intends to explain how the Conseil d'Etat has slowly but surely reduced the category of actes de gouvernement since the first case law which was traditionally accepted as the starting point of the emergence of the acte de gouvernement theory in 1822.[32] As Lord Roskill said about prerogative powers, actes de gouvernement are certainly 'the clanking of medieval chains of the ghosts of the

27. § 79.
28. *See* M. Virally, *supra*, p. 318: 'Without any reasons given to the claimant of the non-justiciablity of *acte de gouvernement*, should the court be guilty of a major crime: the miscarriage of justice?'.
29. *R (Miller & others) v. Secretary of State for Exiting the European Union* [2017] UKSC (*Miller 1*); R (*Miller & others*) *v. The Prime minister; Cherry and others v. Advocate General for Scotland* [2019] UKSC 41 (*Miller 2*).
30. *R v. Secretary of State for Foreign and Commonwealth Affairs, ex parte Bancoult (No 2)* [2008] UKHL 61.
31. The recent French doctrine adopts a different attitude. The political questions theory was the subject of an excellent PhD thesis in comparative law written by Claire Saunier in 2019: *La doctrine des questions politiques. Étude comparée: Angleterre, France, États-Unis*, Thèse Université Paris II-Panthéon Assas, 2019, 720 p., dir. D. Baranger.
32. CE, 1 May 1822, *Laffite*, Rec. p. 371.

past'.[33] But this legal theory has not totally collapsed and it seems to be an irreducible part of decisions taken by the Executive which can't be challenged before courts.

1 THE IRRESISTIBLE DECLINE OF A LEGAL CATEGORY

Because of the lack of definition of the actes de gouvernement, the better way to understand them is to set out the emblematic cases which are traditionally mentioned.

The Conseil d'Etat judgment analysed by the doctrine as the first one dealing with the actes de gouvernement dates back to 1822. In 1821, a famous bank asked the Ministry of Finance to refund the arrears of a government bond previously handed over by Pauline Bonaparte. The administration dismissed the application. This decision was challenged before the Conseil d'Etat. Only six years after the exile of Napoleon, France was still deeply divided. The Bourbon Restoration in 1814-1815 was followed by tough measures against the Bonaparte family and their closer allies. Due to this particular political context, the Conseil d'Etat refused to be involved in it. In their order, the judges concluded that the challenge against the ministry's decision was 'a matter of policy of which resolution only depended on the Government's jurisdiction'.[34] Thirty years later, there was another litigation between the Bonaparte family and the last French king who governed France (Louis-Philippe d'Orléans) which enriched the actes de gouvernement case law. The Conseil d'Etat judged that a decree which commanded the restitution of goods owned to Louis-Philippe's sons to the State property is 'an acte de gouvernement of which execution and effects can't be challenged in court'.[35] Two further cases involved the Orléans family. In 1867, the fifth son of Louis-Philippe (the Duke of Aumale) published a book on the History of the Princes of Condé. The Second Empire administration decided to confiscate all copies. The higher administrative court considered these decisions to be 'political acts which cannot be reviewed'.[36]

This first part of the acte of gouvernement history must be understood as an illustration of significant judicial self-restraint. For two-thirds of the nineteenth century, the Conseil d'Etat, in its judicial functions, was not totally independent from the Executive. The theory of justice retenue (justice upheld by ministers on administrative matters) was still dominant until 1872 when an act of Parliament created the system of justice déléguée (delegated administrative justice) which allowed the Conseil d'Etat to uphold a judgment in its own name. Since then, and since the leading precedent Sieur Cadot,[37] the Conseil d'Etat has carefully extended its control over governmental decisions. In 1875, the supreme administrative court limited the scope of the theory of actes de gouvernement. At the beginning of the Third Republic, the name of a general who served under the Second Empire was crossed off the official military officers list by the minister for war. Associated with regime change, this decision was similar to the

33. *Council of Civil Service Unions v. Minister for the Civil Service* [1985] AC 374, [1984] UKHL 9, § 417.
34. *Laffite*, above.
35. CE, 18 June 1852, *Famille d'Orléans v. Le domaine de l'État*, Rec. p. 252.
36. CE, 9 May 1867, *Duc d'Aumale et Michel Lévy*, Rec. p. 472.
37. CE 13 December 1889, *Cadot*, no. 66145, Rec. p. 1148.

cases mentioned above. But, for the first time, following the opinion of its commissaire du Gouvernement (who is a judge independent from the Executive power despite her or his appellation and whose name now is rapporteur public), René David, the Conseil d'Etat, allowed the judicial review and accepted its own jurisdiction. Though the judges did not quash the administrative act, non-justiciability based on evasive political justifications was rejected. Since the *Prince Napoléon* case, the legal category of actes de gouvernement has been specified and progressively restricted.

In its judgment of 1875, the Conseil d'Etat tried to identify a criterion to justify non-justiciability. It limited the scope of the political reasons previously retained in its case law. Because the political argument could be identified in too many Government decisions, the Conseil d'Etat considered that the non-justiciability was exceptional and depended on an interpretation of the Constitution and the law which assigned to the Government a wide margin of appreciation based on the 'superior interest of the State'.

The real specificity of actes de gouvernement is due to the fact that they don't depend on exceptional circumstances (states of emergency, war, etc.). Judicial immunity is recognised in 'normal times' as an act whose purpose is closely linked to high policy matters of the State even if the political motive has not been sufficient to justify non-justiciability.[38] On this basis, the case law about actes de gouvernement is focussed on two governmental activities: the relationships with other constitutional powers and foreign affairs. But even in these fields, the number of actes de gouvernement has dramatically decreased.

In the first category (relationships with other constitutional powers), a Prime Minister's decree which nominates a member of Parliament to an administrative function is subject to review because it is removable or detachable from constitutional relationships between the Executive and the Parliament.[39] The same reasoning based on 'detachability' is applied when a litigant challenges the Government's refusal to use Article 37 al. 2 of the French Constitution which confers the power to the Executive to deem an act illegal when is outside legislative competence (limited by Article 34).[40] By definition, this decision is purely administrative because of parliamentary incompetence. As such, it is subject to review. More recently, the Conseil d'Etat held that the appointment of the chairman of a Parliament committee in charge of the electoral boundaries created by the Constitution is subject to review.[41]

The prerogative of the president of the Republic to give pardon (Article 17 of the Constitution) is not an acte de gouvernement despite its constitutional basis and the

38. Moreover, today, an administrative decision opposed to an individual can't be based, in principle, on a political argument. This kind of decision is quashed for abuse of power or error of law (CE, 28 May 1954, *Barel*, Rec. p. 305; *see* M. Long et al., *Les grands arrêts de la jurisprudence administrative*, Dalloz, 23rd ed., 2021, p. 19).
39. CE, 25 September 1998, *Mégret*, Rec. p. 340.
40. CE, 3 December 1999, *Association ornithologique et mammologique de Saône-et-Loire et Rassemblement des opposants à la chasse*, Rec. p. 379.
41. CE, 13 December 2017, *Président du Sénat*, Rec. p. 372. *See also* CE, 15 December 2017, *Brillault*, Rec. p. 372.

discretionary power to exert it.[42] The dismissal of the Conseil d'Etat's jurisdiction is now justified by the judicial nature of this prerogative.[43]

The fall in the number of actes de gouvernement is even more important in the second type related to the Executive's action in foreign affairs. These actions are understood as diplomatic decisions which, in principle, cannot be reviewed. In French public law, the Constitution gives a large margin of appreciation to the Executive to conduct international relations. According to Article 5, the head of state is the custodian of national sovereignty, territorial integrity and the observance of treaties. The Executive has discretionary power to nominate ambassadors and to negotiate international agreements. This constitutional rule is close to the general principle identified in British constitutional law. As Lord Oliver explained it in the *Tin Council* case, 'On the domestic plane, the power of the Crown to conclude treaties with other sovereign states is an exercise of the royal prerogative, the validity of which cannot be challenged in municipal law.'[44] But the traditional approach was progressively limited.

The criterion of 'detachability' is also operable on the matter of foreign relations. All administrative decisions which are necessary to give legal effect to a treaty in domestic law can be reviewed (decree of publication, decision of ratification ...[45]). The criterion is finally retained when the administration enjoys a wide discretion relative to its international obligations. A decree to extradite signed pursuant to an international agreement is not an acte de gouvernement,[46] even when the decree is made on the request of the foreign State.[47]

The most emblematic evolution was certainly the Conseil d'Etat's judgment by which it was accepted to interpret on its own a treaty without referring to the Foreign Office.[48] In this leading case, the influence of the European Convention on Human Rights (ECHR) was clear.[49] The commissaire du gouvernement Abraham also raised an argument of comparative law underlining the fact that such a referral to the Executive before a judgment did not exist in other European legal systems.[50] But an exception was maintained pursuant to Article 55 of the Constitution. A bilateral treaty has a superior legal value to another piece of legislation if there is reciprocity in its enforcement. For a long time, the Conseil d'Etat has judged that the appreciation of the reciprocity was a power which was vested in the hands of the Executive. The ECHR

42. The power to give pardon was an *acte de gouvernement* until 1947 (CE, 30 June 1893, Rec. p. 544 and CE, 28 March 1947, *Gombert*, Rec. p. 138).
43. CE 30 June 2003, *Section française de l'Observatoire international des prisons*, Rec. p. 296.
44. *J.H. Rayner (Mincing Lane) Ltd v. Department of Trade and Industry* [1990] 2 AC 418, §§ 499E-500D. *See also Blackburn v. Attorney-General* [1971] 1 WLR 1037, 1040; *R v. Foreign Secretary, ex p. Rees-Mogg* [1994] QB 552.
45. CE, 3 October 1964, *Société Prosagor*, Rec. p. 497; CE, 18 December 1998, *SARL du Parc d'activités de Boltzheim*, Rec. p. 483.
46. CE, 28 May 1937, *Decerf*, Rec. p. 534; 3 July 1996, *Koné*, Rec. p. 255.
47. CE, 15 October 1993, *Royaume-Uni de Grande-Bretagne et d'Irlande du Nord et gouverneur de la colonie royale d'Hong-Kong*, Rec. p. 267.
48. CE, 29 June 1990, *GISTI*, Rec. p. 171.
49. Rony Abraham based his opinion on the Article 6 (concl. *in AJDA* 1990, p. 621). A few years later, the ECHR will uphold the *Conseil d'Etat*'s decision (24 November 1994, *Consorts Beaumartin v. France*, no. 15287/89).
50. *Ibid.*

condemned France[51] for this case law and the Conseil d'Etat changed its position in 2010,[52] despite the difficulty for a court to concretely value the condition of reciprocity.[53]

To conclude, since 1875, there have been a lot of reasons to explain why the Conseil d'Etat has expanded its control. The first reason was its growing institutional role since the 1872 Act which put an end to justice retenue. The second one is the indirect influence of the development of the constitutional review by the Conseil constitutionnel since 1971 (with the leading case by which fundamental rights are legally enforceable before the Conseil) and the capacity of administrative courts to declare a French law incompatible with European Union (EU) law or international law since 1989.[54] Indeed, since all Acts of Parliament are subject to review, it is more difficult to justify that some administrative decisions cannot be challenged in court. The third explanation is undoubtedly the influence of the ECHR and more particularly its Articles 6 § 1 and 13 which sanction the right to a fair trial before an independent and impartial tribunal and the right to an effective remedy.

The progressive decline of actes de gouvernement, even their extinction, is deeply sustained by an important part of French public law scholars who are mostly legal normativists or in favour of the extension of courts' jurisdiction. They notably consider that the law is always above politics. Even executive prerogative traditionally considered as non-justiciable could be challenged before courts which could at least scrutinize procedural requirements. For instance, Article 12 of the French Constitution regulates the President's prerogative to dissolve the National Assembly. If this is a personal prerogative of the head of State who doesn't have a constitutional duty to explain the purposes and motives for which he uses it, there are a few procedural requirements, especially to consult the Prime Minister and the presidents of the Senate or the National Assembly. In fact, procedural requirements are often imposed on the President of the Republic when he wants to use his personal prerogatives (Article 16 about temporary regime of confusion of powers to overcome a major crisis, e.g., a military invasion of the national territory; and Article 11 to hold a legislative referendum).[55]

In theory, the argument to extend the court's power on highly political decisions could be seen as a major progress of the Etat de droit. But it raises some real difficulties and could provide too much power to the courts in a democracy. From a constitutional point of view, the survival of actes de gouvernement is justified by different kinds of legitimacy in a modern democracy, the separation of powers, and the specialization of each branch of government. The balance of powers is not only a concept applicable to the Legislative and the Executive, but also to the court system. The theory of actes de gouvernement in French administrative law could also be seen as a French illustration of the opposition between green and red light theories in English administrative law.[56]

51. ECHR, 13 February 2003, *Chevrol v. France*, no. 49636/99).
52. CE, 9 July 2010, *Mme Chérier-Benseghir*, Rec. p. 251.
53. *See* CE, 19 July 2019, *Association des Américains accidentels*, Rec. p. 297.
54. CE, 20 October 1989, *Nicolo*, Rec. p. 190.
55. *See* section 2 below.
56. C. Harlow & R. Rawlings, *Law and Administration*, 14th ed., CUP, 2022, p. 32.

The Executive needs a large discretionary power to be efficient in a few limited circumstances (particularly in foreign relations or to resolve a major national or international political crisis). That is why, despite the constant problems brought up by the theory of actes de gouvernement and the necessity to confine it in the name of Etat de droit, the Conseil d'Etat refuses to put a definitive end to it.

2 THE POLITICAL IRREDUCIBILITY OF A LEGAL CATEGORY

There are two categories of administrative acts which benefit from a judicial immunity: relationships between constitutional powers, and international affairs. In the first group, most of the discretionary presidential powers listed in Article 19 of the Constitution are not subject to review. The decision to dissolve the National Assembly (Article 12),[57] to nominate the Prime Minister (Article 8.1),[58] to nominate the president and a member of the Conseil constitutionnel (Article 56.3 and 56.1)[59] and to refer a matter to this competence (Article 61.2)[60] are not amenable for review.

For these specific presidential powers, a crucial question arises. If the President of the Republic does not respect a procedure imposed by the Constitution (e.g., by overlooking some non-mandatory advice by another institution), can the use of these powers be subject to review? The case of the presidential decision to summon the electorate for a referendum on the basis of Article 11 is a very interesting one. This article is considered by legal scholars as a way to pass a bill through referendum, but it excludes amending the Constitution because Article 89 deals with the specific procedure which must be followed to revise the Constitution. This *lex specialis* overrides the *lex generalis*. This view was held by the Conseil d'Etat in 1998, even if its judgment did not deal with the lawfulness of the use of Article 11.[61] Regardless, de Gaulle used this Article in 1962 to change the Constitution and to introduce the election of the President of the Republic by direct universal suffrage because Article 11 allows the Executive to put to the citizen's vote a question related to 'public powers' (in French, the expression of pouvoirs publics is a synonym of institutions ruled by the Constitution). The statute approved by referendum was exceptionally challenged before the Conseil constitutionnel, not the Conseil d'Etat. The former ruled that, as a judge invested by the Constitution to control all operations organizing a national referendum (Article 60), it can review presidential decrees related to this matter. In

57. CE, 20 February 1989, *Allain*, Rec. p. 20.
58. CE, 16 September 2005, *Hoffer*, Rec. tables, p. 691.
59. CE, 9 April 1999, *Mme Ba*, Rec. p. 124. *See also* Ord. CE, 21 January 2022, *M. A.*, no. 460456, *AJDA* 2022, p. 192 (nomination of a member of the Conseil constitutionnel by the President of the National Assembly).
60. CE, 7 November 2001, *Tabaka*, Rec. tables, p. 789.
61. CE, 30 October 1998, *Sarran et Levacher*, Rec. p. 368: 'Considérant qu'il ressort de ces dispositions que seuls les référendums par lesquels le peuple français exerce sa souveraineté, soit en matière législative dans les cas prévus par l'article 11 de la Constitution, soit en matière constitutionnelle comme le prévoit l'article 89, sont soumis au contrôle du Conseil constitutionnel.'

1962, the Conseil constitutionnel held that it had no jurisdiction to hear the case.[62] However, in 2000, it accepted to review the constitutionality of three decrees which planned a referendum on the basis of Article 89. It accepted control of the formal procedure, not the scope of the question in itself.[63] In 2005, the Conseil constitutionnel passed a new step. The judge accepted control of the constitutionality of the Treaty establishing a Constitution for Europe through the review of the presidential decree which summons the electorate for a referendum on the basis of Article 11.[64] Although this precedent is seen as an argument in favour of a substantial review of the constitutionality of law adopted by referendums, it is not clear that it means the Conseil constitutionnel will explicitly accept it in the future. First of all, the Conseil constitutional decisions in 2000 and 2005 were exceptional and subject to limited conditions.[65] Then, the Conseil constitutionnel acted as an electoral judge. Finally, its substantial review is limited and not really developed. It would be understandable as a 'review without control'.[66] That is why some lawyers remain cautious with this precedent and make the point that it would put democracy in danger if a judge prevented an institution elected by the people to consult them on a constitutional matter - a procedure which is considered as an expression of the popular sovereignty. Moreover, in 1962, the interpretation of the Constitution by de Gaulle was sanctioned by political responsibility: a motion of defiance was adopted against his government led by Georges Pompidou.[67]

The same kind of purely theoretical configuration could arise concerning Article 16 of the Constitution. Decrees taken on the basis of this article aim to proclaim a temporary executive dictatorship when there is a major threat to the integrity of the National Territory or the working of the institutions (war, terrorism, massive epidemic or a huge natural or industrial disaster for example[68]). This is a personal prerogative of the President of the Republic which is not subject to review.[69] If there was a willingness to avoid the constitutional procedure, different political configurations would occur: a change of political regime, a resignation of the President of the Republic after a major opposition to his decision, or civil troubles. A court intervention, even formal, against the will to establish a long-lasting dictatorship illustrated by the breach of Article 16 would be pointless in these contexts.

Non-justiciability is also understandable for all decisions which deal with the legislative process: to present or to withdraw a bill to or from Parliament, to summon

62. Dec. n° 62-20 DC, 6 November 1962, *Loi relative à l'élection du Président de la République au suffrage universel direct, adoptée par le référendum du 28 octobre 1962*, Rec. p. 27. *See also* dec. n° 92-313 DC 23 September 1992, *Maastricht III*, Rec. p. 94.
63. Dec. n° 2000-21 REF, 25 July 2000, *Hauchemaille I*, Rec. p. 117.
64. Dec. n° 2005-31 REF, 24 March 2005, *Hauchemaille et Mayet*, Rec. p.
65. *See* M. Fatin-Rouge Stefanini, 'Jurisprudence du Conseil constitutionnel, Contentieux des actes préparatoires au référendum', *Rev. fra. de droit constitutionnel* 2005, p. 606; La décision du Conseil constitutionnel du 24 mars 2005, *Hauchemaille et Meyet*: un nouveau pas en matière de contrôle des référendums, *RFDA* 2005, p. 1040.
66. S. Roussel & C. Nicolas, above.
67. The French people voted in favour of the constitutional reform and gave a huge majority to the Gaullists after the general elections following the defiance motion.
68. Article 16 is in competition with other constitutional or legal states of emergency.
69. CE, 2 March 1962, *Rubin de Servens*, Rec. p. 143.

Congress (the gathering of the two assemblies to revise the Constitution on the basis of the Article 89),[70] and to promulgate an act of Parliament.[71]

In the second category (international affairs), case law is abundant. For instance, all Executive decisions related to the negotiations of a treaty,[72] decisions to enter into diplomatic relations or severance of diplomatic relations,[73] to resume nuclear tests,[74] to commit armed forces abroad,[75] or to not repatriate French citizens from the civil war in Syria[76] are not up for review.

It is not clear what the legal position of the Conseil d'Etat would be in case of a judicial review against the decision of the Executive to notify the European Counsel of the French intention to withdraw from the EU ('Frexit'). There are a lot of uncertainties about the different constitutional ways to get Frexit done ... and the role of the Conseil d'Etat and the Conseil constitutionnel depends on them.[77] But, before notification, the most likely option would be a revision of the Constitution to repeal all articles related to the relationship between France and the EU, perhaps after a referendum on the basis of Article 89, the procedure of which gives Parliament a major role. In this constitutional context, there would be little chance that the notification could be reviewed, because there would be no constitutional limits to an Executive power to begin negotiations with the EU to concretize a withdrawal from it. Even if the case were submitted to the Conseil d'Etat, the notification would surely be considered as an acte de gouvernement. If the Constitution were not modified before the notification (which is possible in theory), the Conseil d'Etat could have two options: because the notification can be withdrawn before Frexit, this decision remains an act linked to foreign affairs not amenable for review. The second interpretation would consider that a notification without a revision of the Constitution is unlawful. In this exceptional case, the judgment of the Conseil d'Etat would be similar to *Miller 1*.

All these decisions raise highly political matters and a review by the courts depends on the design of the separation of powers and the demarcation between law and politics in democracy. Whatever the design of these aspects, there will always be a 'grey area' of non-justiciability, essential to protect the most sensitive state affairs, preserve the separation of powers and protect the political accountability of the Executive before the Parliament and the citizens which are as fundamental as judicial control on administrative decisions. The difficulty for the judge is to find the happy medium between Etat de droit and judicial activism.

70. CE, 22 February 2005, *Hoffer*, Rec. p. 691.
71. CE, 27 October 2015, *Fédération démocratique alsacienne*, *AJDA* 2015, p. 2374.
72. CE, 13 July 1979, *SA Coparex*, Rec. p. 319.
73. CE, 2 March 1966, *Cramencel*, Rec. p. 157.
74. CE, 29 September 1995, *Assoc. Greenpeace France*, Rec. p. 347.
75. CE, 5 July 2000, *Mégret*, Rec. p. 291.
76. Ord. CE, 23 April 2019, *Mme C and Mme D*, no. 429668, *AJDA* 2019, p. 1644; 9 September 2020, *Mme C and Mme D*, n° 439520, *AJDA* 2020, p. 2373.
77. S. Sydoryk, 'Conditions et conséquences constitutionnelles d'un éventuel Frexit: entre inconnues constitutionnelles et évolutions jurisprudentielles', *Politeia* 2018, n° 32, p. 331.

The limitation of justiciability is not always in contradiction with the rule of law or the Etat de droit.[78] As for all principles, Etat de droit has its exceptions which are justified by non-legal considerations. Our analysis points to the fact that the theory of the actes de gouvernement must not be seen as a negation of the Etat de droit but as a realist approach to the relations between powers in democracy. The political irreducibility of actes de gouvernement is constructed from a legal starting point which is the principle of justiciability of administrative decisions. The principle/exception divide evolves for political and societal reasons, not on the basis of a clear and absolute partition between legal and high policy matters. That is why case law surrounding actes de gouvernement can be understood with a better knowledge of the societal, political, cultural, even economic context. As Alexander Bickel wrote about 'political questions' in the United States, actes de gouvernement are an illustration of 'passive virtues'.[79] The Conseil d'Etat has a range of possibilities to control administrative decisions (a kind of 'sliding scale of judicial control' from non-justiciability to the control of proportionality, by way of a self-restraint on the substantive motives of an administrative decision). Between an in-depth control of proportionality like 'the balancing test'[80] and the refusal to adjudicate an act, there is a wide spectrum of judicial technic and powers developed by the judge to take into account different constraints: public utility, individual interests, citizens' rights and liberties, interests of the Administration and efficiency of its action, balance of power and societal context. Indeed, there is no absolute rule or principle which can precisely determine in abstracto and a priori the clear boundary of the judicial adjudication on a specific legal matter. The only certain element is that the judge has powers as limited as the other constitutional powers.

These limits are determined by the Constitution, Acts of Parliament and case law. This is why the theory of actes de gouvernement is perfectly justified in an Etat de droit and is not entirely 'a relic of past age'.[81] To plagiarize Lord Neuberger in *Miller 1* about prerogative, 'that description [by Lord Reid] should not be understood as implying that the royal prerogative is either anomalous or anachronistic'.[82] It is a result of a constitutional framework and a legal culture which evolved in a constant search for a better balance of powers in a democracy. But we must keep in mind that all institutions try to increase their power to the detriment of the others. The question is not 'are actes de gouvernement justified in a democracy?', but if the recognition of non-justiciability or, on the contrary, the justiciability of administrative decisions by the Conseil d'Etat, leads to a profound imbalance of powers. In parliamentarian democracies where the Executive is dominant, judicial decisions of justiciability or non-justiciability can be

78. *See*, for instance, T. Endicott, 'The Reason of the Law', *American Journal of Jurisprudence*, 2003/48, p. 83.
79. *The Least Dangerous Branch: The Supreme Court at the Bar of Politics*, Yale University Press, 2nd ed., 1986, p. 110.
80. *See supra* n. 5.
81. As Lord Reid appreciates the prerogative in *Burmah Oil case* (*Burmah Oil Co (Burma Trading) Ltd v. Lord Advocate* [1965] AC 75, § 101).
82. *Miller 1*, § 49.

analysed through a risk of an increase of the Executive power or a decrease of the Parliament's role which can also be weakened by courts activism.

Today, case law in France seems to be well balanced, all the more since the Conseil d'Etat has accepted to engage in no-fault state liability when an acte de gouvernement causes harm to an individual.[83] Finally, the large majority of the Conseil d'Etat decisions about actes de gouvernement is understandable in light of the previous remarks. Despite the tendency of the growth of the judicial empire in Western democracy by 'converting political questions into legal ones',[84] it seems to be fundamental not to set in opposition judicial adjudication and politics, but to reconcile them by keeping in mind, as lawyers, that the judge is not always the best way to resolve conflicts. As Lord Sumption underlines in his famous speech 'The limits of the law', while accepting 'judicial lawmaking is unavoidable', 'the judicial resolution of major policy issues undermines our ability to live together in harmony by depriving us of a method of mediating compromises among ourselves'.[85]

83. CE 27 June 2016, *M. C.*, Rec. tables p. 935.
84. Lord Sumption, 'The Limits of Law', 27th Sultan Azlan Shah Lecture, Kuala Lumpur, 20 November 2013, p. 6.
85. *Ibid.*, p. 15 and p. 13. For a discussion of this position, *see* N.W. Barber, Richard Ekins & Paul Yowell (eds), *Lord Sumption and the Limits of the Law*, Bloomsbury – Hart Publishing, 2016, 231 p.

CHAPTER 12

Les cours suprêmes dans l'espace juridique européen: Hommage à Patrick Birkinshaw

Bernard Stirn

Les cours suprêmes dans l'espace juridique européen, par Bernard Stirn, président de section honoraire au Conseil d'Etat, membre de l'Institut de France.

Par nature, les cours suprêmes interviennent dans le périmètre d'un Etat. Il leur revient de veiller à l'unité du droit dans un pays et d'assurer les évolutions de jurisprudence dont le droit national a besoin. Aussi auraient-elles pu paraître fragilisées par l'internationalisation croissante du droit, qui se manifeste par l'autorité renforcée des traités internationaux et par le rôle accru des juridictions internationales. Le phénomène est particulièrement marqué en Europe, où se conjuguent le droit de l'Union européenne et le droit de la convention européenne des droits de l'homme et où, par le dynamisme de leur jurisprudence, les deux cours européennes, la Cour de justice de l'Union, qui a son siège à Luxembourg, et la Cour européenne des droits de l'homme, installée à Strasbourg, confèrent toute leur portée à ces deux branches, interactives et souvent entremêlées, du droit européen.

Mais l'espace européen a aussi ouvert aux cours suprêmes nationales de nouveaux horizons. Avec des exigences d'indépendance et d'impartialité davantage affirmées, elles ont vu leurs propres garanties renforcées et elles sont appelées à jouer un rôle accru pour veiller au respect de ces exigences par les juridictions placées sous leur autorité. Elles apportent leur contribution à la construction d'un droit public européen et elles remplissent une mission éminente dans le dialogue des juges qui s'établit pour en définir les contours. Souvent les décisions qu'elles rendent rencontrent une audience qui va bien au-delà de leur propre pays. Aussi, loin d'être victimes de l'inscription du droit dans l'espace européen, sont-elles plutôt des acteurs engagés et des partenaires bénéficiaires de ce mouvement : l'espace européen les conforte sur le plan institutionnel et élargit leur office jurisprudentiel.

1 L'ESPACE EUROPÉEN CONFORTE LES COURS SUPRÊMES SUR LE PLAN INSTITUTIONNEL

Du point de vue institutionnel, la construction d'un espace juridique européen s'est accompagnée d'un accroissement du nombre des cours suprêmes et d'un renforcement de leur autorité.

1.1 Un nombre accru

Certaines cours suprêmes sont les héritières d'une longue histoire. Tel est le cas en France du Conseil d'Etat, dont l'évolution accompagne celle des institutions politiques depuis l'Ancien Régime et auquel la constitution du Consulat a donné en l'an VIII sa forme moderne. Tel est de la même manière le cas de la Cour de cassation, qui s'inscrit dans la descendance du Parlement de Paris de la monarchie puis du Tribunal de cassation institué en 1790. Mais la famille des cours suprêmes s'est agrandie dans les années récentes et la construction d'un espace juridique européen y est pour beaucoup : elle a joué un rôle déterminant dans la multiplication des cours constitutionnelles et dans l'apparition de nouvelles cours suprêmes.

Né aux Etats-Unis avec l'arrêt Marbury c/ Madison rendu en 1803 par la Cour suprême, le contrôle de constitutionnalité des lois a mis beaucoup de temps à traverser l'Atlantique. Aux lendemains de la première guerre mondiale, il apparaît, sous l'influence de Kelsen et dans le contexte de la disparition de l'empire austro-hongrois, dans la constitution autrichienne de 1920, qui crée une cour constitutionnelle. Mais le cas autrichien demeura une exception en Europe et il fallut attendre les idéaux affirmés après la victoire sur le nazisme pour que les cours constitutionnelles s'y implantent plus largement. Leur institution est liée au rétablissement de la démocratie et à la volonté de la consolider. Une cour constitutionnelle est créée en Italie en 1948, la Loi fondamentale allemande de 1949 met en place la cour de Karlsruhe. Avec le retour du Portugal et de l'Espagne à la démocratie, le lien entre contrôle de constitutionnalité et démocratie se renforce : une cour constitutionnelle est prévue par la constitution portugaise de 1976 comme par la constitution espagnole de 1978. Après la chute du Mur de Berlin et l'éclatement de l'Union soviétique, un mouvement comparable s'observe en Europe de l'Est, y compris en Russie où la Cour constitutionnelle est instituée en 1991. Même si de grandes démocraties continuent d'ignorer la justice constitutionnelle, comme le Royaume-Uni, le Danemark, les Pays-Bas, la Norvège, la Suède ou la Suisse, un modèle européen de cour constitutionnelle, distincte des cours suprêmes judiciaires et administratives, se dessine et se différencie du modèle américain de cour suprême unique. Dans les nombreux pays européens où elles existent désormais, les cours constitutionnelles rejoignent les cours suprêmes classiques, qui jugent les affaires en dernier ressort. Si, d'un pays à l'autre, les articulations entre les traditionnelles cours suprêmes et les nouvelles cours constitutionnelles varient, la catégorie générique des cours suprêmes nationales s'enrichit, avec les cours constitutionnelles, d'une nouvelle composante.

Les cours suprêmes elles-mêmes deviennent plus nombreuses. En Allemagne, cinq cours fédérales sont spécialisées dans les domaines civil et pénal, administratif, financier, social et du droit du travail. Elles ont chacune la qualité de cour suprême de leur ordre de juridiction, même si la cour constitutionnelle de Karlsruhe peut être saisie de recours qui mettent en cause le respect par leurs décisions des principes énoncés par la Loi fondamentale. Particulièrement caractéristique du développement des cours suprêmes est la récente création de la Cour suprême du Royaume-Uni. Traditionnellement le rôle de juridiction suprême revenait au Judicial committee de la Chambre des Lords, composé de douze Law Lords. Choisis parmi les juristes les plus éminents du pays, ils siégeaient à la fois comme parlementaires à la Chambre des Lords et comme juges de dernier ressort au Judicial committee. Cette organisation, héritée de l'histoire mais très singulière au regard de la séparation des pouvoirs, a pris fin avec le Constitutional reform act de 2005, adopté sous le gouvernement de Tony Blair. Effectivement installée le 1er octobre 2009, la nouvelle Cour suprême a rapproché les institutions britanniques des standards européens et elle a immédiatement pris place parmi les grandes cours dont les jurisprudences ont un écho au-delà des frontières nationales. Elle revêt aussi une dimension mondiale puisqu'elle a aussi hérité des attributions du Conseil privé à l'égard des pays du Commonwealth qui continuent d'accepter sa juridiction de dernier ressort.

Plus nombreuses, plus diversifiées, les cours suprêmes ont une autorité qui s'affirme davantage.

1.2 Une autorité renforcée

Traditionnelle aux Etats-Unis, où la Cour suprême a joué de longue date un rôle déterminant pour trancher de grandes questions de société, fin de la ségrégation raciale[1], encadrement de la peine de mort[2], acceptation de l'interruption volontaire de grossesse[3], affirmation du droit au recours pour les détenus de Guantanamo[4], reconnaissance du mariage pour tous[5], l'intervention des cours suprêmes dans les débats juridiques et politiques est de plus en plus largement reconnue en Europe.

L'exemple du Conseil constitutionnel français est significatif à cet égard. Conçu au départ comme une institution chargée de garantir les prérogatives du gouvernement face au Parlement - le professeur Rivero le qualifie de « chien de garde du parlementarisme rationalisé »-il s'est progressivement affirmé comme une véritable cour constitutionnelle. Par sa jurisprudence, il a incorporé dans son contrôle la conformité des lois aux principes du Préambule à partir de sa décision du 16 juillet 1971 relative à la liberté d'association. L'ouverture de sa saisine à soixante députés ou soixante sénateurs en 1974 puis l'introduction en 2008 de la question prioritaire de constitutionnalité, qui le rend accessible aux citoyens, ont parachevé l'évolution. Une montée en puissance

1. Cour suprême des Etats-Unis, 1954, *Brown v. Board of education of Topeka.*
2. Cour suprême des Etats-Unis, *Atkins v. Virginia*, 2002 et *Roper v. Simmons*, 2005.
3. Cour suprême des Etats-Unis, 21 janvier 1973, *Roe v. Wade.*
4. Cour suprême des Etats-Unis, *Rasul v. GW Bush*, 2004.
5. Cour suprême des Etats-Unis, 28 juin 2013, *US v. Windsor* et 26 juin 2015, *Obergefell v. Hodges.*

comparable se retrouve en Belgique où la cour d'arbitrage, créée en 1980, a pris le nom de cour constitutionnelle en 2007.

De son côté, la nouvelle Cour suprême du Royaume-Uni s'est reconnue compétente pour trancher des questions constitutionnelles de grande portée lorsqu'elle a jugé que le Brexit ne pouvait, eu égard à ses conséquences pour les droits et libertés des citoyens britanniques, être décidé sans un vote du Parlement de Westminster mais que l'accord des assemblées locales d'Ecosse, du Pays de Galles et d'Irlande du Nord n'était en revanche pas requis[6]. Puis elle n'a pas hésité à censurer la décision du gouvernement de Boris Johnson de suspendre pendant cinq semaines les travaux du Parlement pour avoir les mains plus libres dans la négociation de l'accord de retrait avec l'Union européenne[7].

Devant les impératifs de la lutte contre le terrorisme comme face aux mesures nécessaires pour combattre l'épidémie de covid-19, la conciliation entre état d'urgence et état de droit a été assurée par la jurisprudence des cours suprêmes, qui, saisies de questions analogues, leur ont donné des réponses comparables. En France, la procédure de référé liberté, issue de la loi du 30 juin 2000, a ainsi permis au juge des référés du Conseil d'Etat d'intervenir dans de très brefs délais et de donner un cadre jurisprudentiel à l'état d'urgence, de 2015 à 2017, comme à l'état d'urgence sanitaire en 2020 et 2021. Le souci d'assurer une stricte proportionnalité des mesures prises aux exigences de la situation a conduit, durant l'état d'urgence, à encadrer les assignations à résidence[8] et les perquisitions administratives[9]. Le même souci s'est retrouvé, pendant l'état d'urgence sanitaire, en particulier dans les décisions en matière de liberté de manifestation[10], d'enregistrement des demandes d'asile[11], de surveillance par les drones[12], d'ouverture des lieux de culte[13], de nécessité de la présence de l'accusé devant la cour d'assises[14].

L'autorité des cours suprêmes s'accroît aussi au travers du renforcement des garanties dont elles disposent et du rôle qui leur est de plus en plus confié de veiller à l'indépendance de leur ordre de juridiction. En France, la révision constitutionnelle du 23 juillet 2008 a ainsi fait passer la présidence du Conseil supérieur de la magistrature du président de la République au premier président de la Cour de cassation et au procureur général près cette cour, selon qu'il s'agit de débattre de questions intéressant les magistrats du siège ou les magistrats du parquet. Le vice-président du Conseil d'Etat préside de même le Conseil supérieur des tribunaux administratifs et des cours administratives d'appel. Ces évolutions ne sont pas étrangères à la décision par laquelle le Conseil d'Etat a jugé que si un décret avait pu confier à l'Inspection générale de la justice des compétences pour examiner la gestion administrative et financière des

6. Cour suprême du Royaume-Uni, 24 janvier 2017, *Miller*.
7. Cour suprême du Royaume-Uni, 24 septembre 2019.
8. CE, 11 décembre 2015, Cédric Domenjoud et autres.
9. CE, 6 juillet 2016, Napol et Thomas.
10. CE, 13 juin 2020, Ligue des droits de l'homme et autres.
11. CE, 30 avril 2020, ministre de l'intérieur.
12. CE, 18 mai 2020, Association la Quadrature du net.
13. CE, 18 mai 2020, Fraternité sacerdotale Saint-Pierre et autres ; 29 novembre 2020, Association civitas et Confédération des évêques de France.
14. CE, 27 novembre 2020, Association des avocats pénalistes.

juridictions judiciaires, sans s'immiscer bien sûr dans l'appréciation des décisions rendues, il avait, en revanche, illégalement inclus la Cour de cassation dans le champ de son contrôle. Des garanties particulières, qui n'avaient pas été prévues, s'imposaient en ce qui la concerne, eu égard à sa mission, au sommet de l'ordre judiciaire, et au rôle confié par la constitution à son premier président et à son procureur général à la tête du Conseil supérieur de la magistrature[15].

Confortées du point de vue institutionnel, les cours suprêmes nationales exercent aussi, dans l'espace européen, un office jurisprudentiel élargi.

2 L'ESPACE JURIDIQUE EUROPÉEN ÉLARGIT L'OFFICE JURISPRUDENTIEL DES COURS SUPRÊMES

L'espace juridique européen élargit l'office jurisprudentiel des cours suprêmes d'une double manière : il leur confère des attributions qui soulignent les spécificités de leur intervention ; elle les conduit, en dépit de difficultés, d'incertitudes, de tensions qui apparaissent dans certains pays et à propos de certaines décisions, à rendre des arrêts qui dépassent le cadre de leur Etat pour contribuer, par des échanges au-delà des frontières, à dégager des principes partagés et à concourir ainsi à poser ensemble les pierres d'un droit global. Organisées en réseau, les cours suprêmes jugent au-delà des frontières.

2.1 Le réseau européen des cours suprêmes

Dans l'espace européen, les cours suprêmes exercent un office renouvelé. A leur rôle de juge de dernier ressort, au sommet d'un ordre de juridiction, vient s'ajouter celui de représentant particulièrement qualifié de la justice de leur Etat dans un univers élargi où les juges des différents pays ont à échanger pour coordonner leurs jurisprudences.

Dès le traité de Rome de 1957, une distinction apparaît entre les cours suprêmes et les autres juridictions : alors que ces dernières peuvent, en cas de difficulté sérieuse sur l'interprétation du droit de l'Union ou la validité d'une norme de droit dérivé, saisir la Cour de justice d'une question préjudicielle, les cours suprêmes ont l'obligation de le faire. La particularité des cours suprêmes est plus marquée encore dans la procédure introduite par le protocole n°16 à la convention européenne de droits de l'homme : entré en vigueur en 2018, ce protocole réserve aux cours suprêmes des pays qui l'ont ratifié la possibilité de saisir la Cour européenne des droits de l'homme d'une demande d'avis consultatif sur une question de principe relative à l'interprétation ou à l'application de la convention. Les cours suprêmes nationales participent enfin au choix des juges européens. L'article 255 du Traité sur le fonctionnement de l'Union européenne a ainsi créé un comité, composé d'anciens juges ou avocats généraux de la Cour de justice et de membres des cours suprêmes nationales, qui apprécie l'aptitude des candidats proposés par les Etats à exercer les fonctions de juge à la Cour de justice et au Tribunal de l'Union européenne ainsi que d'avocat général à la Cour. S'inspirant

15. CE, 23 mars 2018, syndicat Force ouvrière magistrats et autres., Cédric Domenjoud et autres.

de ce précédent, le comité des ministres du Conseil de l'Europe a décidé qu'un « panel », réunissant d'anciens juges de la Cour européenne des droits de l'homme et des membres des cours suprêmes nationales, donnerait un avis sur la qualification des candidats aux fonctions de juge à la Cour européenne des droits de l'homme.

L'association des cours suprêmes nationales à la désignation des juges européens s'inscrit dans la perspective qui fait de ces cours les acteurs principaux du dialogue des juges en Europe. Elles participent aux associations qui facilitent les échanges par des rencontres, des réseaux de diffusion de la jurisprudence, des forums internet. Elles entretiennent entre elles des liens bilatéraux souvent fort étroits. Elles sont les participants naturels du dialogue régulier avec les deux cours européennes. Ainsi la Cour européenne des droits de l'homme réunit-elle chaque année, pour un séminaire de travail, les présidents des cours constitutionnelles et des cours suprêmes des Etats membres du Conseil de l'Europe.

Au travers du réseau de juges, par une écoute attentive, par un croisement des jurisprudences, de nombreuses questions délicates sont résolues grâce à des logiques conciliatrices, comme celle qui permet d'articuler la suprématie de la constitution dans l'ordre interne et la primauté du droit international et européen. Prononçant en 2014 le discours de rentrée de la Cour européenne des droits de l'homme, Andreas Vosskuhle, alors président de la cour de Karlsruhe, expliquait que le droit en Europe ne se décrivait plus à partir de la pyramide de Kelsen mais se comparait davantage à un mobile de Calder, dont les éléments, sans cesse en mouvement, trouvent leur équilibre dans leur interaction permanente et réciproque. Ce mouvement est animé par les cours suprêmes et leur rôle au-delà des frontières.

3 JUGER AU-DELÀ DES FRONTIÈRES

Ecoutées par leurs homologues comme par les juridictions internationales, les décisions des cours constitutionnelles et des cours suprêmes ont, par là même, une audience qui dépasse le cadre national. Plus encore les solutions qu'elles retiennent ont des conséquences sur de grands débats et trouvent souvent en conséquence de forts échos bien au-delà de leurs frontières.

Le rôle que joue la cour allemande de Karlsruhe est à cet égard particulièrement caractéristique. Gardienne vigilante des droits fondamentaux et des équilibres démocratiques garantis par la constitution allemande, elle est en même temps engagée dans la construction européenne. L'équilibre qu'elle trace entre exigences constitutionnelles nationales et avancées de l'édifice européen donne à sa jurisprudence une importance primordiale pour l'Union dans son ensemble. Par une décision du 30 juin 1989, elle juge ainsi que la ratification du traité de Lisbonne ne nécessite pas une révision de la constitution allemande mais implique que la loi fédérale rappelle les impératifs de démocratie, les responsabilités du Parlement et les exigences de respect des droits fondamentaux. Elle autorise la création du Fonds européen de stabilité financière[16] comme la ratification du traité sur la stabilité, la coordination et la

16. Cour de Karlsruhe, 7 septembre 2011.

gouvernance en Europe[17], tout en soulignant que le Bundestag doit conserver le contrôle de la politique budgétaire. Saisie de la question du rachat des dettes souveraines sur le marché secondaire par la Banque centrale européenne, elle pose, pour la première fois, une question préjudicielle à la Cour de justice de l'Union européenne[18]. Eclairée par la réponse de la Cour[19], elle juge le dispositif conforme aux exigences constitutionnelles allemandes[20]. Mais elle précise ensuite que la Banque centrale européenne doit justifier, par une analyse compréhensible et précise, de la conformité des rachats de dette publique à son mandat et de la proportionnalité de ses interventions[21]. A l'occasion de ces différentes décisions, la cour de Karlsruhe a tenu dans son prétoire une part de l'avenir de la construction européenne. Au-delà du droit constitutionnel allemand, les décisions qu'elles a rendues ont eu un écho et une portée dans toute l'Europe, à qui elles ont permis de franchir des étapes et de surmonter des crises, sans négliger les caractéristiques constitutionnelles de l'un de ses principaux Etats membres.

Des principes partagés se dégagent des jurisprudences combinées des cours constitutionnelles et des cours suprêmes. Les deux cours européennes en assurent une forme de synthèse. Des standards de procédure sont définis pour assurer un recours effectif devant un juge indépendant et impartial et assurer le bon déroulement d'un procès équitable. Des notions communes s'affirment, proportionnalité, sécurité juridique, confiance légitime, subsidiarité. Des valeurs s'expriment, non-discrimination, dignité de la personne humaine, prééminence du droit, exigences de la démocratie.

Des difficultés et des tensions sont inévitablement présentes. Au sein de l'Union européenne, les réformes de la justice en Pologne et en Hongrie ont fait naître des inquiétudes sur l'indépendance des magistrats. Des décisions sont lourdes de menaces pour les libertés, comme l'arrêt du 22 octobre 2020 par lequel le Tribunal constitutionnel polonais réduit presque à néant le droit à l'interruption volontaire de grossesse. A l'intérieur du Conseil de l'Europe, l'évolution de la Turquie après le coup d'Etat manqué de l'été 2016 porte atteinte aux libertés essentielles, avec des arrestations arbitraires et une méconnaissance délibérée de l'indépendance des juges. En 2022, la guerre d'Ukraine, qui a entraîné l'exclusion de la Russie du Conseil de l'Europe, est venue rappeler que les rapports de force et le recours aux armes peuvent l'emporter sur le respect du droit et l'autorité des juges. Mais, de façon moins tragique, la mise en cause par les régimes illibéraux de la légitimité des interventions des juges, comme les tentatives de reprise en main des cours constitutionnelles et des cours suprêmes, sont aussi, comme un hommage du vice à la vertu, le reflet du pouvoir des juges dans l'univers mondialisé. Des excès se trouvent heureusement tempérés par les interventions de la Cour de justice à l'égard des Etats membres de l'Union et de la Cour européenne des droits de l'homme pour ce qui concerne les pays du Conseil de l'Europe. Ainsi le gouvernement polonais a revu la réforme de sa cour suprême après

17. Cour de Karlsruhe, 12 septembre 2012.
18. Cour de Karlsruhe, 14 janvier 2014.
19. CJUE, 16 juin 2015, Gauleiter.
20. Cour de Karlsruhe, 21 juin 2016.
21. Cour de Karlsruhe, 5 mai 2020.

que la Cour de justice, accueillant une action en manquement engagée par la Commission, avait constaté qu'elle méconnaissait les droits fondamentaux garantis par l'Union[22].

Au-delà de ces difficultés, un fonds commun se constitue à partir des décisions des cours constitutionnelles et des cours suprêmes nationales. Pour les deux cours de Luxembourg et de Strasbourg, il constitue une base à partir de laquelle elles construisent une jurisprudence qui vient synthétiser les éléments apportés par chaque droit national. La Cour de justice de l'Union européenne dégage ainsi des principes généraux à partir des traditions constitutionnelles communes aux Etats membres. La Cour européenne des droits de l'homme recherche de son côté si un consensus apparaît entre les différents Etats du Conseil de l'Europe, auxquels elle reconnaît une marge d'appréciation d'autant plus large que le consensus est faible.

Par les échanges entre elles, par l'édification commune d'un corpus jurisprudentiel dont la portée dépasse les frontières étatiques, les cours suprêmes nationales interviennent au total dans un horizon plus large et avec des perspectives plus étendues. Devenues des acteurs essentiels d'un univers juridique élargi, elles contribuent à donner tout son assise au droit global nécessaire à sa régulation. Loin de réduire leur office, l'espace juridique européen leur confère, en dépit des tensions et des conflits, de nouvelles missions, renforce leur indépendance, accroît leur autorité et fortifie leur vitalité.

22. CJUE, 17 décembre 2018.

CHAPTER 13

Ius Publicum Europaeum and the Use of Comparative Law by the CJEU: Unity in Diversity?

Constantinos Kombos

1 INTRODUCTION

Jean Rivero famously identified the tendencies towards a common European administrative law and urged public lawyers to 'talk about an administrative ius commune'.[1] That was a groundbreaking proposition because it pointed to the analysis of the evolution of public law as a multilevel legal phenomenon and as a matter of a Pan-European legal space that exists beyond and yet within the national context. Patrick Birkinshaw was one of the first to explore that route and became one of the pioneers[2] that promoted the study of European public law as a fluid legal phenomenon

1. J. Rivero, 'Vens un droit commun europèen: nouvelles perspectives en droit administrative', in M. Cappelletti (ed.), *New Perspectives for a Common Law of Europe* (Florence: Publications of the EUI, 1978), volume 1, p. 389.
2. J. Schwarze, *European Administrative Law* (London: Sweet and Maxwell, 1992); P. Birkinshaw, *European Public Law* (London: Butterworths, 2003); J. Schwarze (ed.), *Administrative Law under European Influence* (London/Baden-Baden: Sweet & Maxwell/Nomos, 1996); Y. Galmot, 'Réflexions sur le recours au droit comparé par la Cour de justice des Communautés européennes' (1990) 6 *Revue française du droit administratif* 254 ; P. Beaumont, C. Lyons and N. Walker (eds), *Convergence and Divergence in European Public Law* (Oxford: Hart Publishing, 2002); J. Beatson and T. Tridimas (eds), *New Directions in European Public Law* (Oxford: Hart, 1998); G. Anthony, 'The Europeanization of United Kingdom public law' (2000) 14 *Yearbook of European Studies* 83; G. Anthony, *UK Public Law and European Law* (Portland: Hart Publishing, 2002); T.A. Bőrzel, 'Member State Responses to Europeanization' (2002) 40(2) *Journal of Common Market Studies* 193; L. Conant, 'Europeanization and the Courts: Variable Patterns of Adaptation among National Judiciaries', in M.G. Cowles, J.A. Caporaso and T. Risse (eds), *Transforming Europe: Europeanization and Domestic Change* (Ithaca, NY: Cornell University Press, 2001), p. 97.

with multidirectional influence[3] between legal orders. That forms part of his academic legacy and a valuable contribution to legal science, especially since it took place in the English legal context that was traditionally entrenched in its approach to foreign systems of law.[4]

The groundbreaking work of the forerunners paved the way for a new research field within which the participants seek to describe, understand and analyse how, why and when national and supranational legal orders in Europe interact.[5] Within that discussion and with reference to the Court of Justice of the European Union (CJEU), it has been argued that the role of comparative law is instrumental and 'has a special meaning and place in the EU'.[6] Comparative law serves as a tool that contributes to the attainment of the delicate balance between the competing elements of 'unity' and 'diversity' that are dynamically connected in the Union's motto ('unity in diversity'). Therefore, 'the law of the EU must be read in a way that accommodates that dynamic balance. To that end, the authors of the Treaties vested the ECJ with the constitutional

3. J. Bell, 'Mechanisms for Cross-Fertilisation of Administrative Law in Europe', in J. Beatson and T. Tridimas (eds), *New Directions of European Public Law* (Oxford: Hart Publishing, 1999), p. 147; T. Tridimas, 'Fundamental Rights, General Principles of EU Law, and the Charter' (2014) 16 *Cambridge Yearbook of European Legal Studies* 361; X. Groussot, J. Hettne and G.T. Petursson, 'General Principles and the Many Faces of Coherence: Between Law and Ideology in the European Union' in S. Vogenauer and S. Weatherill (eds), *General Principles of Law European and Comparative Perspectives* (Oxford: Hart, 2017), p. 77.
4. For example, C. Himsworth, 'Convergence and Divergence in Administrative Law', P. Beaumont, C. Lyons and N. Walker (eds), *Convergence and Divergence in European Public Law* (Oxford: Hart Publishing, 2002), p. 99. Cf. G. Anthony, 'Community Law and the Development of UK Administrative Law: Delimiting the "Spill-Over" Effect' (1998) 4 *European Public Law* 253; G. Anthony, 'EC Law, UK Public Law, and the Human Rights Act 1998: A New Integrative Dynamic?' (1999) 2 *Cambridge Yearbook of European Legal Studies* 417; C. Harlow, 'Export, Import: The Ebb and Flow of English Public Law' (2000) *Public Law* 240; C. Hilson, 'The Europeanization of English Administrative Law: Judicial Review and Convergence', (2003) 9 *European Public Law* 125.
5. For example, H.C.H Hofmann, 'Mapping the European Administrative Space' (2008) 31(4) *West European Politics* 662; H. Siedentopf and B. Speer, 'La Notion d'Espace Administratif Européen', in J.-B. Auby and J. Dutheuil de la Rochère (eds), *Droit Administratif Européen* (Bruxelles: Bruylant, 2007), p. 299; J. Trondal and G. Peters, 'A Conceptual Account of the European Administrative Space', in M. Bauer and J. Trondal (eds), *The Palgrave Handbook of the European Administrative System* (London: Palgrave MacMillan, 2015), p. 79; R. Widdershoven, 'European Administrative Law', in R.J.G.H. Seerden (ed.), *Administrative Law of the European Union, its Member States and the United States: A Comparative Analysis*, 3rd ed. (Cambridge: Intersentia, 2012), p. 245; R. Widdershoven and M. Remac, 'General Principles of Law in Administrative Law under European Influence' (2012) 2 *European Review of Private Law* 381; J. Trondal and G.B. Peters, 'The Rise of European Administrative Space: Lessons Learned' (2013) 20(2) *Journal of European Public Policy* 295; H.C.H. Hofmann and B.C. Mihaescu, 'The Relation Between the Charter's Fundamental Rights and the Unwritten General Principles: Good Administration as the Test Case' (2013) 9 *European Constitutional Law Review* 73; G. Martinico and G. Repetto, 'Fundamental Rights and Constitutional Duels in Europe: An Italian Perspective on Case 269/2017 of the Italian Constitutional Court and Its Aftermath' (2019) 15(4) *European Constitutional Law Review* 731; F. Nicola, 'National Legal Traditions at Work in the Jurisprudence of the Court of Justice of the European Union' (2016) 64 *American Journal of Comparative Law* 866; G. van der Schyff, 'The Constitutional Relationship Between the European Union and Its Member States: The Role of National Identity in Article 4(2) TEU' (2012) 37 *European Law Review* 563.
6. K. Lenaerts and K. Gutman, 'The Comparative Law Method and the Court of Justice of the European Union: Interlocking Legal Orders Revisited', in M. Andenas and D. Fairgrieve (ed.), *Courts and Comparative Law* (Oxford: OUP, 2015), p. 141, at p. 141.

authority to engage in a comparative study of the laws of the Member States. The comparative law method is thus a valuable interpretative tool that serves to strike that dynamic balance'.[7]

Therefore, the purpose of this paper is to explore the way the CJEU has made use of comparative law. In this light, the paper pays tribute to the work of Patrick Birkinshaw by adopting as a methodological tool the position that European Public Law is concerned 'with the impact of EU law and the ECHR on the laws of the Member States, and the impact in turn, of the law of Member States on EU law, in particular, as well as on each other'.[8] Within this definition, the function of comparative law is important, since it is one integral component of the interaction between legal orders and their courts in specific. Comparative law is relevant to the CJEU's problem-solving (gap-filling and interpretation), the rationale justification used and the persuasiveness of the judicial argumentation. At the same time, comparative law is instrumental in the process of adoption, modification and transmission of legal principles, concepts and approaches in public law. The CJEU is arguably the most significant factor in the preceding system and the present contribution focuses on the utilization of comparative law by the Court.

In this context, two preliminary clarifications must be made. Firstly, the ECtHR and the national courts are important parameters for European Public Law, but the emphasis is for practical reasons herein limited to the CJEU. National courts also make use of comparative law,[9] arguably in a manner not dissimilar to that of the CJEU's, and are at the same time in the unique position of having to follow the jurisprudence of the CJEU after it has made use of comparative law.[10] This is especially interesting when a national court that has internally crystalized its legal approach to a specific issue, has to follow the approach of the CJEU that has made reference to the preceding national approach when formulating the European Union's (EU) approach.[11] The CJEU's process of selective borrowing, modifying and applying leads to a final product that is

7. K. Lenaerts, 'The European Court of Justice and the Comparative Law Method' (2017) 25(2) *European Review of Private Law* 297, at p. 298.
8. P. Birkinshaw, 'Does European Public Law Exist?', *Queen' Paper on Europeanisation No. 9/2001*, available at http://www.qub.ac.uk/ies/onlinepapers/poe9-01.pdf, at p. 4; P. Birkinshaw, *European Public Law* (London: Butterworths, 2003), at p. 3.
9. For example, E. Mak, 'Reference to Foreign Law in the Supreme Courts of Britain and the Netherlands: Explaining the Development of Judicial Practices' (2012) 8(2) *Utrecht Law Review* 20; A. Barak, 'Comparative Law, Originalism and the Role of a Judge in a Democracy: A Reply to Justice Scalia', speech for the Fulbright Convention, 29 January 2006, http://www.fulbright.org.il; T. Kadner Graziano, 'Is It Legitimate and Beneficial for Judges to Compare?', in M. Andenas and D. Fairgrieve (eds), *Courts and Comparative Law* (Oxford: OUP, 2015), p. 24.
10. The ECtHR represents a different example with the margin of appreciation being an integral element of the approach. *See* J. Gerards, 'Margin of Appreciation and Incrementalism in the Case Law of the European Court of Human Rights' (2018) 18(3) *Human Rights Law Review* 495; I. Villa, 'Subsidiarity, Margin of Appreciation and International Adjudication Within a Cooperative Conception of Human Rights' (2017) 15 *International Journal of Constitutional Law* 393.
11. *See* G. Martinico, 'Exploring the Platonic Heaven of Law: General Principles of EU Law from a Comparative Perspective' (2020) 3 *Nordic Journal of European* Law 1, at pp. 10 et seq. where analysis is made of the principle of proportionality before the Bundesverfassungsgericht in *PSPP*, 5 May 2020, Case No. 2 BvR 859/15, https://www.bundesverfassungsgericht.de/SharedDocs/Entscheidungen/EN/2020/05/rs20200505_2bvr085915en.html with reference to the CJEU's decision in Case C-493/17, *Weiss and Others* EU:C:2018:1000. The German Court in §127 stated

an autonomous concept of EU's law, one that came about by parthenogenesis (virgin-birth) and with its origins not being clearly traceable anymore. According to Martinico,[12] this is what meant by Tridimas when arguing that general principles were 'children of national law, but as brought in front of the Court, they became enfants terribles'.[13] In this framework, antagonism between courts cannot be excluded as for example the age discrimination saga has shown.[14]

Secondly, this paper will not focus on the classic debates about the nature and functions of comparative law.[15] Instead, the comparative law method is in the specific context understood as the ways in which the CJEU 'looks to the rules, principles, and traditions of the Member States, as well as that of other jurisdictions to varying degrees, for the purposes of adjudicating the various types of cases provided for in the Treaties'.[16] It is noted that such outlook is outward looking and it refers to exogenous sources that are formally speaking external to the EU's legal setting, in the sense that they have no binding normative effect. It is also noted that the Court has broadened[17] the scope of available sources to include the law and case law of systems like 'regional and international organizations and tribunals,[18] as well as that of third (non-EU) States, such as the US'.[19]

'The specific manner in which the CJEU applies the principle of proportionality in the case at hand renders that principle meaningless.'

12. *Ibid.*
13. T. Tridimas, *The General Principles of EC Law* (Oxford: Oxford University Press, 1998), at p. 4 (as quoted from Martinico, *supra* n. 11, at p. 10).
14. Case C-144/04, *Mangold* [2005] EU:C:2005:709. *See*: M. Schmidt, 'The Principle of Non-discrimination in Respect of Age: Dimensions of the ECJ's Mangold Judgment' (2005) 7 *German Law Journal* 506; A. Masson and C. Micheau, 'The Werner Mangold Case: An Example of Legal Militancy' (2007) *European Public Law* 587. *See also* the Supreme Court of Denmark Højesteret, decision no. 15/2014 *Dansk Industri acting for Ajos A/S*, https://domstol.dk/hoejesteret/english /supremecourt/nyheder/pressemeddelelser/Documents/Judgment%2015-2014.pdf; C. Jacqueson, 'The Clash: The Danish Supreme Court Defies the CJEU in the Ajos Case' (2017) 4 *Revue de droit comparé du travail et de la sécurité sociale* 250; D. Elkan, R. Holdgaard and G.K. Schaldemose, 'From Cooperation to Collision: The ECJ's Ajos Ruling and the Danish Supreme Court's Refusal to Comply' (2018) 55(1) *Common Market Law Review* 17.
15. For example, O. Kahn-Freund, 'Comparative Law as an Academic Subject' (1966) 82 *Law Quarterly Review* 40; B. Markesinis, 'Comparative Law. A Subject in Search of an Audience' (1990) 53 *Modern Law Review* 1; G.P. Fletcher, 'Comparative Law as a Subversive Discipline' (1998) 46(4) *The American Journal of Comparative Law* 683; R. Michaels, 'The Functional Method of Comparative Law', in M. Reimann and R. Zimmermann (eds), *The Oxford Handbook of Comparative Law* (Oxford: Oxford University Press, 2006) 339; R. Michaels, 'Explanation and Interpretation in Functionalist Comparative Law – A Response to Julie de Coninck' (2010) 74(2) *The Rabel Journal of Comparative and International Private Law* 351.
16. Lenaerts and Gutman, *supra* n. 6, at p. 144.
17. *Ibid.*
18. *Ibid.*, n. 15 cites, *inter alia*, the International Criminal Tribunal for Rwanda and the International Criminal Court that were referred to in Opinion of AG Poiares Maduro in Joined Cases C-514/07 P, C-528/07 P, and C-532/07 P *Sweden and Others v. API and Commission* [2010] ECR I-8533, point 26.
19. *See* K. Lenaerts, 'Interpretation and the Court of Justice: A Basis for Comparative Reflection' (2007) 41 *International Lawyer* 1011, at pp. 1027-1028; K. Lenaerts and K. Gutman, 'The Comparative Law Method and the European Court of Justice: Echoes Across the Atlantic' (2016) 64 *American Journal of Comparative Law* 841; P. Herzog, 'United States Supreme Court Cases in the Court of Justice of the European Communities' (1998) 21 *Hastings International and Comparative Law Review* 903; L.F. Peoples, 'The Use of Foreign Law by the Advocates General

Overall, the CJEU has from the very beginning[20] and throughout[21] emphasized the autonomy of EU law and has ruled that its interpretation of the relevant legal norms is not bound by national perceptions or by the rulings of the ECtHR. The Court is instead inspired, in specific circumstances, by such external sources because it opts to do so or because the Treaties so require in certain instances (Article 6(3) Treaty on European Union (TEU), Article 340 Treaty on the Functioning of the European Union (TFEU)). However, even in the latter cases, it must be noted that the Treaties do not direct the Court as to how the constitutional traditions or general principles common to the Member States are to be considered. The Court remains free to select, evaluate and use those elements originating from external systems, as well as to decide which systems are to be taken into account, subject to certain overriding considerations like the advancement of the EU project, the degree of acceptability of the solutions endorsed and the autonomy of the legal order of the Union.

Therefore, the question posed is how and why the CJEU makes use of comparative law in the public law sphere broadly understood. The answer proposed states that the use of comparative law by the CJEU is much wider than it appears and must become more transparent. The numerous extrajudicial writings by members of the CJEU offer a rare insight and exegeses of the approach to comparative law that is nonetheless not equally present in the case law. It appears to an external observer that the Court applies 'a pick-and-choose' tactic from an array of possible legal options forming a depository of available approaches and solutions. There exists the element of selectivity that is prone to unpredictability and subjectivism and as a corollary the issue of non-transparency arises. Comparative law is therefore both a tool and a method of interpretation for the CJEU and it is intrinsically linked with the need to persuade specific constituencies, primarily national courts, about the reasoning deployed, while simultaneously attaining the Union's objectives. It is exactly this combination of factors that points to the direction of the cognizance of comparative law based on the 'pick-and-choose' approach. Nevertheless, it is argued that the Court's approach is not as random or arbitrary as it appears; it is, instead, a pseudorandom approach: it appears to be random while being produced by a deterministic process. The process of

of the Court of Justice of the European Communities' (2008) 35 *Syracuse Journal of International and Comparative Law* 219; L.F. Peoples, 'The Influence of Foreign Law Cited in the Opinions of the Advocates General on Community Law' (2009) 28 *Yearbook of European Law* 458. Certain notable examples of reference to such sources: Opinion of AG Poiares Maduro in Joined Cases C-402/05 P and C-415/05 P, *Kadi and Al Barakaat International Foundation v. Council and Commission* [2008] ECR I-6351, points 33-34; Opinion of AG Cruz Villalón in Joined Cases C-293/12 and C-594/12, *Digital Rights Ireland and Seitlinger and Others* EU:C:2014:238, point 52; Opinion of AG Poiares Maduro in Case C-305/05, *Ordre des barreaux francophones and germanophone and Others* [2007] ECR I-5305, point 2.

20. Case 26/62, *NV Algemene Transport en Expeditie Onderneming van Gend & Loos v. Netherlands Inland Revenue Administration* [1963] ECR 1; Case 6/64 *Flaminio Costa v. E.N.E.L.* [1964] ECR 585.
21. *See* Opinion 2/13 *re EU Accession to the ECHR* EU:C:2014:2454. *See*: D. Halberstam, '"It's the Autonomy, Stupid!" A Modest Defense of Opinion 2/13 on EU Accession to the ECHR, and the Way Forward' (2015) 16 *German Law Journal* 105; P. Eeckhout, 'Opinion 2/13 on EU Accession to the ECHR and Judicial Dialogue: Autonomy or Autarky' (2015) 38(4) *Fordham International Law Journal* 955.

de-randomization has been explained extrajudicially by members of the Court, yet that exegesis needs to find its way into the case law.

In terms of structure, the paper is divided into three parts. The first part examines the internal setting of the Court that contributes to the use of comparative law and to the lack of visibility of all the instances when that takes place. The second part focuses on the legal bases for the use of comparative law by the CJEU, which partly reveals the rationale of the Court. The third part assesses the extrajudicial views of judges of the CJEU as to the use of comparative law.

2 THE CJEU'S INTERNAL STRUCTURE

In the EU's judicial framework, the comparative law method is applied by CJEU in its full institutional setup that includes the Court of Justice, the General Court[22] and the specialized courts. The focal point of this contribution is the Court of Justice for three interconnected reasons: (a) its jurisdiction in preliminary references from which very significant rulings arise;[23] (b) its appellate jurisdiction vis-à-vis the General Court and especially under Article 340 TFEU;[24] (c) the institutional connection of the Court of Justice with the Advocates General.[25]

In relation to the Advocates General,[26] their role has been instrumental in the application of comparative law. Formally, the Advocates General are part of the Court (Article 19(2) TEU; Article 252 TFEU) and are tasked with delivering reasoned opinions on how the pending case is to be resolved, thus offering valuable assistance to the Court. The role of the Advocates General of the CJEU has been described as sui

22. *See*, e.g., the General Court in Joined Cases T-125/03 and T-253/03, *Akzo Nobel*, paras 170-172, 176.
23. For example, State liability and Joined Cases C-6/90 and C-9/90, *Francovich and Others* [1991] ECR 1-5357; Joined Cases C-46/93 and C-48/93, *Brasserie du Pecheur and Factortame* [1996] ECR I-1029. For overall analysis of the preliminary reference procedure, *see* the classic T. Tridimas, 'Knocking on Heaven's Door: Fragmentation, Efficiency and Defiance in the Preliminary Reference Procedure' (2003) 40 *Common Market Law Review* 9.
24. *See* the saga leading to Case C-58/12 P, *Groupe Gascogne v. Commission*, EU:C:2013:360. For analysis *see* P. Verbruggen and K. Kryla-Cudna, 'The Union's Liability for Failure to Adjudicate Within a Reasonable Time: EU Tort Law after Gascogne, Kendrion and ASPLA' (2020) 57(1) *Common Market Law Review* 191.
25. Article 19(2) TEU; Article 252 TFEU.
26. Generally, on the AG of the CJEU *see*: A. Dashwood, 'The Advocate General in the Court of Justice of the European Communities' (1982) 2 *Legal Studies* 202; K. Borgsmidt, 'The Advocate General at the European Court of Justice: A Comparative Study' (1988) 13 *European Law Review* 106; T. Tridimas, 'The Role of the Advocate General in the Development of Community Law: Some Reflections' (1997) 34 *Common Market Law Review* 1349; F. Jacobs, 'Advocates General and Judges in the European Court of Justice: Some Personal Reflections', in D. O'Keefe and A. Bavasso (eds), *Judicial Review in European Union Law* (The Hague: Kluwer, 2000), p. 17; E. Sharpston, 'The Changing Role of the Advocate General', in A. Arnull, P. Eeckhout and T. Tridimas (eds), *Continuity and Change in EU Law: Essays in Honour of Sir Francis Jacobs* (Oxford: Oxford University Press, 2008), p. 20; N. Burrows and R. Greaves, *The Advocate General and EC Law* (Oxford University Press, 2007); M. Bobek, 'A Fourth in the Court: Why Are There Advocates General in the Court of Justice?' (2012) 14 *Cambridge Yearbook of European Legal Studies* 529; A. Albors-Llorens, 'Securing Trust in the Court of Justice of the EU: The Influence of the Advocates General' (2012) 14 *Cambridge Yearbook of European Legal Studies* 509.

generis[27] in the sense that the Opinion assists the Court without being binding on it and with the Advocate General being a member of the Court but without participating in the deliberations leading to the judgment.[28]

From an early stage, the Advocates General adopted an approach of bringing to the attention of the Court, via the Opinion, a spherical account of the legal issues and of the various approaches to them; within that, comparative law has been frequently present and rather visible in its utilization.[29] In that regard, comparative law 'more often appears in the Opinions of the Advocates General than in the judgments of the Court of Justice'.[30] That relates to what Martinico[31] has described as the CJEU's style of judgments whereby the Court condenses 'the legal reasoning of very revolutionary cases in pretty short decisions', thus making it 'very difficult to understand the real importance of the comparative argument in the economy of the judicial outcome and introduces another element of non-transparency in the legal reasoning'.[32] Moreover, CJEU's Judge Thomas von Danwitz has also pointed out that 'the rather short references which are contained in the Court's judgments indeed only constitute the "tip of the iceberg" and are based on extensive considerations contained in the conclusions of the Advocate General and on preliminary research done by the internal service of the Court'.[33]

It has also been explained[34] that the Advocates General 'may utilize the comparative law method as part of setting out the general background or context of the case',[35] could 'highlight or advocate a particular approach, which may or may not be taken up by the Court', or may 'highlight a difference in approach, in particular by explaining certain issues by contrasting what the EU is not'.[36] Therefore, the Advocates General make use of comparative law for various reasons. Because of the secrecy of the

27. Lenaerts and Gutman, *supra* n. 6, at p. 146; N. Fennelly, 'Reflections of an Irish Advocate General' (1996) *Irish Journal of European Law* 5.
28. On the fair trial and the role of the AG *see*: Case 309/99, *Wouters*; Case184/01, *Hirschfeldt*; C-209/01, *Fleck-Schilling*; Case 147/02 *Michelle K. Alabaster*; Case 181/02 P, *Kvaerner Warnow Werft*; Case 466/00, *Kaba II*.
29. Selectively: Opinion of Advocate General Mischo, Joined Cases 46/87 and 227/88, *Hoechst v. Commission* [1989] ECR I-2875, points 48-126; Opinion of Advocate General Léger, Case C-224/01, *Köbler v. Austria* [2003] ECR I-10243, points 91, 96; Opinion of Advocate General Stix-Hackl, Case C-36/02, *Omega* [2004] ECR I-9611, points 82-84; Opinion of Advocate General Kokott, Case C-550/07 P, *Akzo Nobel Chemicals and Akcros Chemicals v. Commission* [2010] ECR I-8301, points 47, 89-91, 101-104; Opinion of AG Jacobs, Case C-148/02, *Garcia Avello* [2003] ECR I-11613, points 5-22; Opinion of Advocate General Poiares Maduro in Case C-305/05, *Ordre des barreaux francophones and germanophone and Other*s [2007] ECR I-5305, point 71.
30. Lenaerts and Gutman, *supra* n. 6, at p. 147.
31. G. Martinico, 'Exploring the Platonic Heaven of Law: General Principles of EU Law from a Comparative Perspective' (2020) 3 *Nordic Journal of European* Law 1, at p. 4
32. *Ibid.*
33. T. von Danwitz, 'The Rule of Law in the Recent Jurisprudence of the ECJ' (2014) 37 *Fordham International Law Journal* 1311, at p. 1317. The reference to 'tip of the iceberg' is attributed to P. Pescatore, 'Le recours, dans la jurisprudence de la Cour de justice des Communautés européennes, à des normes déduites de la comparaison des droits des Etats membres' (1980) 32(2) *Revue internationale de droit comparé* 337, at p. 358.
34. Lenaerts and Gutman, *supra* n. 6, at p. 147.
35. *Ibid.*
36. *Ibid.*

deliberations of the Court,[37] as well as the absence of dissenting judgments, and due to the often condensed[38] legal reasoning of the Court, the degree of influence of the Opinions on the Court is not always detectable.

In addition, the composition of the Court plays a role in the utilization of comparative law. Judges and Advocates General come from different areas of the legal profession (judiciary, academia, civil service, Union institutions) and represent different legal traditions and training. The enlargement waves have contributed further to that diversification and in combination with the multilingualism of the texts[39] and within the Court, the institutional setting of the CJEU is cosmopolitan and a 'major comparative law laboratory'.[40] It has therefore been argued that 'each deliberation gives rise to a "mixing" of mentalities, cultures, and legal constructions. A judgment will thus tend to be the result of "cross" contributions of different legal systems and ways of legal reasoning. The origin of these contributions will not always be identified and may sometimes even be unidentifiable.'[41] Furthermore, the parties to the proceedings,[42] as well as national courts making preliminary references,[43] have increasingly included comparative law in their argumentation and background analysis.[44]

Overall, 'the comparative law method 'permeates the daily activities' of the Union courts in many ways'[45] and that is quite often less visible than it is present in the reasoning of the Court. The legal bases authorizing the use of comparative law are also important for mapping out the approach of the CJEU.

37. Article 35 Statute of the CJEU; Article 32(1) Rules of Procedure of the Court of Justice of 25 September 2012, [2012] OJ L265/1, as amended on 18 June 2013, [2013] OJ L173/65 (ECJ Rules of Procedure).
38. Martinico, *supra* n. 31, at p. 4.
39. G. Van Calster, 'The EU's Tower of Babel-The Interpretation by the European Court of Justice of Equally Authentic Texts Drafted in more than one Official Language' (1997) *Yearbook of European Law* 363; E. Ioriatti, 'Comparative Law and EU Legal Language: Towards a European Restatement?' (2021) 21(2) *Global Jurist* 305.
40. M. Hilf, 'The Role of Comparative Law in the Jurisprudence of the Court of Justice of the European Communities', in A. de Mestral et al. (eds), *The Limitation of Human Rights in Comparative Constitutional Law* (Cowansville: Les Éditions Yvon Blais Inc., 1986), p. 549, at p. 550; M. Graziadei, 'The European Court of Justice at Work: Comparative Law on Stage and Behind the Scenes' (2020) 13 *Journal of Civil Law Studies* 1, at p. 1; K. Lenaerts, 'Interlocking Legal Orders in the European Union and Comparative Law' (2003) 52(4) *International and Comparative Law Quarterly* 873, at p. 876; Lenaerts and Gutman, *supra* n. 6, at p. 149.
41. K. Lenaerts, 'Interlocking Legal Orders in the European Union and Comparative Law' (2003) 52(4) *International and Comparative Law Quarterly* 873, at p. 876.
42. Lenaerts and Gutman, *supra* n. 6, at p. 148. *See, e.g.*, Case C-550/07 P, *Akzo Nobel Chemicals* [2010] ECR I-8301; Joined Cases T-125/03 and T-253/03, *Akzo Nobel*; Case C-321/95 P, *Greenpeace and Others v. Commission* [1998] ECR I-1651.
43. Lenaerts and Gutman, *supra* n. 6, at p. 148, citing Case C-453/99, *Courage v. Crehan* [2001] ECR I-6297, paras 13, 15; Case C-168/00, *Leitner* [2002] ECR I-2631, para. 12 (the Austrian court cited German law and case law).
44. Lenaerts and Gutman, *supra* n. 6, at p. 148.
45. *Ibid.*, at p. 149.

3 LEGAL BASES FOR THE USE OF COMPARATIVE LAW BY THE CJEU

At first, there must be a clarification as to whether the Treaties authorize the CJEU to make use of comparative law and if yes, in what way that authorization is framed. The authorization is linked to the legitimacy of the Court and to the provision of a justification basis for the approach of the CJEU. In response, it can be argued that the Treaties do provide for the use of comparative law by the Court, and they do so in a variety of ways but without actually and in essence constraining the CJEU as to how comparative law is to be used.

On the legal bases for the use of comparative law, there seems to be a divergence of opinion among the members of the Court, even if the more recent approaches seem to converge. On the one hand, there is the view expressed by Judge Kakouris[46] that sees the Treaties as not expressly and in general terms providing for the use of comparative law by the CJEU. This must be construed as not generally and expressly authorizing the Court to horizontally make use of comparative law during adjudication proceedings. Such an approach could, in contrast, be found in Article 38(1)(c) of the Statute of the International Court of Justice.[47] The Treaties, therefore, lack an expressis verbis general authorization clause for the use of comparative law by the CJEU.

On the other hand, the preceding is a formally correct yet incomplete conclusion. The Treaties have been construed[48] as providing for an overarching yet implied general clause for the use of comparative law that is directly linked to the mission[49] of the Court to ensure that in the implementation and application of the Treaty, the law is observed.[50] In specific, what is now Article 19(1) of the TEU provides for that. This provision has been characterized as 'the most important provision of the Treaty'[51] and

46. C.N. Kakouris, 'Use of the Comparative Method by the Court of Justice of the European Communities' (1994) 6 *Pace International Law Review* 267, at p. 270.
47. Article 38 of the Statute of the International Court of Justice, 26 June 1945: 'The Court, whose function is to decide in accordance with international law such disputes as are submitted to it, shall apply:
    a. international conventions, whether general or particular, establishing rules expressly recognized by the contesting states;
    b. international custom, as evidence of a general practice accepted as law;
    c.*the general principles of law recognized by civilized nations*;
    d. subject to the provisions of Article 59, judicial decisions and the teachings of the most highly qualified publicists of the various nations, as subsidiary means for the determination of rules of law.'
48. *See*, the classic example: Joined Cases 7/56 and 3/57 to 7/57, *Algera and Others v. Common Assembly* [1957] ECR 39, §55: '[u]nless the Court is to deny justice it is therefore obliged to solve the problem by reference to the rules acknowledged by legislation, the learned writing and the case-law of the member countries'.
49. On the mission versus task phraseology *see* N. Fennelly, 'Legal Interpretation at the European Court of Justice' (1996) 20 *Fordham International Law Journal* 656, at pp. 662-663.
50. *See* the progression of Articles 164 European Community Treaty (ECT), 220 ECT, 19(1) TEU.
51. T. Tridimas, 'The European Court of Justice and the Draft Constitution: A Supreme Court for the Union?', in T. Tridimas and P. Nebbia (eds), *EU Law for the 21st Century: Rethinking the New Legal Order* (London: Hart Publishing 2004), p. 113, at p. 116.

is connected to the 'sacred task, indeed the core function of the judge'[52] to interpret and apply the law. This has been understood as constituting 'a primary source of authority or a general legal basis authorizing the Union courts to utilize the comparative law method'[53] because 'the law' must include the laws of the Member States. This is connected to upholding the rule of law due to the classic adjudication duty of the courts (Rechtsfindung),[54] according to which a case before them must be decided regardless of gaps in the normative context. Algera[55] is a classic and early example of such a situation, with the Court expressly stating that 'unless the [ECJ] is to deny justice it is therefore obliged to solve the problem by reference to the rules acknowledged by the legislation, the learned writing and the case-law of the [Member States]'.[56] Therefore, the Court has construed Article 19(1) TEU and its predecessors (Article 164 European Community (EC), Article 220 EC) as establishing the Court's 'overriding general mission statement'[57] and an overarching[58] obligation to resolve the pending case. That is a matter of compliance with the rule of law, and if need be, with resources to the comparative method. This has been confirmed in Brasserie du Pêcheur[59] and by numerous Opinions of the Advocates General.[60] Formally, this is an implied authorization resulting from the interpretation of the provision, yet of enormous significance.

Three important elements interact within the provision. Firstly, the obligation of the Court to ensure the observance of the law that is intrinsically linked with the delivery of judgment under the Treaties. Secondly, the distinction between implementation and application of the Treaty. In this context, the interpretative obligation is understood as 'the means to achieve judgment'[61] and includes the subsequent application of the law. Thirdly, the meaning of 'law'. Judge Kakouris has eloquently explained that meaning:

> By virtue of Article 164,[62] the written law of the Treaty, which is supreme among the provisions of Community law, has above it 'the Idea of Law', to use Plato's terminology. The Court must ensure observance of that Law. 'The Idea of Law' must guide the Court as the polar star guides sailors, to use Stammler's beautiful imagery.[63]

52. K. Lenaerts, 'Interpretation and the Court of Justice: A Basis for Comparative Reflection' (2007) 41 *International Lawyer* 1011, at p. 1011.
53. Lenaerts and Gutman, *supra* n. 6, at p. 150.
54. K. Lenaerts, 'The European Court of Justice and the Comparative Law Method' (2017) 25 *European Review of Private Law* 297, at p. 299.
55. *Supra* n. 48.
56. *Ibid.*
57. Lenaerts, *supra* n. 52, at p. 1015.
58. With reference to Article 19(1) TEU, Lenaerts and Gutman, *supra* n. 6, at p. 150.
59. Joined Cases C-46/93 and C-48/93, *Brasserie du Pêcheur and Factortame and Others* [1996] ECR I-1029, §27.
60. For example, Opinion of AG Kokott in Case C-550/07 P, *Akzo Nobel Chemicals and Akcros Chemicals v. Commission* [2010] ECR I-8301, point 92.
61. Lenaerts, *supra* n. 52, at p. 1013.
62. Applicable to what is now Article 19(1) TEU.
63. Kakouris, *supra* n. 46, at p. 273.

Therefore, Article 19(1) TEU is itself the object of teleological interpretation and within it the use of comparative law emerges as an integral part of the actual essence of the function of the Court.

Furthermore, President Lenaerts has argued that the 'authors of the Treaties vested the ECJ with the constitutional authority to engage in a comparative study of the law of the Member States'.[64] The authority for the Union courts is both 'general and specific'[65] and 'for the purposes of their interpretive and law-making functions'.[66] This is an important statement for an additional reason: it represents one of the rather rare instances where a member of the Court is forthcoming with the recognition that the Court also makes law.[67]

Additionally, the Treaties were gradually amended as to establish a thematically specific legal basis for using comparative law in relation to human rights. What is now Article 6(3) TEU states that 'Fundamental rights, as guaranteed by the European Convention for the Protection of Human Rights and Fundamental Freedoms and as they result from the constitutional traditions common to the Member States, shall constitute general principles of the Union's law.' This provision represents a codification of the case law of the Court in the field of human rights,[68] as does Article 52(4) of the EU Charter.[69]

Finally, there is also the express legal basis of Article 340 TFEU providing that 'In the case of non-contractual liability, the Union shall, in accordance with the general principles common to the laws of the Member States, make good any damage caused by its institutions or by its servants in the performance of their duties.' In this context, the Treaty directs to the formulation of general principles for non-contractual liability,[70] while simultaneously creating a normative lacuna as to the content of such principles that is to be filled-in in the manner prescribed by the provision and without that implying that the approach of any Member State has specific and greater weight in the sense that the CJEU is bound to follow it.[71]

Beyond the preceding legal bases found in the Treaties, it must be noted that the Court has had to function within an incomplete or dynamic treaty framework, a traité

64. K. Lenaerts, 'The European Court of Justice and the Comparative Law Method' (2017) 25 *European Review of Private Law* 297, at p. 299.
65. Lenaerts and Gutman, *supra* n. 6, at p. 150.
66. *Ibid.*
67. *Ibid.*, also pp. 167-170. *See also* K. Lenaerts and K. Gutman, '"Federal Common Law" in the European Union: A Comparative Perspective from the United States' (2006) 54 *American Journal of Comparative Law* 1.
68. Case 29/69, *Stauder v. City of Ulm;* Case 11/70, *Internationale Handelsgesellschaft;* Case 4/73, *Nold;* Case 44/79 *Liselotte Hauer.*
69. 'In so far as this Charter recognises fundamental rights as they result from the constitutional traditions common to the Member States, those rights shall be interpreted in harmony with those traditions.'
70. C. *Hilson, 'The Role of Discretion* in EC Law on Non-Contractual Liability' (2005) 42 *Common Market Law Review* 677; L. Antoniolli, 'Community Liability', in H. Koziol and R. Schulze (eds), *Tort Law of the EC* (Vienna: Springer, 2008), p. 213.
71. Lenaerts, *supra* n. 41, pp. 887-893.

cadre,[72] that is 'imbued by teleology'.[73] Along those lines, President Leanerts has argued that 'in the activities of the Community judge, the comparative approach is a "quasi-compelling" method of interpretation of Community law, intrinsically linked to the continuous integration process which characterises the European construction'.[74] Nevertheless, it must also be remembered that the practical need for resorting to the use of comparative law is not self-referential but balanced with the autonomy, effectiveness and uniformity of EU law; these are primary considerations in the search for solutions to the legal gaps and interpretation needs. Comparative law thus arose as a necessity within the operation of the CJEU, a pragmatic consideration for problem-solving that goes beyond the legal bases authorizing the use of comparative law and to the heart of the judicial function.[75]

What must be further noted is that the legal bases on which the use of comparative law may be justified are flexible enough as: (a) to not impose an obligation to follow specific foreign approaches; (b) to not attribute binding effect to external solutions and/or hierarchy between them; (c) to not constrain the CJEU as to the use it makes of comparative law. As a consequence, the use of comparative law by the CJEU transcended the authorizing legal bases found in the Treaties and became a result-oriented tool, an interpretation technique and a justification device for balancing the unity with the diversity. In that regard, it has been argued by Koskelo that 'for the Court of Justice, just like for national courts, the use that is made of comparative law is pragmatic and instrumental rather than scientific … [and] serves the same ultimate purpose, namely the search for an appropriate solution to a given problem of interpretation'.[76] Comparative law is thus used by the CJEU in a manner similar to that used by the national courts, 'as part of a search for arguments and appropriate solutions rather than part of an exploration of obligatory legal material'.[77]

The margin of discretion for the CJEU when using comparative law is therefore quite broad and it is significant to take into consideration the numerous positions adopted extrajudicially by judges of the Court.

72. B. Davies and F.G. Nicola, 'Introduction: Supranationalism and Foreign Law at the Court of Justice of the EU' (2016) 64(4) *The American Journal of Comparative Law* 797, at p. 798; Lenaerts, *supra* n. 52, at p. 1017.
73. T. Tridimas, 'The Court of Justice and Judicial Activism' (1996) 21 *European Law Review* 199, at p. 205.
74. Lenaerts, *supra* n. 41, at pp. 878-879.
75. G. Benos, 'The Practical Debt of Community Law to Comparative Law' (1984) *Revue Hellenique de droit international* 251.
76. *See* P. Koskelo, 'Report of P. Koskelo, President of the Supreme Court of Finland (2007), at p. 25, available at: https://eur-lex.europa.eu/resource.html?uri=cellar:de4d38f2-300c-442e-aee5-1ec55dfae686.0001.03/DOC_1&format=PDF.
77. *Ibid.*

4 EXTRAJUDICIAL VIEWS OF JUDGES OF THE CJEU AS TO THE USE OF COMPARATIVE LAW

In relation to the use of comparative law by the CJEU, there are numerous extrajudicial writings of current and former members of the Court,[78] to an extent that is impressive when compared with other aspects of the jurisprudence of the Court of Justice. This gives a valuable insight into the judicial perception of the use of comparative law that goes well beyond the express references to it in the case law. The analysis is limited to four judicial accounts that are partly interconnected and illustrate the evolving understanding of the approach by the members of the CJEU.

4.1 Teleology, Comparative Law and the Court as the Consciousness of Europe

Judge Kakouris[79] has explained that comparative law forms part of the judicial function and is being used by courts as a method of interpreting the law which is in force. Courts

78. P. Pescatore, 'Le recours, dans la jurisprudence de la Cour de justice des Communautés européennes, à des normes déduites de la comparaison des droits des Etats membres' (1980) 32(2) *Revue internationale de droit comparé* 337; C.N. Kakouris, 'Use of the Comparative Method by the Court of Justice of the European Communities' (1994) 6 *Pace International Law Review* 267; T. Koopmans, 'The Birth of European Law at the Crossroads of Legal Traditions' (1991) *American Journal of Comparative Law* 500; J. Mertens de Wilmars, 'Le droit comparé dans la jurisprudence de la Cour de justice des Communautés européennes' (1991) *Journal des Tribunaux* 37; Y. Galmot, 'Réflexions sur le recours au droit comparé par la Cour de justice des Communautés européennes' (1990) 6 *Revue Française de Droit Administratif* 255; W. Van Gerven, 'Comparative Law in a Texture of Communitarization of National Laws and Europeanization of Community Law', in D. O'Keeffe and A. Bavasso (eds), *Judicial Review in the European Union – Liber Amicorum in Honour of Lord Slynn of Hadley*, vol. I (The Hague: Kluwer Law International, 2000), p. 433; K. Lenaerts and K. Gutman, 'The Comparative Law Method and the Court of Justice of the European Union: Interlocking Legal Orders Revisited', in M. Andenas and D. Fairgrieve (eds), *Courts and Comparative Law* (Oxford: OUP, 2015), p. 141; F.G. Jacobs, 'Comparative Law and European Union Law', in M. Reimann and R. Zimmermann (eds) *Oxford Handbook of Comparative Law*, 2nd ed. (Oxford University Press, 2019), p. 525; K. Lenaerts, 'The European Court of Justice and the Comparative Law Method' (2017) 25(2) *European Review of Private Law* 297; K. Lenaerts, 'Interpretation and the Court of Justice: A Basis for Comparative Reflection' (2007) 41 *International Lawyer* 1011; K. Lenaerts and K. Gutman, 'The Comparative Law Method and the European Court of Justice: Echoes Across the Atlantic' (2016) 64 *American Journal of Comparative Law* 84; K. Lenaerts, 'Interlocking Legal Orders in the European Union and Comparative Law' (2003) 52(4) *International and Comparative Law Quarterly* 873; K. Lenaerts and K. Gutman, '"Federal Common Law" in the European Union: A Comparative Perspective from the United States' (2006) 54 *American Journal of Comparative Law* 1; K. Lenaerts, 'Interlocking Legal Orders or the European Union Variant of E Pluribus Unum', in G. Canivet, M. Andenas and D. Fairgrieve (eds), *Comparative Law Before the Courts* (British Institute of International and Comparative Law, 2004), p. 99; K. Lenaerts, 'How the ECJ Thinks: A Study on Judicial Legitimacy' (2013) 36 *Fordham International Law Journal* 1302; K. Lenaerts and J.A. Gutiérrez-Fons, 'To Say What the Law of the EU Is: Methods of Interpretation and the European Court of Justice' (2014) 44(2) *Columbia Journal of European Law* 2; S. Rodin, 'Constitutional Relevance of Foreign Court Decisions' (2016) 64(4) *American Journal of Comparative Law* 815; T. von Danwitz, 'The Rule of Law in the Recent Jurisprudence of the ECJ' (2014) 37 *Fordham International Law Journal* 1311.

79. C.N. Kakouris, 'Use of the Comparative Method by the Court of Justice of the European Communities' (1994) 6 *Pace International Law Review* 267.

are not engaging into an abstract quest for the law but rather have to interpret 'vague notions or fill lacunae in written law by recourse to the unwritten law which is already in force, by using a "cognitive" approach. This difference in approach is not theoretical, but real and fundamental'.[80]

Therefore, there is connection between judicial interpretation and comparative law that arises in concrete cases of vagueness or legal lacunae and with the aim of bringing the pending case to a conclusion by recourse to unwritten law. Unwritten law refers in this context as the existence of legal approaches relevant to the matter under examination that are not formally legally binding on the Court.

Judge Kakouris argued that the CJEU makes use of comparative law as a method of interpretation, with 'interpretation' including 'the filling of gaps in the written law which is a cognitive process since it adds nothing to the law in force, but merely transposes unwritten law into written case-law'.[81] According to Judge Kakouris, in relation to the non-contractual liability of the Union and the relevant express authorization ('in accordance with the general principles common to the laws of the Member States') the CJEU has not resorted 'to any sort of mechanistic interpretation'.[82] The approach of the Court is not based on the arithmetic logic either in the form of endorsing the majority view arising from the comparative analysis in the Member States or in the form the highest common denominator. The Court remains free to choose the most appropriate rule in the given case thus moving away from a mechanistic[83] or 'arithmetical'[84] use of comparative law. This is an argument that has appeared early in the case law, with a classic example being the Opinion of AG Lagrange in Case 14/61, Hoogovens:

> the case law of the Court, in so far as it invokes national laws (as it does to a large extent) to define the rules of law relating to the application of the Treaty, is not content to draw on more or less arithmetical 'common denominators' between the different national solutions, but chooses from each of the Member States those solutions which, having regard to the objects of the Treaty, appear to it to be the best or, if one may use the expression, the most progressive. That is the spirit, moreover, which has guided the Court hitherto.
>
> Beyond the non-contractual liability of the Union, Judge Kakouris argued that the Court 'uses the comparative method ... in the service of teleological interpretation',[85] with teleological interpretation being crucial in the approach of the CJEU and being understood as the 'meaning of law in the light of its purpose, its 'telos''.[86] Teleological interpretation is also utilized as a guide for the interpretation of vague notions, as well as a guide to fill legal lacunas with reference to the general principles of law.[87] Therefore, for Judge Kakouris comparative law becomes part of teleological interpretation to the extent that 'the comparative

80. Kakouris *supra* n. 79, at p. 269.
81. *Ibid.*
82. *Ibid.*, at p. 270.
83. *Ibid.*
84. Per Advocate General Lagrange in his Opinion in Case 14/61, *Hoogovens* [1962] ECR 277, at p. 283.
85. Kakouris *supra* n. 79, at p. 273.
86. *Ibid.* Note that telos finds its origin in the Greek word that translates to 'end'.
87. Kakouris *supra* n. 79, at p. 273.

method is in the service of teleological interpretation'.[88] This is an important point that has remained a constant in subsequent accounts by judges of the CJEU (*see infra*).

Judge Kakouris proceeds to offer an explanation as to the way in which the Court uses the comparative method: it takes place in two stages and in order 'to arrive at criteria by reference to the beliefs and common values of the people of Europe'.[89] It can be argued that this is the Achilles' heel of the account because the identification of 'the beliefs and common values of the people of Europe' is vague enough to enable extreme selectivity. It is also antithetical to the premise that the Court has to make use of comparative law in order to adjudicate certain cases and in doing so it remains unconstrained by the arithmetic logic of the common denominators. Camouflaging the selection of the optimal in the circumstances solution as the expression of the European beliefs and values is problematic and unnecessary because it idealizes the role of the Court and presents its approach as being value driven. It must also be remembered that the CJEU will be inspired and then would adjust and apply the solution to the problem as an EU principle or approach. Therefore, the autonomy of EU law already justifies the distancing from national perceptions, not only in terms of those that are bypassed but also in terms of those that form the foundation for the Court's approach in a specific case.

This part of the account by Judge Kakouris is also problematic in relation to the two stages of the use of the comparative method. During the first stage, 'the Court refers to the legislation of the Member States in which those beliefs and convictions are reflected. If the first method does not bring results, the Court then refers directly to the convictions, beliefs and spiritual attitudes of the peoples of Europe. The first stage is the legal application of the comparative method'.[90] Judge Kakouris argues that this two-stage approach is the result of the diversity between States in relation to the same shared and same fundamental conceptions about humanity.[91] Accordingly, 'these differences must be respected. This multicultural approach also imbues the work of the Court. Each case requires the Court to identify what constitutes the resultant vector of those differences, the 'telos' which will guide its decision. In this respect the Court must act as though it were the consciousness of Europe'.[92] It is noted that this idea of 'unity in diversity' has remained a relevant point in subsequent judicial accounts.[93]

4.2 Comparative Law as Informed Choice and as Matter of Ontology

Judge Rodin[94] has developed an alternative and theoretically sophisticated account for the use of comparative law by the CJEU. That account starts with the recognition that the use of exogenous legal sources in constitutional adjudication is structurally integrated into the supranational legal system of the EU.[95] Therefore, the underlying

88. *Ibid.*
89. Kakouris, *supra* n. 79, at p. 274.
90. *Ibid.*
91. *Ibid.*
92. Kakouris, *supra* n. 79, at p.274 (emphasis added).
93. For example, K. Lenaerts, 'The European Court of Justice and the Comparative Law Method' (2017) 25(2) *European Review of Private Law* 297.
94. S. Rodin, 'Constitutional Relevance of Foreign Court Decisions' (2016) 64(4) *American Journal of Comparative Law* 815.
95. *Ibid.*, at p. 816.

question is 'whether the legal rules and social standards of other states and legal systems are or should become operational in domestic legal systems through the agency of judges'[96] and if yes, on the basis of what criteria.

The argument sees the role of comparative law as being specifically limited by intra-systemic factors: 'judicial cognizance of comparative law is restrained by reasons of integrity, autonomy, and efficiency, the reasons for which are instrumental to the construction of the identity of the legal system within which judges operate'.[97] Accordingly, the full exclusion of foreign law is logically difficult because during the adjudication process the judge is not detached from the knowledge basis that forms part of the judicial function. The CJEU judge has an understanding of foreign law that can be relevant to a given case and has the choice to rely on an external source but 'only to the extent that it does not undermine systemic values and the ontological identities on which those values are based'.[98] Therefore, Judge Rodin places the CJEU judge within the EU's constitutional environment that entrenches specific principles, values and qualities that morph the Union's constitutional core. As a corollary, the CJEU is the interpreter and developer of the systemic values and standards of the Union's society and those are inextricably embedded in the liberal essence of the EU.[99] They act as the framework of operation for the judge and guide the use of comparative law.[100] It follows that 'while the comparative law method evidently remains as part of referential framework of judges, its value as a formal element of adjudication seems to be close to zero'.[101]

Judge Rodin thus draws a distinction between 'the application of foreign law as a formal element of adjudication, furnishing either its legal basis or justifying a result, from its application as part of the referential framework of judges. While the former can be easily identified by looking at explicit references to legal sources cited in the text of a judicial decision, the latter enters the equation as an internalized element of judges' reasoning'.[102] In either case, the exercise of that option is governed by the ontological core of the Union and comparative law is 'relevant only to the extent that it does not undermine systemic values and the ontological identities on which those values are based'.[103] In the alternative, the result would be external hierarchical imposition on the Union's legal order and without synchronization with the driving forces behind that legal order. That would lead to transplantation incompatible with the fabric of the recipient system, hence 'there is no reason why that essential content of the European

96. *Ibid.*, at p. 818.
97. *Ibid.*, at p. 816.
98. *Ibid.*, at p. 822.
99. *Ibid.*, at p. 821.
100. *Ibid.*, at pp. 819-820: This approach makes use of Schlag's key ontological identities 'which define the Legal Basis, the Act, the Agent, and the Legitimacy of the social arrangement under which constitutional interpretation operates' (P. Schlag, 'Empty Circles of Liberal Justification' (1997) 96 *Michigan Law Review* 1). In relation to the EU, those are by analogy to the American context as follows: Legal basis the Founding Treaties; Act the ongoing process of construction; Agent the Member States and the peoples of Europe; Legitimacy the consent of the Agents: Rodin, *supra* n. 94, at p. 820 Table 1.
101. Rodin, *supra* n. 94, at p. 823 (emphasis added).
102. *Ibid.*, at p. 817.
103. *Ibid.*, at p. 822.

Union's constitutional ontology should be relinquished to an authority that rests on different ontological assumptions'.[104]

In terms of the formal element of adjudication and comparative law, it is concluded that 'in the judicial process, the judge controls which issues will be considered legal and which factual, and that both facts and law are constructed', therefore 'there is little difference whether the law of the member states is treated as fact or law. Whether fact or law, parties are entitled to plead it before the court, even if the court raises the issue on its own motion'.[105] In terms of the referential framework of adjudication whereby foreign law becomes relevant through the agency of the judges, Judge Rodin argues that 'foreign law is considered fact, both law and fact operate in the same way – by cognition'.[106] Foreign law is knowledge that cannot be side-lined and is incorporated in the referential framework of the judge either discreetly or overtly.[107] Discreet incorporation of foreign law refers to the implicit drawing from foreign sources and results from the general knowledge and understanding[108] of the judges; their 'reasoning is, inextricably, influenced by their knowledge of law and facts, which becomes amalgamated with their decision, with or even without specific reference to its foreign source'.[109] On the other hand, overt reference to foreign sources refers to such sources in a clearer way 'but falls short of recognizing in foreign law any normative value'[110] and accordingly, the law of the Member States can play two different roles: (a) it informs the Court how to fill lacunae in EU law; (b) it serves as a justification for normative choices made by the CJEU.[111]

In the first case, Article 19(1) TEU is construed as a general interpretation clause enabling use of foreign sources 'where necessary to render a decision and avoid a non liquet situation'.[112] Comparative law is therefore a gap-filling tool and does not substitute the normative value of EU law.[113] In the second case, 'when sufficient justification cannot be found in EU law itself, the CJEU refers to the law of the member states'[114] and incorporates through a process of inspiration those general principles of law that are common to the constitutional traditions of the Member States.[115]

Judge Rodin identifies specific limits to the way in which comparative law is used by the CJEU. Firstly, there are limits related to the unity in diversity issue. There are inherent tensions 'between, on the one hand, the quest for autonomy, integrity, and efficiency in EU law that the CJEU is pursuing as the agent of the construction of the key ontological identities and, on the other, an appreciation of the legal diversity of the

104. *Ibid.*, at p. 823.
105. *Ibid.*, at p. 828.
106. *Ibid.*, at p. 828.
107. *Ibid.*, at pp. 829-830.
108. *Ibid.*, at p. 830.
109. *Ibid.* Examples cited: self-executing acts and Case 26/62, *van Gend en Loos*; the strict scrutiny test and Joined Cases C-293/12 and C-594/12, *Digital Rights Ireland*; principle of equality and Case C-555/07, *Seda Kuöcuökdeveci.*
110. Rodin, *supra* n. 94, at p. 831.
111. *Ibid.*
112. *Ibid.*, at p. 832.
113. *Ibid.*
114. *Ibid.*
115. *Ibid.*

system within which European adjudication operates'.[116] The balancing can be difficult but the Court 'developed a response that resulted in the crystallization of autonomous concepts of EU law in a process which is cognitively open but normatively closed to national legal rules'.[117] Therefore, the normative value of external sources is non-existent and they are limited to being sources of inspiration and justification arguments that can support the chosen path.

Secondly, the functional comparative method is inadequate in the context of the CJEU because the Court is not concerned with identifying the functional equivalent of national norms, since the integrative functions of EU law take precedence. Therefore, the Court does not engage into the socio-legal function of the rule in its domestic framework because the integrative functions of EU law are the guiding factor and are different. The Court seeks:

> to identify the law of the member states that is relevant for a given area of regulation in the European Union, either because it interferes with it or because it fills a certain lacuna or because it justifies certain judicial choices. In any case, the point of this exercise is not to derive a norm from any comparative legal system, but to find an independent solution under EU law that can be justified by comparative references or, at least and where possible, a solution that does not manifestly encroach upon them.[118]
>
> This is a clear acknowledgement that the centre of gravity always remains with the CJEU and the Union's goals, with the external sources being utilized where that is useful and to the extent that it is beneficial. The autonomy of EU law has a crucial role in that process and Judge Rodin concludes that 'It is ontology, not teleology, that informs the interpretation of European legal rules. It does not happen as a matter of necessity but makes us aware of the choice between belief in European ontology and the redundancy of European adjudication.'[119]
>
> Surmising, the use of comparative law seems to be inevitable but always subservient to the Union's set of ontological considerations. Comparative law is a choice to be exercised in a constrained manner and when beneficial to the argumentation of the Court. It does not arise out of necessity or as part of the teleological interpretations but rather as selective application of judicial cognizance. This process is driven by the notion of autonomy of EU law and is clearly selective in nature. This is a very pragmatic approach that places comparative law at the service of the Court, and it is by implication subservient to the goals that the Court pursues. In that respect, the Court is not the promoter of the European values as Judge Kakouris has argued, but rather the promoter of the Union's goals as interpreted and developed by the Court.

4.3 More Transparency, More Comparative Law

Judge von Danwitz[120] has touched upon the use of comparative law by the CJEU in a paper about the rule of law jurisprudence of the Court.[121] The account analyses the

116. *Ibid.*, at p. 833.
117. *Ibid.*
118. *Ibid.*, at p. 834.
119. *Ibid.*, at p. 839.
120. T. von Danwitz, 'The Rule of Law in the Recent Jurisprudence of the ECJ' (2014) 37 *Fordham International Law Journal* 1311.
121. *Ibid.*, at pp. 1317-1321.

development of the general principles of law and of the rule of law in the jurisprudence of the CJEU and highlights the particular importance attributed to comparative law considerations.[122] Nonetheless, 'it appears regrettable from an outside perspective that the methodology which the Court applies is not made fully transparent'.[123] This is due to the fact that the case law makes rather short references to comparative law and those represent the tip of the iceberg of the overall consideration given to comparative law.[124] That is related to the discretion exercised by the CJEU when using comparative law and the intention to safeguard the autonomy of the general principles of law. Nonetheless:

> in order to protect the authority of the Court's judgments, it becomes more and more vital to base judicial decision-making on comparative insights. Since the enlargement of the European Union goes along with an increase of legal orders which have to be taken into consideration when it comes to the recognition of general principles of EU law, the importance of comparative analysis is equally enhanced and the discretion which the Court has to exercise in this respect certainly becomes more delicate.[125]

Moreover, Judge von Danwitz points to a series of developments that must be considered: (i) the changing trend to make increasing use of comparative law in domestic legal orders; (ii) the concept of 'multilevel cooperation of courts';[126] (iii) the rise of 'a growing judicial cosmopolitanism';[127] (iv) the equivalent protection for human rights in conjunction with the EU Charter.

Judge Von Danwitz concludes that the importance of comparative law will continue to increase and:

> will become more and more an indispensable condition for legal reasoning in the multi-layered system of judicial protection in Europe. Today, the authority of our judgments requires that they appear convincing to judges in all European Member States who are primarily rooted in a particular national legal tradition and not familiar with the case law of the Court. It is therefore a prerequisite for any further legal integration in Europe that the Court communicates on the basis of a legal reasoning which is, if not familiar, at least easily understandable to all its judicial counterparts.[128]

This account makes a call for a clearer and more transparent exegesis of the ways in which comparative law is used by the CJEU. There is clearly a much deeper and wider utilization of the comparative method by the Court that nevertheless remains part of the internal knowledge and at the possible detriment of the persuasiveness of the justifications put forward by the Court. It is in relation to the dismissal of the

---

122. *Ibid.*, at p. 1317.
123. *Ibid.*
124. Citing as examples: Case C-29/76, *LTU v. Eurocontrol* [1976] ECR 1541, §5; Joined Cases C-56-60/74, *Kampffmeyer* [1976] ECR712, §6; Joined Cases 46/87 and 227/88, *Hoechst v. Commission* [1989] ECR 2919, §17; Case C-224/01, *Gerhard Köbler* [2003] ECR I-10290, §48; Case C-36/02, *Omega* [2004] ECR I-9641, §§33, 35.
125. von Danwitz, *supra* n. 120, at p. 1318.
126. *Ibid.*
127. *Ibid.*
128. *Ibid.*, at p. 1346.

perception of randomness that the numerous accounts by Judge Lenaerts aim (next subsection).

4.4 The Account(s) of President Lenaerts

Judge Lenaerts, currently the President of the CJEU, has written extensively on the use of comparative law by the Court.[129] These accounts are valuable as they offer an insight into the approach of the Court, because they classify and explain the uses of comparative law by the CJEU and they are spread over a long period of time. Moreover, the line of argumentation is detailed and consistent, as well as theoretically oriented and spherical.

4.4.1 Balancing the Best Solution in the Circumstances with the Acceptability of Decisions

In a lengthy article published in 2003[130] Judge Lenaerts recognized the important role that comparative law plays in the case law of the CJEU as one of the methods of interpretation and in order to establish the rule of law in the Union's legal order as required under the then Article 220 EC. It was recognized that the use of comparative law by the Court is extensive and 'permeates the daily activities of the Court',[131] yet for the external observer this is unclear since the case law rarely contains express, explicit and extensive references to comparative law. In contrast, the early case law of the Court was more inclusive of the term comparative law than subsequent jurisprudence; one such notable example is the Algera judgment.[132]

Judge Lenaerts explains the internal set-up of the Court as conducive for comparative law (multilingualism, professional backgrounds, Advocates General, legal traditions) and highlights the existence of authorization in the Treaties for the use of comparative law (then Articles 220 and 288(2) EC, 6(2) and 46 TEU). The account then turns to the way the Court makes use of comparative law (its teleology):

> the comparative law method is driven by a single Leitmotiv, and that is to find through the examination of other legal orders the solution which best suits the objectives of the Community-namely European integration in a 'Community based on the rule of law'-as well as its structure, and which is acceptable for the different national legal orders responsible for implementing Community law.[133]

Therefore, the emphasis is on identifying the optimal solution that is the most appropriate in the present circumstances and which at the same time will attract the acceptability by the national legal orders; this is the delicate balance that the Court

129. *See supra* n. 78.
130. K. Lenaerts, 'Interlocking Legal Orders in the European Union and Comparative Law' (2003) 52(4) *International and Comparative Law Quarterly* 873.
131. *Ibid.*, at p. 876.
132. Joined Cases 7/56 and 3/57 to 7/57, *Algera and Others v. Common Assembly* [1957] ECR 39.
133. Lenaerts, *supra* n. 130, at p. 879.

'instinctively'[134] aims for. In this way, the objective is to preempt or contain resistance in order to protect the effectiveness and uniformity of Union law. Judge Lenaerts characteristically states the purpose of the Court:

> is not just to fill lacunae in the Community construction, but rather, after having carefully 'taken the pulse' of the national legal systems, to find the best solution in the 'middle-line' or compromise solution, which should enjoy credibility and acceptability in the Member States and which will ensure the effectiveness of Community law.[135]

The account proceeds to offer a typology of the situations in which the Court makes use of comparative law: (a) when a legal lacuna exists in a pending case; (b) when dealing with the interpretation of a concept of Union law; (c) when assessing the compatibility of a provision or 'solution' of national law with Union law. It is reasonable to argue that Judge Lenaerts is forthcoming both in relation to the strategic positioning of the Court vis-à-vis the use of comparative law and in relation to the way that it is applied in different instances. This contributes a welcomed element of transparency in the rationale of the Court, and it must be assessed against the legal certainty and predictability of the outcome. The account seems to be elevating the acceptability of a judgment as a defining factor in the thought process of the Court and that is something that later accounts by Judge Lenaerts have followed.

4.4.1.1 *When a Legal Lacuna Exists in a Pending Case*

After the identification of the legal lacuna in the Union order, the quest for the solution takes place through the comparative method. When a legal concept or rule is common to all the Member States, like in Case 25/70, Köster and Case T-192/99, Dunnett and Others,[136] the Court, according to Judge Lenaerts, 'may, without risking opposition in the national legal orders, promote it to a concept or rule of the Community legal order'.[137] It is important to note that the Court may, but is not obliged, to follow such an approach, while at the same time the actual formulation of the content of the rule could in fact evolve by the Court. It is also noted that the primary consideration is the opposition to the judgment, while the best solution in the circumstances is served by the filling-in of the gap.

Alternatively, when there is strong but not total convergence of national solutions, the CJEU is again in a position where the risk of reaction by national courts is very limited.[138] In such circumstances, the Court 'will not hesitate to give preference to the biggest common denominator of the traditions of the Member States, to the highest

134. *Ibid.*, at p. 883.
135. *Ibid.*, at p. 906.
136. Case 25/70, *Köster* [1970] ECR 1161; Case T-192/99, *Dunnett and Others v. EIB* [2001] ECR II-817.
137. Lenaerts, *supra* n. 130, at p. 884.
138. *Ibid.*, at p. 886.

standard of protection, or to the most performing law, in order to improve the level of judicial protection within the Community'.[139]

This is an important point in the account because the arithmetical approach is something that has been rejected by Judge Kakouris (*see supra*) who insists on the criterion of the best, most appropriate solution. Judge Lenaerts has incorporated that in the balancing exercise that guides the Court when using comparative law. However, the account has also left space for the arithmetical logic in limited circumstances and is always subject to the discretionary power of the Court to choose to do so; it is consequently an option and not an obligation.

Moreover, when there is a dominant idea in the national legal systems with certain divergences as to details, the Court, according to Judge Lenaerts:

> guided by such general legal tendency ... will mould, in the image of the attitude adopted by the national legal orders, a 'custom-made' Community solution taking into account the priorities of the Community legal order, the objectives of the Treaty and the particularities of the Community structures and of Community law.[140]

Such an example is provided by the case law on the non-contractual liability of the Union and the State liability of the Member States and the policy limitations on liability, as well as in relation to the expansion of the idea of public liability that existed in national systems and in Article 288 EC to the Member States.[141]

Furthermore, when the comparative method reveals deep contradictions between the national legal systems, the Court, according to Judge Lenaerts, 'will prefer not to impose a solution which would not meet sufficient support in some Member States to ensure a uniform and effective application of Community'.[142] Again, the criterion of national reaction is crucial and in Case C-249/96, Grant is offered as an example where cohabitation between persons of the same sex was not recognized as fully equivalent to cohabitation between heterosexuals in the (then) present state of the law within the Community and in most Member States.[143]

Finally, the Court may opt to adopt or 'import' a solution known to one Member State if that would best serve the interests of the Community legal order;[144] such notable examples are the principle of proportionality[145] and the protection of legitimate expectations[146] that were borrowed from the German legal order.

Overall, in the context of a legal lacuna, the use of comparative law by the Court points to available solutions that are balanced on the basis of the reaction they could

---

139. *Ibid.*, citing the example of Case 222/84, *Johnston* [1986] ECR 1651.
140. Lenaerts, *supra* n. 130, at p. 887 (emphasis added).
141. *Ibid.* citing the example of State liability: Joined Cases C-6/90 and C-9/90, *Francovich and Others* [1991] ECR I-5357; Joined Cases C-46/93 and C-48/93, *Brasserie du Pecheur and Factortame* [1996] ECR I-1029; Case C-5/94, *Hedley Lomas*. And the non-contractual liability of the Union: Case 5/71, *Zuckerfabrik Schoppenstedt* [1971] ECR; Case C352/98 P, *Bergaderm and Goupil v. Commission*.
142. Lenaerts, *supra* n. 130, at p. 894 citing the example of Case C-249/96, *Grant* [1998] ECR I-621.
143. Case C-249/96, *Grant* §§32, 35.
144. Lenaerts, *supra* n. 130, at p. 894.
145. Case 11/70, *Internationale Handelsgesellschaft* [1970] ECR 1125.
146. Joined Cases 205 to 215/82, *Deutsche Milchkontor* [1983] ECR 2633.

trigger and of the effectiveness of EU law. This is not a problematic area, according to Judge Lenaerts, with the Court prioritizing the acceptability of the available and chosen solution.

4.4.1.2 When Dealing with the Interpretation of a Concept of Union Law

The use of comparative law could also arise in the case of dealing with the interpretation of a concept of Union law; here the Court is less open to national solutions. The interpretation of EU law is intrinsically linked to the principle of autonomy and the Court will detach its approach from any alternatives offered by national legal orders or courts.[147] Insufficiently precise provisions of EU law could, by way of exception according to Judge Lenaerts, be construed with having in mind national legal systems and converging approaches (Case 155/79, *AM & S v. Commission* and the body common criteria in national systems for the protection of professional confidentiality).[148]

Judge Lenaerts makes an important point in relation to the interpretation of EU provisions and comparative law when stating that 'the Community courts can also find an excuse in the profound divergences among national interpretations of a given concept in order to establish an autonomous interpretation of Community law'.[149] Nonetheless, in such cases the element of acceptability of the approach of the Court is factored in, as was done in Case 59/85, Reed[150] which in effect reached a conclusion on the basis of the lack of European common ground. There and in the context of derivative rights for members of the family of a worker, the meaning of spouse[151] was construed by the Court as to include unmarried partners in a stable relationship. The Court took note of the fact that any interpretation would affect all Member States and stated that the interpretation must take into account the situation in the whole Community, not merely in one Member State.[152] The CJEU held that '[i]n the absence of any indication of a general social development which would justify a broad construction, and in the absence of any indication to the contrary in the regulation, it must be held that the term 'spouse' in Article 10 of the Regulation refers to a marital relationship only'.[153]

4.4.1.3 When Assessing the Compatibility of a Provision or 'Solution' of National Law with EU Law

According to Judge Lenaerts, in a situation where the Court assesses the compatibility of national law or approach with EU law, usually in the context of preliminary

147. Lenaerts, *supra* n. 130, at p. 894.
148. *See* Case 155/79, *AM & S v. Commission* [1982] ECR 157 §§21-22.
149. Lenaerts, *supra* n. 130, at p. 895 (emphasis added).
150. Case 59/85, *Reed* [1986] ECR 1283.
151. Article 10 of Council Regulation No 1612/68 of 15 October 1968 on freedom of movement for workers within the Community (OJ, Special Edition, 1968 (II), 475).
152. Case 59/85, *Reed* §13.
153. *Ibid.*, §15.

references or infringement actions, it will 'gauge the temperature' of the national legal orders in order to determine the acceptability of its decision.[154] In such type of case, the Court by making use of comparative law can reach a conclusion that the national and EU law are compatible. This is characterized as a 'reconciliation process'[155] by Judge Lenaerts and the example of Case C-126/97, Eco Swiss[156] is given. There, in a preliminary reference concerning the interpretation of the then Article 81 EC, the Court held that the three-month time limit prescribed in Dutch law for lodging an annulment action against an arbitral award was not excessively short compared with those prescribed in other Member States[157] and did not excessively restrict rights conferred under EC law. Judge Leanerts argues that the Court 'was anxious' not to impose a rule which would go against a general principle of law recognized in all the Member States (res judicata),[158] thus comparative law enabled the prevention of national reaction.

It is also possible that the Court could find the national and EU law as being incompatible and Judge Lenaerts once again offers an insight into the workings of the Court when explaining that even in such cases comparative law is internally taken into account. The example of Factortame[159] is provided and it is stated:

> even if this does not come to the surface in the judgment, the analysis of comparative law contained in the Opinion of Advocate-General G. Tesauro certainly assured the Court of Justice of the rightness of the solution to set aside the application of the contested British measure. It follows indeed from this analysis that there exists in all the legal systems of the Member States (the Danish system constitutes a partial exception), however diverse may be the forms and requirements connected with the duration of the proceedings, [. . .] provision for the interim protection of rights denied under a lower ranking provision but claimed on the basis of a provision of a higher order.[160]

In conclusion, Judge Lenaerts recognizes the importance of the use of comparative law for the Court, highlights the extent of that use and offers an exegesis of the mechanics of that application in a typology of cases. It is concluded that the comparative approach 'becomes an exercise in 'psycho-diplomacy' for the Community courts' and the bricks upon which an ius commune is built.[161]

4.4.2 Overarching Interpretative Principle, Comparative Law and European Federal Common Law

In 2007 Judge Lenaerts published an article[162] that revisited the use of comparative law by the Court in the context of comparing with the United States (US) Supreme Court.

154. Lenaerts, *supra* n. 130, at p. 898 (emphasis added).
155. *Ibid.*
156. Case C-126/97, *Eco Swiss* [1999] ECR I-3055.
157. *Ibid.*, §45.
158. Lenaerts, *supra* n. 130, at p. 899.
159. Case C-213/89, *Factortame and Others* [1990] ECR 1-2433.
160. Lenaerts, *supra* n. 130, at p. 901.
161. *Ibid.*, at p. 906.
162. K. Lenaerts, 'Interpretation and the Court of Justice: A Basis for Comparative Reflection' (2007) 41 *International Lawyer* 1011.

The account explains that interpretation is a core element of the judicial function and is connected to upholding the rule of law and ensuring the objectives of the legal order.[163] Interpretation also constitutes the means to achieve judgment[164] and is thus linked with the overarching interpretative principle[165] found in the then Article 220 EC which guides the CJEU, forms its mandate and radiates through all the methods of interpretation at the disposal of the Court.[166]

Therefore, Judge Lenaerts argues, there is an important distinction between the 'overarching interpretative principle guiding the approach of the CJEU and the various methods, techniques, and sources used pursuant thereto'.[167] This elevates the overarching interpretative principle above the tools used to serve it and the three primary methods of interpretation (literal, contextual and teleological). At the same time, the teleological method of interpretation 'commands a prominent place in the Court'[168] due to the programmatic and functional nature of the Treaties. In that context, comparative law performs an instrumental role and the sources of inspiration include national systems, the Convention and even third-country systems.

What is interesting is that Judge Lenaerts, building on earlier work,[169] defines 'European Federal Common Law' as 'Union and Community concepts, principles and rules of decision formulated by the Court of Justice that are not clearly suggested from the face of a provision of primary or secondary Community law'.[170] This involves gap-filling in a broad sense and includes all gaps perceived to preclude the attainment of the aims of the Union. It is also 'essentially submerged within the analysis of its methods of interpretation, particularly its teleological approach'.[171] Therefore, it can be argued that the use of comparative law is entangled with European Federal Common Law and is utilized to that effect, thus raising the question about transparency in the use of comparative law and the need for clearer justification of how and when it is used.

4.4.3 *Revisiting Interlocking Legal Orders*

In 2016 Judge Lenaerts and Kathleen Gutman published an important paper[172] on the use of comparative law by the CJEU that revisited earlier writings. The paper starts with the growing academic interest in the use of comparative law by the Court that cuts across numerous debates about constitutional and EU law (general principles, human

163. *Ibid.*
164. *Ibid.*, at p. 1013.
165. *Ibid.*, at p. 1015.
166. *Ibid.*, at p. 1016.
167. *Ibid.*, at p. 1015.
168. *Ibid.*, at p. 1017.
169. K. Lenaerts and K. Gutman, ''Federal Common Law' in the European Union: A Comparative Perspective from the United States' (2006) 54 *American Journal of Comparative Law* 1.
170. Lenaerts, *supra* n. 162, at p. 1029.
171. *Ibid.*
172. K. Lenaerts and K. Gutman, 'The Comparative Law Method and the Court of Justice of the European Union: Interlocking Legal Orders Revisited', in M. Andenas and D. Fairgrieve (eds), *Courts and Comparative Law* (Oxford: OUP, 2015), p. 141.

rights, constitutional pluralism, federal common law, etc.). The authors argue that the study of comparative law in the Court exceeds the theoretical or academic exercise and goes 'at the heart of the relationship between the Union and the national legal orders and the dialogue between the Union courts and the national courts in particular, as well as the Union's relations with the international community in general, which are essential to the functioning and evolution of the European project, now more than ever'.[173]

The comparative law method is used by the Court 'as an aid to interpretation, which is used alongside or in the service of the other such methods, such as consistent or teleological interpretation' and as a tool for European federal common law.[174] In this context, the authors place the use of comparative law as being underpinned by 'the overarching aim or approach ("teleology")'[175] that seeks to find the solution that 'best suits' the objectives of the Union and which is 'acceptable' for the national legal orders.[176]

It must be noted that Article 19(1) TEU is characterized as the overarching duty of the Court[177] that is different than the overarching approach for comparative law that is unfortunately labelled as teleology. This creates conceptual and terminological confusion, especially since in the earlier version of the account reference was made to that teleology for comparative law as being 'a single Leitmotiv'[178] that included the balance between the best solution and its acceptability. It needs therefore to be clarified that the reference to teleology is not referring to the teleological method of interpretation, nor does it necessarily coincide with the overarching duty of the Court to uphold the law which is a broader mission than the tools used to achieve it.

This functions as the link with the first account examined under this subsection,[179] which is now complemented in various ways due to developments in the case law and institutionally. For example, the approach is described as functional[180] and applied on a case-by-case basis, with detachment from the arithmetical criterion related to a common denominator or majority view in the national legal orders. The Court does however take into account national approaches and is cautious in the event of divergences, with the assessment of the results of comparative law vis-à-vis the overarching aim/teleology being open to different assessments within the Court. The authors give the example of Fabbrica italiana accumulatori motocarri Montecchio SpA (FIAMM)[181] that concerned the non-contractual liability of the Union in the absence of

173. *Ibid.*, at p. 143.
174. *Ibid.*, at p. 150.
175. *Ibid.*, at p. 152.
176. *Ibid.*
177. *Ibid.*, at p. 150.
178. K. Lenaerts, 'Interlocking Legal Orders in the European Union and Comparative Law' (2003) 52 *International and Comparative Law Quarterly* 873, at 879.
179. *Ibid.*
180. Contrast with the ontological approach by Judge Siniša Rodin, *supra* n. 94.
181. Joined Cases C-120/06 P and C-121/06 P, *FIAMM and Others v. Council and Commission* [2008] ECR I-6513.

unlawful acts or conduct. The General Court[182] had introduced no-fault liability under specific conditions and on appeal the CJEU held that the General Court erred in law,[183] because, *inter alia*, of the assessment of the principles in the Member States and of the union law as it stands:

> although the principles in the legal systems of the Member States governing the liability of public authorities for damage caused to individuals by legislative measures varied considerably, it was still possible to state that such authorities can only exceptionally and under special circumstances incur liability for such measures, which served as the basis for a strict approach taken to Union liability based on the fulfilment of certain requirements.[184]

Moreover, and in the same case, Advocate General Maduro took a different view and stated that the Court can take inspiration from certain elements of national law, even if those representing the minority view if the objectives of the Union are best served.[185] From this example, the authors point to the endorsement and application of the overarching aim/teleology approach, by the CJEU, the General Court and the Advocate General,[186] albeit with different results.[187] Nonetheless, it can be argued that

182. Case T-69/00, *FIAMM and FIAMM Technologies v Council and Commission* [2005] ECR II-5393 and in a series of other similar cases: Case T-383/00, *Beamglow v. European Parliament, Council and Commission* [2005] ECR II-5459; Case T-151/00, *Laboratoire du Bain v. Council and Commission* [2005] ECR II-23.
183. Joined Cases C-120/06 P and C-121/06 P, *FIAMM and Others v. Council and Commission* [2008] ECR I-6513.
184. Lenaerts and Gutman, *supra* n. 172, at p. 154, §§170-174 judgment in *FIAMM.*
185. Opinion of AG Poiares Maduro in Joined Cases C-120/06 P and C-121/06 P, *FIAMM and Others*, points 55-63. At §55: 'But should the second paragraph of Article 288 EC be read as authorising an approach regarding the public authorities' non-contractual liability to be incorporated into Community law only if it is shared by all of the Member States? Can the discovery of a 'general principle common to the laws of the Member States' stem only from the almost mechanistic superimposition of the law of each Member State and the retention of only the elements that match exactly? I do not think so. Such a mathematical logic of the lowest common denominator would lead to the establishment of a regime for Community liability in which the victims of damage attributable to the institutions would have only a very slim chance of obtaining compensation. Although the Court of Justice must certainly be guided by the most characteristic provisions of the systems of domestic law, it must above all ensure that it adopts a solution appropriate to the needs and specific features of the Community legal system. In other words, the Court has the task of drawing on the legal traditions of the Member States in order to find an answer to similar legal questions arising under Community law that both respects those traditions and is appropriate to the context of the Community legal order. From that point of view, even a solution adopted by a minority may be preferred if it best meets the requirements of the Community system. To be persuaded that this is so, one need only recall the example of the "*Vertrauensschutzprinzip*" which was enshrined in Community law even though it occurred only in German law. Hence, the fact that only Spanish and French law provide for the public authorities to incur liability by reason of a lawful legislative act cannot prevent such liability being recognised in Community law.'
186. *Ibid.*, §56 of Opinion: 'The decisive question is whether such a solution would best meet the specific needs of the Community legal system. That does not mean that the principle of public authorities' liability for a lawful legislative act should be enshrined in the Community legal order inasmuch as it would appear to be the best legal solution, and as such must be adopted in the Community legal order. Its enshrinement in Community law can only be the result of a comparison of the mechanisms adopted in this respect by the different national legal systems in order to identify the solution best suited to the particular requirements of the Community legal order.'

the reaching of different outcomes through the use of the comparative method under the overarching aim/teleology approach, leads to uncertainty and points to the elasticity and the discretion in the assessment of the use of comparative law. That is, however, not an arbitrary thinking process due to the description of the outcome of the national laws after the comparative study, yet such references were not detailed and followed an approach of announcing the outcome rather than the facts and the process of assessing them. It is in this respect that transparency in justification could be enhanced.

The authors also revisit the typology of the situations in which the Court makes use of comparative law: (a) when a legal lacuna exists in a pending case; (b) when dealing with the interpretation of a concept of Union law; (c) when assessing the compatibility of a provision or 'solution' of national law with Union law. Recent developments in the fields of discrimination on grounds of age are then examined and according to the authors point to the Mangold case[188] as application of the overarching aim/teleology.[189]

Respectfully, this exactly highlights the problems associated with the lack of transparency in the use of comparative law by the Court. It is reminded that in Mangold the Court ruled that 'Directive 2000/78 does not itself lay down the principle of equal treatment in the field of employment and occupation. Indeed, ... the source of the actual principle underlying the prohibition of those forms of discrimination being found, as is clear from the third and fourth recitals in the preamble to the directive, in various international instruments and in the constitutional traditions common to the Member States.'[190] Instead, 'the principle of non-discrimination on grounds of age must thus be regarded as a general principle of Community law'.[191] Subsequently, the ruling came under heavy criticism both from the academia[192] and Advocates General of the Court,[193] with one of the arguments against it being the inaccuracy of the claim that age discrimination is being found in various international instruments and in the constitutional traditions common to the Member States.[194]Advocate General Tizzano in his Opinion in Mangold did not engage in a visible comparative analysis, neither has the Court in its judgment. Therefore, the question of accuracy or inflation of the

187. Lenaerts and Gutman, *supra* n. 172, at p. 155.
188. Case C-144/04 *Mangold* [2005] ECR I-9981.
189. Lenaerts and Gutman, *supra* n. 172, at pp. 160-163.
190. *Mangold* §74.
191. *Ibid.*, §75.
192. *See supra* n. 14.
193. *See*: Opinion of Advocate General Geelhoed in Case C-13/05, *Chacón Navas* [2006] ECR I-6467, points 46 to 56; Opinion of Advocate General Sharpston in Case C-227/04 P, *Lindorfer* [2007] ECR I-6767, points 52 to 58; Opinion of Advocate General Advocate General Mazák in Case C-411/05, *Palacios de la Villa*, points 87 to 97 and points 132 to 138; Opinion of Advocate General Sharpston, Case C-427/06, *Birgit Bartsch* [2008]; Opinion of Advocate General Ruiz-Jarabo Colomer in Case C-267/06, *Maruko*, point 78.
194. Only in Finland (Article 6(2) Finnish Constitution) and Portugal (art. 59(1) Portuguese Constitution) was discrimination on grounds of age expressly prohibited. Neither the International Covenant on Civil and Political Rights (ICCPR), the European Convention on Human Rights (ECHR), nor the European Social Charter contains an express prohibition of discrimination on grounds of age.

justification arises, but the authors respond that the embodiment in Article 21(1) of the EU Charter suffices:

> the Mangold case law evidences the Court's overarching approach of finding a solution that upholds the needs and fundamental objectives of the Union legal order and that accords with the general trend underpinning the constitutional values and traditions of the Member States taken as a whole, here embodied in the Charter, in the process of formulating general principles of EU law on the basis of the comparative law method, even if at the time it was decided such a principle could be found in the laws of only a small number of Member States.[195]

As a corollary, the lack of transparency is magnified in this example and at the detriment of the acceptability of the judgment element of the overarching approach. The authors proceed to discuss the judgment in Akzo Nobel Chemicals[196] as an explanation of the approach in Mangold. In specific, the issue of professional privilege as defined in Case 155/79 AM & S Europe was revisited on the basis of the claim of the appellants that the legal landscape has changed to cover in-house legal advisers and their clients. The General Court had held[197] that no predominant trend could be detected: 'specific recognition of the role of in-house lawyers and the protection of communications with such lawyers ... is relatively more common today than when the judgment in AM & S was handed down, it is not possible, nevertheless, to identify tendencies which are uniform or have clear majority support in that regard in the laws of the Member States'.[198]

Moreover, the General Court proceeded to state that:

> a comparative examination of laws shows that a large number of Member States still exclude in-house lawyers from protection under LPP. In addition, in certain Member States, the issue seems not to have been decided unequivocally or definitively. Furthermore, various Member States have aligned their regimes with the Community system, following upon the judgment in AM & S. Secondly, such an examination shows that a considerable number of Member States do not allow in-house lawyers to be admitted to the Bar or Law Society and, accordingly, do not recognize them as lawyers established in private practice. In fact, in a number of countries, to be a lawyer employed by a person who is not a lawyer in private practice is incompatible with the status of 'avocat'. Moreover, even in countries which do permit this possibility, the fact that in-house lawyers are admitted to a Bar or Law Society and are subject to professional ethical rules does not always mean that communications with such persons are protected under LPP.[199]

Therefore, the General Court went into detail to describe the findings of its comparative analysis and on appeal the CJEU, as well as Advocate General Kokott, agreed. The authors rely on the Opinion by Advocate General Kokott as illustrative of the explanation to Mangold, in the sense that in points 94-96 of the Opinion reference

195. Lenaerts and Gutman, *supra* n. 172, at pp. 162-163.
196. Case C-550/07 P, *Akzo Nobel Chemicals and Akcros Chemicals v. Commission* [2010] ECR I-8301.
197. Joined Cases T-125/03 and T-253/03, *Akzo Nobel*, paras 170-172, 176.
198. *Ibid.*, §170.
199. *Ibid.*, §171.

is being made to the method used by the Court in developing general principles. Specifically, it was stated that recourse to common constitutional traditions or legal principles is not necessarily subject to the precondition that the practice in question should constitute a tendency which is uniform or has clear majority support. It depends rather on an evaluative comparison of the legal systems which must take due account, in particular, not only of the aims and tasks of the EU but also of the special nature of European integration and of EU law.[200] Accordingly, it is by no means inconceivable that even a legal principle which is recognized or even firmly established in only a minority of national legal systems will be identified by the Courts of the EU as forming part of EU law. This is the case in particular where, in view of the special characteristics of EU law, the aims and tasks of the Union and the activities of its institutions, such a legal principle is of particular significance, or where it constitutes a growing trend.[201]

In relation to Mangold, it was stated that the Court held:

> the prohibition of discrimination on grounds of age to be a general principle of EU law, even though, at that time, that prohibition did not appear to constitute a tendency which was uniform or had clear majority support in the national legal systems or even in the constitutional law of the Member States. However, that principle was consistent with a specific task incumbent on the European Union in combating discrimination (Article 19 TFEU, formerly Article 13 EC) and had also been given specific expression by the Union legislature in the form of a directive; moreover, it mirrored a more recent trend in the protection of fundamental rights at Union level, to which the European Parliament, the Council and the Commission had jointly given expression on the occasion of the solemn proclamation of the Charter of Fundamental Rights (*see*, in particular, Article 21 thereof).[202]

Nonetheless, this line of reasoning is unconvincing. The Court was in effect ahead of its time in opting to introduce a new general principle that promoted the overall aims of the Union regardless of the lack of European common ground on the matter. This constitutes an after-the-fact justification that could have perhaps stood if it was advanced in the same detail at the time of the judgment. This relates to the transparency and the completeness of justification, while at the same time the approach does not sit well with the 'acceptability' of the judgment at the time of its formulation. Theoretically, the overarching approach could cover such cases provided that the transparency and justification are such as to neutralize the acceptability problem. Finally, the reasoning (General Court, Court of Justice of the European Union, Opinion) in Akzo Nobel Chemicals actually points to the preferable direction of the approach that is founded on transparency and persuasive justification. Put differently, the more there is lack of support from comparative law, the more is expected in terms of the explanation of the overarching principle.

In conclusion, the authors see the overarching approach as the exegetical device for the use of comparative law and it involves 'a subtle, and increasingly delicate, balancing exercise between upholding the fundamental interests and objectives of the

200. Opinion in *Akzo Nobel*, point 94.
201. *Ibid.*, point 95.
202. *Ibid.*, point 96.

Union legal order and respecting as much as possible the rules, principles, and traditions of the Member States.'[203] The approach 'is both a functional and fluid one, not only depending on the weighing of these two components, but also taking account of social and legal developments occurring at the national and Union levels'.[204] Nonetheless, the crucial point arising from the assessment of the account is the need for clearer, more transparent justification as to the manner in which comparative law is used. This will remove the impression of randomness and selectivity and will project the analytical detail of extrajudicial writings in the justification of the jurisprudence. The process need not be secretive, mystic and internal, but open and a celebration of the use of comparative law.

5 CONCLUSION

The CJEU's use of comparative law has a long history and a bright future. There must first be a distinction between implicit and express use of comparative law by the Court. The latter is evident in the case law in certain examples, but the implicit use seems to be much broader due to the mechanics of operation of the CJEU. The internal setup of the CJEU (no dissenting opinions, the multilingualism and cosmopolitanism of its composition, the role of the Advocate Generals) has created a fertile ground for comparative law and that is manifested either in a clear manner or primarily in a hidden way. This has also contributed to the creation of the rather unusual situation where judges of the CJEU have written extensively on the use of comparative law, thus offering a rare insight into the internal point of view, that is from the perspective of the Court itself. Therefore, numerous positions adopted extrajudicially by judges of the CJEU are revealing of the way comparative law is perceived and used. It appears that the Court applies 'a pick-and-choose' approach from an array of possible legal options forming a depository of available approaches and solutions. The Court does not necessarily apply the common denominator or even the majority view as that emerges from the other legal orders. Therein exists the element of selectivity that is prone to unpredictability and subjectivism; the role of the judge is not limited to being the bouche de la loi[205] and consequently the issue of non-transparency arises. Comparative law is therefore both a tool and a method of interpretation for the CJEU and it is intrinsically linked with the need to persuade specific constituencies, primarily national courts, about the reasoning deployed. This is a pragmatic consideration for the CJEU that must balance between the obligation arising from Article 19(1) TEU ('shall ensure that in the interpretation and application of the Treaties the law is observed') and certain predominant considerations like the advancement of the EU project, the acceptability of the solutions endorsed and the autonomy of the legal order of the Union. Autonomy is fundamental for the adoption, definition and modification of legal principles and approaches because it enables the Court to establish its understanding and to formulate the EU's substantive content of legal rules. It is exactly this

203. Lenaerts and Gutman, *supra* n. 172, at p. 176.
204. *Ibid.*
205. *See* discussion in constitutional relevance p. 818.

combination of factors that points to the direction of the cognizance of comparative law on the basis of the 'pick-and-choose' approach.

Nevertheless, it is argued that the Court's approach is not as random or arbitrary as it appears; it is, instead, a pseudorandom approach: it appears to be random while being produced by a deterministic process. The process of de-randomization has been explained extrajudicially by members of the Court, yet the overall lack of transparency in the thinking process creates the impression of the 'pick-and-choose' use of comparative law. As a result, more transparency is needed in order to remove the impression of selectivity and randomness and in order to enhance the persuasiveness of the reasoning and the solidity of the conclusions reached. Explaining in more detail and comprehensively the supporting use of comparative law in a specific case, and not just in extrajudicial writings, will minimize the reaching of questionable conclusions. In effect, the call is for a more open use of comparative law that would shed light on why and how the Court uses comparative law in each case.

CHAPTER 14

The Right to Judicial Protection and Administration on the EU Periphery: The Fading Mirage of European Legal Convergence

Marton Varju[*]

1 INTRODUCTION

From the lawyers' perspective, the integration into Europe of post-socialist Central and Eastern European countries, including Hungary, promised a real possibility of convergence of European legal systems, possibly towards common, higher standards, in particular in the legal protection of individuals. This promise was based on the availability of cross-national legal frameworks, such as the European Convention on Human Rights (ECHR) and its law, as well as European Union (EU) law, which were assumed to have a genuine capacity to infiltrate and fertilise national legal systems with their requirements. Until the mid-2000s, legal convergence was fuelled directly by the political and policy conditionality of the decade-long accession process to the EU. After acceding to the EU, the normative character of EU obligations, as set out in the EU Treaties, EU legislation, individual EU administrative decisions, and the judgments of the EU Court of Justice, was supposed to enable and guarantee the proliferation of common legal standards and requirements among the different national laws. These developments seemed organically intertwined with the process of the liberal

* I first met Patrick at the job interview in 2005 which secured me a teaching assistantship at the University of Hull, Law School. Patrick was a rigorous supervisor of my PhD research, who was also very supportive, and who was also ready to overlook the academic trespasses of a young researcher. Working with him on my research, and teaching with him several different modules on United Kingdom and European public law were the most transformative experiences of my professional life.

transformation of law and government in these countries started in the 1990s, which was expected to put the rule of law and its different concrete manifestations at the heart of both the public and the private domain. In particular, judicial review and the protection of the individual before the law against the state were introduced in the law as essential components within these parallel processes for integrating with Western Europe and its values. The right to a fair trial and an effective legal remedy under Articles 6 and 13 ECHR and the EU's parallel right to effective judicial protection were available to play a decisive role in the latter development.

However, in the case of Hungary, with the rise of a now deeply entrenched novel political paradigm, legal convergence with Western Europe seems to have lost its attraction as well as its practical feasibility, in particular in the domain of judicial review and the judicial protection of the individual against the state and its administration. Grown out of the particular political, social and geo-economic conditions of a state on Europe's Eastern periphery, this paradigm prioritises executive discretion and administrative responsiveness, and a political instead of a policy or an administrative-managerial logic, among others in steering and administering the national economy, over the particular rights and the legally protected interests of individuals or certain social groups, and their effective legal protection. In legal-constitutional terms, the new paradigm favours what could be labelled as illiberal constructions and solutions, which are characterised in particular by the rolling back of the rule of law as a constraint on public powers. In contemporary Hungary, in strategically significant or politically sensitive areas judicial review against administrative decisions has deliberately been excluded in law, which evidently restricted the possibilities of individuals to seek judicial protection. Furthermore, public authorities have developed practices in policing certain administrative infringements or deciding certain types of administrative cases which directly undermined the rights of the individuals affected as well as their legal protection. This chapter will first explore the European requirements which are supposed to influence judicial review and legal protection against the state and its administration in national law. Then, it will provide an overview of the earlier mentioned rolling back of judicial protection in Hungary under the new political regime established after 2010. The chapter will be closed with an analysis of the European and domestic jurisprudence in which the latter developments were exposed to the relevant European requirements.

2 EUROPEAN REQUIREMENTS, THE RIGHT TO A FAIR TRIAL AND THE RIGHT TO JUDICIAL PROTECTION

Article 6 ECHR provides the right to a fair trial, which includes the right and access to a court, certain requirements imposed on courts as institutions, and certain requirements imposed on the procedure before courts. The right of access to a court, which is a principle inherent in the rule of law, includes the right to have any claim brought before a court or tribunal, and the right of litigants to have an effective judicial remedy enabling them to assert their rights.[1] In order for the right of access to a court to be

1. *Běleš and Others v. the Czech Republic*, § 49; *Golder v. the United Kingdom*, § 36.

effective, the opportunity to challenge 'an act that is an interference with his rights' must be 'clear, practical',[2] in particular the applicable procedural rules or their application must not prevent litigants from using an available remedy.[3] The right to a court also includes the right to obtain a determination of the dispute by a court, preventing a denial of justice from the individual.[4] The earlier mentioned institutional requirements inherent in Article 6 ECHR include the rule that the court in question must have full jurisdiction, which demands that its review is effective and it is able to exercise every element of its judicial function.[5] Fundamentally, the court must have jurisdiction to examine all questions of fact and law relevant to the dispute before it.[6] For example, it must be able to rule independently on issues of fact which are crucial to the settlement of the dispute before it,[7] and it must have jurisdiction to determine the central issue of the dispute.[8] The prompt implementation of a final and binding judicial decision also forms part of the right to a court.[9] In judicial review proceedings, the latter entails not only the annulment of the challenged administrative decision, but also the removal of its effects by the public authority in order to protect the individual effectively and to restore legality.[10]

As further institutional requirements, the court must be established by law, and it must be independent and impartial. The latter principle imposes a holistic obligation on the state and state bodies to respect and abide by the judgments and decisions of the courts, even if they do not agree with them.[11] The central requirement concerning judicial procedures is fairness, which is a fundamental principle of any democratic society, and which applies to procedures in their entirety requiring above all that the interests of the parties and those of the proper administration of justice are secured.[12] The principle of a fair trial denotes primarily the right of the parties to be heard in the procedure, as well as the proper participation of the parties in the procedure.[13] It incorporates the right to adversarial proceedings[14] and the principle of 'equality of arms', the idea of a 'fair balance' between the parties in the procedure.[15] The right to adversarial proceedings means the opportunity for the parties to have knowledge of and to comment on all evidence adduced or observations filed with a view to influencing the court's decision.[16] The equality of arms demands that each party must be afforded a reasonable opportunity to present his case – including his evidence –

2. *Bellet v. France*, § 36.
3. *Zvolský and Zvolská v. the Czech Republic*, § 51.
4. *Beneficio Cappella Paolini v. San Marino*, § 29.
5. *Beaumartin v. France*, § 38; *Obermeier v. Austria*, § 70; *Chevrol v. France*, § 63.
6. *Terra Woningen B.V. v. the Netherlands*, § 52.
7. *Ibid.*, §§ 53-55.
8. *Tsfayo v. the United Kingdom*, § 48.
9. *Hornsby v. Greece*, § 40.
10. *Ibid.*, § 41.
11. *Agrokompleks v. Ukraine*, § 136.
12. *Pretto and Others v. Italy*, § 21; *Stran Greek Refineries and Stratis Andreadis v. Greece*, § 49; *Nideröst-Huber v. Switzerland*, § 30.
13. *Kraska v. Switzerland*, § 30; *Kerojärvi v. Finland*, § 42.
14. *Werner v. Austria*, § 66.
15. *Feldbrugge v. the Netherlands*, § 44.
16. *Ruiz-Mateos v. Spain*, § 63.

under conditions that do not place him at a substantial disadvantage vis-à-vis the other party.[17] As further procedural requirements, litigants have a right to a public hearing and the right for cases to be heard within a 'reasonable time'. As an additional requirement, which may be absorbed by the rights provided by Article 6 ECHR, Article 13 ECHR demands that there are effective remedies before national authorities, including courts, for the violation of ECHR rights and freedoms. It may be essential that the remedy is of judicial nature,[18] but the availability of judicial redress is not an absolute requirement. The remedy must be effective in the sense that it must be capable of directly remedying the impugned situation.[19] In case of judicial remedies, the scope of scrutiny and review by the national court must be sufficient to guarantee protection.[20]

The right to effective judicial protection is a traditional general principle of EU law[21] which has played an instrumental role in the EU's decentralised system for the enforcement of the legal obligations undertaken by the Member States.[22] It forms part of the EU Charter of Fundamental Rights (EUCFR), which in Article 47 provides the right to an effective remedy and to a fair trial. According to the text of Article 47, the right to an effective remedy covers the right to remedy before an independent and impartial court of law (tribunal) for the violation of the rights and freedoms guaranteed by EU law, in a procedure which is fair and where the rights of the defence are respected. Crucially, the right to effective judicial protection has served as a legal instrument to ensure the implementation of Member State obligations in the deep layer of national institutional frameworks, in particular before the national judiciary, and through the judiciary in the national administration. As interpreted by the EU Court of Justice, the right and the principle of effective judicial protection in EU law stands in particular for the 'effective judicial review designed to ensure compliance with EU law' in the Member States before national courts, which 'is of the essence of the rule of law'.[23] It entails the obligation of every Member State to ensure that national courts in the fields covered by EU law 'meet the requirements of effective judicial protection'.[24] In the formulation of Article 19(1) of the Treaty on European Union (TEU), the Member States are specifically obliged to 'provide remedies sufficient to ensure effective legal protection in the fields covered by Union law'.

The right to effective judicial protection includes in particular the right of access to a court.[25] In the context of the effective application of EU law at the national level, which falls predominantly in the domain of domestic administrative law, this entitlement refers most commonly to the right of individuals to challenge administrative

17. *Dombo Beheer B.V. v. the Netherlands*, § 33.
18. *Ramirez Sanchez v. France* [GC], §§ 165-166.
19. *Pine Valley Developments Ltd and Others v. Ireland*, Commission decision, 1989.
20. *Hatton and Others v. the United Kingdom* [GC], 2003, §§ 141-142.
21. Case 222/84 *Johnston* [EU:C:1986:206], para. 53; Case 222/86 *Heylens* [EU:C:1987:442], paras 14 and 15.
22. *Inter alia* M. Dougan, *National Remedies Before the Court of Justice* (Oxford, Hart 2004).
23. Case C-64/16 *Associação Sindical dos Juízes Portugueses* [EU:C:2018:117], para. 36.
24. *Ibid.*, para. 37.
25. Case C-562/13 *Abdida* [EU:C:2014:2453], para. 45.

decisions in judicial review.[26] As it also follows from Article 47 EUCFR, the entitlements covered by the right to a fair trial are also included in the right to effective judicial protection; namely the impartiality and independence of tribunals, a fair and public judicial process, the procedure being closed within a reasonable time, the right to be defended and advised, the conditional right to legal aid, as well as the equality of arms and the rights of the parties to access and comment on the case file and the submissions of the other party. The right of the individual concerned to turn to a tribunal with its case is an essential component of the right to effective judicial protection, and in domains covered by EU law it follows from EU law itself obliging national courts to establish their jurisdiction in the case and to examine that case despite the contrary provisions of national law, or of the silence of national law on the matter.[27] The right of access to a court cannot be made dependent on requiring the individual to pursue a particular conduct, such as a prior violation of a legal rule or of its legal obligations,[28] or to exercise the right which the individual is aiming to contest in the court proceedings.[29] Procedural deadlines regulated in national law as a specific condition of launching judicial proceedings have been assessed under the principles of effectiveness and equivalence, which are principles specific to EU law's engagement with national procedural rules and remedies, and which are applied instead of the right to effective judicial protection but to a similar practical effect.[30]

The right of access to a court under EU law does not entail an absolute entitlement to vindicate rights derived from EU law in a distinct judicial avenue.[31] In particular, the Member States are not required to establish separate judicial avenues and remedies in their national laws for the assessment of the specific question of whether national regulation is compatible with EU law, provided that other national procedures and remedies enable – possibly as an additional component – the effective examination of that issue.[32] In *Unibet*, the Court of Justice confirmed that this requirement may be satisfied – in the absence of a specific procedure for contesting the compatibility of a national rule with a higher-ranking provision of law – by a claim submitted to a tribunal for damages in tort, or when in an administrative or criminal procedure initiated against the individual the tribunal seized in the case can examine the compliance with EU legal requirements of the applicable national rule.[33] In this context, the preference of the individual to pursue certain procedural avenues and remedies, when an alternative, effective judicial procedure is available, may be

26. Case C-682/15 *Berlioz Investment Fund* [EU:C:2017:373], para. 55.
27. Joined Cases C-924/19 PPU and C-925/19 PPU *Országos Idegenrendészeti Főigazgatóság Dél-alföldi Regionális Igazgatóság* [EU:C:2020:367], para. 140.
28. Case C-432/05 *Unibet* [EU:C:2007:163], para. 64; Joined Cases C-245/19 and C-246/19 *The State of Luxembourg* [EU:C:2020:795], paras 67–69.
29. Case C-214/16 *King* [EU:C:2017:914], paras 37, 41 and 47.
30. *Inter alia*, Joined Cases C-698/18 and C-699/18 *Raiffeisen Bank and BRD Groupe Société Générale* [EU:C:2020:537]; Case C-38/16 *Compass Contract Services* [EU:C:2017:454]; Case C-327/15 *TDC* [EU:C:2016:974]; Case C-8/14 *BBVA* [EU:C:2015:731].
31. *See* Case C-432/05 *Unibet* [EU:C:2007:163].
32. *Ibid.*, paras 37–44.
33. *Ibid.*, paras 56–65.

irrelevant.[34] However, when the alternative judicial avenue is materially unsuitable for addressing the claim pursued by the individual, for example the review by the tribunal seized is restricted in regulation to certain issues, and is thus unable to cover the claim, the failure to provide a direct avenue for judicial redress will constitute a violation of the right of access to a court.[35]

The right of access to a court includes - apart from the right to launch legal proceedings before a tribunal - the guarantee that the court seized has jurisdiction to examine every question of fact and law that are relevant to the case.[36] As well-known, in *Johnston* the Court of Justice made it clear that the right to effective judicial protection in EU law demands that the national court examines - without being restricted by a provision of national law - the violation of the individual's right brought before it in the case.[37] In a similar vein, national legal provisions which restrict the review exercisable by the national court and thus exclude matters relevant in the legal dispute from judicial scrutiny are contrary to the right to effective judicial protection.[38] In addition, the right of access to a court requires that the individual is provided with all relevant information, in particular a detailed statement of reasons by the public authority, which are necessary for launching judicial proceedings, and for the national court seized in the case to examine and review the claimed violation of the law and/or the rights of the individual.[39] In case this information is protected by overriding reasons in the general interest, such as national security considerations, access to it can be restricted; however, the individual must still be provided sufficient information so as to enable a decision whether to initiate judicial proceedings, and subsequently to enable the court seized in the case to exercise its jurisdiction.[40] Fundamentally, national courts - either by virtue of national legislation or by way of exercising their jurisdiction - must have the necessary competences and must be enabled in the circumstances of the given case to provide the judicial protection required by EU law.[41]

3 ILLIBERALISM ON THE EU PERIPHERY AND THE ROLLING BACK OF JUDICIAL PROTECTION IN HUNGARY

After a 20-year period following 1989, which can arguably be characterised as a period of transition hallmarked by democratisation, the anchoring of the rule of law, and by establishing a liberal foundation for public and private life, the triumphant emergence of a novel political paradigm has pushed Hungary, as a state on Europe's periphery in geographical, political, social and economic terms, towards a different direction. The

34. Case C-223/19 *YS* [EU:C:2020:753], para. 95.
35. Case C-379/18 *Deutsche Lufthansa* [EU:C:2019:1000], paras 65-71.
36. *Inter alia*, Case C-433/18 *Aktiva Finants* [EU:C:2019:1074], para. 36.
37. Case 222/84 *Johnston* [EU:C:1986:206], paras 19 and 20.
38. Case C-414/16. *Egenberger* [EU:C:2018:257], para. 59; Case C-396/17 *Leitner* [EU:C:2019:375], paras 62-66.
39. Case C-682/15 *Berlioz Investment Fund* [EU:C:2017:373], paras 82-84 and 89.
40. Case C-300/11 *ZZ* [EU:C:2013:363], paras 58-59.
41. Joined Cases C-924/19 PPU and C-925/19 PPU *Országos Idegenrendészeti Főigazgatóság Dél-alföldi Regionális Igazgatóság* [EU:C:2020:367], para. 39.

political and socio-economic system that was established gradually after the 2010 elections has been characterised as a 'plebiscitary leader democracy', which denotes a centralised, highly hierarchical system of government based on the practically unlimited political mandate of the political leader, the prime minister.[42] Policy-making and governance are extensively centralised, and are characterised by a radical concentration of discretionary decision-making powers at the highest level in government, which are not subject to a system of internal and external checks and balances.[43] The system rejects the plurality of viewpoints, interests and needs, which in liberal regimes would be safeguarded by the legal rights of the individual and would be underpinned by extensive possibilities of legal protection, in particular by courts, and ignores possibilities for consensus-building and deliberation.[44] The state and its administration, which prioritise executive discretion and responsiveness in steering and administering among others the national economy,[45] are a predominantly political operation following a logic of political voluntarism, instead of a policy or an administrative-managerial logic.[46]

With the particular rights and the legally protected interests of individuals having been deprioritised in the regime in post-2010 Hungary, unless government politics endorses them for its particular purposes, opportunities for their legal protection and for the parallel restraining of public powers, as required by the rule of law, have also been consciously rolled back, in particular when dictated by the strategic significance or the political sensitivity of the administrative area. This could take place by national legislation explicitly excluding judicial review against certain administrative decisions, or by way of adopting legislation which removes certain decisions from the domain of administrative decision-making and makes them a matter for legislation as adopted in the discretion of the government or the responsible minister. In the latter case, the individual decision, which is formally no longer an administrative decision, but a legislative measure, may only be challenged before the Constitutional Court on constitutional grounds, and not in regular judicial review. As an example, when the new Hungarian Energy and Public Utilities Regulatory Authority was established, the relevant Act XXII of 2013 explicitly excluded judicial review against the regulations of the authority, which could address issues affecting individual market participants, such as the amendment of the network code concerning long-term capacity allocation, or the determination of a network access tariff. There is also the Act LIII of 2006 which authorises the government to declare – in order to decrease their regulatory and administrative burden – certain investment projects as having special economic importance, which decision is not open to being challenged in judicial review.

42. A. Körösényi *et al.*, *The Orbán Regime: Plebiscitary Leader Democracy in the Making* (Abingdon, Routledge 2020).
43. Gy. Hajnal, Illiberalism in the Making: Orbán-Era Governance Reforms in the View of the Administrative Elite, in: P. Kovač & Gy. Gajduschek (eds.), *Contemporary Governance Models and Practices in Central and Eastern Europe* (Bratislava, NISPAcee 2015), pp. 133–156, at 139.
44. A. Körösényi, *The Orbán Regime.*
45. In governance, effectiveness and efficiency have become the dominant – possibly exclusive – priorities, Gy. Hajnal, Illiberalism in the Making, at 140.
46. A. Körösényi, 'The Theory and Practice of Plebiscitary Leadership: Weber and the Orbán Regime', 2019 33(2) *East European Politics and Societies*, 280–301, at 299.

The Act on Competition (Act LVII of 1996) was amended to include an explicit restriction on the availability of judicial review in competition matters. Its Section 24/A provides that the government can declare in a regulation that the merger of certain undertakings is of strategic importance for the national economy and is thus exempt from the usual administrative authorisation of the Competition Authority, which is normally provided in an administrative decision amenable to judicial review. Under Section 65 of another act, Act XLIX of 1991, the government can declare in regulation that specific undertakings are of strategic importance for the national economy and are thus exempt from the normally applicable rules on corporate insolvency procedures. Their winding up is controlled specifically by the state-owned National Reorganisation Non-profit Ltd. In connection with Hungary's controversial application of the safe third-country principle and the resulting restrictive asylum practice of Hungarian authorities, which meant that third-country nationals were effectively detained in the so-called Röszke transit zone set up between the Hungarian and Serbian borders, the applicable Hungarian rules also delimited the judicial protection available by allowing the third-country nationals to challenge the return decision only by means of a procedure before an administrative authority the decisions of which were not amenable to judicial review. In the area of asylum law, where the Hungarian state has been following a policy and practice that fundamentally contradict those promoted and pursued within the EU framework,[47] the legal protection of individuals also faced a challenge from national authorities repeatedly refusing to follow and implement the judgment of the court acting in judicial review of their asylum decisions. This conduct of the Hungarian authorities was helped by the regulation of judicial review in asylum cases, which was modified as a manifestation of the earlier mentioned restrictive policy direction, and which excluded that the review court – beyond examining its lawfulness – modifies the asylum decision, and thus brings it in line with the applicable legal rules.

4 THE ENFORCING OF EUROPEAN REQUIREMENTS

The previously mentioned restricted possibilities of judicial redress against the Hungarian Energy and Public Utilities Regulatory Authority's powers of regulation were challenged by the Commission in an infringement procedure. When the case reached the judicial phase, the Court of Justice established that determining of network access tariffs in a regulation, and not in an administrative decision, which as a genuine form of legislation adopted in delegated powers could only be challenged before the Constitutional Court on constitutional grounds in a constitutional complaint procedure, and not in judicial review before administrative courts on account of their alleged illegality, contravened EU energy market legislation interpreted together with the right to effective judicial protection as guaranteed by Article 47 EUCFR.[48] It ruled that EU law requires that Hungary ensures the effective review of decisions taken by the regulatory authority, which needs to cover (beyond constitutional questions) every relevant

47. *See, inter alia* B. Nagy, 'Hungarian Asylum Law and Policy in 2015–2016: Securitization Instead of Loyal Cooperation', 2016 17 *German Law Journal* 1033–1089.
48. Case C-771/18 *Commission v. Hungary*[EU:C:2020:584], paras 64–65.

question of fact and of law.[49] In reaction to the judgment, the original legislative provision was modified in Act CXIII of 2020, which now provides that network access tariffs are determined in a decision (and not a regulation) of the regulatory authority amenable to judicial review.

In *FMS*, the Court of Justice gave a condemning assessment of the Hungarian rules governing the legal protection of third-country nationals in the context of the restrictive Hungarian policy and practice in granting asylum. It first established that it is contrary to EU law when national legislation allows a third-country national to challenge the decision of the asylum authority only by means of an action brought before an administrative authority, without a subsequent judicial review of the decision of that authority being guaranteed, and it ruled that that the national administrative court when assessing the admissibility of an action for judicial review by such a person against such a decision must declare that it has jurisdiction to hear the case.[50] The Court argued in particular on the basis of its established jurisprudence on the right of access to a court that ensuring the full effectiveness of EU legal provisions, which provide rights to individuals, requires that national courts establish their jurisdiction directly on the basis of those provisions, provide the necessary judicial remedies, including the review of the legality of administrative decisions, when national law fails to do the same and disapply any national provision prohibiting them from proceeding that way.[51] In regard to the detention of asylum applicants or of third-country nationals whose applications for asylum have been rejected in the so-called *Röszke* transit zone set up between the Hungarian and Serbian borders, the Court found that Article 47 requires that Hungary provides effective opportunities for judicial review to challenge the lawfulness of the detention order.[52] In absence of such domestic legal provisions, the national court must establish its jurisdiction to examine the lawfulness of the detention order challenged.[53]

In *Torubarov* and in *PG*, the Court of Justice examined the issue of whether the national court acting in judicial review can modify asylum decisions in its own competences – regardless of the restrictive provisions of national law – and can thus ensure that the decisions comply with the judicial rulings which established their illegality, but which were repeatedly ignored by the Hungarian authorities. The judgment from the Court established that the right to an effective judicial protection under Article 47 EUCFR, as was introduced previously in this chapter, requires that national authorities follow and implement the decisions of national courts that provide a complete assessment in law of the original asylum claim, despite the unavailability of provisions in national law to that effect.[54] Therefore, Hungarian courts must be able to modify the decision of national asylum authorities and substitute their decisions on

49. *Ibid.*
50. Joined Cases C-924/19 PPU and C-925/19 PPU *FMS* [EU:C:2020:367], para. 147.
51. *Ibid.*, paras 144–146.
52. *Ibid.*, para. 290.
53. *Ibid.*, para. 291.
54. Case C-556/17 *Torubarov* [EU:C:2019:626], paras 55–58 and 72-73; Case C-406/18 *PG* [EU:C:2020:216], paras 16–23.

asylum claims with their own decisions.[55] Fundamentally, although EU law does not prohibit national provisions which exclude national courts from amending administrative decisions challenged before them, national courts may disregard any such provisions when they prevent effective compliance with their judgment by the national authority in question. In *PG*, the Court also found that the strict requirement in Hungarian law that the review court must finish its proceedings in 60 days is – not in general – incompatible with EU law. However, when that deadline prevents the national court from applying effectively the substantive and procedural rules afforded by EU law to applicants (asylum seekers), it must disapply that national rule and deliver its judgment outside of the time limit regulated therein 'as promptly as possible'.[56]

In the preliminary reference in the case *Országos Idegenrendeszeti Főigazgatóság and Others*, the referring court questioned among others the compatibility with Article 47 EUCFR the national security exception as regulated in domestic asylum law which allowed for Hungarian authorities to refuse or to withdraw international protection from the person concerned. The question put to the Court asked whether national authorities are obliged to provide access for the individual or that person's legal representative 'to at least the essence of the confidential or classified information or data' which supports the application of that exception. In the original case, the applicant argued that without access to the information or data used to make the withdrawal decision he is unable to challenge that decision in law, and even if access were granted to that information or data, Hungarian legislation prevents their use in the judicial proceedings started by the applicant. The referring court (the Kúria) pointed out that the procedural rights of the applicant should in general be adequately protected by the legislative provision in Hungarian law which enables the review court to inspect the classified information or data collected by the national security services. Nevertheless, the Kúria conceded that it cannot use that information in its proceedings, or make any assessment or finding in relation to it. It observed that without access to the facts and the circumstances supporting the administrative decision review courts are unable to exercise their powers in judicial review effectively. The recent judgment of the Court established that the Hungarian restriction of judicial review contravened EU law. It held that applicants and their legal representatives cannot be denied complete access to the grounds of the asylum decision rejecting or withdrawing international protection, and they cannot be prevented completely from using that information for legal protection.[57]

5 CONCLUSIONS

Following the political, social and geo-economic shift, to which Hungarians as citizens of the EU have been subjected since 2010, convergence towards the legal standards and

55. Case C-556/17 *Torubarov* [EU:C:2019:626], para. 74; Case C-406/18 *PG* [EU:C:2020:216], para. 23.
56. Case C-406/18 *PG* [EU:C:2020:216], para. 37.
57. Case C-159/21 *Országos Idegenrendeszeti Főigazgatóság and Others* [EU:C:2022:708], para. 60.

requirements of Western Europe, as embodied in ECHR and EU law, seems to have lost its assumed priority status in Hungary. Perhaps, in reality legal convergence with Europe has never had that unquestionable value and utility as lawyers and legal academia imagined it. However, currently in a Member State on the Eastern periphery of the EU it is evident that following common European legal standards and requirements is a question of political choice, the outcome of which cannot be predetermined having regard to presumed common principles and expectations, such as respect for the rule of law. The interests as determined in Hungary's extensively centralised and hierarchical system for political decision-making influence foremost whether European requirements are observed and implemented, and the traditional factors of European legal convergence, such as the rights of individuals and their effective legal protection now have a diminished role. When it contradicts the government's political priorities and strategic choices, convergence needs to be enforced in law.

CHAPTER 15

Preliminary Rulings and Acte Clair: National Courts, Advocate General and CJEU

Paul Craig

1 INTRODUCTION

Preliminary rulings are central to the jurisdiction of the Court of Justice of the European Union (CJEU), the jewel in its jurisdictional Crown. The preliminary ruling mechanism has played a key part in the development of European Union (EU) law, being the mechanism through which the CJEU developed core principles of EU law, such as direct effect and supremacy. It is through what is now Article 267 Treaty of Functioning of the European Union (TFEU) that the Court has built a judicial system for the EU, with national courts featuring prominently as courts charged with the enforcement and application of EU law in their jurisdiction.

The circumstances in which national courts have a discretion and an obligation to refer are defined in Article 267, the relevant substance of which has not changed since the inception of the European Economic Community (EEC). Article 267, paragraph 2, provides that any national court has a discretion to refer, if it considers that a decision on a question is necessary to enable it to give judgment. Article 267, paragraph 3, stipulates that where such a question is raised before a national court against whose decisions there is no judicial remedy in national law, then a reference shall be made. There are, nonetheless, exceptions to the obligation to refer by national courts of final resort, which were articulated in CILFIT and subsequent case law.[1]

Cases are significant when they change the status quo ante. They are also significant when they do not. This is more especially so, when the CJEU chooses not to

1. Case 283/81 *Srl CILFIT and Lanificio di Gavardo SpA v. Ministry of Health* [1982] ECR 3415.

do so, notwithstanding a long Opinion by the Advocate General arguing that the area was ripe for reconceptualization. This is what occurred in the recent decision in Consorzio Italian Management,[2] where the CJEU declined the invitation to rethink the acte clair doctrine advanced by Advocate General Bobek.[3]

There is an interesting symmetry between CILFIT and Consorzio Italian Management, insofar as the Court in both cases rejected firm advice from the Advocate General as to the juridical status of the acte clair doctrine. The nature of the advice differed in the respective cases. It is, nonetheless, interesting and instructive to juxtapose the cases, to consider the reasoning of the AG and Court therein and to reflect on the reasons why the Court chose not to follow the Advocate General's Opinion. This is more especially so, given the importance of the issue raised in the cases concerning the EU's judicial architecture.

2 CILFIT: AG, COURT AND JUDICIAL INTENT

2.1 CILFIT: The Criteria

Article 267 TFEU is designed to be used only if there is a question to be answered, which falls into one of the categories in Article 267, paragraph 1. There may be a number of reasons why a 'question' posed by the national court does not necessitate a ruling. The principal categories, as revealed by the Court's jurisprudence, are cases where the question raised is not relevant to the resolution of the dispute; cases where the CJEU has already ruled on the matter, thus obviating the need for a further reference; and cases where the matter is so clear as to render the need for a reference otiose. The issues raised in Consorzio Italian Management were principally concerned with the contours of the last of these exceptions, and the principal authority in this regard was the four-decades-old decision in CILFIT.[4] It is, however, important to remember that Advocate General Capotorti advised against any acceptance of the acte clair doctrine. It is to his Opinion that we turn first.

2.2 CILFIT: The AG

Advocate General Capotorti argued strongly for rejection of an acte clair doctrine. He insisted that a reference could only be declined where the question posed was irrelevant to resolution of the dispute, or where a precedent already existed.

He contended that the very concept of acte clair was associated with a specific Member State, France, and the rationale for its invocation in that jurisdiction was not in any way generalizable for the rest of the EEC.[5] The concept of acte clair did not,

2. Case C561/19 *Consorzio Italian Management, Catania Multiservizi SpA v. Rete Ferroviaria Italiana SpA*, EU:C:2021:799.
3. Case C561/19 *Consorzio Italian Management, Catania Multiservizi SpA v. Rete Ferroviaria Italiana SpA*, EU:C:2021:291, AG Bobek.
4. Case 283/81 *CILFIT* (*supra* n. 1).
5. *CILFIT* (*supra* n. 1) [4] AG Capotorti.

moreover, withstand analytical scrutiny, given that before a provision could be applied to a specific case, it was 'always necessary, from a logical and practical point of view, to determine its meaning and scope, failing which it is impossible to establish whether it is applicable to the case in question or to infer from its terms all the implications for that case', with the consequence that 'it is inconceivable for a provision to be applied without there being any need to interpret it'.[6]

This conceptual and analytical critique of acte clair was complemented by an empirical line of argument, to the effect that deployment of the concept by the French courts had been 'anomalous', which was a polite way of stating that they had deemed matters to be acte clair, such as the meaning of the term 'measures having an effect equivalent to a quantitative restriction', which could not by any stretch of the imagination be so regarded.[7] For the Advocate General, this was further proof of the fact that the concept was used by a court of final resort to play fast and loose so as not to refer a case to the European Court of Justice (ECJ) when it did not wish to do so.

2.3 CILFIT: The ECJ

The ECJ, however, declined to follow the lead suggested by the Advocate General. The Court acknowledged that if an existing ruling covered the issue, it could render a reference on the matter unnecessary. It also decided that there could be instances where a reference was unnecessary, even in the absence of a prior CJEU ruling. The criteria that had to be satisfied by the national court before it came to such a conclusion were, however, strictly cast.

The national court 'must be convinced that the matter is equally obvious to the courts of the other Member States and to the Court of Justice'.[8] The existence of such a possibility 'must be assessed on the basis of the characteristic feature of Community law and the particular difficulties to which its interpretation gives rise'.[9]

The national court should be mindful of the fact that 'Community legislation is drafted in several languages and that the different language versions are equally authentic',[10] with the consequence that an interpretation of a provision of Community law thus involved a comparison of the different language versions.

It was also incumbent on the national court to bear in mind that 'even where the different language versions are entirely in accord with one another, that Community law uses terminology which is peculiar to it', and 'that concepts do not necessarily have the same meaning in Community law and in the law of the various Member States'.[11]

It was, moreover, important to recognize that 'every provision of Community law must be placed in its context and interpreted in the light of the provisions of Community law as a whole, regard being had to the objectives thereof and to its state

6. *Ibid.*, [4].
7. *Ibid.*
8. *Ibid.*, [16].
9. *Ibid.*, [17].
10. *Ibid.*, [18].
11. *Ibid.*, [19].

of evolution at the date on which the provision in question is to be applied'.[12] A national court could decline to make a reference where the correct application of Community law was so obvious as to leave no scope for any reasonable doubt, but it could only legitimately reach this conclusion if the preceding criteria had been met.

2.4 CILFIT: Judicial Intent

The CILFIT ruling generated considerable discussion as to the ECJ's intent when it issued the judgment. We cannot know for certain what animated this decision, but two principal arguments have the ring of veracity.

The first was articulated by Mancini and Keeling, Advocate General and Secretary of the Court respectively.[13] They endorsed and built on the earlier analysis by Rasmussen,[14] who characterized the ruling as being one of 'give and take'. Some national courts had in reality been declining to refer cases on the ground that the answer was clear cut. Mancini and Keeling built on this insight. They argued that the Court recognized that it could not coerce the national courts into accepting its jurisdiction. It therefore conceded the right to the national court not to refer if the Community measure was clear, but then restricted the circumstances in which the clarity of the provision could legitimately be sustained to cases so rare that the nucleus of its own authority was preserved intact:[15]

> The objective of the Court is plain: by granting supreme courts the power to do lawfully that which they could in any case do unlawfully, but by subjecting that power to stringent conditions, the Court hoped to induce the supreme courts to use willingly the 'mechanism for judicial cooperation' provided by the Treaty. The result is to eliminate sterile and damaging conflicts and to reduce the risk that Community law might be the subject of divergent interpretations.

The second rationale for the ECJ's acceptance of the acte clair concept is rather different. Thus, even if we accept the Mancini/Keeling thesis as to the Court's purpose, the effect is to leave 'clear' cases that fall within these conditions to the national courts. For such cases, the national courts operate as delegates of the Court for application of EU law. The CJEU can then utilize its time to resolve more problematic cases. The conditions in CILFIT help to ensure that national courts will not readily regard cases as acte clair unless they really are free from interpretive doubt, although it is doubtless true that national courts can interpret these conditions rather differently. This qualified approval could be regarded as rational on cost/benefit terms. The fact that a national court might, on occasion, misapply the criteria, intentionally or unintentionally, did not render the exercise a failure. These error costs had to be balanced against the benefits: straightforward cases could be disposed of expeditiously by national courts. There are in addition 'safety' devices built into the system, independently of the

---

12. *Ibid.*, [20].
13. GF Mancini and DT Keeling, 'From CILFIT to ERT: The Constitutional Challenge Facing the European Court' (1991) 11 YEL 1.
14. H Rasmussen, 'The European Court's Acte Clair Strategy in CILFIT' (1984) 9 ELRev 242.
15. Mancini and Keeling (*supra* n. 13) 4.

conditions in CILFIT. The concern is that a national court may refuse to make a reference, even though the conditions in CILFIT are not met. A national court minded to do this intentionally would, however, be aware of damages liability.[16] There is the further possibility that the Member State might be subject to an enforcement action under Article 258 TFEU. In any event, the matter might still come before the Court via a different court from the same legal system, or from a different legal system. It would also be open to the Court to correct aberrant interpretations by national courts, in the context of a case on a related point that has come before it.

3 CILFIT TO CONSORZIO ITALIAN MANAGEMENT: INTERVENING YEARS

This is not the place for detailed exegesis on the acte clair jurisprudence in the years between CILFIT and Consorzio Italian. Suffice it to say that there was no shortage of suggestions that the CILFIT conditions should be liberalized.

Thus, Advocate General Jacobs argued that national judges should not have to consider all official language versions of EU acts,[17] a view shared by Advocate General Stix-Hackl.[18] This view was echoed by the Association of the Councils of State and Supreme Administrative Jurisdictions of the EU, which contended that the conditions in CILFIT should be applied in a 'common-sense' way, and that comparing all language versions was no longer realistic or feasible. It argued that CILFIT should be applied so that the national court would determine whether the case was worth the burden of a preliminary reference.[19]

Judicial opinion was echoed in the academic literature. Rasmussen developed themes from his earlier article, and argued for a 'CILFIT II', which would 'give the initiative back to the judges of the Member States, trusting them to solve on their own far more questions of interpretation of Community law, including those which are not straightforward', with consequence that the scope of issues that would be deemed acte clair would be expanded.[20] Fenger and Broberg focused on the changed nature of the EU in the intervening years. The number of states had expanded considerably from the original six, and the legal order was less vulnerable than when CILFIT had originally been decided. They argued for differentiation between general questions of interpretation, and more specific issues of application:

> To our mind, there is still a need to limit strictly the possibility for a national court to avoid a preliminary reference in cases concerning general questions of interpretation that go beyond the confines of a single case. Indeed, in such cases there is a genuine need for uniform interpretation that should be established by the Court

16. Case C-224/01 *Köbler v. Austria* [2003] ECR I-10239.
17. Case C-338/95 *Wiener v. Hauptzollamt Emmerich* [1997] ECR I-6495.
18. Case 495/03 *Intermodal Transports BV v. Staatssecretaris van Financiën* [2005] ECR I-8151, [98]-[99].
19. Report of the Association of the Councils of State and Supreme Administrative Jurisdictions of the EU, June 2008, 7; D Sarmiento, 'Amending the Preliminary Reference Procedure for the Administrative Judge' (2009) 2 Rev. Eur. Admin. L. 29.
20. H Rasmussen, 'Remedying the Crumbling EC Judicial System' (2000) 37 CMLRev. 1071, 1109.

> of Justice. In contrast, taking into consideration both the interests of the parties to the main action and the need to keep the Court's caseload at a workable level, it seems less obvious that the same strict conditions should apply in cases where the issue of interpretation is unlikely to arise again, but instead is confined to the particular factual situation before the national court. In this latter situation, we suggest that it should be sufficient for acte clair to apply that the national court finds that the result does not give rise to appreciable doubt, but without requiring that the national court is equally convinced that all other courts find the matter to be equally obvious or requiring an examination of all the language versions of the relevant text.[21]

4 CONSORZIO ITALIAN MANAGEMENT: AG, COURT AND JUDICIAL INTENT

4.1 Consorzio Italian Management: AG Bobek

The preceding quotation provides a fitting link to the Opinion of Advocate General Bobek. There had, as seen above, been previous AG opinions that questioned CILFIT, but the critique had been relatively brief. By way of contrast, AG Bobek's Opinion extended to 39 pages, and constituted an in-depth challenge to the conceptual foundations of CILFIT. The Opinion is erudite and deserves close attention, notwithstanding difficulties with certain aspects of the reasoning.

The facts of the case were complex, but the essence of the question posed by the national court was as follows. It asked whether a national court, whose decisions were not amenable to appeal, was required, in principle, to make a reference for a preliminary ruling on a question concerning the interpretation of EU law, even where the question was submitted to it by one of the parties after that party had lodged its initial pleading, or even after the case had been set down for judgment for the first time, or even after a reference had already been made to the CJEU for a preliminary ruling.

The central core of AG Bobek's argument shares common terrain with Fenger and Broberg, being grounded on the distinction between interpretation and application:[22]

> [T]he process of adaptation suggested requires a major paradigm shift. The logic and the focus of the duty to refer and the exceptions to it ought to change from the absence of any reasonable doubt as to the correct application of EU law in an individual case, evidenced by there being subjective judicial doubt, to a more objective imperative of securing uniform interpretation of EU law across the European Union. In other words, the duty to refer a question for a preliminary

21. N Fenger and M Broberg, 'Finding Light in the Darkness: On the Actual Application of the *Acte Clair* Doctrine' (2011) 30 YBEL 180, 212. *See also*, A Kornezov, 'The New Format of the *Acte Clair* Doctrine and Its Consequences' (2016) 53 CMLRev. 1317; A Limante, 'Recent Developments in the Acte Clair Case Law of the EU Court of Justice: Towards a More Flexible Approach' (2016) 54 JCMS 1384; S Gervasoni, 'CJUE et cours suprêmes: repenser les termes du dialogue des juges?' (2019) AJDA 150.
22. Case C561/19 *Consorzio Italian Management*, EU:C:2021:291 (*supra* n. 3) [4], AG Bobek italics in the original.

> ruling should not be focused primarily on the correct answers, but rather on identifying the right questions.

The Opinion contains a number of strands that are woven together to form the complex argument. The principal elements were as follows.

4.1.1 Article 267: The Status Quo and National Courts

AG Bobek acknowledged that a request for a preliminary ruling could be made at any time, irrespective of a previous preliminary ruling of the Court issued within the same proceedings, as long as the referring court took the view that the Court's answer was necessary to enable it to deliver a judgment. That decision was always to be taken by the national court, in the light of any reasonable doubt that it might still have regarding the correct application of EU law in the case before it.

However, the AG took the view that the matter could not be resolved so easily, and that in reality the reference raised deeper questions concerning the nature and extent of the obligation to refer. Whether any such root and branch rethinking of CILFIT was required, and if so the nature of any such reform, was disputed by those who submitted evidence to the CJEU.[23]

4.1.2 Article 267: Text and Normative Foundation

AG Bobek rightly noted that the text of Article 267 contained, on its face, no exceptions to the duty to refer on a court of last resort. Thus, from a purely textualist perspective it might be argued that the Treaty did not countenance any exceptions to the duty.[24] However, this position clearly did not cohere with the Court's interpretation of Article 267 from the very inception of the EEC. It was, therefore, necessary to consider the normative foundation for the duty to refer cast on courts of final resort.[25]

> The structural reason for the obligation incumbent on courts of last instance was stated early on in Hoffmann-Laroche: 'to prevent a body of national case law [that is] not in accordance with the rules of EU law from being established in any of the Member States'. In other words, the special purpose of the third paragraph of Article 267 TFEU is the need 'to prevent the occurrence within the [Union] of divergences in judicial decisions on questions of [Union] law'. The limitation of that obligation to last-instance courts is specifically justified by the fact that 'a court adjudicating at last instance is by definition the last judicial body before which individuals may assert the rights conferred on them by EU law. Courts adjudicating at last instance have the task of ensuring at national level the uniform interpretation of rules of law'.

23. *Ibid.*, [39]-[41].
24. *Ibid.*, [47]-[48].
25. *Ibid.*, [51].

4.1.3 *Article 267: Problems with CILFIT*

AG Bobek surveyed some of the recent jurisprudence on Article 267, and concluded that it was not easy to reconcile the reasoning or result in the respective cases.[26] This then provided the foundation for analysis of problems associated with CILFIT.

The principal critique was conceptual, connoting the mismatch between the CILFIT exceptions and the Hoffmann-La Roche rationale for the duty to refer. For AG Bobek, the 'logic behind such a duty to refer is clearly structural and focused on uniform interpretation across the European Union', with the consequence that the triggering point and nature were 'objective, focusing on the case law in general, not merely on the individual case before the referring court'.[27] By way of contrast, the focus of the acte clair exception in CILFIT was 'the individual case and the subjective judicial hesitations in that specific case'.[28] This was, for AG Bobek, 'where the real problem lies'.[29] The acte clair exception 'remained centred around the absence of any reasonable doubt as to the outcome of an individual case',[30] even though the 'requirement to check the correct application of the law in each individual case is a very tall order'.[31]

The conceptual critique was then complemented with more empirically grounded criticism based on the feasibility of applying the CILFIT criteria, drawing on earlier AG Opinions and academic articles.[32] This led AG Bobek to conclude that 'the lack of any reasonable guidance as to the logic or application of the CILFIT criteria is not only reflected in the (surprisingly consistent) criticism given by the past Advocates General over the years', coupled with the fact that 'among those tasked with applying that obligation, and in particular those who are actually enforcing it, no one appears to be following the guidance of the Court'.[33]

This was followed by a temporal challenge to CILFIT. The EU had changed markedly in the years since that decision, both in terms of number of Member States, and range of subject matter covered by the EU. For AG Bobek, it was then ironic that 'in the midst of this vastly altered legal landscape stands the motionless Titan of a long bygone era, CILFIT, insisting that references be made by courts of last instance in every case where any form of reasonable doubt exists'.[34]

4.1.4 *Article 267: The Proposed Reform*

The AG's proposed reform of CILFIT flowed naturally from the preceding critique. It was predicated on curing the mismatch between CILFIT and Hoffmann-La Roche:[35]

26. *Ibid.*, [69]-[87].
27. *Ibid.*, [91]. italics in the original.
28. *Ibid.*, [92], italics in the original.
29. *Ibid.*, [93].
30. *Ibid.*, [96], italics in the original.
31. *Ibid.*, [97].
32. *Ibid.*, [99]-[110].
33. *Ibid.*, [110].
34. *Ibid.*, [123].
35. *Ibid.*, [133]-[134], italics in the original.

> [T]he focus of the duty to refer must change, from there being no subjective reasonable doubt as to the correct application of EU law in respect of the outcome of the specific case, to there being, an objective divergence detected in the case-law at the national level thereby threating the uniform interpretation of EU law within the European Union. In this way, the focus also moves from establishing the correct answer in the case before the national court to the identification of the right kind of questions.
>
> Following that logic, I would suggest that, under the third paragraph of Article 267 TFEU, a court or a tribunal of a Member State against whose decisions there is no judicial remedy under national law is to refer the case to the Court of Justice provided that it raises (i) a general issue of interpretation of EU law (as opposed to its application); (ii) to which there is objectively more than one reasonably possible interpretation; (iii) for which the answer cannot be inferred from the existing case law of the Court of Justice (or with regard to which the referring court wishes to depart from that case law).

AG Bobek elaborated on these criteria. Thus, in relation to the first criterion, he stressed that the duty to refer ought to be triggered whenever a national court of last instance is confronted with an issue of interpretation of EU law, 'formulated at a reasonable and appropriate level of abstraction'.[36] The level of abstraction was 'logically defined by the scope and purpose of the legal provision at issue'.[37] However, he acknowledged that 'mere application may quickly turn into interpretation, provided, for instance, that the referring court were to invite the Court to narrow, broaden, qualify, or depart from the definition already provided'.[38] He also acknowledged that there was no clear border 'between where interpretation ends and applications starts and vice versa', while nonetheless continuing to maintain that the 'aim of the duty to refer is to ensure the uniform interpretation of EU law, not the correct application of that law',[39] such that the uniformity sought should be in relation to the legal rules to be applied.

The second criterion was the existence of more than one possible reasonable interpretation. Central to this aspect of the AG's analysis was the contrast between what he regarded as the 'inherently internal and subjective uncertainty in the form of any reasonable doubt as to the outcome of an individual case', which he felt characterized the CILFIT approach, as compared to the 'existence of plausible alternatives that place similar considerations on a more external and objective footing'.[40] On this view there had to be more than subjective doubt or absence of knowledge to justify a duty to refer. There had to be plausible alternative interpretations, as exemplified by situations where different interpretations had been taken by national courts of final resort.[41]

36. *Ibid.*, [145].
37. *Ibid.*, [145].
38. *Ibid.*, [146].
39. *Ibid.*, [149].
40. *Ibid.*, [150], italics in the original.
41. *Ibid.*, [151]-[153].

The third criterion for the duty to refer was that the answer to the inquiry could not be inferred from the existing case law of the CJEU. This was the least problematic of the criteria, since it built on the well-established principle that a national court of last instance is not obliged to refer a question of interpretation of EU law if the same provision had already been interpreted by the Court. This was equally so where previous CJEU decisions in whatever type of proceedings had already provided sufficient interpretative guidance to allow the national court to settle the issue on the basis of existing case law.[42] For AG Bobek, what was to be established or inferable from the existing case law was the EU law rule to be applied, not the outcome of the specific case.[43]

A national court of final resort could still refer if it wished to do so, notwithstanding that the preceding criteria were not met. The absence of a duty to refer did not imply the absence of discretion to make a reference.[44] The AG also reiterated a point made earlier in the Opinion, to the effect that his analysis referred to the contours of the duty to refer on matters of interpretation. The national court was, by way of contrast, under a strict duty to refer in relation to issues of validity.[45]

There is an important fourth dimension to the AG's analysis, which is the duty to provide reasons. It does not feature directly in the previous quotation, but it is nonetheless central to his suggested approach. Thus, if a national court of final resort is minded not to refer because it feels that it is not necessary in the light of the previous criteria, it must provide adequate reasons for its conclusion that the case before it does not fall under the obligation to make a reference pursuant to the third paragraph of Article 267 TFEU.[46] It followed that a 'general, vague, and largely unsubstantiated reference to "acte clair" or CILFIT, without any real and case-specific reasoning being provided as to why exactly there is no duty to refer on the merits of the case in question, does not meet that minimal requirement'.[47] Interpretative problems could not therefore be 'swept under the carpet' without proper reasoning.[48]

4.2 Consorzio Italian Management: CJEU

The Grand Chamber of the CJEU declined the invitation from AG Bobek to engage in a root-and-branch rethink of CILFIT, although it did, as will be seen, modify the criteria to some degree. The reasons for this approach by the CJEU will be considered in the next section. The present analysis is concerned with the CJEU's reasoning.

The CJEU regarded the case as raising the issue of whether a court of final resort had an obligation to refer a question concerning the interpretation of EU law to the CJEU where that question is put to it by a party at an advanced stage of the proceedings,

42. *Ibid.*, [160].
43. *Ibid.*, [162].
44. *Ibid.*, [137].
45. *Ibid.*, [138].
46. *Ibid.*, [167].
47. *Ibid.*, [169].
48. *Ibid.*, [170].

after the case has been set down for judgment for the first time or where a reference for a preliminary ruling has already been made in that case.[49]

The Court emphasized the centrality of the preliminary ruling mechanism to the EU judicial system, and its importance in securing the uniform interpretation of EU law.[50] It was for the CJEU to furnish national courts with the points of interpretation to enable the latter to apply EU law in the cases that came before them.[51] The CJEU reiterated orthodoxy as to the threefold circumstance in which a national court of final resort could be relieved of the obligation to refer. This could occur where the question raised was irrelevant; where the EU law provision in question had already been interpreted by the Court; or where the correct interpretation of EU law was so obvious as to leave no scope for any reasonable doubt.[52] In cases where a previous ruling existed, the authority of an interpretation already provided by the Court under Article 267 TFEU could deprive the obligation in the third paragraph of Article 267 TFEU of its purpose and thus empty it of its substance, although a reference could still be made if the national court sought clarification as to meaning of the earlier ruling.[53] Subject to this, it was for the national court to decide whether a reference was warranted.[54]

The CJEU then revisited the third type of case where a national court could be relieved of the obligation to refer as laid down in CILFIT, the correct interpretation, rather than application, of EU law was so obvious as to leave no scope for any reasonable doubt. The CJEU, nonetheless, largely reiterated orthodoxy. It emphasized that the national court or tribunal of last instance must be convinced that the matter would be equally obvious to the other courts or tribunals of last instance of the Member States and to the CJEU.[55] The issue had to be 'assessed on the basis of the characteristic features of EU law, the particular difficulties to which the interpretation of the latter gives rise and the risk of divergences in judicial decisions within the European Union'.[56] The national court must therefore bear in mind that EU legislation was drafted in several languages and that the different language versions were all equally authentic.[57] The CJEU acknowledged that a national court of final resort could not be required to examine all language versions, but 'the fact remains that it must bear in mind those divergences between the various language versions of that provision of which it is aware, in particular when those divergences are set out by the parties and are verified'.[58] It was also incumbent on the national court to recognize that EU law used its own terminology and concepts, which did not necessarily bear the same meaning as national concepts with the same name.[59] It was, moreover, necessary to ensure that 'every provision of EU law must be placed in its context and interpreted in

49. Case C561/19 *Consorzio Italian Management*, EU:C:2021:799 (*supra* n. 2) [26].
50. *Ibid.*, [27]-[28].
51. *Ibid.*, [30].
52. *Ibid.*, [33].
53. *Ibid.*, [36]-[38].
54. *Ibid.*, [35].
55. *Ibid.*, [40].
56. *Ibid.*, [41].
57. *Ibid.*, [42].
58. *Ibid.*, [44].
59. *Ibid.*, [45].

the light of the provisions of EU law as a whole, regard being had to the objectives thereof and to its state of evolution at the date on which the provision in question is to be applied'.[60] It was only where the preceding criteria were met that a national court of final resort could legitimately conclude that a reference was not necessary.[61]

However, the mere fact that a provision of EU law could 'be interpreted in another way or several other ways, in so far as none of them seem sufficiently plausible to the national court or tribunal concerned, in particular with regard to the context and the purpose of that provision as well as the system of rules of which it forms part',[62] was not sufficient for the view to be taken that there is a reasonable doubt as to the correct interpretation of that provision. The existence of divergent lines of case law in the courts of a particular Member State, or across the courts of different Member States, should, nonetheless, make a national court of final resort 'particularly vigilant in its assessment of whether or not there is any reasonable doubt as to the correct interpretation of the provision of EU law at issue', given that the objective of the preliminary ruling procedure was to secure uniform interpretation of EU law.[63]

The CJEU emphasized the importance of reason-giving when a national court of final resort was minded not to refer. If the national court was inclined to take this view, the statement of reasons for its decision must show either that the question of EU law raised was irrelevant for resolution of the dispute, or that there was prior case law covering the point, or, in the absence of such case law, that the interpretation of EU law was so obvious to the national court or tribunal of last instance as to leave no scope for any reasonable doubt.[64]

Subject to this, it was for the national court to decide whether a reference should be made, and whether it was necessary at the particular stage of the national proceedings. The fact that it was asked to make a reference by a party to the dispute did not compel it to do so. The system of cooperation between national courts and the CJEU was independent of any initiative by a party to the case, and Article 267 did not therefore constitute a means of redress for the parties to the national dispute.[65]

While the principal contours of the CJEU's reasoning echo those found in previous cases, there are nonetheless changes. The Court drew on the juridical technique whereby process reinforces substantive obligations. In this context the salient substantive obligation is the duty incumbent on national courts of last resort to refer unless one of the three established grounds for not doing so is present. Reason-giving is crucial in this respect, as emphasized by Gentile and Bonelli.[66]

> It follows that national courts of last resort must provide a statement of reasons to justify their decision not to refer to the CJEU. The duty of statement of reasons is

60. *Ibid.*, [46].
61. *Ibid.*, [47].
62. *Ibid.*, [48]
63. *Ibid.*, [49].
64. *Ibid.*, [51].
65. *Ibid.*, [52]-[59].
66. G Gentile and M Bonelli, 'La jurisprudence des petits pas: C-561/19, *Consorzio Italian Management, Catania Multi Servizi SpA v Rete Ferroviaria Italiana SpA*, *REALaw.blog*, available at https://realaw.blog/2021/11/26/780/, 2.

of central importance in EU law. It is provided for under the Treaties (*see* Article 296 TFEU with reference to EU institutions) as well as under Article 47 of the EU Charter. With Consorzio, the CJEU has aligned its case law with that of the ECtHR: the latter court had long-established a duty to state reasons for national courts of last instance when deciding not to refer to the CJEU in light of Article 6 of the European Convention on Human Rights.

4.3 Consorzio Italian Management: Judicial Intent

There is, as noted at the outset, a symmetry between CILFIT and Consorzio Italian Management, insofar as strident Opinions by the AG were rejected by the Court. There is perforce nothing odd or untoward in the fact that the Court declines to follow a line of reasoning suggested by the Advocate General. It is also readily apparent that the arguments presented by AG Capotorti and AG Bobek in the respective cases were very different. It was nonetheless interesting to inquire as to what might have motivated the Court to reject the view of AG Capotorti in CILFIT, and it is equally interesting to press the same inquiry in the context of Consorzio Italian Management. This is more especially so given that AG Bobek undertook a lengthy critique of the legal status quo, coupled with detailed proposals for the way in which the issue should be reconceptualized. The Court, sitting as a Grand Chamber, did not follow this lead, it did not advert to the AG's reasoning and it largely reiterated the status quo. We should then inquire why this was so. There is, as might be expected, more than one possibility in this regard.

4.3.1 Rationale 1: Let Sleeping Dogs Lie

The first possible rationale is to 'let sleeping dogs lie'. AG Bobek referred to this metaphor twice. It 'bookends' his Opinion. Thus, at the outset he stated that:[67]

> [T]he exceptions to that duty [to refer], and above all its enforcement, have been the metaphorical sleeping dogs of EU law. We are all aware that they are there. We are all able to discuss or even write scholarly treatises about them. However, in real life, it is best that they be left undisturbed.

The Advocate General returned to this metaphor at the end of his Opinion, where he duly noted that the Court was unlikely to engage in root and branch rethinking of the CILFIT criteria.[68]

> Indeed, having read the compelling Opinions of all my learned predecessors quoted throughout this Opinion, it is clear that the Court is not likely to reopen that file lightly. Moreover, with tongue in cheek, it could be suggested that, since CILFIT has not worked for 40 years, a few more years or decades will make no difference. There is also a certain beautiful simplicity and wisdom in inertia, particularly once the system, as a whole, finds some sort of equilibrium. Indeed,

67. Case C561/19 *Consorzio Italian Management*, EU:C:2021:291 (*supra* n. 3) [2], AG Bobek.
68. *Ibid.*, [174].

> returning to the metaphor used in the introduction to this Opinion, it may be wiser to let sleeping dogs lie. If they should wake, no one knows whom they may bite.

This first rationale may well have played a part in the CJEU's reasoning and decision. This is more especially so, given that there are in reality a number of related, albeit distinct, reasons for not waking the sleeping hound.

There is, on the one hand, the concern as to fallibility. No court likes to acknowledge that doctrine that has been on the 'books' for a long period was misconceived. AG Bobek was inviting the CJEU to recognize that doctrinal precepts that had been central to the regime of preliminary rulings for 40 years were misconceived. It is unsurprising that it should be reluctant to concede this error. The CJEU does change track, often subtly, sometimes explicitly, as in the context of the case law on the free movement of goods and the separate treatment accorded to selling conditions. The CJEU would, nonetheless, have to have been really convinced of the error of its past jurisprudence in order to follow the AG's lead. The very fact that it restated the key contours of that jurisprudence in its judgment signifies that it had not been convinced in this respect.

There is, on the other hand, contestation as to the existence of a problem. AG Bobek's Opinion is predicated on the assumption that the current law relating to CILFIT and the manner in which it was interpreted by national courts was a real practical problem. The national courts of final resort could not meet the CILFIT criteria. They could not look at all language versions. They remoulded the test as to whether a reference was required into something that worked for them. The CJEU may, nonetheless, have been willing to let sleeping dogs lie, in part because it did not think that there really was a practical problem that required root and branch doctrinal reform. There had not been a chorus of pressure to this effect from national courts. Most Member States did not submit detailed submissions on the issue in the instant case, indicating that they were not unduly concerned. The AG mentions four players that did do so. It is noteworthy that the two most powerful players, the Commission and Germany, argued that the CILFIT criteria should not be modified in any way, and that they had stood the test of time.[69] The suggestions for reform from the Italian government were modest.[70] It was only the French government that came close to the change of direction for which AG Bobek pressed.[71] The CJEU could then conclude that sleeping dogs could lie, or to mix metaphors, if it 'aint broke why fix it'.

4.3.2 Rationale 2: Substantive Disagreement – General

The second possible rationale for the CJEU not taking up the 'baton of change' presented by the AG is at the other end of the spectrum: it did not agree with the AG's reasoning. This rationale may well have explanatory force. It is, moreover, clear that insofar as the CJEU may have felt intellectual disquiet with the AG's reasoning, this

69. *Ibid.*, [39].
70. *Ibid.*, [40].
71. *Ibid.*, [41].

would not surface in the body of the CJEU's judgment, and rightly so. The CJEU judgment is not a forum for detailed academic debate between the AG and the Court as to the merits and demerits of different doctrinal positions. The CJEU is tasked with delivering a judgment, having come to its view on what that should be, albeit with the assistance of the AG and arguments by the parties.

If the CJEU substantively disagreed with the AG and therefore declined the invitation to recast CILFIT as he wished, it would logically have been because of disagreement with the central tenets of the AG's argument.

He was pristinely clear as to his desired direction of travel. The cornerstone of the argument was the need for fit or symmetry with the rationale for the duty to refer in Hoffmann-La Roche, viz. that the duty on national courts of final resort was there to prevent a body of case law contrary to EU law from building up in a Member State. This was the foundation for the central proposition.[72]

The logic and the focus of the duty to refer and the exceptions to it ought to change from the absence of any reasonable doubt as to the correct application of EU law in an individual case, evidenced by there being subjective judicial doubt, to a more objective imperative of securing uniform interpretation of EU law across the EU. In other words, the duty to refer a question for a preliminary ruling should not be focused primarily on the correct answers, but rather on identifying the right questions.

This in turn led to AG Bobek's three-part test. There had to be a general issue of interpretation of EU law, as opposed to its application; to which there was objectively more than one reasonably possible interpretation; and for which the answer could not be inferred from the existing CJEU case law.[73]

4.3.3 *Rationale 2: Substantive Disagreement – General Interpretation and Application*

The divide between general interpretation and application is central to the AG's reasoning. There are, however, difficulties with this line that lies at the core of the argument. AG Bobek acknowledged that it was not possible to demarcate this divide with pristine certainty, but underestimated the difficulties in this respect.

First, it is very hard, in conceptual terms, to decide on the level of abstraction that should be regarded as falling within the remit of 'interpretation', and the level of specificity that comes within 'application'. It requires identification of the characteristics, factors or features that can be regarded as part of the abstract definition of the relevant legal term, as compared to matters of concrete detail that concern its application.

Second, in the context of the duty to refer, this determination resides with the national court of final resort, which will be under a duty to refer under AG Bobek's schema if it decides that the question posed goes to general interpretation, and the other criteria are met, but not if it relates to concrete application. We can then crudely

72. *Ibid.*, [4], italics in the original.
73. *Ibid.*, [134].

posit 'good' and 'bad' national courts. The former will bona fide struggle to divine the divide between general interpretation and application, since there will inevitably be uncertainty as to whether they should refer or not, this being the second-order consequence of the fragile divide between interpretation and application. The latter, the 'bad' national courts, will be tempted to use the division between general interpretation and application as a shield to justify not sending references.

Thirdly, a rigid line between general interpretation and concrete application would almost certainly not be desired by the CJEU. It often wishes to maintain control over the direction of a body of EU law, precisely by fine-tuning the application of a more abstract interpretive proposition. The CJEU would not, therefore, wish to instantiate a revised CILFIT doctrine that rendered it more difficult for it to do this. This is so notwithstanding the fact that the divide between interpretation and application is part and parcel of Article 267 TFEU. It is for the CJEU to decide on the interpretation of EU, and it is for the national courts to decide on the application of this concept in a particular case. It is, nonetheless, generally acknowledged that the CJEU uses various juridical techniques to maintain control over the legal development of an area. It may choose to construe the question of interpretation raised in a very specific manner, thereby leaving little or nothing for the national court to do under the guise of application, other than execute the CJEU ruling. It may in other contexts content itself with the elaboration of principles, but then give 'guidance' to national courts as to their application in a particular case. The CJEU has used this technique repeatedly in the context of, for example, state liability in damages, where it has elaborated the criteria for liability and the factors that are constitutive of a serious breach, and then provided guidance to the national court as to the application of those criteria to the instant case.

Finally, the idea that fidelity to the Hoffmann- La Roche rationale for the duty to refer on the national court of final resort, viz. that it is there to prevent a body of case law contrary to EU law from building up in a Member State, demands the shift advocated by AG Bobek is not self-evident. It is certainly true that this danger could be realized if such a court refused to refer on a question of interpretation and then answered that question in a manner contrary to other Member States, or contrary to how the CJEU would have decided if the matter had been referred. However, this danger could, in substance, be equally present if the national final court refused to refer in a number of cases concerning 'application' and then gave what were felt to be aberrant rulings in such cases. To put the same point in another way, erroneous rulings on 'application' of a more abstract 'general interpretive' concept could do as much damage to the uniformity of EU law across the Member States as if the national court had given a different interpretive meaning to the concept itself.

4.3.4 *Rationale 2: Substantive Disagreement – Objective and Subjective*

The line between 'subjective' and 'objective' views as to the existence of more than one possible reasonable interpretation of EU law features prominently in AG Bobek's Opinion. The legal status quo of CILFIT is characterized in terms of subjectivity, in the sense that it suffices that the national court or judge just feels that the answer to the correct application of EU law in the instant case is clear or unclear. The desired direction of travel is characterized in terms of objectivity, in the sense that it is for the national court or judge to show objectively that there is more than one possible view as to the meaning of a general issue of interpretation of EU law, the acid test in this regard being the advancement of plausible alternatives.

The difficulties between a focus on general interpretation and application have been charted above. It is questionable whether the language of subjectivity/objectivity adds anything in this regard. There is, with respect, little to substantiate the conclusion that national courts that apply CILFIT systemically reach the conclusion as to the existence of reasonable doubt through mere subjective belief, as opposed to some data that could be regarded as objective. Nor is there any normative linkage between subjectivity/application or objectivity/interpretation. Thus, even if one were minded to categorize an issue before a national court as coming within the realm of application, there is no a priori or contingent reason why the national court would make the relevant evaluation subjectively as opposed to objectively.

5 CONCLUSION

The Grand Chamber of the CJEU was presented in Consorzio Italian Management with the invitation to recast the circumstances in which a national court of final resort would have an obligation to refer. It declined to do so, notwithstanding the lengthy critique by Advocate General Bobek. The reasons that might have motivated the Court were considered above, as were those that inclined the Court not to accept the very different Opinion of Advocate General Capotorti a generation earlier. The criteria in CILFIT, as modified by subsequent case law and by Consorzio Italian Management, will continue to provide the guide for national courts for the foreseeable future.

CHAPTER 16

Is Democracy Sufficiently Safeguarded under the UK's Unwritten Constitution?

Sir Jeffrey Jowell KC[*]

Patrick Birkinshaw has played an important part in public law in the United Kingdom (UK) and in Europe. He is a pioneer in the development and promotion of all that a liberal democracy stands for.

I want here to ask, in effect, whether our unwritten constitution is worth the paper it is not written on. At least to the extent of upholding those qualities of liberal democracy that this country has professed to live by but are increasingly disparaged internationally.

I shall consider four questions. First, do we have a constitution, and if so, where do we find it? Secondly, what kind of a constitution is it? Thirdly, is it upholding democracy? Fourthly, is it time to repair the constitution or to write it down in one document?

Do we have a constitution?

It is true that in the UK there is no supreme law, written down and available to all, that sets out the framework principles and rules for the governance of our nation. This lack of codification makes us an outlier, together only with New Zealand and Israel. In all other countries a constitution can be found in one place, is written down, and guides and constrains all branches of government, including the legislature.

The lack of such a constitution may not suit those of us who would prefer to have access to the rules of the game in a convenient way. It has, however, suited our governments as it gives them freedom to make things up as they go along. Divine qualities have been attributed to that flexibility – such as Mr Podsnap in Dickens' Our Mutual Friend who told a foreign visitor 'We Englishmen are very proud of our Constitution… It was bestowed upon us by Providence'.

* A much shorter version of this paper was delivered as the Rothschild/Foster Human Rights Lecture, in King's Place, London on 2 November 2022.

The late Queen was more straightforward about our constitution. She said simply that the UK Constitution 'has always been puzzling, and always will be'.[1]

Many in this country assume that since our constitution is not written down, in one document, we just don't have one. But surely there must exist some source that confers power to make, interpret and enforce laws- as in countries which do have a single written constitution?

During Liz Truss' short reign as Prime Minister (PM) an exasperated conservative Member of Parliament (MP) cried out to a television interviewer that 'we must stop all this nonsense and start governing again under our constitution'.

However, where is this elusive and obscure thing to be found? What does it say? Most constitutional experts contend that our constitutional edifice rests on just one foundational rule, which is: 'what the King-in-Parliament enacts, is law.' In ordinary language this simply means: 'whatever parliament says, goes' because the monarch, although formally empowered to refuse Royal assent to laws, has not, by convention, done so since 1708.

But can our complex system of governance be fuelled by just one rule, encapsulating parliament's 'sovereignty' which itself is not set out in any authoritative document?

Those who think it can point to a series of authoritative dicta that they say provides a 'mountain of evidence' demonstrating that parliamentary sovereignty is the 'current orthodoxy'.[2] They cite a number of dicta of judges over the years who proclaim that orthodoxy. And they invariably turn to the work of Professor Albert Venn Dicey, of All Souls Oxford who, in 1885, in his book *The Law of the Constitution*, declared that our prime constitutional principle (rather than a rule) was what he called 'the sovereignty of parliament'.

Dicey took this notion to some extreme. He asserted that parliament could make or unmake any law whatsoever, allowing only one exception: that parliament could not make a man into a woman and a woman into a man (a power that parliament is perhaps no longer willing to forgo).

Dicey's notion of parliamentary sovereignty could be interpreted as having authoritarian connotations. Could parliament really decree 'anything'? Even, to use the stock example invariably debated by the students, to decree that all blue-eyed babies be killed? Could parliament really enact a law permitting it to rule indefinitely without any future election? Could parliament dispense with courts of law, or even prohibit any challenge to official decisions by abolishing judicial review? Or create a one-party state? Or disenfranchise any one group or gender? Is that really what our constitution permits?[3]

---

1. P. Hennessy, *The Hidden Wiring* (1995) p. 33.
2. J. Goldsworthy, *Parliamentary Sovereignty: Contemporary Debates* (2010) p. 97.
3. For a view that Goldsworthy's evidence is counteracted by other equally persuasive evidence to the contrary, *see* M. Elliott, 'Parliamentary Sovereignty in a Changing Constitutional Landscape' in J. Jowell and C. O'Cinneide, *The Changing Constitution* (9th ed. 2019). For a recent discussion, see J. Goldsworthy, 'Is Parliamentary Sovereignty Alive, Dying or Dead?' [2023] Public Law 126; M. Loughlin and S.Tierney, 'The Shibboleth of Sovereignty, (2018) 81(6) MLR 989; N. Barber, *The United Kingdom Constitution,* (2021), Chapter 7.

However, let me defend Dicey from that charge of authoritarianism, because in that same book he frequently decries what he calls 'despotism'. Furthermore, his championing of parliament was surely in the cause of democracy, rather than against it (however imperfect democracy was in his time).

It bears noting that when Dicey wrote his book the franchise had been considerably extended by means of the Reform Acts of 1832, 1867 and 1884 (the year he was writing it). This surely for Dicey legitimised the ultimate vesting of sovereign power in those chosen by the electorate to represent them in parliament. True representative government had arrived, never mind the fact that at that time no women could vote (and that Dicey argued passionately, that women's enfranchisement would be 'a calamity to the nation'[4]!).

Representative government is of course a central feature of any democracy, allowing those who are freely and fairly elected to make policy decisions in what they see as the public interest.

And another important function of the sovereign parliament is to hold the executive (the Prime Minister and cabinet) to account.

So Dicey recognised at least the beginnings of a system of government which justified ultimate power residing in the elected legislature which held the executive to account. But more than that, he also foresaw, and here rests his genius, that majority rule alone is a thin form of democracy and he therefore proposed too a second constitutional principle, the rule of law, as a constraint on raw parliamentary power.

He thus divined what we now know, particularly from the history of Germany and the Soviet Union in the twentieth century, where freely elected governments demonstrated how unconstrained sovereignty could transform into tyranny. Isaiah Berlin wrote about this in his book, The Crooked Timber of Humanity,[5] noting:

> the ideological storms that have altered the lives of virtually all mankind: the Russian Revolution and its aftermath – totalitarian tyrannies of both right and left and the explosions of nationalism, racism, and, in places, of religious bigotry, which, interestingly enough, not one among the most perceptive social thinkers of the nineteenth century had ever predicted.

By proposing and identifying a constraint on unbridled majoritarianism, Dicey sensed this possibility, in a way that others of his time simply did not. And although he was not in favour of an entrenched bill of rights, he believed that the rule of law (his original expression), should temper and constrain the grant or exercise of overweening power. The rule of law could not authorise judges to overrule parliament's legislation, but it did provide at least as a moral imperative that laws should not confer arbitrary power, and that law should be obeyed, that law should be applied equally, that it should be accessible and certain, and that official decisions should be amenable to challenge in the ordinary courts by an independent judiciary.[6]

---

4. R.S. Rait, *Memorials of Albert Venn Dicey* (1925), pp. 121-122.
5. (1990), p. 1.
6. *See* the various 'ingredients' inherent in the rule of law as outlined by T. Bingham, *The Rule of Law* (2010).

Dicey also identified another aspect of democracy which is often forgotten, namely that to be successful-to really cohere and be sustainable – it must be grounded in a culture of democracy. And that such a culture depends not only on public opinion, and requires adherence not only to high principles and rules, but also to what he called 'constitutional conventions'. Such conventions were for him rooted in behaviour which, like the rule of law, would be expected both to realise efficient governance and also to constrain the misuse of power.

One hundred and thirty-seven years after Dicey's book was published, we can quarrel with a great deal of his detailed justification of his principles and their reach in his and our time. However, his notion of our three constitutional fundamentals remains largely intact, namely: parliamentary sovereignty, moderated by the rule of law and sustained by constitutional conventions.

But these are high principles and so to have a practical effect, over time both parliament and the courts have added layers of decision-making institutions and standards. These have an enabling and disabling effect. They enable or empower various instruments of government to carry out various decisions and they also disable or constrain that power so to prevent its abuse, thus buttressing and deepening the democratic quality of our constitution.

Just some examples of these buttressing features include electoral laws; judicial review of official decisions; powers conferred on the devolved nations and regions; access to information, anti-corruption laws and the Human Rights Act of 1998, which incorporates into our law most of the provisions of the European Convention of Human Rights. And we should add to this some of the international treaties which we are obligated to enforce.

So in answer to the first question, yes we do have a constitution. It is a scattered constitution, not written down in any one place or entrenched, but a constitution nonetheless.

What kind of constitution?

As the distinguished historian Linda Colley says, constitutions are not neutral or innocent.[7] They further different political and ideological goals. Some openly seek an autocratic system, by placing ultimate power in the party, or in an individual dictator. Others are popular rather than representative in design. There can be no doubt however that ours, for reasons stated above, is a democratic constitution in the sense not only of embracing representative government but also by buttressing majority rule by means of different institutional constraints and through fidelity to the rule of law and human rights.

However, unlike entrenched written democratic constitutions, any or all of the buttressing constraints are vulnerable (at least under the unmodified conception of parliamentary sovereignty) to being swept away by an all-powerful parliament, like a leaf in a storm.

Is the constitution upholding democracy?

---

7. L. Colley, *The Gun, the Ship and the Pen* (2021), *see* esp. pp. 401 ff.

Let us turn now to the third question: Is this opaque, scattered constitution fit for the purpose of safeguarding our democracy?

While the advantage of an unwritten constitution may be its flexibility, its corresponding weakness is its inherent uncertainty, which militates against the stability required by the rule of law. Uncertainty also militates against what might be called a constitutional approach; constitutional thinking.

There are two stark examples of how constitutional uncertainty resulting in the lack of constitutional thinking creates misconceptions and confusion. First, in the autumn of 2022 we witnessed the confusion about procedures for the election of our prime ministers. After Boris Johnson abided by the convention that if a Prime Minister loses the confidence of the House of Commons he should resign, Liz Truss was elected to the office of Prime Minister by a tiny proportion of the electorate – some conservative party members, overriding the majority of the conservative MPs, whose preference was for Rishi Sunak. That Tory MPs were forced to accept a choice that was not theirs could be seen to contradict the notion of representative government. The opposition and others called for a general election, on the ground that the country as a whole should have its say in the choice of a new leader. A similar claim was made earlier by government minister Jacob Rees-Mogg, who asserted that if Boris Johnson were forced by parliament to resign, a new election would have to be called.

The short answer to both these calls for a general election is that ours is not a presidential system, where the president has his or her own mandate, independent of parliament and can be held personally to account. By convention, the Prime Minister is the leader of the largest party and is responsible to parliament but not directly to the electorate. An election is therefore not constitutionally required, but this may seem somewhat counter-intuitive, since in practice these days we tend to vote for a prime minister (as much, if not more, than a particular MP). You might also expect the choice of a new PM to be supported by the majority of their own party in parliament.

The second example of constitutional confusion relates to the status of a referendum, held in 2016 about whether to remain in or leave the European Union ('EU').[8] Leaving the EU was a decision of the most profound constitutional import. After all, in 1972 Parliament had conferred authority on EU institutions to make laws for the UK. Brexit would cancel that major source of law, as well as the hundreds of EU laws effective in the UK. But the referendum was authorised without any consideration of its constitutional implications and impact. In virtually any country with a written constitution (exceptions are very rare) a rupture of this magnitude would have required a special procedure – perhaps a 'super-majority', majority by both parliament and referendum (either or both with a special majority) and acquiescence by all the entities in a federal system. The Venice Commission has made clear that these or other mechanisms should ideally be employed so as to make a constitution more difficult to change than ordinary legislation.[9]

8. Under the terms of the European Union Referendum Act 2015.
9. *See* the Venice Commission Report, *On Constitutional Amendment*, European Commission for Democracy Through Law, CDL-AD(2010)001, para. 6: 'In almost all constitutions ... change is more difficult than with ordinary legislation, and typically requires either a qualified parliament

This lack of constitutional due diligence was amplified by the fact that the question put to the people was not suitable to address the different ways in which Brexit might be achieved (within or out with the customs union, with or without an Irish border, etc.).[10]

In large part due to neglect of its constitutional significance, Brexit has caused a number of after-shocks, beginning with the two famous cases where the executive sought to usurp the rightful power of parliament fearing that parliament might renege on the referendum's result.

The first of those concerned whether the then Prime Minister, Theresa May, or parliament, had the power to trigger Brexit. Article 50 of the Treaty on European Union provides that any member state which decides to withdraw from the Union must notify the European Council 'in accordance with its own constitutional requirements'.

But here again, our 'constitutional arrangements' were unclear and deeply contested. Teresa May announced her intention to withdraw from the EU under what are known as prerogative powers exercised by the executive, in this case in the area of international affairs. In other words, she claimed that a decision to cancel an international treaty was for her. Gina Miller, a brave citizen, challenged her power to do so without the authority of an act of parliament.

A majority of the Supreme Court sided with Mrs Miller[11] on the ground, briefly, of Brexit's enormous constitutional significance for reasons just mentioned. The Court also stressed that as Brexit would result in a loss of a number of domestic rights, these could only be changed by parliament (under the principle of parliamentary sovereignty) - and not by the executive.

The second case[12] (also initiated by Gina Miller and Joanne Cherry MP in its Scottish version) involved Mr Johnson's invoking the Queen's prerogative power to prorogue parliament - to suspend it for a period - in this case for 34 days. This would have allowed the executive to negotiate exit from the EU without parliamentary oversight. A full and unanimous Supreme Court held that the suspension of parliament would frustrate, without reasonable justification, the ability of parliament to carry out its constitutional function as a legislature and as the body responsible for the supervision of the executive.

In both those cases we see the principle or rule of parliamentary sovereignty upheld, but upheld against the executive branch of government.

---

majority, multiple decisions, special time delays or a combination of such factors. Sometimes ratification by popular referendum is required, and in federal systems sometimes ratification by the entities.'

10. A further peculiarity of the referendum process was that the terms of the 2013 Referendum Act in no way required the result of the referendum to be binding upon the government or parliament. As was said in *Miller* 1 (*see* note 11 below). Any interpretation that it did so was therefore purely a 'political' rather than a 'legal' interpretation. Compare the Parliamentary Voting System and Constituencies Act 2011 which authorised a referendum on the subject of an alternative vote system in Parliamentary elections and was intended to bind parliament.
11. *Secretary of State for Exiting the European Union v. R (Miller)* [2017] UKSC 5. Henceforth: *Miller 1. See* J. Jowell, 'Brexit Judicialised: *Crown v Parliament Again*', The UK Supreme Court Yearbook, 8 (2016-2017), p. 238.
12. *R (Miller) v. Prime Minister; Cherry v. Advocate General* [2019] UKSC 41 ('*Miller 2*').

There is another aspect of the first Miller case which bears mention, namely, the government's disregard of a constitutional convention which, as we have seen, Dicey rightly regarded as the cultural glue that binds the constitution. Ours is now a multi-layered constitution, albeit not quite a federal structure because in each of the devolution settlements, a section provides that the powers devolved to the relevant legislature 'does not affect the power of the Parliament of the United Kingdom to make laws for [Northern Ireland, Wales or Scotland]'.[13] However, there is a convention, as stated by Lord Sewel (the Minister of State in the Scotland Office in the House of Lords who was responsible for the progress of the Scotland Bill in 1998), that 'we would expect a convention to be established that Westminster would not normally legislate with regard to the devolved matters in Scotland without the consent of the Scottish Parliament'.[14] It was acknowledged by the UK Supreme Court in Miller that this expectation has been observed over the years.[15]

The Sewel Convention, however, has more recently received statutory recognition through section 2 of the Scotland Act 2016, which alters section 28 of the Scotland Act 1998 that governs the law-making powers of the Scottish Parliament to read:

This section does not affect the power of the Parliament of the UK to make laws for Scotland.

But it is recognised that the Parliament of the UK will not normally legislate with regard to devolved matters without the consent of the Scottish Parliament.

In Miller 1, the Government of Scotland submitted that the Sewel convention should be judicially endorsed and enforced. The Supreme Court did not 'underestimate the importance of constitutional conventions, some of which play a fundamental role in the operation of our constitution'.[16] However, it held that their validity cannot be the subject of judicial proceedings. As for the Sewel convention, it operates only as a 'political restriction' on the activity of the UK Parliament, even though it was reduced to statutory form since 'the purpose of the legislative recognition of the convention was to entrench it as a convention'.[17] In other words, not as a legal rule.

If the purpose of section 2 of the Scotland Act 2016 was to codify, or legalise, the Sewel Convention, Miller 1 sanctions the executive simply to ignore it nevertheless, as the courts will not subject a convention to review.

At the time of writing this chapter, the executive continues to assert its primacy. Some of the instances that follow may have been modified or withdrawn by the time this volume is published, but they will remain as examples of the kind of disregard for constitutional propriety that an unwritten constitution allows.

The first example concerns a parliamentary bill called the Retained EU Law (Revocation and Reform) Bill which received its second reading in November 2022. The Bill's intention is to revoke or replace more than 2,400 EU-derived regulations by the end of 2023. These are the 'retained laws' that, after Brexit, were kept on the statute

13. Northern Ireland Act 1998, section 5(6); Government of Wales Act 2006, section 107(5); Scotland Act 1998, section 28(7).
14. HL Deb 21 July 1998, vol. 592 col 791.
15. *Miller* (1) [137].
16. *Ibid.*, [151].
17. *Ibid.*, [149] (emphasis added), [136].

book, to ensure continuity – at least for a while. The minister in charge of the bill, Jacob Rees-Mogg pronounced that the bill would finally rid us of the 'sovereignty of EU law', but the bill seeks to give the power to revoke, revise or retain any of the EU regulations to the executive, rather than to parliament.

Some delegated legislation to the executive may sometimes be necessary in a fast-moving, time-constrained parliament or in the case of a public emergency such as during the COVID-19 pandemic lockdowns. However, this bill gives more than disproportionate legislative power to the executive. There is no provision for public consultation, and at most only a two- hour debate in parliament for MPs to say yes or no. Hardly sufficient scrutiny for a myriad of laws such as the level of radioactive substances in water, the designation of wildlife habitats, regulations about protecting our rivers, controls of pesticides in foods, protection of part-time workers, minimum requirements for maternity pay, ban on trafficking of illegal weapons, etc.

This is rank usurpation of parliament's power to make law on these matters that are important to so many. It is also a violation of the rule of law insofar as the public and businesses have no idea what government intends to do.

Another example arose in respect of respect for the rule of law in the international sphere. As Tom Bingham contends in his book The Rule of Law,[18] the rule of law must be complied with not only in the domestic, but also in the international order. The adherence to the rule of law in the international order used to be required under the Ministerial Code, a set of practices, first published by John Major in 1992 to guide the executive branch of government. The Code has no legal status and is enforced at the discretion of the Prime Minister. It initially imposed an overarching duty on ministers to comply with the law 'including international law and treaty obligations'.

However, in 2015 it was amended by excising the reference to international law and simply providing that ministers must uphold 'the law'. In defence of that deletion it was disingenuously argued that 'the law' included international law, so why waste words? But the omission is surely a telling signal from the executive at that time that regard for the rule of law in the international order was to be softened.

The handling of the Northern Ireland Protocol to the EU Treaty is one example of disrespect for international law. Despite assertions to the contrary by Boris Johnson during the Brexit negotiation, the eventual Brexit treaty did create a customs border between the UK and Northern Ireland. This has since been a bitter bone of contention. When subsequent negotiations with the EU to relax the border control stalled, the Government decided to introduce a bill in Parliament unilaterally to breach their previously signed agreement with the EU.

Amazingly, the UK minister responsible for Northern Island conceded in parliament that the Bill would indeed breach international law, but 'only in a very specific and limited way'.

It was only after one of the government's prominent law officers resigned in protest – as did the head of its legal department – that the government withdrew those provisions.

18. (2010).

However, another bill was then submitted to break the agreement. The then Solicitor General, Suella Braverman, prepared the ground by claiming that it was ('painfully') necessary to legislate to cancel the Northern Ireland Protocol because the EU had created a trade barrier in the Irish sea, and that the Protocol was 'unreasonable and disproportionate'. This despite the fact that the UK had voluntarily signed up to the deal.

Incidentally, these were clearly political justifications from someone whose role as Attorney General was to provide independent advice to the government.

The bill in its latest iteration is justified by a spurious 'doctrine of necessity', which, in the words of another recent Solicitor General who also resigned his office, Alex Chalk KC, attempts to 'defend ... the indefensible'. Surely the House of Lords' Constitution Committee is right to have said, on more than one occasion that it is 'not appropriate for Parliament acting unilaterally to reinterpret an international treaty to which the UK has been a party'.

Let me now turn to government attitudes towards our judiciary and the Human Rights Act. After the first Miller case in the Divisional Court the judges who held against the government were pilloried as 'enemies of the people' by the Daily Mail and other newspapers, but with the fingerprints of the government all over the attacks. Beneath that headline the papers accused the judges of lack of impartiality on the ground of their 'European connections'. And even remarked that one of the judges at first instance was 'openly gay'. Gina Miller and her fellow claimants were also derided and belittled.

The Lord Chancellor of that time was Liz Truss who had a statutory duty, under the Constitutional Reform Act, to support judicial independence and the rule of law. However, after taking some time to react, she expressed only general support for both judicial independence and the freedom of the press. In a later letter to the Times she expressed confidence in the judges in the case, but refused to go further to avoid interfering with the freedom of the press or to 'censor headlines' which she did not believe had 'imperilled' judicial independence.

However, according to the Chief Justice of the time, Lord Thomas, the reaction was such that he had to order additional security for the judiciary.[19]

In respect of the second Miller case, relating to the prorogation of parliament, Boris Johnson did comply with the judgment, and parliament immediately reconvened. But he nevertheless commented that the court had 'got it wrong'.

His then attorney General Geoffrey Cox threatened parliamentary scrutiny of judicial appointments and his next Attorney General, yes, Suella Braverman, wrote, even before she was formally appointed, that 'judges have made a chronic and steady encroachment on the political arena', urging parliament to 'take back control'.

Over the past few years these attacks on the judiciary, probably the most competent, impartial and independent in the world, have increased. As have criticisms of various provisions of the Human Rights Act, and the judgments of the European

19. In an interview with the respected legal journalist, J. Rozenberg. For a full account *see* his book: *Enemies of the People* (2020), Chapter 2

Court of Human Rights in Strasbourg, which adjudicates infringements of Convention rights.

Two independent commissions were set up. One under Lord Faulks, to consider whether judicial review in general goes too far;[20] and another, under Sir Peter Gross, a retired Court of Appeal judge, to consider the Human Rights Act.[21] Both have been impeccably thorough and both have suggested only minor amendments, which, in relation to judicial review, have already been passed into law.

However, when Dominic Raab became justice secretary in Johnson's final cabinet his new bill included proposals which the Independent Rights Commission did not think necessary – such as, making it more difficult for claimants of human rights such as Gina Miller to bring cases, and some other weakening of rights. Raab's bill has returned at the time of writing under the Sunak administration. Although Raab's bill did not advocate withdrawal from the Convention, it does propose the repeal of the Human Rights Act which incorporates Convention rights into UK law, and proposes that our courts could diverge to a greater extent from the judgments of the European Court of Human Rights. This again could amount to a breach of one of the UK's international treaty obligations.[22]

We should note here the Judicial Power Project, run by a think tank called Policy Exchange which is close to the government. The purpose of this project is to strengthen parliamentary sovereignty and reduce what they call 'judicial overreach'. It is led by the Oxford Professor Ekins who, in October 2022, issued a paper in which he said that there is a powerful case for withdrawal from the European Convention, on the ground that our domestic common and statute law perfectly well safeguarded human rights before the Human Rights Act came into force.[23]

This I am afraid is simply not so. There were of course decisions which furthered liberty and civil rights, but looking back to those years we see umpteen cases where people's rights were not recognised in our law but were protected only when they petitioned the Strasbourg court. Under parliamentary sovereignty our courts lacked the power to review legislation which might breach human rights, which could only be protected through petition to the Strasbourg court. Let us remember too that until we incorporated the European Convention into our law in 1998, the UK was held to be one of the worst offenders in Europe by the Strasbourg Court. It reversed decisions of the UK courts – such as those which had denied rights of gay men and women to join the army,[24] or denied Ugandan Asians entry to this country (despite their British citizenship),[25] or which censored the Sunday Times to reveal the detail of the thalidomide scandal,[26] or which permitted corporal punishment in schools,[27] and many more.

20. *The Independent Review of Administrative Law 2020.*
21. *The Independent Human Rights Act Review 2021.*
22. *See* T. Hickman, 'A UK Bill of Rights?' London Review of Books, 44(6), 24 March 2022, p. 32.
23. R. Ekins, *The Limits of Judicial Power, Policy Exchange* (2022).
24. *Smith and Grady v. United Kingdom* (2000) 29 EHRR 493.
25. *East African Asians v. United Kingdom* (1973) 3 EHRR 76.
26. *Sunday Times v. United Kingdom* (1979) 2 EHRR 245.
27. *Tyrer v. United Kingdom (1979-80)* 2 EHRR 1.

Professor Ekins also proposes in that paper that the Lord Chancellor should refuse to appoint judges who cast doubt on parliament's authority to 'make or unmake any law', harking back to Dicey's extravagant pronouncement in 1885. One might think that that degree of interference in judicial decision-making by the executive is unthinkable in a democracy properly so-called.

The Judicial Power Project also urges the government to prevent the courts from refusing to implement 'ouster clauses'. These are provisions in a statute which empower a body exercising public functions but then proceed to seek to preclude the courts from reviewing whether the body had acted within the scope of those powers. Following ancient case law, the Supreme Court has recently held that an ouster clause violates the rule of law insofar as it permits the body established by parliament to define the limits of its own powers. But the decision is one of a number that the present government, following the lead of the Judicial Power Project, wish to reverse.[28]

Another murky area in our constitutional arrangements concerns ethical standards. A recent document by the excellent Constitution Unit at University College London[29] has developed a list of constitutional values, some of which I have already alluded to and which rightly includes 'integrity and standards'. In the past few years various mechanisms have been put in place to achieve this, and I have already referred to the Ministerial Code of Practice.

The Code's potentially most enforceable provision is the one that states that 'ministers who knowingly mislead parliament' will be expected to offer their resignation to the Prime Minister. This is an important provision because parliament's authority to hold ministers to account is toothless if misleading information leads to no sanction. Yet enforcement has been slack, as we saw with the allegations of bullying against the then Home Secretary Priti Patel, which led to the resignation in protest of the relevant civil servant. Suella Braverman, when she was Home Secretary under the brief administration of Liz Truss, confessed to breaking the ministerial code and resigned. However, she was re-appointed as Home Secretary the following week by the new Prime Minister, Rishi Sunak.

While on the subject of integrity, mention has to be made of the House of Lords. Credit must be given to the Lords for the high quality and often independence of their scrutiny of legislation, which may or may not justify its swollen numbers (over 800) and its retention of 85 peers who are there by virtue of birth, the hereditary peers, all of them men.

There is also of course a question of the legitimacy of our being governed, albeit with limited powers, by those whom we don't elect and we cannot remove.

---

28. The case is *R (Privacy International) v. Investigatory Powers Tribunal* [2019] UKSC, 22. I declare an interest as a counsel in that case. *See* J. Jowell QC and D. Rose QC, 'Beyond *Anisminic*: The Rule of Law and Ouster Clauses after *Privacy International*', 10, The UK Supreme Court Yearbook (2018-2019), p. 140. Professor Ekins wrote of this case that three of the four judges 'asserted an intention in the future openly to disobey statute', which he considered 'warranted removal from office in accordance with the terms of the Senior Courts Act'. *See* Jowell and Rose, above, p. 143.
29. M. Russell, Al. Renwick and L. James, *Protecting Constitutional Principles: What Are They and Why Do They Matter?* Constitution Unit, October 2022.

Attempts to reform the Lords have failed largely because the Commons fear competition if the upper house is made more acceptable. But surely the most offensive aspect of the Lords is the practice of appointing peers on the basis of their contribution to the coffers of one political party or another. According to one account (and I have not been able to check this) 22 of the Tory party's largest donors who together have donated GBP 54 million have been appointed to the Lords in the last 10 years. What does this say about the integrity of our system of governance?

I'm afraid there is more: Our impartial civil service is a much-valued feature of our constitutional landscape. But here too we note the recent attempts to politicise the civil service by securing the dismissal of various senior officials who were viewed as displaying any significant independence, as shown by the then Chancellor of the Exchequer, Kwasi Kwarteng's, dismissal of the permanent secretary in the Treasury.

And there have been other attacks on the independence of institutions which are key to our constitutional structures in one form or another. These include the electoral commission, a move described by a former chief justice as 'repugnant'. For one brief moment it seemed that the Bank of England was also seen as dispensable, not to mention the Office of Budget Responsibility.

There are many, many other uncertainties in our system that cause confusion such as the status of our overseas territories and Crown Dependencies. Post-colonial structures and attitudes need addressing to preclude the injustice inflicted on the inhabitants of the Chagos Islands, who were exiled from their own islands and sent to Mauritius, as outlined in Philippe Sands' recent book on the subject.[30]

This litany of constitutional slippage, of democratic die-back, somewhat like the present plague on the country's ancient ash trees, is I believe deeply concerning. It reverses a trend which since the second world war has deepened our democracy in many ways, including increased opportunity to challenge decisions made about our lives, through judicial review, but also through quasi-legal methods such as the ombudsman, tribunals and inquiries. And then by allowing better access to information, incorporating the provisions of the European Convention on Human Rights, promoting more local decision-making, and introducing regulation of standards in public life, making the appointments of judges independent, introducing regulation on standards of integrity in public life, deepening the devolutions settlements, and so on.

This is all in stark contrast to recent lapses from democratic standards which are not due to fits of absentmindedness – but reflect a persistent and flagrant disregard of democratic fundamentals.

To summarise: We have in very recent years seen the desirable fluidity and flexibility of an unwritten constitution being revealed as containing an underbelly which is dominated by uncertainty, confusion and the ability to evade democratic fundamentals. Sovereignty of parliament over the executive has been severely confronted until saved by the courts in the two Brexit cases. The rule of law in the national and international sphere has been disregarded and the enforcement of ethical

30. *The Last Colony* (2022).

standards has been lax. It seems that we can no longer rely on constitutional conventions, codified or not, to be honoured.

The international dimension

Such constitutional muddle should not be viewed from the domestic perspective alone. As we have seen in respect of our economic decisions, we are not isolated from the world at large. And here we should not ignore the mighty existential battle raging between democracy and the forces of authoritarianism and tyranny. So many countries which for a while embraced democracy from the 1990s are being undermined by nationalism, religious extremism and corruption.

Former success stories for democracy, such as Turkey, are now imprisoning critics and marginalising minorities. Places like Hungary and Poland are forsaking the rule of law and human rights under the banner of being 'illiberal democracies'. The Arab Spring turned into a desolate winter, especially in Syria. It's one democratic aspiration, Tunisia, is again asserting its former despotic tendencies. Russia has reverted to its tyrannical past.

It may be too early to judge the performance of recent governments of Italy and Sweden or whether the pattern has been decisively reversed in Brazil. China, under the iron rule of Chairman Xi Jinping, has forsaken any pretence of democracy and, because of its economic success, is providing a model for the developing world of autocratic capitalism through trade and investment.

This is not the time for the oldest democracy to be seen to be flouting the rule of law both domestically and internationally. And particularly not to trash the European Human Rights Convention which has been so successful in binding together 46 disparate countries into a common human rights law. Some of those countries may be diminishing their commitment to the Convention's rights, but compare Europe now to when the Convention first came into effect after World War II. What sort of a signal does it give if we renounce the Convention entirely, or even make the arrogant decision to cherry-pick its rights or judgments? And if we leave the Convention, as our Home Secretary would like, we will only be in the European company of Russia and Belarus.

Time for a written constitution?

There is little question that many of the attributes of a well-written constitution would benefit us. It would bring at least a greater degree of certainty than we have now. It would certainly bring about greater understanding of the way we are governed. It would, as Tom Bingham put it, 'provide a map and compass in a trackless desert'.[31]

However, there has to be real doubt as to whether what has been called a 'constitutional moment' has arrived; a moment which impels a country to come together and proclaim a new order sealed with a root-and-branch written constitution. Linda Colley's book[32] shows convincingly how the sound of guns and the cost of ships led to new constitutional settlements in the countries she describes. Most of those constitutions begin in effect: 'Never Again', seeking to sweep away an unsatisfactory

31. T. Bingham, 'A Written Constitution?', *Lives of the Law* (2011), p. 97.
32. *Supra* note 7.

past. As did the constitutions in the post-Soviet era, or the post-apartheid South African constitution.

As far as the UK is concerned, even the constitutional turbulence of the recent past seems unlikely in itself to have brought us to that 'constitutional moment' when various interests drop their weapons and come together in a national constitutional convention to write a foundational document. Realistically, there is no present political steam behind constitutional codification and no leadership to encourage it. If Scottish or Welsh independence were imminent, that might create the necessary trigger, perhaps.

So if that moment has not arrived, what do we do? Sit on our hands and, like Beckett's characters Vladimir and Estragon wait for the Godot who may never arrive? I would rather hope that constitutional reform now might in some way avert the adversity that usually precedes a constitutional moment.

And while an overriding constitutional code may well be the best way to achieve constitutional ground rules so as to make our system understandable, transparent, accessible, coherent and firmly located within democratic strictures, in the meantime more straightforward measures might achieve these aims, at least in part. This could be achieved in the form of a Constitutional Reform Act, or a series of acts, along the model of the major spate of constitutional reforms of the late 1990s and early 2000s.

These started with the devolution settlements, the human rights act and freedom of information act. It continued to the Constitutional Reform Act of 2005, which among other things, altered the role of the Lord Chancellor and created a system for independent appointment of judges. Most importantly, it incorporated in statute for the first time what it called 'the existing constitutional principle of the rule of law'.

If cross-party consensus could be achieved, the process of reform could be guided by a running commission, along the lines of the Joint Parliamentary Committee on Human Rights, or the House of Lords Constitution Committee.

By one means or another, it is surely time to wave away the smoke and remove the mirrors that obscure constitutional reality (and hide offences against democratic standards) and to seek clear answers to burning questions such as:

> How best can we restrain breaches of the rule of law on the national and international level? Should a change of prime ministers now require support from their political party? Or the wider electorate? Should the ministerial code be independently enforceable? Should it contain more stringent penalties? Should the role of civil society organisations in challenging official decisions in which they have an interest be entrenched? Should there be a right to judicial review? Should other institutions receive greater entrenchment, such as the National Health Service, BBC, Bank of England? Should the use and procedures of referendums be clarified? Should the role of the attorney general be made less political? Is it right, in international law or simple morality, to export to other countries our obligations to asylum-seekers that reach our shores? Should we continue to be the most centralised country in Europe rather than a properly federal state, through more financial or other autonomy conferred on devolved nations and regions or cities? What should be the limits of subordinate legislation? Should representation in the House of Lords be on the basis of regional representation? Should appointment to the Lords be allowed on the basis of a financial contribution? Has the time come to codify the presently unenforceable conventions, by way of a new constitutional

> arbitrator[33]? Should we, as many written constitutions do, identify and celebrate our fundamental constitutional principles and values that underlie our democratic order? Should these include not only to representative government and the rule of law, but also integrity, equality, and solidarity or even 'levelling up'? What should our relationships with the Overseas Territories and Crown Dependencies look like? And perhaps most fundamentally, do we really feel comfortable about living in a country which allows, even as an unlikely hypothetical risk, never mind atrocities against blue-eyed babies, but which allows more immediate prospects, such the politicisation of our judiciary, or the weakening of our fundamental rights, including to challenge decisions in the courts?

There may be some who think it best to treat those issues with benign neglect, with faith that pragmatic British common sense will resolve them in the end. But surely the length of this list alone, and the fact that so many of the issues are unresolved, are stark indications that we should confront them head on. This becomes all the more urgent when we see that trust in our institutions, and in democracy as a whole, is at an historic low. A recent poll shows that six out of 10 people aged 18-44 think a good way to run this country is 'a strong leader who does not have to pay attention to parliament'.[34] This statistic above all others should jolt us into action.

The structure and fabric of our democratic house are in a state of neglect. As any householder knows, deferred maintenance invariably leads to compound and exponential damage down the line. If the time is not now ripe for a root and branch rebuilding, there is a burning case for immediate refurbishment. It is at our peril that we neglect the care and attention that our constitutional democracy deserves; for the sake of our future – at home, and in the world at large.

33. Lord Sumption, a former Justice of the Supreme Court, has recently suggested that conventions be regulated through a committee of the Privy Council (provide the source in article in the Times).
34. YouGov poll December 2020.

PART III Law's Promise

CHAPTER 17

Why Also the ECJ Needs to Be Controlled?

Peter M. Huber

1 THE RULE OF LAW IN EU-LAW

1.1 Need to Put the Concept in Concrete Terms

Just like its Member States, the European Union (EU) is, as is explicitly set out in Article 2 Treaty on European Union (TEU), founded on the rule of law. This finding does, however, not provide for any further guidance on what the rule of law entails or requires in detail. In fact 'the rule of law' is an open legal concept that needs to be put in concrete terms, but in doing so, it cannot be filled with just any arbitrary content. Concepts, especially in constitutional law, are – figuratively speaking – not just 'smoke and mirrors' but they define a certain perception of reality. To reformulate it in the words of Georg Wilhelm Friedrich Hegel: What cannot be put into a concept does not exist.[1]

The fact that a legal term is undefined does not mean that it lacks a substantive content or that it can be interpreted at one's sole discretion.[2] Rather, it is primarily the responsibility of the bodies in charge of, and for, a legal system to reduce the vagueness of legal terms and to develop some guidance for its understanding and interpretation. Therefore, it is in the first place the task of the constituent power or the legislator amending the constitution and – at the level of the EU – a task of the Member States as Masters of the Treaties. In second place it is the task of the ordinary legislator designated as first interpreter of the constitution, i.e., the Treaties and ultimately it is

1. *Georg W. F. Hegel*, Die Verfassung Deutschlands (1800–1801), in: *ibid.* (ed.), Werke 1, Frühe Schriften, 1971, p. 450 (460).
2. *Peter M. Huber*, Art. 2 EUV als Grundlage des Staaten- und Verfassungsverbundes der EU, in: Lisso/Strzelbicki/Poznanskie (eds), Pánstwo a gospodarka, Ksiega Jubileuszowa dedykowana Profesir Bozenie Popowskiej, 2020, p. 41.

a task of the judiciary designated as final interpreter of the law. Thereby, it is of course not for the judiciary to dispose of the content of legal terms. Judges – at the Union level as well as in the national context – are rather bound to the rules on competences and procedures as well as to the substantive legal requirements, which they have to apply to the specific case within recognised legal methods. In doing so, courts are not only integrated into a system of multiple instances on a national level and in a network of courts on a European level (*Rechtsprechungsverbund*) – in particular constitutional and supreme courts together with the European Court of Justice (ECJ) and the European Court of Human Rights (ECtHR; *Verfassungsgerichtsverbund*) – but they are also subject to an intensive rationality control by the academia which supplements or replaces the general social and political control by the public (cf. thereto § 169 GVG[3], § 17 BVerfGG[4]).[5]

More than 70 years after the beginning of European integration, apparent contours of a European understanding of the rule of law have been shaped and can also be operationalised in practice. The existence of a procedure under which, *inter alia*, an infringement of the rule of law can be sanctioned (Article 7 TEU) – and which in German is not by chance called '*Rechtsstaatsverfahren*'[6] – as well as the introduction of the so-called rule of law mechanism as a tool to withhold funds from Member States breaching the rule of law demonstrate that there is at least some accord on certain elements of the rule of law.

Taking the common constitutional traditions of the Member States, on which the legal order of the EU and thus also the correct understanding of Article 2 TEU is based,[7] as a starting point, there are in particular with regard to the judiciary common requirements for the organisation, procedure and functioning of courts, which are generally recognised in the European legal area[8] and, therefore, must also determine the understanding of the rule of law on the level of the EU. Those common requirements have partially been cleared by rulings of the ECJ on the organisation of the court systems in the Member States since the decision *Associação Sindical dos Juízes Portugueses*[9] or on the rule of law mechanism,[10] but also by decisions of the ECtHR[11]

3. Courts Constitution Act (*Gerichtsverfassungsgesetz*).
4. Act on the Federal Constitutional Court (*Bundesverfassungsgerichtsgesetz*).
5. *Peter M. Huber*, Rechtsprechung und Rechtswissenschaft, JZ 2022, 1 (7).
6. Cf. *Christoph Möllers/Linda Schneider*, Demokratiesicherung in der Europäischen Union, 2018, pp. 45 ff.; earlier already *Thomas Pforr*, Die Allgemeine Unionsaufsicht, 2004.
7. *Peter M. Huber*, Die gemeinsamen Verfassungsüberlieferungen der Mitgliedstaaten – Identifizierung und Konkretisierung, EuR 57 (2002), 145 (151).
8. Cf. *Stefan Storr/Sebastian Unger/Ferdinand Wollenschläger* (eds), Der Europäische Rechtsraum, 2021.
9. More recently, ECJ, Judgment of. 27.2.2018, Case C-64/16, ECLI:EU:C:2018:117, paras 41 et seq. – *Associação Sindical dos Juízes Portugueses*; Judgment of 6.3.2018, Case C284/16, ECLI-:EU:C:2018:158, para. 34 – *Achmea*; Judgment of 25.7.2018, Case C 216/18 PPU, ECLI-:EU:C:2018:586, paras 35, 45 et seq. – Minister for Justice and Equality (shortcomings of the judicial system in Poland).
10. ECJ, Judgment of 16.2.2022, Case C-156/21, ECLI:EU:C:2021:97 *Hungary v. European Parliament a Council of the European Union*.
11. Cf. ECHR, Judgment of 24.11.1994 – No. 15287/89, para. 38 – *Beaumartin v. France*, para. 38; Judgment of 28.5.2002 – No. 46295/99, para. 78, – *Stafford/UK*; Judgment of 6.5.2003 – Nos 39343/98, 39651/98, 43147/98 and 46664/99, paras 193 et seq. – *Kleyn and others/Netherlands*;

and national constitutional courts such as the Federal Constitutional Court of Germany.[12]

1.1.1 *Checks and Balances as an Element of the Rule of Law*

The rule of law entails, *inter alia*, the principles of legal certainty and the protection of legitimate expectations, proportionality, the principle of equality and effective legal protection by independent courts.[13] It also includes the principle of separation of powers in the national context (e.g., Article 20 paragraph 2 sentence 2 GG[14])[15] and in the context of the EU its functional equivalent: the institutional balance. Both - the principle of separation of powers and the institutional balance - aim at a moderation of state or supranational power through a separation and mutual control of organs. In this respect, a system of checks and balances - as described by Montesquieu with regard to Great Britain in the 18th century[16] - is part of the indispensable institutional design of every constitutional state or organisation based on the rule of law.[17]

1.1.2 *Checks and Balances as the Core Element of the Separation of Powers*

Taking Germany as an example, Article 20 paragraph 2 sentence 2 GG stipulates that the state power emanates from the people and is primarily exercised by special bodies

Helen Keller/Cedric Marti, Der EGMR als Schöpfer von Verwaltungsprozessrecht, in: v. Bogdandy/Huber/Marcusson (eds), Ius Publicum Europeaum, Vol. 8 (IPE IX), 2021, § 154 paras 62, 64, 75 with further references.

12. For Germany, cf. e.g., BVerfGE 149, 346 ff. - European Schools; BVerfGE 163, xx - European Patent Office.
13. ECJ, Judgment of 27.2.2018, C-64/16, ECLI:EU:C:2018:117, para. 31 f. - *Associação Sindical dos Juízes Portugueses*; Judgment of 6.3.2018, Case C-284/16, ECLI:EU:C:2018:158, para. 36 - *Achmea*; Judgment of 25.7.2018, Case C-216/18 PPU, ECLI:EU:C:2018:586, para. 48 f. - *Minister for Justice and Equality* (shortcomings of the judicial system in Poland).
14. Basic Law of the Federal Republic of Germany.
15. *Peter M. Huber*, Rechtsstaat, in: Herdegen/Masing/Poscher/Gärditz, Handbuch des Verfassungsrechts, vol. 1, 2021, § 6 Rn. 28 ff. with further references.
16. *Charles de Secondat, Baron de Montesquieu*, De l'Esprit des Lois, 1748, Livre XI, Ch. 6, included in: Caillois (ed.), Montesquieu. Oeuvres complètes, vol. II, 1951, pp. 396 ff.; on this *Max Imboden*, Montesquieu und die Lehre von der Gewaltentrennung, 1959; *Ulrich Lange*, Teilung und Trennung der Gewalten bei Montesquieu, Der Staat 19 (1980), 213 ff. Needless to say that idea already goes back to *John Locke*, Two Treaties of Government, 1689, Book II, pp. 247 ff.
17. On the principle of separation of powers as a 'fundamental structural element [...] of all constitutions of the modern constitution', already *Richard Thoma*, in: Anschütz/Thoma Handbuch des Deutschen Staatsrechts, vol. 2, unchanged, reprint of the 1st ed. 1932, § 71 pp. 111 f.; *Klaus Stern*, Staatsrecht vol. 1, 2nd ed. 1987, § 20 IV 3, p. 792 f.; *Hans-Detlef Horn*, Gewaltenteilige Demokratie, demokratische Gewaltenteilung - Überlegungen zu einer Organisationsmaxime des Verfassungsstaates, AöR 127 (2002), 427 (428); in this sense also *Schmidt-Aßmann*, in: Isensee/Kirchhof (eds.), vol. 2, 3rd ed. 2004, § 26 Rn. 46 f.; *Di Fabio* in: Isensee/Kirchhof (eds.), vol. 2, 3rd ed. 2004, § 27 Rn. 80; *Christoph Möllers*, Gewaltengliederung, 2005, pp. 1, 76 ff.; *Ralf Poscher* in: Hoffmann-Riem/Schmidt-Aßmann/Voßkuhle (eds.), Grundlagen des Verwaltungsrechts, vol. 1, 2nd ed. 2012, § 8 Rn. 8, 19 f.; as well as *Helmuth Schulze-Fielitz*, in: Dreier (ed.) GG, 3rd ed. 2013, Article 20 Rn. 67 according to which the principle of separation of powers is a fundamental idea central to the type of Western constitutional state; *Peter Badura*, Staatsrecht, 7th ed. 2018, p. 425 f.; *Sommermann* in v. Mangoldt/Klein/Starck GG, 7th ed., 2018, Article 20 marginal no. 205; more critical of the common attribution of the separation of powers as an essential element of the principle of the rule of law *Katharina Sobota*, Das Prinzip Rechtsstaat, 1997, p. 70.

of the legislature, the executive and the judiciary. According to the case law of the Federal Constitutional Court, the principle of the separation of powers determines and further shapes the division and mutual control of the legislative, executive and judicial powers with regard to specific aspects. Although Parliament, which is directly elected by the people and which is meant to take all fundamental decisions under the Basic Law, the latter neither provides for a so-called monism of powers granting comprehensive reservation of power for the parliament[18] such as the sovereignty of Parliament nor does it recognise some kind of hierarchy among the constitutional bodies with regard to their democratic legitimacy.[19] The organisational and functional separation and division of powers stipulated in Article 20 paragraph 2 sentence 2 GG rather aims at ensuring that decisions are taken in the best way possible, i.e., by the organs and bodies that are best equipped to take the respective decision in terms of their organisation, composition, function and procedures.[20]

The separation of powers is an essential constitutional principle in all Member States forming the European legal space. Even if the specific design of the balance of powers is by nature historically contingent and differs from one Member State to another, it is in principle common to all constitutional states.[21]

The concept of 'institutional balance' among the institutions of the European Communities, i.e., the EU, however, is a creation of the Court of Justice of the EU. In the late 1980s, at a time when the constitutionalisation of Union law was still in its very beginning, it was a kind of equivalent for the principle of the separation of powers, which was not envisaged in the European treaties and could not without further ado be

18. Cf. BVerfGE 68, 1 (86 f.); 98, 218 (251 f.); 139, 19 (46 para. 53); 150, 1 (99 para. 197) - Census 2011.
19. In this sense *Ernst-Wolfgang Böckenförde/Rolf Grawert*, Sonderverordnungen zur Regelung besonderer Gewaltenverhältnisse, AöR 95 (1970), 1 ff., 25 f., according to which the contrast between the legislative and the executive is only based on direct or indirect legitimation, which is only a difference of degree; on the sufficiency of indirect legitimation, BVerfGE 47, 253 (275); 49, 89 (125) - Kalkar; 77, 1 (40); on the fact that the invocation of the principle of democracy may not override the constitutional order of competences BVerfGE 137, 185 (236) - Export control for arms.
20. Cf. BVerfGE 79, 106 (120); 150, 1 (99 marginal no. 197) - Census 2011; *Fritz Ossenbühl*, in: Isensee/Kirchhof (eds.), vol. 5, 3rd ed. 2007, § 101 marginal no. 61.
21. *Mario Dogliani/Cesare Pinelli*, Grundlagen und Grundzüge staatlichen Verfassungsrecht: Italien, in: v. Bogdandy/Villalón/Huber (eds), Ius Publicum Europaeum, vol. 1, 2007, § 5 paras 120 ff.; *Piotr Tuleja*, Grundlagen und Grundzüge staatlichen Verfassungsrecht: Polen, in: v. Bogdandy/Villalón/Huber (eds), Ius Publicum Europaeum, vol. 1, 2007, § 8 para. 76 f.; *Manuel Medina Guerrero*, Grundlagen und Grundzüge staatlichen Verfassungsrecht: Spanien, in: v. Bogdandy/Villalón/Huber (eds), Ius Publicum Europaeum, vol. 1, 2007, § 11 para. 71 f.; *Gábor Halmai*, Grundlagen und Grundzüge staatlichen Verfassungsrecht: Ungarn, in: v. Bogdandy/Villalón/Huber (eds), Ius Publicum Europaeum, vol. 1, 2007, § 12 Rn. 17 ff.; Stylianos-Ioannis G. Koutnatzis, Grundlagen und Grundzüge staatlichen Verfassungsrecht: Griechenland, in: v. Bogdandy/Villalón/Huber (eds), Ius Publicum Europaeum, vol. 1, 2007, § 3 para. 117; *Ewald Wiederin*, Grundlagen und Grundzüge staatlichen Verfassungsrecht: Österreich, in: v. Bogdandy/Villalón/Huber (eds), Ius Publicum Europaeum, vol. 1, 2007, § 7 para. 98; *Hans-Heinrich Vogel*, Grundlagen und Grundzüge staatlichen Verfassungsrecht: Schweden, in: v. Bogdandy/Villalón/Huber (eds), Ius Publicum Europaeum, vol. 1, 2007, § 9 para. 106; *Jacques Ziller*, Verwaltungsgerichtsbarkeit in Frankreich, in: v. Bogdandy/Huber/Marcusons (eds.), Ius Publicum Europaeum, vol. 8, 2019, § 130 para. 35; *Schulze-Fielitz* in Dreier (ed.), GG, vol. 1, 3rd ed. 2013, Article 20 para. 35.

transferred from the common constitutional traditions of the Member States to the European level.[22] However, since the Treaties had established a functional order among the institutions, which can - *mutatis mutandis* - certainly be understood as a system of checks and balances, the ECJ resorted to the equally innocuous and versatile concept of institutional balance and assigned itself the task:

> (...) to ensure that the provisions of the Treaties concerning the institutional balance are fully applied and to see to it that the Parliament's prerogatives, like those of the other institutions, cannot be breached without it having available a legal remedy, among those laid down in the Treaties, which may be exercised in a certain and effective manner.[23]

The separation of powers and the institutional balance are not just mere legal principles. They are of such an importance for the rule of law that their core content may by no means be affected. In Germany, the separation of power is one of the principles of Article 20 GG, which must not be derogated pursuant to Article 79(3) of the Basic Law; in Austria, it is one of the main pillars (Baugesetze) of the Federal Constitution within the meaning they have received by Article 44(3) of the Austrian Federal Constitution and at the European level, it is one of the core values enshrined in Article 2 TEU, which are - so to speak - the 'business basis' (*Geschäftsgrundlage*) for the membership of a state in the EU. Against this background, modifications to the principle of separation of powers are in principle inadmissible, unless they pursue a legitimate objective - such as the change from a presidential to a parliamentary system of government or vice versa - and the means used are proportionate with regard to the objective pursued.[24] Similar considerations apply to the concept of the institutional balance.

1.2 The Traditional Perspective on the Judiciary Within the Separation of Powers

The principle of separation of powers equally applies to the division and mutual control of the legislative, executive and judicial branch of powers. Although, constitutional thinking and theory typically focus on the role of parliament and its influence on the executive[25] it is not less relevant for the role of the judiciary as the third branch of power. In most states of the European legal space, (constitutional) jurisdiction is equipped with a right to annul legislative acts. For the most part this function, also

22. *Peter M. Huber*, Das institutionelle Gleichgewicht zwischen Rat und Europäischem Parlament in der künftigen Verfassung für Europa, EuR 38 (2003), 574 (576).
23. ECJ, Judgment of 4.10.1991, Case C-70/88, [1990] ECR I-2041 et seq. para. 25 - *Parliament v. Council (Chernobyl)*.
24. ECtHR, Judgment of 18.2.1999, No. 26083/94, para. 59 with further references - *Waite and Kennedy v. Germany*; Urt. v. 6.1.2015, No. 415/07, para. 62 - *Roland Klausecker v. Germany*; BVerfGE 149, 346 (365 para. 39) - Europäische Schulen.
25. As for example the Federal Constitutional Court establishing an obligation of the legislator to take all essential decisions (*Wesentlichkeitsdoktrin*), BVerfGE 150, 1 (96 ff. marginal nos 190 ff.) - Zensus 2011.

designated as 'negative legislation'[26] – following the terminology of Hans Kelsen[27] – is either welcomed or at least accepted laconically. However, in France there has been a long tradition of fearing a 'gouvernement des juges'[28] and also in Germany, particularly since the 1980s, warnings about a *'Richterstaat'* or a *'Rechtswegestaat'* – i.e., a state directed by judges or trapped in the complex system of judicial review – arose[29] especially with regard to the Federal Constitutional Court.[30]

In the national context, the courts of the European space seem to be well aware of their limits. Almost every important constitutional or supreme court decision and many decisions of courts of lower instances, have to elaborate on the – not (fully) reviewable – margins for assessment and discretion with regard to statutes, regulations, administrative acts etc. of the first and second powers and thus necessarily implicitly always deal with the principle of the separation of powers. This also applies to the Court of Justice of the EU, which, however, typically applies a far lower standard of control vis-à-vis the other organs, bodies and institutions of the EU[31] compared to the standard applied vis-à-vis the Member States, where the approach of a strict substantial control dominates.[32]

26. Cf. for the term *Karl August Bettermann*, Richterliche Normenkontrolle als negative Gesetzgebung?, DVBl 1982, 91 ff.; *Christoph Gusy*, Parlamentarischer Gesetzgeber und Bundesverfassungsgericht, 1985, p. 40 f. *Christoph Grabenwarter* in: v. Bogdandy/Grabenwarter/Huber (eds), IPE VI, 2016, § 102 Rn. 101, 115 ff.; rejecting the functional description of constitutional court jurisdiction as 'negative legislation' *Joachim Wieland*, in: Dreier (ed.), GG, vol. 3, 3rd ed. 2018, Article 94 Rn. 27; likewise *Stefan Korioth* in: Schlaich/Korioth, Das Bundesverfassungsgericht, 12th ed. 2021, marginal no. 119 with further references.
27. *Hans Kelsen*, Wesen und Entwicklung der Staatsgerichtsbarkeit, VVDStRL 5 (1929), 30 (56).
28. The formulation goes back to the work published in 1921 entitled 'Le Gouvernement des juges et la lutte contre la legislation sociale aux Etats-Unis', by Edouard Lambert; on this *Christian Hillgruber*, Gouvernement des juges – Fluch oder Segen? – an introduction, in: ders. (ed.), Gouvernement des juges – Fluch oder Segen?, 2014, p. 11 f.
29. *Otto Rudolf Kissel*, Sorgen um die Justiz, DRiZ 1981, 219; *ders.* Grenzen der rechtsprechenden Gewalt, NJW 1982, 1777 (1779); *Horst Sendler*, 40 Jahre Rechtsstaat des Grundgesetzes – Mehr Schatten als Licht?, DÖV 1989, 482; *Rüdiger Zuck*, Blick in die Zeit, MDR 1989, 418 (420); on this already *Peter M. Huber*, Verfassungsstaat und Finanzkrise, 2014, p. 37 f.; in detail *Bernd Rüthers*, Die heimliche Revolution vom Rechtsstaat zum Richterstaat, 2014; on the concept of the 'Rechtswegestaat' also *Christian Starck*, Der demokratische Verfassungsstaat, 1995, p. 253.
30. *See Matthias Jestaedt / Oliver Lepsius / Christoph Möllers / Christoph Schönberger*, Das entgrenzte Gericht, 2011.
31. Vis-à-vis the Union legislator: ECJ, Judgment of 13.11.1990, Rs. C-331/88 – ECR 1990, I-4023, paras 14 et seq. – *FEDESA et al.*; Judgment of 11.7.1989, Rs. C-265/87 – ECR 1989, 2237, para. 22 – *Schräder*; Judgment of 17.10.1995, Rs. C-44/94, ECR 1995, I-3115, paras 567 ff. – *Fishermen's Organisations et al.* 26.11.1996, C-68/95, [1996] ECR I-6065, paras 54 ff. – *T. Port/BLE*; Case C-491/01, ECLI:EU:C:2002:741, para. 123 – *British American Tobacco*; Case C-58/08, ECLI:EU:C:2010:321, para. 52 – *Vodafone*; Case C-508/13, ECLI:EU:C:2015:403, para. 29 – *Estonia v. Parliament and Council; v. Commission*, Case C-508/13, ECLI:EU:C:2015:403, para. 29 – *Estonia v. Parliament and Council*, 15.6.1974, Case C-74/74, ECR 1975. 533, 547, para. 19/23 – *CNTA*; Case C-136/77, ECR 1978, 1245, 1256, para. 4 – *Racke*; Case C-50/74, ECLI:EU:C:2015; *Council*; v. 25.10.1977, Case C–26/76, para. 45 – *Metro/Commission*; *Thomas von Danwitz*, Verwaltungsrechtliches System und Europäische Integration, 1996, p. 333; vis-à-vis the European Central Bank (ECB): ECJ, Judgment of 16.7.2015, Case C-62/14, ECLI:EU:C:2015:400 – Gauweiler; Judgment of. 11.12.2018, Case C-493/17, ECLI:EU:C:2018: 1000 – *Weiss*.
32. ECJ, Judgment of 15.5.1986, Case C-222/84, [1986] ECR 1651, para. 18 f. – *Johnston v. Royal Ulster Constabulary*; crit. already *Peter M. Huber*, Recht der Europäischen Integration, 2nd ed., 2002, § 8 para. 72.

In essence, these questions signify a control of the first and second branch of powers by the third. They do not address the control of the judiciary itself. However, the functioning of the concept of a separation of powers or the resilience of the institutional balance evenly depends on an effective control of the judiciary by the other branches of power, especially by the legislature.

1.3 The Need for Democratic Legitimation of the Judiciary

Contrary to what the curtailed quotation attributed to Montesquieu might suggest, the judiciary in Continental Europe has never been never 'en quelque facon nulle'[33] - not even in the 18th century - and the judge has always been more than '*la bouche qui prononce les paroles de la loi*'.[34] Furthermore, there has always been an awareness that some vagueness and ambiguity are necessarily attached to every legal term, that it is impossible to foresee every potential aspect of real life, and that it would overstrain the abilities of the legislator to expect that it could solve all potential conflicts in a society in a general and abstract way in advance. Hans Kelsen therefore rightly understood that process of 'finding the law' (*richterliche Rechtsfindung*) necessarily implies some sort of concretisation of the legal provisions applicable in the specific case, the legislator thereby merely forming the 'framework' of the decision. This procedure is structurally comparable to what the legislator or the executive do within the framework of the constitution or a statute, whose decisions - laws or administrative acts - can equally be understood as a (political) concretisation of legal provisions applicable to the respective situation.[35]

Against this background, judgments, decisions and injunctions prove to be the concrete decision of a normative framework, and this means in substance the exercise of power. From this perspective, it makes sense that the judiciary is called the third branch of power. Therefore, it must not only provide a certain level of democratic legitimation, but must also be integrated into the system of separation of powers or the institutional balance respectively.

Therefore, despite the fact that the Basic Law in Article 20(3) seems to bind the executive and the judiciary to law and justice without distinction, it doesn't provide for identical functions when tying the judiciary to legal boundaries but pursues a different concept or set, at least a different accent than that tying the executive branch: While the requirement of lawfulness of administrative action or the principle of legality are intended to protect the freedom and property of citizens from an encroachment by the

33. *Charles de Montesquieu*, De l'Esprit des Lois, 1748, Livre XI, Ch. 6, in: Caillois (ed.), Montesquieu. Oeuvres complètes, vol. II, 1951, p. 401, with a view to eighteenth century Britain.
34. *Charles de Montesquieu*, De l'Esprit des Lois, 1748, Livre XI, Ch. 6, in: Caillois (ed.), Montesquieu. Oeuvres complètes, vol. II, 1951, p. 404. On the context of this formulation and its reception, again *Regina Ogorek*, De l'Esprit des légendes, RJ 2 (1983), 277 (288 f.); *ibid.*, Die erstaunliche Karriere des 'Subsumtionsmodells' oder wozu braucht der Jurist Geschichte?, in FS Klaus Lüderssen, 2002, 127 ff.; *Michael Guttner*, Rechtsprechung und Vertrauensschutz, Diss. Munich 2021, p. 213 f. (manuscript).
35. *Hans Kelsen*, Reine Rechtslehre (1934), pp. 101 ff. Reine Rechtslehre (2nd ed. 1960), pp. 423 ff., 597 et. seq.

government or the administration and to limit the political power of the executive, binding the judiciary rather aims at tying the latter to the choices made by the democratic majority and thus provide the judiciary with democratic legitimation.

Under German constitutional law doctrine there are three ways in which state action acquires democratic legitimation: firstly through either a direct election of the person exercising a state function or an appointment, which can ultimately be traced back to voters through an uninterrupted chain of acts of appointment (personal legitimacy), secondly through their binding to laws, ordinances and other instruments by which parliament or its majority determine, steer or at least influence state action (content legitimacy), and thirdly through an endowment of certain institutions by the constitution or the European Treaties themselves, such as courts (e.g., Article 97 GG, Article 19 TEU)[36] or central banks (e.g., Article 88 sentence 2 GG, Article 127 paragraph 1 Treaty on the Functioning of the European Union (TFEU)),[37] providing those mostly independent organs or bodies with a special legitimation (institutional legitimacy).[38] In the outcome, it is decisive that an overall sufficient level of democratic legitimation is provided for a specific state action and that it can be traced back to parliament and the people at least in a broader sense.[39]

In contrast to what applies to government and administration, for which the submission to law and justice, in the words of Otto Mayer, the father of modern German administrative law, is primarily about 'containing the flooding mass of administrative activity' in order to protect citizens from encroachments of their rights and liberties,[40] binding the judiciary to law and justice is primarily about limiting its power and binding it to the will of the legislator (Parliament). It is true that courts can also interfere with (fundamental) rights – e.g., when issuing an arrest warrant or when

36. *See Horst Dreier*, in: *ibid.* (ed.), GG, vol. 2, 3rd ed. 2015, Article 20 (Democracy) marginal nos 139 ff.; *Bernd Grzeszisk*, in: Maunz/Dürig, GG, Article 20 II. (as of 2010) marginal nos 244 ff.; *Michael Sachs*, in: ders. (ed.), GG, 9th ed. 2021, Article 20 Rn. 35, 45; in detail *Andreas Voßkuhle/Gernot Sydow*, Die demokratische Legitimation des Richters, JZ 2002, 673 (676 ff.); *Axel Tschentscher*, Demokratische Legitimation der dritten Gewalt, 2006, pp. 56 f., 186; *Michael Guttner*, Rechtsprechung und Vertrauensschutz, Diss. Munich 2022, pp. 302 ff. (manuscript).
37. *Horst Dreier*, in: *ibid.* (ed.), GG, vol. 2, 3rd ed. 2015, Article 20 (Democracy) marginal no. 131; *Bernd Grzeszisk*, in: Maunz/Dürig, GG, Article 20 (as of 2010) marginal no. 145; *Karl-Peter Sommermann*, in: v. Mangoldt/Klein/Starck, GG, vol. 2, 7th ed. 2018, Article 20 marginal no. 178; *see also Hermann-Josef Blanke/Stefan Pilz*, in v. Mangoldt/Klein/Starck, GG III, 7th ed. 2018, Article 88 marginal nos 22 et seq.
38. Cf. *Ernst-Wolfgang Böckenförde*, Demokratie als Verfassungsprinzip, in Isensee/Kirchhof (eds), Handbuch des Staatsrechts der Bundesrepublik Deutschland, vol. 2, 3rd ed. 2004, § 24 Rn. 9 ff.; *Horst Dreier*, in: ders. (ed.), GG, vol. 2, 3rd ed. 2015, Article 20 (Democracy) marginal nos 109 ff.; *Bernd Grzeszisk*, in: Maunz/Dürig, GG, Article 20 II. (as of 2010) marginal nos 120 ff.; *Michael Sachs* in: ders. (ed.), GG, 9th ed. 2021, Article 20 marginal no. 35; *Karl-Peter Sommermann*, in: v. Mangoldt/Klein/Starck, GG, vol. 2, 7th ed. 2018, Article 20 marginal nos 163 ff.
39. Cf. BVerfGE 83, 60 (72) – Right to vote for non-Germans II; 93, 37 (67) – Participation Schleswig-Holstein; 107, 59 (87) – Lippeverband; 119, 331 (366) – Hartz IV-Arbeitsgemeinschaften; 130, 76 (124) – Vitos Haina; 136, 194 (262 para. 168) – Wine Levies; 137, 185 (232 para. 131) – Arms Exports; 147, 50 (127 f. para. 198) – DB AG and BaFIn; 151, 202 (291 para. 129) – European Banking Union.
40. *Otto Mayer*, Deutsches Verwaltungsrecht, Vol. I, 2nd ed., 1914, p. 95.

handling procedural requirements.[41] As a rule, however – as is shown by Article 19 paragraph 4 GG[42] as well as by Article 6 European Convention on Human Rights (ECHR) or Article 47 Charter of Fundamental Rights (CFR) – courts act as guardians of individual (fundamental) rights, not as a threat to them. Against this background, Article 20 paragraph 3 GG by binding the judiciary to law and justice, primarily attributes substantive legitimation to its judgments and orders and thus provides for its control by the legislature.

Limiting the power of the judiciary is already a challenge at the national level. There, however, it is mitigated or contained by the possibilities that the legislator has to overrule a jurisdiction by issuing a statute or in relation to the constitutional jurisdiction through an amendment of the constitution, by the embeddedness of judges in a dense network of communication with other powers, the public, the professional and academic world, by reasonably homogeneous qualification requirements, predictable rationality requirements, a sophisticated system of legal remedies, specific regulations for the civil service and much more.

At the level of the EU in contrast, there are at best only rudiments of comparable constraints. This is a widely neglected problem.[43]

2 THE UNDEFINED ROLE OF THE JUDICIARY IN THE INSTITUTIONAL BALANCE OF THE EU

2.1 Exclusive Focus on Legal Protection

The guarantee of effective legal protection implies that every act of power potentially violating the law may be subject to judicial review in fact and in law.[44] Access to a judicial decision on the merits must therefore – subject to inherent constitutional limits – not be excluded, factually rendered impossible or made more difficult in an unreasonable manner that cannot be justified by legitimate reasons.[45] According to the case law of the ECJ, the ECtHR and the Federal Constitutional Court, it is part of the very essence of the legal protection guaranteed in Article 6 of the ECHR, Article 47 of the Charter and Article 19 paragraph 4 GG that the courts granting it must be independent of the bodies on whose legal acts they have to adjudicate and that also personal independence of the judges must be guaranteed. In this respect, national

41. *Peter M. Huber*, in: v. Mangoldt/Klein/Starck, GG, vol. 1, 7th ed. 2018, Article 19 marginal nos 440 ff.; *Andreas Voßkuhle*, Rechtsschutz gegen den Richter, 1993, pp. 1 ff., 255 ff.; *see also* already *Dieter Dörr*, Rechtsschutz gegen vollzogene Durchsuchungen und Beschlagnahmen im Strafermittlungsverfahren, NJW 1984, 2258 (2261 f.).
42. For violations of rights under private law, Article 2(1) in conjunction with Article 20(3) of the Basic Law gives rise to a so-called right to justice. Article 20 (3) of the Basic Law. Cf. *Peter M. Huber*, in: v. Mangoldt/Klein/Starck, GG, vol. 1, 7th ed. 2018, Article 19 marginal nos 354 et seq.
43. General *Frank Schorkopf*, Legislation by Supreme Courts and Parliaments. Zu Anspruch und Versuch einer gewaltenübergreifenden Korrektur von Rechtsprechungsrecht, AöR 144 (2019), 203 (211, 215).
44. Cf. BVerfGE 149, 346 (363 marginal no. 34) – European Schools.
45. Cf. BVerfGE 149, 346 (363 marginal no. 34) – European Schools.

constitutions, the ECHR and the Charter, which must be taken into account reciprocally by every court interpreting a question on fundamental rights,[46] broadly concur.

With regard to the ECJ the focus on legal protection when addressing the institutional balance is almost exclusive. As the quotation from the Chernobyl case (cf. above)[47] and its later decisions on institutional balance and the rule of law prove, its reasoning time and again deals with the question to what extent effective legal protection must be available to contest decisions of the legislature and the executive on national and Union level as well as around the widest possible application of Article 267 TFEU. Furthermore, by using Article 19 paragraph 1 sentence 2 and Article 2 TEU, the ECJ has tried to optimize judicial control by Luxembourg and to exercise control over the organisation of the national judiciary.[48] Framing it as an instrument to safeguard the rule of law in Poland is a clever way the ECJ has tried to immunise this approach against any criticism. Nevertheless, as the organisation of the national court system falls within the institutional and procedural autonomy of the Member States and there is no empowerment of the EU to harmonize it. This approach remains, legally speaking, an artifice.

2.2 Lack of Checks and Balances with Regard to the ECJ

As set out before, courts do not only control the other two (state) functions, but judgments, decisions and interim injunctions are also exercises of sovereign power and therefore require a sufficient level of democratic legitimation.

2.3 Weak Determination Contentwise

Under the aspect of content legitimacy (as set out before), the democratic legitimation of the jurisprudence of the Luxembourg Court is rather weak – just similar as it is the case with national constitutional courts or the ECtHR. The Treaties contain an abundance of abstract principles, general objectives and discretion for decision-making, which make it considerably difficult to tie the European judiciary back to the will of the contracting parties. This finding becomes even more troublesome considering that the Treaties are understood as 'living instruments', which means that the point of reference for their interpretation and application is not primarily their wording in 24 authentic languages (Article 55 TEU), but what the respective objectives allegedly demand under the social, political and economic conditions at a given time.[49] This opens up an almost unlimited leeway for decision-making by the ECJ.

46. Cf. BVerfGE 158, 1, marginal nos 69 ff. – Ökotox.
47. ECJ, Judgment of 4.10.1991, Case C-70/88, [1990] ECR I 2041 et seq., paras 25 et seq. – *Parliament v. Council (Chernobyl)*.
48. ECJ, Judgment of 27.2.2018, Case C-64/16, ECLI:EU:C:2018:117, para. 31 f. – *Associação Sindical dos Juízes Portugueses*; Judgment of. 6.3.2018, Case C-284/16, ECLI:EU:C:2018:158, para. 36 – Achmea; Judgment of. 25.7.2018, Case C-216/18 PPU, ECLI:EU:C:2018:586, para. 48 f. – Minister for Justice and Equality (shortcomings of the judicial system in Poland).
49. *Dieter Grimm*, Auf der Suche nach Akzeptanz. Über Legitimationsdefizite und Legitimationsressourcen der Europäischen Union, Leviathan 43 (2015), 325 (328 ff.).

This leeway for decision-making is further widened by the structure of the EU and the organisation of the ECJ: the high thresholds for amending the Treaties, in particular the requirement of unanimity, renders it practically impossible to overrule decisions of the ECJ even by the Masters of the Treaties if a majority disapproves. Furthermore, the decisions on the common organisation of the market in bananas[50] and in the Pupino case, [51] the second opinion on the accession of the EU to the ECHR[52] as well as the refusal to establish specialised courts contrary to the fact that they are explicitly provided for in Article 257 TFEU, a move that has been instigated by the ECJ,[53] show that even if there is a sufficient accord to determine a question on a primary law level, the ECJ case law does not necessarily adhere to it. Moreover, the Commission's monopoly to initiate legislative acts makes it particularly difficult to amend secondary legislation and delegated legal acts, which leads to an extensive petrifaction of case law,[54] which the European legislator – the Council and the European Parliament – can only revise in exceptional cases.

2.4 Lack of Embeddedness

Additionally, the ECJ lacks what can be described as 'embeddedness': the integration into a political, legal and judicial culture that makes the public, and especially the professional and academic community, kind of a 'public superintendent'[55] over the courts. While national courts cannot escape severe criticism, Luxembourg's Kirchberg is far away. Criticism, to the extent it actually occurs, is usually nationally fragmented and can thus be easily dismissed from the ECJ's perspective as some sort of irrelevant national position. In this respect, the reactions to the second opinion on the accession of the EU to the ECHR, which triggered criticism throughout Europe – at least in expert circles – were somewhat exceptional.[56] However, they are hardly comparable with

50. ECJ, Judgment of 5.10.1994 – C-280/93, ECR I-4973 – *Banana Market*.
51. ECJ, Judgment of 16.6.2005 – C–105/03, ECR I-5285 – *Pupino*.
52. ECJ, Opinion 2/13 of 18.12.2014, ECLI:EU:C:2014:2454 – *ECHR Accession II*; previously Opinion 2/94 of 28.3.1996, ECR 1996, I-1759 – *ECHR Accession I*.
53. *Peter M. Huber*, in: Streinz (ed.), EUV/AEUV, 3rd ed., 2018, Article 257 marginal no. 2 m. w. N.
54. *Dieter Grimm*, Europa ja – aber welches?, 2016, pp. 18, 41; *Fritz W. Scharpf*, Legitimacy in the Multi-level European Polity, in: Dobner/Loughlin (eds), The Twilight of Constitutionalism?. Oxford 2010, pp. 89 et seq., (100); *Klaus Messerschmidt*, Gesetzänderung in der Europäischen Union, in: Kloepfer (ed.), Gedächtnisschrift für Thilo Brandner, 2011, p. 29 ff.; cf. already *Mauro Cappelletti/Monica Seccombe/ Joseph H. H. Weiler*, Integration Through Law: Europe and the American Federal Experience, A General Introduction, 1985, p. 40.
55. The German literature frequently uses 'Oberaufsicht des Publikums' which is a quote from the German version of *Jeremy Bentham's*, Tactik oder Theorie des Geschäftsgangs in deliberierenden Volksversammlungen, 1817 (nach dessen hinterlassenen Papieren bearbeitet von E. Dumont), S. 11.
56. *Adam Łazowski/ Ramses A. Wessel*, When Caveats Turn into Locks: Opinion 2/13 on Accession of the European Union to the ECHR, German Law Journal 16 (2015), 179 (211); *Piet Eeckhout*, Opinion 2/13 on EU Accession to the ECHR and Judicial Dialogue: Autonomy or Autarky?, Forthham International Law Journal 38 (2015), 955 (992); Ágoston *Mohay*, Back to the Drawing Board? Opinion 2/13 of the Court of Justice on the Accession of the EU to the ECHR – Case note, Pécs Journal of International and European Law – 2015/I. 28 (35 f.); *Steve Peers*, The CJEU and the EU's accession to the ECHR: a clear and present danger to human rights protection, EU Law

reactions following, e.g., the German Federal Constitutional Courts Crucifix ruling – an order annulling a legal provision according to which crucifixes had to be placed in every classroom in public schools in Bavaria – that saw 40,000 people protesting on the Odeonsplatz in Munich.[57]

In addition, the academic discipline of European law obviously stands under the long shadow of Pierre Pescatore[58] and shows a self-conception that can be described as almost clerical. Instead of raising fundamental questions and discussing them in an unprejudiced and unbiased manner, it appears to believe that it is its primary task is to support any decision of a European institution and limits itself putting the decisions of the ECJ into the right boxes. Fundamental scepticism towards any act of power as well as generally questioning institutions and arguments, which is supposed to be an indispensable attribute for any legal scholar, can be readily found on the national level but is rather sought in vain with regard to the European level in general and the ECJ in particular.

This has contributed to a considerable level of self-referentiality in Luxembourg as well as in Brussels, which repeatedly has failed to adequately grasp the complexity of a legal order of an association of 27 Member States. This situation causes considerable risks for the acceptance of EU law and in the medium and long run also of European integration as such.

The most striking example evidencing that observation is the debate on the precedence of application (not primacy) of EU law and its limits, a debate that has been going on for over 60 years now. Summarising its abundant case law, the Federal Constitutional Court in the decision on the Unified Patent Court II in June 2021 has once again underlined in this respect:

> Yet this precedence of application only exists by virtue of, and within the limits set by, its constitutional foundations [...]. The openness of the domestic legal order to EU law, which has its basis in the design of the Basic Law and is given effect by the legislator deciding on European integration matters, is subject to limits that derive not only from the European integration agenda (Integrationsprogramm), for which the legislator bears responsibility, but also from Germany's constitutional identity enshrined in the Basic Law (Art. 23(1) third sentence in conjunction with Art. 79(3) GG), which is beyond the reach of both constitutional amendment and European integration. The precedence of application of EU law only applies to the

Analysis 18.12.2014; http://eulawanalysis.blogspot.com/2014/12/the-cjeu-and-eus-accession-to-echr.html; *Sionaidh Douglas- Scott*, Opinion 2/13 on EU accession to the ECHR: a Christmas bombshell from the ECJ, Verfassungblog, 24.12.2104, https://verfassungsblog.de/opinion-213-eu-accession-echr-christmas-bombshell-european-court-justice-2/; *Stian Oby Johansen*, Opinion 2/13: A bag of coal from the CJEU, PluriCourts Blog, https://www.jus.uio.no/pluricourts/english/blog/stian-oby-johansen/opinion-213-a-bag-of-coal-from-the-cjeu.html.

57. Cf. BVerfGE 93, 1 – Crucifx; *Heribert Prantl*, Aufstand der Aufgeregten. 20 Jahre Kruzifix-Urteil, Süddeutsche Zeitung, 19.8.2015, available at http://www.sueddeutsche.de/politik/jahre-kruzifix-urteil-aufstand-der-aufge-regten-1.2613635 (4.8.2022).
58. *Vera Fritz*, Activism on an Off the Bench: Pierre Pescatore and the Law of Integration, CMLR 57 (2020), 475 (476, 477, 498, 500).

> extent that the Basic Law and the domestic act of approval permit or provide for a transfer of sovereign powers ....[59]

Although similar provisions and decisions can be found in almost all Member States[60] and although the treaties obviously justify this position (Article 4 paragraph 2, Article 5 paragraph 1 sentence 2, paragraph 2, Article 48, Article 49, Article 50 TEU etc.), it has been ignored by the ECJ. The European Commission too was obviously not aware of this established line of jurisprudence. It seems to consider it sufficient to orientate itself towards the Luxembourg case law and to ignore approaches that do not fit into its concept or interests thus failing to properly understand the legal reality in the Union it has to serve. This might explain why the European Commission in the aftermath of the Federal Constitutional Court's decision of 5 May 2020 on the Public Sector Purchase Programme (PSPP) once again threatened to initiate an infringement proceeding against Germany with merely the same line of arguments it had already used in 1974 with regard to a possible infringement procedure following the Solange I decision of the Federal Constitutional Court[61] though this decision has turned out to be a landmark in the development of fundamental rights protection on the European level. The files have also been closed this time but the press communication of the European Commission accompanying that step makes one doubt whether it is willing to accept the EU as it is.

3 PROBLEMS CONCERNING THE INNER STRUCTURE OF THE ECJ

The organisation of the ECJ gives rise to further doubts concerning its insertion into a functioning system of checks and balances.

59. BVerfGE 158, 210 (239 f. marginal no. 73 f.) - Unified Patent Court II, with reference to BVerfGE 37, 271 (279 f.) - Solange I; 58, 1 (30 f.) - Eurocontrol; 73, 339 (375 f.) - Solange II; 75, 223 (242) - Kloppenburg; 89, 155 (190) - Maastricht; 123, 267 (348 ff., 402) - Lisbon; 126, 286 (302) - Honeywell; 129, 78 (99); 134, 366 (384 para. 26) - OMT referal; 140, 317 (336 para. 40) - Identiätskontrolle I; 142, 123 (187 f. para. 120) - OMT; 154, 17 (89 f. para. 109) - PSPP.
60. Kingdom of Belgium: Constitutional Court, Ent. No. 62/2016 v. 28.4.2016, para. B.8.7.; for the Kingdom of Denmark: Højesteret, Urt. v. 6.4.1998 - I 361/1997 -, para. 9.8.; Judgment of. 6.12.2016- I 15/2014 -; for the Republic of Estonia: Riigikohus, Urt. v. 12.7.2012 - 3-4-1-6-12 -, paras 128, 223; for the French Republic: Conseil Constitutionnel, DC v. 27.7.2006, No. 2006-540, para. 19; DC v. 9.6.2011 No. 2011-631, para. 45; DC v. 31.7.2017, Ent. No. 2017-749, paras 9 et seq.; Conseil d'État, Ent. v. 21.4.2021, No. 393099, para. 5; for Ireland, Supreme Court of Ireland, Judgment 9.4.1987, Crotty v. An Taoiseach, (1987), I.R. 713 (783); S.P.U.C. (Ireland), Judgment v. 19.12.1989, Ltd. v. Grogan, (1989), I.R. 753 (765); for the Italian Republic: Corte Costituzionale, Judgment of 18.12.1973, No. 183/1973, paras 3 et seq. - Frontini; Judgment of. 8.4.1991, No. 168/1991, para. 4; Judgment of 23.11.2016 No. 24/2017 para. 2; for Latvia: Satversmes tiesa, Urt. v. 7.4.2009 - 2008-35-01 -, para. 17; for the Republic of Poland: Trybunał Konstytucyjny, Judgment of. 11.5.2005 - K 18/04 -, paras 4.1., 10.2.; Urt. v. 24.11.2010 - K 32/09 -, marginal nos 2.1. ff.; Urt. v. 16.11.2011 - SK 45/09 - para. 2.4., 2.5.; for the Kingdom of Spain: Tribunal Constitutional, Declaration v. 13.12.2004, DTC 1/2004; for the Czech Republic: Ústavní Soud, Judgment v. 31.1.2012 - 2012/01/31 - Pl. ÚS 5/12 - para. VII; for Croatia: Ustavni Sud, Ent. v. 21.4.2015 - U-VIIR-1158/2015 - para. 60.
61. Letter from the European Commission to BM *Hans-Dietrich Genscher* dated 18 December 1974; letter from the President of the Federal Constitutional Court *Walter Seuffert* to Federal Chancellor *Helmut Schmidt* dated 25 March 1975 (available at BArch, B 136/31083 and B 136/17928).

The unlimited possibility to renew the six-year term of the office for judges and advocates general (Article 19 para. 2, third subparagraph, second sentence, TEU) fosters the establishment of power structures within the Court, favoring those who are reelected time and again and impeding newcomers. It does not encourage the discourse on the correct interpretation and concretisation of Union law and the openness to put a line of jurisprudence into question if it turns out to be outdated or even misguided. It should therefore raise concern that the main dogmatic tools of Union law haven't changed much since the 1980s: the precedence of application, the autonomy of the Union's legal order which is an offspring of the aforementioned discussion, the principles of the 'effet utile' and of equivalence and art. 267 TFEU; those tools have been applied to every angle of life but have remained more or less unchanged in substance as is demonstrated by the C.I.L.F.I.T case.[62] The lack of specialisation within the ECJ too nurtures a tendency to rather sweeping grand formulas, which may be no longer appropriate for a (partial) legal order encompassing not only the realisation of the common market as in earlier times.

Other problems are the virtually unlimited discretion of the President of the ECJ in assigning cases to the rapporteurs and the lack of transparency and plurality in the recruitment of judges and advocates general. Though there is a committee under Article 255 TFEU which gives advice on candidates proposed by the Member States to the council, the whole process is far from being intelligible for the public and thus prevents the gradual emergence of embedded judges from the offspring. In addition it could be a reasonable debate whether it makes sense to appoint judges who previously often pursued careers in the ministerial administrations of the Member States. They may be fabulous lawyers but experience shows that if people are socialised in a hierarchical system they behave differently from professional judges or legal scholars, who as a rule, have benefitted from personal independence all their professional life.

Finally, the case law of the ECJ suggests that the court was a monolithic bloc and may remind one of the 10 commandments of Moses. Considering that there are 15 judges sitting in the Grand Chamber, this can hardly reflect the content and outcome of the deliberations, provided the judges really engage in these. This is quite a threshold for an open debate on the improvement of EU law, alternatives and its further development. 'Two lawyers, three opinions' – this joke should also apply to European law and describes the circumstance that in every case there is theoretically more than one solution. The opinions of the advocates general only offer a weak substitute in this regard.

4 THE DIALOGUE WITHIN THE NETWORK OF CONSTITUTIONAL COURTS AS SOME SUBSTITUTION

Given that it is practically impossible to overrule and therefore correct the case law of the ECJ even if it deviates from the will of the Masters of the Treaties – especially with

62. ECJ, Dec. of 6 October 1982 – C-283/81, ECLI:EU:C:1982:335.

regard to the principle of conferral – constitutional and supreme courts of the Member States are for the time being the only resort which to a certain extent is in a position to limit the power of the ECJ and its self-serving interest as the 'engine of integration'.

Checks and balances with regard to the ECJ's jurisdiction can practically be neither realised through the (rather theoretical) possibility of a treaty amendment according to Article 48 TEU nor by the hardly (less theoretical) possibility of the European Commission, Council and European Parliament overruling the case law by a legislative decision, especially if the ECJ has impregnated a solution by using arguments from primary law, but through the – necessarily contentious – cooperation with constitutional and supreme courts. In this Network of Constitutional Courts (*Verfassungsgerichtsverbund*)[63] the 'last word' remains by definition in abeyance which means that the ECJ cannot systematically ignore the position of the constitutional and supreme courts of the Member States without risking its authority and the willingness of the national courts to generally follow its jurisdiction. If several constitutional and supreme courts develop similar lines of jurisdiction – possibly also in close temporal connection – this will also affect the decisions of the ECJ, given that the common principles forming the European legal order must ultimately be based on the common constitutional traditions of the Member States and not on the postulate of an imaginary autonomy of the European legal order.[64]

There are without any doubt, several examples of a fruitful cooperation within this Network that have also helped to adapt the jurisprudence of the ECJ in the Member States. For instance the decisions in Aranyosi and Căldăraru[65] or Taricco[66] mark a (provisional) end to a longer process of clarification on fundamental rights standards between the ECJ and the German *Bundesverfassungsgericht* and the Italian *Corte Costituzionale* respectively. They are by no means exceptional cases[67] but offer proof that the cooperation between the ECJ and constitutional and supreme courts can contribute to reach a balance in different areas of law in the common interest.

As a result, all members of the Network of Constitutional Courts bear a specific responsibility for the success of the EU as a community based on the rule of law. For the constitutional and supreme courts, this responsibility for the success of the EU as a

63. *Christoph Grabenwarter/Peter M. Huber/Raijko Knez/Ineta Ziemele*, The Role of Constitutional Courts in the European Judicial Network, EPL 27 (2021), 43 et seq.
64. ECJ, Opinion 2/13 of 18.12.2014, ECLI:EU:C:2014:2454, para. 158 – *ECHR Accession II*; ECJ, Judgment of. 6.3.2018, Case C–284/16, ECLI:EU:C:2018:158, para. 32 – *Achmea*; ECJ, Opinion 1/17 v. 30.4.2019, para. 109 f. – CETA; cf. also *Weiß*, Die externe Autonomie des Unionsrechts als Schranke für den Investitionsschutz, und weit darüber hinaus? – Zum CETA-Gutachten des EuGH als Ursprung einer überschießenden verfassungsrechtlichen Anforderung, EuR 2020, 621 (626 ff.).
65. ECJ, Judgment of 26.2.2013, Case C-399/11, ECLI:EU:2013/107 – *Melloni*; then: BVerfGE 140, 317 et seq. – *Identity Control I*; then: ECJ, Judgment of. 5.4.2016, C-404/15, C-659/15 PPU, ECLI:EU:C:2016:198 – *Aranyosi and Căldăraru*.
66. ECJ, Judgment of 5.12.2017, Case C-42/17, ECLI:EU:C:2017:936 – *Taricco II*; then: Corte Costituzionale, Judgment of 10.4.2018, No. 24/2017, 115/2018 – *Taricco II*.
67. ECJ, Judgment of 14.10.2004, Case C 36/02, [2004] ECR I-9609 – *Omega Spielhallen/OB Bonn*; Judgment of 12.6.2014, Case C-156/13, ECLI:EU:C:2014:1756 – *Digibet and Albers digibet*; *see* further *Peter M. Huber*, Europäisches und nationales Verfassungsrecht, VVDStRL 60 (2001), 194 (232) m.w. Fn. 301.

whole goes beyond their own intrinsic competences of jurisdiction and can be based on their (constitutional) responsibility for European integration (*Integrationsverantwortung*).[68] With regard to the ECJ such responsibility is set forth in Article 19 TEU and with regard to the ECtHR in Article 19 ECHR.

The necessary cooperation within the network of constitutional courts is demanding, prone to abuse and, of course, also influenced by personal vanities. In the short term, it may be detrimental to legal certainty, in the medium and long run, however, it is indispensable in the interest of an orderly, sustainable and generally accepted process of integration and in the interest of securing of a minimum level of control with regard to the European judiciary. A withdrawal from the EU (as set forth in Article 50 TEU) is no reasonable alternative in this respect – although some people on the Kirchberg in Luxembourg may expect national courts simply to obey and not to question what they are told by the ECJ.[69]

5 CONCLUSION

Cooperation in the Network of Constitutional Courts has so far been erratic, dependent on coincidences. It has not taken place in an orderly procedural framework and goes along with outcomes that are hardly predictable. In a community based on the rule of law, there must however be more to it.

For example, when deciding a case in which the national constitutional identity is at stake (Article 4 paragraph 2 TEU), the ECJ may not – as it did in the Egenberger case[70] – ignore that aspect. It could be rather be obliged under Article 19 paragraph 1 TEU to clarify this question *lege artis*, which ideally presupposes an enquiry to the national court that is ultimately responsible to interpret the constitution and accordingly as to how the constitutional identity must be understood. It might also be reasonable to engage in an enquiry with all constitutional and supreme courts concerned, in particular in cases in which fundamental questions regarding the allocation of competences are concerned in order to avoid respective acts being declared *ultra vires* by the national courts.[71] For example, this could have been the case with regard to the EU's competence to conclude international trade agreements[72] or with regard to the banking union.[73]

The option to involve national constitutional and supreme courts in order to identify what the situation is under the national constitutional law of the Member States is already open to the ECJ *de lege lata* according to Article 24 paragraph 2 of the

68. For Germany, cf. BVerfGE 134, 366 (394 ff. paras 44 ff.) – OMT referral; 135, 317 (393 f. para. 146) – ESM; 142, 123 (180 para. 99) – OMT; 151, 202 (279 f. para. 101) – European Banking Union; 152, 216 (243 para. 67) – Right to be Forgotten II; 158, 1 (37 para. 71) – Ökotox.
69. Cf. the obiter dictum in *GA Tanchev* v. 17.12.2020, C-824/18, ECLI:EU:C:2020:1053, para. 84 A.B. and others /Krajowa Rada Sądownictwa.
70. ECJ, Judgment of 17.4.2018, Case C-414/16, ECLI:C:2018:257 – Egenberger.
71. The Member States would have to designate a competent court in this respect, as is done in other areas.
72. Cf. BVerfGE 143, 65 pp. – CETA e.A.; BVerfG, Beschluss vom 9. Februar 2022 – 2 BvR 1368/16 – vorl. Anwendung von CETA.,
73. Cf. BVerfGE 151, 202 pp. – Europäische Bankenunion.

ECJ Statute. Nevertheless, it has not yet considered such requests and justifies this denial with the – unconvincing – argument that neither the Treaties nor the ECJ Statute do provide for such a request. Compared with the thriving phantasy the court can unfold if it comes to secure its institutional interests, it is understandable that such a step is not likely to be very attractive for the ECJ. It would, on the one hand, force it to recognise that constitutional and supreme courts of the Member States play a special role in the European Constitutional Network and, on the other hand, would increase the burden of reasoning for its decisions. However, both arguments are poor.

De lege ferenda, the masters of the Treaties should therefore amend the TFEU by Article 267a, which obliges the ECJ to make a referral to the respective national constitutional or supreme court in cases in which Article 4 paragraph 2 TEU is at stake or in cases in which fundamental questions with regard to the allocation of competences according to Article 5 paragraph 1 TEU have to be resolved.[74] This would be, so to speak, the keystone in the arch of the Network of Constitutional Courts and of the rule of law in the EU.

74. *Christoph Grabenwarter/Peter M. Huber/Raijko Knez/Ineta Ziemele*, The Role of the Constitutional Courts in the European Judicial Network, EPL 27 (2021), 43 (60).

CHAPTER 18

The Guardianship of the Constitution and Its Legitimacy

Massimo La Torre

1 RULES, PRINCIPLES, AND BALANCING: ARGUMENTATIVE REPRESENTATION

It was in the debate between the powerfully compelling Anglo-American legal philosopher Ronald Dworkin and the German scholar of public law and legal philosophy Robert Alexy that the question of constitutional justice, its limits, and its justification recently came into special prominence within legal theory. But equally interesting, I would suggest, is the more recent debate that on these same topics Alexy was engaged in with the Italian jurist, judge, and legal philosopher Luigi Ferrajoli. For an appreciation of these debates, however, it will be useful to set the stage for them with a few broad notions. And we begin with the distinction between rules and principles, a distinction introduced by Dworkin and then taken up, reworked, and made stricter by Alexy. Rules, according to this distinction, are norms or standards requiring that something be achieved in a definitive manner. Rules cannot conflict with one another and still maintain their validity: if they do contradict one another, one will be valid and the contradictory ones invalid. And which ones will stand and which ones will not depend on criteria of temporality, hierarchy, or speciality (which rule is more recent, which one ranks higher, which one is more specific).

Principles, by contrast, are norms or standards that can all be valid within a given legal order even when they are in conflict with one another. This is because they lack types of action and actuating facts that can trigger them as conditions for them to be applied. So they cannot be slotted into a category of conduct or set of facts under which a specific act or case is to be subsumed. Principles are applied by balancing them. This is what Dworkin says. To which Alexy adds that principles require that something be achieved to the greatest extent possible as a matter of both fact and law. Alexy accordingly describes principles as "optimization commands." So, as Alexy sees the matter, while rules are governed by a deontological logic (where the question is whether they correctly apply to the case at hand, and they either do or they do not), principles are governed by a teleological logic (where the question is how best, or more effectively, to apply them, or to what extent their aims can be achieved). Balancing in this perspective is driven by a strict utilitarian or, if you like, economic rationality.

A further thesis, in view of this distinction, is that constitutional rights are essentially principles. This thesis is defended by Alexy and rejected by Dworkin, who argues that rights are not principles but rules. Indeed, rights, in Dworkin's argument, are strictly deontological: they cannot be interpreted or applied on the basis of a teleological logic. They are not apt for balancing (as if they had "weights") but rather function as trumps, or veto powers, that can be placed against legislative measures, which do, by contrast, operate on the basis of teleological or consequentialist considerations.[1] Alexy disagrees, arguing that constitutional rights, as principles, apply by balancing. There cannot thus be any "absolute" principles, but only ones that, though still applicable in a case, do not have "weight" enough against a competing principle to be considered binding for that case. Though principles do not ever contradict each other, nor could they be derogated from, they can by balancing be waived or strongly de-escalated in their biding force and efficacy.

There is a further fundamental thesis that Alexy defends, arguing that principles are necessarily, and not just contingently, connected to the criterion of proportionality.[2] That is because of the understanding that conflicts among principles are inevitable, precisely because, as noted, there is no logic of contradiction that can be brought to bear in applying principles that can be used as an exclusionary clause for principles' validity. In order to apply principles, it is necessary to take into account what rules lack, namely, the weight of each principle in relation to the case at hand. On this point, Alexy finds himself in agreement with Dworkin. But Alexy takes the point even further by specifying or, better, narrowing down what balancing consists of. He thus stipulates a first law of balancing expressed as follows: the greater the extent to which a principle remains unfulfilled (the greater the detriment to it), the more important it must be to fulfill the competing principle.[3]

Alexy then introduces a second law of balancing, under which he distinguishes two types of discretion in fulfilling a principle: there is a structural discretion and an epistemic discretion. Structural discretion is the kind that is exercised in assessing the weight of the principle, or the gravity (or detriment) that can be assessed depending on the extent to which the principle remains unfulfilled. Epistemic discretion is instead the judgment that needs to be exercised when the facts are unclear or the standard that applies to them needs to be clarified (empirical or normative uncertainty). This is the kind of balancing that needs to be done when it cannot be determined by reasoning or

1. Cf. lately R. Dworkin, *Justice for Hedgehogs*, The Belknap Press, Cambridge, Mass 2011, pp. 412 ff.
2. Cf. R. Alexy, *Constitutional Rights and Proportionality*, in Revus—Journal for Constitutional Theory and Philosophy of Law, Vol. 22, 2014, pp. 51 ff.
3. *See* R. Alexy, *Theorie der Grundrechte*, Suhrkamp, Frankfurt am Main 1986, p. 146.

argumentation which of two competing principles carries greater weight, or which of the two entails a greater detriment when sacrificed to the other. In this framework, judicial review can only be based on an assessment of whether the powers vested in the legislature have been properly exercised. The second law of balancing can be summarized as follows: the greater the detriment to a principle, or the encroachment on a basic right, the more compelling must be the reasons justifying that detriment or encroachment.[4]

For Alexy, a law can pass the test of constitutionality, and can therefore be deemed constitutional, only if it is proportional, considering (a) that principles inevitably come into conflict, (b) that this conflict can only be resolved by balancing, and (c) that the fundamental balancing criterion is that of proportionality. Proportionality is something that, in turn, Alexy conceptualizes by mostly following the doctrine developed in the case law of the German Federal Constitutional Court, which identifies three "moments" or subcriteria for it, namely, necessity, adequacy, and proportionality in the strict sense. This last subcriterion Alexy then offers to construe in an original way in terms of Pareto optimality.

But wouldn't it be possible for this proportionality review to be carried out by the legislature itself? Does it necessarily have to be entrusted to the courts? Alexy argues that it does—that we do need a constitutional court—and in making that argument he points to the teleological nature of principles (and of constitutional rights generally) and the proportionality criterion that governs their use.

But how specifically to argue that it is in fact the courts that need to be entrusted with the task of guaranteeing that constitutional principles (and rights) are applied according to the proportionality criterion that is proper to them? There are at least two arguments, according to Alexy, that can be offered in support of this view. There is in the first place a structural argument, namely, nemo judex in causa sua—no one can be a judge in their own cause—and the same tenet therefore applies to lawmakers judging the validity of their own acts. That judgment needs to be entrusted to an impartial third party. And at any rate, a judicial review of legislative acts is better than no review at all.

There is then a substantive argument to be made. Constitutional justice, Alexy argues, depends on its ability to guarantee the procedural conditions on which rest the democratic state and its legislation. An adequate conception of democracy needs to encompass and ground not only the form of democracy, its decision-makers, and the decisions made (through a system of self-government, or government by majority rule) but also the arguments behind those decisions and their content, or substance. This goes not only for the lawmakers but also for the constitutional judges—except that here, with the constitutional judge, the argumentative aspect, or the content of the decisions made, is essential.

4. This second law of balancing is presented in the *Postcript* to *Theorie der Grundrechte*, English version edited by J. Rivers, *A Theory of Constitutional Rights*, Oxford University Press, Oxford 2002, especially pp. 418-419. Cf. J. Rivers, *Proportionality, Discretion and the Second Law of Balancing*, in *Law, Rights and Discourse: The Legal Philosophy of Robert Alexy*, edited by G. Pavlakos, Hart, Oxford 2007, pp. 167 ff.

Even so, Alexy recognizes that "the existence of good or plausible arguments is enough for deliberation or reflection, but not for representation."[5] It would seem, then, that the content of argumentation cannot make up for the shortcomings of the form of argumentation, that is, for the fact that the argumentation cannot be sufficiently representative in a democracy. How, then, is it possible to justify a decision—however correct it may be in principle—if the person making the decision does not represent everyone and so is not fully accountable to everyone? Alexy thinks that in order to close this gap between representation and argumentation, "the ideal level of argument and correctness must be connected with the real level of actual acceptance."[6] But what does that mean?

A decision handed down by a constitutional court will be democratically legitimate if it can be presumed to be acceptable to the majority of citizens. But this presumption, Alexy argues, needs to be qualified with a further presumption: we need to be able to assume, in other words, that citizens are by and large capable of making a rational assessment of the constitutional court's arguments. The court needs to be able to count on a virtuous audience. Or, as Alexy puts it, there needs to be "a sufficient number of rational persons, that is, persons who are able and willing to accept sound or correct arguments for the reason that they are sound or correct."[7] There needs to be a broad base of what Alexy calls "constitutional persons." It is through this device of an idealized body of persons that constitutional justice gains its legitimacy, enabling the arguments of constitutional justice to carry representative weight.

But now a question comes up. Even if this idealized or transcendental "constitutional person" can be assumed to exist, how can we be sure that this person will accept the court's arguments? To this end, we would have to somehow prefigure and configure a discursive space in which judges meet citizens, and in which the latter can in dissent reject the judges' reasoning and therefore deny the validity of their decisions. Representation implies accountability and the possibility that the representative dignity or quality is challenged and eventually denied or repealed. But nowhere in Alexy's "transcendental" construction is this communicative moment and chance to be found, and so nowhere can we find the possibility of challenging the judge's decisions, even if only argumentatively. Nowhere does Alexy's construction, in its appeal to the quality of arguments, afford a way for this quality to be certified within a discursive framework that is independent of those engaged in the discourse at issue, namely, the courts. Here, reason remains unqualifiedly monological, even if the agent it is ascribed to is a collective one. As much as this agency may be collective, it cannot communicate with anyone, much less persuade them, except through a tautological appeal to the quality of its own work. There is no attempt to thematize discourse, and rationality once more retreats to a place where it cannot be challenged, where the superiority it claims for

5. R. Alexy, *Constitutional Rights, Democracy and Representation*, Rivista di filosofia del diritto, 2015, p. 34. Cf. R. Alexy, *Balancing, Constitutional Review and Representation*, I-Con, 2005, p. 580: "The existence of good or plausible arguments is enough for deliberation or reflection, but not for representation."
6. R. Alexy, *Constitutional Rights, Democracy and Representation*, Rivista di filosofia del diritto, 2015, p. 34.
7. *Ibid.*

itself cannot be verified on any pragmatic basis. It can only be monologically assumed or claimed. Once reason is so insulated—where it can no longer be challenged or falsified—it may be easily used as an ideological device with which to confer on the work of the courts a fairness and legitimacy which they may very well, and often do, lack. This is truly the triumph of the judge as a king, an unaccountable ruler.

2 A CONSTITUTIONALISM OF PROTECTIONS VERSUS A CONSTITUTIONALISM OF PRINCIPLES

It was in response to Alexy that the Italian legal philosopher Luigi Ferrajoli joined the debate, subjecting Alexy's construction to a tightly argued line of criticism. Ferrajoli starts out on a historical note, pointing out the paradigm shift that took place in legal systems across the European continent in the wake of World War II. The war gave way to an intense effort to set the law itself on a legal foundation, that is, to entrench basic rights in the constitution through a rigid constitutionalization of these rights. The constitution restructured the notion and practice of sovereignty by delimiting the sphere of legislative power: it carved out an area of subject matter in which no legislature or majority may make decisions, and another area in which it cannot refrain from making decisions. The political power to make decisions concerning the rights to liberty and autonomy was stripped back, with the constitution prohibiting any governmental restrictions on these rights. But when it came to social rights, political power was by contrast expanded, with the constitution actually requiring the state to intervene in this area.

Ferrajoli underscores that under a system of rigidly protected constitutional rights, we have a deontic bifurcation between two main sources of law, namely, the constitution and statutory law. The process can be described as one in which the principles of natural law are positivized. Modern rigid constitutions "have transformed constitutional norms into laws of reason."[8] It is thus possible to conceive of positivized law that is illegitimate not only formally but also materially. A distinction can accordingly be drawn in the force of law: on the one hand we have the formal validity of law, where the law is in force if it has been properly enacted according to procedure; on the other we have a substantive validity of law, where the validity of law depends not on its having been properly enacted but on its being consistent with the language and the values of the constitution, its own political morality. As a result, a law may be in force but unenforceable, that is, it may be formally binding (regularly enacted) but substantively nonbinding (unconstitutional). The possibility of this deontic disjunction between formal and substantive validity clearly needs to be addressed, in part in view of the need to preserve the certainty of the law, and this is the proper task, and functional justification for, constitutional justice.

But there is also the problem of the political legitimacy of constitutional justice in a democratic system, considering that a constitutional court can strike down an act of

8. L. Ferrajoli, *Diritti fondamentali e democrazia: Due obiezioni a Robert Alexy*, Rivista di filosofia del diritto, 2015, p. 41.

parliament, that is, of a lawmaker democratically voted into office by the people, who are ultimately the basis on which rests the legitimacy of the laws making up the legal system itself. There are two aspects to this problem: an institutional one and a methodological one.

The first aspect relates to the question of the court's democratic credentials: its representativeness. The second one is about the kind of legal reasoning that judicial review needs to embody if it is to account itself as democratic. Here, in this second regard, we have to work out what the appropriate logical or argumentative standard and practice is that courts are to follow in applying the constitutional rights and principles they are entrusted with protecting.

If a rigid constitution is to hold up against any arbitrary act a legislature may decide to do, and if it wants to ensure a coherent and homogenous validity for its provisions, it will need a mechanism for reviewing the constitutionality of the laws enacted by that legislature. At the same time, the constitution, through the basic rights enshrined in it, guarantees the ability of citizens to exercise sovereignty as individuals (uti singuli) rather than only as members of an electorate forming a general will expressed by way of ordinary legislation. Citizens, in other words, can be secure in their ability to exercise the individual sovereignty that is made possible by the basic rights enshrined in the constitution. These basic rights can thus be described as individual units of popular and collective sovereignty. Their individual exercise needs to be legally protected, and that protection is entrusted to constitutional justice.

Even in legal systems, such as the Italian system, under which citizens cannot directly turn to constitutional justice to redress an alleged infringement of a basic right, challenges brought to court seeking to have a law declared unconstitutional mostly proceed from a specific case in which individual rights and interests are at stake. It is more often than not from an individual case, and from the need to protect constitutional rights recognized for individuals, that the process is set in motion for subjecting a law to constitutional review. But here, when it comes to jurisdiction, and constitutional jurisdiction in particular, the notion of democratic representation cannot apply. It would be inaccurate, and indeed misleading, to qualify judges—including constitutional judges—as "representatives" of the people, at least within a legal system premised on the traditional separation of powers. Even if justice is exercised "in the name of the people," this still cannot be taken to mean that judges—including elected ones—are representatives of the people and so are directly accountable to the people.

There are two basic functions of the state that Ferrajoli distinguishes: one is to govern (stewardship) and the other is to guarantee basic rights (protection). This latter function is the sole remit of the courts. Now, as Ferrajoli argues, this rights-protection function can have any democratic legitimacy only if the basis of its exercise can be ascertained as being correct—what Ferrajoli calls the "truth" of its exercise.[9] In the case of constitutional jurisdiction, the only truth that counts is a "legal truth," meaning the courts' correct application of constitutional provisions. The courts can claim a connection to popular sovereignty precisely on the basis that they apply the law and the

9. *Ibid.*, p. 44.

constitution. What confers legitimacy on the courts, including the constitutional court, is the principle of legality and the primacy of the law, or the idea that everyone is subject to the law: in the case of the constitutional court, this means in particular that the court is bound by the constitution, which it must uphold and defend, though it should be added that in a system governed by a rigid constitution, every court is a constitutional court, and the judgment of constitutionality is in a sense understood as one that is spread out across the entire court system.

But what does it mean to be subject to the law? Ferrajoli puts it this way: "Subjection to the law consists in the naming of a legal fact ... through the words of the law."[10] Ferrajoli subscribes to the distinction between rules and principles. But the notion of principle, he argues, is not as extensive and rigid as Alexy and others make it out to be. In fact, a distinction is called for between directive or guiding principles, on the one hand, and regulative principles, on the other.

A directive principle—an example of which is the principle of substantive equality set forth in Article 3(2) of the Italian Constitution—does not single out any specific course of conduct as obligatory but rather offers guidance in the form of an argument that must be taken into account when interpreting and applying statutory provisions. So, while the guidance is mandatory, having the force of a standard, the principle itself cannot be violated: "there is no violation that can be configured for it."[11] Not so with a regulative principle, which does translate into rules expressly requiring us to act in one way or another, such that it can, by contrast, be immediately violated. Now, as Ferrajoli goes on to argue, regulative principles are the source from which many basic rights can be extracted, such that "the majority of basic rights can be reduced to rules," that is, to legal provisions which specifically prescribe a course of conduct, and which can accordingly be framed under a category of conduct or class of situations. These principles will therefore not be applied by weighing and balancing. It is worth noting here that, on this approach, there will not always be conflicts among rights, in the sense that the rights that do come into play in a given case will all be enforceable in that case. In many of these cases, principles can be ranked on a hierarchical scale.

Even so, Ferrajoli does not rule out the possibility of conflicts between principles and rights. In these cases, however, he takes the view that what need to be weighed and balanced are not legal norms but rather "the concrete circumstances that make each case unique and unrepeatable":[12] the balancing happens between the facts of the case and their characteristics. "The weighing is therefore concerned ... not with the legal norms to be applied, but with the distinctive and unrepeatable features of the facts brought to judgment."[13] What is weighed, then, is not legal norms, which do not change from one case to the next, but the circumstances of the case, which do change with each case.

10. *Ibid.*, p. 45.
11. *Ibid.*, p. 46.
12. *Ibid.*, p. 48.
13. *Ibid.*

Looking at the problem in this light, then, we need to rethink the concept of fairness, that is, of justice in the particular case at hand. As Ferrajoli puts it, this situated justice "comes down to our understanding and assessment of the concrete and unrepeatable circumstances and features that distinguish each fact from the whole range of other facts that can all be subsumed under the same legally qualified class of facts."[14] We need to distinguish, Ferrajoli argues, a constitutionalism of principles from a constitutionalism of protections and guarantees: in the former, basic rights and constitutional norms are construed as principles, which need to be balanced in order to be applied; in the latter, these rights and norms are construed as rules, or at least as general rules waiting to be further specified into required courses of action. In either case, what constitutional norms offer are not specific or ready-made prescriptions but arguments to be used as the basis for deciding the case in question. There are three methodological conclusions that Ferrajoli extracts from this framework.

First, for all violations of a constitutional norm, even when it turns out that what has been violated is a rule, this rule can also be construed as a principle, "that is, as an argument which can be used in reasoning through a case and which is always required in interpreting and hence applying the law."[15]

Second, the system of legal norms can always be defined and applied as a hierarchical system, one that accordingly serves as a criterion for their application. As Ferrajoli comments: "In many cases where competing principles are set forth in different constitutional norms, the problem is not one of conflict among such norms but one of subordination, where the application of some norms takes precedence over the application of others." So, it is not so much that basic rights come into conflict as that they are hierarchically ordered, and in figuring out what the proper order is we may have to start out from the specifics of the case and what they amount to.

And third, where balancing does prove necessary, it is not the content of legal provisions that is balanced but the weight or salience of the circumstances the provisions apply to. As Ferrajoli puts it: "Where principles actually come into conflict, what need to be weighed are not the norms through which they are expressed—which norms are always the same—but the cases or facts being judged, each of which is unique and unrepeatable."[16]

On this alternative way of conceptualizing legal principles and their application hinges the contrast between the two kinds of constitutionalism identified by Ferrajoli: a constitutionalism of principles as against a constitutionalism of protections and guarantees.[17]

The first kind of constitutionalism, the principles-based one, confers on principles an expansive force that only the judge can then make effective. It accordingly suggests that the constitutional state needs to be redefined in such a way as to diminish the role of democratic citizenship, which gets upstaged by the paternalism inherent in

14. *Ibid.*, p. 49.
15. *Ibid.*, p. 51.
16. *Ibid.*
17. *See* L. Ferrajoli, *Constitucionalismo principialista y constitucionalismo garantista*, Doxa—Cuadernos de Filosofía del Derecho, Vol. 34, 2011, pp. 11 ff.

a system where decisions are made by bodies with little or no democratic legitimacy. Not so with the second kind of constitutionalism, the protections-based one, under which the constitution—no matter how substantivized through its take-up of material principles—can never be used as a means through which to loosen the review needed to guarantee the rights the document itself enshrines. A principles-based constitutionalism, by contrast, runs the risk of turning the constitution against itself, and in addition does so by thwarting from the start any practical effort to bridge the gap between the material validity of the constitution and the formal validity of the law, even as this gap is necessary to maintaining the dialectic between the constitutional moment and the legislative moment. Without this dialectic, or mutual feedback, democracy as a space within which legal norms are produced and justified would turn into a sort of conveyor belt for constitutional norms conceived as self-enclosed and self-sufficient provisions: democracy would turn merely into a device for correctly applying rules to the cases they cover, and would do so without securing the finality or ultimateness that could only be entrusted to constitutional justice.

3 THE INSTITUTIONAL QUESTION AND THE METHODOLOGICAL ONE: JUSTIFICATORY DISCOURSE AND APPLICATIVE DISCOURSE

As far as the institutional question is concerned, I would suggest that if we want to solve the problem of the democratic legitimacy of constitutional justice, we will have to shift our focus from the constitutional judge to the fact of the court's jurisdiction. If the constitutional court as a governing body struggles to find democratic legitimacy—and can only metaphorically or figuratively be configured as "representative" of the people, or as reflecting the popular will—it is a different scenario that we come upon once the question is framed in terms of constitutional jurisdiction. Here the judge is but one of several other actors, among which a prominent place ought to be accorded to the citizen, for it is the citizen who is the bearer of the basic constitutional rights, and who in asserting these rights exercises a fragment of popular sovereignty. Constitutional jurisdiction thus becomes the place where citizens exercise popular sovereignty as individuals (uti singuli) and as such achieve the democratic principle. It is here that the considerations offered by Ferrajoli prove to be useful.

Alexy's argumentative-representation thesis is not just mystifying but is also liable to collapse the institutional question into the methodological one: it does so by framing the facticity of institutions—a problem of power—as a problem of reason. In this framing, normativity is pushed through a supremely idealistic filter that neglects the phenomenology and pragmatic makeup of a concrete sphere of action. The materiality of this sphere of action thins down to a gossamer web on contact with the blazing light of an idea. Even the meaning of the sphere of action is watered down, for it is reduced to the justice of action, in much the same way that, on some accounts, the meaning of a proposition boils down to its truth-value.

We can now turn to the methodological question, in which regard I like to go back to an old debate, one that took place between Robert Alexy (once more) and Klaus

Günther, professor of criminal law and philosophy of law at the University of Frankfurt, as well as one favorite disciple of Jürgen Habermas.[18] Günther challenges Alexy on the idea that constitutional norms and basic rights are optimization commands. Following a thesis that Joseph Raz also espouses,[19] Günther argues that these norms and rights are instead general rules of very wide scope—meaning that there is no structural or ontological distinction between rules and principles.

The criterion for applying principles as general, broad-gauged rules will not be that of their universalizability, nor will it be a criterion for balancing conflicting norms, but will rather be a criterion of coherence and appropriateness (Angemessenheit).[20] Günther—and then Habermas in agreement—distinguishes two kinds of discourse on the use of norms, arguing that the distinction is structural. There is a foundational discourse, which seeks to confer justification and validity on norms, and the criterion in doing so is in fact one of generality or universalizability. A norm will qualify as valid, in other words, if it can be conceptualized and operationalized as universally valid by all those subject within a given legal order whose interests are put at stake by the norm. Once the norm has been so validated, it can then be applied to a concrete case. Here the discourse that legitimizes the norm's application as correct will no longer hinge on a criterion of universalizability. Indeed, when it comes to the application of a rule to a concrete case, we should not be concerned with its universalizability, but rather consider whether its application is correct or appropriate. In making this judgment of appropriateness, we will need to look at (a) the overall system of relevant norms and at (b) all the circumstances of the case, thereby judging the matter all things considered.

Before us, then, there are two different types of practical discourse: a justificatory one and an applicative one. These two types of discourse, Günther argues, can be found in the sphere of morality as much as in that of the law. Günther and Habermas moreover take this distinction to mean that these two spheres of law and morality are best considered as separate—a thesis that Alexy unequivocally rejects, construing legal discourse as a special case of moral discourse. Indeed, the argument that Günther and Habermas mount in working towards this separation thesis turns a bit murky.

Morality, they claim, underpins the discourse by which norms are justified: what guides morality is the criterion of universalizability, and once a norm is so justified, it becomes a general rule waiting to be applied. But the general rule cannot yet be applied as such, for it is only a prima facie rule, lacking the force it needs to actually guide conduct. Hence the need for an applicative discourse to shape the general rule into a specific rule of concrete guidance, to which end, as mentioned, we need to consider all

18. *See* K. Günther, *Critical Remarks on Robert Alexy's "Special-Case" Thesis*, and R. Alexy, *Justification and Application of Norms*, in Ratio Juris, Vol. 6, 1993. 1972, respectively pp. 143 ff. and pp. 157 ff.

19. *See* J. Raz, *Legal Principles and the Limits of Law*, in The Yale Law Journal, Vol. 81, 1972, pp. 123 ff.

20. *See* K. Günther, *Der Sinn fur Angemessensheit: Anwendungsdiskurse in Moral und Recht*, Suhrkamp, Frankfurt am Main 1989. *See also* K. Günther, *Normbegründung und Normanwendung in Recht und Ethik*, in *Generalisierung und Individualisierung im Rechtsdenken*, edited by M. Herberger, U. Neumann and H. Rüssman, Franz Steiner, Stuttgart 1992.

the aspects of the case in question and correctly fit them into the normative framework in light of the issue they give rise to. At this point the general rule will be valid not prima facie but all things considered. Now, in the positive law—at least when understood as a system through which to concretely determine how people are to act under the law—the criterion of universalizability no longer plays any key role. What counts here, as argued, is instead a criterion of appropriateness, or Angemessenheit—a gauge by which to decide when a norm has been appropriately applied. And to this end we proceed not by balancing one norm against another, but by laying out an argument by which to specify the general norm into a rule that tells us how the case is to be framed. But appropriateness is also about coherence, in that the concrete norm needs to be coherent with the normative history by which the applicative decision is preceded. Here Günther explicitly invokes the ideal of integrity that Dworkin in his account of "law's empire" identifies as an overarching guiding criterion for legal practice.[21]

Specification has an advantage over balancing in that it does not require us to interpret and use norms as teleological precepts, and so does not require us to tread the deontological waters of normative reasoning. At the same time, specification would prevent the judge from bypassing the conditional structure of the legal norm: the judge is thus relieved of the task of having to decide what the aims of the norm are, with the result that the judge cannot be made to bear political responsibility for such a decision. A judge who proceeds by specification would thus be a less "active" and overreaching practitioner of the law than one who resorts to balancing. In this sense, judges can be said to derive their legitimacy above all from the letter of the law, in that they confine themselves to applying the law as stated, staying within the semantic boundaries of its literal meaning.

Indeed, the criticism raised against Alexy's "special case" thesis—with the balancing this thesis entails—revolves around four objections.[22] The first of these is that while the law is rife with conflict and controversy, morality rests on a practice of discussion with a view to finding common ground or some framework of mutual understanding. This would mean that the rules of ideal discourse do not apply to legal reasoning. However, this objection, raised by Ulfried Neumann,[23] is one that Habermas does not see as carrying much weight. Indeed, Habermas recognizes that Alexy has a point in replying that, even if the parties under any system of law are bound to come into conflict, they still have to make a case for their claims, and must do so on the basis of arguments that can be universalized: these arguments, in other words, must be such that judges can accept and use them as such in justifying the decisions they hand down. The parties are forced to couch their interests in the language of rights if they are to be taken seriously by the judge. At issue in any trial is not so much the competing interests of the parties to the suit as what the law requires in that regard, or what counts as good

21. *See* R. Dworkin, *Law's Empire*, Hart, Oxford 1998, Chapters 6 and 7.
22. *See* J. Habermas, *Faktizität und Geltung: Beiträge zur Diskurstheorie des Rechts und des demokratischen Rechtsstaats*, 2nd ed., Suhrkamp, Frankfurt am Main 1994, pp. 283 ff.
23. *See* U. Neumann, *Juristische Argumentationslehre*, Wissenschaftliche Buchgesellschaft, Darmstadt 1986.

law in working out the conflict[24]—an idea that had previously been set out by Dworkin in his "rights thesis."[25]

The second objection to Alexy's "special case" thesis hinges on the indeterminacy of morality. Morality is not equipped to deliver anything like a one right answer to the case at hand. This is a shortcoming that only the law can make up for, with its exceptional ability to positivize its decisions and make them operative through its institutions. But here Alexy convincingly replies that what is at stake is not so much the justice of a legal decision as its claim to justice. That there is no one right answer to any practical problem is something that Alexy recognizes without hesitation, and in so doing he keeps his distance from Dworkin. For what matters here, as mentioned, is the claim to correctness and to justice, where the validity of reasoning remains intact.

Habermas replies by pointing out that if moral argumentation is to be effective in the law, it needs to rely on interpretive techniques that are recognized and well-established in the positive law itself and in the case law. But here, too, Alexy has no problem conceding the point. To which he adds that the role filled by the law as a backstop for morality doesn't mean that the law is diminished or taken out of the picture, as Joseph Raz, for example, would argue with his pre-emption thesis."[26] Rather, the idea is that legal reasoning grafts itself onto moral reasoning and feeds on it, and can at any rate be evaluated in relation to the latter.

Finally, Habermas goes back to the idea of an applicative discourse, noting that this moment is crucial in the law, for unlike what happens in morality, the making of a general norm is an institutionally separate moment from that of its application. And, on top of that, the grounding or justification of the norm can be defective. And so, unless applicative reasoning is bent on fashioning itself into a norm-making discourse, in such a way as to undermine the separation of powers, it cannot attempt to morally validate the norm it is applying. Legal discourse would thus be necessarily decoupled from moral discourse. Here, too, Alexy can concede some ground to Habermas. But he cannot go along with Habermas's final conclusion, namely, the separation between law and morality. For, even if there is no doubt that positive law can be morally flawed and still qualify as law, the consequences of these moral flaws are not just moral but can also be distinctly legal. This is what happens when the norm is so morally flawed that it crosses the threshold of extreme injustice, for in this case the norm, however positive it may be, will find it difficult to gain the acceptance it needs as a practice that continues to rest on a claim to justice, and which therefore always finds itself having to keep its guard up so as to avoid the performative contradiction that takes place when the extreme injustice is so apparent and blatant that it amounts to the law explicitly owning up to it.[27] A court ruling that ended with the statement "and this ruling is unjust" would be self-defeating and immediately open to challenge—at least on

24. *See* J. Habermas, *Faktizität und Geltung.*, 2nd ed., cit., p. 283.
25. *See* R. Dworkin, *Taking Rights Seriously*, Duckworth, London 1978.
26. *See* paradigmatically J. Raz, *Authority, Law and Morality*, in The Monist, Vol. 68, 1985, pp. 295 ff, especially p. 299.
27. *See* R. Alexy, *Begriff und Geltung des Rechts*, Alber, München 1992, and its English version *The Argument from Injustice: A Reply to Legal Positivism*, edited by S.L. Paulson and B. Litschewski Paulson, Clarendon, Oxford 2003.

account of its unreasonableness. Extreme injustice can be argued to be phenomenologically equivalent to an explicitly avowed performative contradiction. And a performative contradiction, as is known, makes invalid the proposition that brings it into being: in the words of John Langshaw Austin, the scholar who theorized this contradiction, the contradiction makes that proposition "infelicitous."[28]

Habermas's criticism can thus be seen to fall short of the more general objective of challenging the connection between law and morality. More cogent, however, and posing a greater threat to Alexy's theory, is the criticism aimed at his thesis that rights are to be understood as principles, and that they therefore need to be balanced against one another. In fact there is more than a grain of truth to this criticism, for it underscores the slippery slope that, with balancing, nudges us toward making utilitarian considerations in pondering the consequences of weighing basic rights, easily crossing the deontological line—the Brandmauer, or firewall, as Habermas calls it[29]—that these very rights are instead supposed to mark, in the manner of rights as trumps or vetoes in Dworkin's account of them.

And no less threatening to Alexy's theory of balancing is the alternative to it that Günther offers in dealing with principles. Once principles are reframed as general norms, rather than as optimization commands, they will have to be applied by specifying their content, to which end, as we saw and as Günther points out, we need to consider the circumstances of the case and whether it is being decided in a way that preserves the overall coherence of the given system of norms and decisions pertaining to it. That there is something to Günther's argument can be appreciated as well from the crisis that the theory of principles as optimization commands has been thrown into from within. This crisis was set off by the critique that Alexy received from his disciple and research assistant Jan Sieckmann, who points out that if an optimization command is in fact a command, it needs to be applied in a definitive manner rather than by balancing.[30] And if that is the case, then principles so defined (as optimization commands) are not liable to balancing.[31]

This is a critique in response to which Alexy has taken several different angles, but the outcome feels less than satisfying. Thus, he found himself having to correct course and say that principles are not optimization commands but "commands to be optimized," leaving us to wonder what the difference is and what we are to make of these latter commands. He subsequently qualified principles as "command-optimization commands," once more giving us a baroque notion that cannot be intuitively grasped. Finally, and most recently, he described principles as "ideal

---

28. *See* J.L. Austin, *How to Do Things with Words*, 2nd ed. by M. Sbisà and O. Urmson, Oxford University Press, Oxford 1983.
29. J. Habermas, *Faktizität und Geltung*, 2nd ed. cit., p. 315.
30. For a criticism in the same tenor, outlining the deontological nature of a "Gebot," the command which Alexy says principles consist of, cf. M. La Torre, *Nine Critiques to Alexy's Theory of Fundamental Rights*, in *Arguing Fundamental Rights*, edited by A.J. Menéndez and E.O. Eriksen, Springer, Frankfurt am Main 2006, pp. 53 ff. Principles thus would remain, as far as they are "commands," though of optimization, standards that are deontoloical, not teleological, and that consequently can be definitively applied without balancing.
31. *See* J. Sieckmann, *Regenmodelle und Prinzipienmodelle des Rechtssystems*, Nomos, Baden-Baden 1990.

ought": they prescribe states of affairs which, at the same time, they do not prescribe, in that they may be satisfied by incompatible states of affairs; principles are therefore apt to be expressed through contradictory precepts, and when that happens, the contradiction will have to be resolved by balancing.[32] We can see, then, that the theory of principles begins to wobble, and instead of giving us a tool with which to clarify how legal reasoning works, it seems to envelop such reasoning in a series of complex lucubrations and artful logical solutions, not to mention that some of these introduce novel logical operators thus far unknown to deontic logic or the logic of norms. And while these operations may all be methodologically legitimate, they can only inject further complexity and confusion into the work of a jurist whose job is to wade through legal materials so as to state what the law is, what reasoning it is governed by, and what justifications it rests on, and to do so in a way that most people will be able to understand and accept.[33]

The crisis of the principles theory that manifests in the list of tweaks and disavowals we just ran through brings Günther's proposal back into play, suggesting that we would gain from an effort to better understand and articulate the normative-application discourse in the realm of legal practice. At the same time, that crisis should prompt us to consider that principles are not necessarily commands or teleological-reasoning entities that can only be operationalized by way of balancing. It wouldn't be unreasonable to treat principles as general norms of very wide scope to be applied not so much by balancing as by specification,[34] not least because specification is something that judges, and in particular constitutional judges, might be able to do without incurring so much political risk and without so much exposure to the charge that they lack democratic legitimacy.

32. *See* R. Alexy, *Ideales Sollen*, in Grundrechte, *Prinzipien und Argumentation: Studien zur Rechtstheorie Robert Alexys*, edited by L. Clérico and J.-R. Sieckmann, Nomos, Baden-Baden 2009, pp. 21 ff. *See also* R. Alexy, *Zur Stuktur der Rechtspinzipien*, in *Regeln, Prinzipien und Elemente im System des Rechts*, edited by B. Schilcher, P. Koller and B.C. Funk, Verlag Österreich, Wien 2000, pp. 31ff.

33. Cf. the astute critical remarks by R. Poscher, *Insights, Errors and Self-Misconceptions of the Theory of Principles*, in Ratio Juris, Vol. 22, 2009, pp. 425 ff. Cf. also R. Poscher, *The Principles Theory: How Many Theories and What Is Their Merit?*, in *Institutionalized Reason: The Jurisprudence of Robert Alexy*, edited by M. Klatt, Oxford University Press, Oxford 2012, pp. 218 ff.

34. *See*, on this type of applicative normative reasoning, Henry S. Richardson, *Specifying Norms as a Way to Resolve Concrete Ethical Problems*, in Philosophy and Public Affairs, Vol. 19, 1990, pp. 279 ff.

CHAPTER 19

Russia's Expulsion from the CoE: The CoE's Reactionto Russia's Non-compliance: Rethinking the System in Light of Human Rights Protection and Accountability[*]

Katarzyna Gromek-Broc & Anna Facchinetti

1 INTRODUCTION

Russia's unjustified and illegal invasion of Ukraine triggered an overwhelming reaction of the international community that stood up for the principles and values of international law. The efforts to stop the war have been in vain so far, but the mobilization of all international actors against the aggressor State has been unprecedented and amounted to some symbolic steps taken against Russia. In fact, the termination of the Russian membership of the Council of Europe (CoE) was manifestly a decisive move to discontinue the Russian presence and its aggressive attitude, potentially dangerous in spreading a wrong example of membership at the European human rights organization. At the same time, Ukraine as a respondent stopped being investigated since the European Court of Human Rights (ECtHR) suspended the examination of the applications against Ukraine until further notice.[1] The termination of the Russian membership by expulsion is a strong standpoint although Russia might argue that the termination followed its own withdrawal, that is not completely unfounded.

* Katarzyna Gromek-Broc wrote sections 1, 2 and 6; Anna Facchinetti sections 3-5.

1. Measures applied in respect of cases in which Ukraine is a respondent or an applicant Government following the military attack of February 2022, ECHR 069 (2022) 02.03.2022, at: https://hudoc.echr.coe.int/eng-press#{%22itemid%22:[%22003-7274040-9908360%22]}.

In the history of the CoE, the expulsion or rather forced withdrawal of a Member State happened only once, in the case of Greece. Greece, although not a founding member of the CoE, accessed in the year of its foundation and was one of the signatories of the European Convention on Human Rights (ECHR). In 1967, following a military dictatorship, Greece was on the point of being expelled but it promptly withdrew in 1969 before the voting on expulsion could have taken place.[2] The situation with Russia seems to present some similarities. In both cases, the Parliamentary Assembly of the Council of Europe (PACE) acted without a delay not leaving to the exiting members much space for manoeuvre. Moreover, in the Russian case, the CoE insisted on the use of Article 8 (expulsion) of the Statute of the CoE,[3] whereas the same Article arguably indicates that Article 7 (withdrawal) is to be used first by stating that a member which violated Article 3 of the Statute may 'be requested by the Committee of Ministers to withdraw under Article 7'.[4]

The issue of sanctions brings to the fore an ongoing debate on how to ensure effective compliance with the rules of the international organization to which the particular State is a party. The CoE provides for the use of sanctions such as expulsion or suspension; but given that they are devastating for the civil society and population of the targeted country, they are rarely applied.[5] In fact, sanctions such as rejecting of the credentials of the delegation, or suspension of voting, or denying the participation in the election of judges and senior CoE personnel have been more frequent. According to Article 8 of the CoE Statute, any member that violated Article 3 may be suspended from its rights of representation whereas Article 9 provides for the possibility of suspending the right of representation in the Council of Ministers.[6]

This contribution will examine the difficult Russia-CoE relationship, the systematic non-observance of the rules of the organization and the rights enshrined in the ECHR as well as the reforms of the CoE machinery to strengthen the procedure on compliance (2). Further, it will look at the CoE's procedural inconsistencies regarding the termination of the Russian membership (3). The following section will address the issue of human rights protection and accountability after Russia's departure (4). Finally, it will consider some comparative examples and the potential lessons to be learnt from other systems of human rights protection (5).

2. Becket, James, The Greek Case Before the European Human Rights Commission, *Human Rights* (1970) 1 (1), 91-117; Kiss, Alexandre Charles and Végléris, Phédon, L'affaire grecque devant le Conseil de l'Europe et la Commission européenne des Droits de l'homme, [The Greek Case Before the Council of Europe and the European Commission of Human Rights]. *Annuaire Français de Droit International* (1971) 17 (1), 889-931.
3. Statute of the Council of Europe, 1949, European Treaty Series No. 1 at https://rm.coe.int/1680306052.
4. *Ibid.*
5. Steininger, Silvia, With or Without You: Suspension, Expulsion, and the Limits of Membership Sanctions in Regional Human Rights Regimes, 2021, 533-566.
6. Statute of the Council of Europe, 1949.

2 RUSSIAN'S PROBLEMATIC MEMBERSHIP OF COE

Russia's CoE's membership has always been turbulent, characterized by a quite systematic non-fulfilment of the obligations incumbent on Russia from that membership. Nonetheless, Russia becoming a part of the CoE machinery had a symbolic meaning, increased the legitimacy of international law and attracted attention to the centrality of human rights and democratic values that had the potential to spread to the non-European part of its vast territory. In the pre-accession period from 1992-1996, Russia had a status of special guest participating in the work of the CoE with some enthusiasm. It engaged in 'political dialogue' with the Council of Ministers and somehow agreed that a political solution needed to be found to the Chechen conflict.[7] The pre-accession and the early years of Russia's membership corresponded to the most friendly in history relationship with the European Union in the hope of strengthening the bonds at least in economic terms.

Nevertheless, Russia was a problematic member of the CoE all the way through its membership. Its accession, in 1996, was openly opposed by other members of the CoE, due to Russian military operations in Chechnya.[8] In the early years of its membership, Russia's unwillingness to observe the rights enshrined in the ECHR forced PACE to impose sanctions on the Russian delegation, prohibiting it to vote in the plenary session of the Assembly in April 2000.[9] Soon after, in January 2001, the credentials of the delegation of the Russian Federation were challenged on substantial grounds under Rule 8 (3) of Procedure and the Assembly decided to refer the issue to the Political Affairs Committee.[10] In response, the Duma found the position of the Assembly 'unjust and unfounded', deciding not to participate in the Assembly's work and requesting to reverse the Assembly's decision.[11] Besides, Russia was the only member which did not ratify Protocol 14 by 2006 and Russian political circles started to openly criticize the judgments of the ECtHR.[12] This Protocol was crucial to enhance the Court's operation and the delivery of judgments, and Russia was the only member State blocking the reforms ratified by every other CoE Member State.[13] Russia's uneasiness to comply with the obligations under the ECHR culminated with the

7. Russia's request for membership of the CoE, Opinion 193 (1996); Assembly debate on 25 January 1996 (6th and 7th Sittings) (*see* Doc. 7443, report of the Political Affairs Committee, rapporteur: Mr Muehlemann; and Doc. 7463, Opinion of the Committee on Legal Affairs and Human Rights, rapporteur: Mr Bindig. Text adopted by the Assembly on 25 January 1996 (7th Sitting), Parliamentary Assembly, at https://pace.coe.int/en/files/13932.
8. Drzemczewski, Andrew, The (Non-) Participation of Russian Parliamentarians in the Parliamentary Assembly of the Council of Europe: Recent Developments. *Journal of the Brazilian Institute of Human Rights*, 20(S.I.), 49-58, dec. 2020, available at http://revista.ibdh.org.br/index.php/ibdh/article/view/420.
9. Report, Doc. 8949, 23 January 2001, Credentials of the delegation of the Russian Federation, http://www.assembly.coe.int/nw/xml/XRef/X2H-Xref-ViewHTML.asp?FileID = 9170&lang = en.
10. *Ibid.*
11. *Ibid.*
12. Mowbray, Alastair, Faltering Steps on the Path to Reform of the Strasbourg Enforcement System, *Human Rights Law Review* (2007) 7(1), 609-618.
13. Council of Europe Press Release 816 (2006), Russian State Duma votes against the ratification of Protocol 14 to the European Convention on Human Rights: Declaration by Council of Europe Secretary General Terry Davis, 22 December 2006.

annexation of Crimea in 2014.[14] The PACE found the Russian occupation of Crimea unlawful, in violation of the Statute of the CoE and consequently applied a series of sanctions, namely a suspension of the voting rights of the Russian delegation, revoked a right to be represented in the Assembly's leading bodies, and a right to participate in election observation missions, which were effective until the end of the 2014 session, in practice till 26 January 2015.[15] It is worth noting that the sanctions against a member's delegation were applied only three times in the history of the organization, each time in relation to Russia.[16] The first time concerned the suspension of the right to vote in plenary due to the second Chechen war in 2000, then in 2014[17] in relation to the illegal annexation of Crimea and in 2015, regarding the continuing occupation of the latter and the conflict in eastern Ukraine.[18] Once again, the Russian delegation decided to boycott the Assembly's work in 2014 and 2015.[19] Moreover, Russia did not make any payments to the CoE budget for a number of years.[20] In addition, from January 2016, until June 2019, Russia did not propose any delegation to PACE, avoiding in this way the sanctions that otherwise would have been imposed.[21] In the end, Russia threatened not to rejoin the PACE unless the possibility to challenge credentials on substantive grounds was removed from the Rules of Procedure.[22] The hostility continued and the CoE's response was to prevent Russia from participating in the election of judges to the ECtHR, the Human Rights Commissioner and senior officials in the organization.[23]

The most significant Russian antagonistic stand was to question the authority of the ECtHR judgments. Between 2010 and 2015, the ECtHR condemned 'Russia 72 times for the non-enforcement of national courts' judgments'.[24] For example, the case *Ilascu and Others v. Moldova and Russia*[25] is one of the early illustrations of Russia's unwillingness to abide by the CoE's system. Similar resistance is well visible in the

14. Roter, Petra, 'Russia in the Council of Europe: Participation à la carte' in Mälksoo, Lauri and Benedek, Wolfgang (eds), *Russia and the European Court of Human Rights: The Strasbourg Effect*, 2018, 26-56.
15. Citing Crimea, PACE suspends voting rights of Russian delegation and excludes it from leading bodies, 10 April 2014 at https://pace.coe.int/en/news/4982.
16. Doc. 8949, Credentials of the delegation of the Russian Federation of 23 January 2001, at para. 2, and Doc. 8956, Credentials of the delegation of the Russian Federation, of 25 January 2001, at para. 1.
17. Schennach, Stefan, Reconsideration on Substantive Grounds of the Previously Ratified Credentials of the Russian Delegation, para. 28, at https://pace.coe.int/en/files/20745.
18. Drzemczewski, Andrew, *supra*.
19. Alì, Antonino, The Parliamentary Assembly of the Council of Europe and Sanctions Against the Russian Federation in Response to the Crisis in Ukraine, *Italian Yearbook of International Law* (2017) 27, 77-92, at 78.
20. Drzemczewski, Andrew, *supra*.
21. *Ibid.*
22. *Ibid.*; Steininger, Silvia, *supra*, at 558.
23. *Ibid.*
24. CoE Commissioner for human rights, As long as the judicial system of the Russian Federation does not become more independent, doubts about its effectiveness remain, 2016, at https://www.coe.int/en/web/commissioner/-/as-long-as-the-judicial-system-of-the-russian-federation-does-not-become-more-independent-doubts-about-its-effectiveness-remain.
25. 004-VII 179; (2005) 40 EHRR 46.

2012 case of *Markin v. Russia*,[26] paving the way to an even more hostile approach following the case of *Anchugov & Gladkov v. Russia*, in which Russia manifestly rejected an unequivocal compliance with the ECtHR judgment.[27] In fact, the situation escalated in 2015, when the Russian Constitutional Court held that the ECtHR judgments, in the case of conflict with the Russian Constitution, could not be enforced.[28] In the same year, a Federal Constitutional Law no. 7-FKZ[29] was enacted, allowing in the Articles 104.4 and 106 for the scrutiny of the ECtHR judgments, which, in the situation of conflict with the Russian Constitution, could not be enforced. Rightly so, Kahn sees this law as a dangerous tool sending a wrong message to other Member States of the organization.[30]

More importantly, the Russian case revived the debate on effective sanctions and led to the establishment of an ad hoc Committee in view of reforming of PACE, in particular in relation to participation and representation of the State parties.[31] At the centre of attention was the credential procedure used as a sanction against the delegation of a Member State.[32] The 2018 report suggested to maintain the credentials procedure used as a sanction, but with a higher quorum for 'initiating and rejecting credentials'.[33] The report also envisaged to 'exempt from the sanction procedure the right to elect judges and senior CoE personnel'.[34] In the end, a compromise was reached between Russia and the CoE and despite the serious violations by the former, representation rights were not going to be withheld.[35] Nonetheless, the work of the ad hoc Committee was not completely in vain and led to the introduction of a new 'Complementary Joint Procedure' applicable in the situation when a Member State

26. ECtHR, *Markin v. Russia*, Appl. No. 30078/06, Judgments of 7 October 2010 (First Section) and 22 March 2012 (Grand Chamber). *See* Kahn, Jeffrey, The Relationship Between the European Court of Human Rights and the Constitutional Court of the Russian Federation: Conflicting Conceptions of Sovereignty in Strasbourg and St Petersburg, *The European Journal of International Law*, (2019) 30(3), 933-959; Nelaeva, Galina A., Khabarova, Elena A. and Sidorova, Natalia V., Russia's Relations with the European Court of Human Rights in the Aftermath of the Markin Decision: Debating the 'Backlash', *Human Rights Review*, (2020) 21(1), 93-112.
27. Human Rights, Tenth Annual Report of the Committee of Ministers (2017), at 59. ECtHR, *Anchugov & Gladkov v. Russia*, Judgment of 9 December 2013. All ECtHR decisions are available at http://hudoc.echr.coe.int/.
28. Leach, Philip, A Time of Reckoning? Russia and the Council of Europe, *European Human Rights Law Review* (2022) 3, 219-227.
29. Russian Constitutional Law No. 7-FKZ, in Kahn, Jeffrey, *supra*, at 945.
30. *Ibid.*
31. PACE Doc. 14621 (2018), Report by Petra de Sutter, 'Strengthening the Decision making Process of the Parliamentary Assembly concerning Credentials and Voting'.
32. *Ibid.*, in Steininger, Silvia, *supra*.
33. PACE Doc. 14621 (2018), Report by Petra de Sutter, 'Strengthening the Decision making Process of the Parliamentary Assembly concerning Credentials and Voting'.
34. *Ibid.*, in Steininger, Silvia, *supra*, at 559.
35. Glas, Lize R., Russia Left, Threatened and Won: Its Return to the Assembly Without Sanctions, *Strasbourg Observers*, 2 July 2019.

seriously violates the statutory obligations of the organization.[36] As the name indicates, the procedure does not replace the existing sanctions but complements them. The procedure aimed to strengthen the coordinated action between the Council of Ministers and the PACE to respond more effectively to any violations of the values and principles of the organization.[37] The main aim of the new procedure is to restore a dialogue and cooperation in view to ensure compliance, while avoiding sanctions.[38] The procedure must be initiated by the Council of Ministers, the PACE or the Secretary General and it includes the report on the procedure and short time limits for the specific actions.[39] For example, four weeks is the timeframe for a mission to the State that violates the rules, and eight weeks for the drafting by the Secretary General and adoption by CoE institutions of the targets to be achieved.[40] Further, the targets need to be implemented within nine months.[41] In case of unsuccessful implementation, the Council of Ministers might trigger the expulsion procedure under Article 8 and such a decision needs to be justified in the PACE report.[42] The procedure illustrates the efforts of the organization to provide a more compelling and transparent system. It underlines the voluntary basis for addressing the violations, nonetheless it does not provide any solution in the situation when the Member State in question does not want to engage with the dialogue.

3 COE'S REACTION TO RUSSIA'S INVASION OF UKRAINE: PROCEDURAL HURDLES

Russia stopped being a member of the CoE on 16 March as the first-ever member expelled from the CoE, apart from the Greek withdrawal in 1969.

On 25 February 2022, immediately after Russia invaded Ukraine, the Committee of Ministers of the CoE, after consultation with PACE, decided to activate the procedure under Article 8 of the Statute of the CoE. As mentioned earlier, in case of non-compliance by a Member State with the fundamental values of the CoE, that provision allows suspension of the Member State's representation rights within the organization, including voting rights; to request the concerned Member State to withdraw from the organization; and, if the request is not satisfied, even to expel the Member State. The fundamental values of the CoE are expressed in Article 3 of the Statute, whereby every member of the CoE must accept the principles of the rule of law and of the enjoyment by all persons within its jurisdiction of human rights and fundamental freedoms, and

36. Steininger, Silvia, *supra*, at 559.
37. Council of Ministers, 129th Session of the Committee of Ministers, Helsinki, 17 May 2019, in Steininger, Silvia, *supra*, at 561.
38. PACE, Resolution 2319 (2020) 'Complementary Joint Procedure between the Committee of Ministers and the Parliamentary Assembly in Response to a Serious Violation by a Member State of its Statutory Obligations'.
39. *Ibid.*, in Steininger, Silvia, *supra*, at 562.
40. *Ibid.*
41. *Ibid.*
42. *Ibid.*

collaborate sincerely and effectively in the realization of the aim of the Council as specified in Chapter I.

Based on Chapter I, the aim of the CoE is 'to achieve a greater unity between its members for the purpose of safeguarding and realising the ideals and principles which are their common heritage and facilitating their economic and social progress'.[43] Peace is a natural precondition of such unity. The CoE was created after World War II precisely to avoid repeating the horrors of war. This intent is apparent from the Preamble of the Statute, according to which 'the pursuit of peace based upon justice and international co-operation is vital for the preservation of human society and civilisation'.[44] Russia's armed attack against Ukraine, condemned by the Committee of Ministers as a violation of international law,[45] could thus not but be regarded by the Committee as a serious breach on the part of the Russian Federation of the fundamental values of the organization, as enshrined in Article 3 of the Statute.[46]

At first, the Committee of Ministers only suspended Russia's participation rights within the Committee and PACE, in accordance with the procedure set out in Article 8. As the armed attack against Ukraine continued, on 10 March the Committee of Ministers decided to consult PACE on the possibility to proceed further on the basis of Article 8 of the Statute. On 15 March, PACE delivered a unanimous decision stating that the Russian Federation had committed such serious breaches of the Statute of the CoE that it could be no longer a Member State of the organization.[47] The Assembly condemned, *inter alia*,[48] Russia's failure to comply with the interim measures ordered by the ECtHR, which had indicated to the government of the Russian Federation to refrain from military attacks against civilians and civilian objects.[49]

Probably aware of the imminent expulsion, the Russian Federation decided to exit the CoE on its own terms: on that same date, 15 March, it announced its intention to withdraw from the CoE and to denounce the ECHR. Russia's withdrawal, however, would not have had immediate effect: a six months' notice is necessary for withdrawals from the ECHR to take place,[50] whereas, according to the Statute of the CoE, withdrawals from the organization become effective at the end of the financial year.[51] Since Article 58(3) ECHR states that 'any High Contracting Party which shall cease to be a member of the CoE shall cease to be a Party to this Convention under the same conditions',[52] withdrawal from the ECHR would have likely taken place at the end of the financial year, thus in December 2022. Another reason why Russia's withdrawal from the Council and the ECHR would not have been necessarily straightforward is that

43. Statute of the Council of Europe, 1949, Article 1.
44. *Ibid.*, Preamble, para. 2.
45. It did so already on 24 February: Committee of Ministers, Decisions of 24 February 2022, CM/Del/Dec(2022)1426bis/2.3, para. 1.
46. Committee of Ministers, Decisions of 25 February 2022, CM/Del/Dec(2022)1426ter/2.3.
47. Parliamentary Assembly of the Council of Europe, Opinion No. 300(2022) on the Consequences of the Russian Federation's aggression against Ukraine, para. 19.
48. *Ibid.*, paras 2 ff.
49. Press release of 1 March 2022, ECHR 068 (2022).
50. Convention for the Protection of Human Rights and Fundamental Freedoms, Article 58(1).
51. Statute of the Council of Europe, Article 7.
52. Convention for the Protection of Human Rights and Fundamental Freedoms, Article 58(1).

it could have raised doubts as to its validity because of lack of national parliamentary approval, as instead required by the Russian Constitution for the conclusion of treaties and based also on the *pro democratia* principle affirmed within the context of other human rights treaties, namely the American Convention on Human Rights.[53] The timing and validity of Russia's withdrawal, however, soon became theoretical issues, as the day later, on 16 March, the Committee of Ministers directly expelled the Russian Federation from the CoE with immediate effect, without waiting for Russia's withdrawal to take place.[54]

By directly expelling Russia from the organization, the Council of Ministers and PACE preferred to send a strong message to Russia, deeming that a Member State in blatant violation of the CoE's values could no longer be a Member State of the organization. However, waiting for Russia's withdrawal from the CoE to take effect – admitted it was considered valid – rather than expelling Russia, would have ensured more continuity in terms of human rights protection, to the benefit of persons under the jurisdiction of the Russian Federation, as will be illustrated in the next section.

4 THE IMPACT OF RUSSIA'S EXPULSION FROM THE COE ON HUMAN RIGHTS PROTECTION AND ACCOUNTABILITY

The expulsion of the Russian Federation from the CoE had an impact also on Russian membership to the ECHR. The reason is that the ECHR links the two memberships to each other: as mentioned above, according to Article 58(3) ECHR, a State party which ceases to be a member of the CoE shall cease to be a party to the ECHR under the same conditions. A plain reading of this provision – in particular, the expression 'under the same conditions' – might suggest that the timeline of expulsion from the CoE would apply also to membership of the ECHR. Following this interpretation, the Russian Federation would have ceased to be a State party of the ECHR with immediate effect. In contrast, in its resolution on the consequences of the expulsion of Russia from the CoE, the ECtHR adopted a purposive interpretation of Article 58(3) ECHR, recalling that

53. Based on Article 106 of the Russian Constitution, 'Liable to obligatory consideration by the Council of the Federation shall be the federal laws adopted by the State Duma on the following issues: [...] d. ratification and denunciation of international treaties and agreements of the Russian Federation [...]'. Although the cause of invalidity set out at Article 46 the Vienna Convention on the Law of Treaties only relates to the stipulation of treaties, and not to their denunciation, it is possible to detect the emergence of a 'parallel principle', requiring that the same internal procedure for conclusion of a treaty also applies to denunciation. The Inter-American Court of Human Rights has recently affirmed this principle in its Advisory Opinion OC-26/20, stating that a domestic decision on the withdrawal from a human rights treaty requires a transparent public debate (Inter-American Court of Human Rights, Denunciation of the American Convention on Human Rights and the Charter of the Organization of American States and the consequences for State human rights obligations, Advisory Opinion OC-26, Series A No 26 (9 November 2020), para. 64). As stated in literature, this translates into a *pro democratia* principle in the law of treaties. *See*: Burgorgue-Larsen, Laurence, Interpreting Articles 78 of the American Convention on Human Rights (ACHR) and 143 of the Charter of the Organisation of American States (OAS): Is There Something Special when the IACtHR Comes to Interpret 'Procedural Clauses'?, *Questions of International Law* (2021) Zoom-in 80, 33-52.
54. Committee of Ministers, 16 March 2022, Resolution CM/Res(2022)2 on the cessation of the membership of the Russian Federation to the CoE.

the object and purpose of the Convention as an instrument of human rights protection called for the interpretation and application of its provisions so as to ensure practical and effective protection to those subject to Member States' jurisdiction.[55] Therefore, the Court decided that the Russian Federation ceased to be a State party to the Convention not immediately, but within a six-month period – the same notice period required in case of denunciation. Therefore, the Russian Federation remained a Member State of the Convention until 16 September, meaning that it is possible to launch applications against the Russian Federation for facts occurred until that date,[56] which seems to include facts which occurred prior to that date but whose domestic remedies are exhausted later.[57] The critical date of 16 September was later confirmed by the Committee of Ministers, which also decided that it will continue to supervise the execution of judgments against the Russian Federation.[58]

With its resolution on the consequences of Russia's exclusion, the ECtHR clearly stated that individuals cannot be deprived of human rights protection from one day to another. This is particularly important not only for individuals living in Russian territory, therefore under the territorial jurisdiction of Russia, but also in light of the armed conflict taking place in Ukrainian territory, where the extraterritorial jurisdiction of Russia could be established. It is true that, in its previous case law on armed conflicts (in particular, in *Georgia v. Russia II*), the ECtHR affirmed that during the active conduct of hostilities States' extraterritorial jurisdiction is not established, because in the battlefield the parties indeed fight to obtain effective control over a territory and persons.[59] At the same time, the issue of jurisdiction during armed conflicts was a novel one for the Court, over which the judges were divided. Therefore, the judgment in *Georgia v. Russia (II)* does not bear a strong precedential value, so that it is not excluded that the Court's case law will change in the future.[60] In its decision on Ukraine's request for provisional measures, the ECtHR has already affirmed that human rights must be respected also in times of armed conflict (and implicitly, during the active conduct of hostilities) by ordering interim measures based on prima facie evidence of violations, on the part of the Russian Federation, of Article 2 (right to life),

55. European Court of Human Rights, Resolution of the European Court of Human Rights on the consequences of the cessation of membership of the Russian Federation to the Council of Europe in light of Article 58 of the European Convention on Human Rights, 22 March 2022, *Considerando* No. 6.
56. *Ibid.*, para. 2 of the Declaration.
57. Dzehtsiarou, Kanstantsin, and Helfer, Laurence, Russia and the European Human Rights System: Doing the Right Thing … but for the Right Legal Reason?, 29 March 2022, *EJIL: Talk!*, at: https://www.ejiltalk.org/russia-and-the-european-human-rights-system-doing-the-right-thing-but-for-the-right-legal-reason/.
58. Committee of Ministers, Resolution CM/Res(2022)3 on legal and financial consequences of the cessation of membership of the Russian Federation in the Council of Europe, CM/Res(2022)3, para. 7.
59. European Court of Human Rights (Grand Chamber), *Case of Georgia v. Russia (II)*, Judgment of 21 January 2021, Appl. No. 38263/08, para. 137.
60. Milanovic, Marko, The Russia-Ukraine War and the European Convention on Human Rights, 1 March 2022, *Lieber Institute West Point*, at: https://lieber.westpoint.edu/russia-ukraine-war-european-convention-human-rights/.

Article 3 (prohibition of torture and inhumane and degrading treatment or punishment) and Article 8 (right to respect for private and family life) of the Convention.[61]

The Court's decision to delay the consequences of Russia's expulsion from the CoE and the ECHR to September 2022 represents a commendable attempt to provide access to justice for victims of the armed conflict. This, however, does not change the fact that Russia's exclusion, albeit a morally justifiable response to Russia's blatant violations of international law and of the fundamental values of the CoE, is detrimental to the protection of fundamental rights. Russia would have exited the Convention in any case, but this would have likely happened in December 2022. Time matters – even more so as the armed conflict is still ongoing at the time of writing this contribution (December 2022). The extension of the protection of the European Convention for three more months could have made a change for victims.

What is worse, Russia's expulsion not only limits the possibility to demand Russia's accountability within the framework of the ECHR and, in more general terms, within the CoE, but does not even pay off in terms of the CoE's ability to change the behaviour of the sanctioned State, which is normally the main objective of sanctions. In fact, the exclusion does not offer any immediate incentive for Russia to stop its war of aggression, as there are no economic advantages connected to membership of the CoE.[62] Moreover, the Russian executive power does not seem to value CoE membership from a reputational perspective, as apparent from its declared withdrawal from the organization, possibly because of Russia's perception of the CoE as a traditionally 'Western States club'.[63] It is true that expulsion in case of non-compliance also serves the function of ensuring that the work of the organization is not blocked by a deviant Member State.[64] Russia's expulsion might have seemed to the Member States of the CoE not only a necessary symbolic measure, but also the only tenable option from a practical perspective in order to prevent Russia from seriously hindering the activity of PACE and the Committee of Ministers. Still, this result could have been reached with the simple suspension of the Russian Federation, and certainly without depriving individuals of human rights protection. There is thus a strong case to reform the CoE system when it comes to the instruments available to react to non-compliance by a Member State.

61. Press release of 1 March 2022, ECHR 068 (2022).
62. Jahn, Jannika, The Council of Europe Excludes Russia: A Setback for Human Rights, 23 March 2022, *EJIL: Talk!*, at: https://www.ejiltalk.org/the-council-of-europe-excludes-russia-a-setback-for-human-rights/. Jahn rightly points out that CoE membership is not required for international cooperation within the framework of the World Trade Organization, the UN or the OSCE.
63. This expression, used by Gavrich, explains why the Russian Federation seems to value membership in the CoE less than membership in organizations of which it is a constituent member, such as OSCE (or the UN, I would add). *See*: Gavrich, Andrea, The OSCE Added Value in Times of Strongest Contestation, in Friesendorf, Cornelius and Wolff, Stefan (eds), *Russia's War Against Ukraine: Implications for the Future of the OSCE*, OSCE Network Perspectives 1/2022, at 29.
64. Jahn, Jannika, *supra*.

5 POSSIBLE LESSONS FROM OTHER INTERNATIONAL ORGANIZATIONS AND HUMAN RIGHTS SYSTEMS

A comparison with the instruments available to the CoE and to other international organizations is, of course, difficult, given the extreme diversity in the nature and aims of each organization. It might be helpful, however, to consider the reaction to Russia's invasion of Ukraine of two organizations of which the Russian Federation is a Member State and whose aims include, *inter alia*, the protection of fundamental human rights, namely: the United Nations – in particular, its Human Rights Council – and the Organization for Security and Co-operation in Europe (OSCE). Lessons can be learnt also from other human rights systems, at the regional and global levels. We will consider, in particular, the Inter-American system of Human Rights.

Within the United Nations framework, particularly relevant with respect to the human rights dimension of Russia's invasion of Ukraine is the reaction of the United Nations General Assembly and the Human Rights Council.[65] This latter is an inter-governmental, subsidiary body established by the UN General Assembly to promote human rights protection, assess human rights violations and make recommendations upon them.[66] It is responsible for the periodic review of UN Member States' situation in relation to human rights and can establish special procedures, such as ad hoc monitoring/investigating commissions, in relation to any Member State of the United Nations. Based on the UN General Assembly's Resolution which established the UN Human Rights Council, the General Assembly can suspend the rights of membership in the Council of a Member State that commits gross and systematic violations of human rights.[67] In response to the war of aggression started by the Russian Federation, the UN General Assembly passed a Resolution suspending Russia's membership of the Council. In protest against such a decision, Russia decided to directly leave the Human Rights Council before the end of its term.[68] Nonetheless, as the Russian Federation remains a Member State of the United Nations, the Human Rights Council will have the possibility to continue monitoring and investigating Russia's conduct in relation to human rights. This is particularly important for the work of the commission of inquiry on the situation in Ukraine, set up by the Human Rights Council in March 2022,[69] which can contribute to the global effort to hold Russia and Russian officials accountable through national and international tribunals. Suspension from the Human Rights Council in reaction to non-compliance with human rights obligations thus does not lead to lack of accountability.

With respect to the OSCE, it is worth noting that this organization stands at the opposite extreme than the CoE in terms of type of States' commitments – which, within

65. The UN Security Council is obviously blocked from taking any action because of the Russian veto.
66. United Nations General Assembly, Resolution of 15 March 2006, A/RES/60/251.
67. *Ibid.*, para. 8.
68. *See*: https://news.un.org/en/story/2022/04/1115782.
69. United Nations General Assembly, Human Rights Council, Resolution of 4 March 2022 on the situation of human rights in Ukraine stemming from the Russian aggression, A/HRC/RES/49/1.

the OSCE, are of political, not legal, binding nature[70] – and structure of the organization – which for the OSCE is markedly inter-governmental, since the organization mainly functions as a platform for dialogue among Governments on security-related issues, including human rights. As consensus among Member States is required for every decision to be taken within the OSCE, it is not even possible to suspend Russia, let alone to expel it in case of non-compliance with the cooperative values of the organization. This voting mechanism is clearly not apt to send a strong message to a non-compliant Member State, and even risks blocking the work of the organization due to Russia's veto. Still, Russia's ongoing participation in the organization has an added value, because it provides States with the possibility to dialogue with Russia for bringing the conflict to an end, and allows for the continuous monitoring of the human dimension of the OSCE (including human rights protection) through the Moscow mechanism. Such mechanism permits any individual Member State of the OSCE to launch investigations concerning another Member State's alleged violations of human rights, by setting up an ad hoc investigative commission composed of independent experts, even without the consent of the accused State.[71] The Moscow mechanism has already been activated three times by coalitions of Member States with regard to Russia's invasion of Ukraine and produced one report documenting Russia's international crimes.[72]

The lessons which can be learnt from these examples is that a form of reaction against serious violations of human rights law is needed to put political pressure on the non-compliant Member State, in order to change its behaviour, but also to send a message to it and the international community that such violations might not go unpunished. In this respect, the CoE is much better equipped than the Human Rights Council and especially the OSCE. This does not mean, however, that the strong message sent through expulsion from the CoE is necessarily effective in changing Russia's conduct, as explained above. Suspending the participating rights of the non-compliant Member State, while monitoring over its conduct, seems to achieve more, at least in terms of accountability if not in terms of ability to influence that State's conduct.

The CoE could draw from the Inter-American system of human rights. The Charter of the Organization of American States provides Member States with the possibility to suspend another Member State's participating rights within the organization,[73] but does not confer them the power to expel a member of the organization, nor is suspension linked to membership in the American Convention on Human Rights. A drawback of this system is that suspension is possible only in case of overthrow of a

70. This does not mean that States' commitments with regard to human rights are only expression of goodwill: they amount to political promises, which, however, are not enforceable in a Court of law. *See*: OSCE Office for Democratic Institutions and Human Rights (ODIHR), OSCE Human Dimension Commitments, Vol. 1 (Thematic Compilation), 3rd ed., 2011, at XVIII.
71. OSCE Office for Democratic Institutions and Human Rights (ODIHR), OSCE Human Dimension Commitments, *supra*, at XX.
72. OSCE Moscow Mechanism's mission of experts, Report on Violations of International Humanitarian and Human Rights Law, War Crimes and Crimes against Humanity Committed in Ukraine since 24 February 2022, 12 April 2022, available at: https://www.osce.org/odihr/515868.
73. Charter of the Organization of American States, Article 9.

democratically elected Government.[74] In contrast, from the perspective of the suggested reform of the Council Europe, obviously it should be possible for the Committee of Ministers, as already the case, to suspend a Member State from the organization for any serious violation of the aims of the CoE, but without this necessarily translating into an expulsion, and in any case without effect on the human rights obligations of that State under the ECHR. Such a solution would protect victims' rights, providing them access to justice when it is most needed.

It is true that a non-compliant Member State which experiences political pressure might always decide to directly withdraw not only from the organization, but also from the relevant human rights treaty, as the Russian Federation did with respect to the ECHR on 15 March. This challenge to human rights might be addressed with a further reform of the CoE system – and, in particular, of the ECHR – by simply eliminating the ECHR provision which currently allows States to denounce the Convention (Article 58). There are already human rights treaties which do not provide for denunciation. For instance, the International Covenant on Civil and Political Rights, which does not contain withdrawal clauses, has been interpreted by its monitoring body, the UN Human Rights Committee, as not permitting denunciation or withdrawals, in light of the continuing nature of human rights obligations.[75] In its view, 'once the people are accorded the protection of the rights under the Covenant, such protection devolves with territory and continues to belong to them', notwithstanding historical changes such as change in government or dismemberment.[76] In other words, people cannot be deprived of the human rights they enjoy. This principle should inspire also a revision of the ECHR.

6 CONCLUDING REMARKS

Undoubtedly, the CoE's almost immediate reaction to the Russian aggression of Ukraine and the decision to expel Russia from the CoE sent a strong message to other contracting parties and to the outside world. As such a reaction is quite novel in the CoE system and there is no established practice that could clarify the subsequent steps or provide guidance in case of a doubt. Russia's termination of the CoE's membership raises some doubts concerning the legal basis. The CoE referred to Article 8 (expulsion), but Article 7 (withdrawal) of the CoE Statute could possibly have been used, given that Russia addressed the communication to the Secretary General on 15 March with its intention to withdraw.[77] The difference in procedures is an important consideration in terms of the time limit left for the effective termination, that is more generous in case of withdrawal.[78]

74. *Ibid.*
75. Human Rights Committee (HRC), CCPR General Comment No. 26: Continuity of Obligations, 8 December 1997, CCPR/C/21/Rev.1/Add.8/Rev.1, para. 3.
76. *Ibid.*, para. 4.
77. Leach, Philip, *supra*; Dzehtsiarou, Kanstantsin and Helfer, Laurence, *supra*.
78. Steininger, Silvia, *supra*.

Nonetheless, the prompt termination of Russia's membership left many uncertainties. The first concerns the application of the ECHR to the pending cases. The Committee of Ministers confirmed that Russia will cease to be a part of the ECHR on 16 September 2022, and the ECtHR will have jurisdiction in cases initiated prior to that date.[79] Article 58(3) of ECHR offers a few options for interpretation that the Committee of Ministers could have followed. Russia loses a judge sitting permanently on the ECtHR panel, although in cases against Russia the ECtHR might rely on an ad hoc judge.[80] On the other hand, however, the CoE reaction, although justified, contradicts to some extent the spirit of the newly introduced Complementary Joint Procedure, which emphasizes dialogue and the avoidance of sanctions.

Looking at the tempestuous Russian membership in the CoE: Russia systematically violated the rights enshrined in the ECHR, did not align with the procedural requirements, and neglected sanctions. We might thus question the merits of such a membership. Conversely, Russia's participation in the human rights organization elevated the place of human rights and international law in the world. Its membership was precious. In fact, Russia was the only superpower ever subjected to the human rights monitoring mechanism.[81] Further, its membership improved human rights' observance in Russia despite its systematic non-compliance and the objection to enforce some ECtHR judgments. Many judgments led to changes of law in Russia, mentioning the decisions in cases such as *Putintseva*, *Bednov*, *Rakevich* or *Malysh and Others*,[82] and promoted, in theory, freedom of association, freedom of expression, protection of property rights, and access to the Court.[83]

In addition, the Russian case evidenced the weaknesses of the CoE sanctions system, in particular the suspension procedure, and forced the organization to re-examine it in view of more accountable and transparent means.[84]

Finally, the biggest losers are the individuals living under the jurisdiction of Russia, including those in occupied territories or otherwise subjected to the extraterritorial jurisdiction of Russia based on the notion of effective control over a person or a territory, because they will not be able to seek redress in case of human rights violations. Continuous membership in the ECHR could have been critical in providing justice to the victims of the Ukrainian conflict, having in mind a post-war scenario – which, we hope, will come soon.

79. Dzehtsiarou, Kanstantsin and Helfer, Laurence, *supra*.
80. *Ibid*.
81. Leach, Philip, *supra*.
82. ECtHR, *Putintseva v. Russia*, Judgment of 10 August 2012, Appl. No. 33498/04; *Bednov v. Russia*, Judgment of 1 September 2022, Appl. No. 21153/02; *Rakevich v. Russia*, Judgment of 24 March 2004, Appl. No. 58973/00; *Malysh and Others*, Judgment of 28 June 2010, Appl. No. 30280/03.
83. Russian Federation Execution of the European Court of Human Rights' Judgments, Main Achievements in Member States, at: https://rm.coe.int/ma-russia-eng/1680a186c0.
84. Steininger, Silvia, An Internal Safety Net for the Council of Europe?, *Verfassungsblog*, 28 December 2019 at https://verfassungsblog.de/an-internal-safety-net-for-the-council-of-europe/.

CHAPTER 20

The Contribution of the Sub-national Authorities to the EU Legality: The Evolution of Article 263 TFEU

Fabio Giglioni

1 THE CAPACITY OF SUB-NATIONAL AUTHORITIES TO INFLUENCE THE EU LAW

In European Union (EU) history the role of local and regional authorities has increasingly got bigger and bigger. This result is firstly due to the amount of powers which have generally been obtained by the Member States, given that these competences are crucial for some important EU objectives. Just to give some examples one can mention the powers they wield for transport and mobility, energy, land-use planning, environment, welfare, public utilities or, more generally, local development. The EU receives an important contribution from them and, even more importantly, also in terms of democracy and citizenship, since they can compensate for the failing trust with the citizens that the EU institutions and the Member States have been recording for the most recent years. In addition, one can consider that about a third of the EU budget is assigned to structural and investment funds through which regional cohesion policies find concrete implementation.

Remaining within this point of view, if you shift the look at the European institutions, you cannot avoid saying a word about the European Committee of the Regions (ECR) with its consulting powers in the legislative procedures and also with its power to bring the legal action before the European Court of Justice (ECJ) if its prerogatives are at stake. More significantly the ECR actually has the ability to appeal to the ECJ even where the subsidiarity principle is infringed so that the annulment action is possible beyond the question concerning the protection of its own procedural prerogatives. In other terms, local and regional authorities have gained room in the EU legal system thanks to the institution which better represents them.

Moreover, we can also find EU institutions within the cities' networks. Over the years cities have built numerous transnational networks throughout the world for several reasons. Most of them are out of the EU scope so that the Covenant of Mayors interestingly appears an exception inasmuch as the EU institutions are involved in application of this pact. Such a development shows a progressive entangled relationship between the EU level and local authorities with no filter of the Member States.

With this in mind, the aim of this contribution is to understand if the alliance between the EU and sub-national authorities could be embedded in a firmer rationale. In other words it would be important to ascertain if the sub-national authorities are endowed with powers allowing them to protect the EU law on their own. In this regard, the thought goes to Article 263(4) Treaty of Functioning of the European Union (TFEU), according to which 'any natural or legal person may, under the conditions laid down in the first and second paragraphs, institute proceedings against an act addressed to that person or which is of direct and individual concern to them, and against a regulatory act which is of direct concern to them and does not entail implementing measures'. Among the legal persons it is not controversial that sub-national authorities are included so that they contribute to the respect of rule of law in the EU legal system. Actually, one of the most recursive positions affirmed by the case law is that of guaranteeing a wide spectrum of legal actions and legitimate claimants for the sake of legality. That is why also the sub-national authorities can contribute to that goal. But the question is: to what extent can sub-national authorities contribute to get the EU aims through legality?

As it is well known, sub-national authorities are not included in the privileged applicants so they are obliged to demonstrate the specific interest that they have to protect when they are willing to bring a legal action.[1] In other terms sub-national authorities are prevented from applying the legal action where the controversy does not clearly regard themselves. From this point of view the first of the three limbs outlined by Article 263(4) is plain enough since the right to lodge an appeal is pacific when the applicant is also the addressee of the controversial act. The only question in this case is to prove the specific interest in bringing proceedings, but it is less relevant to our aims.[2] The conclusion is different when the claimant is not the addressee because the boundary between the subjective and objective reasons which lie in the application is more subtle.[3] It is no coincidence if someone, by referring to the sub-national

1. This is a long-standing case law as the following cases: C-95/97 *Región wallonne v. Commission*, EU:C:1997:184; C-180/97 *Regione Toscana v. Commission*, EU:C:1997:451; C-417/04 *Regione Siciliana v. Commission*, EU:C:2006:282; C-586/11 *Regione Puglia v. Commission*, EU:C:2013:459.
2. *See* for this issue J. Wildemeersch, *Standing Requirements of Private Parties in Actions for Annulment Concerning Regulatory Acts: The State of Affairs 10 Years after the Entry into Force of the Lisbon Treaty*, Max Planck Institute, 2, Special Issue, 2020, 50-54.
3. Even the case has not brought about any specific advantages, it is interesting to consider also the case T-46/18 *Comune di Milano v. Council*, EU:T:2018:131, wherein the GC has declined its competence to rule because the applicant of the city of Milan coincided with the one that the Italian Republic brought before the ECJ. After that the case C-182/18 *Comune di Milano v. Council*, EU:C:2018:445 has ruled that the ECJ already had the opportunity to state that the active

authorities' power to apply, said that they are "atypical" non-privileged applicants.[4] Understanding to what extent the sub-national authorities can introduce objective reasons in the applications lets us grasp the wideness of the contribution that they can give.

2 THE DIFFICULTIES TO OVERCOME A LONG-STANDING CASE LAW

Once the perspective from which the analysis in-depth will be run is made clear, two other observations have to be put forward. The first one is as follows: even if the next considerations are dedicated to all those circumstances where the claimants are public authorities, the parameters that the ECJ demands are the same as the court applies to non-public claimants. That is why the case law I am going to cite involves even findings where the claimant is not a public authority. The second note is that the close examination of what is next takes into consideration the other two limbs of Article 263(4) TFEU separately.

With regard to the second limb, the act, which is the object of the application, has to be of direct and individual concern for the claimant's interests. From this point of view a long-standing case law has ruled that two criteria have to be met for that: (i) the measure must directly affect the legal situation of the individual; (ii) it must leave no discretion to its addressees so as to make implementation purely automatic with no application of other intermediate rules.[5]

For the first condition to be applied, we consider the hypothesis the contested act is turned to individuals other than the applicants. In this case the applicant is expected to demonstrate that its interests are effectively involved. For that aim there are some clear symptoms able to help the applicants. For instance, if they have taken part in a rule-making procedure or if they prove their observations had been taken into consideration by the authority adopting the contested act, there are sufficient grounds that they are directly interested. At that point if the controversial act disadvantages the applicant, the first condition regarding the limitation of the legal situation is ascertained.

If the contested act is a regulation or has the Member States as addressees, the applicant is also called upon to demonstrate that the effects affecting its legal position are directly referred to the same act. That means that the controversial act has no implementing measures or that the implementation is purely automatic.[6] In case the contested act is a (legislative) regulation, there is no problem at all, given that

participation of any person to a procedure which adopted a controversial decision can be an element able to demonstrate the direct concern for the annulment of the contested act. Hence, the city of Milan could be legitimated to bring a legal action against the European institutions in that case, even if an analogous action was promoted by the State Member.

4. *See* the Opinion of AG Bobek in case C-352/19 P *Brussels-Capital Region*, EU:C:2020:588 para. 141.
5. *See, inter alia*, from C-622/16 P to C-624/16 P *Scuola Elementare Maria Montessori v. Commission*, EU:C:2018:873; C-313/19 P *GranoSalus v. Commission*, EU:C:2020:869.
6. *See* the recent case C-872/19 P *Venezuela v. Council*, EU:C:2021:507.

regulation does not need the execution to be effective. In other cases the applicant has to bring evidence that the Member States did not have discretionary power with regard to the implementation of the contested act so that their measures are to be considered automatic. The same conclusion is drawn if the Member States, though they had a margin of choice not to apply the contested act, had decided to execute the controversial act in advance. This evidence is fundamental in order to prove the limitation of the applicant's legal position directly depends on the contested act. Vice versa, if the violation of the claimant's interests comes from the Member States in application of the European act, it is forced to bring the legal action against the domestic act so that the National court could raise a preliminary ruling before the ECJ, pursuant to Article 267 TFEU.[7]

All these conditions, though, are still not sufficient. An additional burden lies on the claimant: it has to prove to be individually affected, meaning that it has such individual qualities or that there are such circumstances through which it is possible to distinguish it from the general public. In other words, the applicant, though not the addressee, has to present conditions as if it was indeed in terms of facts.[8] The same result could be attained if the controversial act contains specific reference to the applicant, even if it is not the final addressee: this way could be the evidence that the applicant has a diverse position from the others. However, these conditions are considered able to limit the *locus standi* right significantly. That conclusion, as law scholars know, originates from the Plaumann case.[9]

The rationale of the EU jurisprudence is clear enough: it seeks to avoid an excessive legitimation of claimants for annulment of the EU acts at the point the entire legal system would not be sustainable anymore. At the same time it is sufficiently obvious that the strict application of the individual test does not adjust to those situations wherein the applicants intend to protect general interests more than their own interests. A classic example is the action for environmental protection. Applying the individual test as if the claimants are the factual addressees of the controversial act does not make sense, because it demands the satisfaction of subjective conditions whereas the applicant has the intention to protect objective interests.[10] However, the ECJ has been unmovable on this point.

7. *See* the recent case C-911/19 *Fédération bancaire francaise v. ACPR*, EU:C:2021:599.
8. There are many cases with this interpretation. *See, inter alia*, T-437/15, *Eden Green Vivai Piante di Verdesca Giuseppe v. Commission*, EU:T:2016:144.
9. *See* the very famous case C-25/62 *Plaumann v. Commission*, EU:C:1963:17. *See also* the joined cases C-408/15 P and C-409/15 P *Ackermann Saatzucht v. Parliament and Council*, EU:C:2016:893 and the case C-594/19 P *Deutsche Lufthansa v. Commission*, EU:C:2022:40 for the same typology of rulings.
10. There is in literature sufficient awareness on this point; *see, e.g.*, A. Albors-Llorens, *Sealing the Fate of Private Parties in Annulment Proceedings: The General Court and the New Standing Rest in Article 263(4) TFEU*, 71 Cambridge Law Journal, 2012, 507; M. Van Wolferen and M. Eliantonio, *The EU's Difficult Road Towards Non-compliance with the Aarhus Convention*, in M. Peeters and M. Eliantonio (eds), *Research Handbook on EU Environmental Law*, Elgar, 2020; G.C. Leonelli, *A Threefold Blow to Environmental Public Interest Litigation: The Urgent Need to Reform the Aarhus Regulation*, European Law Review, 2020, 324.

In the *Armando Carvalho and others v. European Parliament and Council of European Union* case[11] the claimants had expressly asked for the overruling of the Plaumann approach, but the ECJ denied again. This case is particularly interesting. Actually the claimants were individual operators of different countries, including extra-EU countries, in the field of agriculture as well as tourism. They asked for the annulment of some legislative EU acts because of the detachment of the Paris Agreement objectives. For the first thing, they tried to demonstrate that its legal position was different from that of the general public. According to them, insufficient measures against climate change would provoke aggravation of the environmental conditions with risks to their business which are particularly exposed to climate variability. The ECJ ruled that the fact that the effects of climate change could be different for some persons rather than others is not a sufficient element to distinguish them individually from the general public equally affected by climate instability. According to the EU court a contrary conclusion 'would render the requirements of the fourth paragraph of Article 263 TFEU meaningless and would create locus standi for all without the criterion of individual concern referred to in the judgement in Plaumann being fulfilled'. More interestingly, the ECJ rejected the applicants' arguments wherein they had affirmed that they were claiming a fundamental right whose application is fully individual. The ECJ has welcomed the objection of the EU Parliament according to which such an interpretation amounts to saying everyone has the title to bring the legal action against every EU act, since whichever EU general act is potentially able to affect a fundamental right. Therefore, it would be a misinterpretation that to hold the fundamental rights allows to distinguish the individuals from the public.[12]

Once the attempt to prove the Plaumann conditions were met failed, the claimants clearly requested the overcome of the Plaumann case on the ground of a series of motivations, including Article 47 of the Chart of Fundamental Rights (CFR). Particularly, they had argued it was paradoxical that the EU courts constantly state the supremacy of the rule of law as well as fundamental rights without concerning the concrete effects of their findings, given that the strict interpretation of individual tests ends up preventing persons from making legal actions. Such a criticism is enhanced as no Member State applies this test in the domestic law so that it would be wrong to maintain that the test belongs to the general principles of the Member States. Likely, the impediment to apply other legal action from the claimants contradicts the supremacy of the rule of law that the courts continuously repeat. Before all these arguments the ECJ has responded in a formalistic way, by reaffirming the conditions of Article 263(4) TFEU and the importance of avoiding it to be meaningless. With reference to Article 47

11. It is the case C-565/19 P *Armando Carvalho and others v. Parliament and Council*, EU:C:2021:252.
12. It is notable p. 49 where you can read 'an infringement of their fundamental rights, inferring individual concern from that infringement, on the ground that the effects of climate change and, accordingly, the infringement of fundamental rights are unique to and different for each individual, it cannot be held that the acts at issue affect the appellants by reason of certain attributes which are peculiar to them or by reason of circumstances in which they are differentiated from all other persons, and by virtue of these factors distinguish them individually just as in the case of the person addressed'.

CFR, the ECJ notes that although 'the conditions of admissibility laid down in the fourth paragraph of Article 263 TFEU must be interpreted in the light of the fundamental right to effective judicial protection, such an interpretation cannot have the effect of setting aside the conditions expressly laid down in that Treaty'.[13] In other terms, no way for other possibilities.

Within this framework sub-national authorities do not represent an exception,[14] so that the above-mentioned limits for application are also valid for local and regional authorities.

2.1 Little Signals of Change

2.1.1 Despite This Tendency, Something Has Little Changed in Recent Years

The first signal of change regards Article 263(4) TFEU literally. Although it mostly replicates the old Article 230 of Treaty of European Community (TEC), the amendment of Lisbon Treaty has introduced what the previous paragraph has called the third limb. Thanks to this, any natural or legal person can apply legal action even against 'a regulatory act which is of direct concern to them and does not entail implementing measures'. The novelty has confirmed that it was untrue that the EU allowed whichever shape of protection for the sake of rule of law so that the legislator was forced to do such a change.

It is interesting to track back the origins of this change. Article 230 TEC prevented the natural or legal persons from applying against the binding general acts other than the legislative ones where their effects were immediately directed to them without an implementing measure. Such a situation was actually at the origin of a paradox: the interested persons in that case were forced to infringe the EU law in order to bring the legal action against the EU act provoking their prejudices. In the light of this serious vulnerability of the rule of law, the General Court (GC) tried to overcome the long-standing individual test for the sake of legal protection effectiveness.[15] Therefore in the case *Jégo-Quéré v. European Commission*[16] the GC held that the legitimation had to be acknowledged to the persons affected or constrained by direct obligations in a certain and immediate way. The GC shared the opinion of the General Advocate Jacobs

13. It would have to be considered that this position was already expressed by the ECJ: *see* the case T-16/04 *Arcelor v. Parliament and Council*, EU:T:2010:54; C-583/11 P *Inuit Tapiriit Katanami v. Parliament*, EU:C:2013:625; the joined cases C-408/15 P and C-409/15 P *Ackermann Saatzucht v. Parliament and Council*; case T-600/15 *Pesticide Action Network v. Commission*, EU:T:2016:601.
14. *See*, for instance, the cases T-214/95 *Vlaams Gewest v. Commission*, EU:T:1998:77; T-462/13 *Comunidad Autónoma del País Vasco v. Commission*, EU:T:2015:902; from T-227/01 to 229/01, T-266/01 and T-270/01 *Territorio Histórico de Álava, Comunidad Autónomica del País Vasco v. Commission*, EU:T:2009:315; C-455/07 P *Commission v. Ente per le Ville Vesuviane*, EU:C:2009:529; C-524/14 P *Commission v. Hansestadt Lübeck*, EU:C:2016:971; T-66/19 *Vlaamse Gemeenschap and Vlaams Gewest*, EU:T:2019:484.
15. It deserves to bear in mind that even the ECJ was aware of this absurd paradox: *see*, for instance, C-583/11 P *Inuit Tapiriit Katanami v. Parliament*, EU:C:2013:625, with particular regard to paras from 58 to 60.
16. *See* the case T-177/01 *Jégo-Quéré v. Commission*, EU:T:2002:112.

by virtue of the absence in the old Article 230 TEC of any reference to the individual as a key element for *locus standi*. It follows that 'a natural or legal person is to be regarded as individually concerned by a Community measure of general application that concerns him directly if the measure in question affects his legal position, in a manner which is both definite and immediate, by restricting his rights or by imposing obligations on him. The number and position of other persons who are likewise affected by the measure, or who may be so, are of no relevance in that regard'. It was a real attempt to overcome the individual test for legal action legitimation. However, the ECJ reversed the sentence in appeal with arguments which are well known at this point. On the other hand, in the *Union de Pequenos Agricultores v. the European Council*,[17] the ECJ had already held there was no way for an extensive interpretation of Article 230 TEC unless the Treaty had changed.[18]

Therefore, the third limb of Article 263(4) TFEU is the fruit of this story. Since then the protection of natural and legal persons has been widened. The most important contribution of this amendment to the EU law has regarded the focus on acts other than legislative ones. It was the legacy of the failed endeavour of approving the Constitutional Treaty that would have distinguished the legislative acts from the regulatory acts. In spite of this failure, Article 263 TFEU kept this distinction. Thanks to that it is possible to mention that the meaning of the regulatory act has been permitted to include a wide range of acts with potential strengthening of the EU legality. Actually the ECJ has ruled that whichever decision with general binding effects could be considered 'regulatory act', pursuant to Article 263(4) TFEU.[19]

The second signal of change was the *Ville de Paris, Ville de Bruxelles and Ayuntamiento de Madrid v. the European Commission* case.[20] The GC has actually considered valid the legal action promoted by the three European cities against a regulation adopted by the Commission which had raised the tolerated standards of nitrogen dioxide emissions in order to homologate the cars with Euro 6 motors. The

17. *See* the case C-50/00 P *Unión de Pequeños v. Council*, EU:C:2002:462. This ruling was furtherly confirmed with the case C-455/07 P *Commission v. Ente per le Ville Vesuviane*.
18. *See* the comments of this case by L. De Lucia, B. Marchetti, *Il sistema integrato di tutela*, L. De Lucia and B. Marchetti (eds), *L'amministrazione europea e le sue regole*, il Mulino, 2015, 212-215 and G. Falcon, *La tutela giurisdizionale*, M.O. Chiti and G. Greco (eds), *Trattato di diritto amministrativo europeo*, Giuffré, 2007, General Part, II, 731.
19. *See* the cases T-18/10 *Inuit Tapiriit Katanami v. Parliament*, EU:T:2011:419; T-96/10 *Rütgers v. European Chemicals Agency*, EU:T:2013:109; C-583/11 P *Inuit Tapiriit Katanami v. Parliament*; C-274/12 *Telefónica v. Commission*, EU:C:2013:852; C-133/12 *Stichting Woonlinie v. Commission*, EU:C:2013:336; T-219/13 *Ferracci v. Commission*, EU:T:2016:485; T-220/13 *Scuola elementare Maria Montessori c. Commission*, EU:T:2016:484; C-565/19 P *Armando Carvalho and others v. Parliament and Council*, EU:C:2021:252; T-251/18, *IFSUA v. Council*, EU:T:2020:89. *See* again J. Wildemeersch, *Standing Requirements of Private Parties in Actions for Annulment Concerning Regulatory Acts: The State of Affairs 10 Years after the Entry into Force of the Lisbon Treaty*, cit., 54-56. The State aid measures, though, are not equivalent to the "regulatory act" where the content is individual: *see* the case C-594/19 P *Deutsche Lufthansa v. Commission*.
20. *See* the joined cases T-399/16, T-352/16 and T-391/16 *Ville de Paris, Ville de Bruxelles and Ayuntamento de Madrid v. Commission*, EU:T:2018:927 with the comments by *see also* E. Tatí, *Cities' Legal Actions in the EU: Towards a Stronger Urban Power*, European Papers, 3, 2019, 861; É. Chavelier, *Chronique de jurisprudence de l'Union européenne – Pollutions et nuisances*, 4, Revue juridique de l'environnement, 2020, 807-808.

contested regulation was executing Directive 2007/46 concerning the circulation of the motor vehicles, but – according to the applicants – it ended up affecting their power to adopt restrictive measures for fighting the air pollution under Directive 2008/50. This latter allows the Member States to allocate the limiting powers of circulation to the local authorities where the clean air is at risk. It follows that the three cities complained about the interfering effect on their power because of the controversial regulation. There was no doubt that the control of legal action legitimation should have been done on the basis of the third limb of Article 263(4) TFEU. Likely, the type of the contested regulation clearly appeared as a regulatory act, in a sense of general binding non-legislative act.

What remained uncertain, was whether or not the claimants were directly affected by the controversial act without any implementing measures. Relating to the implementing measures, the GC has concluded that the application of the contested regulation did not require any execution and it was self-implementing. On the other hand, the eventual application of sanctions cannot be confused with implementing measures, given that such an interpretation would make completely useless the normative provision of Article 263 TFEU. The real point was to demonstrate the contested regulation effectively impressed on the claimant's interests.

In this regard, the main objection of the European Commission was that the contested regulation had nothing to do with the claimants, given that it was executing the Directive on the authorisation of the cars' circulation. From this point of view the act contributed to the single market of cars with no interference with the claimants. However, the GC had the opportunity to state that a general legislative act is usually able to give wide effects regarding even provisions out of its strict object. In the specific case if the local authorities did not be touched by these acts, a severe consequence would be determined, since every city could adopt restrictive measures regardless of the new standards decided by the controversial act. It is useless to underline that uncertainty would prevail with dangerous repercussions on the motor cars' market. Moreover the Member States can not only prohibit the registration and the sale of the cars complying with the new standard, but also cannot limit the entry into force or circulation on the road of those vehicles so that all the authorities are asked to follow the new definitions of standard. In this regard, the GC recalls the application of the practical effect as a key element of legitimation of the three cities.

In addition, the GC has also faced the question of the real interference with the cities' powers where the contested act is other than the one regarding the clean air protection. Put in that way, the GC has noted that the Member States as well as the sub-national authorities are under whichever general binding EU law so that what is important, is not the adequacy of powers with regard to the origin of assignment but the concrete modality when they wield those powers. In other words, if the execution of power, bestowed on specific objectives, is affected by an act with different aims, it is sufficient enough to state that the limitation is relevant for the legal position of the authority. In the end, the GC held valid the legal action brought by the three cities.

It is really interesting to observe the use of the practical effect that GC made: it has not been used for EU law to prevail over the domestic law, but for embedding the ability of sub-national authorities to protect the EU law without the filter of the Member

States.[21] Basically, what can be drawn from the reasoning of the court is precisely a reflected and indirect dynamic of the practical effect which, in demanding the full application of EU law, ends up imparting a breadth of legal consequentialism that has repercussions on another discipline safeguarding different European objectives and when it is achieved it is the right of every subject, who is in the purview of Article 263(4) TFEU, third limb, to intervene to protect European law. So the absence of the individual test along with the wide recognition of what is the direct concern of claimants let us conclude that sub-national authorities have the right to bring a legal action for annulment even if they mainly apply for objective reasons. The three cities represent all European cities;[22] their appeal could have been brought by any other European city inasmuch as its Member State had assigned the relative power under the EU law. The only aim to protect the EU objectives, e.g. the clean air, has allowed the three cities to access to justice procedure. Significantly this happened when the local authorities were called upon to pursue environmental goals.

The third signal of change was the amendment of the Aarhus Regulation. With the regulation 2021/1767 the EU reformed the previous regulation 1367/2006 on the application of the Aarhus Convention on access to information, public participation in decision-making and access to justice in environmental matters to Community institutions and bodies.[23] As to explain the impact of this amendment, background needs to be shared. According to Article 2(2) of Aarhus Convention, the access to judicial procedure did not include the acts with legislative quality. It would have been followed that all the administrative acts concerning environmental matters would have had to be considered for appeal by the members of public or members of 'public concerned' (Article 2(4) and (5)). However, the Aarhus Regulation was not so faithful to that provision. Article 2(1)(g) laid down that an administrative act is 'any measure of individual scope under environmental law … having legally binding and external effects'. It is not difficult to note that this definition is more restrictive than what could have been prescribed and, above all, this provision presents again the 'individual scope' of the measure.

With no unpredictable result, this solution has opened new conflicts because of the non-governmental organisation's (NGO) attempts to claim the respect of the Aarhus Convention. In *Stichting Natuur* case,[24] the ECJ overruled the GC's decision by reaffirming the necessity to comply with the Aarhus Regulation according to the formalistic way of the ECJ reasoning that we already explored earlier. In the Mellifera

21. *See* the comments I had already proposed: F. Giglioni, *Le città e l'inquinamento atmosferico nel diritto europeo*, 4 Giornale di diritto amministrativo, 2019, 447.
22. *See* E. Tatí, *Cities' Legal Actions in the EU: Towards a Stronger Urban Power*, cit., 869.
23. *See* G.C. Leonelli, *Access to the EU Courts in Environmental and Public Health Cases and the Reform of the Aarhus Regulation: Systemic Vision, Pragmatism and a Happy Ending*, 1 Yearbook of European Law, 2021, 230.
24. *See* the case T-338/08 *Stichting Natuur en Milieu and Pesticide Action Network Europe v. Commission*, EU:T:2012:300 and, then, the joined cases C-404/12 P and C-405/12 P *Council and Commission v. Stichting Natuur en Milieu and Pesticide Action Network Europe*, EU:C:2015:5.

case,[25] the ECJ expressly ruled that any interpretation put forward cannot be a *contra legem* interpretation. The question is always the same: claimants, who represent collective interests, have a few chances to appeal. What we said earlier about Article 263(4) TFEU, confirms this conclusion. In addition, it should be considered that even the slight opening of Article 263(4) TFEU, third limb, is useless when you are in environmental scope, because the regulatory acts almost never lack for implementing measures, given the complexity of the discipline.

For that reason, the reform of the original Aarhus Regulation is an important step forward. Significantly, this change was raised from the finding of the Aarhus Convention Compliance Committee, which held that the Aarhus Regulation had failed to implement the Aarhus Convention just for the aspects above underlined.[26] The main changes are three. The first one is the request for review that now concerns any non-legislative act (or any failure to adopt non-legislative act) with legal and external effects, just in case it contravenes environmental law. In that way any reference to individual scope of act has disappeared. The second variation regards the subjects with the right to access to justice procedure, given that they are all the members of the public which meet one of two following criteria: (i) their rights are prejudiced by the act contravening the environmental law; (ii) they are directly concerned by such an act in comparison with the public at large. On those grounds they are not required to demonstrate that they are directly and individually concerned, but it is sufficient to show they suffer an unjustified restriction to the exercise of their rights or powers. This change seems to regard any natural and legal person, including the sub-national authorities. Differently from the 'three cities case', they have to distinguish their situation from the public at large, but that is basically concentrated on the demonstration they are directly concerned about. The last modification concerns the absence of any reference to the implementing measures so that the EU administrative acts can be objects of appeal without or with implementing measures, even if the latter is both automatic and not automatic. That is true at all the levels: EU level and Member States level.

2.1.2 A Still Long Way to Travel

The discussed changes are not lacking contradictory elements.

In spite of the fact that the EU legislator has introduced the third limb of Article 263(4) TFEU, case law is quite conservative. By the way of implementing measures, for instance, the ECJ has refused to distinguish between automatic and not-automatic implementing measures, although the difference would be substantial.[27] As a result, any implementing measure, even without significant ability to give a real contribution

25. *See* the case C-784/28 P *Mellifera v. Commission*, EU:C:2020:630. *See also* the important case C-240/09 *Lesoochranárske Zoskupenie (Slovak Bear)*, EU:C:2011:125, where the ECJ confirmed its orientation again.
26. *See* the findings and recommendations adopted by the Aarhus Convention Compliance Committee on 17 May 2017.
27. *See* the cases C-15/06 P *Regione Siciliana v. Commission*, para. 31 EU:C:2007:183.

to the regulatory act, has been considered able to stop the application of Article 263(4) TFEU, third limb.[28]

Furthermore, the same access to justice from sub-national authorities has mostly recorded negative findings. In this regard, the *Region de Bruxelles-Capitale v. European Commission* case[29] is epitomising. The sub-national authority appealed against a regulation through which the European Commission had renewed the approval of the active substance of glyphosate for plant-based products. According to the appellant, such a decision had affected its rights for the assignment of relative authorisation. The ECJ, confirming the GC ruling, denied its right to appeal for different reasons. First of all, the claimant tried to apply the Aarhus Convention by arguing that Article 216(2) TFEU obliges the EU institutions to comply with the international agreements that they had stipulated. Still again, though, the ECJ rejected the supremacy of the Aarhus Convention with the reason that the international conventions only prevail on the secondary EU rules, thereby excluding the establishing treaties. Secondly, it would be wrong to deduce a direct concern of the effect through a contrary reasoning rationale. The fact that an eventual missed approval by the European Commission would have stopped the market of plant-based products does not mean that the contrary effect has been brought about in case of approval. As a matter of fact, the holders of authorisation are required to ask for new authorisation in that case, so that national authorities can decide to confirm or not. There is no obligation for confirmation. Thirdly, the ECJ denied the appellant was really affected since under the national law the authorisation of power is given to the national authority. The Region of Bruxelles takes part in the procedure as consultant authority with no binding effects. It is important to stress, however, that the ECJ also underlines that the powers of the sub-national authority did not come from the EU law. In the end, the ECJ also considered insufficient the declared contradiction with the 'three cities case', since the argument did not explain precisely why this alleged contrast would be unlawful by itself. Although the conclusion was opposite to the 'three cities case', the finding seems to correspond to the parameters the GC established in that case.

The Region of Bruxelles actually had powers not coming from the EU law and was not forced to exercise its power, so that any analogy is improper. This boundary is a key element in order to confuse the sub-regional authorities with the privileged applicants.

Unfortunately, the slight opening of the 'three cities case' was overruled by the ECJ at the beginning of 2022. In the joint cases from C-177/19 P to C-179/19 P, the ECJ has been urged to give a decision.[30] The opposite conclusion of the ECJ ruling has not impeded the recognition of the GC's decision on the point that the three cities were

28. *See* for this interpretation T-400/11 *Atladis v. Commission*, EU:T:2013:490; C-274/12 *Teleónica v. Commission*; C-132/12 P *Stichting Woonput v. Commission*. EU:C:2014:100; C-133/12 *Stichting Woonlinie v. Commission*; C-456/13 P *T&L Sugars v. Commission*, EU:C:2015:284; T-397/13 *Tilly-Sabco v. Commission*, EU:T:2016:8; T-434/13 *Doux v. Commission*, EU:T:2016:7; C-384/16 P *European Union Copper Task Force v. Commission*, EU:C:2018:176. *See also* C. Buchanan and L. Bolzonello, *Another Step towards a Definition of 'Implementing Measures'*, 7, European Journal of Risk Regulation, 2016, 225.
29. *See* the case C-352/19 P *Région de Bruxelles_Capitale v. Commission*, EU:C:2020:978.
30. *See* the joint cases from C-177/19 P to C-179/19 P, *Germany v. Commission*, EU:C:2022:10.

affected by the controversial act under a specific perspective. Paragraph 41 has stated that 'Furthermore, it is apparent from paragraphs 59, 74 and 76 of the judgement under appeal that, according to the GC, in so far as the regulation at issue introduces a conformity factor which applies to the values laid down in Regulation No. 715/2007, in order to define the values of pollutant emissions of oxides of nitrogen which cannot be exceeded (not-to-exceed (NTE)) during the Real Driving Emissions (RDE) tests established by Regulation 2016/427, the second subparagraph of Article 4(3) of Directive 2007/46 applies equally to those NTE values, with the result that, on account of the adoption of the regulation at issue, the public authorities could no longer impose restrictions on circulation based on the pollutant emission levels of vehicles which fall into the category covered by Regulation No 715/2007 and which comply with those NTE values. In view of its finding that the regulation at issue thus affects the respondent cities 'own legislative powers in relation to the regulation of the circulation of motor vehicles, the General Court concluded, in particular in paragraphs 50, 76, 80 and 84 of that judgement, that that regulation was of direct concern to them', even if the ECJ subordinates such a conclusion to the merit of other objections of the appeal.

Actually, the court did not welcome the interpretation proposed by the GC about the cross-interference among different EU rules. According to the ECJ, the controversial regulatory act has to be interpreted in the light of the framework within which it has been given birth, including the considerations about its real genesis. It follows that the contested act had to do only with access to the market for motor vehicles. An extensive interpretation about its effects would be hard to justify, according to the ECJ. Interestingly, the ECJ held not to welcome the interpretation put forward by AG Bobek,[31] who, differently from the GC, did not subscribe to the conclusion whereby the cities competences on air protection had been completely crushed, but he admitted that their exercise had been made harder, thereby espousing them to legal conflicts by virtue of different policies they were able to adopt.

It is worth noting that the ECJ has not made use of the concept of practical effect, which was the key element in the GC ruling, by replicating a formalistic approach as we observed in other circumstances. Indeed, with a very hasty wording, paragraph 95 has stated 'no other ground put forward by the respondent cities nor any of the findings made by the GC in the judgment under appeal supports its conclusion that the regulation at issue is of direct concern to the respondent cities'. In this sense this wording appears poor in terms of the necessity of a strict review.

It is also interesting the refusal opposed to the Ayuntamiento de Madrid's argument in paragraph 65. It deserves to be fully referred to: 'Furthermore, after observing that cities play a major role in EU law, the Municipality of Madrid notes the objective of opening up the conditions for bringing direct actions and the fact that the development of the approach taken as regards the admissibility of actions brought by infra-State entities, especially in matters relating to environmental law, may be seen as a corollary to the principle of sincere cooperation laid down in Article 4(3) TEU and

31. *See* the AG Bobek conclusion in the joint cases from C-177/19 P to C-179/19 P *Germany v. Commission*, EU:C:2021:476. For this reason, he expressed the contrary opinion to the overruling.

referred to by the General Court in paragraph 79 of the judgement under appeal. Thus, it might be accepted that infra-State bodies, such as the respondent cities, which by their actions incur the liability of the States to which they belong with regard to the European Union, enjoy a presumption of admissibility, the onus being on the author of the contested act to demonstrate that they are not affected by the contested provisions'. In other words, Madrid asked for a full recognition of the cities to contribute to the EU law, especially where the environmental law is at stake, with a presumption of admissibility. That would have been very crucial for the perspective of this paper, but the ECJ has eschewed this argument, by considering it unfounded. The ECJ reminded that sub-national authorities' role cannot be confused with the Member States.

As for the Aarhus reform, it will take some time before we see what concrete effects it will produce with regard to access to justice, also with regard to the legitimacy of the sub-national authorities. So far, the ECJ has demonstrated a certain ability to skip any innovative interpretation.

3 CONCLUSIONS

In the light of what has been discussed until now one can conclude that there is a large distance between the potential role of the sub-national authorities, particularly cities, and the concrete legal tools they possess to pursue EU objectives. The opening process is very slow, despite the fact that there is evidence of clear flaws in the EU law in order to assure a very complete remedial system. This is particularly obvious where the matters of environmental law are involved.

On the one hand, the peculiar and insuppressible collective nature of these interests is not compatible with the requirements that consider the individual test as a key factor.[32] Now it will be interesting to observe the application of the Aarhus Regulation reform, but it is important to remark on the contribution of the sub-national authorities for that. Besides the clean air directive, it is also relevant to mention the role of sub-national authorities in the energy package and in the Green Deal adopted by the EU Commission. On the other hand, as long as the EU system keeps showing flaws in terms of completeness of the remedial system, particularly with reference to the EU law without or with automatic implementing measures, every effort to improve this result for the sake of the rule of law should be evaluated positively.[33] In this sense the sub-national authorities can offer sufficient guarantees for that aim.

32. This is the main opinion by G.C. Leonelli, *Access to the EU Courts in Environmental and Public Health Cases and the Reform of the Aarhus Regulation: Systemic Vision, Pragmatism and a Happy Ending*, cit., 239.
33. It is no coincidence that many AGs noted the necessity to overcome the well-established case law as Leonelli has remembered: *see* G.C. Leonelli, *Access to the EU Courts in Environmental and Public Health Cases and the Reform of the Aarhus Regulation: Systemic Vision, Pragmatism and a Happy Ending*, cit., 250-251.

CHAPTER 21

The Lisbon Treaty and EU Democracy: A Brief Assessment of Selected Areas

Nikos Vogiatzis

1 INTRODUCTION

Approximately thirteen years have passed since the Lisbon treaty entered into force in December 2009. Carrying the weight of the unsuccessful 'Constitutional treaty', there was a feeling at the time[1] (which has now been confirmed) that this European Union (EU) treaty would last longer than its predecessors. In the meantime, the EU has had to deal with several crises - some of which are ongoing. Most recently, the ecological crisis, the COVID-19 pandemic and Russia's war of aggression against Ukraine have prompted new debates on the direction that the EU (including EU Law) should follow.[2] The rule of law crisis in Hungary and Poland necessitates determination for action (that seems to be missing) by the EU institutions. In parallel to these developments (albeit affected by the pandemic[3]), the Conference on the Future of Europe reflected on the way forward: regardless of one's views about the success or otherwise of this supranational exercise, there is no doubt that the question of EU democracy was central to these debates, and of particular interest to EU citizens who were participating therein.

1. *See*, among others, Michael Dougan, 'The Treaty of Lisbon 2007: Winning Minds, Not Hearts' 45 *Common Market Law Review* 617, at 702-703 (2008); Patrick Birkinshaw and Mike Varney, 'Introduction' in Patrick Birkinshaw and Mike Varney (eds) *The European Union Legal Order after Lisbon* (Kluwer Law International 2010) p. xxiv.
2. Editorial Comments, 'A Jurisprudence of Distribution for the EU' 59 *Common Market Law Review* 957 (2022).
3. It is, however, questionable whether the pandemic was the reason behind the delay: *see* Alberto Alemanno, 'Releasing Europe's Democratic Genie' (2021) available at: https://socialeurope.eu/releasing-europes-democratic-genie (accessed 23 August 2022).

To that end, this chapter, in honour of Professor Patrick Birkinshaw's remarkable career, will illustrate some of the developments and challenges related to EU democracy, taking the Lisbon treaty as a starting (or main reference) point. Of course, as the readers of this volume will be aware, the question of the EU's democratic deficit predates Lisbon (and possibly Maastricht as well, when EU citizenship was introduced[4]). Inevitably, in light of space limitations, there will be considerable selectivity in the areas covered. One crucial consideration that has informed the discussion is, of course, Birkinshaw's leading work. For example, it would have been a notable omission if this chapter had not considered developments regarding access to documents and transparency. Thus, the chapter adopts a broad understanding of EU democracy, which also includes rights (such as access to documents) which are not explicitly mentioned in the so-called 'Provisions on democratic principles' under Articles 9-12 Treaty on European Union (TEU); although the latter provisions, and more specifically Articles 10 and 11 TEU, do refer to the principle of openness. In this context, subsequent sections will explore issues related to access to documents and transparency; the role of the European Parliament (with a particular focus on the European elections and the Spitzenkandidaten process); and probably Lisbon's most debated contribution to EU participatory democracy, the European citizens' initiative (ECI). The concluding remarks will offer an outlook, taking also into account the conclusions of the Conference on the Future of Europe.[5]

2 TRANSPARENCY AND ACCESS TO DOCUMENTS

Access to documents, transparency and openness are essential for democracy: they are means via which the government can be held to account, while also fostering citizens' participation and trust in decision- and policy-making.[6] As already noted, the Treaty at various places underlines the Union's commitment to openness – most emphatically, perhaps, in Article 1 TEU, which states that 'decisions are taken as openly as possible and as closely as possible to the citizen'. Of course, this declaratory aim is often not met. The key piece of legislation is Regulation 1049/2001,[7] which has still not been amended (this matter is briefly returned to below).[8] In addition, the legally binding Charter of Fundamental Rights enshrines the right of access to documents under Article 42, as does Article 15(3) Treaty on the Functioning of the European Union (TFEU). It

4. For an account of its evolution *see, e.g.*, Jo Shaw, 'Citizenship: Contrasting Dynamics at the Interface of Integration and Constitutionalism' in Paul Craig and Gráinne de Búrca (eds) *The Evolution of EU Law* (Oxford University Press 2021) 608.
5. *See*: https://futureu.europa.eu/?locale=en (accessed 23 August 2022).
6. Patrick Birkinshaw, 'Freedom of Information and Openness: Fundamental Human Rights?' 58 *Administrative Law Review* 177 (2006).
7. Regulation (EC) No 1049/2001 of the European Parliament and of the Council of 30 May 2001 regarding public access to European Parliament, Council and Commission documents [2001] OJ L 145/43.
8. Regarding citizens' right to access environmental information, Directive 2003/4/EC of the European Parliament and of the Council of 28 January 2003 on public access to environmental information and repealing Council Directive 90/313/EEC [2003] OJ L 41/26 is the key reference point regarding the Member States.

goes beyond the scope of this chapter to examine the interplay between access to documents, openness and transparency[9] – but it is accepted that the latter two notions are broader than access to documents.

Regarding Regulation 1049/2001, scholarly attention often focuses on the so-called 'mandatory' and 'non-mandatory' exceptions to access,[10] and the rich case law that has been produced, in this respect.[11] Suffice to note here that in the landmark *Turco* judgment the link between democracy and participation was highlighted: 'increased openness ... enables citizens to participate more closely in the decision-making process and guarantees that the administration enjoys greater legitimacy and is more effective and more accountable to the citizen in a democratic system'.[12]

Whereas Article 15(3) TFEU under the Lisbon treaty extends the right of access to documents to all EU institutions, bodies, offices and agencies (the exception under Article 15(3)(4) TFEU is briefly addressed below), while the various references to openness in the treaty would lead an external observer to assume that meaningful steps have been taken towards further transparency, commentators have underlined that there are signs that the tendency is, in fact, in the opposite direction.[13] To begin with, Regulation 1049/2001 has not yet been revised – although advanced discussions on this matter were taking place a few years after its entry into force.[14] One can assume that there is resistance from many Member States and certain EU institutions, in this respect.

In this chapter, two developments may be mentioned, which can also be characterized as persistent problems: the transparency of trilogues; and relatedly, albeit also separately, the scepticism of the Council towards further transparency (a matter that goes beyond trilogues, as will be shown below). As is known, trilogues are informal meetings between the three key institutions involved in EU legislation: the Commission, the European Parliament and the Council. The purpose of these meetings is to find common agreement at an early stage, and they constitute the norm: '[t]oday, the use of trilogues has become a structural feature of the first reading of the legislative process employed in the vast majority of legislative proposals'.[15] As is often the case with debates around transparency, the trade-off here appears to be improving efficiency versus ensuring transparency and accountability. However, the general scholarly (critical) view, to which this author also subscribes, is that trilogues have operated in an unduly secretive way.[16]

---

9. *See also* Birkinshaw, *supra* n. 6.
10. *See* Article 4 of Regulation 1049/2001.
11. For a more recent account *see, e.g.*, Deirdre Curtin and Paivi Leino-Sandberg, 'Openness, Transparency and the Right of Access to Documents in the EU' (2016) Study for the PETI Committee of the European Parliament, PE 556.973.
12. Joined Cases C-39/05 P and C-52/05 P, *Turco v. Council*, EU:C:2008:374, para. 45.
13. Curtin and Leino-Sandberg, *supra* n. 11, at 5.
14. Ian Harden, 'The Revision of Regulation 1049/2001 on Public Access to Documents' 15 *European Public Law* 239 (2009).
15. Maarten Hillebrandt and Päivi Leino-Sandberg, 'Administrative and Judicial Oversight of Trilogues' 28 *Journal of European Public Policy* 53, at 55 (2021).
16. *See*, among others, *ibid.*; Gijs Jan Brandsma, 'Transparency of EU Informal Trilogues through Public Feedback in the European Parliament: Promise Unfulfilled' 26 *Journal of European Public Policy* 1464 (2019).

In 2016, the European Ombudsman (generally one of the most prominent advocates for transparency in the EU[17]) concluded an important strategic inquiry into the transparency of trilogues.[18] Several recommendations were made to improve transparency, on the basis that EU law-making legitimacy would be enhanced as citizens 'must be in a position to scrutinise the performance of their representatives during this key part of the legislative process' and they 'also require information on the topics under discussion during Trilogues to be able to participate effectively in the legislative process'.

In 2018, in an important judgment, the General Court found that trilogues are subject to the principles of transparency, and that limitations to access (while possible) should be interpreted restrictively.[19] It cannot be categorically excluded that the General Court took into consideration the attention and interest that was generated further to the Ombudsman's strategic inquiry.

There have been further inquiries in which the Council has shown reluctance to follow the Ombudsman's recommendations. In another high-profile inquiry, the Ombudsman effectively looked into whether and to what extent the Council was implementing the leading *Access Info Europe* judgment, in which the Court of Justice confirmed the General Court's annulment of the Council's decision to refuse to disclose the identities of Member States in documents related to the legislative process (concerning, in fact, a possible revision of Regulation 1049/2001).[20] The Ombudsman criticized the Council's practice in many respects[21] – and the matter was so serious and important for the Ombudsman's transparency agenda that a special report was submitted to the European Parliament: the most recent special report to date, and the last step that can be taken by the Ombudsman when the institution concerned is unwilling to comply/ and or implement her recommendations. More recently, however, the Ombudsman welcomed the steps taken by the Council to improve legislative transparency.[22]

17. On which *see, generally*, Nikos Vogiatzis, *The European Ombudsman and Good Administration in the European Union* (Palgrave Macmillan 2018) Ch. 5.
18. Decision of the European Ombudsman setting out proposals following her strategic inquiry OI/8/2015/JAS concerning the transparency of Trilogues, available at: https://www.ombudsman.europa.eu/en/decision/en/69206 (accessed 23 August 2022).
19. Case T-540/15, *De Capitani v. European Parliament*, EU:T:2018:167. For a comment *see* Francesca Martines, 'Transparency of Legislative Procedures and Access to Acts of Trilogues: Case T-540/15, *De Capitani v. European Parliament*' 3 *European Papers* 947 (2018).
20. Case C-280/11 P, *Council v. Access Info Europe*, EU:C:2013:671.
21. More specifically, the Ombudsman 'criticised the Council's failure to record systematically the identity of Member States taking positions in preparatory bodies, and the widespread practice of restricting access to legislative documents while the decision-making process is ongoing (the so-called "LIMITE" marking)'; *see* Special Report of the European Ombudsman in strategic inquiry OI/2/2017/TE on the transparency of the Council legislative process, available at: https://www.ombudsman.europa.eu/en/special-report/en/94921 (accessed 23 August 2022).
22. These 'include proactively publishing progress reports on negotiations on draft laws as well as the Council mandate for negotiations with the European Parliament': *see* Press Release 2/2020, 'Ombudsman welcomes steps to make EU law making more accessible to the public', available at: https://www.ombudsman.europa.eu/en/press-release/en/130298 (accessed 23 August 2022).

Developments and/ or concerns about transparency are not confined to the Council - although the latter features prominently in research related to this matter.[23] As noted earlier, Article 15(3)(4) TFEU confines the right of access to documents to the administrative functions of the Court of Justice, the European Central Bank, and the European Investment Bank. The Court may have recently taken steps to stream some of its Grand Chamber hearings[24] (certainly a noteworthy development) - but is there clarity, or even willingness, on the part of the Court, to identify its administrative functions? Recent research indicates that this may not be the case.[25]

3 THE ROLE OF THE EUROPEAN PARLIAMENT

The discussion on the role of the European Parliament in this section may not be viewed as implying that the potential of national parliaments (and the national level, more generally) should not be duly considered as well in the context of discussions on the EU's further democratization. After all, the EU is based on a dual channel of representation (and legitimacy), as is also confirmed by Article 10 TEU.[26] Although space limitations would prevent an examination of the literature related to this path of enquiry, it can briefly be noted that the available research has identified several and varied challenges regarding the actual or potential contribution of national parliaments to EU democracy[27] - including via the so-called 'early warning mechanism' for the monitoring of the subsidiarity principle.

Another crucial element to be noted is that the European Parliament strengthened its overall position in the Lisbon treaty in a number of ways: via the extension of what is now the ordinary legislative procedure, further budgetary powers, control of

23. *See, e.g.*, Stéphanie Novak and Maarten Hillebrandt, 'Analysing the Trade-Off Between Transparency and Efficiency in the Council of the European Union' 27 *Journal of European Public Policy* 141 (2020).
24. Court of Justice of the European Union Press Release No 63/22, 'Broadcast by Streaming of Hearings and the Handing Down of Judgments and Opinions of the Court of Justice' available at: https://curia.europa.eu/jcms/upload/docs/application/pdf/2022-04/cp220063en.pdf (accessed 23 August 2022).
25. Nikos Vogiatzis, 'The Administrative Functions of the Court of Justice of the European Union' 47 *European Law Review* 222 (2022).
26. Article 10(1) TEU is worded as follows: 'The functioning of the Union shall be founded on representative democracy'; while Article 10(2) TEU provides: 'Citizens are directly represented at Union level in the European Parliament. Member States are represented in the European Council by their Heads of State or Government and in the Council by their governments, themselves democratically accountable either to their national Parliaments, or to their citizens.'
27. *See*, among others, Katrin Auel and Thomas Christiansen, 'After Lisbon: National Parliaments in the European Union' 38 *Journal of European Public Policy* 261 (2015) (and the contributions included in that special issue); Diane Fromage, *Les parlements dans l'Union européenne après le traité de Lisbonne: La participation des parlements allemands, britanniques, espagnols, français et italiens* (Editions L'Harmattan 2015); Davor Jancic (ed.), *National Parliaments after the Lisbon Treaty and the Euro Crisis: Resilience or Resignation?* (Oxford University Press 2017); Katarzyna Granat, *The Principle of Subsidiarity and Its Enforcement in the EU Legal Order: The Role of National Parliaments in the Early Warning System* (Hart Publishing 2018); Anna Jonsson Cornell and Marco Goldoni (eds), *EU-Legislative Procedure Post-Lisbon: The Impact of the Early Warning Mechanism* (Hart Publishing 2017).

executive power, among others.[28] If one thinks that the European Parliament directly represents citizens at EU level, one might then be prepared to consider these developments as adding to the democratic credentials of the Union – but this also depends, of course, on one's view of EU democracy more generally. In any event, this section will focus on two areas related to European elections: the Spitzenkandidaten process and the right to vote for EU citizens who have not exercised free movement rights.

As to the former, the exposition should begin by recalling the key (and probably rather ambiguous) provision in the Lisbon Treaty, which prompted the creation of the Spitzenkandidaten process. Thus, Article 17(7) TEU[29] is worded as follows: 'Taking into account the elections to the European Parliament and after having held the appropriate consultations, the European Council, acting by a qualified majority, shall propose to the European Parliament a candidate for President of the Commission. This candidate shall be elected by the European Parliament by a majority of its component members'. This provision therefore outlines the process via which the President of the Commission is to be elected by Parliament; yet, since Lisbon it has been clear that there is a degree of ambiguity on the precise role of the European Parliament in that process: in particular, what the term 'taking into account the elections to the European Parliament' entails is unclear. The two European elections that took place in 2014 and 2019 resulted in establishing (2014), but then effectively backtracking from (2019), the Spitzenkandidaten process, and ultimately in a power struggle between (primarily) the European Parliament and the European Council (and the Member States, more generally).

The process was devised by the European Parliament in the years prior to the European elections of 2014; that is, the first elections after the entry into force of the Lisbon treaty. It is an idea that effectively entails that the European political parties, seen also in light of the reference, under Article 10(4) TEU, that they 'contribute to forming European political awareness and to expressing the will of citizens of the Union', select and nominate a candidate of their choice (a lead candidate) for the post of Commission President. If, following the European elections, that party secures the most seats in the European Parliament, that candidate should become the President of the Commission. Thus, in accordance with this reading of Article 17(7) TEU, Jean-Claude Junker was nominated by the European People's Party (EPP) prior to the 2014 elections and, since the EPP gained the most seats, he was elected and became President in 2014. As commentators have observed, while voices within the European Parliament had called for an 'elected' Commission even before Lisbon (which, after all, introduced – at first glance at least – relatively minor, but rather ambiguous, changes to the wording related to the appointment/ election of the Commission President), the

28. *See* Dougan, *supra* n. 1, at 692. He situated this discussion, however, in the context of what was (rightly) described as 'a relative resurgence in intergovernmental influence within the functioning of the Union' (*ibid.*, p. 698).
29. Article 17 TEU more generally outlines the key role of the Commission, which is to promote the general interest of the Union.

eurozone crisis contributed to the need to appeal to a possibly pan-European audience.[30] It has also been argued that the then President of the European Parliament, Martin Schulz, was rather influential in rendering that mechanism a success.[31] Although this author and many others found potential in this novelty, the possible trade-off should be acknowledged: a balance would have to be found between legitimizing the Commission in the eyes of European citizens, and avoiding a situation whereby the Commission would become unduly politicized. As already mentioned, it is generally understood that the Spitzenkandidaten process is not mandated by Article 17(7) TEU as the latter does not prescribe how the results of the European elections should be 'taken into account' by the European Council.[32] It was, perhaps, a creative interpretation (within the law, but one of many others) of the treaty by the European Parliament: a 'power grab' for some, an important contribution to EU democracy for others.

That process was, however, discontinued in 2019. The election of Ursula von der Leyen (who was not a Spitzenkandidat) as President of the European Commission following the most recent European elections has prompted scholarly commentary as to why the European Parliament 'lost' that process (and, relatedly, why it accepted a different process).[33] Crucially, the question of the Spitzenkandidaten process should be viewed in light of the criticism that European elections are 'second order',[34] a claim that is a key component of the EU's democratic deficit. Although more recent studies show different motivations across voters,[35] the premise of the Spitzenkandidaten process should not be underestimated, namely that the lead candidates would run a campaign across Member States focussing on matters of common EU interest. That is not, of course, in and of itself, sufficient to address the democratic deficit. Could the increase

30. Sara Hobolt, 'A Vote for the President? The Role of *Spitzenkandidaten* in the 2014 European Parliament Elections', 21 *Journal of European Public Policy* 1528 (2014); Thomas Christiansen, 'After the *Spitzenkandidaten*: Fundamental Change in the EU's Political System?' 39 *West European Politics* 992 (2016).
31. Joseph Weiler, 'The *Spitzenkandidaten* Exercise One Year Later – The Unsung Hero' 26 *European Journal of International Law* 311 (2015).
32. Editorial Comments, 'After the European Elections: Parliamentary Games and Gambles' 51 *Common Market Law Review* 1047 (2014).
33. *See, e.g.*, Ben Crum, 'Why the European Parliament Lost the *Spitzenkandidaten*-Process' *Journal of European Public Policy*, https://www.tandfonline.com/doi/full/10.1080/13501763.2022.2032285 (2022). Crucial is also the method (and related shortcomings) via which the European parties select their lead candidate, on which *see, e.g.*, Wouter Wolfs, Gert-Jan Put and Steven Van Hecke, 'Explaining the Reform of the Europarties' Selection Procedures for *Spitzenkandidaten*' 47 *Journal of European Integration* 891 (2021).
34. This theory suggests *inter alia* that European elections are viewed by voters as less important than national elections and/or are dominated by national (as opposed to European) politics and considerations. In addition, the turnout is lower than in national elections. Although several variations of this theory exist, the starting point is the well-known account by Karlheinz Reif and Hermann Schmitt, 'Nine Second-Order National Elections – A Conceptual Framework for the Analysis of European Election Results' 8 *European Journal of Political Research* 3 (1980).
35. Dorian Alt, Erik Brandes and David Nonhoff, 'First Order for Some: How Different Forms of Politicization Motivated Voters in the 2019 European Parliamentary Election' *Journal of Common Market Studies*, DOI: 10.1111/jcms.13376 (2022). *See also* Piret Ehin and Liisa Talving, 'Still Second-Order? European Elections in the Era of Populism, Extremism, and Euroscepticism' 41 *Politics* 467 (2021).

in voter turnout in 2019[36] – for the first time – be attributed, partly at least, to the success and promise of the 2014 experience? This is an open question – but undeniably, the process of election of the Commission President is likely to be of institutional interest and scholarly attention for years to come.[37]

Another development worth mentioning here is what is perhaps one of the most significant contributions of the Court of Justice of the EU to the political dimension of Union citizenship, and the right to vote for the European elections, more specifically. It should be noted that prior to *Delvigne*,[38] it was thought that EU law prohibited discrimination on grounds of nationality regarding the right to vote:[39] it regulated situations in which EU citizens had exercised free movement rights.[40] By contrast, in *Delvigne* we were before a different situation: the applicant, convicted of a serious crime, was unable to vote for the European elections in the Member State of his nationality (France). The Court, drawing a link between Article 39(2) of the Charter and Article 14(3) TEU,[41] found that the right to vote regardless of free movement falls within the scope of EU law, and therefore any restrictions to that right should be proportionate (here, they were).[42]

It is difficult to imagine that the approach of the Court in Delvigne was not influenced by the Lisbon treaty (beyond the legally binding Charter,[43] Articles 10(2) and 14(2) TEU as well).[44] To be sure, the judgment was not unreservedly applauded: for some it confirmed the significance of the political dimension of Union citizenship,[45] while for others (while acknowledging the aforementioned significance) the judgment could also be seen as potentially disrupting the division of powers between the Union

36. According to the European Parliament, the turnout in 2019 was around 50.6%, up from 42.6% in 2014. *See*: https://www.europarl.europa.eu/election-results-2019/en/turnout/ (accessed 23 August 2022).
37. *See also*, in this respect, European Parliament, Constitutional Affairs Committee Press Release, 'Electoral Reform Should Be Addressed Prior to the Next Elections, MEPs Say' (2020) available at: https://www.europarl.europa.eu/news/en/press-room/20200918IPR87433/electoral-reform-should-be-addressed-prior-to-the-next-elections-meps-say (accessed 23 August 2022).
38. Case C-650/13, *Thierry Delvigne v. Commune de Lesparre-Médoc*, EU:C:2015:648.
39. *See* Article 22(2) TFEU: 'every citizen of the Union residing in a Member State of which he is not a national shall have the right to vote and to stand as a candidate in elections to the European Parliament in the Member State in which he resides, under the same conditions as nationals of that State'.
40. *See* Article 21(1) TFEU.
41. Article 14(3) TEU states that the 'members of the European Parliament shall be elected for a term of five years by direct universal suffrage in a free and secret ballot'. Article 39(2) of the Charter is largely aligned with the former provision.
42. *Delvigne*, *supra* n. 38, paras 43-49.
43. On the significance of the Charter *see also* Jo Shaw, 'Prisoner Voting: Now a Matter of EU Law' (2015) available at: https://eulawanalysis.blogspot.com/2015/10/prisoner-voting-now-matter-of-eu-law.html (accessed 23 August 2022).
44. On this *see* Hanneke van Eijken and Jan Willem van Rossem, 'Prisoner Disenfranchisement and the Right to Vote in Elections to the European Parliament: Universal Suffrage Key to Unlocking Political Citizenship?' 12 *European Constitutional Law Review* 114, at 117-118 (2016).
45. *See, e.g.*, Stephen Coutts, '*Delvigne*: A Multi-level Political Citizenship' 42 *European Law Review* 867 (2017); Koen Lenaerts, 'Linking EU Citizenship to Democracy' 11 *Croatian Yearbook of European Law and Policy* VII (2015); van Eijken and van Rossem, *supra* n. 44.

and the Member States.[46] In any event, the case presented the Court with an opportunity to clarify the scope of the right to vote in the European elections - and, in doing so, its constitutional and democratic significance.

4 THE ECI AND CITIZENS' PARTICIPATION

It would be appropriate to include a section on citizens' participation in this chapter, particularly in light of Articles 9-12 TEU and the EU's stated commitment to participatory democracy.[47] Of course, participation can have various manifestations: often a complaint on a policy matter[48] or (more specifically in the EU context) a complaint to the European Ombudsman against an EU institution can be viewed as an instrument of participation.[49] Nevertheless, this chapter will focus on the instrument that - since Lisbon, at least - has received the most scholarly attention: the ECI. The key provision is Article 11(4) TEU, which is worded as follows: '[n]ot less than one million citizens who are nationals of a significant number of Member States may take the initiative of inviting the European Commission, within the framework of its powers, to submit any appropriate proposal on matters where citizens consider that a legal act of the Union is required for the purpose of implementing the Treaties'. The legal framework is further outlined in the so-called ECI Regulation,[50] which has recently been amended. It may briefly be noted that the Commission should decide to register the proposal first, after which point a period of 12 months starts for the collection of signatures; however, under the new Regulation the organisers can activate this period at a later point, but in any case within 6 months, after registration. The proposal is not binding upon the Commission.

The time that has elapsed since Lisbon enables us to look at the ECI from a distance: it is noteworthy that scholarly expectations years before the entry into force of the first ECI Regulation,[51] as well as more recent scholarly assessments of that instrument, do not differ that much. Simply put, there were low expectations then, which have been corroborated more recently, especially with reference to the Commission's practice. Thus, critical accounts have centred on how the Commission

46. Sébastien Platon, 'The Right to Participate in the European Elections and the Vertical Division of Competences in the European Union' in Nathan Cambien et al. (eds), *European Citizenship under Stress: Social Justice, Brexit and Other Challenges* (Brill 2020) 364, in particular 377 et seq.
47. *See*, among others, Joana Mendes, 'Participation and the Role of Law after Lisbon: A Legal View on Article 11 TEU' 48 *Common Market Law Review* 1849 (2011); Armin von Bogdandy, 'The European Lesson for International Democracy: The Significance of Articles 9-12 EU Treaty for International Organizations' 23 *European Journal of International Law* 315 (2012).
48. Birkinshaw has also observed this, for example in Patrick Birkinshaw, 'Grievances, Remedies and the State - Revisited and Re-appraised' in Michael Adler (ed.) *Administrative Justice in Context* (Hart Publishing 2010) 353, at 355-356.
49. Vogiatzis, *supra* n. 17, Ch. 3.
50. Regulation (EU) 2019/788 of the European Parliament and of the Council of 17 April 2019 on the European citizens' initiative, [2019] OJ L 130/55.
51. Miguel Sousa Ferro, 'Popular Legislative Initiative in the EU: *Alea Iacta Est*' 26 *Yearbook of European Law* 355 (2007).

applies the admissibility test,[52] its unwillingness to give meaningful follow-up (effectively to accept the legislative proposal) where appropriate,[53] the overall formality and/or complexity of the instrument – among others. Accordingly, certain EU institutions and bodies (most notably the European Parliament and the European Economic and Social Committee[54]) have also highlighted challenges and submitted recommendations for this participatory instrument.

How, then, to explain such ongoing scholarly attention, in the simultaneous presence of scholarly scepticism and concern? One explanation, perhaps (which is also confirmed by the conclusions of the Conference on the Future of Europe) could be that many citizens, certain EU institutions and academic commentators are really keen to explore the 'democracy question', feeling that the EU can and should do more towards this direction. As such, the concerns about the ECI that have been expressed in the literature and elsewhere could also be seen as a call for the EU institutions and Member States to take democracy in the EU more seriously.

Thus, if one were to pose the question of whether the ECI has managed to meaningfully contribute towards a more participatory EU, the answer would probably be in the negative. As noted earlier, the ECI is not, of course, the only form of citizen participation: the provisions on consultation could also be mentioned, alongside other instruments – although this also depends on how broad an understanding of participatory democracy may be adopted. But arguably, since Lisbon, it has been the instrument that has been discussed most extensively in the literature.

5 CONCLUDING REMARKS

Shortly after the entry into force of the Lisbon treaty, it was observed that the EU's democratic deficit remained 'unsolved'.[55] That stands true today as well. The proposals and conclusions of the Conference on the Future of Europe should be of interest.[56] The EU institutions are presently considering these proposals – which cannot be analysed here in detail.[57] In the closing conference plenary of April 2022, citizens sent among others the following key message:

> Europe needs a more democratic Union. European citizens love the EU, but let's face it: it is not always easy. You called on us to help you and asked us: How

52. James Organ, 'Decommissioning Direct Democracy? A Critical Analysis of Commission Decision-Making on the Legal Admissibility of European Citizens Initiative Proposals' 10 *European Constitutional Law Review* 422 (2014).
53. Nikos Vogiatzis, 'Between Discretion and Control: Reflections on the Institutional Position of the Commission Within the European Citizens' Initiative Process' 23 *European Law Journal* 250 (2017).
54. *See, e.g.*, European Economic and Social Committee, Opinion on 'The European Citizens' Initiative (Review) (Own-Initiative Opinion)', 2016/C 389/05, 21 October 2016.
55. Massimo La Torre, 'Citizenship and European Democracy: European Constitution and Treaty of Lisbon' in Patrick Birkinshaw and Mike Varney (eds) *The European Union Legal Order after Lisbon* (Kluwer Law International 2010) 197, at 209.
56. On the structure and design of the Conference *see* Alemanno, *supra* n. 3.
57. Conference on the Future of Europe, 'Report on the final outcome' (2022) available at: https://futureu.europa.eu/pages/reporting (accessed 23 August 2022).

> should European democracy look like in the Future? And we answered to you: We citizens want a Europe in which decisions are made transparently and quickly, where the unanimity principle is reconsidered and in which we citizens are regularly and seriously involved.[58]

It may be objected that the above statement, framed in rather careful wording, may not fully capture the sentiments that many citizens feel vis-à-vis the EU, even if they may not consider themselves as Eurosceptics. In any case, it is a message that should be taken seriously: the forthcoming months (or years) will reveal more, in this respect.

The preceding discussion could only offer a brief exposition of the democracy question: selective as it may have been, it nonetheless illustrated that such question has various dimensions. There is also the thorny question of treaty revision. The European Parliament is apparently in favour of it,[59] as it has activated the ordinary revision procedure laid down in Article 48 TEU.[60] Without wishing here to enter into discussions on the interplay between democracy and constitutionalism in the EU, it is appropriate – also because it is relevant for the democracy question – to conclude with a thought from Birkinshaw's latest edition of European Public Law, where he observed: '[i]f a movement towards a constitution re-emerged we would be likely to see those visions of a new Europe and a new constitution for Europe either giving full vent to European federalism, or wishing to see the Member States more clearly defined as Masters of the Treaties and limits placed on the competence of the Union institutions'.[61]

58. *Ibid.*, p. 39.
59. European Parliament Press Release, 'Parliament activates process to change EU Treaties' (2022) available at: https://www.europarl.europa.eu/news/en/press-room/20220603IPR32122/parliament-activates-process-to-change-eu-treaties (accessed 23 August 2022).
60. European Parliament resolution of 9 June 2022 on the call for a Convention for the revision of the Treaties (2022/2705(RSP)).
61. Patrick Birkinshaw, *European Public Law: The Achievement and the Brexit Challenge* (Kluwer Law International 2020) 762.

CHAPTER 22

Reasons to Be Grateful: Government, Information and the Development of the Law in the United Kingdom

Mike Varney

> A moment's thought should make us appreciate that we have always been an information society. Anyone who has studied the constitutional history of Britain will appreciate that a major factor in the struggle between Crown and Parliament was the latter's desire to be informed about who counselled and advised the monarch in the formulation of policy ... What is novel in our society, however, is the heightened awareness of the use, collection, dissemination or withholding of information. Such functions are facilitated by artificial intelligence systems, advanced information technology and the opportunities which exist to influence public opinion through ever more sophisticated broadcasting, telecommunications and information technology networks.[1]

1 INTRODUCTION

The quote set out above sets out part of the prescient introduction to the second edition of Patrick Birkinshaw's book on *Freedom of Information*. It seems certain that even though he would have had far more insight than most into the impact of information and its use on government, the exercise of executive power and the ability to influence the public sphere, even then it would have been impossible to predict how profound

1. Patrick Birkinshaw *Freedom of Information: The Law, the Practice and the Ideal* (2nd ed., Butterworths, 1996), pp. 6-7.

some of the changes have been in the subsequent quarter of a century. We have seen an enormous growth in government gathering, processing and use of information with further expansion planned in the future,[2] as well as increasing and profound concerns about the impact of the use of social media and the dissemination of information on social media on the functioning of the public sphere.[3] The challenges faced by legal systems when seeking to encourage transparency and access to information on the one hand, while regulating its use to preserve privacy and to protect the operation of the public sphere are manifold.

This short chapter aims to offer an overview of some key issues in government and information management in current scholarship, reflecting on the significant contribution to this field made by Patrick Birkinshaw. The chapter will conclude by offering some reflections on future directions for research and will also offer some personal reflections on the contribution that Patrick has made to scholarship in the field and the development of those who have been fortunate enough to have had the opportunity to work with him.

2 THE COMMON LAW AND INFORMATION

> When discussing openness and the courts, it must be appreciated that the theme is subject to various interpretations. It may refer to the openness of the courts themselves … the phrase can refer to the role of the courts in helping achieve openness or fuller provision of information … [or] the expression can refer to the role of the courts in resolving disputes between parties over property rights in information or over the use of information acquired in a variety of circumstances.[4]

It is not possible to explore all of the judicial developments in the three fields outlined above in this paper, but an important aspect – the role of the courts in promoting openness and further provision of information will be examined. There might be several different facets to this role of the courts. The most important include the imposition of a duty to give reasons for administrative decisions, the requirement that government should provide data or information that it holds in order to permit public

2. *See, e.g.*, Central Digital and Data Office *Transforming for a Digital Future: 2022 to 2025 roadmap for Digital and Data* (2022) https://www.gov.uk/government/publications/roadmap-for-digital-and-data-2022-to-2025/transforming-for-a-digital-future-2022-to-2025-roadmap-for-digital-and-data.
3. *See, e.g.*, Emma Goodman 'Online Political Advertising in the UK 2019 General Election Campaign' (2019) Media@LSE Blog, https://blogs.lse.ac.uk/medialse/2019/12/12/online-political-advertising-in-the-uk-2019-general-election-campaign/ and Cristian Vaccari, Andrew Chadwick & Johannes Kaiser (2022) 'The Campaign Disinformation Divide: Believing and Sharing News in the 2019 UK General Election' *Political Communication* DOI: 10.1080/10584609.2022.2128948.
4. Patrick Birkinshaw *Freedom of Information: The Law, the Practice and the Ideal* (1st ed., Weidenfeld and Nicolson, 1988), pp. 173-174.

participation in consultation processes and the requirement of reasons and accompanying data to justify decisions taken in cases of substantive judicial review.

3 THE DUTY TO GIVE REASONS

The duty to give reasons for administrative decisions has long been recognised as an important part of the administrative process, serving important process values.[5] In English law, a duty to give reasons for decisions might be imposed by legislation[6] or by the courts. It is well-known that the courts have been reluctant to impose a general duty to give reasons for all administrative decisions.[7] Over time, the common law approach has moved to a situation summarised by Elias LJ as 'it may be more accurate to say that the common law is moving to the position whilst there is no universal obligation to give reasons in all circumstances, in general they should be given unless there is a proper justification for not doing so'.[8] In this case, Sales LJ took a more cautious approach, noting that 'In my view, the common law should only identify a duty to give reasons where there is a sufficient accumulation of reasons of particular force and weight in relation to the particular circumstances of an individual case.'[9]

The common law duty to give reasons remains somewhat uncertain in its scope, despite an acknowledgement from the Supreme Court that the giving of reasons is often crucial to the fairness of administrative decision-making.[10] The duty's contours remain uncertain, particularly where the common law duty is to be shaped by interpretation of powers granted by legislation. The *Hoverspeed* case required that reasons be given for a customs search where legislation said that vehicles could be searched where there were 'reasonable grounds to suspect' that the vehicle was being used to transport goods on which customs duties had not been paid.[11] The legislation permitting these searches was subsequently amended to permit searches where they are deemed to be 'necessary'. The decision in *Karia* held that 'necessity' in a case such as this related to the system of search that was to be adopted, rather than to decisions to search individuals, so no reasons need to be given or recorded for searches of individual

5. For an overview, *see, e.g.*, Patrick Birkinshaw and Michael Varney *Government and Information Rights: The Law Relating to Access, Disclosure and Their Regulation* (5th ed., Bloomsbury, 2019), Chapter 10, or Mark Elliott 'Has the Common Law Duty to Give Reasons Come of Age Yet?' (2011) *Public Law* 56.
6. *See, e.g.*, SI 2011/1824 The Town and Country Planning (Environmental Impact) Regulations 2011, reg. 24(1) or the United Kingdom Internal Market Act 2020, section 36(4) and (5).
7. *See, e.g.*, *R v. Secretary of State for the Home Department, ex parte Doody* [1994] 1 AC 531 and *Oakley v. South Cambridgeshire District Council* [2017] EWCA Civ 71.
8. *Oakley*, *supra* n. 7 at [30].
9. *Ibid.*, at [76].
10. *Dover DC v. Campaign to Protect Rural England (Kent)* [2017] UKSC 79, per Lord Carnwath at [54]-[55].
11. *R (on the application of Hoverspeed Ltd) v. Customs and Excise Commissioners* [2002] EWCA Civ 1804.

passengers.[12] This demonstrates that the duty to give reasons, even where administrative actions or decisions are made that have significant impacts on individuals, will not always be required.

When considering the providing of reasons for the adoption of policy choices we should note that the subject has been tested in a number of recent cases. In *Manchester Airports Holdings*,[13] the High Court held that the duty to give reasons did not impose requirements beyond those already satisfied by the government when it produced an impact assessment for the movement of countries between different categories of travel restrictions due to COVID-19.[14] The judgment makes plain that the court must always balance the burden on administrative authorities should reasons be demanded, with the putative benefits of the imposition of the duty. The claimant's submission that the duty to give reasons may also be expanded to a broader common law duty of transparency is rejected by the court, emphasising that the uncertain scope of such a common law duty would have the potential to impose excessive burdens on decision-makers.[15]

There is no doubt that the common law duty to give reasons has expanded over recent years and has become more comprehensive in its scope. However, recent cases render apparent continuing limitations to the duty and uncertainties in its application. Despite its development, Elliott argues that *Oakley* maintains the position that there is no general duty to give reasons, although such a development 'may now be at least in judicial contemplation'.[16] Since the decision in *Oakley*, the decision in *CPRE Kent*[17] emphasised the link between the duty to give reasons and a broader principle of fairness in administrative decision-making and the *Manchester Airports Holdings*[18] case has rejected a broader common law duty of transparency. The concepts and their integration are ripe for further development in future case law, building on the substantial developments of previous years.

4 INFORMATION PROVIDED AS PART OF CONSULTATION EXERCISES

An important element of transparency of government is the provision of information to the public during consultations prior to policymaking or the development of secondary legislation. The famous summary of the requirements of the law on consultation in *ex parte Gunning* make it clear that where the executive is required to undertake a

12. *R (on the application of Karia) v. Secretary of State for the Home Department* [2018] EWCA Civ 1673.
13. *R (on the application of Manchester Airports Holdings Ltd) v. Secretary of State for Transport* [2021] EWHC 2031 (Admin).
14. *Ibid.*, at [33].
15. *Ibid.*, at [40]-[44].
16. Mark Elliott '*Oakley v. South Cambridgeshire District Council*: The Maturing of the Common Law Duty to Give Reasons' *Public Law for Everyone* 22 February 2017. Available at https://publiclawforeveryone.com/2017/02/22/oakley-v-south-cambridgeshire-district-council-the-maturing-of-the-common-law-duty-to-give-reasons/.
17. *Supra* n. 10.
18. *Supra* n. 13.

consultation exercise by legislation prior to making policy or secondary legislation, a core requirement is that adequate information is provided to consultees to allow them to understand the details of the proposals and to make an adequate response.[19] This has been followed by subsequent decisions that require consultation processes to be accompanied by the publication of relevant government research and data where this would assist respondents,[20] though the precise position in respect of the requirement of disclosure of reports and information produced for government in advance of a consultation process is not clear cut. As Lord Hoffmann observed in *Edwards*, where a claimant is arguing that the common law duty of fairness requires disclosure of internal working documents, some consideration needs to be given to the legislative framework and also the danger that requiring extensive disclosure of all internal data and working documents could provide for a substantial lengthening of consultation processes:

> When the whole question of public involvement has been considered and dealt with in detail by the legislature, I do not think it is for the courts to impose a broader duty ... If the Agency has to disclose its internal working documents for further public consultation, there is no reason why the process should ever come to an end.[21]

Despite these concerns, the common law duty of fairness has led to an expectation of substantial transparency during consultation processes. The *Moseley* case illustrates that in a consultation process, a public authority may be required to disclose not only its preferred policy choice, but also the possible alternatives, in order to allow participants in the consultation to offer an intelligent response.[22] The precise scope of this obligation to disclose alternative policy options and the underlying information that might justify these remains uncertain,[23] though it is plain that over time the expectation of disclosure has expanded, should the expectations of the common law as to fairness be met. All the same, we can see both in the requirements of the law in terms of the giving of reasons for decisions and the duty to consult, the principle of fairness has been developing and has enhanced expectations of disclosure.

5 INFORMATION, EVIDENCE AND REASONS IN THE SUBSTANTIVE REVIEW OF ADMINISTRATIVE DECISIONS

It has long been held that the failure to give reasons for a decision, or to give reasons that are not adequate to justify a decision[24] or support a decision by reference to

19. *R v. Brent London Borough Council, ex p Gunning* (1985) 84 LGR 168.
20. *R v. Secretary of State for Transport, ex parte London Borough of Richmond Upon Thames and others* (1995) *The Times*, 11 May.
21. *R (on the application of Edwards and another) v. Environment Agency and others* [2008] UKHL 22; [2008] 1 WLR 1587 at [44].
22. *R (on the application of Moseley) v. Haringey London Borough Council* [2014] UKSC 56, though N.B. the reservations of Lord Reed JSC on the scope of the requirements of the common law principle of fairness on the scope of the duty to consult.
23. *See, e.g., Electronic Collar Manufacturers Association v. Secretary of State for the Environment, Food and Rural Affairs* [2019] EWHC 2813 (Admin) and *R (on the application of Article 39) v. Secretary of State for Education* [2022] EWHC 589 (Admin); [2022] 1 WLR 4240.
24. *See, e.g., Padfield v. Minister of Agriculture, Fisheries and Food* [1968] A.C. 997.

supporting evidence[25] can render the decision to be unlawful or *ultra vires* on substantive grounds. This form of control has no doubt extended as the approach of the courts to substantive review of administrative action has developed in its sophistication. The demand for reasons and justifications for decisions and that these reasons should be adequate has expanded notably since the Human Rights Act 1998 came into force, and the proportionality test used under the 1998 Act and the concurrent development of the common law test for rationality have meant that the courts are increasingly vigilant in their requirement for justification of interference with fundamental rights, with a number of cases making clear that reasons and factual evidence would need to be demonstrated in support of administrative action, both to justify the action taken under the proportionality test and to facilitate effective judicial review of such administrative action.[26]

More recent cases have again reiterated the need for adequate reasons in support of administrative decisions or policymaking to be offered in order for such decisions to be lawful, with a careful examination of the supporting evidence in order to determine legality in appropriate circumstances. In *Caroopen*, the Court of Appeal considered the practice of the Secretary of State in issuing letters supplementary to immigration decisions where the immigration decision was challenged in tribunal or by means of judicial review. The Court of Appeal acknowledged that these letters tended to serve two important purposes from the perspective of transparency and justification – to provide further reasons for the initial decision and to put forward or address new evidence adduced since the initial decision.[27] The court accepted the intrinsic value of both purposes and was open to such supplementary letters being considered,[28] though the issuance of such supplementary reasons and evidence should always have its context to the original decision explained[29] and there must be caution to ensure that the supplementary reasons are not inconsistent with the initial decision:

> even in a case where there was no explicit statutory duty to give reasons the courts should approach attempts to rely on subsequently-provided reasons with caution; ... particularly so in the case of reasons put forward after the commencement of proceedings and where important human rights are concerned.[30]

The decision of the High Court in *Friends of the Earth*[31] also serves to illustrate the importance of the provision of reasons and supporting evidence to the subsequent

---

25. *R v. Monopolies and Mergers Commission, ex parte South Yorkshire Transport Ltd* [1993] 1 WLR 23 (Commission found to have acted lawfully in this case due to disclosure of complex reasoning and justification for decision) and *R v. Ministry of Agriculture, Fisheries and Food, ex parte. First City Trading Ltd* [1997] 1 CMLR 250 at [70] (state aid scheme found to be justified in light of reasons and ministerial statements offered in support).
26. *See, e.g., Secretary of State for the Home Department v. Rehman* [2001] UKHL 47; [2001] 3 WLR 877 and *R (on the application of Farrakhan) v. Secretary of State for the Home Department* [2002] EWCA Civ 606; [2002] QB 1391.
27. *Caroopen v. Secretary of State for the Home Department* [2016] EWCA Civ 1307; [2017] 1 WLR 2339.
28. *Ibid.*, [61]-[62].
29. *Ibid.*, per Underhill LJ at [62] and Beatson LJ at [94]-[95].
30. *Ibid.*, [30].
31. [2022] EWHC 1841 (Admin).

consideration of the rationality of decision. Section 14 of the Climate Change Act 2008 imposed a duty on the Secretary of State to draw up a 'carbon budget', designed to limit the amount of carbon emissions and to bring about a gradual reduction of carbon emissions, until the United Kingdom (UK) reaches a 'net zero' position.[32] In respect of the carbon budget, section 14(2)-(4) of the Climate Change Act 2008 requires disclosure of the proposals for meeting the carbon budget, the time scales over which they operate, the economic impact of the proposals and details of how the carbon budgets applicable to different sectors will be credited to the overall target. The claimants in the case argued that the Secretary of State had acted unlawfully by failing to disclose reasons for the conclusion that the proposed budget would deliver the necessary reductions in carbon emissions, the impact (where quantifiable) of the budgets applied to each sector and the timescales for delivering the reduction.[33] The requirement in section 14 is that the report produced by the Secretary of State should be laid before Parliament, rather than disclosed to the public.[34]

Holgate J. found that the Secretary of State had acted unlawfully in failing to disclose the information required, with there being '... no justification for the legal adequacy of a s. 14 report required in the context of Parliamentary accountability to be materially lower than that of a report issued for public consultation, certainly not when dealing with the core legal requirements for reports relating to climate change policy. In both instances, the legal object of the reports is to enable its readers to understand and assess the adequacy of the Government's policy proposals and their effects. Furthermore, a report under s. 14 is also required in the interests of public transparency'.[35] The carbon budget was thus unlawful insofar as suitable information had not been provided to permit Parliamentary and public scrutiny.

It is interesting to note that this case was one where the Secretary of State sought recourse to section 31(2A) of the Senior Courts Act 1981, which provides a 'makes no difference' provision and prevents the court from granting a remedy in judicial review if it is 'highly likely that the outcome for the applicant would not have been substantially different if the conduct complained of had not occurred'. Holgate J. held that in light of the absence of the reasoning and information that should have been provided under section 14, it was not possible for the court to determine the extent of the legal error made by the Secretary of State, so relief should not be refused under section 31(2A).[36] A failure to engage with requirements of transparency or disclosure of reasons may well impede public participation in decision-making, or lead to a situation where the courts are unable to determine the substantive legality of an administrative decision. In such circumstances, it appears unlikely that a remedy will be denied under the 'makes no difference' provisions.

---

32. *See also*, s. 4 of the Climate Change Act 2008.
33. *See R (on the application of Friends of the Earth Limited, Clientearth, Good Law Project and Joanna Wheatley) v. Secretary of State for Business, Energy and Industrial Strategy* [2022] EWHC 1841 (Admin). A summary of the grounds for the claim can be found at [16].
34. *See* section 14(1) of the Climate Change Act 2008.
35. *Friends of the Earth, supra* n. 33 at [245].
36. *Ibid.*, at [278] and *see also R (on the application of Swainsthorpe Parish Council) v. Norfolk CC* [2021] EWHC 1014 (Admin).

6 ALGORITHMS, REASONS AND RATIONALITY

The growth of administrative decision-making using computer algorithms gives rise to numerous concerns in relation to transparency, reason-giving and the public and judicial understanding of how decisions are made.[37] Judicial review cases concerning challenges to algorithmic decision-making or the use of algorithms to make decisions by public authorities remain scarce. The decision of the Court of Appeal in *Bridges* concerned the adoption of facial recognition technology by South Wales Police in order to identify 'persons of interest'.[38] Numerous challenges to the legality of the use of such technology were brought, including a claim that its use was unlawful in light of the 'Public Sector Equality Duty' found in section 149 of the Equality Act 2010, as South Wales Police had failed to consider whether the algorithm used discriminated against individuals on grounds of their race, ethnic origin or gender.

In the case, the expert witnesses who had appeared before the High Court were unable to reach a clear conclusion on this issue because the algorithm used had not been disclosed for reasons of commercial confidentiality.[39] The Court of Appeal issued a declaration, finding that the use of the facial recognition technology was contrary to the Public Sector Equality Duty as South Wales Police had been unable, due to ignorance of the way that the algorithm operated, to determine the neutrality or otherwise of its operation.[40] This decision illustrates some of the notable challenges that exist where algorithmic decision-making takes place. It may not be possible for the public or the judiciary to have a true appreciation of the operation of the algorithm and even where expert witnesses are called upon, commercial confidentiality may render opaque some or all of the operation of the algorithms. This has the potential to pose substantial challenges for judicial review in these contexts and there is no doubt that this will be the subject of some important litigation in the future.

7 'OPEN GOVERNMENT': THE IMPACT OF FREEDOM OF INFORMATION AND CHALLENGES

> Open government is a more demanding objective than freedom of information … Open government places its emphasis upon the opening up of the channels of government decision-making, and the provision of information is one feature of local government … With a subject matter that is inevitably complex, the provision of brute information is not adequate in itself. One needs to see 'outside'

---

37. *See* the concerns raised by Lord Sales 'Algorithms, Artificial Intelligence and the Law' *Sir Henry Brooke Lecture for BAILII* (19 December 2019), available at https://www.supremecourt.uk/docs/speech-191112.pdf.
38. *R (on the application of Bridges) v. Chief Constable of South Wales Police* [2020] EWCA Civ 1058; [2020] 1 WLR 5037.
39. *Ibid.*, at [196]-[199].
40. *Ibid.*, at [210].

> personnel with a sufficient degree of skill, expertise and independence in assessing the information.[41]

The above passage, from the first edition of *Freedom of Information*, provides important insight into the approach to 'open government' and some of the challenges that transparency and the publication of information might provide. It was illustrated above that over time, the concepts of fairness and rationality imposed by the courts in judicial review cases have become more sensitive not only to the provision of reasons and information to support administrative decision-making, but also to the quality of that information. More broadly, we can identify several significant moves within the legal system in England and Wales that have fostered the development of open government. One of the most notable is the Freedom of Information Act 2000, a piece of legislation to which Professor Birkinshaw made a significant contribution as special adviser to the House of Commons Select Committee on Public Administration during its consideration of the legislative proposals. The impact of the Act and the freedom of information regime is far greater than anticipated, as illustrated by Tony Blair's memoirs, where he says 'Freedom of Information. Three harmless words. I look at those words as I write them, and feel like shaking my head till it drops off my shoulders. You idiot. You naive, foolish, irresponsible nincompoop. There is really no description of stupidity, no matter how vivid, that is adequate. I quake at the imbecility of it.'[42] One might imagine that given the challenges faced by subsequent governments, these thoughts must not be isolated only to the Prime Minister who led the government that introduced the legislation.

The Freedom of Information Act 2000 has done much to allow those who wish to have access to government information to obtain it, with a number of notable challenges for government, including the start of the famous Members of Parliament's expenses scandal, triggered by freedom of information requests.[43] It has enabled journalists and the media to access government information hitherto unavailable and also facilitates accountability of public authorities through the ability to request information. It is not possible in this chapter to examine all of the facets of the Act, but this has been covered in great depth elsewhere.[44]

8 PUBLICATION SCHEMES AND TRANSPARENCY

A number of important challenges remain in terms of the effective application of the Act insofar as it requires proactive transparency. One might argue that the provisions

41. Birkinshaw, *supra* n. 4 at 235.
42. A. Blair *A Journey* (Hutchinson, 2010), p. 516.
43. For an account, *see* B. Worthy 'Freedom of Information and the MPs Expenses Crisis', in J. van Heerde-Hudson (ed.) *The Political Costs of the 2009 British MPs' Expenses Scandal* (Palgrave MacMillan, 2014).
44. *See, e.g.*, P. Birkinshaw *Freedom of Information: The Law, the Practice and the Ideal* (4th ed., Cambridge University Press, 2012), P. Birkinshaw and M. Varney *Government and Information Rights: The Law Relating to Access, Disclosure and Their Regulation* (Bloomsbury, 2019) and P. Coppel *Information Rights: A Practitioner's Guide to Data Protection, Freedom of Information and other Information Rights* (Bloomsbury, 2020).

on publication schemes, contained in section 19 of the Act have remained relatively static since the Act was passed. The publication scheme regime has potential to drive an expanding concept of open government in public authorities, but the classes of information contained in the various model publication schemes have changed little over time and necessarily define the information that must be published at a very generic level.[45] As the adoption of the model publication schemes is now mandated, public authorities are unable to seek the approval of a publication scheme that is more expansive than that published by the Information Commissioner's Office (ICO). Publication schemes have been the subject of complaints to the Information Commissioner on a relatively infrequent basis (with a search of the ICO database revealing only 23 complaints out of some 13,500 decisions), suggesting that the imposition of a model scheme that can be easily adopted has delivered some consistency in its use. There are some recent examples of the ICO finding public authorities in breach of section 19 through failure to adopt a publication scheme and publish it,[46] or by relying on a scheme adopted by a parent department of government.[47]

One important issue that may arise in future situations is the question of whether where the model publication scheme provides that public authorities will publish 'decision making processes and records of decision' and 'enforcement actions and sanctions', this may require the publication of reports into investigations undertaken by public authorities where there is no express legislative power to publish the reports concerned in the legislation that grants the power to investigate. In *Vote Leave*,[48] the Electoral Commission undertook an investigation into the compliance with statutory rules on the financing of referendum campaigns during the Brexit referendum. It found irregularities and issued sanctions and fines in a number of cases, publishing the report of its findings on its website. The claimant argues that this disclosure of the report was unlawful as there was no express statutory power to publish the report. The Court of Appeal held that the publication was lawful, as it was incidental to the carrying out of enforcement functions under the Political Parties, Elections and Referendums Act 2000.[49] This finding rendered the need to determine whether the adoption of the publication scheme under section 19 of the Freedom of Information Act 2000 granted the power to publish unnecessary. However, in respect of this argument, Underhill LJ said:

> When I first read the papers I found that argument unpersuasive. Mr Coppel in his oral submissions strove to shift me from that first impression, but the exercise succeeded only to the extent of satisfying me that a proper treatment of the

45. Version 1.2 of the generic model publication scheme (2015), approved by the Information Commissioner. This is available at: https://ico.org.uk/media/for-organisations/documents/1153/model-publication-scheme.pdf.
46. *See, e.g.*, *General Teaching Council for Northern Ireland* IC-45233-L6H9.
47. *The Traffic Commissioner for the West Midlands Traffic Area* FS50357622.
48. *R (on the Application of Vote Leave Ltd) v. Electoral Commission* [2019] EWCA Civ 1938; [2019] 4 WLR 157.
49. *Ibid.*, at [31]. It is interesting to note that Underhill LJ notes at [24] and [31] that the publication of the report is an important route through which the Commission can give reasons for its findings.

> question would require a careful analysis, both of the statutory provisions and of the Commission's publication scheme ....[50]

It may well be that the publication scheme cannot give rise to independent powers of disclosure that are not otherwise provided for, but the argument at least illustrates that publication schemes may have the potential to have a broader impact on transparency than might be immediately apparent.

9 PRIVATE COMMUNICATION OF INFORMATION

The wide range of easily available mechanisms of private communication available to government ministers and public officials gives rise to concerns under both freedom of information and data protection legislation. Platforms such as WhatsApp and LinkedIn, along with the multitude of easily accessible free-of-charge email providers give the potential for private communication of the work of government with increasing ease. It is plain that the use of private communications channels such as these carry some security and data protection implications, but may also put important information relating to government decisions outside official records and thus not available through freedom of information requests, though the ICO's guidance is clear that information held in private email accounts can still be information covered by the Freedom of Information Act if it relates to the official business of the public authority.[51] However, where there is no record of the information or communications having taken place, it may well be that such information would not be found should a freedom of information request be made.[52] Though in the ICO's investigation into the use of private channels of communication it was illustrated that government ministers and officials often forwarded some or all of these communications to official accounts for the purposes of record keeping, there is clear potential for inconsistency and omission.[53]

The Cabinet Office issued guidance in 2013 on the use of private email by government ministers and officials.[54] Paragraph 7 of this Code provides that 'The originator or recipient of a communication should consider whether the information contained in it is substantive discussions or decisions generated in the course of conducting Government business and, if so, take steps to ensure the relevant information is accessible (e.g. by copying it to a government email address).' Compliance with such requirements, given the wide range of different communication platforms avail

50. *Ibid.*, at [33].
51. Information Commissioner's Office *Official information held in private email accounts* (2017). Available at: https://ico.org.uk/media/for-organisations/documents/1147/official_information_held_in_private_email_accounts.pdf.
52. A point illustrated by the discussion in Information Commissioner's Office *Behind the screens – maintaining government transparency and data security in the age of messaging apps*, available at https://ico.org.uk/media/about-the-ico/documents/4020886/behind-the-screens.pdf, pp. 10-12 and 22.
53. *Ibid.*, pp. 21-22.
54. Cabinet Office *Guidance to Departments on the Use of Private Email* (2013). Available at: https://assets.publishing.service.gov.uk/government/uploads/system/uploads/attachment_data/file/207131/Private_Email_guidance.pdf.

able, will always be difficult to monitor. There is strong evidence that the use of private communication platforms has been common in recent UK governments,[55] yet the Ministerial Code, which governs the behaviour of government ministers does not set down any specific guidance on this issue, either from the perspective of transparency or information security. Paragraph 2.14 of the Code provides that ministers must maintain the security of government business[56] and Suella Braverman MP resigned after sending government policy documents to and from her private email account, making it clear in a subsequent letter that she believed that the Code had been breached by these actions.[57] However, the precise obligations under the Ministerial Code in relation to the use of private email and other communications networks remain unclear and it is notable that as it stands at the moment, the primary focus of the Code is on information security, with lesser consideration of transparency.[58]

The analysis above has sought to demonstrate that considerable concerns remain about the impact of the use of private communications channels in the business of government. Guidance exists, but it is fragmented and to some extent dated, in the sense that it focuses on the use of email, when social media networks and their inbuilt and often non-permanent modes of communication may generate stronger concerns in respect of transparency.

10 CONCLUSIONS

This short paper has sought to examine some important issues in relation to government and information, demonstrating the prescience and enduring relevance of Patrick Birkinshaw's work in that area. Judicial review and the approach of the courts to reason-giving, information provided in consultation and rationality review where transparency or reasons are involved are all critical elements of an effective system of open government. It is plain that over the decades, the courts have developed a more sophisticated view of the impact of transparency and reason giving on the fairness and legality of administrative decisions, though the concept of 'fairness' as it applies in this context requires further development if it is to display a true coherence.

55. A useful account can be found in T. Durrant, A. Lilly and P. Tingay *WhatsApp in Government How Ministers and Officials Should Use Messaging Apps – And How they Shouldn't* (Institute for Government, 2022). Available at: https://www.instituteforgovernment.org.uk/sites/default/files/publications/whatsapp-in-government.pdf. See also, *R (Good Law Project)* v. *The Prime Minister and Others* [2022] EWCA Civ 1580.
56. Cabinet Office *Ministerial Code* (December 2022). Available at: https://assets.publishing.service.gov.uk/government/uploads/system/uploads/attachment_data/file/1126632/Ministerial_Code.pdf.
57. Letter from Suella Braverman MP to Dame Diana Johnson MP, 31 October 2022. Available at: https://assets.publishing.service.gov.uk/government/uploads/system/uploads/attachment_data/file/1114666/311022_HASC_letter.pdf.
58. Although NB para. 1.3(d) of the *Ministerial* Code, which states that 'Ministers should be as open as possible with Parliament and the public, refusing to provide information only when disclosure would not be in the public interest.'

In many areas of government and information, new technologies give rise to substantial concerns. Algorithmic decision-making has the potential to have a deleterious effect on transparency and reason-giving, particularly insofar as many of the algorithms may be commercially sensitive and developed and owned by the private sector. In relation to communication between government ministers and officials, the use of private email accounts and social media networks gives rise to both freedom of information and data protection concerns and also illustrates a perpetual challenge – the pace of innovation and the development of different networks and modes for the communication and storage of information often outpaces the development of guidance and regulation for their use.

What is without a doubt is that if one steps back and looks at the field of government and information law in England and Wales, the impact of Patrick Birkinshaw's work has been profound. His book *Freedom of Information* was a trailblazing work, opening up a substantial new field of enquiry for academic lawyers. Patrick has gone on to make a substantial contribution to the law and practice in the field and continues to do so.

A Personal Tribute to Patrick Birkinshaw

All of the contributors to this excellent volume have had the fortune to engage with Patrick during his academic career. I regard myself as being one of the most fortunate of all, having been taught by him as an undergraduate student and then having him as the supervisor of my PhD thesis. I then worked with him, teaching public law and allied subjects, until his retirement from the University of Hull Law School. Throughout that time, I found Patrick to be extremely supportive, generous with his time and always willing to use his knowledge, expertise and networks to foster opportunities for others. Throughout all of my dealings with him, Patrick is warm and has always had a great sense of humour. His contribution to the University of Hull Law School was immense – he was Head of School during an exceptionally successful period both in terms of its teaching and research and taught many generations of students who speak with fondness and respect of his impact on their legal education. I know that many contributors to this volume have benefited similarly from their friendship with Patrick and we are all richer for knowing and working with him.

CHAPTER 23

Whistleblowing, Freedom of Expression and the Public's 'Right to Know' in the ECHR

Dimitrios Kagiaros

> Accountability is based upon reliable information. If we or our representatives do not know what government is doing, how meaningful is accountability? Without information, accountability will merely be the shadow of an idea lacking any substance.
>
> Patrick Birkinshaw, 'Freedom of Information and Openness: Fundamental Human Rights?' (2006) 58 Administrative Law Review 177, 194.

1 INTRODUCTION

Patrick Birkinshaw was one of the first scholars to argue that access to government-held information through freedom information (FOI), openness[1] and transparency[2] should be viewed as fundamental human rights. His scholarship outlined how these concepts are intrinsically important by noting how FOI in particular 'fulfils that relationship of trust that government must have in the people'[3] and ensures that everyone is treated 'with equal concern and respect by power wielders'.[4] However,

1. Patrick Birkinshaw, 'Freedom of Information and Openness: Fundamental Human Rights?' (2006) 58 Administrative Law Review 177, 194.
2. Patrick Birksinshaw, 'Transparency as a Human Right' in Christopher Hood and David Heald (eds), *Transparency the Key to Better Governance?* (Oxford University Press / British Academy, 2006).
3. Patrick Birkinshaw, 'Freedom of Information and Openness: Fundamental Human Rights?' (*supra* n. 1) 203.
4. *Ibid.*, at 214.

Professor Birkinshaw also placed emphasis on the instrumental value of these concepts. For Birkinshaw, FOI, transparency and openness of government serve as prerequisites for meaningful democratic participation and a well-functioning democracy. As he argued in his work, access to information is necessary to ensure that those in power are held accountable for their actions; to guarantee efficiency in government; and to expose financial irregularities or other forms of wrongdoing committed by public officials.[5]

Professor Birkinshaw explored in remarkable detail the extent to which robust FOI frameworks can contribute to a well-functioning democracy and an informed citizenry.[6] FOI regimes, however, sometimes fail to capture instances of government misconduct, abuses of power and corruption. Instead, in many cases, wrongdoing has been brought to the public's attention through unauthorised disclosures of government-held information by whistleblowers.

Whistleblowers are increasingly recognised for their contribution to combating corruption and for ensuring that public (but also private) organisations are held accountable for wrongdoing. The term is commonly used to describe 'any person who reports or discloses information on a threat or harm to the public interest in the context of their work-based relationship, whether it be in the public or private sector'.[7] The Council of Europe (CoE) has recognised that 'without whistleblowers, it will be impossible to resolve many of the challenges to our democracies',[8] including corruption, the misuse of personal data, activities that harm the environment or other threats to public health. However, the disclosure of organisational wrongdoing can expose whistleblowers to retaliation, especially when they publicly report misconduct to the press. This retaliation can take the form of employment-related sanctions or penalties under criminal law for disclosing what may sometimes be confidential information.[9] In an increasing number of states across Europe,[10] whistleblowers are afforded legal protections that are aimed at shielding them against such retaliatory action. In addition to such protections usually found in domestic employment law frameworks, whistleblowers in Europe can also claim protection under human rights law, and specifically freedom of expression.

The protection for free speech under Article 10 of the European Convention on Human Rights ('the ECHR' or 'the Convention'), includes the right 'to receive and impart information and ideas without interference'.[11] This right to impart information

5. *Ibid.*
6. For his in-depth study of the United Kingdom's (UK) FOI regime *see* Patrick Birkinshaw, *Freedom of Information, the Law, the Practice, and the Ideal* (4th ed., Cambridge University Press, 2010).
7. Council of Europe, Recommendation CM/Rec(2014)7 of the Committee of Ministers to Member States on the protection of whistleblowers (adopted 30 April 2014).
8. Council of Europe, Parliamentary Assembly Resolution 2300 (2019) on 'Improving the protection of whistle-blowers all over Europe' [4].
9. For an in-depth account of the retaliation whistleblowers commonly face *see* Fred Alford, *Whistleblowers: Broken Lives and Organizational Power* (Cornell University Press, 2001).
10. For a country by country overview of domestic frameworks for whistleblower protection *see* https://www.eqs.com/compliance-blog/whistleblower-protections-across-europe-legal-context/.
11. Council of Europe, European Convention for the Protection of Human Rights and Fundamental Freedoms, as amended by Protocols Nos 11 and 14, 4 November 1950, ETS 5, Article 10.

is the basis on which the European Court of Human Rights ('the ECtHR' or 'the Court') has relied to find that 'blowing the whistle' is an activity that falls within the protective scope of Article 10.[12] In practice, this means that any detriment to which a whistle-blower is subjected for bringing public attention to misconduct must satisfy the test established in Article 10 §2 in order to be Convention-compliant. More specifically, any restriction to whistleblowers' speech must be prescribed by law, it must serve one of the legitimate aims mentioned in Article 10, and it must be 'necessary in a democratic society'.

The chapter examines the ECHR framework for whistleblower protection under Article 10 and analyses the relationship between whistleblowing, freedom of expression, and the public's 'right to know'. It addresses two distinct but interconnected issues. The first relates to the Court's approach to whistleblowing as a form of expression. The chapter demonstrates that in the Court's understanding, the key justification for bringing whistleblowing into the ambit of Article 10 is the listener's interest in receiving the information that the whistleblower discloses rather than the whistleblower's right to effect change in their institution by blowing the whistle. Much like Professor Birkinshaw's analysis of the instrumental value of access to information, the Court views whistleblower protection under freedom of expression as a means to give effect to the public's 'right to know' and to strengthen democratic deliberation by providing citizens with accurate and reliable information on government misconduct.[13] From this perspective, the whistleblower is better understood as a conduit through which information on misconduct reaches the public, rather than as a traditional speaker who engages in an act of self-expression by 'blowing the whistle'. A key consequence of this approach is that the protection whistleblowers enjoy under Article 10 is not determined on the basis of their individual interest in communicating freely. Instead, the degree of protection the whistleblower receives is largely reliant on whether the public interest in their disclosure outweighs their duties as civil servants towards the government.

This approach to whistleblowing may give rise to certain concerns.[14] The second issue the chapter addresses, delves into one such concern. If whistleblower protection largely hinges on the value of the disclosed information for the recipient audience, are whistleblowers disadvantaged in instances where the ECtHR is deferential to the respondent state when determining the public interest in a specific communication? The chapter demonstrates that one potential consequence of the Court's approach is that whistleblowers could be deprived of effective protection if their disclosure relates to a matter where states enjoy a wide margin of appreciation in the balancing of the

12. *See* indicatively, *Heinisch v. Germany* App. No. 28274/08 (ECHR, 21 July 2011) and *Matúz v. Hungary* App. No. 73571/10 (ECHR, 21 October 2014).
13. *Guja v. Moldova* [74].
14. I have noted elsewhere the difficulties or dangers for whistleblowers to calculate or predict whether their disclosure will be in public interest. *See* Dimitrios Kagiaros, 'Protecting "National Security" Whistleblowers in the Council of Europe: An Evaluation of Three Approaches on How to Balance National Security with Freedom of Expression' (2015) 19 International Journal of Human Rights 408, 413 et seq. and Dimitrios Kagiaros, 'Reassessing the Framework for the Protection of Civil Servant Whistleblowers in the European Court of Human Rights' (2021) 39 Netherlands Quarterly of Human Rights 220-240.

competing public interests in disclosure and non-disclosure. To illustrate this point, the chapter uses national security whistleblowing as a case study. The term 'national security' whistleblowing will be used in the chapter to refer to whistleblowers whose restrictions to speech were justified on the basis of the legitimate aim of protecting national security.[15] In the ECtHR's case law, states have traditionally enjoyed a great degree of latitude where restrictions to speech on national security grounds are concerned. By engaging with the relevant ECtHR judgments, the chapter demonstrates that, in its earlier case law, the Court seemed to apply this deferential approach to national security whistleblowers, thus seriously undermining the potential of Article 10 to serve as an effective shield against retaliation. In a more recent judgment, however, the Court seems to have evolved its approach and has carried out stricter scrutiny of restrictions attempting to stifle national security whistleblowers' free speech. Additionally, there has been a proliferation of instruments produced by the CoE organs that further endorse extensive protections for national security whistleblowers. The paper concludes that these developments show some promise and demonstrate the CoE's increasing recognition of the value of protecting national security whistleblowing. Nevertheless, in future cases, the Court should adopt a clearer and more consistent approach to national security whistleblowing to ensure they are effectively protected.

The subsequent sections develop this discussion following the order in which the two issues were presented above, while the final section offers some concluding thoughts.

2 PART 1: WHISTLEBLOWING AS A FORM OF EXPRESSION

The relationship between whistleblowing and free speech remains an issue that divides academic opinion.[16] A key disagreement in the literature relates to whether the link between whistleblowing and speech is made on the basis of the whistleblower's right to express her moral outrage against the wrongdoing her organisation has committed, or whether free speech protection should be afforded to whistleblowers as a means to an end, namely to ensure that the information they disclose reaches the public without state interference. Under the first understanding, whistleblower protection under free speech is intended to primarily serve the interests of the speaker. The second perspective focuses more on the interests of the recipient audience, namely the public interest in accessing vital information on wrongdoing.

C. Edwin Baker is a notable proponent of the first view. For Edwin Baker, whistleblowing is an attempt to halt corruption and illegal activity in an organisation in order to ensure that it pursues the values the whistleblower holds.[17] Thus, he contends that whistleblowing 'involves using speech directly to make the world correspond to

15. This is one of the legitimate aims for restricting speech mentioned in Article 10§2 ECHR.
16. For a detailed overview of how the various theories of free speech can accommodate whistleblowing *see* Ashley Savage, *Leaks, Whistleblowing and the Public Interest: The Law of Unauthorised Disclosures* (Edward Elgar, 2016) 7-23.
17. C. Edwin Baker, *Human Liberty and Freedom of Speech* (Oxford University Press, 1989) 61.

the speaker's substantive values'.[18] Similarly, Vandekerckhove draws parallels between whistleblowers and dissidents,[19] and frames the whistleblower as an 'individual who wants to be an actor, who wants to reshape the social'.[20] This conception of whistleblowing focuses on the transformative impact of the whistleblower's speech, and views disclosures of information as a means to bring an organisation that has been involved in wrongdoing in line with the whistleblower's values.

Other scholars focus on the benefits of whistleblowing for the audience that receives the information on misconduct. Barendt contends that although free speech is designed to cover 'the interest of both speaker and recipient',[21] in practice, 'the speaker's interest in a particular communication is stronger than that of the audience'.[22] He concedes, however, that where whistleblowing is concerned, basing free speech protection for unauthorised disclosures made in breach of secrecy laws on 'a civil servant's interest in disclosing the contents of government files, is much less attractive'.[23] According to Barendt, the civil servant who discloses classified information in such cases can only be afforded a 'parasitic'[24] free speech claim, as in this instance free speech protection is directed towards the recipient of the information, the audience. Similarly, Benkler suggests that the whistleblower 'serves a *public role*, so the defense [against any retaliation] is public and systemic, rather than individual-rights based'.[25] These views seem to closely align with perspectives on free speech that place great significance on the contribution of freedom of expression to a well-informed citizenry. Schauer for instance, in discussing democracy-based justifications for speech, identifies access to information as a prerequisite for equal participation in the process of government.[26] Raz makes a similar point when arguing that 'the better informed the governed are and the better able they are to evaluate the information at their disposal the stronger the case for heeding their wishes'.[27] Birkinshaw has built on these analyses in his seminal work on freedom of information and openness as human rights. As he argues:

18. *Ibid.* It would be important here to draw a distinction between 'watchdog whistleblowing' and 'protest whistleblowing'. Watchdog whistleblowing involves the disclosure of information that demonstrates that the institution against which the whistle is blown has engaged in misconduct or illegal behaviour. Conversely, protest whistleblowing describes instances where the 'whistleblower objects to a lawful or transparent activity of his employer' *see* Wim Vandekerckhove, *Whistleblowing and Organizational Social Responsibility: A Global Assessment* (Ashgate, 2006) 215. By referring to wrongdoing, the framework the ECtHR only focuses on watchdog whistleblowing.
19. Wim Vandekerckhove, 'Freedom of Expression as the "Broken Promise" of Whistleblower Protection' (2016) 10 Revue des droits de l'homme [59].
20. *Ibid.*
21. *See* Eric Barendt, *Freedom of Speech* (2nd ed., Oxford University Press, 2007) 26.
22. *Ibid.*, at 27.
23. *Ibid.*, at 25.
24. *Ibid.*, at 195.
25. Yochai Benkler, 'A Public Accountability Defense for National Security Leakers and Whistleblowers' (2014) 8 Harvard Law & Policy Review 281, 305 [*emphasis added*].
26. Frederick Schauer, *Free Speech: A Philosophical Inquiry* (Cambridge University Press, 1982) 41.
27. Joseph Raz, 'Freedom of Expression and Personal Identification' (1991) 11 Oxford Journal of Legal Studies 303, 308.

> An informed citizenry is a citizenry better able to contribute to governmental processes sensibly; better able to understand and accept the basis of decisions affecting them; and better able to help shape the context – social, political, and environmental – in which they live.[28]

While it could be argued that these two perspectives are not mutually exclusive, it is the second understanding of the relationship between whistleblowing and speech that seems to have informed the developing framework for the protection of whistleblowers under freedom of expression in international and regional human rights instruments.[29] It is telling that the first reference to whistleblower protection by the United Nations Rapporteur on Freedom of Opinion and Expression was in a report focusing on the then nascent right of access to information.[30] The report identified whistleblowing as another avenue to keep the public informed where more mainstream means of public access to official information have failed.[31] Similarly, the Rapporteur's 2015 Report which was dedicated to the protection of whistleblowers[32] justified the inclusion of whistleblowers in the protective scope of freedom of expression on the basis that '[s]ources of information and whistleblowers are essential for the public's right to know, for the public's participation in political affairs, democratic governance and accountability'.[33]

As the subsequent section demonstrates, the development of whistleblower protection in the ECtHR under Article 10 ECHR was premised on similar justifications.

2.1 Emerging from the Shadows: Whistleblower Protection under Article 10 ECHR

In the earlier case law of the ECtHR, whistleblowers were only indirectly protected under Article 10 ECHR through the protections the ECHR framework offers journalists and the press. More specifically, one of the key safeguards of press freedom under Article 10 is that journalists cannot be compelled by state authorities to reveal their sources.[34] The rationale the Court advanced to justify this specific aspect of press freedom, was that a failure to protect the identity of sources might deter other individuals with access to important information from sharing it with the press.[35] The

28. Patrick Birkinshaw, 'Freedom of Information and Openness: Fundamental Human Rights?' (*supra* n. 1) 204.
29. For an overview of whistleblower protections in international law *see* Dimitrios Kafteranis, 'The International Legal Framework on Whistle-Blowers: What More Should Be Done?' (2021) 19 Seattle Journal for Social Justice 729, especially 732 et seq.
30. United Nations Committee on Human Rights, Report of the Special Rapporteur on the Promotion and Protection of the Right to Freedom of Opinion and Expression (18 January 2000) (submitted in accordance with Commission resolution 1999/36 E/CN.4/2000/63).
31. *Ibid.*, Principle 9.
32. U.N. Secretary-General, Report of the Special Rapporteur on the Promotion and Protection of the Right to Freedom of Opinion and Expression, U.N. Doc. A/70/361 (8 September 2015).
33. *See* factsheet available at https://www.ohchr.org/Documents/Issues/Expression/Factsheet_4.pdf.
34. *See* for instance *Goodwin v. United Kingdom* App. No. 17488/90 (ECHR, 27 March 1996) at [39] and more recently *Voskuil v. the Netherlands* App. No. 64752/01 (ECHR, 22 November 2007).
35. *See Voskuil v. the Netherlands* [65].

Court noted that this would undermine 'the vital public-watchdog role of the press' and its ability 'to provide accurate and reliable information' to the public.[36]

This indirect protection meant that, if the whistleblower remained anonymous, press freedoms could serve as a useful shield to maintain this anonymity and protect whistleblowers from any retaliation for blowing the whistle. The whistleblower, however, remained a shadowy figure. Their protection under Article 10 was, in essence, a by-product of the much stronger protections the ECHR offers the press.

It was not until 2008 that the Court for the first time explicitly dealt[37] with the practice of whistleblowing, in the landmark Grand Chamber judgment in *Guja v. Moldova*.[38] The applicant was a civil servant who was employed as the Head of the Press Department of the Prosecutor General's office in Moldova. He leaked two letters to the press that contained evidence of apparent governmental interference in the criminal justice system. Following the publication of the letters, he was dismissed for breaching official secrecy rules.

The Court's justification for including whistleblowing into the protective ambit of Article 10 is telling. In its submissions to the Court, the respondent government argued that the applicant's actions did not amount to speech, and therefore, Article 10 was not applicable to the circumstances of the case. This was because the applicant had not authored the letters he disclosed, nor had he written the newspaper articles that discussed his allegations. According to the government's argument, the act of leaking official information to the press did not amount to speech.[39]

The ECtHR's Grand Chamber was not convinced by these arguments and rejected the government's claim. The Court held that by leaking the relevant documents, the applicant was 'imparting information', an activity protected under Article 10.[40] It was noted that the Court had extended Article 10 protection to individuals disseminating information from third parties in the past.[41]

In line with perceptions of whistleblowing as an added means of democratic accountability, the Court linked whistleblowing to the public's right to know by noting that government should not only be subject to scrutiny through legal mechanisms but also from 'the media and public opinion'.[42] The Court, in justifying why Article 10 protects whistleblowing, stated that:

> a civil servant, in the course of his work, may become aware of in-house information, including secret information, whose divulgation or publication corresponds to a strong public interest. ... This may be called for where the employee or civil servant concerned is the only person, or part of a small category of persons, aware of what is happening at work and is thus best placed to act in the public interest by alerting the employer or the public at large ....[43]

36. *Ibid.*
37. Jacobs, White & Ovey, *The European Convention on Human Rights* (Oxford University Press, 2010) at 442.
38. App. No. 14277/04 (ECHR, 12 February 2008).
39. *Guja v. Moldova* [50].
40. *Ibid.*, [53].
41. *See* for instance, *Jersild v. Denmark* App. No. 15890/89 (ECHR, 23 September 1994).
42. *Guja v. Moldova* [74].
43. *Ibid.*, [72] and [75]. Emphasis added.

On this basis, the public interest in the disclosed information is a key criterion that features in the Court's reasoning to determine whether a restriction to a whistleblower's free speech will amount to a violation of Article 10.[44] Moreover, in order to ensure that the public is exposed to information that is accurate and reliable, the Court establishes a duty on whistleblowers to take reasonable steps to verify the veracity of the information they disclose.[45] As the Court has stressed, disclosures of information that are 'formulated in bad faith'[46] or contain 'excessively defamatory accusations devoid of foundation'[47] will not be protected.

The Court then weighs this public interest in the disclosure against other interests. More specifically, the Court examines the damage caused by the disclosure to the organisation against which the whistle was blown,[48] it assesses the whistleblower's motives,[49] and whether or not they made any attempts to use less drastic means to raise concern on the wrongdoing they uncovered.[50] Finally, the Court examines the severity of the penalty to which the whistleblower was exposed.[51]

A result of the audience-centred approach to whistleblowing that the Court has adopted is that consideration for the whistleblower's 'right' to self-expression is not included in the Court's reasoning. As Boot notes, in its assessment of the proportionality of the interference with the whistleblower's speech, the Court essentially weighs the public interest in disclosure against the public interest in non-disclosure of the information without considering the whistleblower's right to self-expression as part of this equation.[52] He observes that the language employed in whistleblowing cases to determine whether the restriction to the whistleblower's free speech amounts to an Article 10 violation is 'drifting away from individual rights and towards public goods'.[53] While this is an astute observation, the Court's approach to whistleblowers does not differ from its approach to other speakers who act as information disseminators. For instance, the Court has similarly not focused on the interest in self-expression of the speaker in judgments relating to journalists who faced penalties for publicly disseminating their interviews with controversial subjects.[54] Equally, the interest in self-expression did not feature in the Court's reasoning when finding that Non-Governmental organisations have a right to request and access official information under Article 10 when this is done 'with the intention of imparting that information to the public and thereby contributing to public debate'.[55]

This emphasis on the public interest, however, may raise concerns as to the ECtHR's capacity to effectively protect whistleblowers when their disclosure relates to

44. *Ibid.*
45. *Ibid.*, [75].
46. *Ibid.*
47. *Ibid.*
48. *Ibid.*, [76].
49. *Ibid.*, [77].
50. *Ibid.*, [73].
51. *Ibid.*, [78].
52. Eric R. Boot, 'No Right to Classified Public Whistleblowing' (2018) 31 Ratio Juris 70, 73 et seq.
53. *Ibid.*, 73.
54. *See* for instance, *Jersild v. Denmark* App. No. 15890/89 (ECHR, 23 September 1994).
55. *Magyar Helsinki Bizottság v. Hungary* App. No. 18030/11 (ECHR, 8 November 2016) [131].

an area where the Court's approach is characterised by reluctance to authoritatively determine the public interest in a specific communication. To illustrate this concern, the following section uses national security whistleblowing as a case study. It focuses on three factors that lead the Court to be particularly deferential towards the respondent state and its assessment of the public interest in a disclosure. These are firstly, the fact that the Court has recognised a compelling state interest in preserving official secrecy; secondly, the wide margin of appreciation states enjoy in relation to restrictions to qualified rights on national security grounds; and thirdly, the 'duties and responsibilities' under Article 10 of certain speakers. After highlighting these factors, the chapter assesses whether they have in fact served to disadvantage national security whistleblowers from receiving protection under Article 10.

3 PART 2: NATIONAL SECURITY WHISTLEBLOWING

State secrecy, the margin of appreciation and 'the duties and responsibilities' of the speaker.

Some of the most high-profile unauthorised disclosures of information have been related to security-sensitive issues. From Daniel Ellsberg's leak of 'the Pentagon Papers' to the more recent disclosures by Chelsea Manning[56] and Edward Snowden,[57] 'national security' whistleblowers have brought to light systemic state misconduct and gross human rights violations. Such whistleblowers, typically members of the military or the intelligence and security community, have faced the most severe forms of retaliation for disclosing official information without authorisation. As Scott asserts, '[n]ational security relies upon secrecy'.[58] Therefore, it is not surprising that strict reprisals await those who breach official secrecy rules. In many cases, the duty of secrecy that such individuals owe to their organisation is lifelong,[59] and any disclosure of classified information must go through a rigorous authorisation process.[60]

The Court has recognised that this state interest in preserving official secrecy is legitimate.[61] This interest generates duties of loyalty, moderation and confidence[62] that civil servants in particular owe towards the government of the day. As the Court stresses, 'the mission of civil servants in a democratic society is to assist the government in discharging its functions'[63] and 'the public has a right to expect that they will

56. https://www.theguardian.com/us-news/2018/oct/07/chelsea-manning-wikileaks-whistleblowing-interview-carole-cadwalladr.
57. https://www.theguardian.com/world/2013/jun/09/edward-snowden-nsa-whistleblower-surveillance.
58. Paul F. Scott, *The National Security Constitution* (Hart Publishing, 2018) 193.
59. *See* for instance in the UK, the Official Secrets Act 1989 section 1(1).
60. In the UK *see R (on the application of A) v. B* [2009] UKSC 12 and in the United States, Kevin Casey, 'Till Death Do Us Part: Prepublication Review in the Intelligence Community' (2015) 115 Columbia Law Review 417-460.
61. *Guja v. Moldova* [71]. From the Court's broader case law, *see also Stoll v. Switzerland* App. No. 69698/01 (ECHR, 10 December 2007) [155].
62. *Guja v. Moldova* [70].
63. *Ibid.*, [71].

help and not hinder the democratically elected government'.[64] National security is also one of the legitimate aims on which a state can rely to justify restrictions to speech as long as it can demonstrate that such restrictions are 'necessary in a democratic society'.

That is not to say that such duties of secrecy altogether preclude Article 10 protection for whistleblowers. As the Court has held, the public interest in a disclosure may be so compelling, so as to override even a legally binding duty of confidence the employee owes to their employer.[65] However, how is this public interest to be assessed where national security is at stake, and who should have the final say on where the public interest lies? Courts have been notoriously reluctant to challenge state assertions on the harm caused by certain disclosures of secret information to national security interests. As Nasu eloquently argues:

> recourse to the right of access to public information necessarily involves value judgements, which may well be quite arbitrary at times, in weighing competing interests to assess what is necessary and proportionate ... . This arbitrariness is further exacerbated by the ambiguity of the 'public interest'.[66]

Thus, protection for national security whistleblowers can be undermined by the fact that national security assessments where the disclosure of state secrets is concerned are complex, and an international court like the ECHR may not be best placed to make them.

Additionally, the ECtHR has traditionally granted states a wide margin of appreciation where restrictions to qualified rights on national security grounds are concerned.[67] The margin of appreciation doctrine which is linked to the principle of subsidiarity[68] maintains that contracting parties to the Convention are 'entitled to certain latitude in resolving the inherent conflicts between individual rights and national interests'.[69] In practice, this translates to significant judicial self-restraint on the part of the Court as 'it serves to trace the dividing line between judicial law-making in Strasbourg and the proper responsibility of the democratic institutions of the ECHR countries'.[70]

Apart from the wide margin of appreciation doctrine that usually applies in security-related cases, another significant factor that results in judicial restraint is the duties and responsibilities that apply to certain categories of speakers. National security restrictions to speech are most invoked against members of the armed forces

64. *Ibid.*
65. *Ibid.*, [74].
66. Hitoshi Nasu, 'State Secrets Law and National Security' (2015) 64 *International and Comparative Law Quarterly* 365, 395.
67. *See* I. Cameron, *National Security and the European Convention on Human Rights* (Martinus Nijhoff Publishers, 2000).
68. On this *see* Alastair Mowbray, 'Subsidiarity and the European Convention on Human Rights' (2015) 15 Human Rights Law Review 313-341.
69. E. Benvenisti, 'Margin of Appreciation, Consensus and Universal Standards' (1998-1999) 31 NYU Journal International Law & Policy 843.
70. P. Mahoney and L. Early, 'Freedom of Expression and National Security: Judicial and Policy Approaches under the European Convention on Human Rights and Other Council of Europe Instruments' in J. Fitzpatrick et al. (eds), *Secrecy and Liberty: National Security, Freedom of Expression and Access to Information* (Martinus Nijhoff Publishers, 1999) at 116.

or intelligence agencies. Article 10 is the only Convention right that mentions the 'duties and responsibilities' that rights-holders have when exercising a right. The Court has interpreted these duties as an added reason to be deferential towards the state where certain speakers are involved. For instance, in *Engel and others v. Netherlands*,[71] disciplinary action was taken against two soldiers for writing and distributing material in their army base that was thought to undermine military discipline. In finding that the disciplinary action did not violate Article 10, the ECtHR assigned particular weight to the special duties and responsibilities under Article 10 that were incumbent on military personnel.[72] The applicants argued that facing harsher restrictions to their free speech on the basis of their military status was discriminatory, as civilians distributing similar material would not be subject to comparable sanctions. In rejecting this claim, the Court held that the dissimilar treatment 'is explicable by the differences between the conditions of military and of civil life and, more specifically, by the "duties" and "responsibilities" peculiar to members of the armed forces in the field of freedom of expression'.[73]

This was affirmed in *Hadjianastassiou v. Greece*,[74] a judgment concerning an aeronautical engineer employed by the Greek Air Force who had provided a technical study on guided missiles to a private company. While the Court acknowledged that freedom of expression 'applies to servicemen just as it does to other persons',[75] it attached significant weight to the special duties and responsibilities that are part of military life.[76] Furthermore, the Court reiterated that contracting parties to the Convention enjoyed a wide margin of appreciation when the protection of national security and the disclosure of military secrets were at stake.[77] This led to a finding of no Article 10 violation.

That is not to say that the Court will not find a violation of Article 10 in all cases where the speaker has heightened duties and responsibilities. In *Grigoriades v. Greece*,[78] for instance, Greece was found in violation of Article 10 for penalising a conscript for sending a letter to his superior in which he frankly expressed his views that the army 'is an apparatus opposed to man and society'.[79] However, it is worth noting that in this instance the ECtHR found that there was no pressing social need to suppress the speech because 'the letter was not published by the applicant or disseminated by him to a wider audience'.[80]

71. App. No. 5100/71, 8 June 1976.
72. *Ibid.*, [100].
73. *Ibid.*, [103]. *See also* I. Cameron, *National Security and the European Convention on Human Rights* (Martinus Nijhoff Publishers, 2000) 370 et seq.
74. App. No. 12945/87, 16 December 1992.
75. *Ibid.*, [39].
76. *Ibid.*, [46].
77. *Ibid.*, [47].
78. App. No. 24348/94 (ECHR, 25 November 1997).
79. *Ibid.*, [14].
80. *Ibid.*, [47].

4 'NATIONAL SECURITY' WHISTLEBLOWERS IN THE CASE LAW OF THE ECTHR AND COE INSTRUMENTS

The analysis in the previous section may paint a disappointing picture for the prospects of national security whistleblowers to rely on Article 10 for protection. Additionally, the paucity of judgments relating to such whistleblowers does not allow us to discern a clear pattern or a consistent approach on how the Court will deal with national security whistleblowing. As this section demonstrates, in the very few judgments where national security served as the legitimate aim for restricting the whistleblower's speech, the Court has been inconsistent in its approach. What is more encouraging in the CoE more broadly, however, is the adoption of multiple resolutions and recommendations from various CoE organs that endorse protection for national security whistleblowers. These will be examined at the end of this section.

Pasko v. Russia[81] was the first ECtHR judgment linked to national security whistleblowing following the establishment of the Court's whistleblower protection framework under Article 10 in *Guja v. Moldova*. The applicant was a naval officer who also served as a journalist for the in-house newspaper of the Russian fleet. Additionally, he worked as a freelance journalist for certain Japanese media. The applicant was convicted and imprisoned for treason and espionage-related crimes after he was caught carrying classified information while preparing to leave the country on an official trip to Japan. He was allegedly planning to share this information with Japanese journalists. The information related to environmental pollution in the Sea of Japan caused by the Russian fleet's dumping of nuclear waste.[82]

In its assessment of the case, the Court attached particular weight to the duties and responsibilities of the applicant as a military officer and the wide margin of appreciation states enjoy in relation to national security.[83] It is quite telling that the significance of the information in question, or its potential to contribute to public debate, did not feature in the Court's reasoning. Without much by way of explanation, the Court also rejected the applicant's argument that he was acting in his capacity as a journalist.[84] This led to a finding of no violation of Article 10. Therefore, in this case, the duties and responsibilities of the applicant along with the wide margin of appreciation led the Court to forego any assessment of the public interest in the disclosure the applicant intended to make.

In the judgment of *Bucur and Toma v. Romania*,[85] a few years later, however, the Court adopted an altogether different approach. The case involved a member of the Romanian intelligence services who revealed information to the press of illegal telecommunication surveillance of journalists, politicians and other public figures. The applicant was prosecuted and given a two-year suspended sentence for gathering and

81. *Pasko v. Russia*, App. No. 69519/01, 22 October 2009.
82. For a more detailed account of the facts of the case *see* the Report submitted to the Parliamentary assembly available at https://assembly.coe.int/nw/xml/XRef/X2H-Xref-ViewHTML.asp?FileID=10312&lang=en.
83. *Pasko v. Russia* [87].
84. *Ibid.*, [87].
85. *Bucur and Toma v. Romania* (App. No. 40238/02, 8 April 2013).

imparting secret information. In its assessment of the interference with the whistleblower's free speech, the Court paid particular attention to the fact that the intelligence services in Romania were engaging in illegal activity that violated rights, notably the right to privacy. The Court reiterated its position against unlawful state surveillance and concluded that the public interest in being informed about irregularities that threaten the democratic foundations of the state outweighed the competing considerations of national security and maintaining public confidence in the intelligence services.[86] When reaching its conclusion on the public interest, the Court also considered that information on illegal state surveillance 'was of particular importance in a society which during the communist regime had known a policy of close surveillance by the secret services';[87] Additionally, the Court noted that domestic courts had not taken into account the public interest in the disclosure.[88] Finally, the Court placed emphasis on the fact that the respondent state had not presented sufficient evidence to demonstrate how the disclosures at issue would harm national security or the institutions against which the whistle was blown.[89] These considerations are specific to the facts of this case, and therefore it is difficult to glean whether they signal a new approach towards unauthorised disclosures of information that purportedly harm national security. This judgment, however, does constitute a welcome development for national security whistleblowers. Importantly, and in stark opposition to the Pasko judgment, the Court mentioned the applicant's duties and responsibilities under Article 10 only in passing.[90] These duties were not found to override the public interest in the disclosure.

The more nuanced approach the Court developed in its judgment in Bucur has been accompanied by further positive developments for national security whistleblowers. Since the Pasko judgment in 2009, Various CoE organs have adopted multiple recommendations and resolutions that have emphasised the significance of national security whistleblowing. For instance, CoE Parliamentary Assembly Resolution 1729 (2010) on the protection of whistleblowers, included members of the armed forces and special services in its ambit of protection.[91] The CoE's Parliamentary Resolution 1838 (2011) 'On the Abuse of State Secrecy and National Security' also provided support for national security whistleblowers by noting that:

> The media ... rely heavily on the co-operation of 'whistle-blowers' within the [intelligence and security] services of the state. The Assembly reiterates its calls for adequate protection ... for whistleblowers.[92]

86. *Ibid.*, [115].
87. *Ibid.*, [101].
88. *Ibid.*, [104].
89. *Ibid.*, [114].
90. This is mentioned in [93], where the Court cites [70]-[78] from the *Guja* judgment.
91. Council of Europe, Parliamentary Assembly Resolution 1729 (2010) on the 'Protection of Whistleblowers' at 6.1.2.
92. Council of Europe, Parliamentary Assembly Resolution 1838 (2011) on 'Abuse of state secrecy and national security: obstacles to parliamentary and judicial scrutiny of human rights violations', text adopted 6 October 2011 at 8.

Similarly, the CoE's Venice Commission report on the 'Democratic Oversight of the Intelligence and Security Services' included whistleblowers in the means of keeping the services accountable and called for procedures to protect whistleblowers who raise concern outside their organisation.[93] Finally, Parliamentary Assembly Resolution 1954 (2013) aimed at providing guidance on how states should balance National security and access to information, provided that '[a] person who discloses wrongdoings in the public interest (whistle-blower) should be protected from any type of retaliation, provided he or she acted in good faith and followed applicable procedures'.[94] This Resolution endorsed the Tshwane Principles on access to information that 'are designed to give guidance to legislators and relevant officials … with a view to reaching an appropriate balance between public interests both in national security and in access to information'.[95]

While these instruments are not legally binding on the Court or the CoE Member States, they represent a growing consensus among states in Europe on the significance of whistleblower protection for national security whistleblowers. The Court commonly relies on such instruments to identify emerging trends in human rights standards across Europe.[96] These instruments can empower the Court to carry out stricter scrutiny of speech restrictions on national security whistleblowers. This approach would be fully in line with the rationale underpinning the inclusion of whistleblowing into the protective scope of Article 10. If the justification for offering Article 10 protection to whistleblowers is the audience interest in their speech, the Court should not deprive whistleblowers of sharing particularly sensitive information on wrongdoing from such protection.

5 CONCLUSION

The ECtHR has offered whistleblowers across Europe an added layer of protection from retaliation under Article 10 ECHR. The chapter has demonstrated that in the ECHR context the whistleblower is best understood as a distinctive type of speaker, one who draws protection from the audience interest in her speech. Whistleblowing is viewed as an act of imparting information on matters of public concern, and as a result, the public interest in the whistleblower's disclosure plays a central role in the Court's reasoning. The Court has demonstrated some reluctance in assessing the public interest in a

93. European Commission for Democracy through Law (Venice Commission), 'Report on the Democratic Oversight of the Security Services' (2007) 146.
94. Council of Europe, Parliamentary Assembly Resolution 1954 (2013) on 'National Security and Access to Information', text adopted on 2 October 2013 [9.7.].
95. *Ibid.*, [7]. On balancing free speech and national security whistleblowing *see* Ioannis Kampourakis, 'Protecting National Security Whistleblowers in the U.S. and in the ECtHR: The Limits of Balancing and the Social Value of Public Disclosures' (2020) https://papers.ssrn.com/sol3/papers.cfm?abstract_id = 3576036.
96. On this *see* Kanstantsin Dzehtsiarou, *European Consensus and the Legitimacy of the European Court of Human Rights* (Cambridge University Press, 2015) 45 et seq.

disclosure that purportedly prejudices national security. However, in more recent judgments, the Court has been willing to more confidently challenge state assertions on the harms caused by a disclosure to security interests. This approach finds further support in COE instruments that increasingly recognise the significant contribution of all whistleblowers to transparency and accountability

PART IV New Bearings

CHAPTER 24
'Courts in Federal Systems'

Stephen Tierney

1 INTRODUCTION

A federal system of government is one which, more than most - given the deep inter-governmental tensions it contains - finds its origins and manifests itself constitutionally through the intimate interplay of law and politics. The balance of power between the authority of law and the practice of politics can shift radically from system to system and over time as each federal system develops, and in the face of underlying or new tensions in the life of the polity.

History tells us that the long-term outcome of the law-politics interplay has, in many federal systems, been the consolidation of a strong central authority and a weakening of the real power of the constituent territories. The question then arises as to how this process occurs; how is it that changes in political mood lead to constitutional change or redirection? One answer of course is formal constitutional amendment, but as we know constitutions change, often fundamentally, in processes that do not involve such textual transformation, or in ways in which changes in constitutional culture supplement formal constitutional change to reconfigure constitutional reality.[1] A principal agent of change which combines both formal and a deeper cultural dimension of change is the judiciary. In this chapter I address the role played by top courts in multi-level systems. I begin by trying to identify what we understand by the federal idea itself, and from there I consider how the courts in a select number of systems have played a crucial role either in articulating and developing the federal idea or in undermining it in favour of a dominant central authority.

1. B. Ackerman, *We the People I: Foundations* (Cambridge, MA: The Belknap Press of Harvard University Press, 1991); G. Jeffrey Jacobsohn, *Constitutional Identity* (Cambridge: Harvard University Press, 2010).

This enquiry rests upon a further, anterior question: what is federalism and how does its nature reflect the interplay of law and politics? Astonishingly, the nature of federalism as a constitutional idea is one that has rarely been addressed by systematic study, even after several decades in which it has been the focus of intense consideration within political science and constitutional law. In recent work I have tried to unpack the federal idea. A key premise of my work is that the essence of federalism can only be properly understood through the register of constitutional theory, and that much of the confusion that surrounds the nature of federalism is a consequence of it being defined through the prism of political science. I return shortly to the role of constitutional theory in how we understand federalism but I would begin with a definition of federalism itself. I take federalism to be a specific genus of constitutional government for the modern state which, in the act of constitutional union, gives foundational recognition and accommodation to the state's constituent territorial pluralism. The purpose of the federal constitution is both to foster this foundational pluralism and to maintain the constitutional relationship between pluralism and union in the creation and reconciliation of different orders of government.[2] My contention is that to understand the role of top courts in a federal system as agents of constitutional change – and therefore as crucial actors within a broader constitutional-political reflexivity,[3] we need to focus upon the constitutional essence of federalism as a fundamental commitment to the legal-normative significance of territorial pluralism. My key question therefore is, to what extent have top courts respectively fulfilled or frustrated this constitutional function?

My approach, with its focus upon the constitutional essence of federalism, therefore depends upon an anterior point of context. Given that I am tying the very idea of federalism to constitutional theory, it is first necessary to locate the federal idea conceptually within a broader account of modern constitutional theory. It is notable that some have sought to extract federalism from the generic story of modern constitutionalism, addressing it as a form of government, or indeed as a form of state, sui generis and hence as one that in many ways need not trouble general accounts of constitutional rule. A number of accounts,[4] including very recent accounts,[5] treat federalism not really as part of the modern democratic constitutional turn of the late eighteenth century but more as an exotic outlier which should be addressed as a categorically distinct form of statehood. My contention is that this approach is misconceived. Federalism is very much part of one generic story of modern constitutionalism, emerging and in fact shaping, through the United States (US) constitution, that very story. It is challenging for the way in which it offers an alternative form of constitution to the unitary constitution, but it is very much a form of modern

2. S. Tierney, *The Federal Contract: A Constitutional Theory of Federalism* (Oxford: Oxford University Press, 2022).
3. E. Christodoulidis, *Law and Reflexive Politics* (New York: Springer, 1998).
4. O. Beaud, *Théorie de la Fédération* (Paris: Presses Universitaires de France, 2009); M. Forsyth, *Union of States: The Theory and Practice of Confederations* (New York: Leicester University Press, 1981).
5. S. Rehling Larsen, *The Constitutional Theory of the Federation and the European Union* (Oxford: Oxford University Press, 2021).

government for coherent states; a departure from a monistic mindset within *constitutionalism* but not within statehood.

What makes federalism distinctive is the approach it takes to the foundations and ensuing legitimacy of constitutional rule. On this register it is fundamentally different from unitary foundations and the premises of unitary rule; unitary constitutions are founded upon the a priori recognition of individual subjecthood and it is this idea that sustains their authority and the legitimacy that underpins them; federal constitutions on the other hand are premised upon a foundational constitutional commitment to the salience of territorially located citizenship; this is the essence of its authority and the leitmotif that remains a constant referent for the legitimacy of that authority.

A key feature of the process of modern state-building from the eighteenth century onwards was both the unification of disparate groups within one constitutional order and the husbanding of all political power under the authority of one sovereign order of rule. In this context federalism, which recognises a plurality of constitutionally salient territories, and embeds their various governments within the constitution of the state, irritates against and in some ways directly contradicts, the core assimilationist purpose of the modern constitution.

Constitutional theory (or constitutionalism, which I use in this chapter as a short-hand synonym for constitutional theory) is the study of the specific task performed by constitutions: the transformation of political power into normative authority. The modern state has been built upon this alchemy, allowing political control over territory to acquire the legitimacy of lawful rule. Constitutions perform this task for specific purposes - for example, to protect individual rights and to limit the scope of government to that end: the classic purpose of liberal constitutionalism. But since federalism is a distinct order of rule for the modern state, it follows that it must be understood as transforming political power into legal authority *for a particular purpose* and one that differs from default or monist constitutionalism. This purpose recognises that the federal constitution is founded through constituent territories and is fashioned to accommodate this foundational territorial pluralism, reconciling the constitutional recognition and ongoing autonomy of the constituent territories with the forging of a union of the two orders of government that together constitute the governmental matrix of the state.

This definition of federalism may sound like a truism but I would submit that only the methodology of constitutionalism can reveal the true significance of such a foundationally discrete purpose: as a constitutional commitment and not just a political observation. Constitutionalism performs various roles: it has proven to be a key device in giving a modern legally ruled polity its - and citizens within it their - very identity; it also provides the polity with its foundational and ongoing legitimacy: power within it taking on legal validity; and it categorises a hierarchy of norms, providing law-making and executive functions across different levels with the essential legal-normative referent that warrants their exercise and demarcates their respective sites of authority. A federal constitution therefore has a foundationally different identity from a unitary constitution; it is one premised upon territorial constituent power which prioritises the constitutional status, symbolically and substantively, of its constituent territories. It is the *consent of these territories* rather than the citizenry as an undiffer entiated whole that gives the constitution its foundational and ongoing legitimacy and which operates within the constitution to condition fundamentally the constitution's authority.

In short, it is the centrality of territorial pluralism to the federal idea that makes it a discrete genus of rule within the constitutional species. Federalism can only be properly understood as a particular form of government if this purpose is uncovered and explained, and such a process of uncovering and explanation can only be done through the register of constitutionalism, taking full account of the foundationally fundamental step that is taken in the process of constitutionalisation and the ongoing significance of a constitution as the shaper and conditioner of the polity's very existence, legitimacy and governmental efficacy. From this core starting point – the legal-normative significance of a constitution – we can say that a federal constitution is crucial to the consolidation of territorial pluralism as the polity's purpose, for three main reasons:

> First, it gives foundational constitutional status to the respective levels of government created by the constitution. It does so across four registers: recognition, autonomy, associational government and reciprocity. The pluralisation of government, upon which any federal constitution is founded, must be understood in this way. Notably, this commitment is not just about autonomy or territorially focused constitutional prerogatives. The role of the constitution is to embed the federal project as a whole, from the recognition of pluralism as the core purpose of the constitution, to a matrix of rule that involves cooperation and contestation in the portmanteau of authority across the polity: union as the essential corollary of pluralism; the constitutional principles of associational rule and reciprocity supplementing those of recognition and autonomy.
>
> A second feature is entrenchment and a particular approach to constitutional change. The process of changing a federal constitution, like most constitutions, typically involves a complex process but federal change takes on its own particular characteristic. In a federal system this typically involves a particular role for the constituent territories either directly or indirectly. It is also the case that constitutional amendment can be a particularly vital issue within a federal constitution precisely because it is the core institutional device that guarantees both the central place of territories within the constitutional fabric and because it is in guarding this process of change that the federal constitution can maintain its distinctive character. The salience of this dimension of the federal constitution is evident for example from the protracted debates about the amendment formula in Canada from the 1950s onwards.
>
> Third, entrenchment gives a significant role to the top courts. Federal constitutions are typically difficult to change through formal channels, largely due to the super-majority and multi-step processes which this can involve. On this basis the courts can become key levers of change, not only managing the

> boundaries between powers within the constitution, but, through interpretation of the constitution, developing these boundaries to reflect social, economic and political changes. Therefore, as we focus upon the role of the court in a federal system we need to do so in the context both of federalism as a constitutional idea and the impact of constitutionalism upon the framework of authority that is the institutional manifestation of that idea.

One other point should be made as we turn to some examples of how the approach taken to federalism by top courts has developed. This is arguably a direct consequence of the federal constitution being subsumed within a generic way of thinking about modern constitutionalism, with its discrete nature obscured or indeed subverted by a singular narrative of authority within the state. This neglect or indeed over-riding of federalism's specificity is essentially the product of a particular political ideology: one that views the purpose of any constitution, including a federal constitution, as being to provide a bulwark for the consolidation of a unifying and ultimately centralising state. In this way the constitution operates as an instrumental device that works towards more integrated statehood. It is in the extension of this generic idea about modern constitutionalism in general to federalism in particular that in many respects the essential commitment within federalism to territorial pluralism has largely been lost. In short, federalism has come to be seen as just another form of division or separation of powers, promoting restrained government within a unified state, rather than a foundationally and categorically different way of structuring normative authority within the state that makes it a genuinely pluralistic approach to the allocation of constitutional competence.

Having laid the groundwork to explain the constitutional specificity of federalism as genus of both constitutional idea and practice, we can turn to the role of the courts in a federal system with benchmarks through which to analyse whether they have acted to consolidate the former or latter view and whether they have been key agents in the political transformation of foundational constitutional commitments. In this endeavour I will briefly discuss the constitutional trajectory of the US, Canada and the United Kingdom (UK). In the space available this can be no more than a series of vignettes.[6]

2 FEDERALISM AS A CONSTITUTIONAL ORDER

The role of a top court in a federal system emerged within the first modern federal system created by the US Constitution: 'The Judicial Power of the United States, shall be vested in one supreme Court, and in such inferior Courts as the Congress may from time to time ordain and establish.'[7] Subsequent systems have also established processes of constitutional adjudication. Canada relied upon the Judicial Committee of the Privy Council for final decisions until the Supreme Court of Canada (SCC), created by the British North America Act 1867, became the court of final resort in 1949. The High

6. I discuss this further in Chapter 10 of the Federal Contract.
7. Article III, section 1.

Court of Australia was established in 1901 by section 71 of the Constitution, sitting after the passage of the Judiciary Act in 1903. Since then, judicial review has been key to the development of federalism across many constitutional systems.[8]

One way in which the allocation of authority within a federal system is often explained is in terms of a division between levels: central and regional. If such a categorisation is accepted, a question arises as to how we conceive of the location of the top court. One formulation is to see it as part of the central level of government. This is how it appears within the American constitution: the third branch of the central or federal tier. I would submit that if we allude to federalism's foundational purpose – a real commitment to territorial pluralism – then such a conceptualisation is not consistent with the federal idea. The nature of federal courts is tied up in understandings of the federal project as a whole; it is there to arbitrate on the constitution's foundational commitment to territorial pluralism, not as part of one branch of that pluralism.

A useful aid to this conceptualisation of the top court's role is Hans Kelsen's theory of federalism. Kelsen conceived of federalism as a particular type of state. As noted, I contest such an approach methodologically, with its focus upon the idea of the federal state rather than the federal constitution. I also take the view that Kelsenian positivism is in the end not capable of explaining the nature of ultimate authority, or sovereignty, within a constitutional system.[9] Nonetheless, Kelsen did explain that the nature of federal authority was in an important way, if not fundamentally, distinct from unitary constitutionalism.

Kelsen concluded that the institutionalisation of pluralism inherent in, and the decentralised nature of, the federal polity required its own account within the theory of the state. Kelsen took the view that this was encapsulated in the idea of the 'three-branch federal state'. Within a federal polity there are three levels of rule: the sub state territories and the central state, and above these there is the federal state itself which ought not to be elided with the central institutions of the state. For Kelsen, as Grimm puts it, this was 'the common state, which was the actual federal state and an expression of the unity of the whole'.[10] For Kelsen, ultimate authority rested in this third level – the federal state itself.

Therefore, we do indeed need to conceive of the federal constitution as a discrete order of rule. I would submit that within a properly functioning federal constitution a top court that is assigned the role of arbitration on federal matters must adopt a mind-set that separates it from either level of government, that sees itself as part of a third level of rule: part of the constitutional apparatus itself rather than the different levels of government created by that apparatus.

8. T.O. Hueglin and A. Fenna, *Comparative Federalism: A Systematic Enquiry* (Broadview Press: Peterborough, Ont., 2006), 275.
9. Tierney, Federal Contract, Chapters 3-5.
10. Grimm, 66.

3 TOP COURTS AND THE FEDERAL IDEA

3.1 United States of America

The American Supreme Court rarely confronts deep theoretical questions at the heart of the federal idea and when it does we find different visions as to how the foundation of the American constitution should be conceived. An example is the *Term Limits* case in 1995. In this case the Supreme Court ruled that States cannot impose qualifications for prospective members of the US Congress which are stricter than those specified in the Constitution. It is significant however for the fact that different judges set out their understanding of the constitutional origins of the polity, presenting starkly contrasting approaches.

For Justice Kennedy, the foundational moment was demotically unifying: 'the whole people of the United States asserted their political identity and unity of purpose when they created the federal system'.[11] We find a similar understanding among contemporary academic commentators.[12] By contrast, however, Justice Thomas stated: the 'ultimate source of the Constitution's authority is the consent of the people of each individual State, not the consent of the undifferentiated people of the Nation as a whole'.[13] This dispute in fact reflects the Federalist Papers themselves, including one paper by James Madison that seems to express both of these views at once.[14] It is notable that over two hundred years later the nature of the American demos at the foundational moment was still a source of dispute in the Term Limits case, leading to fundamental disagreement about the nature of the identity and ultimate source of authority of the polity.

The overwhelming story of American constitutionalism has however been nationalisation rather than territorial pluralism. And to this end the establishment of a top court within the federal branch has been crucial. Madison himself expressed the view that 'the tribunal which is ultimately to decide, is to be established under the general government'.[15] As one commentator puts it: 'This model presupposes that there exists a national political community transcending the separate peoples of each state.'[16]

The US Supreme Court assumed the national role for itself that Madison had intended, and this has grown extensively over time. The familiar story is of course how *Marbury v. Madison* began a long process of judicial review. But another crucial decision in the early period of the US' constitutional development was *McCulloch v. Maryland* in which the Supreme Court positioned itself as the arbiter of the division of

11. *U.S. Term Limits, Inc. v. Thornton,* 514 U.S. 779, 838 per Kennedy J.
12. A.R. Amar, 'Of Sovereignty and Federalism', (1987) 96 *Yale Law Journal* 1425-1520; A.R. Amar, 'Philadelphia Revisited: Amending the Constitution Outside Article V', (1988) 55 *University of Chicago Law Review* 1043-1104.
13. *U.S. Term Limits, Inc. v. Thornton* per Thomas J.
14. J. Madison, 'The Federalist No. 49', C. Rossiter, ed., *The Federalist Papers* (New York: New American Library, 1961).
15. J. Madison, Letter to Edward Everett, 31 August 1830.
16. J. Read, 'John C Calhoun's Federalism and Its Contemporary Echoes' in Ashgate Research Companion 245-260, 247.

federal powers within the constitution. In this way a branch of the federal government asserted kompetenz-kompetenz in relation to disputes between this branch and the several States. In *Cohens v. Virginia* the Court also emphasised its jurisdiction to decide on powers of the states.[17] As LaCroix puts it in relation to Chief Justice Marshall's position in Cohens: 'The basis of the American union was divided authority, with the Court taking upon itself the role of the dividing authority.'[18]

We assume today that a top court is the natural institution to manage federal relations. But this was not so in 1787. And in fact, the empowerment of the Supreme Court created an in-built institutional bias towards centralisation: 'The Philadelphia delegates' decision to use courts rather than legislatures as the principal mechanism to balance multiplicity with union gave concrete, institutional meaning to the emerging federal vision.'[19]

Another consequence of elevating the role of judges was of course the juridification of the constitution. The American system has cast another shadow over federalism by the way in which the American system has come to be so heavily judicialised. This is a consequence of a number of factors. First, little attention was paid to the allocation of powers in the drafting process, in contrast to the design of federal institutions. Secondly, the constitution is itself a very brief text in which very few powers were enumerated to the central state.[20] Thirdly, there was considerable ambiguity in the drafting of the constitution as to the intended balance between general federal powers and a residual power to the States. And finally, the constitution contained an amendment process that has over time made political change to the constitution extremely difficult. These different factors have allowed the Supreme Court and other federal courts to facilitate a massive accrual of power to the centre through the very liberal interpretation of laconic constitutional provisions such as the 'necessary and proper' clause and the 'general welfare' clause. All in all: 'judicial interpretation [has] played havoc with the original design'.[21]

In this task of course, the court was largely reflecting social developments. America after the Civil War was a country in which national identity grew and state-based territorial identities significantly declined in salience. The Madisonian promise of an American nation reached fulfilment in the post-Civil War era. The ratification of the 14th amendment was key to this. And it is no coincidence that it is precisely this instrument which the federal courts have used to consolidate the power of the federal government, to the point where Feeley and Rubin state: 'what now passes for federalism in the United States is actually managerial decentralization'.[22] While

17. A.L. LaCroix, *The Ideological Origins of American Federalism* (Cambridge, MA: Harvard University Press, 2011), 218-219.
18. LaCroix, 219.
19. *Ibid.*, 221.
20. T.O. Hueglin and A. Fenna, *Comparative Federalism: A Systematic Enquiry* (Broadview Press: Peterborough, Ont., 2006); (2nd edn, Toronto: University of Toronto Press, 2015), 153.
21. Hueglin and Fenna, 156.
22. M. Feeley and. E Rubin, *Federalism: Political Identity and Tragic Compromise* (Ann Arbor: University of Michigan Press, 2008), Preface, ix. Also: 'Federalism Is No longer an Operative Principle in the United States', Preface, ix. *See also* R. Nagel, The Implosion of American Federalism, Daniel J. Hopkins, ed., *The Increasingly United States: How and Why American*

there have been periods where the Court has reined back federal governmental power, in recognition of state authority, the overwhelming trajectory since 1865 in particular has been towards the centralisation of power.

What then can we say about the interaction of law and politics? On the one hand we could assert that the US Supreme Court has been the driver of change, taking a territorially pluralised polity and transforming it unilaterally in a homogenistic way. But this is too simple a story. The federal courts have been, in many ways, instruments themselves of deeper attitudinal change; in many ways responding reflexively to changing societal realities; Feeley and Rubin's wider point is that the political mentality of the US is no longer really federal and that the courts have simply recognised this and adapted the meaning of the constitution to reflect a territorially homogenised American national identity. It would therefore be wrong to criticise the court for failing to enforce a 1787 territorial reality within twentieth and twenty-first-century America. Courts in the end are a mirror of power: 'a centralist or noncentralist stance often (but not necessarily) reflects the centralization gradient of the federal system'.[23]

3.2 Canada

An intriguing and very different story emerges when we turn to the approach taken to federalism by the Canadian judiciary. One important conditioning factor is Canada's long association with the UK which left ultimate adjudicatory competence in the hands of the Judicial Committee of the Privy Council until the elevation of the SCC to the position of final appellate court in Canada for all matters in 1949. Both courts have been instrumental in shaping the meaning of Canada's constitutional arrangements and ultimately in interpreting how federalism ought to be understood. It is impossible to explain this complex story briefly, but it has often been argued that the Judicial Committee of the Privy Council (JCPC) was in general largely protective of the constitutional position of the Provinces, restricting attempts by the federal government to expand its jurisdiction into areas of provincial competence. One explanation is that the JCPC saw itself as an essential balance to protect the Provinces, in particular Quebec, from a constitution which, unlike its American equivalent, enumerated very extensive powers for the federal government. As Popelier puts it, 'courts are more inclined to take a noncentralist stance when representation of subnational governments at the federal level is weak'.[24] Another is that the JCPC, as a UK-based court, saw itself as overseer of the whole Canadian constitution, rather than an actor on behalf of either internal level. Insofar as it had an interest it was principally that of the British Empire or commonwealth as the 'federal' unit. In this way, more by accident than design, it took on the third-level role identified by Kelsen.

Political Behavior Nationalized (Chicago, IL: University of Chicago Press, 2018); and A. Fenna, 'The Centralization of Australian Federalism 1901-2010: Measurement and Interpretation', (2019) 49 *Publius: The Journal of Federalism* 30-56, https://doi.org/10.1093/publius/pjy042.

23. P. Popelier, 'Federalism Disputes and the Behavior of Courts: Explaining Variation in Federal Courts' Support for Centralization', (2017) 47 *Publius* 27-48, 44.
24. *Ibid.*, 44.

The role of the SCC is more complex, arguably swinging from a very centralising approach in the 1980s and early 1990s towards a more federal approach since then.[25] It should also be observed that the Court has had to adjudicate during a very fraught period in Canadian federal history, between the time of patriation of the constitution in 1981-1982 up to the Quebec referendum on sovereignty in 1995 and its aftermath. It has been widely argued that the Court, in a series of cases in the early part of this period, failed to give sufficient recognition to the centrality of federalism to the Canadian constitution, and in particular to Quebec's particular place within Canadian federalism.[26] The issue at stake was the patriation of the amendment process. The Court in adjudicating upon this issue found that amendment was largely a matter of constitutional convention. Having decided this, it took the view that it was not the Court's place to give legal effect to conventions. It did however seek to articulate the content of the convention of provincial consent to constitutional change, and it was in relation to this that the Court came in for criticism. The Court's ultimate conclusion was that there was a convention of substantial provincial consent in relation to constitutional amendment in Canada but that this did not necessarily require the consent of Quebec specifically. This bolstered the federal government's claim that it could secure the patriation of the constitution and the creation of a new amendment formula within the patriated constitution without Quebec's consent.

Although the Court in this case was criticised for not properly articulating the real nature of Canadian federalism, in particular the salience of the French fact or binational or plurinational nature of the country, the issue was difficult given how constitutional conventions are treated within Westminster constitutional systems. The Court is also widely perceived to have retrieved much of its lost credibility in its Secession Reference opinion in 1998. In this the Court gave a wide-ranging account of the origins and foundations of the Canadian constitution, its evolution over time, the meaning of subjecthood and of the dynamics of constitutional change on the most fundamental feature of all, secession from the federation itself.[27] In doing so, it gave federalism a preeminent place within the iconography of Canadian constitutionalism, emphasising the country's foundational constitutional commitment to territorial pluralism.

In this way the SCC has come to see itself arguably within the third or constitutional level of the polity, rather than as a branch of either level of the state. It can also be argued that the role of the judiciary since the nineteenth century has been one that has helped sustain the constitutional commitment of Canada to territorial pluralism far more than has the US Supreme Court has in relation to America. But again, we must consider how law reflects politics. Canada is a country in which federalism reflected territorial pluralism in large part to guarantee the French fact in Canada. Within Quebec French-Canadian identity was stubbornly maintained and has in fact grown since the 1960s. The SCC has therefore in large part merely responded

25. R. Schertzer, *The Judicial Role in a Diverse Federation: Lessons from the Supreme Court of Canada* (Toronto: University of Toronto Press, 2016).
26. P. Oliver, 'Canada, Quebec, and Constitutional Amendment', (1999) 49 *The University of Toronto Law Journal* 519-610.
27. Reference *Re Secession of Quebec*, [1998] 2 SCR 217.

both to this and to the generally stronger focus which Canadians place upon federal rule than is the case in many other 'uni-national' federal systems.

3.3 United Kingdom

The UK is not usually defined as possessing a federal constitution but the degree to which its constitution now accommodates the country's territorial pluralism calls into question such a formalistic approach to constitutional categorisation. The role of the courts in managing its territorial arrangements is still at an early stage given that the implementation of devolution itself dates only to 1999. Only a limited number of competence disputes have come before the top court: first the JCPC and since 2009, the UK Supreme Court. In the few that have come from Wales it is generally considered that the court has been generous in its treatment of devolved competence. The court has not in general engaged in broad reflections upon the nature of the constitution and its relationship to the territorial nature of the state in any way comparable to the Canadian Secession Reference. Devolution was a huge change in the UK's constitutional arrangements. Unusually among federal-type constitutions it is heavily asymmetrical, not only in relation to the very different arrangements it makes for each of Scotland, Wales and Northern Ireland,[28] but in the fact that England, the largest nation of the state, was not accorded any measure of self-rule. Despite this the Supreme Court has tended to take a fairly narrow, positivist approach to adjudicating on the boundaries of devolved competence.[29]

The 2014 referendum on Scottish independence, and the closeness of the result (55-45 voting No to separation) was a shock to the system which led to the devolution of further powers in the Scotland Act 2016. This measure also introduced two notable changes in terms of constitutional structure. One concerned the interface between autonomy and shared rule – the so-called Sewel convention. By this convention the UK Parliament will not normally legislate in devolved areas without the consent of the devolved legislature. The Scotland Act 1998, as amended by the 2016 Act, now gives statutory recognition to this convention but does not turn it into a legally enforceable rule. Secondly, the Scotland Act also now confirms the permanence of the devolved Scottish Government and Scottish Parliament, neither of which can be removed without a referendum in Scotland. The role of the courts in interpreting these two provisions is an interesting question, and one which in the longer term could lead to a fuller articulation of how the court sees the UK constitution.

Other strains upon the constitution have also drawn the Supreme Court into considering fundamental features of the system. In the *Miller I* case which arose from the Brexit referendum, the Supreme Court was asked if the convention extended to

28. Although Welsh devolution has moved closer to Scottish devolution in recent statutory changes.
29. Notable in cases involved the Scotland Act 1998 – *Martin v. Most* [2010] UKSC 10; *Imperial Tobacco Ltd v. Lord Advocate* [2012] UKSC 61; (UK Withdrawal from the EU (Legal Continuity) (S) Bill 2019 SC (UKSC) 13; *Attorney General and Advocate General Reference on the United Nations Convention of the Rights of the Child (Incorporation) (Scotland) Bill and the European Charter on Local Self-Government (Incorporation)(Scotland) Bill* [2021] UKSC 42.

prevent the UK Parliament from legislating to notify the European Union (EU) of its intention to withdraw. The court found that the Sewel convention, even with statutory recognition, constituted no more than 'legislative recognition' of a 'political convention' that 'operates as a *political* restriction on the activity of the UK Parliament'.[30] It is certainly the case that by everything we know about constitutional conventions within the UK system of government the court could not have treated the Sewel convention as a legal restriction, nor did it even emphasise its status as a constitutional rule moderating behaviour but falling short of a law – the normative *via media* by which conventions are given salience within our uncodified constitution.[31] There was little evidence that the Court's consideration of the larger issue left it inclined to see the territorial dimension of the constitution as particularly significant.

The issue of the permanence of the devolved institutions has not arisen before the courts and would only do so directly in light of the unthinkable process of Parliament legislating to remove them. But there are other issues, such as the legality issues surrounding a future referendum on independence, which might well prompt the Supreme Court to articulate more fully its understanding of the territorial pluralism of the UK constitution. At the time of writing the Scottish Government has proposed a Bill which it hopes to introduce in the Scottish Parliament to hold a second referendum on independence. It has referred this Bill to the Supreme Court, asking the Court to rule on its competence. Core to this question is whether the fact that 'the Union of the Kingdoms of England and Scotland' is reserved to the UK Parliament precludes a referendum on this issue being held by the Scottish Parliament without the consent of Westminster.[32] Other federal courts have been unequivocal in denying any unilateral right to hold secession referendums and in doing so have taken the opportunity to articulate their understanding of the nature of the federal system as indivisible[33] or divisible only by the consent of the federal system as a whole.[34] In this they confirm the two core dimensions of federalism, autonomy and union, and assert that the former cannot trump the latter or the very constitutional commitment to union, inherent in the constitutional idea of federalism, makes no sense. The UK Supreme Court has accepted the Lord Advocate's reference and will adjudicate on the matter in the autumn of 2022. We wait to see if the Court will articulate more definitively its understanding of the territorial nature of the constitution.

30. *R (on the application of Miller and another) v. Secretary of State for Exiting the European Union* [2017] UKSC 5.
31. The majority of the court in *Miller* stated at [151] that the policing of the scope and the manner of operation of political convention 'does not lie within the constitutional remit of the judiciary, which is to protect the rule of law'. This is undoubtedly true, but courts can recognise the existence and salience of conventions: e.g., *Attorney-General v. Jonathan Cape Ltd and Others* [1976] QB 752; *Reference Re Resolution to amend the Constitution* [1981] 1 SCR (Canada) 753.
32. Reference by the Lord Advocate of devolution issues under para. 34 of S6 Scotland Act 1998; 15 July 2022, UKSC 2022/0098.
33. America: *Texas v. White* [1868] 74 U.S. 700; Germany: 2 BvR 349/16, BVerfG 16 December 2016.
34. Spain: Constitutional Court of Spain, Judgments 76/1988, 247/2007, 31/2010, 42/2014.

4 CONCLUSIONS

In this chapter I have argued that federal constitutions should be understood and located within a wider conceptualisation and narration of modern state constitutionalism in general. In this process courts have been important. Federal constitutions, even more than unitary constitutions, tend to be hard to change. We have also now entered an era of particularly rigid constitutionalism, with ever more detailed constitutions and with arguments for unamendable constitutional provisions. These contextual factors give courts an even more important role. What we have seen in a number of systems such as that of the US is a propensity to use this role to augment a monistic conception of the demos and a nation-building dynamic equivalent to that in unitary states (other examples not addressed here include Australia, Germany and India). To this end, it is clear that rather than being developed as a discrete constitutional theory of federalism, the federal idea has instead been subsumed within political ideology, particularly that which has inspired and bolstered the strong democratic state – liberalism. The methodological individualism that characterises liberalism finds itself at odds with what I argue is the definitive feature of federal constitutionalism: the a priori significance of territorial pluralism.

Of course, it can be argued that certain models of institutional design are significant in judicial approaches to centralisation. One issue is appointment of judges. Popelier argues that low representation of states in the selection of judges or in the composition of the courts would appear to encourage courts to be more centralist in disposition.[35] Another is whether judges from the territories see themselves as somehow representative of these regions.[36] In terms of the allocation of competences, Cheryl Saunders for example suggests the single list of 'federal' powers model is most likely to lead in a centralising direction. 'The experience of both the United States and Australia suggests that the brief statement of federal power itself offers little effective limit to its scope in the absence of competing powers expressly assigned to the states.'[37] She refers to the commerce clause in America ('raising questions about the existence of any judicially enforceable limits on this power'[38]) and to Australia and the federal powers to legislate with respect to 'trading ... and financial corporations' or 'external affairs'.

I would question, however, how significant these factors really are. Such a trajectory does not happen by magic; it requires the intervention or at least the acquiescence of federal courts in the accrual of central power. Notably the Canadian constitution was designed to be more centralising than that of the US, which by the mid-1860s seemed to show the perils of excessive state power. But in fact the trajectory of the 1867 Act, bolstered by the JCPC, has tended towards protections for provincial

35. P. Popelier.
36. R. Schertzer, 'Quebec Justices as Quebec Representatives: National Minority Representation and the Supreme Court of Canada's Federalism Jurisprudence', (2016) 46 *Publius: The Journal of Federalism* 539-567.
37. C. Saunders, 'Commonwealth of Australia', in John Kincaid and G. Alan Tarr, eds, *Constitutional Origins, Structure, and Change in Federal Countries, Volume 1* (Montreal-Kingston: McGill-Queens University Press, 2005), 12-47.
38. *Ibid.*

prerogatives. When the US Supreme Court chose to interpret a single list of central powers a particular way, such as the commerce clause, necessary and proper clause etc., it could have gone in a very different direction than it did. There is surely no doubt that the US Supreme Court acted as a mirror of wider political and demotic trends that saw less and less salience in territorial demarcations across the country. The trend towards court power shows that even very detailed constitutions do not inoculate a system against judges as constitution-makers. The Canadian constitution is much more detailed than the American but it has not led to fewer federalism cases; the same can be said of India or Germany where both courts are busy and have been activists in shaping the federal polity.[39] And it is also the case that despite an approach to drafting the Canadian constitution that sought a stronger central government in 1867 than that which had prevailed in the US before the Civil War, the courts have in fact not significantly constrained the development of the Canadian constitution in a decentralising direction.

The UK Supreme Court has also recognised the very asymmetrical nature of the UK territorial constitution and it has not played a determinative role as yet either in a centralising or decentralising direction. In fact, the political constitution has itself played this role, leading to more and more autonomy for the devolved territories and as yet few significant constitutional disputes before the courts have required judges to take a strong stand on the issue of the federal principle.

The British experience is it would seem instructive, suggesting that federal polities develop better through the political institutions by the state, rather than by way of judicial engineering. Courts are neither by expertise nor constitutional legitimacy suited to shaping the nature of a polity. They tend to be more comfortable making decisions based upon the letter of the law and are not sites for meaningful, democratic deliberation. It is also the case that a supreme or constitutional court within a modern constitution, even a federal constitution, can find it difficult to distinguish its position from that of the federal level of government. On that basis the political realm remains the preferred site through which a federal system should navigate the relationship between law and politics. The political interaction between a federal constitution's constituent subjects and between them and the central organs of the polity remains the more appropriate way through which the constitutional life of the federal idea can develop from place to place in response to the shifting political moods of the polity.

39. Hueglin and Fenna, 43.

CHAPTER 25

Consultations, Politics and Reform of Judicial Review

David Feldman

When developing policy, governments have wide discretion as to whether, when, whom and how they consult (unless constrained by law). This chapter examines the consultations concerning moves by the Conservative Government of the United Kingdom (UK) under Boris Johnson (2019-2022) to reform judicial review (JR) in England and Wales.

For some years, UK governments have promulgated guidance on consultations. In 2002, Tony Blair's Labour Government made a 'Compact' (renewed by the Conservative-Liberal Democrat coalition Government in 2010) with representatives of 'civil society organizations' (CSOs) to foster good working relationships between them and public bodies.[1] The Government undertook to give early notice of consultations to CSOs and, where appropriate to enable meaningful engagement, to conduct 12-week formal, written consultations, otherwise explaining why a shorter period or informal process is adopted.[2] The Government would consider providing feedback on how respondents had influenced (or not influenced) policies, programmes and services, and assess their implications for CSOs.[3] Subsequent governments, while not expressly renewing the Compact, have produced more general guidance. A *Code of Practice on Consultation*, first introduced by the Blair Government in 2000 with an amended

1. HM Government, *The Compact: The Coalition Government and Civil Society Organisations Working Effectively in Partnership for the Benefit of Communities and Citizens in England* (London: Cabinet Office, 2010). Accessible at https://assets.publishing.service.gov.uk/government/uploads/system/uploads/attachment_data/file/61169/The_20Compact.pdf, last visited 25 July 2022).
2. *Ibid.*, section 2.4.
3. *Ibid.*, sections 2.5, 2.6.

version being published by Gordon Brown's Labour Government in 2008,[4] set out the Government's policy on dialogue with 'stakeholders' through formal, time-limited, public, written consultations. In 2013 the Coalition Government replaced it with a shorter, less glossy document, *Consultation Principles*,[5] not limited to written consultations, discussing, among other things, how to decide whether to consult and what form of consultation would be appropriate in different circumstances. This in turn was replaced by Theresa May's Conservative Government in 2018 with a less discursive statement of 11 principles, by reference to which the JR consultation process may be evaluated:[6]

(a) consultations should be clear and concise;
(b) consultations should have a purpose and be carried out at a formative stage in developing plans or policies;
(c) consultations should give enough information to ensure that consultees understand the issues and can give informed responses;
(d) consultation is an ongoing process which may include informal, iterative consultation as well as formal consultation;
(e) consultation should last for a proportionate amount of time (although an earlier general starting point of a minimum of 12 weeks in normal circumstances in the 2008 Code of Practice, or 2 to 12 weeks in the 2013 version of the Principles, is absent from the 2018 Principles);
(f) consultations should be targeted towards specific groups if appropriate;
(g) consultations should take account of the pressures on different consultees (but suggested periods to be allowed for holiday periods were dropped from the 2018 version);
(h) consultations should receive collective ministerial agreement before publication, especially in relation to new policy proposals, and published on gov.uk;
(i). consultations should accommodate scrutiny by publishing the government's response to the consultation on the same web page as the original consultation, explaining consultees' responses and their number and how they informed policy;
(j) the Government's response should be published within 12 weeks of the end of the consultation, or the reason for not doing so should be explained, with appropriate time between closing the consultation and implementing policy or legislation;

4. London: Better Regulation Executive, Department for Business, Enterprise and Regulatory Reform, 2008, accessible at https://assets.publishing.service.gov.uk/government/uploads/system/uploads/attachment_data/file/100807/file47158.pdf (last accessed 25 July 2022).
5. *Consultation Principles*, accessible at https://assets.publishing.service.gov.uk/government/uploads/system/uploads/attachment_data/file/255180/Consultation-Principles-Oct-2013.pdf (last accessed 25 July 2022); for relationship to the *Code of Practice on Consultation, see* the first paragraph on p. 1,
6. *Consultation Principles 2018*, accessible at https://assets.publishing.service.gov.uk/government/uploads/system/uploads/attachment_data/file/691383/Consultation_Principles__1_.pdf (last accessed 25 July 2022).

(k) consultations should not normally be launched during national or local election periods.

The reform of JR became a Conservative priority because of a string of judicial decisions quashing government decisions and actions which some ministers and the Judicial Power Project (an off-shoot of Policy Exchange, a right-leaning think-tank) regarded as evidence of judicial over-reach, hosting on its website critiques of controversial judgments.[7] JR was not the Conservatives' only target; they were also unhappy about the Human Rights Act 1998 (HRA). Commitments to reform or repeal it had been in the party's general election manifestos since 2005.[8] Their manifesto for the 2019 General Election[9] responded to two interventions by the Supreme Court in the process of the UK's withdrawal from Europe: the first holding that the Government could not use the royal prerogative power of international relations in 2016-2017 to trigger the process without statutory authorization;[10] the second holding that the Prime Minister's advice to the Queen to prorogue Parliament in November 2019 to facilitate reaching an agreement with the European Union (EU) was unlawful.[11] They exacerbated irritation about use of the 'principle of legality' as a ground of JR of decision-making by the Attorney General and the Investigatory Powers Tribunal despite statutory provisions aimed at preventing such review, and of regulation-making by Ministers.[12] The manifesto undertook to 'update' both the Act and administrative law 'to ensure that there is a proper balance between the rights of individuals, our vital national security and effective government' in the light of complaints that courts and

7. *See* https://judicialpowerproject.org.uk/.
8. *See, e.g.*, reference to 'our review of the Human Rights Act' at p. 22 of the Conservative Election Manifesto 2005, *Are You Thinking What We're Thinking? It's Time for Action*, p. 22, accessible at http://newsimg.bbc.co.uk/1/shared/bsp/hi/pdfs/CON_uk_manifesto.pdf (last accessed 1 December 2021), 2010 manifesto, *Invitation to Join the Government of Britain* (London: Conservative Party, 2010), p. 79: 'we will replace the Human Rights Act with a Bill of Rights'. Accessible at https://general-election-2010.co.uk/2010-general-election-manifestos/Conservative-Party-Manifesto-2010.pdf, last accessed 1 December 2021. *See also* Commission on a Bill of Rights, *A UK Bill of Rights – The Choice Before Us* (London, 2012), 2 vols; *Strong Leadership, a Clear Economic Plan, a Brighter, More Secure Future* (London: Conservative Party, 2015), the manifesto for the 2015 election, accessible at https://www.theresavilliers.co.uk/sites/www.theresavilliers.co.uk/files/conservativemanifesto2015.pdf (last accessed 1 December 2021) (with talk of a Bill of Rights at pp. 58, 60); the manifesto for the 2017 election, Conservative and Unionist Party, *Stronger, Together: Our Plan for a Stronger Britain and a Prosperous Future* (London: Conservative Party, 2017), p. 37.
9. *The Conservative and Unionist Party Manifesto 2019, Get Brexit Done, Unleash Britain's Potential* (London: Conservative and Unionist Party, 2019), accessible at https://assets-global.website-files.com/5da42e2cae7ebd3f8bde353c/5dda924905da587992a064ba_Conservative%202019%20Manifesto.pdf, last accessed 1 December 2021.
10. *R. (Miller) v. Secretary of State for Exiting the European Union (Birnie intervening)* [2017] UKSC 5, [2018] AC 61.
11. *R. (Miller) v. Prime Minister; Cherry v. Lord Advocate* [2019] UKSC 41, [2020] AC 373.
12. *See particularly R. (Evans) v. Attorney General* [2015] UKSC 21, [2015] AC 1787; *R. (Privacy International) v. Investigative Powers Tribunal* [2019] UKSC 22, [2020] AC 491; *R. (UNISON) v. Lord Chancellor* [2017] UKSC 51, [2020] AC 869. For critique of the use of the 'principle of legality' for this purpose, *see* Jason N. E. Varuhas, 'The Principle of Legality' (2020) CLJ 578-614.

the HRA had skewed 'the relationship between the Government, Parliament and the courts'.[13]

To avoid appearing to meddle with constitutionally important institutions for party-political purposes, the Conservatives envisaged establishing a Constitution, Democracy and Rights Commission to examine 'broader aspects of our constitution', including inter-institutional relationships, 'the functioning of the Royal Prerogative; the role of the House of Lords; and access to justice for ordinary people' as well as the 'ability of our security services to defend us against terrorism and organised crime'.[14] This grand plan was overtaken by events, especially the COVID-19 epidemic. Instead, the Government established two more narrowly focused panels to review JR and the HRA respectively.

The review of JR, launched in July 2020, aimed 'to guarantee that judicial review is available to protect the rights of the individuals against an overbearing state, while ensuring that it is not abused to conduct politics by another means or to create needless delays'.[15] The terms of reference were to examine trends in JR, particularly of central government's policies and decision-making, and consider how citizens' legitimate interest in testing the lawfulness of executive action could be balanced with effective government under the law, particularly considering codification of non-justiciability and grounds of review, remedies for different kinds of errors, powers and subject-matters, and measures to streamline JR. The judges subsequently invited the panel to consider ending JR of Upper Tribunal decisions concerning permission to appeal, so-called *Cart* reviews.[16] The terms of reference ignored other means of accountability and redress, and the complementary role of JR where political accountability failed. The panel later quoted Lord Reed's observation that litigation over Brexit had come at a time when the working relationship between the Government and Parliament had not been operating smoothly enough to offer other systems of accountability and redress.[17]

13. The Independent Review of Administrative Law (IRAL) panel later noted that its establishment 'was in part a response to the Supreme Court's decisions in the two Brexit cases' and concerns influenced by the Judicial Power Project: *The Independent Review of Administrative Law*, CP 407 (London: HMSO, 2021), para. 20.
14. *Get Brexit Done, Unleash Britain's Potential*, *supra* n. 9, p. 48.
15. https://www.gov.uk/government/groups/independent-review-of-administrative-law last accessed 3 December 2021. Concern about litigation challenging democratic processes (e.g., Attorney General Suella Braverman, 'Accountability and the Constitution', speech to the Public Law Project Conference, Judicial Review Trends and Forecasts 2021, on 19 October 2021, accessible at https://www.gov.uk/government/speeches/judicial-review-trends-and-forecasts-2021-accountability-and-the-constitution, last accessed 6 December 2021) is taken into account by judges (e.g., *R. (SC) v. Secretary of State for Work and Pensions* [2021] UKSC 26, [2022] AC 223) but underestimates the importance of allowing marginalized people and groups compensating for weaknesses in the democratic process (e.g., David Feldman, 'Public Interest Litigation and Constitutional Theory in a Comparative Perspective' (1992) 55 *MLR* 44-73).
16. *R. (Cart) v. First-tier Tribunal* [2011] UKSC 28, [2012] 1 AC 663, SC.
17. *The Independent Review of Administrative Law*, paras 25 and 29, referring to HL Constitution Committee, Annual Evidence Session with the President and Deputy President of the Supreme Court, 4 March 2020, p. 2.

Required to report to the Lord Chancellor by 31 January 2021, making the review a rushed job, the panel[18] published a call for evidence on 7 September 2020 and also sent Government Departments a questionnaire giving generous opportunities to highlight perceived problems with JR. Conscious that the review 'was in part a response to the Supreme Court's decisions in the two Brexit cases' and concerns voiced by the Judicial Power Project,[19] the panel sought evidence on the practice of JR, including 'notable trends' and the impact and effectiveness of courts' rulings.[20] The closing date for evidence was 19 October 2020,[21] allowing six weeks for responses. This was later extended by one week, but was still less than the 12 weeks regarded as normal by the Code of Practice on Consultation in 2008 and a very short period given the importance and complexity of the subject.[22] Responses nevertheless came from 16 central government Departments, the Scottish and Welsh Governments, the Crown Prosecution Service, NHS Resolution, Ofsted, Planning Inspectorate and Serious Fraud Office, two county councils and seven local authorities. Submissions were also received from 35 individuals and 173 groups and non-governmental organizations. The panel did not publish the evidence, but some individuals and organizations made their evidence available on their own websites or on the website of the UK Administrative Justice Institute.[23] The panel and its secretariat worked wonders in the time available to analyse the material and prepare a balanced, judicious report supported by a mass of valuable data, although statistics relating to *Cart* reviews required to be supplemented in the Government's response to the report.

In its report, the panel noted that its review formed 'a small part of a debate that has smouldered, and sometimes burst into flames, over many years', that there 'is not, never has been and is unlikely to be, a fixed idea of the "appropriate place" of judicial review in the constitution',[24] and that adjudicating between individuals' grievances and effective government was only part of JR's task. JR also contributed to good government under the law more generally; responses from Departments did not

18. Members were Lord Faulks QC (Chair), barrister and cross-bench peer (but formerly former a Minister of State for Justice under David Cameron between 2013 and 2016 who had resigned in protest over Theresa May's decision to appoint Liz Truss, a non-lawyer, as Lord Chancellor and Secretary of State for Justice); Professor Carol Harlow QC (LSE); Vikram Sachdeva QC, a barrister with practice including public law; Professor Alan Page (University of Dundee); Celina Colquhoun, a barrister specializing in planning and environmental law; and Nick McBride, Lecturer in Law (Pembroke College, Cambridge).
19. *The Independent Review of Administrative Law*, CP 407 (London: HMSO, 2021), para. 20.
20. Call for evidence, p. 4. The panel examined only UK-wide and England and Wales matters (although inevitably it had to take account of the implications of judicial review of UK-wide powers and duties diverging from that of devolved functions for the law in devolved jurisdictions): *ibid.*, and *see* the report, *The Independent Review of Administrative Law*, CP 407 (London: HMSO, 2021), Ch. 5.
21. IRAL Secretariat, Ministry of Justice, *Does judicial review strike the right balance between enabling citizens to challenge the lawfulness of government action and allowing the executive and local authorities to carry on the business of government?*
22. *The Independent Review of Administrative Law*, para. 1.
23. https://ukaji.org/2020/11/04/collection-of-responses-to-the-independent-review-of-administ rative-law-iral/ (last accessed 7 August 2022).
24. *The Independent Review of Administrative Law*, Introduction, p. 11, paras 21-22.

evidence disproportionate cost or inconvenience arising generally from JRs.[25] The panel thought that the case for major changes, such as putting the grounds of JR on a statutory footing, or defining the conditions for non-justiciability or for judicial treatment of parliamentary processes, had not been made out. The disadvantages of codification would outweigh the advantages,[26] and, while Parliament could of course legislate as it pleased (for example, to reverse the effect of individual decisions), it would not be practicable to legislate to set out the circumstances in which judges should exercise restraint in conducting review.[27] Ouster clauses were justifiable in particular circumstances, although they would face critical scrutiny in Parliament and would need to be carefully drafted to overcome judicial suspicion of them on constitutional grounds.[28] Standing and time limits should not be tightened; indeed, the requirement for proceedings to be brought 'promptly' even within the three-month period might usefully be removed.[29]

The panel recommended parliamentary legislation on only two matters: to prevent *Cart* reviews by protecting Upper Tribunal decisions on permission or leave to appeal through a suitably drafted ouster provision;[30] and to allow courts (if courts do not achieve it themselves) to suspend quashing orders for a set period in order to provide flexibility in certain cases.[31] It also recommended that there should be guidance on when interveners should be permitted,[32] and that the Civil Procedure Rules Committee should consider removing the requirement that, within the three-month time limit for applying for JR, there should be no requirement to act 'promptly',[33] and providing for an extra step in the process of filing a Reply, to be filed within seven days of receipt of the Acknowledgement of Service.[34]

Responding to the report in March 2021, the Lord Chancellor, Robert Buckland, announced that the Government accepted the panel's recommendations for only limited change,[35] and reassuringly endorsed the panel's view of the importance of mutual respect and confidence between politicians and judges.[36] He accepted that legislating to define grounds of review and areas which would be non-justiciable would be likely to be excessively complex without producing greater clarity. He noted, however, that, if the development of new grounds of review and restriction of the scope of non-justiciable matters continued, the Government would need to consider 'whether proposing legislation on these and other broader constitutional questions was

25. *Ibid.*, p. 16, paras 34-36.
26. *The Independent Review of Administrative Law*, Ch. 1.
27. *Ibid.*, Chs 1 and 2.
28. *Ibid.*, Ch. 2.
29. *Ibid.*, Ch. 4.
30. *Ibid.*, Ch. 2.
31. *Ibid.*, Ch. 3.
32. *Ibid.*, para. 4.108.
33. *Ibid.*, paras 4.148-4.149.
34. *Ibid.*, para. 4.158.
35. Ministry of Justice, *Judicial Review Reform: The Government Response to the Independent Review of Administrative Law*, CP 408 (London: HMSO, 2021), para. 10.
36. *Ibid.*, paras 119-120, endorsing the panel's comments, *The Independent Review of Administrative Law*, Conclusions, para. 15.

needed'.[37] His moderation was out of step with the wishes of other Ministers, including the Prime Minister Boris Johnson. Mr Buckland's reluctance to push ahead with more radical restrictions of JR led the Prime Minister to dismiss him from the post of Lord Chancellor and Secretary of State for Justice in September 2021 and appoint Dominic Raab, a long-standing critic of the HRA and JR, in his place.

Mr Raab quickly suggested that the Government might introduce wider legislative changes to JR in the Judicial Review and Courts Bill. He specially mentioned courts' involvement in the planning of major infrastructure projects, a desire to make the Supreme Court the ultimate arbiter of rights under the European Convention on Human Rights (ECHR) to the exclusion of the European Court of Human Rights (although without withdrawing from the Convention system, so leaving the UK potentially in breach of international law), and a wish to 'protect Parliament' from what he called 'judicial legislation' by allowing ministers to reverse judicial decisions with which they disagree (although it is not clear whether this would be prospectively by way of primary legislation or, far more worryingly, retrospectively and perhaps even by way of subordinate legislation over which Parliament would have little control).[38]

The Government's increasingly robust stance led to a further consultation on suggestions for clarifying the effect of ouster provisions by reversing some effects of the expansive interpretation given to 'jurisdictional error' in the decades after *Anisminic Ltd. v. Foreign Compensation Commission*,[39] and legislating to provide for most errors of law in the form of misuse, rather than absence, of power to make decisions voidable rather than void, including breach of the 'principle of legality' as that was used in the *UNISON* case[40] and standard grounds of review (apparently including breach of natural justice).[41] The Government sought a way of drafting effective ouster clauses and clarifying what might amount to a sufficient justification for and limits to them.[42]

Another possibility was to provide for judicial remedies to have only prospective, not retrospective, effect. This was a more significant threat to the rule of law than merely suspending the effect of a remedy until the period of suspension ended. It would greatly increase the risk of a person being denied an effective remedy for harm flowing

37. Ministry of Justice, *Judicial Review Reform: The Government Response to the Independent Review of Administrative Law*, CP 408 (London: HMSO, 2021), para. 46.
38. *See* The Sunday Telegraph, 17 October 2021. For commentary, *see* Mark Elliott, 'Undermining the Rule of Law? A Comment on the Justice Secretary's Sunday Telegraph Interview', accessible at https://www.youtube.com/watch?v = MfOWpnmo8Rw (last accessed 2 December 2021). *See also* Tom Newton Dunn and Jonathan Ames, 'Boris Johnson Plans to Let Ministers Throw Out Legal Rulings', *The Times*, 6 December 2021.
39. [1969] 2 AC 147. *See, e.g.*, discussions in *Pearlman v. Keepers and Governors of Harrow School* [1979] QB 56, CA, *per* Lord Denning MR; *In re Racal* [1981] AC 374; *Boddington v. British Transport Police* [1999] 2 AC 143 at 154 *per* Lord Irvine of Lairg LC; *R. (Lumba) v. Secretary of State for the Home Department (JUSTICE and others intervening)* [2011] UKSC 12, [2012[1 AC 245 at para [66] *per* Lord Dyson; *R (Privacy International) v. Investigatory Powers Tribunal* [2019] UKSC 22, [2020] AC 491.
40. *R. (UNISON) v. Lord Chancellor* [2017] UKSC 51, [2020] AC 869.
41. Ministry of Justice, *Judicial Review Reform: The Government Response to the Independent Review of Administrative Law*, CP 408 (London: HMSO, 2021), para. 81.
42. *Ibid.*, paras 89, 91, 92, quoting Laws LJ in *R. (Cart) v. Upper Tribunal* [2009] EWHC 3052 (Admin) at [99] and Lord Sumption and Reed in *R. (Privacy International) v. Investigatory Powers Tribunal* [2019] UKSC 22 at [210].

from unlawful governmental action. The Government's main aim, however, was to make it more difficult to challenge subordinate legislation to uphold constitutional principles or support a class of vulnerable people. Such challenges can have significant implications for public finances and government policy, so there is a respectable argument for giving remedies prospective effect only. The Government suggested a presumption that any remedy in challenges to statutory instruments should have only prospective effect, but also, less justifiably, that quashing orders should always be suspended in all JRs or at least that there should be a presumption in favour of suspending them.[43]

Consulting on these further ideas showed transparency about the Government's thinking and indicated openness to argument despite the strength of some Ministers' views. This new consultation ran for six weeks to 29 April 2021, bringing the time devoted to formal, written consultations over the process as a whole to 13 weeks, more than the norm of 12 weeks suggested in the Code of Practice for Consultations in 2008. The Ministry of Justice also conducted a series of online round tables with experts from the UK and some other common-law jurisdictions and within the civil service.

In July 2021, the Government published its response,[44] at the same time introducing to the House of Commons the Judicial Review and Courts Bill. Responses had convinced it not after all try to legislate for theoretical matters such as the scope of nullity. On the other hand, it had decided to press ahead with its plan to allow judges to make quashing orders prospectively only, with a general presumption in favour of making any quashing order either suspended or prospective-only, not limited to JR of statutory instruments. The Government also favoured making the ouster clause to *Cart* JRs a model for effective ouster clauses in those circumstances where there is a sufficient justification for them. Yet even after the Bill was published the Government continued to consult experts on its provisions by way of an online round table on its provisions.

In the Second Reading debate,[45] the clauses on JR were immediately a focus of controversy. Angela Crawley (Scottish National Party) described them as 'part of a broader drive to increase the power of the Executive, to limit oversight, and to reduce the ability to seek judicial remedy in the courts and to hold this Government and Governments after them to account'.[46] Clause 1 proposed to insert new section 29A into the Senior Courts Act 1981 extending courts' powers by allowing them to suspend quashing orders or limit their retrospective effect. Courts would have to take into account factors in new section 29A(8) including the interests and expectations of litigants and third parties and 'any other matters which appear to the court to be relevant'. A prospective-only quashing order would be made only if the successful litigant still received an effective remedy; such cases were likely to be rare. A suspended quashing order would have full retrospective effect once the period of

43. Ministry of Justice, *Judicial Review Reform: The Government Response to the Independent Review of Administrative Law*, para. 11.
44. Ministry of Justice, *Judicial Review Reform Consultation: The Government Response*, CP 477 (London: HMSO, 2021).
45. HC Hansard, 26 October 2021, vol. 702, col. 189 ff.
46. *Ibid.*, col. 218.

suspension expired, unless also made prospective-only. Other JR remedies were unaffected. The impact on effectiveness of JR seemed limited. The previous day David Davis MP (Conservative) had written in *The Guardian* that the provisions 'tip the scales of law in favour of the powerful',[47] but they were mild in their effects compared with measures which 10 Downing Street and Mr Raab himself would have preferred.

More troubling was the proposed statutory presumption that quashing orders would be suspended or given only prospective effect. Subsections (9) and (10) of new section 29A would have provided that, in cases where the court has decided to make a quashing order but 'it appears to the court' that suspending the order or making it prospective only 'would, as a matter of substance, offer adequate redress in relation to the relevant defect', the court would have been obliged to suspend the quashing order and/or make it prospective only 'unless it sees good reason not to do so', taking account of the considerations listed in new section 29A(8). Fears were expressed on all sides of the House that the presumption could deprive victims of redress.[48]

Clause 2 also generated criticism. It proposed to insert a new section 11A into the Tribunals, Courts and Enforcement Act 2007 providing that a decision or purported decision by the Upper Tribunal to refuse permission or leave to appeal 'is final, and not liable to be questioned or set aside in any other court' (proposed new section 11A(2), (7)). Furthermore, the Upper Tribunal 'is not to be regarded as having exceeded its powers by reason of any error made in reaching the decision', and 'the supervisory jurisdiction does not extend to, and no application or petition for judicial review may be made or brought in relation to, the decision' (proposed new section 11A(3)). This triple attack on JR was supplemented with proposed new section 11A(6) which prevented litigants from evading the preclusive provision by seeking JR of the First-tier Tribunal.

It was informed by provisions proposed by the then Labour government in the Nationality and Immigration (Treatment of Claimants, etc.) Bill in 2003-2004, but not ultimately enacted, to exclude courts from most immigration matters. In *Privacy International* the majority had regarded those provisions as having made the exclusion of JR abundantly clear.[49] But that provoked concern on two counts: first, constitutional objections to excluding access to courts on questions of law; second, concern that the Government would use the formula to exclude JR in many contexts without offering criteria for assessing whether an ouster clause would be justifiable in different circumstances, risking unnecessary and over-extensive protection for public administrators from judicial accountability.[50] Nevertheless, the Bill received its Second Reading by 321 votes to 220.

---

47. David Davis, 'Be Warned: This Government Is Robbing You of Your Right to Challenge the State', *The Guardian*, 25 October 2021, accessible at https://www.theguardian.com/commentisfree/2021/oct/25/judicial-review-peoples-right-fight-government-destroy-courts-undemocratic.
48. *See, e.g.*, Sir Robert Neill (Con), HC Hansard, vol. 702, at col. 205; Anne McLaughlin (SNP), *ibid.*, at cols 210-211.
49. *R. (Privacy International Ltd) v. Investigatory Powers Tribunal* [2019] UKSC 22, [2020] AC 491 at [111] *per* Lord Carnwath, [165] *per* Lord Lloyd-Jones.
50. *See, e.g.*, Jeremy Wright (Con), HC Hansard, vol. 702, at col. 212.

Scrutiny by the Public Bill Committee included a further stage of public consultation. The Committee received written evidence on JR from 17 individuals and organizations and heard oral evidence from 16 individuals in sessions on 2 November 2021.[51] Discussion focused again on fears that clauses 1 and 2 would, in different ways, reduce effectiveness of remedies for victims of unlawful governmental action. The presumption in favour of suspending quashing orders or giving them only prospective effect attracted criticism on practical as well as principled grounds. As it would be an unusual case in which it would be appropriate not to give a remedy to people who had been held to have suffered as a result of unlawful action, and the presumption was anyway weak in view of conditions for and exceptions from its operation, it was not clear what its point was beyond signalling the Government's unhappiness about judicial intervention. Lord Anderson would later describe the provision in the Lords as 'a curious and misshapen thing'.[52] As Dr Jonathan Morgan argued, the provision would be more legitimate if monetary compensation were available to claimants instead of a quashing order,[53] but not all unlawfulness can be financially compensated.

Clause 2, the ouster to end *Cart* JRs, was again criticized as an assault on the rule of law and for denying justice to a significant number of vulnerable individuals. But some Conservative members wanted the Government to go still further. Sir John Hayes proposed new clauses to reverse the effect of *Privacy International* in order to reassert the power of Parliament over the courts.[54] Andy Slaughter (Labour) pointed to the threat that proliferation of such clauses would:

> risk undermining the UK's constitutional framework and the protection against abuses of Executive power. Judicial review is generally available only where there is no other recourse to an alternative remedy. The effect of ouster clauses is therefore often to shut down all routes to challenge a decision, even if the decision has been based on a misinterpretation of the law .... [T]he Executive should not be able to go beyond their legal limits without the potential for accountability in the courts.[55]

But James Cartlidge said that the Government were considering an ouster clause to reverse *Privacy International*, and were 'not closed-minded to the possibility of going further on judicial review .... [M]y right hon. Friend says we do not go far enough; I would say that we go this far at this time'.[56]

The Government saw off all amendments to clauses 1 and 2 until Third Reading in the Lords, when Lord Anderson's amendment to remove the presumption from the

51. Written evidence is accessible from https://bills.parliament.uk/bills/3035/publications and transcripts of the oral evidence sessions are at https://publications.parliament.uk/pa/bills/cbill/58-02/0152/PBC152_JudicialReview_1st-11th_Compilation_23_11_2021_REV.pdf (last accessed 8 August 2022).
52. HL Hansard, 27 April 2022, vol. 821, col. 284.
53. Jonathan Morgan, 'In Praise of Flexibility: Clause 1 of the Judicial Review and Courts Bill (2021)', UK Const L Blog (23 September 2021) and 'IRAL's Missing Remedy: Compensation for Unlawfulness', UK Const L Blog (12 October 2021) (both available at http://ukconstitutionallaw.org/).
54. HC Hansard, 23 November 2021, vol. 704, cols 401-405.
55. *Ibid.*, cols 408-409.
56. *Ibid.*, cols 413, 414.

Bill was passed and the Government decided not to reverse it in the Commons.[57] Lord Anderson commented that the proposal had been so odd 'that I did wonder when moving against it whether it was always intended to be the hunk of meat that would be thrown off the back of a sledge to distract the ravening wolves'.[58] That is by no means impossible.

The threat of further incursions on JR, however, is clear. What are now sections 1 and 2 of the Judicial Review and Courts Act 2022 do not exhaust the Government's ambitions. In August 2022 *The Guardian* newspaper reported a leaked Ministry of Justice document setting out possible options for Mr Raab who is said to be 'minded to consult on further reforms to judicial review', including adjusting the intensity of review to be applied in different situations, imposing a costs penalty on claimants who are held to lack standing, and reversing the effect of controversial cases such as *Evans* and *Privacy International*.[59] It is at least reassuring that there would be a further round of consultation.

This account of consultations on reforming JR seems to me to paint a generally encouraging picture, whether or not one agrees with the measures which have so far emerged. Despite the Government's clear predisposition to rein in JR, well understood by respondents to the consultations, the Consultation Principles were well implemented. Referring issues to a specially appointed, independent panel went beyond the requirements of the Principles; it was necessitated by the recognition of the constitutional importance of JR, the desire to avoid appearing to be meddling with the constitution on party-political grounds, and the stalled manifesto commitment to a Commission to conduct a more wide-ranging review of the constitution. Despite its unpromising terms of reference and what some regarded as loaded consultation questions, the panel produced a balanced report, engaging clearly with consultees through a variety of channels and giving appropriate weight to evidence and experience. Consultees understood the issues, and on the whole (as the 2008 Code of Practice, paragraph 3.2, suggested) it was reasonably clear where there was room to influence policy development and what had already been decided. The Government's response and second round of consultation made even clearer the Government's thinking and what scope there was to influence it. The Government's measured response to the second consultation and the substance of clauses 1 and 2 of the Judicial Review and Courts Bill showed that they had listened to and to some extent been influenced by the consultees' comments, and the Public Bill Committee's evidence-taking added a third stage of consultation. Throughout the process, various methods of consultation were used to reach different audiences and attract a range of opinions and types of expertise and experience. The total period devoted to consultation during the

57. The Lords removed the presumption on Third Reading, HL Hansard, 6 April 2022, vol. 820, cols 2089 et seq. *See also* Commons' consideration of Lords' amendments, HC Hansard, 26 April 2022, vol. 712, cols 601 et seq.
58. HL Hansard, 27 April 2022, vol. 821, col. 284.
59. Haroon Siddique, 'Leaked Report Suggests Dominic Raab Trying to Curb Judges' Powers', *The Guardian*, 7 August 2022, accessible at https://www.theguardian.com/politics/2022/aug/07/leaked-report-suggests-dominic-raab-trying-to-curb-judges-powers (last visited 19 August 2022).

iterative process was well in excess of 12 weeks, albeit that the proposals subject to consultation changed somewhat over the course of it. The Ministry of Justice's receptiveness to consultees' views was particularly impressive in view of the strength of feeling in some other parts of Government and the Conservative Party more generally that JR was out of hand and needed to be tightly controlled.

This does not mean that the process was apolitical. The consultations took place against a background of the Government's determination not only to be seen to be doing something to limit judicial interference in politics and public administration but to give additional, effective protections to politicians and administrators against JR where that could be justified. This aim could be said to have had electoral support; despite some concern about the effect on the rule of law, the changes discussed here could not be said to be excessively draconian (except perhaps in the removal of *Cart* JRs) or undemocratic. But this is not the end of the story. Political pressure is likely to lead to a further round of legislation with a Lord Chancellor less inclined to listen to criticisms than was Mr Buckland, who lost his job because of his openness to argument. The next stage of consultation might prove to be more dominated by political steers than the previous rounds.

The Government has given fair warning.[60] Mr Johnson as Prime Minister was reported to have wanted the Judicial Review and Courts Bill to reverse the effects of the two Brexit judgments of the Supreme Court and make more radical reforms.[61] Lord Howard of Lympne, Conservative former Home Secretary and party leader, criticized as 'deeply disappointing' the Bill's 'minimalist' character, and hoped that it was not the Government's last word on reform of JR.[62] Mr Johnson, Mr Raab and the then Attorney General, Suella Braverman, were said to favour legislation allowing Ministers to change the law, perhaps retrospectively, to relieve themselves of decisions which they dislike.[63] Ms Braverman has spoken of wanting to ensure that we do not ignore 'the single most important decision-maker in our system: the British people'.[64] This suggests that she considers the Government to represent and be accountable to the people rather than Parliament, replacing parliamentary sovereignty with a form of populist ministerial supremacy as a justification for reducing the powers of the judiciary.

The consultations on JR described here show that the process can work well but that outcomes depend significantly on the views of individual ministers and on pressure of other events. It will be interesting to see how future consultations are conducted and whether Rishi Sunak as Prime Minister gives high priority to reform of human-rights law and further adjustments to JR under changing economic, social and political conditions.

60. *Judicial Review Reform*, para. 46; above, text at *supra* n. 37.
61. Tom Newton Dunn and Jonathan Ames, 'Boris Johnson Plans to Let Ministers Throw out Legal Rulings', *The Times*, 6 December 2021.
62. HL Hansard, 7 February 2022, vol. 818, col. 1360.
63. Tom Newton Dunn and Jonathan Ames, 'Boris Johnson Plans to Let Ministers Throw out Legal Rulings', *The Times*, 6 December 2021.
64. Rt Hon Suella Braverman MP, 'Accountability and the Constitution', speech to the Public Law Project Conference, Judicial Review Trends and Forecasts 2021, on 19 October 2021, accessible at https://www.gov.uk/government/speeches/judicial-review-trends-and-forecasts-2021-accountability-and-the-constitution (last accessed 6 December 2021).

CHAPTER 26

State Aid in the Prism of Public Interests. For a Renewed Approach

Mario P. Chiti

1 INTRODUCTION

The notion of State aid, as elaborated in decades of Community law and jurisprudence, deserves a profound revision; both by taking occasion from the banking events that I have been investigating in recent researches and by reconsidering its objective and subjective significance in general.

The considerations made below on the current notion of State aid therefore start from the crises of some European banks in the last decade; but it goes beyond banking. In particular, by examining the unexpected intersection between the economic fallout of the COVID-19 pandemic and the issue of State aid. Within the limits of this essay we will try to configure a new meaning of aids of State capable, on the one hand, of jointly covering the subjects concerned by subsidies and various "State" incentive measures; on the other hand, brought back to a delimited value as unequivocally provided for by the letter of the European Treaties; since the European Economic Community (EEC) Treaty of Rome in 1957.

We are aware that it seems unlikely to question an (apparent) solid jurisprudence of the judges of the Union on State aid; but upon careful analysis, the same jurisprudence appears more varied and open than what is apparent from the dominant vulgate, as will be exemplified with sentences of particular importance, even in the banking sector. Furthermore, the fact that legal science continually returns to these issues in a problematic way is not only a foregone confirmation of the importance of the issue of State aid, but also of a partial dissatisfaction with the dominant notion.

The themes examined here in the perspective of banking crises are mainly five, with some related themes which we will briefly mention: (a) the "opacity" of the notion of State aid; (b) the continuing tension of the issue of State aid with Italian Constitution;

(c) the criticalities of the system of European sources of State aid; (d) the limits of the judicial protection of the interested parties in the current context; also with regard to compensation for damage; (e) the overwhelming role of the European Commission in relation to other institutions (especially the Council and the European Central Bank) and to national authorities.

2 THE LIMITS OF THE TRADITIONAL NOTION

Starting from the way in which State aid is understood in European Union (EU) law, with direct effects on the laws of the Member States, it should be noted that the generic notion of State aid—such as to cover any public measure capable of distorting competition—badly suited to the provisions of the Treaties; questioning the first criterion for the interpretation of the "law," which also in EU law is the literal one. This interpretative criterion is aimed at understanding the meaning of a provision on the basis of the words and linguistic formulas used; acknowledging that, as noted by the Court of Justice, EU law may use a terminology that is its own and which may also have a different meaning from that of the same terms in domestic law.

The current Treaty on the Functioning of the European Union (TFEU) provides for provisions on State aid (Articles 107-109) that are almost identical to those contained in the 1957 Treaty (Articles 92-94) establishing the European Economic Community. One of the very few cases of continuity in the discipline of a subject in the decades of the progress of European integration.

Reading these provisions, the four conditions emerge from the EEC Treaty which the jurisprudence has then refined to ascertain which of the public aids must be considered "State aid." They are, as is well known: the reference of the resource to the State, even indirectly; the existence of an economic advantage for the beneficiary, including the issue of aid selectivity; the harm that resources can cause to competition; the further damage that these resources may cause to trade between Member States. It is never useless to remember that, in order to be able to speak of State aid, such conditions must exist cumulatively.

2.1 The Letter of the Treaties and the Broad Interpretation of the Commission

The reference to the literal data of the Treaties—as mentioned, substantially unchanged since 1957—is not superfluous because if those provisions were examined today by Robinson Crusoe's "Man Friday," unaware of the Community events, they would inevitably be read by him as provisions applicable to limited cases of resources granted by the State, which correspond to the four conditions mentioned above; given their rigorous definition and the necessary cumulative nature. Basically, "Friday" would have the well-founded impression that State aid, as provided for in the Treaties, represents only a part of public aid, which in general remains subject to the rule of free granting of public subsidies, under the conditions provided for by national regulations. The interpretation of "Friday" would therefore collide with that of Crusoe, his mentor, who instead developed his knowledge in the cultural context of the EEC, first, and then of the Union; where the literal interpretation of this part of the Treaty has always been disregarded.

Beyond the metaphor, the literal formulation of the grid of conditions provided for by the Treaties to be able to qualify public subsidies as State aid suggests (rectius should, given what was then the dominant reading) that public subsidies are not in themselves prohibited; especially when they are aimed at safeguarding the stability of the markets. In any case, the possible State aid must be ascertained from time to time, with an assessment subject to the judicial review of the European courts.

A clear confirmation, again based on the literal data of the Treaties, is the discipline in the field of competition of agreements between companies. Agreements are always prohibited; public subsidies are referred to only when they can be configured as State aid when the four conditions are met.

On the other hand, the Commission has taken a broad interpretation of State aid since the first experience following the 1957 Treaty of Rome. The major measures taken by the Commission have in fact always assumed implicitly, without specific demonstration, that the measures were public aid; so as to extend the objective scope of the notion to almost any type of subsidy (with the exception, here insignificant, of their quantitative dimension). The same happened for the subjective sphere, tracing almost all public subsidy measures to the "State"; even when provided by "eccentric" subjects with respect to the State.

In this way the precise subjective and objective perimeter of the notion has been dispersed. The famous *Tercas* case is exemplary in banking matters for the delimitation of the subjective sphere, in which the Commission has—illegitimately, as ascertained by the judges of the Union—attributed to the State the rescue measure decided by the Interbank Fund deposit protection. The multiple measures taken by the Commission to regulate State subsidies to businesses to counter the economic consequences of the COVID-19 pandemic are exemplary then, for the delimitation of the objective scope; immediately (the Communication of March 13, 2020, Com 2020-112 final, is a few days after the full-blown start of the pandemic) the Commission considered these measures as State aid, when a reading by every sensible person would have brought the pandemic event back to the category of "exceptional events" (Article 107, paragraph 2, letter b) which, as such, allow the granting of subsidies that remain outside the scope of State aid.

2.2 A Full Spectrum Functional Notion

The Commission's extensive practice in configuring State aid has been substantially suffered by the Member States and not effectively opposed by the Court of Justice, as regards both the area of aid and the exercise of discretion by the Commission. In fact, the assertion that "the Commission has a wide discretionary power, the exercise of which implies evaluations of an economic and social nature that must be made in a community context, is constant. The Court, in carrying out the review of the legality of the exercise of this freedom, cannot substitute its own assessment on the matter for that of the competent authority, but must limit itself to establishing whether the latter is not vitiated by a manifest error or by misuse of powers" (case C-88/03). The assessment of the compatibility of aid measures with the internal market, pursuant to Article 107(3) TFEU, falls within the exclusive competence of the Commission, which acts under the control of the judges of the Union (*see* judgment of November 21, 2013, *Deutsche Lufthansa*, C 284/12, paragraph 28; and others similar, including the judgments of September 11, 2008, *Kronofrance*, C 75/05 P and C 80/05 P, paragraph 59; March 8, 2016; *Greece v. Commission*, C 431/14, paragraph 68).

There remains the only limit of a specific verification, case by case. Indeed, even in the matter under consideration, the adoption of a communication such as that on the banking sector of 2013 does not release the Commission from its obligation to examine the exceptional circumstances that a Member State invokes in order to request the direct application of Article 107, paragraph 3(b) of the TFEU and, where appropriate, to justify its refusal to grant such a request (judgment cited on March 8, 2016, *Greece v. Commission*, C 431/14 P, paragraph 72).

Basically, the notion of State aid is good for everything and functional to the interests of the Commission, which in this way extends its role also to preventive control over national support policies for businesses, without even waiting for the full deployment of national measures. But it is also functional, it should be noted, in the interest of the Court of Justice—the community institution par excellence, together with the Commission—to ensure the "useful effect" of EU law in this field as well.

The consolidated situation is however showing progressive criticalities. The most striking case is that, already mentioned, of the policies to combat the negative economic effects of the COVID-19 pandemic. The absorbing reason is that the pandemic is in itself, without misunderstanding, an "exceptional event" that keeps public subsidies outside the State aid discipline, by express provision of the Treaties (the aforementioned Article 107, paragraph 2, letter b). In the same sense, it is also worth noting that the pandemic is a general phenomenon by definition, which affects the whole of Europe and beyond; in the face of the pandemic, the States have tried to support companies everywhere in crisis. These were not measures to distort competition, but aimed at preservation—for as much as possible—of the pre-pandemic situation, stabilizing the markets.

However, contrary to the provisions of the Treaties, even in the very significant case of the pandemic the Commission took action (*see* the Communication of March 19, 2020) even before the States decided the first measures; thus giving rise to an *ex ante* control over national economic policies, substantially to condition them (but in an inadmissible way) even when they want to involve redistributive measures completely outside the perimeter of State aid.

For such cases, with great meta-juridical wisdom and Manzoni-like words, Natalino Irti observed: "It is time for historical crises, whether they are financial or social or health, when individuals realize they are alone, and look into tall with wet and pleading eyes (…). Individuals and businesses seek refuge in the unitary structures of coexistence (…). What on earth can the State do if not help?"[1]

3 STATE AID AND THE ITALIAN CONSTITUTION

The second theme for reflection concerns the continuing tension between the principles of our Constitution and the issue of State aid; as well as the relevance of recent constitutional jurisprudence that rebalances the relationship between our legal system and that of the Union.

It is undisputed that at the time of the Constituent Assembly (1946-1947) the topic of subsidies was not directly dealt with for the unexpressed, but shared by all, the idea that public subsidies were a necessary part of the country's reconstruction and modernization policies. Moreover, public intervention in that period was common to all European States, winners and losers; implemented with substantially similar formulas in the new Constitutions (such as the German Grundgesetz).[2]

Considering that only ten years later the Treaty establishing the EEC was approved with original rules, such as in terms of competition, it is legitimate to consider that the Community innovations should be compared and dimensioned with the interventionist welfare State model of some founding countries of the EEC, such as Italy and Germany.

It is therefore not surprising that the issues of State aid and competition have entered the Italian constitutional debate and the jurisprudence of the Constitutional Court very slowly. It is a phenomenon not of cultural and institutional backwardness, but of progressive awareness of the various developments of the EU and of the original jurisprudence of the Court of Justice, on general principles including the primacy of European law, which with some reluctance the Constitutional Court had to give space starting since the *Granital* judgement (n. 170/1984). The decisive thrust finally came from the constitutional reform of 2001 (Constitutional Law No. 3/2001) with the specific reference to the notion of competition. The issues of State aid and competition have been reported by the Constitutional Court mainly in Article 41 of the Constitution, combining the freedom of enterprise with the public governance of the economy and with "social utility," under the watchful control of the Constitutional Court.

Approximately a decade followed, in which constitutional jurisprudence and the courts of last resort followed the positions of the judges of the Union without particular specificity (at this stage not only of the Court of Justice, given the increasingly frequent disputes for direct appeal to the Court pursuant to Article 263 of the TFEU).

---

1. N. Irti, *Preface*, in E. Bruti Liberati, M. De Focatis & A. Travi (eds.), *State Aid, General Profiles and Energy Issues*, Wolters Kluwer, Milan, 2020, XVII.
2. M. Luciani, *State Aid in the Italian Constitution and in the European system*, in E. Bruti Liberati, M. De Focatis & A. Travi (eds.), *State Aid, General Profiles and Energy Issues*, Wolters Kluwer, Milan, 2020

3.1 The Principle of Primacy in Recent Constitutional Jurisprudence

This situation of jurisprudential and scientific "calm" has gradually succumbed to the configuration of a more articulated relationship between the two legal complexes, for two main reasons: a rethinking of the characteristics and scope of the principle of the primacy of EU law; the upheavals caused by the great financial and economic crisis that opened in 2008.

The principle of the primacy of EU law over the law of States, posed by dating back to the Court of Justice case law (starting from the *Costa* case, C-6/64), even though it is not consolidated in the Treaties, is one of the most important general principles for the European legal system; indeed, it represents the architrave. In the Declaration no. 17 annexed to the Lisbon Treaty, it is reported the opinion of the Council Legal Service dated 22.7.2007, according to which "it is clear from the jurisprudence of the Court of Justice that the primacy of Community law is a fundamental principle of Community law itself. According to the Court, this principle is inherent in the specific nature of the European Community. At the time of the first ruling of this consolidated jurisprudence (*Costa v. Enel*, 15.7.1964, case 6/64) there was no mention of primacy in the Treaty. The situation remains unchanged to this day. The fact that the principle of primacy will not be included in the future treaty does not in any way alter the existence of the principle itself and the existing jurisprudence of the Court of Justice."

The Constitutional Court had—as mentioned—progressively adapted to the principle of primacy and to all its various implications; after initial resistance. However, she had been sensitive to the theory of "counter-limits," according to which the primacy does not apply when the law of the Union puts at risk the fundamental principles of our Constitution or the rights of individuals. Exceptional hypotheses, but still possible as demonstrated also by recent cases (the so-called *Taricco* jurisprudence: ord. Constitutional Court n. 115/2018).

Recently, the reference to the theory of counter-limits—which concerns specific situations, not casting doubt on the principle of primacy in general—has however been integrated into the jurisprudence of the Constitutional Court by a more articulated approach to EU law. This orientation appears entirely acceptable as the counter-limits theory appears dated with respect to the evolution of the relations between the EU legal system and the legal systems of the Member States. In the direction of better defining the scope of the principle of the primacy of EU law, to be valid only for European norms of a constitutional nature in a formal or objective sense. Because not everything that is provided for in the Treaties can simplistically be considered the constitutional right of the Union.

As the German jurist Dieter Grimm pointed out, EU law "suffers" from an excess of constitutionalism (over-constitutionalism).[3] When can a Constitution be defined as such when it is formed, as in EU law, by three acts (Treaty on European Union (TEU),

3. D. Grimm, 'The Conquest of Constitutionalism and Its Perspectives in a Transformed World', *Science & Politics*, 2018, 131.

TFEU and Charter of Fundamental Rights), a complex of 466 articles (the TFEU alone has 358 articles)? Not to mention the many Protocols, which also have primary rank.

The principle of primacy must therefore be valid only for European norms of an objectively constitutional nature (a part of the primary norms) and for those disciplines that are directly implemented; but not for everything that has been regulated on this basis.

The main effect of this jurisprudence is—frankly speaking—that the Constitutional Court has reduced the scope of the principle of primacy because it goes beyond the theory of counter-limits. In fact, it constantly intends to verify the absoluteness of the European principle with reference to our relevant constitutional principles in the case under examination. Therefore, in the joint examination of the interests at stake, of the Union and our constitutional system, the prevalence of the former is not a given and inevitable.

The reference to these general developments is not an eccentric parenthesis with respect to the issue under consideration, because it entails a direct consequence, unexpected by many: the issue of State aid is not legally to be resolved only in EU law.

The recent crises of these first two difficult decades of the new century have highlighted problematic knots in the national law/EU law relationship that must be considered according to the new approach followed by the Constitutional Court. Suffice it to think, for banking law, of the effects that the new regulation established with the European banking union has determined for principles and rights of primary constitutional importance, such as property rights. Likewise, for the measures to combat the economic consequences of the pandemic due to the tension between the limits set by the Commission with the communications limiting State aid and the principles of social solidarity and equality.

From this point of view, therefore, new scenarios are opening up for State aid, to be considered not only in the perspective of EU law but in that of the not strictly hierarchical combination with constitutionally relevant national public interests.

4 THE ATYPICAL SOURCES OF THE STATE AID FRAMEWORK

A third exemplary theme to confirm the need for a revision of the notion and scope of State aid is the sources of the matter.

Examining the decades-long experience of the State aid discipline, an apparently surprising fact emerges: the clear prevalence of atypical acts, in particular of "communications," compared to primary legislative acts and other typical acts (obviously the parameter of typicality is the provisions of Treaties, especially the TFEU: Articles 288 et seq.).

One explanation lies in the structural characteristics of the legal acts of the Union, when placed in the context of State aid measures. Regulations and directives are legislative acts for which the Treaties provide for complex approval procedures, which are usually quite slow. They are therefore not very suitable for disciplining problems that require rapid measures that are open to equally rapid changes. The other typical acts (recommendations and opinions) also have, albeit to a limited extent, the same procedural problems; above all they are almost never appropriate to regulate matter. On the other hand, atypical acts are the most suitable, because they usually arise from simple and quick procedures (almost all carried out within the Commission); for this reason they can be easily amended or replaced. They are often configured as acts with binding effects, even if this is the most debatable issue as we will now see.

Among the atypical acts, the Commission's "communications" are the most commonly used also in terms of State aid. Communications are a *genus* only in the name, given that, as demonstrated for some time,[4] they can have a very different content: interpretative, recognition, additive, regulatory, self-limited the powers of the Commission, binding or not, etc. In particular, there is a diversity of purposes—which translates into a different objective context—between communications that provide for *ex ante* incentive measures, with "rewards" for actions to be performed (therefore a propulsive nature) and communications for *ex post* checks, of compensatory character in the face, for example, of natural disasters or other exceptional events (such as now the pandemic).

Experience shows that for communications the qualification of soft law acts is not valid to distinguish them as non-binding acts from binding acts, but to reiterate only the atypical character. Most of the communications, as configured by the Commission, are of a binding nature because they are directly prescriptive for the recipients or because they pose significant procedural and motivational constraints.

4.1 Use and Abuse of Communications

It is precisely banking matters that demonstrate these characteristics of most of the Commission's communications, with some cases of communications of genuine organic discipline on the subject; widely used for State aid, as they allow very rapid interventions; as demonstrated by the repeatedly cited Communication from the Commission of March 19, 2020 relating to measures to combat the foreseeable economic consequences of the COVID-19 pandemic, e.g., Communication 2016/C-262/01) and the conditions under which State aid can be considered compatible with the internal market (e.g., Communication 2019/C-247/01).

Such a continuous and incisive use of communications by the Commission, especially in terms of State aid, however, calls into question essential principles of European law and the common constitutional heritage of the Member States; such as the rule of law, in its implications on the sources of law (Article 2 TEU), the effectiveness of judicial protection (Article 19 TEU and Article 47 Charter of Fundamental Rights), the same principles of democracy (Article 2 TEU), because any intervention by the European Parliament and the other institutions is normally excluded in the communication processing procedure. It is therefore an abuse of the communication tool, which cannot be accepted supinely.

4. M. Antonioli, *Communications of the European Commission and National Administrative Acts*, Giuffrè, Milan, 2000.

Member States have not so far reacted significantly to this practice; the circumstance does not find a convincing explanation. Individuals, natural and legal persons, have instead used the protection tools offered by the Union system for the protection of their rights, either with direct appeals pursuant to Article 263 TFEU which with the preliminary reference procedure pursuant to Article 267 TFEU.

The Court of Justice intervened with significant judgments, which pointed out the characteristics of communications compatible with the system of EU law. For the matter examined in this book, the *Kotnik* judgment (19 July 2016, C-526/14) is exemplary, according to which: "the adoption of the rules of conduct contained in the aforementioned communication had a limited effect on the Commission's self-limitation exercising its discretion, in the sense that, if a Member State notifies the Commission of a State aid project which complies with those rules, the latter must, in principle, authorize such a project. On the other hand, the Member States retain the right to notify the Commission of State aid projects that do not meet the criteria set out in that communication and the Commission may authorize such projects in exceptional circumstances."

"It follows—continues the Court—that the communication on the banking sector is not suitable for creating autonomous obligations on the part of the Member States, but is limited to establishing conditions that aim to ensure compatibility with the internal market of State aid granted to banks in the context of the financial crisis, which the Commission must take into account in exercising the wide margin of discretion which it has under Article 107(3)(b) TFEU.

Taking into account the foregoing considerations, the first question must be answered by declaring that the communication on the banking sector must be interpreted as meaning that it has no binding effect on the Member States." The conclusion has a general character on the subject of the possible binding value of communications, beyond banking matters.

Despite these clear principles, the Commission continued to issue regulatory and binding communications, violating the prerogatives of the Court of Justice which, pursuant to Article 19 TEU, is responsible for ensuring compliance with the law in the interpretation and application of the Treaties; as well as the principle of sincere cooperation between the institutions.[5]

Finally, a decisive intervention by the Court is expected to bring the Commission back within its own enclosure, configuring communications as acts primarily aimed at self-limiting the discretionary powers of the Commission itself, rather than addressed to the Member States and interested parties.

Even from the point of view of the sources of the State aid discipline, the traditional vulgate therefore appears worthy of reconsideration.

5. M.P. Chiti & V. Santoro (eds.), *The Palgrave Handbook of European Banking Union*, Palgrave Macmillan, New York, 2019.

5 THE JUDICIAL PROTECTION OF THE INTERESTED PARTIES: OPEN QUESTIONS

After the cue occasioned by the theme of the Commission's "communications," the question of the protection of interested parties at the source of decisions on State aid is worth further reflection.

In principle, all the acts of the institutions and bodies of the Union are subject to the judicial review of the European judges. The related discipline is, as is well known, provided for in the Treaties, in the related protocols and in various regulatory acts. The model of judicial protection provided for in the Union is particularly complex; therefore rightly considered with full positivity by the national constitutional courts, including our Court (*see* judgment no. 142/2018): "system of judicial protection of the Union, founded on two levels—European and national—communicating with each other, which it must be considered complete and coherent, where it must be recognized that the private individual who has an interest in it benefits, in any case, (at least) from a procedural remedy to assert the illegality of the Commission's decisions."

However, with regard to the effectiveness of the protection, experience shows serious problems. The standing to appeal is subject to significant limitations, despite the positive modification of Article 263 TFEU intervened with the Lisbon Treaty and greater flexibility in the management of the "*Plaumann* jurisprudence" (from the homonymous judgment C-25/62). The timing of the judgment is a serious problem, considering that the average time of a ruling on a preliminary reference is one and a half years (but entering into national proceedings that have been suspended in the meantime) and that the same time is the average of a direct appeal (to the General Court, if presented by natural and legal persons). The precautionary measures are taken by the judges of the Union with extreme selectivity.

These characteristics are in themselves sources of concern from the perspective of the right to effective judicial protection ensured in principle by the Charter in Article 47; yet they are already negative in the matter considered here.

5.1 The *Tercas* Case

The *Tercas* case is exemplary. Appeals at first instance before the Court pursuant to Article 263 TFEU (T-98/16, 196/16 and 198/16) against the Commission decision 2016/1208 of December 23, 2016, took more than two years to reach a judgment (March 19, 2019) and pending the decision there had been the conditions for interim measures. The Commission then appealed and the second judgment (C-425/19) came to an end (March 2, 2021) almost five years after the contested decision; when the story had reached an irreversible point.

It has been said by many commentators that the Commission has decided the fate of a significant piece of the Italian banking system with a decision that the Community judges have legally demolished. Very true, also because in the meantime the Interbank Fund could not be used as it could (and should) be and the banking crises have taken on resolution procedures different from the one that the "Fund model" could wisely ensure. Furthermore, from the perspective of the right to effective judicial protection, the limits of the current EU procedural system have clearly emerged, which do not appear adequate to the importance and urgency of the situations that can be determined in banking matters. The Court itself recognized the problem in the aforementioned *Tercas* judgment, when (paragraph 55) it observed that the blocking of support by the Fund prevented other similar interventions. This is all the more serious because, as will be seen shortly, the margins for obtaining compensation for the unjust damage suffered for non-contractual liability of the Commission are very limited even in the event of a positive outcome of the appeals.

The issue of State aid, as it is now concretely managed by the Commission and poorly conditioned by the judges of the Union, therefore represents an important opportunity to initiate a reform of the procedural rules of the Union, especially with special, accelerated and super accelerated rites. The reform model can be found precisely in some European administrative justice systems which have with success adapted the general model to the emerging needs in the economic sector (public contracts and other issues), with very rapid procedures, [remedies///] in simplified form, etc., ensuring appropriate times for pressing and evolving situations; just what the EU procedural system does not ensure.

In addition to the aspects now considered, judicial protection is conditioned by the limited degree of appreciation made by the judges of the Union. It is in fact a criterion constantly affirmed by the Community jurisprudence that in the matter of State aid the Commission has a wide technical discretion, before which the judge must limit itself to establishing whether the Commission's assessment is vitiated by manifest error and misuse of powers.

5.2 The Role of National Judges

For excellent substantive reasons (to ensure effective protection for the interested parties) it has been proposed[6] (among others, by R. Caranta and C. Schepisi) that national judges assume a greater role than the current one; which mainly focuses on the verification of the notification obligations of aid projects by the Member States and on compliance with the obligation not to provide aid until the decision of the Commission. In particular, on the basis of recent rulings of the Italian Constitutional Court, such as n. 142/2018, it was highlighted that national courts could explicitly identify State aid by interpreting Article 107, paragraph 1, TFEU; if necessary by contacting the Commission for clarification or by raising questions for a preliminary ruling to the Court of Justice. Going beyond the provisions of the Commission's 2009 Communication on the application of State aid legislation by national courts (2009/C-85/01).

6. Among others by R. Caranta, *The Control by the Administrative Judge on Compliance with the Obligation of Prior Notification and Standstill*, in E. Bruti Liberati, M. De Focatis & A. Travi (eds), *State Aid, General Profiles and Energy Issues*, Wolters Kluwer, Milan, 2020, XVII. C. Schepisi, 'The Compatibility Assessment of State Aid: Some Reflections on the Compatibility and Limits of the Commission', *Riv. Reg. Mercati*, 2019, 319.

Still, according to consolidated case law, the implementation of the State aid control system falls, on the one hand, to the Commission and, on the other, to national judges, with distinct but complementary roles. If the Commission has the exclusive competence to assess the compatibility of State aid with the market, the national courts, on the other hand, "ensure the protection of the rights of individuals in the event of non-fulfillment of the obligation of prior notification of State aid to the Commission." Article 107 TFEU, in fact, does not enjoy direct effect, so that "individuals cannot [...] by virtue of Art. 92 (TEC, now Art. 107 TFEU) contest the compatibility of aid with Community law before national courts, nor ask the latter to rule, principally or incidentally, on any incompatibility."

It is true, as recognized in the cited sentence no. 142/1968 of the Constitutional Court, that in the matter of qualification and admissibility of State aid there is an "exclusive competence of the Commission, which operates under the control of the EU judge, with the consequence that national courts are not allowed to rule on point," but it is no less true that "national courts can interpret and apply the notion of aid and the State to assess whether a measure adopted without following the prior checking procedure should be subject to it or not, without prejudice, in case of doubt, the possibility of asking the Commission for clarification or, alternatively, of referring the question for a preliminary ruling to the Court of Justice." This means that the violation of the constitutional parameters invoked must be excluded if the private individual concerned is not individually prejudiced by the Commission decision, but is simply part of a wider category which is affected by it. This subject "may in any case contest, regardless of the deadline for the action for annulment, its validity before the national courts so that they ask the Court to rule on the matter with a preliminary request."

In spite of everything, a wider role of national courts in State aid matters remains conditioned by the concentration of competences in the Commission; operating therefore at the European level. Whereas in the nearby issue of competition there is a more articulated relationship between the competences of the Commission and the national authorities. The allocation of decision-making powers directly reverberates on the jurisdiction, European or national.

5.3 The Limited Effectiveness of the Damage Action

A further problematic aspect of the current State aid discipline is given by the limited possibilities of compensation for the damage unjustly suffered by the interested parties, before the Union or national courts.

Firm and constantly reiterated by the Court of Justice that the interested parties have the right to take action to obtain compensation for the damage, the examination of European jurisprudence shows that cases in which the interest of the plaintiffs has actually been satisfied are very rare. Both for procedural reasons and for the restrictive attitude of the judges; especially with regard to the recognition of legitimate expectations by the beneficiaries of the aid. Equally in national jurisprudence.

As for the damage actions against the EU, the disappointing results so far are mainly due, as mentioned, to a restrictive position of the European judges; despite that

Article 340, paragraph 3, TFEU is in itself unexceptionable and recalls the general principles common to the law of the Member States (which do not pose particular obstacles to action for damages). In turn, actions for damages against the State—quite frequent in relation to public measures provided as a result of natural disasters—have clashed with a rigid view of the judges regarding the legitimate expectations of the interested parties; almost always denied.

In the banking sector, the *Tercas* case fully exemplifies these criticalities. The two judges of the Union sanctioned the aforementioned 2016 Commission decision as illegitimate because the Commission was unable to demonstrate with legal certainty the transferability of the Fund's measures to the State. As already mentioned, this decision was the direct cause of the irreversibility of the crisis of that Bank and wider effects beyond; the two trials before the judges of the Union did not come to an end before the situation of irreversibility of the crisis took place. These are "school conditions" to hypothesize a damage action against the Union (the Commission), given the ascertained serious and manifest violation of Union law. In reality, in the face of the unsatisfactory jurisprudence of European judges, it seems unrealistic that any damage action could have a positive outcome.

6 SOME COLLATERAL PROBLEMS

Other issues relating to State aid deserve to be examined as they compete with the questioning of the traditional notion; but we can only briefly mention them here.

Thus, the unresolved relationship between the Commission and the European Central Bank on the subject of State aid; considering at least that the European Central Bank (ECB), albeit a technical institution par excellence, does not seem to have a direct influence on Commission decisions. Similarly, the relationship between the Commission and the Member States does not appear appropriate; in this case with an absolute imbalance in favor of the former, where it would seem necessary to have a new articulated model not very different from that envisaged for the competition.

In this regard too, it is necessary to call into question the criterion that the State aid discipline is addressed to the Member States and not to companies, as in competition. In fact, this is only formally true, given that in substance the States are the intermediary with respect to the position of the companies concerned, the true recipients of the rules.

Another subject that has not been thoroughly investigated so far, on which it is worthwhile to reflect is that of the relations between the Commission and the Council on the subject of the discipline of State intervention in banking matters. The proposed solution[7] could be to follow the procedure pursuant to Article 118, paragraph 4, and Article 109 which leaves the decision on the categories of State aid that can be exempted from the procedures provided for in paragraph 3 of Article 108.

Then, an issue worthy of further study is the anomalous tension for the development of the European banking union, with its articulated organizational and

7. L. Scipione, *State Aid and Banking Crisis*, Giappichelli, Turin, 2022.

procedural forms, and the continuing "monopoly" of the Commission on the subject of State aid. This issue is partly similar to that already mentioned in the Commission/ECB relations, but which goes even further by investing the role of the other subjects of the European banking union, including the "competent national authorities." One of the most critical aspects of this unresolved relationship is the discipline of banking "resolutions," where the decisions of the ECB and the Single Resolution Board seem to have no influence on those of the Commission in terms of State aid.

7 CONCLUSIONS

From the overview of the major problems of the current State aid discipline, it can be confirmed that the notion of aid which has long been consolidated must necessarily be revised.

This applies in particular to the following points: a better definition of the notion of State aid, such as to overcome its current "opacity"; a more correct use of the sources of the matter, especially with reference to the "communications" of the Commission; a decision-making procedure for State aid in which, without prejudice to the centrality of the Commission, there is dialog with the ECB and with the national authorities; improvement of the forms of protection of the interested parties, especially in the procedural aspects; a more incisive jurisprudence of the judges of the Union both to enforce the principles they have established in the matter and to broaden the conditions for compensation for unjust damage.

CHAPTER 27

Regulate the Use of Algorithms in the Administration: Why? How?

Jean-Bernard Auby

In Tribute to Patrick Birkinshaw

One of the major challenges administrative law has to face nowadays—and Patrick Birkinshaw has for long been quite aware of that[1]—is about determining and conceptualizing the consequences of digitalization in administration.

Everyone can observe the impressive development of digitalization in the functioning of public entities. Then we are realizing that such evolution raises a lot of legal issues, and among them some which the law will not master easily.

Such are some of the impacts of the increasing use of algorithms in administration (section 1). This move is clearly leading to various difficulties, concerning either the algorithms considered by themselves (section 2), or the insertion of algorithms in the administrative processes (section 3). And it appears that the existing law can only partially solve these difficulties (section 4). Therefore, making some additional regulation seems to be an unavoidable step (section 5).

1 THE INCREASING USE OF ALGORITHMS IN ADMINISTRATION

One can say that the digitalizing move in public administration has been following a triple path: one towards the digitalization of administrative procedure and of the relationship between public institutions and citizens, another one towards a pervasive

1. Patrick Birkinshaw and Mike Varney, *Government and Information Rights: The Law Relating to Access, Disclosure and Their Regulation*, 5th ed., 2019.

presence of data and the associated mechanism of algorithms, a third one towards some "macro" phenomena like platforms, networks, smart cities and the like.[2]

Within this overall evolution, algorithms occupy a singular position because, in fact, their use produces effects right inside decisional processes. It tends to shift the decisional logics by substituting to the usual purely human—whether individual or collective—judgment for an assessment of situations and determination of solutions which are partially based upon a formal analysis usually shaped in mathematical formulas intended to become computer programs.

(1) We are witnessing a dramatic increase in the use of algorithms in administration. One can bet that in the long term, all public institutions will be led to use algorithms to carry out one task or another. At present, however, it is in the performance of certain administrative functions especially that the use of algorithms manifests itself in the most apparent way.

Financial and especially fiscal administrations were pioneers. They notably use today algorithms in the context of the fight against tax evasion.[3] Similarly, public services in charge of security are constantly increasing users of algorithms to deal with various risks: crime, natural risks, fires, etc. They use it, for example, to fight against terrorism.[4]

The ambit of education is also home to the use of algorithms. In France, everyone has heard about "Parcoursup," an algorithm that has been used for several years to guide the orientation of applicants for access to universities. This algorithm has even also given rise to litigation, concerning both the possibility of having it communicated and about its substantive legality.[5]

The use of algorithms to process certain health data is also developing in order to inform public decisions in this field.[6] Actually, regret has been expressed by many experts that it was not used more in the fight against COVID-19.

Algorithms are also sometimes used in the preparation and performance of administrative contracts. Administrative contractual procedures are increasingly digitized. At the stage of contract formation, algorithms can analyze the documents provided by companies. They are likely to be used soon to assess tenders. They could also help anti-corruption authorities to detect corruption in the award of public contracts.

The use of algorithms should also appear in the implementation of public contracts by combining blockchain and smart contract technology in order to better identify—and lock in—the obligations of each party and, if necessary, allow for the automatic application of penalty clauses or even termination clauses.

2. Jean-Bernard Auby et al., Smart Cities, *European Review of Digital Administrative Law*, 2021, vol. 2, Issue 1 ; Anthony Townsend, *Smart Cities*, Norton & Company, 2013.
3. *See, e.g.*: Caroline Lequesne-Roth, Algorithmes et finances publiques, in Jeremy Bousquet, Thibault Carrère and Sabrina Hammoudi (eds.), L'action publique algorithmique, Mare & Martin, 2023.
4. In the French law, this is explicitly permitted by article L.851-3 of the internal security code.
5. Even before the Constitutional Court: April 3, 2020, n° 2020-834 QPC.
6. Antony Taillefait and Maximilien Lanna (eds.), *Smart Cities et Santé*, Institut Universitaire Varenne, 2019.

Administrative justice, whose operation is already highly digitized, is on the threshold of the use of algorithms as tools to assist in judicial decision-making. For example, the French Conseil d'Etat is experimenting with an algorithm project that could contribute to the identification of litigation series.[7]

(2) Public institutions have recourse to various types of algorithms. In this regard, several points are worth emphasizing.

The first one is that sometimes—and even, it seems, more and more often—public entities use "self-learning" algorithms, that is to say whose internal logic is enriched with information that is drawn from realities that the algorithm helps to regulate. An algorithm for detecting tax evasion, for example, feeds on the cases of fraud that its use makes it possible to detect: its internal logical skeleton is refined as a result. In the same way, a facial recognition algorithm feeds on the identifications it allows.

The second one is that, also more and more often, the logic on which algorithms operate is probabilistic rather than causalistic. Contemporary algorithms—especially those used by the private sector, it is true—are concerned with establishing unambiguous correlations rather than enlightening all causality chains in what they help analyze.

The third one is that the data on which public algorithms feed (we must never forget that algorithms are only useful when there is a need to decide on the basis of complex data) can be personal data: especially in the health, social, tax, etc. domains.

(3) The legal difficulties raised using algorithms in public action can only be correctly apprehended by distinguishing the various scenarios of their insertion into administrative processes

It should first be noted that algorithms are sometimes used by administrations to help them collect data. Video surveillance tools, for example, can be equipped with algorithms that allow them to identify certain realities that they are asked to screen specifically: this is obviously the case when these tools are used for facial recognition.

Then, of course, public algorithms also serve—possibly after fulfilling the previous function—as administrative decision support instruments. They inspire decisions, which can be to launch a tax audit procedure, tighten police surveillance of a place at risk, offer a range of possible university registrations, etc.

2 LEGAL ISSUES ARISING FROM THE USE OF ALGORITHMS IN ADMINISTRATION: ISSUES CONCERNING THE ALGORITHMS CONSIDERED BY THEMSELVES

2.1 Some of These Issues Are Related to the Creation of Algorithms

Among corresponding questions is that of determining who, in a particular public institution, has the power to decide that an algorithm will be designed to solve a given problem.

7. *See* Timothée Paris in Jeremy Bousquet, Thibault Carrère and Sabrina Hammoudi, 2023.

Other issues impact the making of algorithms. These can be crafted within the administration that feels the need for them if it has the corresponding expertise—data scientists in particular. But this expertise often remains absent and the making of the algorithm must then be outsourced, entrusted to a specialized entity. This will be done on the basis of a contract. An important question in the relationship between the designers of the algorithm and the commissioning administration, notably in terms of intellectual property rights on the algorithm: we will come back to this a little later on.

Whether the algorithm is developed within the administration concerned or outsourced, a question of major importance is how one checks that it does not contain faults, in particular that it does not harbor any biases, or misinterpretation of the texts that it helps to implement.

2.2 Various Issues Affect the Very Content of Algorithms

There is one of explainability. Among implications of the principle of transparency, there is the fact that the algorithm must be explainable: that is to say that the authorities which use it are able to explain the approach it follows in order to solve the problem which prompted its making.

Naturally, this is more or less easy depending on the complexity of the algorithm and the level of expertise of the administrative agents. But the logic followed by the algorithms must, in principle always be explicable. A particularly delicate hypothesis, here, is obviously that of "self-learning" algorithms, because the approach they follow to identify the problem they help to deal with evolves in interaction with the realities to which they are applied.

Quite delicate is also the issue of biases. One of the most frequent criticisms of algorithms, and especially public algorithms, is that they may contain non-apparent biases. Examples have been given by authors and sometimes relayed in the public debate: among them, the story of a Chicago school teacher evaluation algorithm, which turned out to harbor a design flaw.[8] The most egregious cases that have been noted concern "self-learning" algorithms, which have been trained with skewed data sets. This type of instrument needs to be explained what it is being asked to identify: if one wants an algorithm to identify cancerous cells, one must first show it images of tumors which will be told to be cancerous or not. If the training data is distorted, the algorithm risks making serious identification errors.

The issue of algorithmic biases should not be viewed too naively, though. As Aurélie Jean,[9] who teaches algorithmic science at the Massachusetts Institute of Technology (MIT), explains very well,[10] any social apprehension of reality inherently

---

8. Cathy O'Neil, *Weapons of Mass Destruction: How Big Data Increases Inequality and Threatens Democracy*, Penguin Books, 2017.
9. Aurélie Jean, *De l'autre côté de la Machine. Voyage d'une scientifique au pays des algorithmes, Editions de l'Observatoire, 2019—Les algorithmes font-ils la loi ?*, Editions de l'Observatoire, 2021.
10. Jean-Bernard Auby, Digitalization as a Challenge for Administrative Law, Administrative Law Facing Digital Challenges, *European Review of Digital Administration & Law*, 2020, vol. 1, Issue 1-2, pp. 7-16 and Jean-Bernard Auby et al., Smart Cities, *European Review of Digital Administrative Law*, 2021, vol. 2, Issue 1

contains biases. Algorithms are developed to solve problems. They are therefore designed according to the way in which their promoters and designers approach the problem. They are inherently biased.

Then some biases are unacceptable This is particularly the case for those who introduce into the algorithms discriminations that the law generally bans: those based on sex, race, social origin, etc. (except of course in cases where these criteria are the basis of a positive discrimination accepted by law).

2.3 Other Issues Related to Transparency of Algorithms

Two questions are to be raised, here. The first one is whether people directly affected by algorithms—essentially addressees of decisions based on them—have access to them, either pursuant to general rules on freedom of information or upon specific rules.

The second one is whether public entities using algorithms are constrained to publish the algorithms they are using, independently from the particular decisional processes within which they do so.

2.4 Finally, There Is What Surrounds the Rights over the Algorithm

Firstly, apart from the rights that interlocutors of administrations may assert in application of transparency, one must question possible encroachments on privacy in algorithmic processes.

In terms of economic rights, secondly, algorithms are sometimes very sophisticated intellectual constructs, which have an objective value commensurate with the help they provide in solving certain problems. The question arises as to whether they are correlatively potential objects of property rights, which would be of an intellectual property nature.

The algorithm itself, the mathematical formula that translates it, cannot be subject to intellectual property because it does not meet the conditions of originality and concreteness required to fall within its scope, but this does not apply to the source code into which the algorithm is translated to make it operable by the computer: it can be protected by a copyright.

3 LEGAL ISSUES ARISING FROM THE USE OF ALGORITHMS IN ADMINISTRATION: ISSUES RELATED TO THE INSERTION OF ALGORITHMS IN ADMINISTRATIVE PROCESSES

"Public" algorithms also give way to various legal problems at the stage of their implementation, whether they are used for data collection (section 3.1) or as decision-making tools (section 3.2). Some specific questions surround the hypothesis of "automatic decisions" (section 3.3) as well as the use of algorithms in the preparation and execution of government contracts (section 3.4), and their position in administrative litigation (section 3.5).

3.1 The Use of Algorithms for Data Collection

Here, what is especially problematic is the collection of personal data that are more or less sensitive in terms of privacy protection: this is especially true when the algorithm is used as part of a surveillance or intelligence system.[11]

These problems are accentuated when algorithm-assisted surveillance is used as a basis for decisions concerning individuals: then, the intrusion into privacy is reinforced by risks of bias and other malfunctions in the algorithm.

Such concerns apply to video surveillance and drones. Video surveillance devices are not necessarily equipped with algorithms: they may simply be visualization tools. But it is increasingly common for them to include algorithmic tools to help identify certain realities. Drones used as surveillance and data collection tools are always algorithmically driven. In both cases, abovementioned risks are particularly present.

As to facial recognition, it necessarily presupposes that the corresponding surveillance tool contains an appropriate algorithm—usually of the "self-learning" type—and the presence of this algorithm creates a particular risk not only of invasion of privacy, but also of misidentification that may have disgraceful consequences—in relations with police, judicial, and so on.

3.2 The Use of Algorithms as Decision-Making Tools

Among the numerous issues which can be raised, here, is, firstly, the determination of when administrations may and may not use algorithms to inform their decisions. Is the use of algorithms restricted to the preparation of individual administrative decisions or can it be extended to the preparation of regulatory decisions or plans? Are there limits to the amount of decision-making content that can be entrusted to the algorithm?

Secondly, it is possible that the use of certain types of algorithms would be restricted: what about "self-learning" algorithms in this respect?

Thirdly, there are issues concerning the influence of the algorithm on the final decision. What may have taken place before the algorithm was decided upon and the time it was requested is important, of course, because it determines, in short, the part of its competence that the administrative authority submits to algorithmic processing: everything depends on what the former has already determined. But the more sensitive aspect is about what happens once the algorithm has been implemented. To what extent will the administrative authority rely on it and adopt the decision it suggests? Or will it question what the algorithm proposes, even call for a collegial deliberation?

11. Eleni Kosta, Algorithmic State Surveillance: Challenging the Notion of Agency in Human Rights, *Regulation & Governance*, 2020.

3.3 Here We Find Ourselves in Front of the Intriguing Hypothesis of "Automatic" Decisions Based on an Algorithm

The idea that digitization of public action would lead to a proliferation of "automatic decisions" is put forward somewhat indiscriminately in the literature. Yet, it must be handled with caution.

Strictly speaking, it is about decisions that would be the direct result of computer processing—which may be the source code of an algorithm—without any human intervention—individual or collective—being likely to verify what the processing induces and to correct it if necessary before the decision is taken.

In practice, this seems to happen quite rarely. The opposite impression comes from the fact that, as soon as computers are involved in decision-making processes, there is a feeling that the latter are by nature "automated." Of course, they are automated to a certain extent—the extent to which the computer is needed—but this part may be very limited, it may be restricted to a few intermediate calculations that the computer will make faster than a human being.

That said, there are many cases in which administrations rely totally or almost totally on what an algorithm they have inserted into their decision-making mechanisms suggests. This is particularly true in the case of decisions based on profiling the individuals targeted by these decisions: the simple fact of entering a "box" can then lead to a certain type of decision on the granting of aid, authorization, registration, etc.

It is obvious that this kind of procedural arrangement cannot be accepted without strong caution since it entails the risk of biases or erroneous decisions without any final human supervision susceptible to correct them.

3.4 The Use of Algorithms in Public Contracting

The use of algorithms in the preparation and performance of administrative contracts is also the source of some more or less difficult issues.

Their intervention at the stage of contract formation needs to be regulated notably in order to guarantee both transparency and confidentiality.

In the implementation of public contracts, the use of blockchains should reasonably be submitted to express legal permission since it substitutes the formal traditional fixing of obligations with a kind of "autonomous" one.[12]

3.5 Algorithms and Administrative Litigation

In the relations between algorithms and administrative litigation, two groups of issues are progressively appearing: some are about the treatment of disputes arising from the use of algorithms by administrative authorities, others are about the use of algorithms in the functioning of administrative justice.

12. Kelvin Law and Eliza Mik, Pause the Blockchain Revolution, *International and Comparative Law Quarterly*, vol. 69, January 2020, pp. 135-175.

On the first side of the coin, there is, firstly, the question of whether algorithms can in and by themselves be the subject of an action before the courts. Obviously, it can only be resolved if there is agreement on the legal nature of algorithms. Are they in and by themselves administrative acts? It is difficult to admit because, even in the case of "automatic" decisions, the algorithm does not decide anything: it produces an effect only because the decision-making authority has included it in the process of its decision. Algorithms more probably belong to some kind of "guidelines".

Then, secondly, there are a series of issues concerning the legality review of decisions based on algorithms. In the context of which appeals can this challenge take place? The most probable answer is that, since the algorithm has been inserted into the procedure for drawing up the decision, it is quite simply in the direct appeal against it that it can be discussed.

Thirdly, questioning moves on to the aspects from which the algorithm may be criticized in the context of an appeal against the final decision. This question can be addressed, first of all, in terms of external legality. It will have to be determined, for example, whether the administration has not committed a negative incompetence if it has waived the task of guiding its decision too largely on the algorithm: without having taken sufficient care to surround its design with preset criteria. The question may also be asked whether the way in which the algorithm was used in the preparation of the final decision was not the cause of a procedural defect. For example, because it was used in a case where it should not have been. Or because there was a lack of transparency, for example by not letting parties know that an algorithm was used.

What about internal legality control? Various questions may also be asked here. The algorithm used in the procedure for elaborating an administrative decision is part of the reasoning behind the decision: it is part of its motivation. If the algorithm cannot be explained, is there not an infringement of reason-giving rules? If the algorithm misinterprets the legislation or regulation it helps to apply in the decision-making process, is there not an error of law? Or, if the algorithm oversimplifies the situations it is used to analyze and decide on, is there not a failure to apply rules requiring special consideration to circumstances?

The algorithm may also have flaws that could lead to a violation of the rule of law in the final decision. If it misinterprets the law or regulation it is helping to apply, it may cause the final decision to be directly contrary to that law or regulation. If it has a particular bias, this may lead to the final decision being in breach of the principle of equality.

Then, fourthly, dysfunctions in algorithms can cause damages and might lead to administrative liability. The latter should certainly be attached to the final decision and not to the algorithm itself, of which it is hard to see how it could cause damage without being linked to a decision-making mechanism—even if it is "automatic." It would nevertheless be possible to ground the liability upon the algorithm's imperfections in so far as they would have contaminated the decision.

Which liability regime should apply to such a scenario. When the defectiveness of the algorithm—or perhaps of the data on which it is fed—is clearly established, liability for fault may be envisaged if it can be shown that this defectiveness was indeed the cause of the damage caused by the final decision. Is it conceivable that, in certain cases, fault could be presumed? Perhaps in cases where, without a clear explanation—for example because the algorithm, being of the "self-learning" type, has drifted in its logical content in a way that has not been controlled—the algorithm has led to aberrant decisions, grossly discriminatory for example. Can we imagine cases of no-fault liability? Perhaps in cases where the use of an algorithm was particularly prone to aberrant decisions. But these conjectures may prove useless, because they correspond to hypotheses in which the final decision is illegal and therefore a source of fault-based liability.

4 SHORTCOMINGS OF THE EXISTING LAW[13]

Based on the limited comparative information available, it can be said that the regime of "public" algorithms in general still leaves room for many gaps.

What does exist has essentially a threefold origin. At the international level, it is mainly European law that provides solutions, both substantial and insufficient. In national legislation, the issues relating to algorithms and, more broadly, to digital administration are to be found either in more general legislation or in specific texts: Italy, for example, has a "code of digital administration." There is still some rather exploratory case law here and there.

The resulting diagnosis reveals three groups of issues.

(1) Some are relatively well covered by existing law. This mainly concerns two of them.

Firstly, there is the issue of citizens' access to the algorithms used by the administration. This access is often guaranteed, either by general laws on access to public data or by specific texts.

In French Law, for example, since 2016, the general administrative procedure act—"code des relations entre le public et l'administration"—contains two related provisions, one concerning individual access to algorithms, the other concerning their publication. Article L.311-3-1 of the code provides that "an individual decision taken on the basis of algorithmic processing includes an explicit mention by informing the person concerned. The rules defining this processing as well as the main characteristics of its implementation are communicated." And, Article L.312-1-3 imposes on "administrations ..., with the exception of legal persons whose number of agents or employees is less than a threshold set by decree, (to) publish online the rules defining the main algorithmic treatments used in the performance of their missions when they are the basis for individual decisions."

Secondly, what is also already regulated enough is the protection of personal data collected by means of algorithms or used in the context of decision-making processes using algorithms. In European law, this protection is ensured both by the European Convention on Human Rights and by the 2016 Regulation on Data Protection.

National laws—or even national constitutions—often add their own rules.

13. Jean-Bernard Auby, Digitalization as a Challenge for Administrative Law, Administrative Law Facing Digital Challenges, *European Review of Digital Administration & Law*, 2020, vol. 1, Issue 1-2, pp. 7-16.

(2) Issues that should not be too difficult to master

(a) It is to be expected that laws—of democratic states at least—will succeed without too much difficulty in regulating the mere recourse to algorithms by administrative authorities and the type of algorithms they may use.

In some jurisdictions, for example, limits have already been placed on the use of self-learning algorithms. Thus, the French Constitutional Council indicated that the use of this type of algorithm in the elaboration of an individual decision should be accompanied by a control of its evolution by the data controller: "the data controller must ensure control of the algorithmic processing and its evolution in order to be able to explain, in detail and in an intelligible form, to the data subject the manner in which the processing has been implemented in his or her regard. As a result, algorithms that are likely to revise the rules they apply themselves, without the control and validation of the controller, cannot be used as the sole basis for an individual administrative decision."[14]

(b) Limits to the possible use of "automatic" decision-making mechanisms have started to be established. Both European and various domestic laws have laid down a principle of prohibition of decision-making mechanisms that are based exclusively on automated processing when they lead to decisions affecting personal rights.

The Council of Europe Convention of January 28, 1981, for the Protection of Individuals with regard to Automatic Processing of Personal Data establishes a principle of prohibition. It is taken up in European Union (EU) law by the General Data Protection Regulation of 2016, Article 22 of which states: "The data subject shall have the right not to be subject to a decision which is exclusively based on automated processing, including profiling, and which produces legal effects concerning him or her or significantly affects him or her in a similar way."

Article 22(4) of the Regulation makes the prohibition absolute when sensitive data within the meaning of Article 9 are involved, i.e., "personal data revealing racial or ethnic origin, political opinions, religious or philosophical beliefs or trade-union membership, as well as the processing of genetic data, biometric data for the purpose of uniquely identifying an individual, data concerning health or data concerning the sex life or sexual orientation of an individual." It accepts some exceptions otherwise, though.

(c) Issues created by the intervention of algorithms in contractual contexts do not seem insuperable, provided that means be found in order to combine transparency and confidentiality.

By contrast, the use of blockchains to frame performance of public contracts could be difficult to reconcile both with the necessity of an administrative supervision of that performance and with principles admitted

14. Conseil Constitutionnel, 12 juin 2018.

by case law in order to deal with incidents in the implementation of public contracts.

(d) With time, judges in charge of administrative litigation could become familiar with reviewing efficiently decisions taken on the basis of algorithms.

They will have to pronounce on the legal nature of algorithms, but this does not seem to be too tricky. After having ruled that they were by themselves administrative acts, Italian administrative courts changed their mind[15] and now seem to prefer what is apparently the most reasonable view, i.e., that they are like guidelines.

Then, courts will have to determine what rules of procedure apply to the use of algorithms; German courts, for example, have excluded it when it would deprive concerned citizens of a right to participate in the making of the decision.[16]

They will have to decide how to exercise their review on decisions' motivation, as well as on whether the interpretation of the law conveyed by the algorithm is correct.

They will have to design the conditions under which defects in algorithms can lead to administrative liability.

3. The most challenging problems

(a) It is difficult to accept that algorithms used in administrative decisional processes would remain non-understandable by the administration, judges and concerned citizens.

When an algorithm is elaborated, it is important that administrative authorities that have ordered it are strongly associated with its drafting and, finally, remain able to explain to the public the main lines of reasoning the algorithm follows on the problem it is meant to help solve.

As to the judges, they can be assisted by experts, but it is probably also necessary that they receive a sufficient training for them to grasp the broad outlines of algorithms logics.

(b) A delicate question laws will have to cope with is to decide what part of their discretion they can give up to the algorithms.

(c) Another sensitive issue is related to possible use of algorithms in administrative justice as an aid to judicial decision-making.

The functioning of administrative courts is nowadays highly digitized in most of our countries: opening of databases, communication on the Internet, information for

15. Giorgio Mancosu, "Deterministic Public Algorithms Through the Prism of the Italian Case of Teacher Mobility," Revue générale du droit (www.revuegeneraledudroit.eu), Studies and reflections, 2018; Roberto Cavallo Perin and Diana-Urania Galetta (eds.), *Il diritto dell'amministrazione pubblica digitale*, G.Giappichelli editore, 2020.
16. Karen Yeung and Martin Lodge (eds.), *Algorithmic Regulation*, Oxford University Press, 2019.

litigants on the status of their case, dematerialization of access to the courtroom, internal databases, and so on.
But there are also prospects for the use of algorithmic techniques as substantive tools to assist in court decisions.
The most sensitive question, here, is to what extent administrative justice will convert to the use of "predictive" justice methods. This could involve, for example, using algorithms to base judgments on the multitude of precedents concerning the quantification of compensation in matters of liability. Or to use algorithms to facilitate the non-judicial settlement of disputes.

5 REGULATIONS TO BE PUT IN PLACE[17]

Part of pending issues could find their solutions through case-law. Administrative courts seem to be quite aware of the size of the task to be achieved, and they have started to provide solutions, more or less abundantly depending on the country.

But it is clear that some of these issues can only be approached by legislation, in particular when—which is obviously rather frequent—protection of citizens' rights is at stake.

In EU countries, a strategic question is how far it is possible to rely on EU law. It is clear that Member States tend to expect much from the EU, which has already strongly grasped digital issues—with the Data Protection Regulation—and is preparing other pieces of regulation, on artificial intelligence and the like. Yet, sometimes, the fear is expressed that the States would expect too much from the EU, at the point to hesitate to legislate by themselves.

One issue on which they should not wait for EU intervention is the organization of controls exercised on the making of algorithms and on their implementation, especially in view of combating unacceptable biases and legal misinterpretation.

It is regularly proposed that the algorithms—at least those that are the most sensitive in terms of threats to privacy or possible discrimination—be subject to external controls before—if necessary also during—their implementation. This could take the form of audit procedures or certification mechanisms.

17. Fotis Fitsilis, *Imposing Regulation on Advanced Algorithms*, Springer, 2019; Alejandro Huergo Lora (dir.), *La regulacion de los algoritmos*, Thomson Reuters Aranzadi, 2020; Lena Ulbricht and Karen Yeung (eds.), Algorithmic Regulation, *Regulation & Governance*, vol. 16, Issue 1, January 2022, pp. 1-354

CHAPTER 28

Digital Transition of Public Administration in Italy and the EU Right to a Good Administration: Problems and Prospects Also in the Perspective of the Implementation of Italy's Recovery and Resilience Plan

Diana-Urania Galetta

1 INTRODUCTORY REMARKS

In order to be able to address the question of what challenges are imposed on public administration today by the so-called digital transition, it is first necessary to have a clear idea of what 'digital transition' means and what steps it actually entails for our public administrations.

Summing up here what I have discussed in greater detail elsewhere,[1] digital transition implies the use of Information and Communication Technologies (ICT) within public administrations, with the aim of providing services that meet the needs expressed by citizens in a society that has changed profoundly especially thanks to the use of such technologies.[2]

1. This contribution is partly based on previous papers of mine, published over the last five years and to which I will therefore refer by quoting them, from time to time. A previous, Italian version of this paper has been published in Federalismi.it (9 March 2022), at https://www.federalismi.it. All translations from Italian (or other languages) into English are mine and solely my responsibility.
2. *See* D.U. Galetta, *Information and Communication Technology and Public Administration: Through the Looking-Glass*, in D.U. Galetta, J. Ziller (eds), *Information and Communication Technologies Challenging Public Law, Beyond Data Protection*, Nomos Verlagsgesellschaft, 2018, 119.

As it was already explicitly stated in the 2003 EU Commission Communication on the role of eGovernment for Europe's future 'Information and communication technologies (ICT) can help public administrations to cope with the many challenges. However, the focus should not be on ICT itself. Instead it should be on the use of ICT combined with organisational change and new skills in order to improve public services, democratic processes and public policies. This is what eGovernment is about'.[3]

This means that the digital transition is not (and should not be conceived) as an end in itself, to be achieved 'whatever it takes'. ICT are to be seen as a useful means to an end, which clearly needs to be identified in advance.

The introduction of ICT in the context of administrative procedures must serve, first of all, the objective of making public administration more efficient, improving on the one hand the quality of public services provided to citizens and, on the other hand, reducing the related costs for the community, at least in a medium to long term perspective.[4] With this in mind, the reference model is that of *e-commerce*, whose essential value is, precisely, its efficiency.[5]

The introduction of ICT is therefore seen as being closely related to the objective of modernising public administration: ensuring greater efficiency, but also transparency and simplification of its activities and, consequently, improving the quality of relations with citizens, as well as the service provided to them.[6]

In the perspective of this paper, however, the aim identified as an objective would be that of guaranteeing a better satisfaction/realisation of that right to good administration whose reference parameter is Article 41 of the Charter of Fundamental Rights of the European Union (EU). With this in mind, it is necessary to verify whether and to what extent a public administration that makes use of ICT is (or can be) a better public administration in the sense of being more compliant with the canons of good administration codified therein.

In order to do this, it is obviously necessary to examine – also on the basis of concrete examples – the various and numerous problems and critical issues linked to the so-called digital transition of public administration.

3. *See* Commission Communication of 26.09.2003, The role of eGovernment for Europe's Future, Doc. COM(2003) 567 final, at https://eur-lex.europa.eu/LexUriServ/LexUriServ.do?uri=COM:2003:0567:FIN:EN:PDF, 4.
4. *See* W. Sheridan, T,B. Riley, *Comparing e-Government vs. e-Governance*, in *Geospatial World*, 2010, 1.
5. Among others: C. Zotta, R. Amit, J. Donlevya, *Strategies for Value Creation in E-commerce: Best Practice in Europe*, in *European Management Journal*, Vol. 5, 2000, 463.
6. On this point *see* D.U. Galetta, *Public Administration in the Era of Database and Information Exchange Networks: Empowering Administrative Power or Just Better Serving the Citizens?*, in *European Public Law*, Vol. 25(2), 2019, 171.

2 THE DIGITAL TRANSITION OF PUBLIC ADMINISTRATION: THE NECESSARY STEPS AND RELATED ISSUES

2.1 The Dematerialisation of Documents Held by Public Administrations

In order to be able to identify the potentialities and problematic issues related to the use of ICT in the context of public administration, it is first of all necessary to clarify – albeit quickly – the fundamental steps to be taken in order to achieve the so-called 'digital transition'

The very concept of transition (from the Latin *transire*, i.e., 'to pass') identifies 'a change or shift from one state, subject, place, etc. to another'.[7] Therefore, once this transition has been completed, one should, in theory, find oneself before a new and different (better?) public administration than the one from which one started.

The first step of this transition, however, already implies an enormous amount of work, which consists in transforming traditional paper documents and archives into electronic documents and archives;[8] and in abandoning, for the future, the production of 'paper native' documents and opting instead for 'digital native'[9] documents.

Dematerialisation is, in fact, a *conditio sine qua non* to be able to improve efficiency and control of documents, easy sharing of documents and data, storage and security of information, allowing (at least in perspective) savings in time and resources.

Digital files are considered better than traditional paper documents (or those anchored to a physical medium) insofar as they do not take up 'physical' space in offices, can be easily retrieved and copied, and individual contents can be extracted much more efficiently than from paper documents.

However, this is only true in principle. As the complex story of the creation of the National Register of Resident Population (*Anagrafe Nazionale della Popolazione Residente* (ANPR)) in Italy clearly shows: the national database into which all the 7,903 municipal registers have gradually converged since 21 October 2016.[10]

Even more so, as to the creation of the Electronic Health Record (*Fascicolo Sanitario Elettronico* (FSE)).[11] According to Article 12, paragraph 1 of Decree-Law 179/2012, the FSE is 'the set of data and digital documents of a health and social-health nature generated by present and past clinical events concerning the patient, also referring to services provided outside the National Health Service'.[12]

7. *See* at https://www.merriam-webster.com/dictionary/transition.
8. *See* S. Armenia, D. Canini, N. Casalino, *A System Dynamics Approach to the Paper Dematerialization Process in the Italian Public Administration*, in A. D'Atri et al. (eds), *Interdisciplinary Aspects of Information Systems Studies*, Physica-Verlag HD, 2008, 399.
9. That is, obtained using word processing software and transformed directly into PDF (and not by scanning a paper document).
10. At 31 December 2021, only the municipality of San Teodoro, in the province of Messina, was still missing. *See infra*, section 4.2.
11. *See* M. Moruzzi, *La sanità dematerializzata e il fascicolo sanitario elettronico. Il nuovo welfare a 'bassa burocrazia'*, 2014.
12. Decree-Law 179/2012, converted with amendments by Law no. 221 of 17 December 2012 (in Official Gazette no. 208 of 18 December 2012, no. 294).

Apart from the specific problems related to the content of the FSE and its concrete implementation[13] (*infra,* section 4.2.), if one considers the way in which most of the information contained in citizens' Electronic Health Records was initially transferred from a paper file to an electronic one, one finds out that this is in itself an obstacle in achieving the objective of immediate availability of relevant patient information. Dematerialisation has in fact mostly been achieved, at least in the first phase, through the mere scanning of paper documents, which are then converted into non-indexable[14] pdf files. Whereas, in order to allow a real usability of the information contained in the EHF, the indexing of the files certainly represents an essential step.

2.2 The Creation and Necessary Maintenance of Digital Documents and Archives

Even if, with a burst of optimism, one would disregard the problems linked to the dematerialisation of documents mentioned above and imagine a public administration that – having successfully completed the transition to a full and complete dematerialisation of the documents in its possession – has happily moved from paper to digital documents, the problems would still not be over.

If public administrations were capable of producing only truly digital documents (i.e., not merely scanning paper documents), one could eliminate paper archives and mitigate the problems related to the managing of 'physical space' in public offices.[15]

However, computer archivists[16] warn us that digital archives also have their own specific (and relevant) problems. The continually ongoing process of technological change threatens management and maintenance of digital records.

The resulting problems are obviously many and not insignificant. They concern both the accessibility over time of the contents of the digital document and the integrity of the documents themselves,[17] which are in fact much more vulnerable than classic paper documents.[18]

---

13. *See* di Guarda, R. Ducato, *From Electronic Health Records to Personal Health Records: Emerging Legal Issues in the Italian Regulation of E-health, in International Review of Law,* Computers & Technology, 2016/9, 271.
14. An 'image' PDF whose text will not be 'searchable' unless Optical Character Recognition (OCR) software is used to scan it (to detect text within a digital image), resulting in an optical character recognition process.
15. To give just one example of such problems: for Italy Ministerial Decree 9/3/2007 sets a number of limits on the total amount of paper that can be stored per unit of space in order not to incur a high fire risk. *See* the document at the link: https://www.vigilfuoco.it/allegati/PI/DisposizioniGeneraliPI/COORD_DM_09_03_2007-DM_16_02_2007_RESISTENZA_AL_FUOCO.pdf.
16. *See* in particular M. Guercio, *Archivistica informatica. I documenti in ambiente digitale,* Rome, 2002.
17. M. Guercio, *Archivi digitali. Principi, metodi e criticità organizzative,* in *Treccani,* https://www.treccani.it/enciclopedia/archivi-digitali_%28XXI-Secolo%29/.
18. *See* D. Bearman, *Reality and Chimeras in the Preservation of Electronic Records, D-Lib Magazine,* Vol. 5(4), 1999; P. Dwivedi, *Archive – Where It Started and the Problems of Perpetuity,* in *Proceedings of the Eighteen IEEE Symposium on Mass Storage Systems and Technologies,* 2001, at http://storageconference.us/2001/papers/p10dwive.pdf, 353, which well underlines how 'The

To mention just a few of the critical situations that may arise:[19] the software that originally could read the file format may no longer exist; the medium on which the file was stored may be lost or destroyed. This explains the meaning of the discussion about the need for public administrations[20] to 'move to the cloud': a move that is, however, neither simple nor risk-free.[21]

In addition to this, an enormous problem is that the data contained in electronic documents are not physically 'attached' to their media (as ink is to paper documents).

For analogical 'documentary sources' the passing of time determines therefore, in principle, that they remain largely unaltered, so that it is possible to ensure the conditions for verifying authenticity (e.g., by analysing the support, the writing materials, the structure of the document, the type of annotations etc.).[22] On the contrary this is not at all true for electronic documents, which can easily be modified. More attention needs therefore to be paid to the issue of their integrity, authenticity and reliability.[23]

Together with the problem of the inevitable (and rapid) obsolescence of hardware and software, this means that the 'once-for-all principle' that applied to the archiving of paper documents no longer applies to the archiving of electronic data.[24] Thus, one must rather speak of an 'all-the-time principle' with regard to digital archiving,[25] which implies an endless commitment, also and above all financially. Adequate financial resources have to be constantly made available in order to meet the (ordinary) costs of system administration, updating of technologies, adaptation of human resources, etc. The important consequence of this is that, at the end of the day,

new era has instigated a major change for archivists from a world of "human-readable" data to one of "computer-ciphered" data, introducing a completely new set of issues and processes' (354).

19. In addition to those already quoted *see* I. Boydens, *La conservation numérique des données de gestion (Numéro spécial 'Archivage et perennisation')*, vol. 8, no. 2, Paris, Hermès Sciences, 2004, 13.
20. In this regard, the Three-year Plan for IT in public administration 2021-2023 published by AGID in October 2021 explicitly refers, among the guiding principles, to the 'cloud first' principle: public administrations, when defining a new project and developing new services, adopt the cloud paradigm first, taking into account the need to prevent the risk of lock-in (para. 5). *See also* the relevant information at https://cloud.italia.it/.
21. *See* the 2012 AGID document, Raccomandazioni e proposte sull'utilizzo del Cloud Computing nella Pubblica Amministrazione (Recommendations and proposals on the use of cloud computing in public administration), https://www.agid.gov.it/sites/default/files/repository_files/documenti_indirizzo/raccomandazioni_cloud_e_pa_-_2.0_0.pdf.
22. M. Guercio, *Archivi digitali*, cit.
23. The literature on this point is as complex as it is extensive. Among the many authors *see* K. Stranacher, V. Krnjic, B. Zwattendorfer, T. Zefferer, *Evaluation and Assessment of Editable Signatures for Trusted and Reliable Public Sector Data*, in *Electronic Journal of e-Government*, 2013, 360; M. Runardotter, C. Mörtberg, A. Mirijamdotter, *The Changing Nature of Archives: Whose Responsibility?*, in *Electronic Journal of e-Government*, 2011/1, 68; G. Buccafurri, G. Caminiti, G. Lax, *Threats to Legal Electronic Storage: Analysis and Countermeasures*, in K. Normann Andersen et al. (eds), *Electronic Government and the Information Systems Perspective* (Proceedings of the Second International Conference, EGOVIS 2011, Toulouse, France), Berlin, Heidelberg, 2011, 68.
24. *See* M. Dečman, *Long-Term Digital Archiving – Outsourcing or Doing It*, in *The Electronic Journal of e-Government*, Vol. 5 (2007), 136.
25. *See* M. Dečman cit. previous note.

digital archiving is much more vulnerable to reductions in the budgets available to public administrations for current expenditure; and it is completely incompatible with the very idea of zero 'maintenance' costs.

So, it is evidently necessary to start asking now what might happen in a post-National Recovery and Resilience Plan (NRRP)[26] scenario. Given that the recent trend in Italy has been what I have elsewhere described as 'zero-cost reforms': that is, reforms that come to light accompanied by that notorious 'financial invariance clause' according to which no new or greater burdens on public finances should result from their implementation.[27]

2.3 New 'Social Needs' and the Temptation of Outsourcing (The Different Choice of the NRRP)

Studies by sociologists of public administration also alert us to the fact that the use of ICT and e-governance is developing in a social environment populated by increasingly demanding 'clients' (citizens, professionals and private sector companies).[28] This, in turn, implies having more financial resources to meet and satisfy these 'social' needs and, therefore, greater budgets to offer services related to these new 'social needs'.[29] The paradox, however, is that while they are increasingly demanding as citizens in terms of the facilities and services expected from the public administration, at the same time they appear, as taxpayers, less and less willing to pay for these services.

In order to overcome the dilemma that this inevitably creates for public administrations that are constantly underfunded and increasingly overloaded with tasks and burdens, there is a strong temptation for them to turn to the private sector and outsource these 'services'.[30] This is particularly true in the United Kingdom (UK) context and in the United States; but in reality, it is a widespread phenomenon in our national administrations too, partly because of the enthusiasm about resorting to the private sector (outsourcing) that has characterised the Italian 'institutional scene'[31] for a long time, now.

26. The Italian Recovery and Resilience Plan (NextGenerationItaly), can be read at https://www.governo.it/sites/governo.it/files/PNRR.pdf.
27. *See* on this point in D.U. Galetta, *Trasparenza e contrasto della corruzione nella pubblica amministrazione: verso un moderno panottico di Bentham?*, in *Diritto e Società*, Vol. 1 (2017), 43, paras 6 s. But *see also* in D.U. Galetta, *La trasparenza, per un nuovo rapporto tra cittadino e pubblica amministrazione: un'analisi storico-evolutiva in una prospettiva di diritto comparato ed europeo*, in *RIDPC*, 2016/5, para. 5.8, 1054.
28. *See* S. Ho Ha, M. Jung Lee, *E-Government Services Using Customer Index Knowledge*, in K. Norman Andersen et al. (eds), *Electronic Government and the Information System Perspective* (First International Conference, EGOVIS 2010, Bilbao, Spain, 31 August-2 September 2010, Proceedings), Berlin, Heidelberg, 2010, 174.
29. *See* H. Chesbrough, *Toward a Science of Services*, in *Harvard Business Review*, 2005, 16.
30. *See* on this point M. C. Lacity, R. Hirschheim, *Information Systems Outsourcing; Myths, Metaphors and Reliabilities*, John Wiley & Sons Ltd, England, 1993; E. S. Savas, *Privatizing the public sector: How to shrink government*, Chatham House, 1982.
31. As for Italy, paradigmatic in this respect is the 2013 document to be found on the website of the Presidency of the Council of Ministers, Department of the Civil Service, at http://qualitapa.gov.it/sitoarcheologico/relazioni-con-i-cittadini/utilizzare-gli-strumenti/outsourcing/index.html.

However, the 'outsourcing solution'[32] raises a number of critical issues, not least for the fact that it does not actually reduce public spending, while it throws 'smoke and mirrors' at citizens with the idea that 'shrinking' the administrative apparatus is the solution to the 'costs problem'.[33]

The only sure outcome, in my eyes, is that the public administration takes a step backwards from its fundamental task of guardian of the public interest. With all the related consequences. In general, but even more so where outsourcing refers to services of dematerialisation and digital archiving of public documents, with the well-known (and very important) problems of security and protection of the personal data of all those involved.

In this sense, I very much welcome the strategy outlined in the Italian Recovery and Resilience Plan,[34] which I see moving in a different direction. In fact, there are huge resources invested by the Plan for public administrations, with the aim of creating the internal 'resources' – in terms of civil servants, 'cutting-edge and 4.0 technologies' and training in their use – capable of allowing Italian public administrations to quickly proceed along the path of 'digital transition'.

However, an important question remains in the background: what will (or could) happen about all this in a post-NRRP scenario, in which the available financial resources will necessarily be smaller?

3 THE RIGHT TO GOOD ADMINISTRATION AND ITS LINK WITH THE DIGITAL TRANSITION

3.1 The Origins of the Right to Good Administration

In this regard, the starting premise is so obvious that, perhaps, it would not even be necessary to recall it here. As is now well-known, since the adoption of the Charter of Fundamental Rights, in the context of the EU the so-called good administration is characterised not only as a duty of the public administration[35] but as a new fundamental right of the individual:[36] the right to good administration, as written and detailed in Article 41 of the EU Charter.[37]

32. Outsourcing is the contraction for 'outside resourcing'.
33. *See* J.A. O'Looney, *Outsourcing State and Local Government Services: Decision-Making Strategies and Management Methods*, Quorum Books, London, 1998, 22.
34. *See* at https://www.governo.it/sites/governo.it/files/PNRR.pdf.
35. C.G. Falzone, *Il dovere di buona amministrazione*, Milan, 1953.
36. The first to have clearly identified it as a new fundamental right (and no longer as a mere 'guiding principle' of administrative action) is A. Zito, *Il 'diritto ad una buona amministrazione' nella Carta dei diritti fondamentali dell'Unione europea e nell'ordinamento interno*, in *RIDPC*, 2002, 433. *See also* C. Marzuoli, *Carta europea dei diritti fondamentali, 'amministrazione' e soggetti di diritto: dai principi sul potere ai diritti dei soggetti*, in Vettori (Ed), *Carta europea e diritti dei privati*, Padua, 2002, 255. (265).
37. *See* for all: D.U. Galetta, *Il diritto ad una buona amministrazione europea come fonte di essenziali garanzie procedimentali nei confronti della pubblica amministrazione*, in *RIDPC*, 2005/3, 819-857.

Its legal notion coincides with the philosophical idea best expressed by the Iberian philosopher *Rodríguez-Arana* who underlined that 'A good public administration is one that objectively serves the citizenry ..., that carries out its work rationally, justifying its actions and that is continuously oriented towards the general interest. A general interest which, in the social and democratic State governed by the rule of law, lies in the permanent and integral improvement of people's living conditions'.[38]

I believe that this approach can be shared by all, whatever the concept of 'improving living conditions' may be and regardless of one's political/ideological orientation.

In other words, I believe that there can be a 'common understanding' among public administration scholars on this basic idea.

As to the concrete content of the provision of the EU Charter, according to Article 41(2), the right to good administration includes in particular:

(1) the right of every individual to be heard before an individual measure adversely affecting him or her is taken;
(2) the right of access to his/her file;
(3) the obligation of the administration to give reasons for its decisions.

However, this list should not be considered as exhaustive of everything that may be included in the right to good administration. The most general notion is to be found in Article 41(1) of the Charter: it is the right of every person 'to have his or her affairs handled impartially, fairly and within a reasonable time by the institutions, bodies, offices and agencies of the Union'.

The EU Court of Justice has now clearly and explicitly stated that 'the right to good administration, enshrined in Article 41 of the Charter, reflects a general principle of EU law, which is applicable to Member States when they are implementing that law'.[39] Moreover, for Italian law scholars Article 41 of the Charter expresses the same idea as Article 97 of the Italian Constitution, with respect to the need for impartiality and good performance of the public administration.[40]

In fact, the two provisions complement each other: an administration whose public offices are organised in such a way as to ensure good performance and impartiality is also the only one capable of guaranteeing fair and impartial treatment of

38. J. Rodríguez-Arana, *La buena administración como principio y como derecho fundamental in Europa*, in *Derecho y Ciencias Sociales*, N° 6, 2013, 23 (26), at https://dialnet.unirioja.es/descarga/articulo/5167578.pdf).
39. *See* most recently Court of Justice, judgment of 10 February 2022, in Case C-219/20, *LM*, ECLI:EU:C:2022:89, para. 37. *See also* CJEU, judgment of 24 November 2020, in joined cases C-225/19 and C-226/19, Minister of State for Foreign Affairs and Security. C-225/19 and C-226/19, Minister van Buitenlandse Zaken, ECLI:EU:C:2020:951, para. 34 and case-law cited therein. For further discussion on this issue *see* D.U. Galetta, *Il diritto ad una buona amministrazione nei procedimenti amministrativi oggi (anche alla luce delle discussioni sull'ambito di applicazione dell'art 41 della Carta dei diritti UE)*, in *RIDPC*, 2019/2, 165.
40. *See*, among many others: P. Calandra, *Efficienza e buon andamento della pubblica amministrazione* (voce), in *Enciclopedia Giuridica Treccani*, vol. XVIII, Rome, 2009; A. Andreani, *Il principio costituzionale di buon andamento dell'amministrazione pubblica*, Padua, 1979.

matters affecting the people it administers, as required by Article 41 of the EU Charter. Similarly, an administration whose public offices are organised in such a way as to ensure good performance appears to be the only one capable of guaranteeing compliance with the 'reasonable time' (for handling an affair/taking a decision) referred to in Article 41 of the EU Charter.[41] In other words, the principle of good performance certainly also encompasses a need for efficiency in public administration.[42]

3.2 The Link Between the Digital Transition and the Right to Good Administration and the Central Role of the 'Public Officer in Charge of the Procedure' (Responsible Officer[43])

Turning to the specific issue at hand, the question is whether and how the use of modern ICT, including algorithms[44] and Artificial Intelligence,[45] can (or cannot) contribute to the goal of 'good administration'.

In order to be able to provide an adequate answer to this crucial question it is necessary to bear in mind that, in Italian law, the best translation of the good administration's canons is Law 241 of 1990 on administrative procedure.[46] This law is in line with the idea expressed at the time by our best doctrine regarding the need to 'proceduralise' impartiality and good performance.[47] This idea has also been taken up and emphasised by our Constitutional Court[48] which, although it has never accorded constitutional status to the principle of 'due process' in the context of administrative

41. *See* more extensively on this point D.U. Galetta, *Digitalizzazione e diritto ad una buona amministrazione (Il procedimento amministrativo, fra diritto UE e tecnologie TIC)*, in R. Cavallo Perin, D.U. Galetta (Eds), *Il Diritto dell'Amministrazione Pubblica digitale*, Giappichelli, Turin, 2020, 85.
42. On this subject, *see* most recently S. Pignataro, *Il principio costituzionale del 'buon andamento' e la riforma della pubblica amministrazione*, Bari, 2012, *passim*. *See also* L. Iannuccilli, A. de Tura, *Il principio di buon andamento dell'amministrazione nella giurisprudenza della corte costituzionale*, published in https://www.cortecostituzionale.it/documenti/convegni_seminari/STU_212.pdf, which contains a very useful selection of fundamental rulings of the Constitutional Court in this regard.
43. This is the expression used in the ReNEUAL Model rules. *See* at http://reneual.eu/projects-and-publications/reneual-1-0. It is referred to as 'responsible member of staff' in the European Parliament resolution of 9 June 2016 for an open, efficient and independent European Union administration (2016/2610(RSP)), at https://www.europarl.europa.eu/doceo/document/TA-8-2016-0279_EN.pdf?redirect.
44. An algorithm can be defined as a precise set of instructions or rules, or a methodical series of steps that can be used to make calculations, solve problems and make decisions. *See* R. Benítez, G. Escudero, S. Kanaan, D. Masip Rodó, *Inteligencia artificial avanzada*, Barcelona, 2013, 14.
45. Artificial intelligence systems use computers, algorithms and various techniques to process information and solve problems or make decisions. In this regard, it is interesting to read a recent judgment of the Italian Council of State, sec. III, 4 November 2021, no. 7891, which discusses the distinction between algorithm and Artificial Intelligence, drawing a whole series of consequences in terms of legal reasoning.
46. For a non-official translation into English *see* at https://www.legislationline.org/download/id/5393/file/Italy_Law_Administrative-procedure_1990_am2010_en.pdf.
47. *See* for all G. Berti, *La pubblica amministrazione come organizzazione*, Padova, Cedam, 1968, *passim*.
48. *See* in particular Judgments Nos. 40 and 135 of 1998.

procedure,[49] has however progressively overcome the negative attitude linked to concerns of reduced 'functionality' of an administration tied to 'excessively detailed rules of conduct'.[50] And it has ended up favouring the thesis of those who linked administrative procedure to the objectives of transparency, publicity, participation and timeliness of administrative action, understood as essential values in a democratic system.[51]

At least since the beginning of the 1990s, the principles of impartiality and good performance have also been linked to the need to modernise the 'administrative machinery' and to carry out an adequate reorganisation of it.[52] It is precisely in this perspective that the fundamental role that ICT can play in the context of public administration has been strongly highlighted. It is, in fact, no coincidence that the version of Article 3-bis of Law 241 on administrative procedure – as innovated by the 'Simplification Decree' No. 76/2020 – provides that 'In order to achieve greater efficiency in their activities, public administrations shall act by means of computer and telematic tools, in their internal relations, between the different administrations and between these and private parties'.[53]

The provision – which in its current version seems to me to imply a real obligation for public administration to act 'by means of computer and telematic tools'[54] – does not, however, specify in any way how and with what resources (economic and instrumental) each and every public administration would be required to implement it. Therefore, it has been identified in the doctrine as a largely useless provision, with merely programmatic content.

In addition to what I will explain later (*infra*, section 4.) – regarding the positive impact that the NRRP may have in this context, net of the risks linked to the temporally limited duration of such resources – it appears evident to me that the provision of Article 3-bis of L. 241/90 is addressed, in the first place, to the responsible officer: in the specific perspective of his/her task of ensuring 'the proper and prompt conduct' of the

49. Initially denied in various judgments. *See, e.g.*, Constitutional Court, judgment no. 23 of 1978: 'It should be recalled, first of all, that the so-called principle of due process (in view of which private individuals should be able to present their reasons, before measures limiting their rights are adopted) cannot be considered as constitutionalised'.
50. The Italian Constitutional Court observed in judgement no. 234 of 1985 that 'with excessively detailed rules of conduct imposed on the public administration, far from always obtaining an effective guarantee, there could, on the contrary, be disadvantages, even serious ones, of stagnation'.
51. More precisely, the Constitutional Court's judgment No. 262 of 1997 states that 'By means of the above-mentioned system (*see* Law No. 241 of 1990 and subsequent additions and, as regards the Veneto Region, *see* Regional Law No. 1, Chapter IV of 10 January 1996) the legislator wished to give general application to rules – largely already set out in case law and doctrine – which are the implementation, albeit not exhaustive, of the constitutional principle of good administration (Article 97 of the Constitution) in the objectives of transparency, publicity, participation and timeliness of administrative action, as essential values in a democratic system'. *See also* Constitutional Court judgment no. 104 of 2006.
52. *See* (well before that) the fundamental remarks of M. Nigro, *Studi sulla funzione organizzatrice della pubblica amministrazione*, Milan, 1966, *passim*.
53. Decree-Law No 76 of 16 July 2020, Urgent measures for simplification and digital innovation.
54. *See* already in D.U. Galetta, *Digitalizzazione e diritto ad una buona amministrazione* cit., 93.

investigation phase of the administrative procedure; a task expressly assigned to him/her by Article 6 letter b) of the Italian Law (241/90) on administrative procedure.

I would even go so far as to say that Article 3-bis of Law 241/90, in its 2020 amended version, gives rise to a real obligation for the responsible officer to act by means of computer and telematic tools 'in order to achieve greater efficiency'. In particular, with a view to being able to carry out an adequate and prompt preliminary investigation in the context of the administrative procedure.

The provision of Article 3-bis is in fact directly linked to Article 12 of the Italian Digital Administration Code:[55] which links the use of ICT by the public administration with the aim of 'autonomously organising its own activity', in order to achieve 'the objectives of efficiency, effectiveness, cost-effectiveness, impartiality, transparency, simplification and participation'. Whereas, of course, Article 3-bis of Law 241/1990 has a field of application that clearly goes far beyond the mere scope of the internal organisation of administrative activities.

In this sense, the link with the right to good administration enshrined in the EU Charter is very clear. In the case-law it has in fact been made clear how Article 41 of the EU Charter means in particular, that 'all factual and legal information available' must be taken into consideration in such a way as 'to apply due diligence in the decision-making process and to adopt its decision on the basis of all information which might have a bearing on the result'.[56] This fully coincides with the need to carry out an adequate investigation in the administrative procedure, which Article 6 letter b) of Italian Law 241/90 expressly attributes as his/her task to the responsible officer. This implies, in turn, in a scenario characterised by the availability of sophisticated ICT, the necessity of using (also) all instruments allowing, today, the public administration, to easily acquire not only documents, but also all that information which can be acquired through sensors and monitoring instruments of various types, which are now widely available to them.[57]

In essence, it is about 'giving back' to the figure of the responsible officer the central role that it deserves, also with a view to fully exploiting its potential in this renewed scenario of digitalised administration.[58] In fact, beyond the task already attributed to him/her by Article 41 paragraph 2 of the Italian Digital Administration

55. The Italian Digital Administration Code can be read at https://www.normattiva.it/uri-res/N2Ls?urn:nir:stato:decreto.legislativo:2005-03-07;82.
56. Judgment of the Court of First Instance (First Chamber) of 19 March 1997. *Estabelecimentos Isidoro M. Oliveira SA v Commission of the European Communities*, Case T-7395, ECLI: EU:T:1997:39, point 32.
57. In this regard, reference should be made, for example, to the document of the Italian Ministry of Public Works, General Inspectorate for Circulation and Road Safety, on the Traffic Monitoring System and in particular its appendix B, Systems and technologies for road traffic monitoring, which can be read at https://webcache.googleusercontent.com/search?q=cache:i7TV8OuULKYJ:https://trafficlab.eu/bfd_download/linee-guida-del-monitoraggio-del-traffico/+&cd=1&hl=en&ct=clnk&gl=en&client=firefox-b-d.
58. *See amplius* in D.U. Galetta, *Digitalizzazione e diritto ad una buona amministrazione (Il procedimento amministrativo, fra diritto UE e tecnologie TIC)* cit., 88.

Code, of preparing the so-celectronic file,[59] there is room for the responsible officer to play a much more crucial role.

In the context of a truly digitalised public administration (the so-called public administration 4.0[60]) the responsible officer should in other words be the guarantor, first and foremost, of respect for those principles of fairness and impartiality in the investigation phase of the administrative procedure to which both Article 41 of the EU Charter and Article 97 of the Italian Constitution refer.[61]

From a practical point of view this implies that, within the framework described, he/she also takes on the task of adopting concrete organisational solutions. With the aim of avoiding discrimination between citizens on the basis of their different levels of 'computer literacy' and their different availability of IT tools (and access to the network), i.e. taking on the negative consequences linked to the so-called *digital gap/digital divide.*[62]

In addition to this, it seems clear to me that, in the context of the obligation to manage administrative procedures 'using ICT' established by Article 41 of the Italian Digital Administration Code, it is up to the responsible officer to break the veil of the so-called 'algorithmic neutrality'.[63] It is up to him/her to assess whether the possible use of Artificial Intelligence algorithms in the investigation phase of the administrative procedure, rather than favouring the objective of good administration (a fairer and more impartial decision, as well as a faster one), may instead lead to the result of discriminating – which becomes systematic, if inserted in an algorithm![64]– between different categories of citizens.

On this last point, it should be pointed out in conclusion that, if in the context of their 'power of self-organisation' it is appropriate to allow public administrations to make use of all the tools made available by ICT today, the use of such tools is conditional, first of all, on the circumstance that their use actually allows 'improving

59. On which *see* S. D'Ancona, *Il documento informatico e il protocollo informatico*, in R. Cavallo Perin, D.U. Galetta (Eds), *Il diritto dell'amministrazione pubblica digitale* cit. 159. (187 ff).
60. *See* D.U. Galetta, J.G. Corvalán, *Intelligenza Artificiale per una Pubblica Amministrazione 4.0? Potenzialità, rischi e sfide della rivoluzione tecnologica in atto*, in *Federalismi.it* (http://www.federalismi.it), 3/2019 (6 February 2019), 1.
61. *See also* D.U. Galetta, *Public Administration in the Era of Database and Information Exchange Networks: Empowering Administrative Power or Just Better Serving the Citizens* cit. 171.
62. On the 'digital divide', *see* S. D'Ancona, Provenzano, *Gli strumenti della Carta della cittadinanza digitale*, in R. Cavallo Perin, D. U. Galetta (Eds), Il diritto della amministrazione pubblica digitale cit., 226. *See also* D. Donati, *Digital divide e promozione della diffusione delle TIC*, in F. Merloni (Ed), *Introduzione all'eGovernment: pubbliche amministrazioni e società dell'informazione*, Turin, Giappichelli, 2005, 209.
63. On which *see*, among many others, M. Airoldi, D. Gambetta, *On the myth of algorithmic neutrality*, in *The* Lab's Quarterly, 2018, 25.
64. On this point *see*, among others: D. Freeman Engstrom, D. E. Ho, *Algorithmic Accountability in the Administrative State*, in *Yale Journal on Regulation*, 2020, also available at https://papers.ssrn.com/sol3/papers.cfm?abstract_id=3551544; L. Ayre, J. Craner, *Algorithms: avoiding the implementation of institutional biases*, in *Public Library Quarterly*, 2018, 341.; K. M. Altenburger, D. E. Ho, *When Algorithms Import Private Bias into Public Enforcement: The Promise and Limitations of Statistical Debiasing Solutions*, in *Journal of Institutional and Theoretical Economics*, 2018, 98.; S. B. Starr, *Evidence-Based Sentencing and the Scientific Rationalization of Discrimination*, in *Stanford Law Review*, 2014, 803.

the quality of services rendered to citizens and users'.[65] So, if it is true – as *Jean Bernard Auby* recently put it – that algorithms are a way of managing complexity,[66] then it is certainly necessary for the public administration to make use of them! At the same time, however, one must be careful not to be lulled into the illusion that algorithms are the tool through which it is possible to correct the imperfections inherent in the cognitive processes and choices adopted by human beings/public officials (bias, preferences, partiality, etc.).[67] It is therefore necessary that the use of these tools brings with it a *guarantee* (and not just a vague promise!) of a more complete preliminary investigation in the administrative procedure, one which is more in keeping with the principles of impartiality and good performance; and that all this also takes place in a context of compliance with the principle of transparency.

In fact, even with regard to the so-called robotised administrative procedures, the Italian administrative courts have not per se excluded the possibility of resorting to them;[68] however, what is certainly excluded is the possibility of accepting 'the non-intelligibility of the operations carried out'[69] on the basis of the use of such algorithms.[70]

The principle of transparency[71] – compliance with which the public officer responsible for the procedure must guarantee in his relationship with the addressee of the measure adopted – implies also full knowledge of the existence of any automated decision-making processes and of the algorithms used[72] for that purpose.

In this framework, one must certainly move in the direction of models of *by-design* transparency and *by-default* transparency: in the logic of a digitalised administrative procedure, but which is at the same time respectful of all those principles that must govern administrative action as specified in Article 1 of Italian Law 241/90.[73] And also the right to the protection of personal data of private subjects involved in the administrative procedure plays here a very important role; therefore,

65. Thus Cons. Stato, judgment 5 December 2019, no. 8472, point 8.1. in https://www.giustizia-amministrativa.it.
66. As stated by J-B. Auby, *Il diritto amministrativo di fronte alle sfide digitali*, in *Istituzioni del Federalismo*, 2019/3, 619.
67. On cognitive biases and their consequences on choices made by public administrations *see* most recently S. D'Ancona, *Contributo allo studio della progettazione in materia di appalti e concessioni. Una prospettiva dalle scienze comportamentali e cognitive*, Torino, 2021.
68. *See* in particular Cons. Stato, judgment of 5 December 2019, no. 8472 cit.
69. Cons. Stato, sez. VI, judgment 21 January 2021, no. 799, in https://www.giustizia-amministrativa.it.
70. *See* on this point the remarks of C. Coglianese, D. Lehr, *Transparency and Algorithmic Governance*, in *Administrative Law Review*, 2019 (SSRN: https://ssrn.com/abstract=3293008).
71. *See* to this regard the interesting remarks of P. Birkinshaw, *Information: Public Access, Protecting Privacy and Surveillance*, in Sir J. Jowell, C. O'Cinneide (Eds), *The Changing Constitution*, Oxford, 9th Ed., 2019, 358.
72. *See* in particular Cons. Stato, sez. VI, judgment 8 April 2019, no. 2270, in https://www.giustizia-amministrativa.it.
73. *See* D.U. Galetta, *Algoritmi, procedimento amministrativo e garanzie: brevi riflessioni, anche alla luce degli ultimi arresti giurisprudenziali in materia*, in RIDPC, 2020/3.

one could certainly imagine to go in the direction of those principles of privacy *by design* and privacy *by default* contained in the GDPR.[74]

To conclude on this point, in the perspective of the transition towards the so-called Administration 4.0,[75] the figure of the responsible officer, far from being obsolete, seems to me to represent the essential pivotal point in the relationship between the digitalisation of public administration and good administration. In fact, it is only thanks to an appropriate 'enhancement' of this figure that the use of ICT, from a tool in the investigation phase of the administrative procedure aimed at a mere 'efficiency' of the administrative activity, can become an instrument of greater guarantee and, therefore, of general improvement of the relationship between public administration and citizens. Indeed, it is certainly not by chance that this 'figure' has also attracted the attention of the European Parliament, which expressly mentions it in the context of its Resolution of 9 June 2016 on a regulation for an open, efficient and independent EU administration.[76] Nor is it a coincidence that the NRRP has so emphatically highlighted the need to invest in the selection, training and career development's paths of civil servants.[77]

4 PROSPECTS OPENED BY THE NRRP

4.1 Public Administration Reform and Digital Transition

In the NRRP sent by the Italian Government to the EU Commission at the end of April 2021 – and definitively approved, by means of an Implementing Decision of the Council, on 13 July (2021) – it is underlined that the 'weak administrative capacity' of the Italian public sector has been an obstacle to the improvement of services offered and to public investment in recent years. And it is stated that 'the NRRP addresses this rigidity and promotes an ambitious reform agenda for the public administration'.[78]

The NRRP also highlights how, faced with growing numerical, demographic and training constraints[79] the Italian public administration finds itself managing a set of extremely articulated and complex rules and procedures that have been progressively stratified over time in an uncoordinated and often conflicting manner at different administrative levels (national, regional and local).[80]

In this respect, there is an interesting reference to those Country Specific Recommendations that are formulated every year by the European Council – and subsequently adopted by the Council of the European Union (obviously on a proposal

74. The well-known 'General Data Protection Regulation', EU Regulation 2016/679, at https://gdpr.eu/tag/gdpr/.
75. D.U. Galetta, J.G. Corvalán, *Intelligenza Artificiale per una Pubblica Amministrazione 4.0?* cit.
76. *See* European Parliament Resolution of 9 June 2016 on a regulation for an open, efficient and independent European Union administration cit.
77. *See.* NRRP cit., 4, but especially 44.
78. NRRP cit., 44.
79. In this regard, the NRRP expressly refers to blocking turnover and cutting education and training expenditure for civil servants (an average of EUR 48 per employee).
80. NRRP cit., 45.

from the Commission) in the form of a Recommendation addressed to the different Member States.

The Recommendation of the Council of the European Union for 2020-2021, addressed to Italy,[81] recommends to 'improve (...) the effectiveness of public administration' (recommendation no. 4), stating that 'An effective public administration is crucial to ensure that the measures adopted to address the emergency and support economic recovery are not slowed down in their implementation', while, as far as Italy is concerned, 'Weaknesses include lengthy procedures (...), the low level of digitalisation and weak administrative capacity'.[82] It also points out that 'Digitalisation across public administrations was uneven prior to the crisis' and that 'Online interaction between authorities and the general public was low' with a 'share of administrative procedures managed by regions and municipalities that can be started and completed entirely digitally' which remains low.[83]

The NRRP therefore makes available substantial economic resources for the 'digital transition',[84] with the aim of 'profoundly transforming the public administration through a strategy centred on digitalisation', which is seen as 'a transversal necessity'.[85]

4.2 The Problem of Interoperability and the Necessary Creation of 'Databases of National Interest'

The Council of the European Union's Recommendation 2020-2021 for Italy also stresses – quite significantly – how in our country the crisis 'has also exposed the lack of interoperability of public digital services'.[86]

According to the definition provided by international dictionaries, interoperability is 'the ability of a system or component to function effectively with other systems or components'.[87]

In this regard the problem is that, as a starting point, the technological infrastructure of the (Italian) public administration was the least suited to guaranteeing interoperability, since it had been developed and organised over the years in a haphazard manner, leaving decisions to the initiative of each individual administration and without an overall vision, coordination and planning.

81. EU Commission, Recommendation for a Council Recommendation on Italy's 2020 National Reform Programme and delivering a Council opinion on Italy's 2020 Stability Programme, 20 May 2021, Doc. COM/2020/512 final, at https://eur-lex.europa.eu/legal-content/EN/TXT/?uri =CELEX%3A52020DC0512.
82. Point 24 of the Council Recommendation on Italy's 2020 National Reform Programme cit.
83. *Ibid.*
84. As much as 27% of the NRRP resources are dedicated to digital transition, as explicitly stated on 16 of the NRRP.
85. Mission 1, Component 1of the NRRP cit.
86. Point 24 of the Council Recommendation on Italy's 2020 National Reform Programme cit.
87. Webster's New World College Dictionary, 4th ed., 2010.

The result was that a jungle of thousands of small autonomous data processing centres (DPCs) had been created:[88] so that, already within the Three-Year Plan for Information Technology in public administration 2017-2019[89] launched by the Agency for Digital Italy (*Agenzia per l'Italia digitale* (AGID)), *a specific path dedicated to digital infrastructures had been launched, as part of a more general process of digital transformation of the country.*

The aim was to rationalise the system.

On the subject of interoperability, AGID had stressed that the use of the so-called 'Application Cooperation'[90] between public administrations is a key element: because it is a technical solution that makes it possible to automatically exchange information between information systems and allows services[91] to be shared.

In order to identify a common solution on interoperability based on homogeneous and shared standards, AGID had already issued a couple of 'technical documents' in the past few years, setting out the design and functioning of an application-cooperation-infrastructure between public administration.

The idea is that interchange should be aimed at providing services to citizens and businesses, so as to simplify the interaction between them and the public administration.

More recently, the move is being made from the 'Application Cooperation' model to a new system of interoperability in which the IT systems of the public administration must be connected to each other and, to put it simply, 'speak the same language', making information available immediately where it is needed.[92]

From a technical point of view, last October AGID adopted the 'Guidelines on the technical interoperability of public administrations' and the 'Guidelines on technologies and standards for the security of interoperability through APIs of information systems'.[93] The aim is to ensure that all public administrations comply with such guidelines, so as to guarantee the interoperability of their own systems with those of other subjects and to favour the overall implementation of the Public-Administration-Information-System (PAIS).[94]

---

88. This description of the 'state of the art' was made a few years ago by AGID itself, the Agency for Digital Italy (*see* at https://www.agid.gov.it/it).
89. Which can be read at https://docs.italia.it/italia/piano-triennale-TIC/pianotriennale-TIC-doc/it/2017-2019/index.html.
90. 'Cooperazione applicativa', which is a specific technical solution adopted in order to enhance interoperability.
91. *See* para. 10 of the Three-year Plan for Information Technology in Public Administration 2017-2019, cit.
92. *See* in this regard Determination no. 406/2020 of 9 September 2020 – Adoption of the Circular containing the guideline on technical interoperability and AGID Circular no. 1 of 9 September 2020 – Guideline on technical interoperability, both at https://trasparenza.agid.gov.it.
93. Determination no. 547 of 1 October 2021 Adoption of the 'Guidelines on Technologies and Standards for the Security of Interoperability through APIs of Information Systems' and the 'Guidelines on Technical Interoperability of Public Administrations', in https://www.agid.gov.it/sites/default/files/repository_files/547_dt_dg_n_547_1_ott_2021_adozione_lg_interoperabilit_tecnica_e_sicurezza.pdf.
94. *See* at https://www.agid.gov.it/it/infrastrutture/sistema-pubblico-connettivita/il-nuovo-modello-interoperabilita.

This new interoperability model is a cornerstone of the Three-Year Plan for IT in public administration 2020-2022[95] and is also the basis for the strategies and objectives included in the 2021-2023 update of the plan.[96]

A concrete example of interoperability is the already mentioned 'National Register of Resident Population' (*supra*, section 2.1.), which is part of the six 'Databases of national interest' pursuant to Article 60, paragraph 3-bis of the Italian Digital Administration Code, which in paragraph 1 defines as databases of national interest 'the set of information collected and managed digitally by public administrations, homogeneous in type and content and whose knowledge is relevant to the performance of the institutional functions of other public administrations ...'.

AGID specifies further that the databases of national interest are 'reliable databases, homogeneous in type and content' and that they 'constitute the backbone of the public information heritage' that has to be made available to all public administration, in order to facilitate the exchange of data and avoid asking citizens or businesses for the same information several times.[97]

Unlike some of the other 'Databases of national interest' mentioned in Article 60 of the Italian Digital Administration Code, the 'National Register of Resident Population' already exists. While until a few years ago the personal data of citizens were scattered among almost 8,000 different municipal registers (7,903, to be precise!), as of 17 January 2022 all Italian municipalities have in fact become part of the National Register of Resident Population.[98] This will enable the public administrations to communicate efficiently with each other, having a single and certain source for citizens' data; and in the near future citizens will not have to communicate their personal data or change of residence again and again to every public administration office they reach out to.[99]

It will therefore finally be possible (at least in theory) to go beyond the 'self-certification model', shortening and automating all the procedures relating to personal data.[100]

In the same vein, it will be essential to work towards the complete digitalisation of health services, in particular through the 'Electronic Health Record'. The goal is, as the NRRP expressly states, 'the creation of a homogeneous electronic health record at

95. *See* at https://www.agid.gov.it/sites/default/files/repository_files/piano_triennale_per_linformatica_nella_pa_2020_2022.pdf.
96. *See* at https://www.agid.gov.it/sites/default/files/repository_files/piano_triennale_per_linformatica_nella_pubblica_amministrazione_2021-2023.pdf.
97. https://www.agid.gov.it/it/dati/basi-dati-interesse-nazionale.
98. On 17 January 2022, with the addition of the Sicilian municipality of San Teodoro, the process of bringing all Italian municipalities into the National Register of Resident Population was completed. *See* at https://www.anagrafenazionale.interno.it/tutti-i-comuni-italiani-sono-in-anpr/.
99. *See* at https://www.anagrafenazionale.interno.it/il-progetto/i-vantaggi/.
100. The access to the National Register of Resident Population takes place after the signing of a 'User Agreement' with the Ministry and the identification and selection of the 'use cases' among those provided for and corresponding to the regulatory framework applicable to the body/public administration concerned. C. Saggini, *Accesso ai dati anagrafici con Anpr: stato dell'arte, sviluppi e risvolti pratici*, at https://www.agendadigitale.eu/cittadinanza-digitale/anagrafe-unica/accesso-ai-dati-anagrafici-con-anpr-stato-dellarte-sviluppi-e-risvolti-pratici/.

national level, which will become the single point of access for citizens and residents to their clinical history and to the services offered by the National Health System'[101] (*supra*, section 2.1.).

The 'Electronic Health Record' (EHR) was initially regulated by Decree 2015/178;[102] while the Ministerial Decree of 4 August 2017, amended by the Decree of 25 October 2018, regulated the national interoperability between regional health records.[103] Finally, following the changes introduced by Decree Law 34/2020 (the so-called Decreto Rilancio), the EHR is now activated by law and automatically fed with data.[104]

However, in order to guarantee maximum interoperability, it will be necessary to complete the creation of the 'National Register of Patients' (*Anagrafe Nazionale degli Assistiti* (ANA)), which is also a database of national interest pursuant to Article 60, paragraph 3-bis of the Italian Digital Administration Code.[105] The verification of the personal data of the patient who is to receive a health service from a 'regional domain' (*dominio regionale*) is in fact the necessary precondition for the proper implementation of interoperability processes.[106]

In conclusion, it must be emphasised that the interoperability of databases and systems implies a strong unitary direction at the level of the central government. Nor is it conceivable that single local administrations can alone bear the enormous costs associated with the management and technical design of the necessary technological infrastructures.

4.3 Digitalisation of the Administrative Procedure and the 'Once-Only' Principle, Between National and Supranational Level

As regards the digitalisation of administrative procedures, the operational tool offered by AGID in this respect is the platform called 'Management System of Administrative Procedures' (*Sistema di Gestione dei Procedimenti Amministrativi* (SGPA)).[107]

101. NRRP cit., 31.
102. Decree of the President of the Council of Ministers of 29 September 2015, no. 178, *Regulation on the electronic health record*.
103. Ministerial Decree of 4 August 2017, as amended by the Decree of 25 October 2018, Amendment of the Ministerial Decree of 4 August 2017, concerning the technical modalities and telematic services made available by the national infrastructure for the interoperability of the Electronic Health Record (ESF), at https://www.gazzettaufficiale.it/eli/id/2018/11/06/18A07058/sg.
104. Decree Law No. 34 of 19 May 2020, Urgent measures on health, support for work and the economy, and social policies related to the epidemiological emergency from COVID-19, at https://www.gazzettaufficiale.it/eli/id/2020/05/19/20G00052/sg.
105. This database of national interest, which was established by Article 62-ter of the Italian Code of Digital Administration and is aimed at managing the administrative data of NHS patients, is owned jointly by the Ministry of Economy and Finance and the Ministry of Health. *See* in this regard at https://docs.italia.it/italia/daf/pianotri-schede-bdin/it/stabile/ana.html.
106. In this regard, it is clearly underlined in the pages of the AGID website dedicated to the Electronic Health Record that, pending the establishment of the ANA, the national reference registry is represented by the TS System and that it is therefore required that regional and business registries correctly use the services provided by the TS/ANA System. *See* at https://www.fascicolosanitario.gov.it/it/4.1.Identificazione-Assistito.
107. *See* at https://www.agid.gov.it/it/piattaforme/sistema-gestione-procedimenti-amministrativi.

The SGPA platform deals with document management in the context of administrative procedures, with the aim of guaranteeing proper management of documents 'from production to preservation'.[108]

The connection with the second aspect of the digital transition – the one that the NRRP places alongside the topic of interoperability – emerges clearly: namely, the need to introduce the principle (and objective/standard of the EU) of the 'once-only', i.e., the idea that citizens and businesses have to provide their information to public administrations only once.[109]

There is no doubt that the 'once-only' principle (or objective) necessarily presupposes the digitalisation of administrative procedures. In fact, the idea of the single-access-point involves two key concepts in digital-public-administration-law: the concept of electronic document[110] *and the concept of* document flows and IT protocol.[111]

In this regard, there are three necessary steps to be taken:

(1) The registration of incoming and outgoing documents in the protocol and their assignment to the organisational units (and the issue of administrative organisation and of the necessary changes in this regard is therefore certainly a crucial one, as well[112]).
(2) The dematerialisation of the processing of document flows, both incoming and outgoing (but total dematerialisation, as the 'blended mode' certainly does not work).
(3) The definition of the process of preservation of electronic documents, electronic files and archives as well as copies.[113]

This all involves dealing also with the very sensitive topic of the tools available to citizens to enable their identification. There is in fact a close correlation between digital identity, online services (Article 64 of the Italian Digital Administration Code) and digital procedures (Article 65 of the Italian Digital Administration Code).[114] And it is clear that a real digital transition should also imply investing in this and putting as

108. *See* document quoted in the previous note.
109. *See* NRRP cit., 17.
110. Article 1 of the Italian Digital Administration Code defines the *electronic document* as the 'computerised representation of legally relevant acts, facts or data' (Article 1, letter p) as opposed to the analogue document which is the 'non-computerised representation of legally relevant acts, facts or data' (Article 1, letter p-bis).
111. *See* S. D'Ancona, *Il documento informatico e il protocollo informatico* cit., 159.
112. On this point *see* J. Burn, G. Robin, *Moving towards e-government: a case study of organizational change processes*, in *Logistics Information Management*, 2003, 25.; R. Gil-Garcia, *Enacting e-Government Success: An Integrative Study of Government-wide Website, Organizational Capabilities and Institutions*, Berlin, Heidelberg, 2012; N. Nurdin, R. Stockdale, H. Scheepers, Organizational Adaptation to Sustain Information Technology: The Case of E-Government. Nurdin, R. Stockdale, H. Scheepers, *Organizational Adaptation to Sustain Information Technology: The Case of E-Government in Developing Countries*, in *Electronic Journal of e-Government*, 2012, 70.
113. Steps 2 and 3 (and the related issues) have already been discussed in section 2, *supra*.
114. For more details on the subject *see* S. D'Ancona, Provenzano, *Gli strumenti della Carta della cittadinanza digitale* cit. 234.

many citizens as possible in a position to have a digital identity and to be able to benefit from the advantages it brings.

A final clarification: the 'National Administrative Procedures Management System' is implemented through the definition, by AGID, of the rules for the interoperability of document flows that public administrations implement in order to join the system.[115] But what about the management of procedures at the level of 'non-national' administrations? How and to what extent is it possible to guarantee the same level of digitalisation and compliance with the same standards?

The investment envisaged in this regard by the NRRP implies, first and foremost, the development of the 'National Digital Data Platform' (*Piattaforma Digitale Nazionale Dati* (PDND), provided for by Article 50-ter of the Italian Digital Administration Code), in order to enable (all) administrations to make their information available through digital APIs (Application Programming Interfaces).

There is also a second project that takes especially into account the supranational perspective: it is the 'single digital gateway' (provided for in Regulation (EU) 2018/1724[116]) and which aims to enable harmonisation between Member States and the digitalisation of procedures and services in the EU market.

The implementation of the single digital gateway is expressly provided for within the 'Digitalisation, Innovation, Competitiveness and Culture' mission of the Italian Recovery and Resilience Plan.[117]

5 ONCE-ONLY OR ONCE-AGAIN? CONCLUDING REMARKS ON HOW TO 'NOT DIGITALISE THE COMPLICATION'

In the chapter of the Italian Recovery and Resilience Plan devoted to the reforms to be undertaken (chapter 2), it is stressed out that 'One of the most valuable legacies of the NRRP must be the permanent increase in the efficiency of the public administration and its decision-making capacity'; and 'digitalisation of processes and services' are identified as fundamental to this perspective.[118]

However, as the new president of our Council of State, Franco Frattini, rightly pointed out, in this process of 'digital transition' we must avoid the mistake of 'digitalising the complication',[119] i.e., duplicating all the byzantine complexities of analogue/paper administration.[120]

115. *See* at https://www.agid.gov.it/it/piattaforme/sistema-gestione-procedimenti-amministrativi.
116. Regulation (EU) 2018/1724 of the European Parliament and of the Council of 2 October 2018 establishing a single digital gateway to provide access to information, to procedures and to assistance and problem-solving services and amending Regulation (EU) No 1024/2012. *See* at https://ec.europa.eu/growth/single-market/single-digital-gateway_it.
117. NRRP cit., 83.
118. NRRP cit., 44.
119. This expression was used by the President of the Italian *Consiglio di Stato* Franco Frattini in the context of the conference on 'New perspectives for Administrative Law' organised at the TAR Lazio (Rome) on 24 January 2022 and chaired by him.
120. In this regard, I refer to my remarks in D.U. Galetta, *Technological Transition in response to COVID. Scattered Thoughts on the possibility of a (Technological) transition to a Digitalized*

As I have tried to explain in the previous paragraphs, the transition from traditional administration to a truly 4.0 digital administration[121] is certainly not automatic. A favourable regulatory environment and technological adaptation of administrative structures, thanks also to the resources of the NRRP, are not in themselves sufficient. What is also needed is for the rules to be applied and for the technologies to be properly used.

For this to happen, it is necessary to be fully aware of the potential of ICT and to be able to use these innovative technologies to improve the *overall* quality of public administrations.[122]

At the moment, this is certainly not the case.

One of the major problems that has emerged in recent years – and which is likely to greatly limit the potential that the digitalisation of public administrations could have in terms of achieving 'good administration' – concerns the very way in which the documents held by public administrations are usually stored and which leads to fragmentation, as well as to a multiplication of 'information *silos*'.

The same information is repeated several times and stored in an incongruous and/or totally inconsistent way by different administrations.

The possibility of errors due to the use of outdated or even erroneous data is thus multiplied. This, moreover, corresponds to a completely opposite logic to the one already highlighted in the 2017-2019 Three-Year Plan for Information Technology in Italian public administration, which stressed that 'Data must be understood as a common good, shared freely between public administrations for institutional purposes', with a view to enhancing the value of public information assets as a strategic objective for the public administration.[123]

In this perspective, the creation of the already mentioned 'databases of national interest' provided for in Article 60 of the Italian Digital Administration Code[124] is of utmost importance.

The NRRP itself, in its introductory part (the part on 'general objectives and structure of the plan'), states that it is necessary 'to speed up full interoperability between public bodies and their information bases, which will make it possible to streamline public procedures thanks to the full realisation of the principle (and EC objective/standard) of "once-only",[125] an e-government concept whereby citizens and

---

Public Administration in Italy, with the help of the Recovery and Resilience Plan, in *CERIDAP*, 4/2021, https://ceridaeu (16 November 2021), 154.

121. D.U. Galetta, J.G. Corvalán, *Intelligenza Artificiale per una Pubblica Amministrazione 4.0?* cit.
122. *See* M. Bombardelli, *Informatica pubblica, E-Government e sviluppo sostenibile*, in *RIDPC*, 2002/5, 991.
123. *See* in the 2017-2019 Three-Year Plan for Information Technology in Public Administration about the objective of 'rationalising and enhancing the information assets of the public administration by overcoming the "silos logic" in order to "exploit the potential of the immense wealth of data collected and managed by public administrations"' (paras 4 and 4.1), https://docs.italia.it/italia/piano-triennale-TIC/pianotriennale-TIC-doc/it/2017-2019/index.html.
124. *See* section 4.2 above.
125. The origin of the 'once-only' principle is in fact to be found in the EU Regulation on the single digital gateway, which aims at simplifying and improving the effectiveness of interactions with public administrations of different Member States for citizens and businesses, also avoiding duplications (total or partial) for the same information. Regulation (EU) 2018/1724 of the

businesses must be able to provide their information to authorities and administrations "once only"'.[126]

This need has also been clearly stated in the Italian 2020-2022 Three-Year Plan for Information Technology in public administration, one of the guiding principles of which is 'once-only', i.e., public administrations must avoid asking citizens and businesses for information they have already provided.[127]

However, an objective observation of reality forces one to note that this is exactly the opposite of what currently happens when interacting with almost all Italian public administrations. Interaction with our (semi or poorly digitalised) public administrations consists in fact – essentially and mostly – in a large number of (complicated) forms to be filled in online, with blocked 'fields' and thus lacking any possibility of adaptation to the specific case, should the need arise.[128] Such online forms are usually to be accompanied by plenty of documents (to be attached online, of course), most of which contain data and information that the public administrations already possess.[129] In other words, the whole thing looks much more like a 'once-again interaction' than a 'once-only interaction'! It is no coincidence, in fact, that in the Digital Economy and Society Index (DESI) – the index that summarises the indicators on digital performance and tracks the progress of EU countries – Italy is underperforming in the EU context also in relation to the amount of pre-filled data in the online forms available for access to services.[130]

In conclusion, it seems clear to me that there is an urgent need to address (and hopefully solve) those issues I have briefly mentioned here, as well as many other problematic issues that the 'digital transition' in/of the public administration necessarily entails.[131] In fact, without wishing to indulge in 'neo-Luddite' attitudes – which certainly cannot be shared – it seems evident to me that the only way to avoid being 'swept away' by the flood of a public administration that has gone (or rather 'is going') digital is for us, as administrative law scholars, to deal (albeit with difficulty) also with the essential 'technicalities' related to the public administration's digital transition.[132] This is the only way in which administrative law scholars can be able to give a proper

European Parliament and of the Council of 2 October 2018 establishing a single digital gateway for access to information, procedures and assistance and problem-solving services and amending Regulation (EU) No 1024/2012 and, in particular, recitals 12., 40, 55, 63, 72; Article 14 para. 2.

126. NRRP cit., 17.
127. Three-year plan for information technology in public administration 2020-2022, 9.
128. I am referring to the fact that the forms available to be filled in directly online usually do not allow any flexibility in the input of information and block the filling in of the 'next field' in the event that even one of the data required in the 'previous field' is missing, even though it may not be relevant in the case at hand.
129. Copies of personal documents, identity cards, etc.
130. *See* at https://digital-strategy.ec.europa.eu/en/policies/desi.
131. On this point, *see* already G. Duni, *L'amministrazione digitale. Il diritto amministrativo nell'evoluzione telematica*, Milan, 2008; D. Marongiu, *L'attività amministrativa automatizzata*, Rimini, Maggioli, 2005.
132. In this regard, it is very useful to read, for example, the two volumes by J-C. Heudin, *Comprendre le deep learning: Une introduction aux réseaux de neurones*, Paris, 2016 and Id., *Intelligence Artificielle. Manuel de survie*, Science-eBook, 2017.

contribution in the direction of exploring not just the full potential of 'public administration 4.0' in terms of greater efficiency (which is the perspective emphasised also in the Italian NRRP), but also in the perspective of acknowledging the risks that this new kind of public administration certainly entails for the citizen and the need to control such risks and correct mistakes.

The potential of the digital transition of public administration has in fact to be investigated with full awareness of the technical issues and of their implications; and in the perspective of exploring how much it can deliver also in terms of a better satisfaction/realisation of that right to a good administration provided for by Article 41 of the Charter of Fundamental Rights of the European Union.[133]

133. This right - as already mentioned above, para. 3.1. - 'reflects a general principle of EU law, which is applicable to Member States when they are implementing that law'. So CJEU, judgment of 10 February 2022, in case C-219/20 cit., point 37.

CHAPTER 29

The European Offices of the UK Local Authorities and Devolved Administrations in Light of Patrick Birkinshaw's Concept of European Public Law

Carlo Panara

1 INTRODUCTION

I had the honour and the pleasure of being Professor Birkinshaw's colleague at The University of Hull from 2006 to 2009. I still remember the excitement of meeting with him for the first time in his bright professorial office at the end of the corridor, on the fourth floor of the Wilberforce Building where the entire Law School was located at the time. Professor Birkinshaw was during my time in Hull, and remained throughout my whole career, a role model and source of inspiration. The teaching emanating from his book *European Public Law* (Butterworths LexisNexis, 2003), and from other works, guides my understanding of the reciprocal influences between the domestic and European Union (EU) legal systems. In this chapter, I will discuss the role of the Brussels-based offices of the United Kingdom (UK) local authorities and devolved administrations in light of the concept of European Public Law (EPL) put forward by Birkinshaw in the aforementioned landmark book. These offices are often referred to as the European offices of the UK regions and so will they be hereafter.

According to Birkinshaw, 'European public law is concerned with the development of the public law of European states and their influence upon, and their influence in turn by, the developing law of the European Community or European Union as it is increasingly called.'[1] This concept of EPL is relevant to this study. Among the *raisons*

1. P. Birkinshaw, *European Public Law* (Butterworths LexisNexis, 2003), p. 3. *See also* the third edition of the book published by Wolters Kluwer in 2020, p. 7.

d'être of the European Brussels-based offices of the regions, both those from the UK before Brexit and those from EU Member States, there are the monitoring of European legislation and policy, and the influencing through lobbying of legislation and policies relevant to the regions. It is therefore apparent that the role of these offices is linked to and is a by-product of the influence of EU law on European states, as well as of the impact of the Member States and, by extension, of their substate units, on the law of the EU.[2]

The referendum vote of 23 June 2016, and the subsequent exit of the UK from the EU, altered this pattern fundamentally. Having left the EU, the UK can now repeal and replace legislation originating from the EU.[3] Accordingly, not only the previously described notion of EPL appears prima facie redundant, but there also seems to be no need for UK substate authorities to seek to influence EU legislation and policy, for the simple reason that these regulatory sources are no longer relevant to them. I believe, however, that the supposed irrelevance in the UK of the law of the EU tells us only a part of the story and that, whilst the law emanating from the EU institutions lost its supremacy, direct and indirect effect, and all the other mechanisms to ensure compliance, this still remains an influential factor in the UK. The influence of EU law is not limited to what Birkinshaw calls the 'legacy of EPL', by which he means the survival in UK public law of principles and rules originating from the EU and from the case law of the European Court of Justice.[4]

Pursuant to the Northern Ireland Protocol, Northern Ireland remains effectively in the EU Single Market for goods. A range of EU rules concerning, *inter alia*, anti-discrimination measures, the standards of certain goods, value added tax (VAT) and excises, the electricity market, and state aid, continue to apply to that region.[5] At the same time the Court of Justice of the EU retains jurisdiction over the interpretation of these rules.[6] Scotland has chosen to remain aligned with EU laws by giving its ministers the power to pass regulations that mirror the EU rules on environmental protection, animal health and welfare, plant health, equality, non-discrimination and human rights, and social protection.[7] These examples show how the impact of Brexit in the UK is asymmetrical, with some countries maintaining an alignment to some of the rules originating from Brussels. Another aspect to consider is that the EU, with its 450 million people-strong single market, is the UK's largest trading partner by far. The quality standards and trade arrangements applicable to the 27 Member States have an

2. P. Birkinshaw, *European Public Law* (Butterworths LexisNexis, 2003), p. 565. On the contribution of the substate units to European multilevel constitutionalism, *see* I. Pernice, 'Multilevel Constitutionalism in the European Union', Walter Hallstein-Institut, Paper 5, July 2002, p. 11.
3. This follows from the repeal of the European Communities Act 1972 by the European Union (Withdrawal) Act 2018.
4. P. Birkinshaw, *European Public Law* (Wolters Kluwer, 3rd ed. 2020), pp. 829-830.
5. Annexes from 1 to 5 to the Northern Ireland Protocol attached to the Brexit Withdrawal Agreement of 24 January 2020. On 14 June 2022 the UK government published legislation that could override parts of the Protocol and limit the scope of application of EU law in Northern Ireland. *See* https://bills.parliament.uk/bills/3182 and a commentary by Mark Elliott https://publiclawforeveryone.com/2022/06/13/the-northern-ireland-protocol-bill/ (both accessed July 2022).
6. Article 12 of the Protocol.
7. Part 1 of the UK Withdrawal from the EU (Continuity) (Scotland) Act 2021.

influence beyond the bloc. Accordingly, in addition to the impact of EU law on Northern Ireland and Scotland, there might be a significant although less immediate impact of EU standards of quality and other rules on the rest of the UK.

Using the European offices of the UK regions as a case study, this chapter attempts to demonstrate the continuing relevance, albeit more limited in scope and pervasiveness than in the past, of EPL in the UK after Brexit. The next section will discuss the landscape before Brexit and, more specifically, will touch upon the history of the offices and their functions. The following section will look at the current situation, both in terms of number, size and structure of the existing offices (section 3.1), as well as in terms of the most significant developments instigated by Brexit (section 3.2). This section draws on a review of emerging documentation and interviews conducted in 2021 and 2022 with actors engaged in representing the interests of UK localities and devolved administrations. The reporting of the findings respects the anonymity requested by the interviewees. The final section will lay out the concluding remarks concerning the continuing relevance of the offices and of the concept of EPL.

2 AN EXCURSUS OF THE EUROPEAN OFFICES OF THE UK SUBSTATE AUTHORITIES PRIOR TO BREXIT

The first UK region to open a liaison office in Brussels was Birmingham in 1984, followed in the same year by Strathclyde. In 1994 there were 20 substate offices from the UK, 18 of which were established between 1988 and 1994.[8] These became 29 by 2009, a year that marks the beginning of the crisis of the Eurozone.[9] By 2016, though, shortly before Brexit, their number had already decreased to 15.[10] This fluctuation mirrors the deepening of European integration arising from the Single European Act of 1986, which completed the Single Market, and from the Treaty of Maastricht six years later, which established the EU as an umbrella organisation. These developments increased the reasons for the UK regions to engage with the institutions in Brussels.

In the UK, however, in coincidence with the Eurozone crisis that began in 2009, a significant portion of the public opinion became increasingly disenchanted with the EU or turned against membership of the EU. This led to the questioning by citizens of the cost to the taxpayer and value for money of the European offices.[11] It is also

8. J. Mawson (ed.), P. John, J.E. Birnie, D.M.W.N. Hitchens & E. Nel, 'Policy Review Section', *Regional Studies*, 1994, Vol. 28, No. 7, pp. 739-759, p. 740.
9. Committee of the Regions, 'Associations/Bureaux de Representation Regionale et Communale a Bruxelles: Repertoire' (Committee of the Regions, 2009); J. Greenwood, *Interest Representation in the European Union* (Palgrave Macmillan, 3rd ed. 2011), p. 186.
10. C. Panara and M.R. Varney, 'Multi-level Governance in the EU and EU Democracy: Democratic Legitimacy, Democratic Accountability and Transparency of the European Offices of the English Local Authorities', *Regional & Federal Studies*, 2017, Vol. 27, No. 2, pp. 153-170, p. 155. The authors counted 11 offices from England, plus the representations of the Scottish local authorities and of the three devolved administrations.
11. *See, e.g.*, the Freedom of Information request addressed to Northamptonshire County Council by a citizen on 5 September 2011: https://www.whatdotheyknow.com/request/office_in_brussels (accessed July 2022).

noticeable how the size of some UK offices became smaller in terms of number of staff and funding.[12]

Prior to Brexit, the Brussels-based offices of the UK regions had generally a fourfold function: promoting the image of the region in Brussels; seizing opportunities, particularly funding opportunities, arising from the EU for businesses and organisations from the region;[13] networking with other regions; and monitoring and attempting to influence, for example through lobbying, policy and legislative developments in Brussels.[14] The second function (attracting EU funding to the region) used to be the most important role of the European offices of the English local authorities before Brexit. The fourth function (monitoring and influencing policy), however, was the most relevant to EPL theory, in that it reflects the proactive role of substate units from EU Member States in adapting to policy and legislative developments originating from Brussels, as well as in attempting to influence these developments.

Lobbying and networking were prior to Brexit the most common approaches by the European offices of the English regions to attempt to influence EU decision-making. Lobbying regarded primarily the Commission and the Members of the European Parliament (MEPs), particularly those, irrespective of the Member State of origin, who were chairs or rapporteurs of relevant committees of the European Parliament.[15] The offices also used to talk to and work closely with the UK Mission to the EU (UKRep). This was effective given that the UK government held a seat in the Council where it could cast its vote. Networking, on the other hand, facilitated the creation of coalitions around agendas relevant to the regions from various EU countries, as well as the sharing of best practice between these regions. The most important networks to this purpose are Eurocities, the European Regions Research & Innovation Network, and the

12. O. Sykes and A. Lord, 'Whither a Europe of the (English) regions? Reflections on the Prospects for the Representation of English Territorial Interests in Europe', *Local Economy*, 2011, Vol. 26, No. 6-7, pp. 486-489.
13. The most important funding schemes for the UK local and regional authorities until Brexit were the European Regional Development Fund, the European Social Fund, the Cohesion Funds, the European Structural and Investment Funds, European Regions Research and Innovation Network, Interreg Europe and Horizon. Horizon was particularly important for UK universities and research institutions.
14. On the UK regions, *see* S. Macneill, C. Jeffery and J. Gibney, 'Changing Dynamics of Regional Representation in Brussels: A Case Study of Birmingham and the West Midlands, 1984-2004', *Regional Studies*, 2007, Vol. 41, No. 3, pp. 403-414, pp. 406-407. On the European regions in general, *see* G. Marks, R. Haesly and H. Mbaye, 'What Do Subnational Offices Think They Are Doing in Brussels?', *Regional and Federal Studies*, 2002, Vol. 12, pp. 1-23; M. Callanan and M. Tatham, 'Territorial Interest Representation in the European Union: Actors, Objectives and Strategies', *Journal of European Public Policy*, 2014, Vol. 21, pp. 188-210; M. Tatham, 'Networkers, Fund-Hunters, Intermediaries, or Policy Players? The Activities of Regions in Brussels', *West European Politics*, 2017, Vol. 40, pp. 1088-1108; M. Tatham, 'The Rise of Regional Influence in the EU – From Soft Policy Lobbying to Hard Vetoing', *Journal of Common Market Studies*, 2018, Vol. 56, pp. 672-686.
15. C. Panara and M. Varney, *A Study on the Transparency and Accountability of the European Offices of the English Local Authorities in Brussels: Synthetising and Developing Good Practice Guidance* (Liverpool and Hull, 9 June 2017, available from the author); C. Panara, *The Sub-national Dimension of the EU: A Legal Study of Multilevel Governance* (Springer, 2015), pp. 144-149.

Conference of Peripheral and Maritime Regions (CPMR).[16] An example of successful collective lobbying activity by some English regions prior to Brexit is the inclusion of the 'transition regions', those with a gross domestic product (GDP) between 75% and 90% of the average EU GDP, in the interventions envisaged by Objective 1 of the European Regional Development Fund.[17]

The establishment by the UK substate units of European Brussels-based offices corroborates the validity of Birkinshaw's EPL theory in a twofold manner. First of all, the offices are a clear response to the impact on domestic law of the law and policies originating from the EU.[18] Their focus on influencing EU legislation and policy illustrates that there used to be a two-way process whereby not only EU law impacted on the UK, but also the UK government and substate units attempted to influence policy and legislative developments in the EU. The regional offices were indeed important vehicles channelling this influence.

Second, the fact that the number and size of the offices varied significantly over time, accompanies and mirrors the evolution of the EU and of the relationship between the UK and the EU over the years. It is not merely by accident that Birkinshaw published his book on EPL in 2003 at the apex of European integration, with the Union that the following year would incorporate ten new states, and following the significant expansion of EU competences in previous years. This period coincides with the time in office of three pro-European prime ministers - John Major (1990-1997), Tony Blair (1997-2007), Gordon Brown (2007-2010). As previously noted, the number of the UK offices, and more specifically of the English offices, multiplied and reached its peak around 2009 also thanks to the funding for the offices and focus provided to English regions by the Regional Development Agencies (RDAs). These were abolished in 2012 by the Cameron government.

3 THE POST-BREXIT SITUATION

3.1 Number, Size and Structure of the Current Offices

At present (July 2022), two years and a half after the UK left the EU, there are nine UK regional offices in Brussels.[19] Three of these offices represent the devolved administrations, accordingly, only six offices represent local government authorities and this

16. Sixteen UK cities, including London, Birmingham, Manchester and Bristol *inter alia*, still retain membership of Eurocities. Scotland and Wales still retain membership of the CPMR.
17. C. Panara, *The Sub-national Dimension of the EU: A Legal Study of Multilevel Governance* (Springer, 2015), p. 151.
18. L. Hooghe and G. Marks, *Multi-Level Governance and European Integration* (Rowman & Littlefield, 2001), pp. 89-90.
19. There are five offices from England:

    (i) Bristol & Bath Brussels Office
    (ii) London European Office
    (iii) Kent County Council in Brussels
    (iv) Greater Birmingham & West Midlands Brussels Office
    (v) Local Government Association.

includes two associations of local authorities (the Local Government Association (LGA), and the Convention of the Scottish Local Authorities (COSLA)). Only five out of the nine existing Brussels-based offices represent local authorities from England.

The number of the Brussels-based offices, therefore, declined substantially compared to the years between the entry into force of the Treaty of Maastricht and the first decade of the 2000s (from 29 to the current 9). The number declined visibly also compared to the period immediately preceding the Brexit referendum (23 June 2016), when there were as many as 15 offices. It is noticeable that a number of English regions traditionally very active in the Brussels arena, such as Liverpool, Manchester, Cornwall, South of England, and East of England, closed their representations, whereas others, such as Northamptonshire County Council, have never followed up on their pre-Brexit plans to establish a liaison office in Brussels.

The current number of the offices is small compared to other countries. Two Member States of the European Free Trade Association (EFTA) in 2021 had more regional representations, in proportion to the respective population, than the UK (Norway, 6; Iceland, 1).[20] This shows how the relationship of a country with the EU has a critical impact on the substate engagement with the institutions in Brussels. Norway, for example, along with Iceland and Liechtenstein, is a member of the European Economic Area (EEA), as well as of the EFTA. EEA membership implies that most Single Market rules, including those concerning the free movements, apply to these countries, although not automatically. This means that these countries have to incorporate any new relevant EU law into their domestic legal systems.[21] By contrast, the UK since the beginning of 2021 is no longer a member of the Single Market and the UK parliament is at least in theory at liberty to diverge from European rules and standards.[22]

The offices have been noticeably downsized too. For example, the Birmingham & West Midlands Office, the oldest UK regional office in Brussels, that counted 17 employees back in the 1990s, currently has only one full-time staff and two interns. Similarly, London's European Office had three full-time staff and one half-time

---

Hampshire County Council's Brussels Office was closed in September 2022 following an Executive decision taken in January 2022.

There are, additionally, four offices from the regions with devolved powers:

(i) Scotland Europa
(ii) Wales in Europe
(iii) Convention of Scottish Local Authorities (COSLA)
(iv) Northern Ireland Brussels Office.

There is also a City of London Brussels Office which, however, represents the City of London Corporation and not a 'region'.

20. C. Panara, 'The Activities in Brussels of the Local and Regional Authorities from European Free Trade Area Countries', *Regional & Federal Studies*, published on 17 February 2021 (open access).
21. *See* C. Baudenbacher (ed.), *The Handbook of EEA Law* (Springer, 2015); C. Baudenbacher (ed.), *The Fundamental Principles of EEA Law: EEA-ities* (Springer, 2017).
22. The Conservative leadership contender Liz Truss MP pledged to diverge from outdated EU law and frameworks if she becomes the next British Prime Minister. *See* 'Liz Truss Vows to Review All EU Law on British Statute', *Financial Times*, 22 July 2022, https://www.ft.com/content/3703d4cc-4071-4f05-a885-b1d273f7766c (accessed July 2022).

administrative support staff in 2017, but only one full-time employee at present. The downsizing of the offices, however, is not solely a by-product of Brexit, but also of the COVID-19 pandemic that led to the reduction of the volume of affairs in Brussels for nearly two years. It is also a result of the significant cuts in central funding transferred to local government.[23]

In terms of size, if one looks at the number of Brussels-based full-time employees, the number of permanent full-time staff for the English offices is usually one full-time staff, occasionally with the support of some interns, with the exception of the LGA's Brussels Office that employs 2.7 permanent staff. The offices of the devolved administrations are bigger, given their wider political agendas, with the Northern Irish representation counting nine staff (seven in Brussels and two in Belfast), Wales in Europe nine including two staff working in a partner office, and Scotland Europe 17 (equating 16.8 full-time equivalent).

The current English offices are either entirely owned by one local authority (Kent County Council Office, and London European Office which is entirely owned by the Greater London Authority), or partnerships between local councils and various stakeholders from the region, such as, the local universities and the chambers of commerce (Bristol & Bath Office, Greater Birmingham & West Midlands Office). This second model was common among Brussels offices of the English regions prior to Brexit.[24] The offices of the LGA and of COSLA are entirely funded by the councils from England and Wales and Scotland, respectively, which are members of these associations. The devolved administrations have representations that are organised as delegations to the EU.

Despite Brexit, therefore, some substate authorities from the UK continue to engage with the EU and this phenomenon is not limited to the devolved administrations. Whilst Brexit clearly had an impact on the engagement of these authorities with the EU, at least some of the 'pull' and 'push' factors to go to Brussels still exist, even though the UK is no longer a member of the EU, nor did it become a member of the EEA or of the EFTA. 'Pull' factors are the opportunities the substate authorities can seize in Brussels (mostly, prior to Brexit, European funding). 'Push' factors are located in the domestic context of regional governance. These concern the constitutional status and powers of the substate authorities.[25] This adds strength to the argument I put forward at the outset that the notion of EPL maintains currency in the present post-Brexit regime, albeit in a more circumscribed manner than in the past.

23. *See* the report by G. Atkins and S. Hoddinott, 'Neighbourhoods Services under Strain: How a Decade of Cuts and Rising Demand for Social Care Affected Local Services', Institute for Government, May 2022, https://www.instituteforgovernment.org.uk/sites/default/files/publications/neighbourhood-services-under-strain.pdf (accessed July 2022).
24. C. Panara and M. Varney, *A Study on the Transparency and Accountability of the European Offices of the English Local Authorities in Brussels: Synthetising and Developing Good Practice Guidance* (Liverpool and Hull, 9 June 2017, available from the author).
25. *See, inter alia*, S. Macneill, C. Jeffery and J. Gibney, 'Changing Dynamics of Regional Representation in Brussels: A Case Study of Birmingham and the West Midlands, 1984-2004', *Regional Studies*, 2007, Vol. 41, No. 3, pp. 403-414, pp. 406-407.

3.2 The Functions of the Existing European Offices

Past research found that the main activities in Brussels of the regions from EU countries concern information-gathering, networking, liaising between the region and the EU, chasing funding and influencing policy. Regions with legislative powers typically engage in lobbying of the EU institutions to influence policy, whereas substate authorities without such powers tend to do so to a far lesser extent.[26] In this paragraph I will attempt to situate the existing European offices of the UK regions according to this knowledge.

An area of work common to all the existing offices concerns the scanning of the policy horizon in Brussels. Although the UK has now left the EU, the EU remains a powerhouse for regulation and trade. Its ability to influence certain sectors of UK law and economy remains strong. One example of this is the rules on vehicle emissions and safety. Whilst in theory the UK could pass its own rules and depart from EU standards, this is unlikely. Lower standards would lead to worse air quality in the UK than in the EU and this might not be politically sustainable in the UK, whereas higher standards would likely meet the opposition of domestic car manufacturers that would endure a competitive disadvantage. The more the regulatory standards on, for example, health, consumer and environmental protection diverge between the UK and the EU, the more frictions to trade are created. If in coming years frictionless trade with the bloc continues to be a political priority for UK governments, this inevitably requires that the UK retains most EU standards.

The influencing of policy and lobbying shrank as expected after Brexit due to a combination of factors. One is certainly the more limited and indirect relevance of EU law in the UK compared to the past. The other has to do with the difficulty of influencing EU decision-making processes. This difficulty originates from being outside the EU, with the result that the EU institutions are less inclined to consider the demands from UK regions. These, however, attempt to overcome the present limitations by remaining active in various European networks, such as, Eurocities and the CPMR, and by forming coalitions within these groupings to influence the EU in relation to common themes.

The UK substate authorities benefit from the EU status of their partners to obtain information which would not otherwise be easily accessible. They also benefit from the political leverage that EU regions, unlike those from third countries, may have on the decision-making processes of the EU institutions. This is significant for multilevel governance theory, traditionally exclusively focused on substate actors from the EU, and confirms the findings of earlier studies that the engagement of substate actors in

26. G. Marks, R. Haesly and H. Mbaye, 'What Do Subnational Offices Think They Are Doing in Brussels?', *Regional and Federal Studies*, 2002, Vol. 12, pp. 1-23; M. Callanan and M. Tatham, 'Territorial Interest Representation in the European Union: Actors, Objectives and Strategies', *Journal of European Public Policy*, 2014, Vol. 21, pp. 188-210; M. Tatham, 'Networkers, Fund-Hunters, Intermediaries, or Policy Players? The Activities of Regions in Brussels', *West European Politics*, 2017, Vol. 40, pp. 1088-1108; M. Tatham, 'The Rise of Regional Influence in the EU – From Soft Policy Lobbying to Hard Vetoing', *Journal of Common Market Studies*, 2018, Vol. 56, pp. 672-686.

the EU is not limited to EU countries.[27] These networking activities are also channels for the sharing of best practice in local government (for example, in relation to waste management systems).

It is important to note, however, that in this context the position of Northern Ireland, Scotland and Wales, the three devolved administrations, differs from that of the other substate authorities from the UK. Northern Ireland remains part of the Single Market for goods, therefore some EU rules remain applicable to that region, which in turn explains why Northern Ireland engages more intensively than other regions in attempting to influence EU law. Scotland on the other hand passed an act that enables the Scottish government to adapt the Scottish legislation to the EU law in some areas. This, again, explains the stronger engagement of Scotland with the EU institutions compared to other parts of the UK. It is important to note that the current Scottish government makes no mysteries about its desire to join the EU as an independent country at some point in the future, and therefore of its desire to retain a close alignment to European rules.[28]

Northern Ireland, Wales and Scotland are regions with a strong constitutional status and with the power to pass primary legislation. These regions, due to the range and importance of their responsibilities and complexity of their interests, tend to engage more with the EU institutions compared to other, merely administrative regions, without primary legislative power, such as, the local government authorities from England. Wales, the only devolved government at present which is both pro-European and in favour of remaining part of Britain, does not have a law promoting the alignment to laws emanating from Brussels, nor is it part of the Single Market. Accordingly, even though it is a region with primary legislative powers, Wales does not have amongst its current priorities the influencing of EU law and policy.

The limited engagement by the English local government authorities in attempting to influence EU policy depends on a number of reasons. One important reason is probably the difficulty to influence effectively EU legislative processes. English local authorities clearly see lobbying as too time-consuming and costly, as well as conducive to meagre results unless there are wider coalitions of substate authorities or other political actors across the EU that support the same positions. Additionally, the English offices representing individual regions (Kent, Bristol & Bath, London, Birmingham & West Midlands), with an average of only one full-time employee, are not adequately staffed for this quite resource-intensive type of activity.[29] The exception in this context is the LGA with its 2.7 full-time employees, although even the LGA does not engage in direct lobbying of the EU institutions. It continues to work with other local government

27. C. Panara, 'The Activities in Brussels of the Local and Regional Authorities from European Free Trade Area countries', *Regional & Federal Studies*, published on 17 February 2021 (open access).
28. *See, e.g.*, 'Nicola Sturgeon's speech launching the case for independence', 14 June 2022, https://www.snp.org/nicola-sturgeons-speech-launching-the-case-for-independence/ (accessed July 2022).
29. The size of the Bristol Brussels Office has not changed significantly compared to prior to Brexit. The Office of Greater London Authority, however, moved from three full-time staff in 2017 to the current one only. Birmingham had 17 full-time staff back in the 1990s and certainly around 10 in 2017, and only one currently. Kent had four full-time staff in 2002 and only one currently.

associations from the EU, when they engage in lobbying in areas that could have an indirect impact on future UK policy, such as, environment and waste, energy and climate change, social and labour laws, public procurement, state aid.

The UK regional offices provide support for funding opportunities emanating from the EU. This stream of activity is prominent in relation to the European offices of substate authorities from the EU,[30] as well as for those from Norway and Iceland which are EFTA-EEA countries.[31] The only funding still available to UK substate authorities post-Brexit, however, is limited to Horizon Europe and to some EU projects funded before Brexit (Kent County Council, for example, will manage some of these projects until 2023). At present (July 2022), however, the association of the UK to Horizon is still uncertain due to the political dispute arising from the stated intention of the UK government to amend unilaterally some essential parts of the Northern Ireland Protocol. Another strand of funding that remains available is the PEACE Programme, although its relevance is limited to Northern Ireland.

4 CONCLUDING REMARKS

Brexit has not marked the end of the engagement with the EU by the UK local authorities and devolved administrations. There are aspects and areas of EU law that are still relevant to the UK since the EU remains (as a representative from one of the existing UK offices effectively described it) a 'regulatory superpower', and because of the legal requirement (Northern Ireland) or decision (Scotland) of a part of the UK to keep an alignment to some EU rules. Some historic (pre-Brexit) functions of the UK offices are still in place, such as, information-gathering, networking with other regions and promoting the image of the region in the EU. Others play a smaller role than in the past, such as chasing funding and influencing policy. Two devolved administrations, Scotland and Northern Ireland, continue to attempt to influence policy. This does not appear to be currently the case in Wales.

The divorce between the UK and the EU does not mark the complete end of the idea of EPL. Not only the UK is still bound to the European Convention of Human Rights through the Human Rights Act 1998,[32] but also:

30. C. Rowe, *Regional Representations in the EU: Between Diplomacy and Interest Mediation* (Palgrave-Macmillan, 2011), pp. 83-125; C. Panara, *The Sub-national Dimension of the EU: A Legal Study of Multilevel Governance* (Springer, 2015), pp. 127-154; C. Panara and M.R. Varney, 'Multi-level Governance in the EU and EU Democracy: Democratic Legitimacy, Democratic Accountability and Transparency of the European Offices of the English Local Authorities', *Regional & Federal Studies*, 2017, Vol. 27, No. 2, pp. 153-170.
31. C. Panara, 'The Activities in Brussels of the Local and Regional Authorities from European Free Trade Area Countries', *Regional & Federal Studies*, published on 17 February 2021 (open access).
32. On 22 June 2022 the UK government introduced the Bill of Rights Bill to repeal and replace the Human Rights Act 1998. If passed into law, the Bill could limit the scope of some Convention rights and diminish the role of the European Court of Human Rights in the UK. *See* M. Elliott, 'The UK's (new) Bill of Rights', 22 June 2022, blog *Public Law for Everyone*, available at https://publiclawforeveryone.com/2022/06/22/the-uks-new-bill-of-rights/ (accessed July 20 22).

- Some EU Law remains applicable to parts of the country directly (Northern Ireland pursuant to the Northern Ireland Protocol) or indirectly (Scotland, pursuant to the UK Withdrawal from the EU (Continuity) (Scotland) Act 2021).
- Even where regulatory divergence can now take place following Brexit, there is still a relevance of EU law in certain areas due to the leading role of the EU as a bloc of 27 states and ca. 450 million people. Areas where EU law is still relevant as benchmarking and guidance include environment and waste, energy and climate change, social and labour laws, public procurement, state aid, *inter alia*.[33]
- Some UK substate authorities have a desire to remain in Brussels and to engage with the EU and with partners from the EU, as well as to promote the image of their regions in Brussels. This instigates a process of cross-fertilisation and the sharing of best practice across the Channel.

Because of its solidity and epistemic value, Birkinshaw's notion of EPL has always been useful to me as an interpretative tool throughout my career as a legal academic whenever I reflected on the relationship between the Member States and the Union. If, as argued in this paper, the notion maintains some currency even after Brexit, my expectation is that it will remain useful to scholars to understand the mutual influences between the laws of the remaining 27 Member States and the EU, as well as the new and still evolving relationship between the UK and the bloc, the effects of any remaining retained EU law in the UK alongside the continuing regard to EU law by UK courts.

33. These are the areas that a number of offices mentioned to me in research interviews I conducted in 2021 and 2022.

CHAPTER 30

Implementing China's Constitution: Democratic Dialogue Model and Its Limitations

Zheng Zhu[*]

1 INTRODUCTION

China's 1982 Constitution is often seen as a unique legal instrument that does not have real impact upon the legal practice. This observation is not true. The Constitution does have influence over the legal system - not through judicial rulings, but through law makings. Different from its Western counterparts, China's 1982 Constitution relies on the legislatures at central and local levels rather than the judiciary to be enforced. However, this does not mean the court's hands are entirely bound. On the contrary, in the face of numerous forms of sub-statutory legal documents, the court is making interpretative efforts to bring all sub-constitutional legislation in line with the Constitution. While normatively deprived of powers to interpret the Constitution, the court is still trying to not only preserve the uniformity of the legal system, but also enforce the Constitution by tabling requests of constitutional review. In doing so, it is holding a dialogue with the legislature over the legality and constitutionality issues, but due to the lack of common law tradition and an effective mechanism that brings the political force to account, China's court rulings are not held in the respect of their English counterparts, which hence further tips the balance in favour of the top legislature. As a result, the court rulings would not be strictly followed by the lawmakers. This explains why the democratic dialogue model that effectively deciphers the British

* I thank Professor Patrick J. Birkinshaw and Dr Michael Varney, who supervised my doctoral thesis from 2013 to 2018. All errors remain mine.

constitutional relationship cannot be effectively employed in examining China's legislative-judicial interactions.

This chapter explores how the 1982 Chinese Constitution is implemented. In order to answer the question, the thesis investigates the normative obstacles holding the Constitution back from taking effect. Moreover, it examines how the dialogue between the legislature and judiciary begins and proceeds in the course of enforcing the Constitution. For many years, China's constitution has been viewed fundamentally differently from its Western counterparts – the People's Republic of China (PRC) had inherited the mainstream Marxism-Leninism ideology from its Soviet progenitor. Until today the ruling Party of China officially claims the country is a socialist state led by the Chinese Communist Party (CCP).[1] Ideological divergence determines that China embraces a distinctive constitutional mechanism from the West – it was on the advice of the former Soviet Union leader Joseph Stalin that China embarked on drafting its first Constitution,[2] and after several revisions, the current 1982 Constitution still provides that 'the socialist system is the fundamental system of the People's Republic of China'. All of this in one way or another demonstrates that China's Constitution is unique.

Indeed, China's Constitution is certainly different. This is nowhere better seen than the discussion of how to enforce the Constitution. After many years of debates and discussion, the calls for setting up a Western-style judicial review system in China are believed to be untenable; the aspiration to implementing the Chinese 1982 Constitution can never be met via a superficial comparison or even conflation with its supposed counterparts in the United Kingdom (UK), United States (US), or any other countries. Instead, the Constitution can only be accurately grasped and successfully enforced by following its own logic. However, this does not mean there is no room to make a comparison between China and the West. On the contrary, parallels can be pressed in some more concrete areas such as how to understand the meaning of the terms 'human rights' and 'justiciability' in the Chinese context, and how does the judiciary engage in the dialogue with the legislature, and how to turn the idea of human rights protection into reality despite various normative and political barriers. After all, even though the idea that China could directly copy the American judicial system has all but disappeared, the objectives behind the PRC Constitution are the same as those embedded in the Western Constitutions, that is, to reaffirm the role of individual in the market, and to protect ordinary citizens' interests.[3]

For these reasons, the ensuing discussion comprises three parts. The first part begins with the Constitutional promises made on human rights, which on the one hand highlights twists and turns that human rights development have witnessed, and on the other lays down a foundation for the overall discussion. This will be followed by an

1. Barry Naughton, 'Is China Socialist?', *Journal of Economic Perspectives*, 2017, 31(1): 3-24.
2. Han Dayuan, *1954 Nian Xianfa Zhiding Guocheng (The Making of the 1954 Constitution)*, (Law Press, 2014), 62-69.
3. Tian Lei, *Jiwang Yiwei Xuzhang (Using Past as Prologue, The Institutional Landscape of Constitutional Politics in China)*, (Guangxi Normal University Press, 2021), Chapter 6.

analysis of several plausible propositions and a detailed exposition of the term 'justiciable' in the Chinese context. By dismissing these propositions, the thesis in its second part will bring forward an alternative but more pragmatic way to enforce the Constitution - implementing the Constitution through legislation. As a supplement to the first part, this part presses ahead with the exploration by filling the gap in the chain of reasoning, and highlights the merits and demerits of the implementation, by comparing it with the UK approach. The whole chapter will conclude in the third part with a reflection upon the two mechanisms and make reference to the democratic dialogue theory arising from the UK Constitution. It would explain why the prevailing UK theoretical tool cannot be effectively used to portray the interplays between the legislature and the judiciary in the Chinese context, nor is it a panacea to the challenges facing China.

2 IMPLEMENTING THE CONSTITUTION: THE BEST WAY?

2.1 The Constitution and Human Rights Protection

As a country with a written Constitution, China has its 1982 Constitution sitting at the top of the legal system, with self-proclaimed highest 'authoritativeness'. In the Preamble to the 1982 Constitution, the last sentence reads: '[the Constitution] is the fundamental law of the state and has supreme legal authority'. As a result, the Constitution provides only the most important contents in the country's legal and political narratives. For example, the main content of the Constitution includes the party's leadership, the state's general principles, the institutions of the state, the national symbols such as the flag, emblem, capital, and most important of all, fundamental rights and duties of its citizens.[4]

In terms of human rights' protection, the 1982 Constitution has two revealing changes from earlier models. First, it has rearranged the structure of the new Constitution by placing the human rights chapter ahead of the chapter on state institutions. This stands in a stark contrast with its three precursors - the 1954, 1975, and 1978 PRC Constitutions, which had long put the state organs prior to the human rights chapter, insisting that the collective interests supersede those of individuals.[5] As noted by commentators, restructuring the 1982 Constitution represents a revolutionary shift in the constitutional thinking,[6] denoting that human rights carry heavier weight than state organs, and the institutions exist only to serve the people. In a deeper sense,

4. Articles 34 to 48, the 1982 PRC Constitution.
5. Mo Jihong, 'Xianfa Jigou Fazhan He Bianqian de 60nian - Xianfa Wenben Zhong Guojia Jigou de Tezheng Kaocha (Constitutional Institution Development and Vicissitude over the 60 Years: Features of the State Instittion in the Constitutional Text)', *Faxue Zazhi (Law Science Magazine)*, 2014, 12: 18. Han Dayuan, 'Xinzhongguo Xianfa Fazhan Licheng (II) (New China's Constitutional Development Path II)', *Falv yu Shenghuo (Law and Life)*, 2015, 05: 64.
6. Han Dayuan, '1982 Nian Xianfa de Renwen Jingshen (The Humanistic Spirit of the 1982 PRC Constitution)' *Fashang Yanjiu (Studies in Law and Business)*, 2012, 03: 9.

it symbolises a significant step towards setting up a human rights-oriented constitutional mechanism, which echoes an ancient natural law philosophy that human rights should be taken as being prior to, rather than derived from, state or any legal order.[7]

The significance of reorganising the Constitution's structure can, however, only be properly understood within the historical background. As mentioned before, since the founding of the new China in 1949, four Constitutions have been issued. Time and again the first PRC Constitution, the 1954 Constitution, has been recognised as an instrument with great merits and a main source of inspiration for the subsequent constitutional iteration.[8] Nevertheless, even in the 1954 Constitution, the chapter in respect of fundamental rights and duties was placed after the chapter on state organs, implying that the state, represented by the institutions, is more important than individuals. Understandably, this thinking was enlarged by the 1975 Constitution during the Cultural Revolution years, when the class conflicts were provoked and the tension escalated.[9] Although the 1978 Constitution in part reinforced the human rights' protection after the frenzied political movement ended in 1976,[10] the ill-designed structure lingered on. It was not until the 1982 Constitution that the structure was eventually put to rest.

The second remarkable change is that a new human rights provision was added to the 1982 Constitution. The provision was ushered in through the 2004 Constitutional Amendment, which read that 'the state preserves and protects human rights'. The clause is often cited as the 'human rights clause', and was applauded as bearing considerable significance in at least three respects. First, compared with the rhetoric of 'citizens' fundamental rights', which only covers 'citizens', the newly added term 'human rights' includes all groups of people, which, noted by some authors, suggests that the scope of rights' protection was greatly broadened.[11] Second, by including a general human rights clause, the 27 concrete 'citizen's rights' enumerated by the following articles are recognised as 'human rights', which implies that social rights are deemed as human rights in China. Perhaps more importantly, it is believed that the

7. Qu Xiangfei, 'Woguo Xianfa Shang de "Ren" yu Renquan Baozhang (Human Being and Human Rights in the Chinese Constitution)', *Renquan (Human Rights)*, 2013, 04: 51. For similar discussion in the UK law, *see* Aileen McHarg, 'Rights and Democracy in UK Public Law' in Mark Elliott and David Feldman (eds), *Rights and Democracy in UK Public Law*, vol 2015 (Cambridge University Press 2015) 116.
8. Tu Siyi, 'Wusi Xianfa Zhi Gongmin Quanli Yiwu Guifan de Tedian (On Features of Citizens' Rights and Obligations in the 1954 Constitution)', *Faxue Pinglun (Law Review)*, 2011, 04: 13.
9. It is worth noting that even in the 1975 and the 1978 Constitutions, two constitutions that made during the chaotic Cultural Revolution period, human rights contents were not completely removed. The remaining parts of human rights include the right to vote, work, education, rest and the right to material assistance, as well as freedom of speech, correspondence, the press, assembly, association, procession, demonstration, religion and the freedom to strike, freedom of person and homes (the 1975 PRC Constitution, Articles 27 to 28; the 1978 PRC Constitution, Articles 44 to 53).
10. Mo Jihong, '1978 Nian Xianfa Zai Renquan Baozhang Zhong de Zhuyao Tezheng Jiqi Zuoyong (The 1978 Constitution's Main Features and Role in Protecting Human Rights)', *Henan Sheng Zhengfa Ganbu Guanli Xueyuan Xuebao (Journal of Henan Administrative Institute of Politics)*, 2005, 02: 11.
11. Han Dayuan, 'Jiben Quanli Gainian Zai Zhongguo de Qiyuan yu Yanbian (The Derivative and Evolution of the Concept of Fundamental Rights in China)', *China Legal Science*, 2009, 06: 15.

human rights clause also refers to rights that do not appear in the 1982 Constitution, which include the rights to life, to strike, and access to justice and so on.[12] Seen in this light, adding a human rights clause to the Constitution is indeed a great progress in protecting human rights.

To recap, the newly added human rights clause and the constitutional restructuring have proved the state's resolution to enhance and protect human rights. As positive as these new changes may sound, a major conundrum revolving around the 1982 Constitution, however, has never been resolved in China, i.e., how to implement the Constitution itself. Clearly, without a clear answer to the question, all promises made therein, however serious they are, are built on sand. For this reason, the ensuing section explicates one way that has been proposed by many analysts for the Constitution to be carried out.

2.2 Dual Meanings of Justiciability in the Chinese Context

A plethora of solutions have been propounded to 'give teeth to the Constitution', i.e., to give effect to the Constitution, the most frequent one being to make the Constitution justiciable.[13] Proponents of this scheme complained that the Constitution has been placed beyond people's reach, and in order to realise the aspiration of the Constitution, they argued that the Constitution should be justiciable so that the provisions of the Constitution may be reflected in reality. In Chinese legal literature, however, what is meant by 'justiciable' is largely under-specified. At first glance, all would agree that 'justiciable' is tantamount to enabling the courts to enforce the Constitution, allowing the rights stipulated in the Constitution to be interpreted and applied by the courts, and serving as a basis for adjudications. However, on a closer inspection, its meaning becomes blurred.

Two formulas of explanations are given to the meaning of 'justiciable'. Some advocated that the Constitution should be invoked directly in litigation so that not only constitutional cases, but also 'ordinary ones'[14] are to be resolved on constitutional grounds – as long as they contain constitutional ingredients.[15] Perhaps this stance is manifestly exemplified in the Qi Yuling case, where Ms Qi attempted to seek financial and spiritual remedies from the defendant, who had stolen Ms Qi's identity and studied

12. *Ibid.*
13. Bao Wanchao, 'Xianzheng Zhuanxing yu Zhongguo Sifa Shencha Zhidu (Constitutional Transformation and the Judicial Review in China)', *Zhongwai Faxue (Peking University Law Journal)*, 2008, 06: 805-827. Zhang Qianfan, 'Sifa Shencha yu Minzhu: Maodun Zhong de Gongshengti? (Judicial Review and Democracy: Symbiosis in Paradox?)', *Huanqiu Falv Pinglun (Global Law Review)*, 2009, 01: 58. Wang Lei, *Xianfa De Sifahua (Constitutional Law Applied in Courts)* (China University of Political Science and Law Press 2000) Chapter 7.
14. The term 'ordinary cases' refers to cases that can be settled on non-constitutional grounds, or cases containing no constitutional disputes.
15. Li Zhong and Zhang Cheng, 'Sifa Jiguan yu Xianfa Shiyong (The Judiciary and Constitutional Applicability)' in Zhang Qianfan (ed.), *Xianzheng Luncong (Constitutionalism Review)*, Vol. 03 (Law Press 2003) 526. Tong Zhiwei, 'Xianfa Sifa Shiyong Yanjiu Zhong de Jige Wenti (Several Issues Concerning Making the Constitution Justiciable)', *Faxue (Law Science)*, 2001, 11: 3-8. Cai Dingjian, 'Guanyu Shenme Shi Xianfa (On the Concept and Nature of the Constitution)', *Zhongwai Faxue (Peking University Law Journal)*, 2002, 01: 97, 99-101.

in school under Qi's name. The court found there was no law applicable except the Constitution, since in the Chinese General Principles of Civil Law (the General Principles of Civil Law (GPCL), Minfa Tongze), no such right as 'the right to education' was enshrined. In a reply to the Shandong Province High Court, the Supreme People's Court of China (SPC) did not explicitly order the case to be resolved on a constitutional ground, but it did clarify that Ms Qi's 'constitutional right' – the right to education – had been infringed, and she was therefore entitled to financial remedies.[16] The case was thus resolved by local courts on constitutional grounds. It was acclaimed by some scholars as a milestone marking the opening of a floodgate for the Constitution to be applied in civil litigations.[17]

Other commentators took the term 'justiciable' differently as indicating that the courts are entitled to review the constitutionality of a statute in the light of the Constitution.[18] This stance may arguably find its trace in the Sun Zhigang case,[19] where Mr Sun, a 27-year-old victim, was detained in an Internment and Deportation Transfer Centre, because he did not have a temporary residence permit. Mr Sun was later battered to death by inmates. According to the then effective Measures for Custody and Repatriation of Urban Vagrants and Beggars (MCR), an administrative regulation, the police in China could detain people if they did not have a residence permit. Obviously, the MCR violated Article 37 of the Constitution by depriving citizens of freedom and imposing restrictions on fundamental rights. In order to make the Constitution justiciable, three law students launched a petition to the National People's Congress Standing Committee (the NPCSC), questioning the constitutionality of the MCR. In review of the case and the petition, the term 'justiciable' was interpreted in terms of reviewing the pertinent administrative regulation in accordance with the Constitution.

For the above two cases, it appears that the term 'justiciable' encompasses at least two important yet barely distinguished connotations: it can refer to applying the Constitution to solve general legal disputes in individual cases, for example, civil or criminal ones; or it may indicate invoking the Constitution to resolve discrepancies between enactments, which is often more precisely termed 'constitutionality review'. The ensuing section will therefore first articulate the plausibility of the reading of the

16. The Legal Reply of the SPC, *Guanyu Yi Qinfan Xingmingquan De Shouduan Qinfan Xianfa Baohu de Gongmin Shoujiaoyu De Jiben Quanli Shifou Ying Chengdan Minshi Zeren De Pifu (Reply Regarding Whether One Who Violated the Constitutionally Protected Basic Rights to Education of the Citizen Should Bear Civil Liability)* (28 June 2001).
17. Wang Lei, 'Xianfa Shishi de Xintansuo – Qi Yuling de Jige Xianfa Wenti (New Exploration of the Way to Implement the Constitution: Constitutional Issues in the Qi Yulin Case)', *Zhongguo Shehui Kexue (Social Sciences in China)*, 2003, 02: 29-35.
18. Chen Zheng, 'Zhongguo Fayuan Jinxing Weixian Shencha de Kenengxing Yu Biyaoxing (The Possibility and Necessity for China's Courts to Make Constitutionality Review)', *Xuexi Yu Tansuo (Study & Exploration)*, 2011, 05: 103. Zhou Yongkun, 'Shilun Renmin Daibiaodahui Zhidu Xia de Weixianshencha (On the Constitutionality Review under the People's Congress System)', *Jiangsu Shehui Kexue (Jiangsu Social Sciences)*, 2006, 03: 120-128. Miao Lianying, 'Zhongguo de Weixian Shencha: Shifou Keneng, Ruhe Keneng? (China's Judicial Review: Is It Possible and How?)', *Zhengzhou Daxue Xuebao (Journal of Zhengzhou University)*, 2004 04: 45-51.
19. Guangzhou Intermedium People's Court, 'The Decision of the Sun Zhigang Case' (2003) http://www.hrol.org/uploads/soft/121217/1-12121F00422.doc, accessed 23 October 2017.

above two cases and then refute the two perceptions proffered. It aims to prove that the 1982 Constitution can perhaps only be implemented in a more practical way.

2.3 The Constitution and the Sub-statutory Legislation

However important the Qi Yuling and the Sun Zhigang cases were, the reasoning is defective and the constitutional weight attached to them is somewhat illusionary. Take the Qi Yuling case first. As already observed, the comments primarily focused on two points: one was that nothing in the GPCL deals with the right to education, and only by referring to the Constitution could the case be settled.[20] Another is that the Reply issued by the SPC appeared to have confirmed the legitimacy of applying the Constitution in resolving ordinary disputes.[21] These two conclusions were further reinforced by the opinion of Justice Huang Songyou, who openly claimed that Qi Yuling was the first constitutional case of its kind in China.[22] Nevertheless, as will be shown, neither of these beliefs was correct.

It is erroneous to claim that only by invoking the Constitution could the dispute be resolved. As some civil law scholars observed, a general clause in the GPCL that 'citizens and legal persons who through their fault encroach upon ... the property or "person" of other people shall bear civil liability'. In broader terms, this could encompass the right to education - the expression 'encroach upon ... the person' should be seen as encompassing all interests of an individual, which naturally includes the right to education.[23] Consequently, by referring to the GPCL the case could be settled.

20. Shen Kui, 'Is It the Beginning of the Era of the Rule of the Constitution? Reinterpreting China's 'First Constitutional Case"', *Pacific Rim Law & Policy Journal Association*, 2003, 12: 199.
21. *See* Wang Lei, *Xianfa De Sifahua (Constitutional Law Applied in Courts)* 6. Wang Lei, '*Xianfa Shishi de Xintansuo – Qi Yuling de Jige Xianfa Wenti (New Exploration of the Way to Implement the Constitution: Constitutional Issues in the Qi Yulin Case)*' Chapter 7. Also *see* Jiang Mingan et al., 'Xianfa Sifa Hua Si Ren Tan (Roundtable Discussion on Judicialisation of the Constitution)', *Nanfang Zhoumo (Southern Weekend)*, (Guangzhou 14 September 2001). Lin Laifan, *Cong Xianfa Guifan Dao Guifan Xianfa (From Constitutional Norms to Normative Constitution)* (Law Press 2001) 100-101.
22. The reason for identifying the case as 'the first case of judicial application of the Constitution' was largely due to the opinion by Justice Huang Songyou after the trial in the SPC's newspaper. Huang was then Chief Judge of the First Civil Division of the SPC who heard the case in person. According to him, 'Qi's right to receive education is a right difficult for civil law theory to cover, and is obviously one of the fundamental rights provided by the Constitution. Had we not directly applied the constitutional provisions, it would have been hard to provide judicial remedies.' *See* Guo Guosong, 'Maoming Shangxue Shijian Yinfa Xianfa Sifahua Diyi An (The Usurpation of Another's Name for School Leads to the First Case of Constitutional Justiciability)', *Nanfang Zhoumo (Southern Weekend)* (Guangzhou, 17 August 2001). Also *see* Huang Songyou, 'Qi Yuling An Xianfa Shiyong De Fali Sikao (Jurisprudential Reflection on Constitutional Justiciability in the *Qi Yuling* Case)' *Fazhi Shidai Zhoukan (Legal Era Weekly of People's Court Daily)* (Beijing 13 August 2001).
23. Yu Fei, 'Jiben Quanli Yu Minshi Quanli De Qufen Ji Xianfa Dui Minfa De Yingxiang (Division Between Fundamental Rights and Civil Rights, and the Constitution's Implication for Civil Law)', *Faxue Yanjiu (Chinese Journal of Law)*, 2008, 05: 49-61. Liang Huixing, 'Zuigao Fayuan Guanyu Qinfan Shou Jiaoyuquan An de Fashi [2001] 25hao (Comments on the Reply of the SPC With Respect to the Statutory Construction of the Infringement Upon a Citizen's Basic Right of

It is equally wrong to simply rely on the SPC's letter of reply to conclude that the Constitution is justiciable. After all, the reply was overturned eight years later by the SPC itself for no reason, which at worst implies a potential flaw in the Reply and at best a doubt of the SPC. In fact, the reason why Qi Yuling is so vital in China's constitutional evolution, as pointed out by Professor Xu Chongde, drafter of the 1982 Constitution, is not because it was the first case where the Constitution was held to be justiciable, but because it set up a misleading counter-example where

the Constitution was wrongfully invoked.[24] In the view of the observers, by no means should the PRC Constitution be cited to resolve ordinary disputes, as the fundamental rights highlighted in the Constitution are different in nature from ordinary rights; the functions of the Constitution do not include ordinary dispute resolution.[25]

Often tagged as a constitutionality review case, Sun Zhigang is problematic to the same degree as well. There are at least two reasons why the case should be interpreted otherwise. For one thing, whilst there was indeed a petition calling on the NPCSC to nullify the egregious MCR, before the National People's Congress (NPC) launched the review, the government moved quickly to repeal the Regulation and replaced it with a new measure. The constitutionality review never had a chance to start. For another, the MCR involved may be claimed to have breached the Law of Legislation 2000 (the LL 2000) and the Law of Administrative Penalty 1996,[26] but it did not fall foul of the 1982 Constitution - at least directly. As a country with a written Constitution and a strict legal hierarchy, China is supposed to draw a clear distinction between legality review and constitutionality review. Legality review stands for reviewing the legality of regulations (Fagui) made by the central government or people's congresses at local levels, and rules (Guizhang) issued by the central government departments or local governments. Constitutionality review refers to reviewing the constitutionality of law (Falv), legislation made by the state's supreme legislature.[27] In the case at hand,

---

Receiving Education [2001] No 25)' (Zhongguo Faxue Wang [China Law Website], 2002) http://www.iolaw.org.cn/shownews.asp?id=41, accessed 18 November 2017.

24. Xu Chongde and Zheng Xianjun, '"Xianfa Sifahua" Shi Xianfaxue de Lilun Wuqu ("Constitutional Justicialibility" is a Misleading Area in Constitutional Law Studies)', *Faxue Jia (The Jurists)*, 2001, 06: 60-63.
25. Yu Fei (*supra* n. 23) 58-61. Also *see* Wang Kai and Hao Xin, 'Lun Jiben Quanli Yu Minshi Quanli de Qubie (On the Distinction between Fundamental Rights and Civil Rights)' *Changsha Tiedao Xueyuan Xuebao [Shehui Kexue Ban] (Journal of Changsha Railway University [Social Science])*, 2014, 04: 72-74.
26. NB, both the Law on Legislation 2000 (Article 8.5) and the Law on Administrative Penalty 1996 (Article 9) prescribe that mandatory measures and penalties involving restriction on the freedom of person shall only be provided by law passed by the Supreme Legislature of the country, but the MCR was a regulation made by the government, so the petitioners rightly argued that the MCR had violated the above two statutes, *see* Yu Jiang, Xu Zhiyong and Teng Biao, 'Guanyu Shencha "Liulang Qitao Renyuan Shourong Qiansong Banfa" de Jianyi Shu (Proposal to Examine 'Mesaures for Custody and Repatriation of Urban Vagrants and Beggars'), (Xu Zhiyong's Blog, 2003) http://xuzhiyong2012.blogspot.co.uk/2012/11/blog-post_14.html, accessed 19 November 2017.
27. Professor Ma Ling has made an in-depth distinction between 'Rule Review', 'Legality Review' and 'Constitutionality review', *see* Ma Ling, 'Sunzhigang An De Qishi: Weixian Shencha Haishi Weifa Shencha (Implication of the *Sun Zhigang* Case: Constitutionality review or Legality Review?)', *Guojia Xingzheng Xueyuan Xuebao (Journal of China National School of Administration)*, 2005, 01: 81-82.

however, the MCR is not a law but merely a regulation made by the central government, which, according to the above explanations, has little to do with the constitutionality review but more to do with the legality review. As a consequence, it would be misguided to claim that Sun Zhigang is a case of constitutionality review.

Despite the defects in these two cases, they do reflect the above two understandings of the implementation of the Constitution – citing the Constitution to resolve disputes or reviewing the legislation in accordance with the Constitution, albeit with various twists. Yet whether these two propositions are feasible is associated with the appraisal accorded to them from a normative point of view. The 1982 PRC Constitution explicitly stipulates that the NPC exercises the power to 'supervise the enforcement of the Constitution' (Article 62.2) and the NPCSC enjoys the power to 'interpret the Constitution and supervise its enforcement' (Article 67.1). It is widely understood that by 'interpret' and 'supervise [the] enforcement' it means that only the NPCSC is authorised to clarify ambiguities in the Constitution and to strike down unconstitutional statutes; no other institutions can wield such a power.[28] This means that the judicatures are clearly banned from exercising any powers to interpret, supervise the implementation of the Constitution, nor are they allowed to amend or repeal primary legislation made by the NPC. This is most evident in the Li Huijuan case, where an assistant judge Ms Li Huijuan ruled in her hearing that the legislation enacted by the local people's congress (LPC) was invalid, due to its incompatibilities with the primary law enacted by the NPCSC. The judge unprecedentedly assumed a power to strike down legislation, which was perceived to be ultra vires. The ruling was subsequently nullified in the appellate proceeding and the judge was suspended from office.[29]

For years Chinese administrative law scholars tended to think in terms of a general dichotomy between abstract and concrete administrative acts. Administrative activities which cannot be classified as the former must be the latter. The division between these two types of acts is central to understanding Chinese Administrative Law. Abstract administrative acts refer to those activities aimed at the general public, while concrete acts stand for those administrative acts aiming at specified events or individuals and can only be carried out once.[30] According to the PRC Administrative Litigation Law 1989 (the 1989 ALL), judges may not review abstract administrative

28. There have been debates over whether the NPC itself can 'supervise the enforcement of the Constitution'. Proponents believe that as the NPCSC is a permanent body within the NPC, the NPC can presumably assume any power enjoyed by the NPCSC, whereas opponents insist that since the Constitution only assigns such a power to the NPCSC, the NPC is not to exercise it, *see* Hu Jinguang and Han Dayuan, *Zhongguo Xianfa* (*The Chinese Constitution*) (Law Press 2007) 125, 147, 163. Zhai Xiaobo, *Lun woguo xianfa de shishi zhidu* (*On Mechanism of Implementing the Chinese Constitution*) (China Legal Publishing House 2009) 53. Huang Mingtao, 'Liangzhong "Xianfa Jieshi" de Gainian Fenye Yu Hexianxing Jieshi de Kenengxing (The Divisions Between the Two Types of Constitutional Interpretations and the Possibility of Making an Unconstitutionality Decision)', *Zhongguo Faxue (China Legal Science)*, 2014, 06: 283-286.
29. Jim Yardley, 'A Judge Tests China's Courts, Making History' (*New York Times*, 2005) http://www.nytimes.com/2005/11/28/international/asia/28judge.html?pagewanted=all, accessed 11 March 2016.
30. Chen Jianfu, *Chinese Law: Towards an Understanding of Chinese Law, Its Nature and Development* (Kluwer Law International 1999) 140.

acts, but only concrete ones.[31] While the newly revised Administrative Litigation Law 2014 (the 2014 ALL, Xin Xingzheng Susong Fa) has loosened such a restriction by allowing certain abstract administrative acts to be reviewed, a review will not be launched unless a concrete complaint is filed.[32] That means that judges in China are prohibited from declaring any legislation or even administrative regulation invalid, as doing so is regarded to be undermining the supremacy of the NPC.[33]

Equally unattainable is the other model of 'justiciability' – applying the Constitution to concrete disputes. Despite the fact that some articles of the Constitution are indeed cited, the official stance on this has always been negative. In a reply to Xinjiang High Court, the SPC made it clear that 'despite its fundamental and "parent law" status, the Constitution itself is banned from being applied to resolve criminal disputes'.[34] This opinion was echoed in another reply to Jiangsu High Court, in which the SPC gave a list of applicable laws and regulations, with the Constitution intentionally or unintentionally left out.[35] Likewise, the SPC's overturning of the reply in the Qi Yuling case may hint at this negative attitude,[36] whose stance on the issue is perhaps because of the normative barriers set by the Constitution itself. As mentioned earlier, the Constitution expressly and exclusively confers 'the power to interpret the Constitution' upon the NPCSC, the permanent body of the supreme legislature, and arguably the NPC itself. Thus, there is little room for the courts to apply the Constitution to litigations, for in the course of adjudicating, the judicatures would inevitably 'interpret' the Constitution to various degrees, which is in and of itself unconstitutional.

It seems appropriate to conclude at this point that all the theoretical efforts enabling the courts to interpret and enforce the Constitution are simply armchair strategies – no institution but the NPCSC is endowed with such a power. However, how

31. Zhang Qianfan, *The Constitution of China: A Contextual Analysis* (Hart Publishing 2012) 164.
32. Article 2, *Zhonghua Renmin Gongheguo Xingzheng Susong Fa (Administrative Litigation Law of the People's Republic of China)* (2014).
33. That said, recent years have heard another voice arguing that by adopting the judicial review model under the UK HRA 1998, the paradox between the supremacy of the NPC and the protection of human rights will be resolved. However, the proposition still runs at odds with the constitutional provision, as when the court declares a statute incompatible with the Constitution, it is none the less interpreting the Constitution, *see* Li Ruiyi, 'Can the Chinese Constitution Draw Inspiration from the HRA?' (The UK-China Public Law Conference 2013: The Rule of Law in Modern Constitutionalism), reported by the UK Constitutional Law Blog, http://ukconstitutionallaw.org/2013/09/13/report-on-the-uk-china-public-law-conference-2013-the-rule-of-law-in-modern-constitutionalism, accessed 31 October 2017. Also *see* Wang Kai, 'Qiang Xingshi Sifashencha Yihuo Ruo Xingshi Sifa Shencha? (Strong-Form Judicial Review or Weak-Form Judicial Review?)', *Qinghua Fazhi Lunheng (Tsinghua Journal of Rule of Law)*, 2013, 02: 160-165. Cheng Xueyang, 'Sifa Shencha de Disantiao Daolu (The Third Road of Judicial Review)', *Gansu Xingzheng Xueyuan Xuebao (The Journal of Gansu Administration Institute)*, 2011, 05: 106-110.
34. The SPC, *Guanyu Zai Xingshi Panjue Zhong Buyi Yuanyin Xianfa Zuo Lunzui Kexing de Yiju de Fuhan (Reply on Declining the Constitution as a Basis to Decide Criminal Cases)* (1955), (Yan zidi 1129 hao) (No 11298).
35. The SPC, *Guanyu Renmin Fayuan Zhizuo Falv Wenshu Ruhe Yinyong Falv Guifanxing Wenjian de Pifu (Reply on How to Cite Law in Making Legal Documents)* (1986), (Fa yan 1986, 31 hao) (*Legal Research* 1986, No 31).
36. The SPC, 'Guanyu Feizhi 2007 Niandi Yiqian Fabu de Youguan Sifa Jieshi (Diqipi) de Jueding (Decision No 7 on Abolishing Judicial Interpretations before the End of 2007)' *Renmin Fayuan Bao (People's Court Daily)* (24 December 2008).

does the NPCSC exercise the power is largely under-specified. On the one hand, since its founding, the NPCSC has never openly declared any laws unconstitutional.[37] On the other hand, there are theoretical contentions over the meaning of the term 'implementing the Constitution'. Present literature contains two opinions: sensu stricto, it refers to rectifying mistakes with respect to the Constitution, in particular striking down unconstitutional legislation, whereas sensu lato it stands for most activities in relation to the Constitution, where law enacting under the Constitution,[38] interpreting and amending the Constitution, and even abiding by the law made in accordance with the Constitution are included.[39]

That said, among the many ways prescribed above to implement the Constitution, the primary one is through legislation.[40] This is because, on the one hand, the Constitution encompasses a large number of provisions delegating power to both the NPC and the NPCSC, designating them to articulate the meaning of the Constitution through legislation.[41] On the other hand, other ways to implement the Constitution, such as through amendments and interpretations, are either too strict in procedure or too normatively unfurnished. Although since its coming into force, the PRC Constitution has had 52 amendments, the procedure for amending the Constitution is so rigid that it requires the NPCSC or one-fifth of the congressmen to propose an amendment and at least two-thirds of the deputies to agree before the Constitution can be revised (Article 65). Moreover, the Constitutional amendments were deemed not only hasty and aimless,[42] but also bringing radical changes (only big issues will trigger constitutional amendments),[43] and sometimes even likely impediments to the authority and stability of the Constitution itself.[44] Moreover, despite the importance of constitutional interpretation, the Constitution remains silent on what kind of procedures are entailed, and what are the legal effects of an interpretation.[45] As a consequence, compared with

---

37. He Xin, 'The Party's Leadership as a Living Constitution in China' in Ginsburg Tom and Simpser Alberto (eds), *Constitutions in Authoritarian Regimes* (Cambridge University Press 2014) 251.
38. Xianfa Xue Bianxie Zu (Constitutional Law Studies Editing Group), *Xianfa Xue (Constitutional Law Studies)* (Higher Education Press and People's Publishing House 2011) 296-297.
39. Ma Ling, 'Weixian Shencha Xiangguan Gainian Zhi Fenxi (Analysis on Relative Concepts of "Review of Constitutionality"', *Faxue Zazhi (Law Science Magazine)*, 2006, 03: 107-110.
40. Lin Yan, 'Constitutional Evolution Through Legislation: The Quiet Transformation of China's Constitution', *International Journal of Constitutional Law*, 2015, 13: 61.
41. For instance, in Article 31, the Constitution empowers the NPC to come up with concrete institutions and rules for the Special Administrative Regions. In Article 59, the Constitution decrees that the number of deputies to the NPC and the procedure of their election are prescribed by law made by the NPCSC.
42. Dong Heping, 'Xianfa Xiugai de Jiben Jingyan yu Zhongguo Xianfa de Fazhan (The Experience of Amending the Constitution and the PRC Constitution's Development)' *Zhongguo Faxue (China Legal Science)*, 2012, 04: 46-50.
43. Ma Ling, 'Xianfa Xiugai Yu Xianfa Jieshi (Amending and Interpreting the Constitution)', *Zhongguo Qingnian Zhengzhi Xueyuan Xuebao (Journal of China Youth University of Political Sciences)*, 2007, 02: 74-77.
44. *See, e.g.*, Xiao Weiyun, 'Weihu Xianfa Quanwei Yu Xiugai Xianfa (Maintaining the Constitutional Authority and Amending the Constitution)', *Faxue Zazhi (Law Science Magazine)*, 2004, 01: 3-4. Zhang Fugang, 'Xianfa de Shengming Yu Quanwei (The Life and Authority of the Constitution)', *Hebei Faxue (Hebei Law Science)*, 2012, 07: 49-51.
45. Wang Zhenmin, *Zhongguo Weixian Shencha Zhidu (China's Constitutional Review System)* (China University of Political Science and Law Press 2004) 285.

other processes, law-making has become a compromising but viable way to instil the constitutional ethos into reality.

Therefore, it seems appropriate to conclude that one possible way to implement the Constitution is through legislation. In a stark contrast to the prevalent mindset that the Constitution will have no force if it is not justiciable,[46] Chinese constitutional values are largely articulated in legislation at sub-constitutional levels, and how well the Constitution is implemented depends on how well statutes under the Constitution are made and carried out. However, solely relying on the supreme legislature to enforce the Constitution is problematic, since on the one hand, the meanings of the constitutional norms such as 'supervise the enforcement of the Constitution' and 'interpret the Constitution' remain vague. This gives rise to controversies in practice. For example, while theoretically speaking, the NPC and its Standing Committee are exclusively authorised to enforce the Constitution, given the overwhelming workload, it is a daunting task that is practically unattainable. The ensuing section will therefore provide a more nuanced account of the difficulties of the system before switching to an alternative way to carry out the 1982 PRC Constitution – implementing the Constitution through statutory construction.

3 IMPLEMENTING THE CONSTITUTION THROUGH STATUTORY CONSTRUCTION?

3.1 The Legislature-Centric Enforcement Model and Its Problems

The normative delineation thus far has been concerned with the constitutional term 'justiciable'. It was agreed that according to the Constitution, the judicatures are deprived of any power to 'interpret the Constitution or supervise the enforcement of the Constitution'. Rather, the implementation of the Constitution is contingent upon the supreme legislature's law-making endeavours. That means relying on the courts to make constitutional adjudication or initiate constitutionality review finds no normative basis under the current constitutional scheme. In fact, the so-called 'Legislature-centric constitutional implementation model' was verified not only in the Li Huijuan and Qi Yuling cases, where the SPC and the LPC blocked the judges' drive to transcend the constitutional boundaries, but also in a profusion of enactments made by the NPC and LPCs, which is considered to be the embodiments of the Constitution.[47] As one record showed, from 1950 to 2009, there have been 1109 pieces of legislation made by the congresses at all levels, and even more delegated legislation, administrative regulations, and local rules made accordingly. In comparison with the stagnant efforts to

46. For example, the Supreme Court of the US has constantly referred back to the Constitution's original ideas in a stream of cases concerning human rights violations, and in the UK, constitutional legislation from the Magna Carta to the HRA 1998 is all legally binding and can be directly referred to in litigations, *see* David Feldman, 'The Nature and Significance of "Constitutional" Legislation', *Law Quarterly Review*, 2013, 129: 343-358, *see Factortame v. Secretary of State for Transport* (No 2) [1991] AC 603 (HL). *Thoburn v. Sunderland City Council* [2003] QB 151 (Div Ct).
47. Lin Yan (*supra* n. 40) 87-89.

make the Constitution justiciable, the accelerated growth of legislation conceivably indicates that the Constitution has been counting on legislation for impetus.[48]

However, while it can be argued that endowing the courts with the power to enforce the Constitution (reviewing constitutionality and making constitutional adjudication) would involve the unacceptable weakening of the NPC as the supreme sovereign body to the judiciary, the above 'Legislature-centric Enforcement Model' is equally problematic. For example, this model spurs legislatures to make new laws, which increases the complexity of keeping the laws in line with the Constitution.[49] For another, under the current legal framework, the NPC is the only body authorised to review primary legislation (Article 97.1 of the LL 2015), and the NPCSC is the only organisation to review secondary legislation, administrative regulations and local rules (Article 97.2 of the LL 2015),[50] but due to the limited time and the shortage of personnel, neither the NPC nor the NPCSC is capable of managing this arduous task. The tensions between the burgeoning legislation and the institutional incompetence have given rise to the epidemic of constitutional violations on the one hand, and arguably paralysed constitutionality review on the other.

In fact, the NPCSC is not completely paralysed in reviewing legislation. Since the conclusion of the Cultural Revolution, the NPCSC has launched several rounds of activity 'clearing up' (Qingli) normative documents of various types.[51] In 2004, in order to facilitate the review work, the NPCSC set up an Office for Recording and Review of Regulations (the ORR, Fagui beian shencha shi) specialising in reviewing regulations.[52] In fact, before 2004 the constitutionality review was readily conducted in a concealed way, statistics showed that from 1993 to 1997, there were 3692 pieces of local legislation presented to the NPCSC for review, and among the 2045 pieces examined, 93 pieces were considered to be inconsistent with the Constitution or primary legislation (not specified which).[53] Despite this, in the wake of booming legislating, the ORR became increasingly overworked, and a 'passive review model' was hence introduced to alleviate the workload. According to this model, unless requested to do

48. Wang Shucheng, *Hexianxing Tuiding Lun: Yizhong Xianfa Fangfa (Presumption of Constitutionality: A Theory Towards Constitutional Jurisprudence)* (Qinghua University Press 2011) 191.
49. *Ibid.*, 193.
50. Wang Zhenmin, 'Zhongguo Weixian Shencha de Zhuti he Chengxu (The Main Bodies and Procedure to Make Constitutional Review in China)', *Zhongguo Falv (China Law)*, 2006, 02: 11-12. Also *see* Fu Chuangyu, 'Woguo Weixian Shencha Moshi de Shixiaoxing Jiangou (Establishing an Effective Mode for China's Constitutional Review)', *Hunan Jingcha Xueyuan Xuebao (Journal of Hunan Police Academy)*, 2017, 01: 77-78.
51. 'Quanguo Renda Changweihui Fazhi Gongzuo Weiyuanhui Guanyu Dui 1978nian Niandi Yiqian Banbu de Falv Jinxing Qingli de Qingkuang He Yijian de Baogao (The LAC of the NPCSC's Report about the Movement Reviewing the Pre-1978 Legislation)', *see* Wang Huaian, *Zhonghua Renmin Gonghe Guo Falv Quanshu (Law Encyclopedia of the People's Republic of China)* (Jilin People's Publishing House 1989) 87.
52. Wen Ye and Zhang Yixuan, 'Quanguo Renda Fagui Shencha Beianshi Xinzhang, Weixian Shencha Haizai Yuanchu (The Openning of the LRO Will Not Bring Constitutional Review Closer)' (Zhongguo Xinwen Zhoukan (China Newsweek), 2004) http://news.sina.com.cn/o/2004-06-28/16162931264s.shtml, accessed 26 October 2017.
53. Liu Zheng, '1982nian Dui Difangxing Fagui Shouci Shencha Ji Youci Xiangdao de (The First 1982 Review and Beyond)', *Zhongguo Renda [The People's Congress of China]*, 2004 http://www.people.com.cn/GB/14576/28320/35193/35204/2674577.html, accessed 26 October 2017.

so, the ORR will not initiate review by itself; legislation passed by the local congresses and authorities will come into effect directly as long as the ORR is informed.

However, this passive model failed to ease the tension. As happened in Sun Zhigang, where the law students filed a petition but did not hear any response from the NPCSC, the ORR has never published a single case where unconstitutional legislation was nullified or rectified. Although Mr Xu Anbiao, the then head of the ORR, in the 2017 Session of the NPC praised his team, describing the ORR's work as 'satisfactory and encouraging' in terms of the hundreds of cases reviewed since 2004, Mr Xu himself conceded that there has not been a single unconstitutional case published as yet.[54] Understandably, the ORR and more broadly the NPCSC are prone to operate under an opaque umbrella in this regard, since on the one hand, the LL 2015 endowed various individuals and groups with a locus standi to bring an action to the NPCSC, making a plea to launch the constitutionality and legality review (Article 99.2 of the LL 2015), and on the other hand, five state organs[55] are authorised to make a request to the NPCSC, which will duly initiate the constitutionality and legality review proceedings (Article 99.1 of the LL 2015). More importantly, the Law on Legislation 2015 added one clause in the old version allowing the Standing Committee to initiate the reviewing process once problems arise. This gives much more discretion to the NPCSC, but should this article be carried out strictly, it would place unbearable workloads on the NPCSC (ORR), thereby impeding legislative progress.[56]

The conflict of interests should also be noted. Given that the NPCSC is a permanent body within the NPC, the NPC is not likely to strike down legislation passed by the NPCSC.[57] Similarly, the LPC and the NPC belong to the same family of congress; unless forced to do so, the NPCSC has no institutional incentive to repeal enactments passed by the local congresses and to publicise such an action. Hence, it can be concluded that the constitutionality review system, while enshrined in the Constitution and the LL 2015, has not taken a de facto effect, at least publicly.

Indeed, for the above realistic and institutional analysis, the legislature-centric review model can hardly be described as effective. However, even if we accept the accuracy of this description, the argument that the defective constitutionality review mechanism would necessarily throw the entire legal system into disorder, and that the Constitution is itself undermined, does not follow as self-evidently as some western

54. Xu Anbiao, 'Fagui Beian Shencha Shangwu Gongkai Chexiao Anli (There Has Never Been a Single Annulement Case)', 2017 http://topics.caixin.com/2017-03-09/101064366.html, accessed 26 October 2017.
55. The five state organs include the Central Government, the SPC, the Supreme People's Procuratorate, the Central Military Office, and the Standing Committees of People's Congress at provincial levels.
56. Hu Jinguang, 'Ruhe Tuijin Woguo Hexianxing Shencha Gongzuo (How to Carry On the Constitutionality review in China)' (Zhongguo Falv Pinglun [China Law Review], 2017), http://www.aisixiang.com/data/106517.html, accessed 26 October 2017.
57. A Symposium was held in 2012 to discuss the current constitutionality review system, and as some officials and legal experts agreed, the special relationship between the NPC and its Standing Committee would hamper the review from being effectively carried out, *see* Xu Anbiao et al., 'Xiaweifa yu Shangweifa Xiangdichu de Jiejue Zhidao (How to Reconcile the High- and Low-level Laws)', *Xingzheng Guanli Gaige (Administrative Reform)*, 2012, 05: 48-56.

scholars might have us believe.[58] Quite to the contrary, in the absence of an effective review system, the fact that the Chinese legal system keeps functioning well per se indicates that there must exist a set of latent rules underpinning the operation, pulling together an array of legislation under the Constitution. In order to decode the secret, it is time to return to the meaning of 'justiciable', which perhaps encompasses another layer of meaning that has not yet been unveiled.

3.2 Dual Meanings of Constitutional Adjudication

The ambiguity of the phrase 'making the Constitution justiciable' became comprehensible upon further reflection in the previous section. As explained above, the phrase could be interpreted as containing two different meanings: constitutionality review and interpreting/applying the Constitution in concrete cases, both of which have been proven to be a cul-de-sac: the Constitution itself clearly bans the judiciary from touching upon the interpretation and exclusively authorises the Standing Committee to interpret and supervise the enforcement of the Constitution. As analysed above, the legislature-centric constitutional implementation design would face difficulties in actuality.

Still, it would be possible to dissect the concept of 'justiciable' and further bifurcate it into two categories; distinctions should be drawn between 'to invoke the Constitution in making judicial reasoning' and 'to issue verdicts on the basis of the Constitution'. The former only takes the Constitution into consideration when weighing which sub-constitutional legislation should be cited, and wherever possible, statutes should be construed to avoid serious doubts about their unconstitutionality, whereas the latter bypasses concrete laws and regulations and directly invokes the Constitution to settle disagreements.[59] Within the Chinese legal context, the former should be termed 'presumption of constitutionality' (the PC, or Hexianxing Jieshi),[60] yet the latter should be categorised as 'constitutional application' (Xianfa Shiyong).[61]

The discrepancies between these two norms were not borne out with any great clarity in the former examination, where the twin interpretations of the term 'justiciable' were limited to constitutionality review and invoking the Constitution directly to resolve disputes in litigation, both of which were clearly demarcated by the Constitution text as the supreme legislature's own territory, on which the judicatures were barred from trespassing. Conceivably, the above new illumination of the norm begs a question concerning the constitutionality of the courts' efforts in interpreting

58. *See, e.g.*, Zhang Qianfan, 'Zhongguo Xianzheng de Lujin yu Juxian (The Path and Limitation of the Chinese Constitutionalism)', *Faxue (Law Science)*, 2011, 01: 70-71.
59. Tong Zhiwei, 'Xianfa Shiyong Ying Yixun Xianfa Benshen Guiding de Lujin (Constitution's Application Should Follow the Road Stipulated by Constitution Itself)', *Zhongguo Faxue (China Legal Science)*, 2008, 06: 23-26.
60. Wang Shucheng, 'Hexianxing Tuiding de Zhengdangxing (Legitimacy of the Presumption of Constitutionality: A Theory Towards Constitutional Jurisprudence)', *Faxue Yanjiu (Chinese Journal of Law)*, 2010, 02: 23.
61. Hu Jinguang, 'Weixian Shencha yu Xiangguan Gainian Bianxi (Review of Constitutionality and Analysis of Concerning Concepts)', *Faxue Zazhi (Law Science Magazine)*, 2006, 04: 22-27.

legislation in a way which is compatible with the Constitution. To answer this question, we need to switch back to the constitutional provisions.

Article 131 of the Constitution and Article 4 of the Organic Law of the People's Court (PC) unequivocally provided that 'the people's courts shall, in accordance with the law, exercise judicial power independently ...'. This is widely believed to indicate that, on the one hand, the Constitution was excluded from the category of legal references that the judiciary can invoke. From a normative standpoint, the term 'constitution' was expressly juxtaposed with the laws as two independent sources everywhere else in the texts, which implies that the courts are precluded from citing the Constitution in ordinary lawsuits.[62] This reading is largely congruent with the above analysis that no institution but the NPCSC and arguably the NPC has the power to apply the Constitution.[63] On the other hand and more revealingly, the constitutional provision demonstrates that the judicatures are under a constitutional duty to apply ordinary laws to resolve disputes.[64] Therefore, so far as it is possible, the courts must read and give effect to the legislation in a way that is compatible with the Constitution. Therefore, there is a sound legal basis for the courts to pursue the PC in adjudications.

In the light of the above normative analyses, it can be summarised that the courts are prohibited from implementing the Constitution, but they are mandated by the Constitution to exert every effort to avoid statutes being construed as unconstitutional. Since the concept and its implications are somewhat complex and interesting, some theoretical points pertinent to the PC are worthy of further clarification.

First, it is widely held among Chinese scholars that the PC is not interpreting the Constitution or applying the Constitution to adjudication. Rather, it only targets ordinary statutes and aims to resolve statutory ambiguity by choosing among several versions of constructions and adopting the one that is (most) compatible with the Constitution, so that unconstitutionality concerns will be mitigated or even eradicated.[65] Intrinsically, the PC should be characterised as a legislature-oriented interpretation endeavour, which is adopted by the courts to remove doubts of unconstitutionality surrounding ordinary legislation. Second, the PC to some extent is one of the

62. Han Dayuan and Wang Guisong, 'Zhongguo Xianfa Wenben Zhong "Fakv" de Hanyi (The Connotation of the Term "Law" in the Chinese Constitutional Context)', *Faxue (Law Science)*, 2005, 02: 43-45.
63. Tong Zhiwei, 'A Comment on the Rise and Fall of the Supreme People's Court's Reply to Qi Yuling's Case Symposium on Constitutionality review in China', *Suffolk University Law Review*, 2009, 43: 673-677.
64. Zhang Xiang, 'Liangzhong Xianfa Anjian: Cong Hexianxing Jieshi Kan Xianfa dui Sifa de Keneng Yingxiang (Two Types of Constitutional Cases: The Presumption of Constitutionality and the Constitutional Implications over the Judiciary)', *Zhongguo Faxue (China Legal Science)*, 2008, 03: 112-114.
65. *See, e.g.*, Cai Lin, 'Hexianxing Jieshi jiqi Jieshi Guize (Interpreting Laws in Accordance with the Constitution and Interpretation Rules)', *Zhejiang Social Sciences*, 2009, 10: 52-55. Huang Hui, 'Hexianxing Jieshi jiqi Lilun Jiantao (Presumption of Constitutionality and its Theoretical Reflections)', *Zhongguo Faxue (China Legal Science)*, 2014, 01: 286-287. Wang Shucheng, 'Hexianxing Tuiding yu Hexianxing Shencha de Gainian Renzhi – Cong Fangfa Lun de Shijiao (Presumption of Constitutionality and Recognising the Concept of "Review of Constitutionality: From A Methodological Perspective")', *Zhengjiang Social Sciences*, 2011, 01: 51-58.

judiciary's self-imposed restrictions, which demonstrates that the judiciary is according deference to the legislature.[66] Understandably, under a mechanism upholding the supremacy of the NPC, allowing the courts to address constitutionality/legality concerns and declare statutes passed by the NPC unconstitutional is unthinkable. Hence, the courts tend to presume that all laws passed by the legislature are constitutional, and if there are multiple understandings, the judges are required to single out the one that is consistent with the Constitution, so that the constitutional validity of the legislation will be upheld.[67]

Doubtlessly, the theoretical debates would continue as to what are the nature and limitations of the PC, what happens if there are multiple interpretations that are constitutional, and how to demarcate the boundaries between the PC and the constitutional interpretation. As a concept borrowed directly from the Western world, the PC was only introduced to the Chinese academic discourse in 2008, with its contents and attributes largely left nebulously defined.[68] In fact, in the midst of academic calls for the judiciary to play a bigger role in implementing the Constitution,[69] the Chinese courts have been actively engaging in the PC, and some even have gone so far as to involve the Constitution in judicial reasoning.[70] For better or for worse, it is unrealistic to expect that all statutes are so neatly drafted and clearly defined that there is no need for the courts to handle unconstitutionality issues. Equally, despite being unconstitutional, it is almost impossible to contain the courts' practical drive to interpret the Constitution when presuming one enactment to be constitutional. However, it should be acknowledged that teasing out one best interpretation out of several possible constitutional options is in and of itself a constitutional judgement, which, if defined broadly, is no less than enforcing the Constitution.[71]

66. For detailed analysis on deference, *see* F. Andrew Hessick, 'Rethinking the Presumption of Constitutionality', *Notre Dame Law Review*, 2010, 85: 1461-1481.
67. Wang Shucheng, 'Lun Hexianxing Jieshi Fangfa (On Constitutional Avoidance Doctrine)' *Faxue Yanjiu (Chinese Journal of Law)*, 2012, 05: 51-53.
68. Although there have been many theses exploring the PC's application in China since 2008, there has been little breakthrough – even the English translation of the PC has not been unified yet, *see, e.g.*, Yao Guojian, 'Lingpi Xijin Haishi Sheben Zhumo? – Ye Lun Hexianxing Jieshi Dui Xianfa Shishi de Yiyi (Finding a New Path or Losing the Substance for the Shadow? Constitutional Interpretation and Its Meaning for Constitutional Implementation)', *Fazhexue yu Fashehui Xue Luncong (Archives for Legal Philosophy and Sociology of Law)* (Peking University Press 2009) 215-217. Zhu Fuhui, 'Falv Hexianxing Jieshi de Zhongguo Yujing yu Zhidu Luoji (The Chinese Context and the Institutional Logic of Constitutionality of Legal Interpretation: The Forms of Application of the Constitution by Courts in China)', *Xiandai Faxue (Modern Law Science)*, 2017, 01: 3-15.
69. *See, e.g.*, Chen Zheng (*supra* n. 18) 105-107. Also Ji Weidong, 'Hexianxing Shencha yu Sifaquan de Qianghua (Constitutionality Review and the Strengthening of Judicial Power)', *Zhongguo Shehui Kexue (Social Sciences in China)*, 2002, 02: 15-16.
70. Empirical studies showed that the Chinese courts have constantly invoked the Constitution in litigations in the post-*Qi* Yuling era, *see* Xing Binwen, 'Fayuan Ruhe Yuanyong Xianfa – Yi Qian Pifu Feizhi Hou de Sifa Shijian Wei Zhongxin (How Do the Courts Invoke the Constitution: Legal Practice After *Qi Yuling*)', *Zhongguo Falv Pinglun (China Law Review)*, 2015, 05: 130-152.
71. Whether the PC should be viewed as a constitutional or statutory construction is contested. Inspired by the Swiss scholars E. Campische and N. Muller, mainstream Chinese scholars have adopted an eclectic stance, which considers the PC as encompassing three types of rule: Interpretation Rule (*Jieshi guize*), Conflict Rule (*Chongtu guize*), and Preserving Rule (*Baoquan guize*). The first two are perceived as remaining within the purview of statutory construction,

It certainly can be argued that making PC would inevitably involve constitutional reinterpretation – ostensibly the courts are construing statutes, but from a teleological point of view, they are in effect bringing the statutes in line with their reading of the Constitution, which nonetheless defies the aforementioned constitutional ban on non-legislative interpreting of the Constitution.[72] However, it is not for this thesis to decide whether the PC is constitutional or not, as the main focus of the exploration here is not to evaluate, but to present how the Chinese Constitution is given effect in reality, and what are the features thereof. In order to accomplish this objective, the remaining part of this section will adopt a comparative perspective, and unveil why the Chinese way of implementing the Constitution stands out among its counterparts.

3.3 PC from a Comparative Perspective

As mentioned above, the concept of PC was introduced to China from the West, where the courts have long been employing this vehicle to keep legislation consistent with the Constitution, and maintain the superiority of the legislature. Perhaps because of its implications, the PC has been a hot topic to which the Chinese comparative legal scholars have devoted attention in recent years. Among the many countries that can be taken as comparators to China, the German and American models are of greatest concern to Chinese analysts. It is believed that, in the German Law, the terms 'Verfassungskonforme Auslegung von Gesetz' (VA, or 'Verfassungskonforme Auslegung') and 'die verfassungskonforme Auslegung des Gesetzes' refer to the notion of 'PC' as prescribed above. As some literature articulated, there has been continuing debate in German legal scholarship over whether constitutional interpretation is qualitatively different from statutory interpretation.[73] In accordance with the literature, should a question of the constitutionality of certain statutes arise, judges should construe the legislation in a way compatible with the 'constitutional command', but within the statute's ordinary linguistic meaning.[74] This can be construed as either that the judges should focus on the statute and are prohibited from interpreting the Constitution, or the courts are accorded a certain margin of discretion to construe the meaning of the Constitution so that unconstitutionality of the statutes can be better eschewed. As a matter of theoretical debate, no agreement has been reached among German academics as yet.[75]

---

whereas the last one is viewed as conducting constitutionality review, *see* Liu Jianlong, 'Hexianxing Jieshi Yuanze de Benxiang yu Zhenglun (The Truths and Controversies of the Presumption of Constitutionality)', Qinghua Faxue (Tsinghua Law Journal), 2011, 01: 114. Also Zhang Xiang, 'Hexianxing Jieshi de Liangge Mianxiang (The Two Dimensions of Legal Interpretation in Accordance with the Constitution)', *Zhejiang Social Sciences*, 2009, 10: 61.

72. Wang Kai, 'Hexianxing Jieshi Zhi Fansi (Rethinking the Constitutionality of Legal Interpretation)', *Faxue Jia (The Jurists)*, 2015, 01: 51-57.
73. Winfried Brugger, 'Legal Interpretation, Schools of Jurisprudence, and Anthropology: Some Remarks from a German Point of View', *The American Journal of Comparative Law*, 1994, 42: 398.
74. *Ibid.*, 400-401.
75. Vgl. Helmut Simon, Die verfassungskonforme Gesetzesauslegung, EuGRZ 1974, 86. Vgl. Claus-Wilhelm Canaris, Die verfassungskonforme Auslegung und Rechtsforbildung im System der

In terms of origination, the term PC was in fact first derived from American constitutional discussions, in which the PC was more frequently phrased as 'constitutional avoidance' (CA), meaning that all disputes, constitutional or otherwise, should preferably be resolved on non-constitutional grounds.[76] It shows that the courts should not lightly construe a statute in a way that makes it unconstitutional if an alternative interpretation is available.[77] Taking such an approach, the courts are paying due respect to 'the wisdom ... of the legislative body, by which any law is passed, to presume in [favour] of its validity, until its violation of the Constitution is proved beyond all reasonable doubt'.[78] As far as the theoretical evolution is concerned, it is argued that Justice Brandeis in Ashwander[79] first outlined the principle systematically, and a host of eminent jurists have provided nuanced accounts and critiques thereof more recently.[80]

Upon a detailed examination of these theoretical debates, the rationales and implications of avoiding unconstitutionality can be summarised as follows. On the one hand, within the American context, the principles such as the separation of powers and judicial independence form a solid foundation upon which the CA proceeds. Specifically, as the four dimensions of judicial powers and functions have been clearly demarcated, the judiciary is prohibited from trespassing on the legislative and executive provinces, the courts should make every effort not to declare a statute unconstitutional, and leave the Congress to deal with it.[81] On the other hand, even though the judiciary is endowed with the power to strike down legislation, judges should exercise restraint. This is not only because the Congress, as a democratic institution (the judiciary is an anti-majority/undemocratic branch), should be superior and be treated with some deference, but also because the rule of avoidance is a self-protection

juristischen Methodenlehre, in: Heinrich Honsell (Hrsg.), Privatrecht und Methode: Festschrift fur Ernst A. Kramer, Helbing & Lichtenhahn, 2004, S. 143. *Andreas VoBkuhle, Theorie und Praxis der verfassungskonformen Auslegung von Gesetzen durch Fachgerichte*, AoR 2000, 180-182. Cited from Wang Kai (*supra* n. 72) 46-48.

76. In fact, the concept of PC was on many occasions phrased as 'interpretation in agreement with the Constitution', 'constitutionality faithful interpretation', 'interpretation in conformity with the Constitution', *see* Tim Koopmans, *Courts and Political Institutions: A Comparative View* (Cambridge University Press 2003) 118, cited from Liu Jianlong (n 71) 110.
77. Caleb Nelson, 'Avoiding Constitutional Questions Versus Avoiding Unconstitutionality', *Harvard Law Review*, 2014-2015, 128: 331.
78. *Ogden v. Saunders*, 25 U.S. (12 Wheat.) 212 at 270 (1827), cited from Joseph Eliot Magnet, 'The Presumption of Constitutionality', *Osgoode Hall Law Journal*, 1980, 18: 93, and James B. Thayer, 'Origin and Scope of the American Doctrine of Constitutional Law' *Harvard Law Review*, 1893-1894, 07: 142.
79. *See Ashwander v. Temnessee Valley Authority*, 297 U.S. 346 (1936).
80. *See, e.g.*, Michael T. Crabb, 'The Executive Branch Shall Construe: The Canon of Constitutional Avoidance and the Presidential Signing Statement', *University of Kansas Law Review*, 2008, 56: 711. Richard A. Posner, 'Statutory Interpretation – In the Classroom and in the Courtroom', *University of Chicago Law Review*, 1983, 50: 800. Lisa A. Kloppenberg, 'Avoiding Serious Constitutional Doubts: The Supreme Court's Construction of Statutes Raising Free Speech Concerns', *University of California Davis Law Review*, 1996, 30: 1.
81. *Ibid.*, 13-16.

mechanism for judges, which keeps the judicatures away from controversial constitutional cases, thereby saving them from confronting reproaches.[82]

4 DEMOCRATIC DIALOGUE MODEL AND ITS LIMITATIONS

4.1 PC and the 1998 Human Rights Act

The comparative studies should be further extended by involving the British narratives. As a country embracing the principle of Parliamentary Sovereignty, the UK does have many facets that bear similarities with those of China – especially in areas such as the supremacy of the legislature, human rights protection and the interplay between the courts and the legislature. Specifically, in order to make a response to the pressures exerted by the European Court of Human Rights (ECtHR), the Labour government in 1998 introduced the Human Rights Act (HRA) whose aim is to 'bring rights home'. Twenty years on, the HRA 1998 has not only successfully enhanced the protection of human rights without weakening the value of democracy, but also managed to engage the legislature and judiciary in protecting human rights. Although in more recent years, there has been an increasing call for replacing the HRA 1998 with a UK Bill of Rights,[83] it is no denying that judges' power has been greatly enlarged when it comes to the circumstance where legislation potentially contravene the European Convention on Human Rights (ECHR).

A detailed analysis of the connotations behind the provisions of the 1998 HRA would be of help for the following comparative studies. According to the orthodoxy observation, section 3 (1) of the HRA imposes an interpretive obligation upon the courts, requiring the British judges to 'read and give effect' to primary and subordinate legislation 'in a way that is compatible with the Convention rights', 'so far as it is possible to do so', and if the interpretive effort under section 3 fails to bring the legislation concerned in line with the Convention, the courts are authorised to issue a 'declaration of incompatibility' (DoI) under section 4. In the section, the declaration by the court 'does not affect the validity, continuing operation or enforcement of the provision in respect of which it is given', but in practice it will mount political pressure on Parliament to modify legislation accordingly.[84]

82. *See* Alexander Mordecai Bickel, *The Least Dangerous Branch: The Supreme Court at the Bar of Politics* (Yale University Press 1986) Chapter 4. For Chinese comments on the CA, *see* Li Songfeng, 'Xianfa Huibi Lilun Jiqi Shiyong Xianzhi (Constitutional Avoidance and its Limitation)', *Tsinghua University Law Journal*, 2017, 02: 120-122, and Zheng Xianjun, 'Meiguo Xianfa Huibi Lilun Tanyuan: Yige Fangfa Lun Qishi (The Origins of the Canon of Constitutional Avoidance in the USA: A Methodological Inspiration)', *Tsinghua University Law Journal*, 2016, 05: 89-93.
83. Justice secretary Dominic Raab has proposed a UK bill of rights, the bill is now in the second reading stage in the House of Commons. *See* https://bills.parliament.uk/bills/3227 (visited on 28 June 2022).
84. For influential discussion of the interplay between the courts and Parliament under the HRA 1998 section 3 and section 4, *see* Alison L. Young, *Democratic Dialogue and the Constitution* (Oxford University Press 2017) Chapter 7.

It was held that by depriving the courts of powers to invalidate legislation but vesting in them the authority to make a declaration of incompatibility, the judiciary will be involved in the human rights protection enterprise, whilst the authority of Parliament will be maintained.[85] As an opposing model to the American strong-form judicial review, which empowers the judiciary to repeal statutes, the British judicial review, however, is categorised as a 'weak-form judicial review', which does not empower courts to nullify law which contravenes human rights but the court's ruling would nevertheless generate similar binding effects over Parliament, thanks to the comity doctrine.[86]

In a deeper sense, it is argued that under the British model, a new form of protection of rights has been set up which promotes dialogue between the legislature and the courts. And the British model, along with those practised in other commonwealth countries, is praised as a better means of protecting rights which finds a middle ground between legal and political constitutionalism.[87] As explained, the dialogue is a better mechanism because it not only spurs inter-institutional interactions, but also 'facilitates deliberation, engages citizens, and acts as an effective dialogue in the UK constitution.[88] As much as the interaction is concerned, it comprises dialogue between Court and Parliament, as well as court-court dialogue between the domestic courts and the European Court of Justice and the European Court of Human Rights.[89] Of course the dialogue would occur in a plethora of areas, but for the sake of comparison, the following illustration would be concentrated on the interplay between courts and legislature.

With respect to the interpretation and the DoI, theorist argues that sections 3 and 4 are to be viewed as engaging the courts to either fill in gaps in a provision or determine its meaning, while the legislature is left to acquiesce or change the interpretation as it deems fit.[90] Based on the case law and literature, it can be deducted a strong interpretative duty from section 3, where there is a heavy duty rests on the courts to read legislation in conformity with Convention rights. After making the maximum use of their interpretative powers in section 3, the court should instead issue declarations under section 4, paying deference to the elected branches of government when it is uncertain about what the correct conclusion should be, or where it would be more appropriate to leave the legislature to make decision.[91] Most commentators agreed that democratic legitimacy is one ground for justifying deference – 'the courts are not democratically elected and should therefore not be too strident in taking

85. Li Ruiyi (*supra* n. 33) 21-29.
86. *See, e.g.*, Mark Tushnet, 'Social Welfare Rights and the Forms of Judicial Review', *Texas Law Review*, 2004, 82: 1909-1912. Mark Tushnet, 'Alternative Forms of Judicial Review' *Michigan Law Review*, 2002-2003, 101: 2782-2788. For New Zealand weak-form judicial review, *see* Janet McLean, 'Legislative Invalidation, Human Rights Protection and S 4 of the New Zealand Bill of Rights Act', *New Zealand Law Review*, 2001, 2001: 444-448.
87. Alison L. Young (n 84), Chapter 2.
88. *Ibid.*, Chapter 4.
89. *Ibid.*, Chapter 7.
90. Aileen Kavanagh, *Constitutional Review under the UK Human Rights Act* (Cambridge University Press 2009) 129.
91. *Ibid.*, 169-170.

legislation to task'.[92] On the whole, it is argued that section 3 gives courts more power, whereas section 4 confers more power to the legislature as the DoI has no impact on the legal force, validity or effect of legislation; the legislature would still have the last say on this.[93]

It appears that the above constitutional design has facilitated democratic dialogue between the legislature and the courts. From a comparative perspective, it is claimed that the democratic dialogue or the commonwealth model covers not only PC or CA in America and Germany under section 3, but also declarations of incompatibility under section 4. This model can be easily seen in Canada, New Zealand, the UK, and Australia, albeit not at a Federal level.[94] Early theorists have been convinced that the model can enable the state to obtain the advantages and minimise the disadvantages of American strong judicial review model and also of a purely parliamentary protection of human rights.[95] More importantly, democratic dialogue effectively combines the advantages of judicial and legislative protections of rights, avoiding giving either the legislature or the court the ability to make final, authoritative determinations of human rights - after all, even though Parliament should be free to disagree with judicial decision of rights, the court may not only make a robust interpretation, but also demonstrate contempt for Parliament through declarations of incompatibility when faced with legislation that cannot be read or given effect in a manner compatible with Convention rights.[96] All in all, due to the potential strength, the commonwealth structure or democratic dialogue has been regarded as a novel structure which is therefore advocated to be borrowed to interpret the legislative-judicial relationship in China.

4.2 Applying Democratic Dialogue to China: Panacea or Placebo?

The constitutional structure has captured the attention of Chinese scholars.[97] It is mainly because in one way or another, academics in China are convinced that the model would not enhance human rights at the expense of the authority of the National People's Congress. As such, the model is said to perfectly dovetail with China's situation, where the judiciary is deprived of powers to strike down legislation while the state needs to make good on its promises of protecting human rights.[98] The aforementioned studies, for example, have pressed parallels between the UK's Parliamentary

92. Gerhard van der Schyff, Constitutional Review under the UK Human Rights Act, *European Constitutional Law Review*, 2010, 6(1), 161. *See also ibid*, 196.
93. Alison L. Young (*supra* n. 84) 4.
94. *Ibid.*, 3.
95. Stephen Gardbaum, *The New Commonwealth Model of Constitutionalism: Theory and Practice* (Cambridge University Press 2013) 16-17.
96. Alison L. Young (*supra* n. 84) 5-6.
97. *See* Li Ruiyi, 'Yihui Zhuquan Xia de Yingguo Ruoxing Weixian Shencha (Weak Form of Constitutional Review in the Context of Parliamentary Sovereignty in the UK)', *Faxue Jia (The Jurists)*, 2013, 02: 164. Li Ruiyi, 'Sifa Shencha Zhidu de Youhua: Minzhu Duihua Lilun (Improving Judicial Review: Democratic Dialogue Theory)', *Faxue Pinglun (Law Review)*, 2013, 01: 17.
98. Li Ruiyi (*supra* n. 33) 21-29.

Sovereignty and China's Supremacy of the NPC, and a modus operandi of the courts thereof.[99] The studies went so far as to claim that democratic dialogue sheds light on the Chinese situation where tensions between state institutions would be alleviated, and the strengths of the SPC and the NPC enlarged.[100]

The proposition may find its statutory underpinning in the 2015 LL and pertinent legislation, where a sound foundation is laid down for the alleged dialogue to proceed. Articles 45 and 104 of the LL stipulate that no state organs but the NPCSC may make 'legislative interpretation'; the SPC and the Supreme People's Procuratorate may make 'judicial interpretation' if it is for the purpose of applying the law in adjudication or procuratorate work. According to the newly revised Law on Legislation, the 'judicial interpretation' should only be targeted at specific articles and it should remain consistent with the goals, principles, and original meanings of legislation. Additionally, the specific interpretations shall be reported to the NPCSC for recording within 30 days of their being released. The statute demarcates the NPCSC's own turf that bars the judiciary from trespassing: (1) the specific meaning of a provision requires further clarification; (2) a new situation arises after enactment of the legislation, thereby requiring clarification of how to apply the legislation. The Supreme Court and the Supreme Procuratorate may certainly make a request to the NPCSC for legislative interpretation, but the NPCSC has the final say on whether and how to make such an interpretation. Also, when the top judicial bodies considered certain sub-primary regulations to contradict the Constitution or laws, they may submit to the NPCSC a written request for scrutinising. After reviewing the requests, the NPCSC may attempt to first negotiate with the enacting body, and if it does not work, the NPCSC may repeal the sub-primary legislation.[101]

From a normative point of view, it seems that dialogue is genuinely held between the Supreme People's Court and the NPCSC – the judiciary is endowed with powers to negotiate with the top legislature over when and how to make legislative interpretation, and when necessary, to table a request for the NPCSC to review constitutionality and legality of sub-primary legislation. Under the design, the SPC and the Supreme People's Procuratorate are expected to be merely focusing on applying law and identifying constitutional breaching, with the privileges to make and repeal law exclusively assigned to the NPCSC. In other words, the supreme judiciaries are required to read or give effect to legislation so as to ensure its compatibility with the goals, principles and original meanings set by the NPCSC, as far as it is possible to do so. If the court is convinced that the provision concerned is simply impossible to fulfil the requirement, the court is obliged to request the NPCSC to make an explication or launch a constitutionality/legality review, and it is up to the NPCSC to accept or refuse the judicial conception. On the facade, it is argued that the legislative-judicial interplay in China parallels the model adopted under the HRA in the UK, in that the Supreme Court is empowered to make judicial interpretation whereas the supreme legislature

99. *Ibid.*, 21-28.
100. *Ibid.*, 18-21.
101. Articles 45, 99 and 104 of the Law of Legislation 2015, and Article 32 of the Law of the PRC on the Supervision of Standing Committees of People's Congresses at Various Levels 2006.

still maintains the final say on the validity of the law. More importantly, it is claimed that by authorising the court to interpret law and initiate constitutionality review, the court is in effect holding a dialogue with the NPCSC. In doing so, not only a better channel for protecting human rights is found, but also a midway course between a legal and a parliamentary protection of human rights is charted, or a mechanism which combines the strengths and weaknesses of legal and political models for the Chinese Constitution to be implemented.[102]

However, the actuality presents a different story. On the one hand, although situations where the Constitution is violated do occur occasionally in China, the SPC and the Supreme People's Procuratorate have never tabled to the NPCSC any request for constitutionality or legality review, nor have other state organs under Article 99 of the 2015 LL made such a request. By record, the NPCSC has never conducted review upon request or petition, it is the NPCSC that does so on its own initiative. Therefore, it would be an exaggeration to describe the interplay between the NPCSC and the supreme judiciary as having a dialogue. On the other hand, the two supreme judicial bodies have issued thousands of 'judicial interpretations', which have been given effect as de facto statutes and strictly followed by the courts at lower levels.[103] In effect, these judicial interpretations are treated as equal as primary legislation, even worse, they would supersede and even twist the primary legislation. Nevertheless, because of the ill-designed recording and review system, the interpretations remain rogue and beyond the NPCSC's reach.[104] While expected to be an oversight body under the NPCSC responsible for reining in rogue sub-statutory legislation, the highest court in China has been acting more like a quasi-lawmaker. This gives rise to a paradoxical situation where the court is stripped of power to apply the constitution in dispute revolution, but provided a justification to break into the territory of the NPCSC – the court often issues a large amount of quasi-legislative interpretations to replace NPCSC's enactments.

Perceived in this light, the democratic dialogue model cannot be directly borrowed to depict the institutional interactions in China. For one thing, the statutory design in China aims to strengthen the authority of the NPCSC rather than to empower the court or to encourage the communications between institutions. Despite the fact that the LL 2015 does allow the Supreme Court to make judicial interpretations and file a request for constitutionality review, the LL 2015 is warier of 'judicial power-grabbing' than engaging the courts in a dialogue with the NPCSC, and all the design is aimed to cement the NPCSC's control and curb judicial drive to make law. After all, the judiciary in China is expected to wield statutory interpretation to ensure the NPCSC's intention is strictly carried out, and the executive does not transgress the scope of power granted

102. Cheng Xueyang, 'The Third Path of Judicial Review: The Rise, Development of Weak-form Judicial Review and Its Significant Implications for China', *Journal of Gansu Administration Institute*, 2011, 05: 109-110.
103. Nie Youlun, 'Lun Sifa Jieshi de Lifa Xingzhi (Judicial Interpretation as Legislation)', *Huadong Zhengfa Daxue Xuebao (East China University of Political Science and Law Journal)*, 2020, 03: 23.
104. Liu Maolin and Chen Minghui, 'Xianfa Jiandu de Luoji yu Zhidu Gouxiang (The Logic and System of Constitutional Supervision),' *Dangdai Faxue (Contemporary Law Review)* 2015, 01: 29.

to it by the top legislature; the court is never allowed to defy the NPCSC's order. Therefore, never have statutory provisions authorised the Supreme Court to make a declaration of incompatibility, nor is the judiciary allowed to make law through precedents. It is the role of the top judiciary to interpret legislation as it is enacted, to ensure that the law as enforced also reflects the wishes of the NPCSC. The SPC has never been attached the same weight as the NPCSC in the Constitution, and different from the UK Constitution which empowers the judiciary and the legislature at the same time, there are no constitutional counter-balancing mechanisms in the 1982 PRC Constitution:[105] the NPCSC is always able to authoritatively resolve rights-issues, since it exercises a sweeping influence over all other state institutions, and it always wins all form of exchange as to the determination of a rights-issue. This can be clearly seen in the recent years' development of constitutionality review, where no state organs but the NPCSC would decide whether a review process should be initiated and no other state organs, the court included, would be able to defy the NPCSC's order.[106] Against this backdrop, the Chinese institutional interactions can hardly be unfolded in the light of the aforementioned commonwealth model.

For another thing and perhaps more significantly, China is not a democratic country by any measure. As most Western commentators observed, although China's current 1982 Constitution attaches significance to the will of the people and promises to attain democracy through the People's Congress system, it is the CCP that actually exerts control over law-making processes and state institutions.[107] Recent studies have shown that while the NPC and its Standing Committee would have their imprints on certain decisions, as long as there is an overall threat to party dominance, the institutional design would fall into desuetude, and the CCP would take the gloves off and be back in the driving seat through formal and informal rules.[108] Against this background, despite the recent years' reforms, the NPCSC never functions as a legislature like the US Congress or the British Parliament that brings political parties to account. On the contrary, the top legislature serves as the Party's 'rubber stamp'.[109] Under the overarching leadership of the CCP, not only is the judicial reasoning heavily influenced by the political will, but the principle of judicial independence is weakened by political opinion. As such, it is unlikely for the NPC with the CCP sitting at its top to hold a dialogue with the court, even less would it modify the provisions of the statute in accordance with the judicial suggestion.

---

105. Alison L. Young (*supra* n. 84), 101.
106. Since 2017, the NPCSC would publish an annual report on constitutionality review. For English explanation, *see* https://npcobserver.com/2019/12/05/recording-review-pt-6-npcsc-launches-online-platform-for-citizens-to-request-legality-or-constitutionality-review/ (last visit 15 July 2022).
107. Murray Scot Tanner, 'The Erosion of Communist Party Control over Lawmaking in China', *The China Quarterly*, June 1994, 138: 403.
108. Ewan Smith, 'On the Informal Rules of the Chinese Communist Party', *The China Quarterly*, November 2021, 248: 160.
109. Tony Saich, The National People's Congress Functions and Membership, Harvard Kennedy School ASH Center for Democratic Governance and Innovation Report, November 2015, *see* https://ash.harvard.edu/files/ash/files/the_national_peoples_congress.pdf (last visit 15 July 2022).

Thus, it can be concluded that the Chinese way of human rights protection is more legislature-centric or even CCP-centric, with the NPCSC best placed to determine the scope and application of human rights. This determines that the judiciary is deprived of power to replace the decisions of the legislature with its own conceptions, and the court in China is not allowed to apply the Constitution in concrete litigations, nor is it authorised to make legality or constitutionality review. Instead, the court may only put all efforts to interpret the statutory provisions in a way that is in line with the Constitution, presuming all enactments to be constitutional. And if the efforts failed, the court may submit to the NPCSC a request for constitutionality and legality review, but the review is only targeted at sub-statutory legislation, legal documents that are inferior in legal force to the statutes enacted by the national legislature.[110] Since the Chinese constitutional text squarely proscribes judicial interpretation of the Constitution, and prohibits the courts from questioning or overturning legislation, authorising the courts to issue a declaration of incompatibility is a flagrant contravention of the Constitution. And even if the courts were allowed to interpret the Constitution or even make a declaration, the UK-China comparison in this regard would nevertheless be ill-placed: (a) the judges under the HRA were asked to interpret legislation to achieve compatibility with the European Court of Human Rights (ECHR) as an international treaty,[111] whereas the Chinese enactments are instructed to be read in alignment with the Constitution as a domestic law. Since its promulgation, the HRA 1998 has been criticised as placing Strasbourg above the Parliament, thereby weakening the legal sovereignty of the UK, but the controversy is not seen in China; (b) in the Chinese political context, where the seeds of democracy were sowed[112] but are yet to sprout, how much impact the court's declaration of incompatibility would have on law making process remains in doubt. Without a common law convention, it is highly unlikely for the legislature to accept the court's decision. And because of the authorisation of the LL 2015, the judiciary exercises the powers in an unrestrained manner by issuing judicial interpretations that function as quasi-legislation.

The Chinese court's hands are bound in litigations and constitutional review, but that does not mean there is no institutional interaction. In fact, the legislative-judicial dialogue occurs in the area of statutory interpretation, particularly the aforementioned PC. Conceivably, the Constitution gives different powers to the legislature and the courts, but both institutions strive to protect human rights, and each would have relative advantages – the NPCSC obtains democratic mandate and the judiciary is more

110. Hu Jinguang, 'Lun Woguo Hexianxing Shencha Jizhi Zhong Butong Zhuti de Zhineng Dingwei (On the Functional Orientation of Different Subjects in China's Constitutional Review Mechanism)', *Fa Xujia* (*The Jurist*), 2020, 05: 81-83. For English discussion, *see* https://npcobserver.com/2020/08/18/recording-review-a-reintroduction/ (latest visit on 18 July 2022).

111. Brenda Hale, 'Argentoratum Locutum: Is Strasbourg or the Supreme Court Supreme?', *Human Rights Law Review*, 2012, 12: 77-78.

112. On 4 May 1919, student participants in Beijing staged protests against the Chinese government, calling for a rejection of traditional values and the adoption of Western ideas of science and democracy, *see* Edward X. Gu, 'Who Was Mr Democracy? The May Fourth Discourse of Populist Democracy and the Radicalization of Chinese Intellectuals (1915-1922)', *Modern Asian Studies*, 2001, 35: 589.

litigation-oriented. This satisfies the requirements of dialogue, where (i) each institution would have a better ability to find the right answer as to the scope and application of human rights, and (ii) there is one institution that makes the authoritative determination of the scope and application.[113] The interpretative approach under the HRA 1998 can be compared with the Chinese statutory interpretation. The courts in the two countries are pushing the boundaries of the statutory construction, making efforts to fill legislative loopholes and bringing statutes in harmony with the Constitution/Convention. In doing so, it is on the one hand presuming the constitutionality of legislation, thereby according deference to the legislature as having the main role in implementing the Constitution,[114] and on the other hand, this is a duty imposed by the Constitution (the HRA 1998 is clearly a constitutional statute)[115] - the court is obliged to uphold the supremacy of the NPCSC and presume all laws passed by the NPCSC to be legal and constitutional.

However, it should be noted that the similarities between the UK and China should not be overstated. For example, if unconstitutionality issue arises, the American and German judges are given the freedom to strike down legislation, and British judges issue a declaration of incompatibility, but the Chinese judges only report to the NPCSC for further consideration. Fundamentally, the UK does not strictly adhere to the pure doctrine of separation of powers, it has set up checks and balances mechanism to bring the public powers to account;[116] so have the USA and Germany, where the courts are empowered to disagree with the legislatures over matters of constitutionality. By contrast, the Chinese court, under the unitary NPC system, is precluded from opining otherwise - it can do nothing but interpret sub-statutory legislation in line with the Constitution or table request to the legislature. From this perspective, the judiciary is in effect holding dialogue with the legislature.[117]

5 CONCLUSION

Elaboration on the subtleties of the dialogue theory could continue, but given the limited space, it is befitting to conclude the discussion at this point with a brief summary. On the whole, the 1982 Chinese Constitution is implemented through

113. Alison L. Young, *Parliamentary Sovereignty and the Human Rights Act* (Hart Publishing Limited 2008) Chapter 5.
114. *See* BVerfGE 101, 158, 218. Also *see* P. Kirchhof, Verfassungsverstandnis, Rechtsprechungsaufgabe und Entlastung des Bundesverfassungsgerichts, in: Bogs, Harald (Hrsg.), Urteilsverfassungsbeschwerde zum Bundesverfassungsgericht: Ein Grundrechts-Colloquium, Baden-Baden: Nomos Verlagsgesellschaft, 1999, S. 71, 74, cited from Wang Kai (n 68) 50.
115. *Thoburn* (*supra* n. 46).
116. Views differ as to whether the doctrine of separation of powers exists in any meaningful form in the UK Constitution, Lord Diplock thought it did, whereas Bagehot argued that the fusion of powers guarantees 'the efficient secret of the English Constitution'. These points aside, it should be conceded that in the UK, there is a substantial overlap between the executive and Parliament, but necessary frictions still exists to prevent the abuse of powers, *see Hinds v. The Queen* [1977] AC 195, 212. Walter Bagehot, *The English Constitution* (Oxford University Press 1928) 12, cited from Mark Elliott and Robert Thomas, *Public Law* (2d ed., Oxford University Press 2014) 61, 93-96.
117. Yao Guojian (*supra* n. 68) 215-217.

legislation, legislature-centric review, and statutory construction and particularly the PC. All of the three channels can be grouped as a legislature-centric way of implementing the Constitution, but the final one has been singled out as a point to make comparative studies. Specifically, for the sake of safeguarding the sovereignty of the NPC, duty of removing discordances and contradictions among statutes is exclusively designated to the NPCSC, with the help of the court. In adjudication, the SPC plays an essential role in bringing legislation in conformity with the Constitution through statutory interpretation. Presuming all legislation to be constitutional, judges make efforts by employing various interpretative skills to avoid pronouncing statutes unconstitutional. If the efforts failed, the Supreme Court is vested with power to table to the NPCSC a request for constitutional review. This is similar to the democratic dialogue model under the HRA 1998, which sheds light on the legislative-judicial interaction under the Chinese Constitution. As pointed above, because of the normative and realistic barriers that hamper the Chinese court from freely questioning and invalidating the legislation, the advice to direct transpose the democratic dialogue models from Britain to China remains largely as a placebo.

CHAPTER 31

The CJEU and Comparative Law in the Creation of New Jurisprudential Principles: A Case of Judicial Manipulation?

Thomas Perroud

Comparative law is obviously not considered a source of law that a court can apply to resolve a dispute (except in the context of a conflict of laws). In the common law world, conversely, courts can absolutely draw inspiration from a foreign solution, because it is not about the source, but about resolving a specific dispute, on the basis of facts. Thus, solutions are borrowed freely, although it is true that this is mostly the case in private law. In these legal systems, there is nothing that prevents transplants.

Administrative law does not follow the exact same reasoning, and anyway, the issues are clearly different. This discipline has deep national roots, as noted by Ulrich Scheuner[1] and Jean Rivero.[2] Firstly, administrative law is one of the areas where 'the national traits of a people and of a state are expressed more strongly'[3] and it is 'to a large extent the expression of national characteristics'.[4] Wouldn't it be shocking if the administration and the administrative court applied a foreign rule to the resolution of a dispute? The contribution of comparative law can therefore only be limited. Thus, administrative law, even less than private law, does not lend itself to comparative law. The absolute rule is that the national administrations must apply national law and the administrative court's main role is to enforce national laws.

1. U. Scheuner, 'Der Einfluss des französischen Verwaltungsrechts auf die deutsche Rechtsentwicklung', DÖV1963, pp. 714 ff. quoted by J. Schwarze, Droit administratif européen, rd ed., Bruylant, pp. 102-103.
2. J. Rivero, Cours de droit administratif comparé, Paris, Les cours de droit, 1957-1958, p. 18 ff.
3. U. Scheuner, 'Der Einfluss des französischen Verwaltungsrechts auf die deutsche Rechtsentwicklung', prev. p. 714.
4. *Ibid.*

The use of comparative law by the court is the subject of intense debate today, but mostly outside France. Meanwhile, the French administrative court now makes extensive use of comparative law, but without making this the subject of scholarly discussion. The circulation of judicial solutions and techniques is not new. As Jean Rivero reports for France: 'The Council of State is open to certain foreign jurisprudences. If we are to believe President Letourneur, manifest error of appreciation has a lot to do with the example of the Swiss Federal Tribunal, and the jurisprudence of the International Tribunal of the ILO; according to President Braibant, it is at the origin of the principle of proportionality'.[5] Thus, while principles and solutions circulate, regarding the contemporary increasing recourse to comparative law, there is no ongoing debate in France. The silence of French administrative scholarship on the topic contrasts sharply with the intensity of the debates across the Atlantic. The extreme position (refusal) is well illustrated by Justice Scalia's dissenting opinion in *Roper v. Simmons* from 2005: 'The Court thus ... purports to take guidance from the views of foreign courts and legislatures. Because I do not believe that the meaning of our Eighth Amendment, any more than the meaning of other provisions of our Constitution, should be determined by the subjective views of five Members of this Court and like-minded foreigners, I dissent.'[6] Further, Scalia adds: 'What these foreign sources "affirm," rather than repudiate, is the Justices' own notion of how the world ought to be, and their diktat that it shall be so henceforth in America. The Court's parting attempt to downplay the significance of its extensive discussion of foreign law is unconvincing.' Following this decision, the Republicans tried, unsuccessfully, to pass a law to prevent the Supreme Court from interpreting the United States (US) Constitution using foreign interpretative aids.

What is this really all about? The position of the originalist Justice is a solution inspired by a kind of legal nationalism, the source of which is obviously not the need to protect the sovereignty of Congress. In reality, he is actually opposed to any development concerning the death penalty. But, having said that, one should not rule out from the outset how deeply shocking the use of comparative law can be a priori in a court decision – except in private international law (choice of law) cases. It is perhaps no coincidence that we are asking ourselves this question at a time when we are witnessing a hatred of democracy[7] and an eclipse of legality,[8] one being of course linked to the other. The use of comparative law by judges (the Council of State has made extensive use of it for several years[9]) reflects a new relationship to the sources of

5. J. Rivero, 'Le droit administratif en droit comparé : Rapport final', RIDC n° 4-1989, pp. 919-926.
6. Roper v. Simmons, 543 U.S. 551, 668 (2005).
7. J. Rancière, *La haine de la démocratie*, la Fabrique éditions, 2005.
8. F. Pennings, F.M. Leonard Besselink, S. Prechal, The Eclipse of the Legality Principle in the European Union, Kluwer Law International, 2010.
9. J.-M. Sauvé, 'Le Conseil d'État et la comparaison des droits', *La comparaison en droit public, Hommage à RolandDrago*, Colloquium organized by the Institut français des sciences administratives and the Société de législation comparée, Conseil d'État, 14 February 2014 (available at: http://www.conseil-etat.fr/Actualites/Discours-Interventions/Le-Conseil-d-État-et-la-comparaison-des-droits); B. Stirn, 'Le droit administratif français, européen et global : bilan et perspectives', ELN Interviews ; *Vers un droit public européen*, coll. 'Clefs', Montchrestien, 2015 ; O. Dutheillet de Lamothe, 'Comparative Law as an Essential Feature of French Public Law: The

law revealing the significant development of judges' powers and the growing entanglement of legal systems; a phenomenon which calls for an increasing use of comparative law in Europe today, which Armin von Bogdandy has studied thoroughly.[10] However, all this said, we can only note that in European Union law, it has always been this way.

As a matter of fact, the Court of Justice has used comparative law at least since the Algera judgment of 1957, and precisely in an area that forms part of administrative law. But the position of the Court is different here, since it takes inspiration from the legal systems involved in its action, thus, it is not inspired by foreign legal systems, as was the intention of the Supreme Court in the case *Roper v. Simmons*; in this sense, Justice Scalia does not object to the use of comparative law to compare the laws of US states. The Court of Justice draws inspiration from the laws of the Member States to identify certain principles, expressly prescribed by the Treaty requiring the Court, for extra-contractual liability, to 'remedy, according to the general principles shared by the laws of the Member States, the damage caused by its institutions or by its agents in the performance of their duties'.[11] Accordingly, within the ambit of fundamental rights, the Court stated in the judgments Nold of 1974 and Hauer of 1979 that 'it has an obligation to draw inspiration from the constitutional traditions common to the Member States'.[12] The Court therefore undertakes this comparative approach as an obligation. It therefore performs, we might say, internal comparative law, which does not prevent it from being inspired by the European Convention of Human Rights, or other relevant international instruments. We will show that this is a traditional technique used by the Court of Justice of the European Union (CJEU). Looking at European administrative law in a restrictive sense, as the law of the administration of the European Union, excluding a complete analysis of the general principles of law that Jürgen Schwarze[13] has already studied thoroughly, establishing, for each, the contribution of comparative law, we will try to show how the CJEU has used comparative law from the outset to improve his techniques, to identify new principles, but that this use is in fact an instrumentalization of these sources, which should be subject to critical assessment.

We will begin by establishing the presence of comparative law in European administrative law. We will then analyse its application, to finally deliver a critical assessment of the role of comparative law in European administrative law.

Influence of the European Union and of the European Convention of Human Rights', in M. Ademas, D. Fairgrieve (eds), Courts and Comparative Law, Oxford University Press; F. Lichère, 'The Use of Comparative Law Before the French Administrative Law Courts: Or the Triumph of Castles over Pyramids', Courts and Comparative Law, prev. (2015), pp. 253 et seq.; A. Bretonneau, S. Dahan, D. Fairgrieve, 'L'influence grandissante du droit comparé au Conseil d'État : vers une procédure juridictionnelle innovante ?', RFDA 2015. 855.

10. A. von Bogdandy, 'European Law Beyond "Ever Closer Union" – Repositioning the Concept, Its Thrust and the ECJ's Comparative Methodology', 22(4) European Law Journal, 519-538, July 2016.
11. Paragraph 340, Article 2 of TFEU. For a fairly complete overview of the sources of the comparison: C.N. Kakouris, 'Use of Comparative Method by the Court of Justice of the European Communities', 6 Pace International Law Review 267 (1994).
12. Case nos 4/73 and 44/79.
13. J. Schwarze, *Droit administratif européen*, coll. 'Droit administratif/Administrative Law', Bruylant, 2009.

1 THE PRESENCE OF COMPARATIVE LAW IN EUROPEAN ADMINISTRATIVE LAW

The CJEU has always invoked comparative law, and administrative law offered a perfect incubator for this, since the first major judgment in European administrative law is a judgment using comparative law. This presence goes way back, to the very origin of the European integration process. It can be traced in both jurisprudence and doctrine.

- Comparative law and the origins of European integration

As Julie Bailleux clearly demonstrated, comparative law has from the outset been closely connected to emerging Community law.[14] At the Liberation, while law was disqualified as a means of bringing peoples together and promoting peace for the benefit of economics and political science, comparative law was quickly invoked. Comparative law is then understood as a social science and its purpose resonates with the imperative of the time: to enhance the mutual understanding of the peoples. Julie Bailleux clearly shows that comparative law was redefined at this very time to deepen this understanding between the peoples, the initial objective of the unification of laws, cherished in the nineteenth century, was therefore abandoned. It becomes indispensable 'for the construction of a peaceful international order'.[15] Accordingly, René David asserts that comparative law is 'the modern form of legal humanism'.[16] Comparative law was therefore on the rise after the war and was widely mobilized for the construction of the European Community. In 1957, the creation of the International Faculty of Comparative Law 'led to a close and lasting collaboration between the members of the Legal Service [of the European institutions] and some of the most eminent representatives of a transnational community of jurists which was about to become institutionalized: comparative law specialists'.[17] The confluence of comparative law and Community law seems quite natural; while the former aims at the approximation of laws, the latter constitutes an indispensable tool for such an undertaking. Marc Ancel thus argues that 'the Treaty of Rome on the European Communities, which presupposes or must bring about a harmonization of the legal, social and judicial institutions of the Member States (...) will increasingly require the systematic comparative study of these different institutions'.[18] The European executive

14. J. Bailleux, *Penser l'Europe par le droit, L'invention du droit communautaire en France*, coll. 'Nouvelle Bibliothèque des thèses', Dalloz, 2014, chap. 1.
15. J. Bailleux, *Penser l'Europe par le droit, L'invention du droit communautaire en France*, prev., p. 86.
16. R. David, 29 janvier 1947, 'Raisons pour lesquelles il est souhaitable de voir créer dans lecadre de l' UNESCO une organisation pour l'étude du droit comparé', Archives of UNESCO, available on the institution 's website, quoted by Julie Bailleux, in *Penser l'Europe par le droit, L'invention du droit communautaire en France*, prev., p. 86.
17. *Ibid.*, p. 258.
18. M. Ancel, 'Cent ans de droit comparé en France', in *Livre centenaire de la Société de législation comparée : un siècle de droit comparé en France*, 1869-1969, quoted by J. Bailleux, *Penser l'Europe par le droit, L'invention du droit communautaire en France*, prev., p. 262.

therefore invested heavily in institutions such as the International Faculty of Comparative Law, the first annual session of which was dedicated to Community law.[19] Julie Bailleux describes the contribution of comparativists as follows: 'The latter very quickly established comparative law studies as an essential resource for the construction of Community law as a symbolic and practical product. Firstly, they mobilized comparative law studies to fill the content of European rules resulting from the (daily) activity of the institutions of the ECSC, then of the EEC and Euratom. ECSC legislation in social matters, for example, was largely drawn up on the basis of studies which, in Michel Gaudet's view, are the results of "comparative social legislation", practised as of 1955 by a group of professors from the different countries of the European Community, brought together by the services of the High Authority.'[20] There is therefore, at the institutional level, a specific Directorate dedicated to the approximation of laws which thus deals with comparative law.

This interest is not specific to the European executive bodies since Julie Bailleux quotes a letter from a judge of the European Court of Justice, Nicolas Catalano, who insists on the need to reflect on the approximation of the laws of the six member states.[21] Maurice Lagrange has theorized this method quite abundantly. For this lawyer, the alternative is the following: 'either the legal order of the ECSC belongs to the international legal order of which it is only a manifestation; or, it constitutes an autonomous, balanced legal order, the rules of which are borrowed from the internal public law of the member states of the ECSC'.[22] He then adds, and this is crucial for us, that the European Court of Justice must render judgements taking into account 'the rules which were quite naturally borrowed from the common fundaments of the six member states'.[23] He thus rejects international law as a source, prioritizing the internal law of the Member States, as the sole source of Community law.[24] The European Court of Justice, he says, 'performs comparative law'.[25] Here is how Maurice Lagrange describes this method: 'If the court is autonomous and must proclaim what the law of the Treaty is, it is easy to imagine that the source of this law can only be drawn from the common legal base of the six States'.[26] It is therefore necessary to discover their 'common denominator' after a comparative law analysis in order to discover 'these

19. J. Bailleux, *Penser l'Europe par le droit, L'invention du droit communautaire en France*, prev., p. 265.
20. J. Bailleux, *Penser l'Europe par le droit, L'invention du droit communautaire en France*, prev., pp. 265-266.
21. Letter from Nicolas Catalano to Pierre Wigny dated 9 November 1959, Archives of the Jean Monnet Foundation, Gaudet collection, Correspondances, quoted by J. Bailleux, p. 266.
22. J. Bailleux, *Penser l'Europe par le droit, L'invention du droit communautaire en France*, prev., p. 266. She quotes here a sentence by Maurice Lagrange taken from the following article: 'L'ordre juridiquede la CECA', *RDP* 1958, p. 843.
23. M. Lagrange, 'La Cour de justice de la Communauté européenne du charbon et de l'acier', *RDP* 1954, p. 434, quoted by J. Bailleux, *Penser l'Europe par le droit, L'invention du droit communautaire en France*, prev., p. 266.
24. M. Lagrange, 'L'ordre juridique de la CECA', *RDP* 1958, p. 843, quoted by J. Bailleux, *Penser l'Europe par le droit, L'invention du droit communautaire en France*, prev., p. 266.
25. *Ibid.*, p. 856.
26. M. Lagrange, 'Une réalité européenne. La cour de justice de la CECA', *Cahiers chrétiens de la fonction publique*, April 1955, p. 20, quoted by J. Bailleux, *Penser l'Europe par le droit, L'invention du droit communautaire en France*, prev., p. 267, note 165.

general principles of law, which give, in reality, although through different paths of thought, the same solution to identical problems'.[27]

We will see this idea in action in case law and doctrine.

- The comparative method at the heart of case-law and doctrine in European administrative law

We will study a few cases here, to analyse the way in which case-law and possibly the opinions of the Advocates General use comparative law. Then, we will also illustrate the use of comparison in an original doctrinal proposal, that of the ReNUAL group, which has drawn up a draft European code of administrative procedure.

1.1 The Comparative Method in the Case Law of the Court of Justice

Many areas of European administrative law have been influenced by comparative law, as Jürgen Schwarze has amply demonstrated in his handbook.[28] Case law has borrowed extensively from national administrative laws; from Germany, for example, the review of proportionality or legitimate expectations.

This point will be illustrated based on the Algera judgment, which offers the advantage of showing the influence of the thinking of Maurice Lagrange. This judgment was rendered on 12 July 1957,[29] based on his opinion. The case concerned the legality of the withdrawal of an administrative act establishing a right (in this case the appointment of a civil servant in public employment). The Court recognizes that the regulation of this question is based on administrative law traditions of the Member States, and the Treaty is silent on this point. The Court then carried out a comparative administrative law study to identify the rules common to the Member States in this field: 'As to the possibility of withdrawing such acts, this is a problem of administrative law, well known in the case-law and doctrine of all the countries of the Community, but for the solution of which the treaty does not provide any rules. The Court, to avoid a denial of justice, is therefore obliged to resolve the case by drawing inspiration from the rules recognized by the legislations, the doctrine and the case-law of the member states.' The Court's analysis leads to the conclusion that, in the six Member States of the Community, the revocability of an illegal administrative act is always possible, within a reasonable time. This conclusion is in accordance with the views of Advocate General Lagrange, who begins by stating that 'Indeed, it is a principle that, when individual decisions comply with the law, they cannot be withdrawn: persons who are the addressees of those decisions derive from them an individual right and they are entitled to require that it should be respected.' Where does the Advocate General get this principle from? He confines himself to explaining the following: 'This solution, which meets the need to ensure the stability of legal relationships and which, in the realm of unilateral public law relationships, corresponds, to the effects of a contract in multilateral relationships, is common to the principles of the law of all six member

27. *Ibid.*
28. J. Schwarze, *Droit administratif européen*, 2nd ed., Bruylant, 2009.
29. Case no. 7/56 and 7/57, Rec. p. 81.

countries.' We can therefore infer that the comparative analysis preceded the drawing up of the opinion, but the Advocate General does not go into more details. On the other hand, the question of the withdrawal of illegal individual decisions is subject to extensive elaboration. The AG first analyses French administrative case-law to show that the withdrawal of such decisions was, at the time, possible when these decisions were illegal; but within the time limit to bring judicial review. Recourse to the French example is questionable in this case, since in the absence of a relevant time limit for review in Europe at the time (this was only introduced by the ruling of the Court on 21 February 1957), the applicants concluded that the acts in question could not be revoked. The Advocate General is therefore faced with a dilemma which leads him to continue his analysis by turning to other legal systems: he notes that France is the only country in which the withdrawal of the illegal act is limited by the time limits applicable for judicial review. In Germany, the inviolability of the acquired rights of civil servants is a fundamental principle of constitutional civil service law in that country, except in certain cases, including cases of illegality. Should we therefore take inspiration from the French solution?

The Advocate General therefore notes:

> 'It will be for the Court to decide whether, when the general time-limit laid down for the application of Article 58 is applicable (it is so now), it intends to lay down case-law modelled on the French case-law which will protect the vested rights of officials. For the time being, all that I would be inclined to accept for my part is the idea of a "reasonable period of time"'. He also notes that this concept of reasonable time is in accordance with German law, as set out in a manual cited by the Advocate General.

In light of the silence of the Treaties, it is the French and German administrative laws that allow the Advocate General and the court to identify the applicable rule. Why does he omit to elaborate on the situation in the legal systems of the other Member States? The use of comparative law thus serves to identify a rule, even if the analysis is not all that thorough.

We can continue this analysis, based on two other judgments which seem particularly emblematic of the approach of the Court in its use of comparative law. These are the 1974 Nold[30] and the 1979 Hauer[31] decisions. In the Nold judgement, a company challenged a Commission decision on the grounds that it violated its fundamental rights, in this case its right to property, by compromising the profitability of its business. At the time, the Treaty was silent on the matter of fundamental rights. The Court starts by declaring that fundamental rights form an integral part of the general principles of law, the observance of which it ensures. But it then adds in safeguarding these rights it 'is bound to draw inspiration from constitutional traditions common to the Member States, and it cannot therefore uphold measures which are incompatible with fundamental rights recognized and protected by the Constitutions of those States'. It adds furthermore that it can also find inspiration in the international instruments for the protection of human rights of which Member States are signatories.

30. Case no. 4-73 of 14 May 1974.
31. Case no. 44/79 of 13 December 1979.

It is thus in the light of these principles that the violation of the right to property by an administrative act must be assessed. It develops its control in a way that is indeed not foreign to the classic review of the violation of a fundamental right. We find the same line of reasoning in the Hauer judgment of 1979.

EU law thus has a particular affinity to comparative law. There is now an increasing use of this method, which can be explained by the culture of the Court, which has the ideal resources to do this work. The composition of the Court makes it a perfect place to carry out comparative analyses, with each judge arriving in Luxembourg bringing their own legal tradition. This is the reason why the opinions of the Advocates General very often contain elaborations on comparative law. Pierre Pescatore mentions in this regard the model developed in the opinion of AG Lagrange in the Assider judgment of 11 February 1955 on the concept of misuse of power.

Jürgen Schwarze unpacks various influences of national administrative law on European administrative law. From the outset, French administrative law has played an influential role in the development of European administrative law, and in particular in the development of judicial review: the cases in which review may be brought are directly inspired by this tradition. German administrative law then played a leading role in the development of the proportionality test and the protection of legitimate expectations. We cannot fail to note that the German inspiration for the proportionality test is a topos of comparative law and deserves further nuancing: the proportionality test has in fact existed in administrative law in France for a long time, in particular in the context of the review of police measures (since the Benjamin case of 19 May 1933), yet it is also true that the German technique, with the three-tier test, is much more elaborate. It is also striking that procedural rights, in particular the right to be heard, are recognized by the Court just one year after the United Kingdom joins the Community. Jürgen Schwarze quotes here the opinion of Advocate General Warner in the *Transocean Marine Paint Association* case.[32] In this case, the Advocate General conducted a detailed analysis of English law, in which this principle of natural justice has existed for a long time. He even refers to the landmark case *Ridge v. Baldwin* of 1964 of the House of Lords.

The importance of comparative law is not only apparent in case-law. It is also clearly discernible from the doctrine.

1.2 Comparative Law and the Development of the European Code of Administrative Procedure

Comparative law is indeed of vital importance in the legislative activity of the Commission, as well as in certain areas of academic work. For example, the draft European Code of Administrative Procedure, initiated by European academics, is strongly inspired by the comparison of laws.

32. CJEC, 23 October 1974, *Transocean Marine Paint Association v. Commission of the European Communities*, n° 17-74.

Herwig C.H. Hofmann and Jens-Peter Schneider explain that they used comparative law to develop the code in two ways: on the one hand, they compared existing rules of procedure in European Union law in the major areas of European policymaking; on the other hand, they carried out a comparative analysis of the administrative procedural principles of each Member State.[33] The comparison did not only focus on the procedural laws of the Member States, since the American example has strongly inspired the drafters in at least one area: the development of acts of general application. Herwig Hofmann and Jens-Peter Schneider explain that national experiences could not be used by the drafting team, because, generally, the procedural codes or laws of EU Member States did not provide for a specific legal regime for these acts. Therefore, the ReNUAL team drew inspiration from American law. It is worth noting that following the American model,[34] the drafters provided for a high degree of transparency, participation and evaluation of draft regulatory acts. The drafters thus carried out an in-depth analysis of American law on this subject in an attempt to identify the difficulties of applying the participatory procedure in the US: 'As to the American rules for drawing up acts of general application, these provide for an information and participation procedure. Following a thorough analysis of American scholarship on the subject, the editors of the working group entrusted with Book II concluded that the risk of "ossification" (that is, the difficulty experienced by US agencies to implement new rules due to complex procedural requirements and the obligation to state reasons imposed by the procedure for drawing up acts of general application), was less due to this procedure as such, than to the rules of standing before the American courts. Consequently, because of the considerable differences between the litigation rules applicable in the United States and in Europe, the drawbacks of the participatory procedure appeared to be less relevant for Europe.'[35] In this case, we may witness real comparative law analysis with the aim of transplanting the American model. The American participatory model is indeed highly criticized for its cumbersome nature, preventing agencies from updating the regulations. The editors found that this risk was not present in Europe due to the particulars of the judicial review procedure, meanwhile, the participatory procedure promised great benefits. It should be noted that in France there is no general rule requiring the participation of stakeholders in the preparation of administrative acts of general application (despite relative progress made by the Code of relations between the public and the administration which provides for such a procedure but at the discretion of the administration)[36] nor is there

33. H.C.H. Hofmann, J.-P. Schneider, 'Administrative Law Reform in the European Union: The ReNEUAL Project and Its Basis in Comparative Legal Studies', S. Rose-Ackerman, P. Lindseth, Comparative Administrative Law, Edward Elgar, forthcoming.
34. *Ibid. See* ReNEUAL Model Rules on EU Administrative Procedure, 2014, Article II-4.
35. C.H. Hofmann, J.-P. Schneider, 'Administrative Law Reform in the European Union: The ReNEUAL Project and Its Basis in Comparative Legal Studies', prev.
36. *See* Title III on involving the public in decisions taken by the administration: 'When the administration decides, apart from cases governed by legislative or regulatory provisions, to involve the public in the design of a reform or in the development of a project or an act, it makes the terms and conditions of this procedure public, makes the relevant information available to

such a requirement in effect in Germany,[37] Italy[38] or Spain.[39] The codification work therefore meant looking to America for the purposes of ensuring a significant degree of transparency in the development of administrative policies at the European level.

Comparative law is therefore a major source of inspiration in the creation of European administrative law, both at the level of jurisprudence as well as of legislation. The fate of the future European code of administrative procedure is undecided, but we can clearly see to what extent comparative law can be useful in creating new procedures.

It is now worth looking at how the court uses comparative law methods in European administrative law.

2 THE IMPLEMENTATION OF COMPARATIVE LAW IN EUROPEAN ADMINISTRATIVE LAW

Does the court apply a particular method? We will see that it is altogether quite unsophisticated. We will also see that comparative law is used by the Court within the context of its teleological method; it is an instrument for finding the principle of law or rule which best serves to achieve the objectives of the treaty. More fundamentally, is comparative law not just a discourse to legitimize jurisprudence, the spirit of which is to base judicial law-making on the law of the Member States and thereby promote a higher acceptance of its judge-made solution? We will first look at the methods used by the Court in comparative law before demonstrating that comparative law forms a part of a teleological reasoning.

2.1 Analysis of the Methods Used

Is there a method that could lead to the conclusion that comparative law is used in a scientific and neutral way? The Court used both quantitative and qualitative methods. I prefer this distinction to that used by Pierre Pescatore, who distinguishes between an analytical method and a synthetic method, the first consisting of bringing together the status quo in the laws of the Member States on a given issue and the second serving to identify a common principle, because it does not quite seem to reflect the reasoning of the judges.[40]

---

the persons concerned, ensures them a reasonable period of time to participate in it and ensures that the results or the envisaged follow-up are, at the appropriate time, made public' (Article L. 131-1).

37. A. Jacquemet-Gauché, U. Stelkens, 'La participation à l'élaboration des règlements administratifs en Allemagne', in Droit comparé de la procédure administrative, J.-B. Auby and T. Perroud (dir.), p. 261.
38. G. della Cananea, 'Administrative Rulemaking in Italy: Theories and Practice', in Droit comparé de la procédure administrative, J.-B. Auby and T. Perroud (dir.), p. 247.
39. C. Velasco, 'La participation à l'élaboration des règlements administratifs : le casespagnol', in Droit comparé de la procédure administrative, J.-B. Auby and T. Perroud (dir.), p. 289.
40. P. Pescatore, 'Le recours, dans la jurisprudence de la Cour de justice des Communautés Européennes, à des normes déduites de la comparaison du droit des États membres', RIDC

2.1.1 *The Quantitative Method*

In liability cases, the Court of Justice used a quantitative method in the FIAMM and Fedon judgments[41] to rule out the existence of a general principle of law in strict liability cases in the absence of unlawful behaviour by the Community. The difference of opinion on the existence of this principle between the Commission, joined by the Court, and Advocate General Maduro highlights the importance of the quantitative factor. We will first analyse the Court's reasoning and then the result, which is based on the comparative law analysis provided by the Commission. Then we will look at how Advocate General Maduro sought to justify his position.

The reasoning of the Court for rejecting such a principle is based on the observation that only seven Member States have this principle in place and apply it only in specific cases so that, under these circumstances, the principle cannot be considered a principle common to the legal orders of the Member States of the Union, in the sense of Article 288(2) (now Article 340(2) of the Treaty on the Functioning of the European Union).[42] Now to the comparative law analysis provided by the Commission: 'examination of the 25 legal orders of the Member States indicates that, in contrast to cases such as expropriation in the public interest or compensation paid by the State for damage caused by dangerous activity on its part or on account of a specific relationship between it and the victim, which are irrelevant here, any obligation to pay compensation as a result of a lawful State act reflecting a broad discretion, on account for example of considerations of solidarity or fairness, is unknown to the law of a large number of Member States. While liability of such a type can be found, in exceptional circumstances, in the legal orders of certain other Member States, it is, as a general rule, limited solely to administrative acts, with the notable exception of French law which alone clearly accepts this type of liability in the case of legislative activity, provided that the damage is unusual, special, serious and direct, that the legislature is not pursuing the common good and that the legislature has not ruled out compensation as a matter of principle. Furthermore, the principle specific to French law cannot be transferred to the Community legal order. While the basis of that principle is the fact that, in France, judicial review by the Conseil d'État (Council of State) of the constitutionality of laws is precluded, Community law provides for review of the legality of measures of the legislature by reference to the Treaty and fundamental principles and for the possibility of the liability of the Community to be put in issue if those higher-ranking norms are infringed.'[43]

---

n° 2- 1980, pp. 352 ff. We find this distinction in the following work : J.F. Delile, *L'invocabilité des accords internationaux devant la CJUE et le Conseil d'Etat français*, Bruylant, 2016, p. 574.

41. Case no. C-120/06, to the opinion of Advocate General Maduro. *See* J.F. Delile, L'invocabilité des accords internationaux devant la CJUE et le Conseil d'Etat franç ais, coll. 'Droitde l' Union européenne', Bruylant, 2016, p. 574 ; A. Arcuri, S. Poli, 'What Price for the Community Enforcement of WTO Law ?', EU I Working Papers Law 2010/01. *See also* A. Barav, '"Injustice normative" et fondement de la responsabilité extracontractuelle de la Communauté économique européenne', in *L'application judiciaire du droit de l'Union européenne : Recueil d'études*, Bruylant, 2015.
42. A. Arcuri, S. Poli, 'What Price for the Community Enforcement of WTO Law?', prev., pp. 19-20.
43. Case no. C-120/06, §151-152.

Advocate General Maduro did not share this view. He tries to override the quantitative argument, since in fact there are only two States in Europe with a principle of strict liability in the absence of an unlawful act, when the act causing harm is a legislative act. The question raised by Maduro is therefore legitimate: 'should the second paragraph of Article 288 EC be interpreted as excluding a solution in matters of extra-contractual liability of public authorities in Community law unless it is shared by all Member States?'.[44] The risk of such an approach is to retain only 'the lowest common denominator', according to Maduro. Advocate General Roemer in the Zuckerfabrik judgment of 2 December 1971 'rejected the application of the "rule of the lowest limit" that would result if it were decided to adopt only rules existing in all the Member States'.[45] He emphasized that there was no need to seek 'the concordance of the legal orders of all the Member States' or even 'of a majority'.[46]

For Maduro, therefore, it is necessary to overcome the quantitative method when using comparative law in order to find the 'legal solution (...) which will be the most appropriate for the context and the needs of the Community legal order'.

The Court's approach is questionable because, as Pierre Pescatore put it, 'the comparative approach is sometimes used to introduce legal concepts of a single Member State into Community law'.[47] Koen Lenaerts has also reflected on the fluctuation of the quantitative method in jurisprudence.[48] Sometimes, the convergence of Member State laws makes it possible to find a solution, but the Court clearly doesn't refrain from transposing purely and simply a technique inspired by one single legal system, such as transplanting the proportionality test or the principle of legitimate expectations from Germany. The quantitative criterion cannot therefore be an authoritative criterion since it has never been consistently used throughout the history of European Union law.

The use of the quantitative method is not uncommon in European administrative law. Yet it is questionable. Another method can also be used, which I will refer to as the qualitative method. This approach was explained by Advocate General Roemer.

2.1.2 The Qualitative Method

Advocate General Roemer, in a 1973 case concerning the definition of the principles governing the Community's extra-contractual liability, made explicit reference to a

44. Item 55.
45. Opinion by AB Maduro in case C-120/06, note 59 which cites AG Roemer's opinion in the case *Zuckerfabrik Schöppenstedt v. Council*, 2 December 1971, n° 5/71, *Rec.* p. 975, in particular p. 991.
46. Opinion in case Werhahn Hansamühle e.a. v. Council and Commission, n° 63/72 to 69/72, 13 November 1973, *Rec.* p. 1253, in particular p. 1258, quoted by Maduro in note 59.
47. P. Pescatore, 'Le recours, dans la jurisprudence de la Cour de justice des Communautés Européennes, à des normes déduites de la comparaison du droit des États membres', R1DC n° 2- 1980, pp. 353-354.
48. K. Lenaerts, 'Le droit comparé dans le travail du juge communautaire', in *L'utilisation de la méthode comparative en droit européen*, F. van der Mensbrugghe (dir.), Pressesuniversitaires de Namur, 2003, pp. 111 ff.

concept developed by the great comparatist Zweigert:[49] the balanced study of comparative law. He explains his approach as follows: 'Rather what is indicated – as always when judicial decisions are arrived at by references to general principles – a process of assessment in which above all the particular objectives of the Treaty and the peculiarities of the Community structure must be taken into account (and in which perhaps it is appropriate that the guideline be the best elaborated national rules)'.[50] He adds in another case that 'What is important in ascertaining the law under Article 215, second paragraph, [on the extra-contractual liability of the Community], is not the unanimity of the legal systems of all Member States, nor a kind of vote ending in a majority finding; no, it is rather a matter of looking at what eminent legal writers (e.g., Zweigert) have called evaluative comparative law. In this connexion what may be highly relevant is to ascertain which legal system emerges as the most carefully considered'.[51]

What does that mean? What is the CJEU method? This is said to be the great comparatist Zweigert's method, referred to as wertende Rechtsvergleichung in German (in English: evaluative comparative law). It is a knowledgeable method of evaluation with the aim, of creating new law, of selecting the legal rule most appropriate to the context: 'Methodically, it is not a functional comparison of legal provisions; it is therefore not a question of analysing the objectives of a provision in a given context. Rather, it is a method of careful selection and elaboration of certain rules on the basis of a prior assessment. The standard used to select the rule includes the setting of a goal which may be to safeguard the highest level of protection, especially in the area of fundamental rights, and the compatibility of the new rule with the objectives and structures of the law of the Union. This method therefore does not consist of a simple transfer of a national rule to the European Union, but of the development of common European standards.'[52] As TP van Reenen puts it, evaluative comparative law is in fact a method of applied comparative law. It is about using comparative law in order to identify the different rules applied in each Member State to a given legal situation and

49. Author of the famous introduction to comparative law: K. Zweigert, H. Kötz, An Introduction to Comparative Law, Oxford, 3rd ed., 1998.

50. Opinion in case 5/71, *Aktien-Zuckerfabrik Schöppenstedt v. Council of the European Communities*, Rec., XVII, p. 991.

51. Opinion in joint cases 63 to 69/72, *Wilhelm Werhahn Hansamûhle e.a. v. Council of the European Communities*, Rec., 1973, p. 1258. *See* J. Kokott, C. Sobotta, 'The Charter of Fundamental Rights of the European Union after Lisbon', EUI Working Paper, AEL 2010/6, Academy of European Law, p. 2.

52. P. Dann, 'Thoughts on a Methodology of European Constitutional Law', in The Unity of the European Constitution, Michal Rynkowski, Philipp Dann, eds., Berlin, 2006, p. 52. The method is also explained this way 'Evaluative comparison' differs from analytical comparison in that, although it identifies differences between the legal orders under comparison, it attempts to level these differences by receiving or re-evaluating the foreign solutions in the own, domestic system. In this regard Eörsi's view that the socialist legislator may adopt the solutions of non-socialist legal systems after they have been 'stripped of their bourgeois elements', is worth mentioning (G. Eörsi, 'Comparative analysis of socialist and capitalist law', 1964 Coexistence, n° 141, 143-145). This kind of comparison implies the involvement of value judgment in addition to the purely cognitive process of analytical comparison. 'Applied comparative law' is, therefore, as a rule, evaluative comparative law' (TP van Reenen, 'Major Theoretical Problems of Modern Comparative Legal Methodology: The Comparability of Positive Legal Phenomena', 28(3) The Comparative and International Law Journal of Southern Africa (November 1995), pp. 407-421, esp. pp. 413-414.

to assess each of these rules in the light of the Community's needs and to retain only the most relevant rule.

Koen Lenaerts explains furthermore that the comparative method is actually associated with the teleological method: 'First, the comparative method provides a range of different possible options for interpretation. Then, the Court chooses the one which is best for achieving the objectives pursued by the Union.'[53] But, as I have shown, comparative law often only provides an argument and is not decisive.

As we can see, despite the development of a few theories, which the judge or the Advocate General never explains, the comparative method is often instrumentalized. Franz C. Mayer and others are therefore correct in arguing that the Court's comparative work in its judgments is not sufficiently transparent, clear, and developed.[54] It is more about practising comparative law in order to achieve the objectives of the Community.

2.2 The Instrumentalization of the Comparative Method

The comparative method is used both by the Advocates General and the Court. As Pierre Pescatore clearly pointed out, there are no objective criteria that would allow us to predict the result of the comparison.[55] Comparative law must make it possible to find the solution which best meets the objectives of the Union. It is about finding the solution best suited to the judge's goals, which is why the comparative study is inserted within the framework of the teleological reasoning of the Court[56] and this is the reason why comparative law can even be used as 'contrast agent', as Pierre Pescatore had pointed out, in the event that the existence of differences between the laws of the Member States could lead the Court to deviate from these rights in order to find the most satisfactory solution.[57]

More fundamentally, one will need to find the solution which represents the least conflict with the interests of Member States. In this regard, it fulfils a diplomatic function. The use of comparative law must enable the optimal articulation of European and national legal orders. Comparative law therefore contributes to 'ensuring the

53. K. Lenaerts, 'La Cour de justice de l'Union européenne et la méthode comparative', Proceedings of the International Days of the SLC, Le droit comparé au XXIe siècle, Paris, Société de législation comparée, 2016.
54. F.C. Mayer, 'Constitutional Comparativism in Action: The Example of General Principles of EU Law and How They Are Made – A German Perspective', 11(4) I-CON 1003-1020, p. 1008 (2013); L. Wildhaber, 'The Role of Comparative Law in the Case-Law of the European Court of Human Rights', in Festschrift Ress, Internationale Gemeinschaft und Menschenrechte: Festschrift für Georg Ress zum 70. Geburtstag am 21. Januar 2005, p. 1101.
55. P. Pescatore, 'Le recours, dans la jurisprudence de la Cour de justice des Communautés Européennes, à des normes déduites de la comparaison du droit des États membres', RIDC n° 2-1980, p. 353 ff. *See also* F.C. Mayer, 'Constitutional Comparativism in Action: The Example of General Principles of EU Law and How They Are Made: A German Perspective', 11(4) I-CON 1003-1020, p. 1007 (2013).
56. C.N. Kakouris, 'Use of Comparative Method by the Court of Justice of the European Communities', 6 Pace Int'l L. Rev. 267 (1994), esp. p. 273.
57. P. Pescatore, 'Le recours, dans la jurisprudence de la Cour de justice des Communautés Européennes, à des normes déduites de la comparaison du droit des États membres', prev., p. 354.

primacy, effectiveness and uniformity of application' of Union law.[58] In light of the scepticism of the German Federal Constitutional Court (in the Solange decision) with regard to the degree of protection of fundamental rights granted by the Court of Justice, we can better understand the need to justify CJEU decisions with reference to the constitutional traditions of the Member States. Comparative law is therefore at the centre of the discourse legitimizing the creative activity of the Court.

However, the case-law of the Court, and in particular the opinions of the Advocates General, are not completely free from a certain bad faith regarding the use of comparative law, and sometimes from a certain condescension towards certain legal systems, because the use of comparative law is sometimes imbued with the idea of progress. Certain judgments on the extra-contractual liability of the Community are very interesting in this respect. These are the judgments Zuckerfabrik of 1971[59] and Werhahn of 1973,[60] both rendered on the basis of the Opinion delivered by Advocate General Roemer. We have seen that in this field, according to the Treaty, the Court settles this question by recourse to comparative law.

Roemer notes that in France, Belgium, Italy and the Federal Republic of Germany the State's liability for the illegality of a normative act is possible, even if differences exist between these States regarding the scope of damages that can be compensated. As demonstrated above, the Advocate General sets himself as a guideline that, for the interpretation of this Article of the Treaty, the approach shouldn't be to retain only rules which exist in all the Member States, since this would have the effect of transposing into Union law only those rules which constitute the 'lowest common denominator'. He thus dismisses the principle of the lowest common denominator. It is clear, that in his choice of comparative law the Advocate General is guided by a legal policy inspired by the idea of progress, of hierarchy. This is what he calls 'proceeding in a critical manner' taking into account the objectives of the Treaty. He thus rejects the rule of the lowest common denominator in favour of a critical approach, which he says is inspired by a reference point: adopting 'the most judiciously elaborated national regulation'. Of course, these standards are extremely subjective. But how does he proceed in the particular case? He begins by noting the particular nature of the Community and, in this case, its democratic deficit due to insufficient parliamentary control. He then details the general economy of the Treaty and of Union law, all of which stand in favour of the Community's liability for the illegality of a normative act, a principle that is by far not shared by all Member States.

However, in the second Werhahn judgment of 1973, the same Advocate General must respond to a criticism formulated by the parties concerning the relevance of his comparative law analysis. The plaintiffs criticize him for having said in his opinion that the principle of state liability under the different national laws was 'widespread'. The Advocate General then clarified that he only meant to say that it was recognized 'in a

58. K. Lenaerts, 'The European Court of Justice and the Comparative Law Method', 25(2) European Review of Private Law 297-312, esp. p. 49 (2017).
59. CJEC, 2 December 1971, *Aktien-Zuckerfabrik Schöppenstedt v. Council of the European Communities*, n° C-5/71.
60. CJEC, 13 November 1973, *Werhahn Hansamuehle e.a. v. Council*, n° 63 to 69-72.

number of states'. He plays with words by adding that 'the idea of "broad application" should therefore only be understood in a geographical sense. Neither the findings, nor the judgment lost sight of the fact that liability for legislative injustice is an unusual situation which only plays a very small role in practice'. In other words, Advocate General Roemer considerably watered down his comparative law analysis in the Zuckerfabrik opinion to arrive at the solution he wanted and his denials in the Werhahn opinion are likely to only have convinced him alone. But what is even more interesting about this second opinion is the question which the Advocate General asks next: should the inclusion of three new Member States in the Community change anything in respect of the rule laid down in the Zuckerfabrik judgment? He asks the question as follows: 'Yet one can already wonder with reason whether it is really necessary to take account of the legal orders of the new Member States for the interpretation of Article 215, paragraph 2' of the Treaty on the extra-contractual liability of the Community. The analysis is narrower, but not devoid of bad faith. After having shown that the principle is not accepted in the new Member States, he confirms that he has not 'however discovered decisive reasons against maintaining the current case-law'. It is thus not necessary to seek a concordance, but to carry out this 'evaluative study of comparative law' described above, with the purpose of deciding which legal system offers the 'best' rule. In this light, he notes that the laws of the new Member States show 'progress in the area of state liability'. Next, AG Roemer assumes the role of a prophet: 'So we can rightly say that the three legal orders which show a largely negative attitude on the point of interest to us at the moment will continue to come closer, in this important field of legal protection, to the orders of the more progressive legal systems, if you will, of the other Member States.' Here we are witnessing an implicit classification of states, reactionary states and progressive states and the Court of Justice is meant to show the way forward.

These findings highlight a fairly clear competition between administrative law traditions for primacy, a competition in which the Court of Justice is the arbiter. Comparative law is therefore not simply an argument, to use Fabrice Melleray's[61] expression, but instrumentalized by the various institutions and the Member States in the competition between the different traditions of European administrative laws to help a certain model of public action succeed.

61. F. Melleray (dir.), *L'argument de droit comparé en droit administratif français*, Bruylant, 2008.

CHAPTER 32

How to Spend (Our) Money Wisely: The SCA and Control of Public Tax and Spend in a Post-Brexit United Kingdom

Andrea Biondi & Maria Kendrick

1 INTRODUCTION

The United Kingdom (UK) Government has recently announced that on 4 January 2023, the new regime regulating the granting of subsidies as provided for by the Subsidy Control Act 2022 (SCA), will enter into full force.[1] This new system will provide the framework for a UK-wide, subsidy control so – according to the UK Government – as to enable public authorities, including devolved administrations and local authorities, to 'deliver subsidies tailored to local needs; to support government priorities such as driving economic growth and to reach net zero'.[2] All extremely laudable aims but the Government is actually even too modest as the new SCA is much more: the new legislation is – together with the UK Internal Market Act[3] – one of the most comprehensive post-Brexit regulatory settlements raising all manner of possible implications and complications; it also represents one of the most extensive domestic legislative regimes in terms of control of public spending – and not to forget the role of tax; because of the model adopted it is bound to have serious repercussions on the UK's public law system, especially as far as the role of public authorities and judicial control are concerned. Finally, it raises crucial questions in terms of solidarity between devolved regions and central government. In short, a whole stable of Professor Birkinshaw's hobby horses.

1. SCA 2022 (c. 23).
2. https://www.gov.uk/government/collections/subsidy-control-regime (accessed 26 October 2022).
3. UK Internal Market 2022 (c. 27).

2 THE SUBSIDY CONTROL ACT

The SCA 2022 received Royal Assent on 28 April 2022 and as mentioned it is expected to enter in full force by the beginning of 2023.[4] At 92 articles and 3 schedules, such an extremely comprehensively detailed regulatory framework was not exactly based on independent political choice. The SCA has been drafted and approved so as to directly comply with specific obligations imposed by the Trade and Cooperation Agreement (TCA hereafter) concluded between the European Union (EU) and the UK which, as is well known, sets out preferential arrangements in various trade and economic sectors.[5] Article 371 of the EU-UK TCA specifically requires both parties to set an 'effective domestic regime of subsidies control'.[6] The effectiveness of such a system would have to be measured against its compliance with the very detailed and lengthy articles of Chapter 3 of the TCA, one of the most extensive examples of subsidies regulation in any kind of international trade agreement. The SCA generally tends to replicate the TCA structure and it strictly adheres to the requirements imposed by the EU-UK TCA in terms of its scope. The SCA is roughly divided into the three broad areas regulated by the TCA: the definition of what constitutes a subsidy; the monitoring of subsidies; and enforcement and remedies in case unlawful subsidies have been granted.[7]

3 A 'MADE IN THE UK' SUBSIDY

3.1 The Four-Limb Test

The definition of what constitutes a subsidy, contained in section 2 SCA, faithfully replicates that of Article 363(1)(b) of the TCA and comprises four limbs. 'Subsidy' means financial assistance which: (a) is given, directly or indirectly, from public resources by a public authority; (b) confers an economic advantage on one or more enterprises; (c) is specific, that is, it is such that it benefits one or more enterprises over one or more other enterprises with respect to the production of goods or the provision of services; and (d) has, or is capable of having, an effect on competition or investment within the UK, and on international trade. The four limbs of the test are cumulative and they all need to be satisfied for a measure to be classified as a subsidy. In terms of scope, these four limbs are very resonant of concepts developed in the context of EU state aid law and World Trade Organization (WTO) regulation on subsidies.[8] However,

4. SCA 2022 (c. 23).
5. Trade and Cooperation Agreement between the European Union and the European Atomic Energy Community, of the one part, and the United Kingdom of Great Britain and Northern Ireland, of the other part OJ L 149, 30.4.2021, p. 10-2539.
6. For a fuller discussion *see* Andrea Biondi and Anneli Howard KC, *Levelling Up a Level Playing Field: Competition and Subsidies in Post-Brexit Britain*, in Adam Lazowski & Adam Cygan (eds), *Research Handbook on Legal Aspects of Brexit* (Edward Elgar, 2022) Ch. 15.
7. The SCA does not of course cover the questions of possible controversies that could arise by possible violations of Chapter 13 TCA. The complex system of arbitration/ retaliation measures is contained in the TCA itself as the Agreement provides for several State-to-State remedies in case of a serious risk of negative effect on trade, subject to a possible arbitration procedure.
8. Biondi and Howard KC, cit. above.

a few comments more related to the likely impact on the perimeter of UK Public Law may be more pertinent here. For instance, the SCA refers to 'public resources' given by 'a public authority'. Curiously, the section 6 definition of 'public authority' is a negative one. It defines which entities are *not* public authorities, such as the Houses of Parliament, leaving the legal as well as the practical responsibility for making decisions on the granting of subsidies to a very broad range of local and devolved authorities and many central government bodies, due to the breadth and negatively worded definition. What constitutes a public authority within the EU context is very much shaped by the imperative of guaranteeing the uniform and effective application of supranational norms and its impact has radically shaped and influenced UK public law as well.[9] This is demonstrable in the well-known formula, that anybody or an organisation, even one governed by private law 'to which a Member State has delegated the performance of a task in the public interest and which possesses for that purpose special powers beyond those which result from the normal rules applicable to relations between individuals'[10] will be considered public.

If we stick to the domestic arena, perhaps appropriately in a post-Brexit scenario, the emphasis is still placed on functionality, therefore, for example, the UK Data Protection Act defines a Public Authority as anybody 'performing a task carried out in the public interest or in the exercise of official authority vested in it'.[11] Furthermore, as the UK system has strongly been characterized by a process of progressive 'privatization' of public functions, questions concerning so-called hybrid authorities are likely to arise in the context of funding and subsidization of certain activities. In this context, analogies may be drawn from the extensive case law on the interpretation of section 6(3) of the Human Rights Act 1998, which defines a 'public authority' as including section 6(3)(b) 'any person certain of whose functions are functions of a public nature' and from principles developed in claims for judicial review. Whilst the latter may be more pertinent, as the later section of this chapter considers, in both the human rights and the judicial review context English courts seem to concur that it is the presence of certain factors which reveal the public nature of the body in question, such as: being publicly funded; exercising statutory powers; taking the place of local authorities or the Government and providing a public service.[12] However, the question to be asked in the context of the SCA should not be whether a certain body carries out a public function or not but the crucial factor will very much depend on the definition of 'public resources'. This is entirely logical because if the definition of subsidy is left entirely to the nature of the body making that grant, the risk would be that government resources could be channelled to entities which do not constitute 'public authorities' so that they

9. Case 222/84 *Marguerite Johnston v. Chief Constable of the Royal Ulster Constabulary*. ECLI: EU: C: 1986:206. *See further* Patrick Birkinshaw, 'English Public Law under European Influence', in Jurgen Schwarze (ed.), *Bestand und Perspektiven des Europäischen Verwaltungsrechts* (Nomos Verlagsgesellschaft mbH & Co. KG, 2008).
10. Case C-413/15 *Elaine Farrell v. Alan Whitty* ECLI: EU: C: 2017:745.
11. UK Data Protection Act 2018 (DPA 2018) section 7(2), Part 2, Ch. 2.
12. *See, e.g., R v. Panel on Takeovers and Mergers ex parte Datafin Plc* [1987] QB 815 and *Aston Cantlow v. Wallbank* [2003] UKHL 37. On this possible analogy *see* Patrick Birkinshaw, *European Public Law: The Achievement and the Brexit Challenge*, 3rd ed. (Kluwer Law International 2021), pp. 449 and ss.

are then made available, at the direction of a public authority, to a beneficiary providing goods or services on the market. Interestingly, the UK Government guidance on the application of the SCA suggests that the notion of public resources should include 'public funds that are administered by the UK government, the devolved administrations or local authorities, whether they are given directly, through other public bodies, or through private bodies'.[13] This leaves open the possibility that even where the entity granting the subsidy does not constitute a public authority under the more traditional Public Law approach, if a transfer of resources is taking place anyway, the measure could be classified as a subsidy. This does not mean that an enquiry on the Imputability of the measure should not be carried out. In EU state aid law, it is a well-established principle that the mere fact that a measure is taken by a public undertaking is not per se sufficient to consider it imputable to the State but it needs to be demonstrated by a 'set of indicators arising from the circumstances of the case and the context in which the measure was taken' such as for instance the presence of factors of an organic nature which link the public undertaking to the State, or the fact that the body could not take the contested decision without taking account of directives coming from the Government.[14] As held by the Court of Appeal in a pre-Brexit state aid case, for the criteria of public resources to be established there should be 'a clear and direct nexus of a relatively formal character between the advantage and the foregoing of revenue'. The link between allowing private use and the possible engagement of State resources cannot be merely 'hypothetical, remote and indirect' and the corresponding alleged aid has to be 'more than an estimation of a diffuse advantage spread across a wide class with no clear share or definition or formality to it'.[15] This is one of the areas where the implementation of the SCA regime can have an impact, perhaps unanticipated, on the development of UK Public Law.

3.2 The Lawfulness of a Subsidy and the Integrity of the UK Market

The most significant innovation in terms of definition is contained in Schedule 1 of the SCA. Schedule 1 lists several principles that need to be verified in order to establish whether a certain measure constitutes a subsidy. These principles need to be replicated *verbatim* here:

> subsidies should pursue a specific policy objective in order to remedy an identified market failure or address an equity rationale (such as local or regional disadvantage, social difficulties or distributional concerns); subsidies should be proportionate to their specific policy objective and limited to what is necessary to achieve it; subsidies should be designed to bring about a change of economic behaviour of the beneficiary; subsidies should not normally compensate for the costs the beneficiary would have funded in the absence of any subsidy; and subsidies should be an

13. Draft Statutory Guidance on the SCA at https://www.gov.uk/government/consultations/statutory-guidance-on-the-subsidy-control-act-2022 (consulted 8 November 2022) pp. 21 and ss.
14. C-482/99, *France v. Commission (Stardust)* ECLI: EU:C:2002:294, para. 55.
15. *British Academy of Songwriters, Composers and Authors (BASCA) v. Secretary of State for Business, Innovation and Skills* [2015] EWHC 1723 (Admin).

appropriate policy instrument for achieving their specific policy objective and that objective cannot be achieved through other, less distortive, means.

These are exactly the principles listed in Article 366 EU-UK TCA. The SCA introduces a further principle: subsidies should be designed to achieve their specific policy objective while minimising any negative effects *on competition or investment within the United Kingdom*. This provision echoes the fourth limb of section 2 on the definition of a subsidy which requires that a measure being classified as a subsidy must, or must be capable of having, an effect on competition or investment either on *international trade* or within *the United Kingdom*. This extra focus on the possible 'internal' distortions of competition and level playing field is extremely welcome because in theory it should work as a guarantee to ensure solidarity between the different parts of the UK. It also fits in with the aspiration of the UK Internal Market Act that aspires to guarantee a free market access on goods and services by removing or preventing any potentially harmful trade barriers within the UK. In this respect, it is also worth noting that the SCA introduces an anti-delocalisation provision in requiring that subsidies should not be 'given to an enterprise subject to a condition that the enterprise relocates all or part of its existing economic activities' and where 'the relocation of those activities would not occur but for the giving of the subsidy'. Relocation subsidies, a very controversial issue within the EU internal market, are therefore prohibited in order to maintain the integrity of the UK internal market. Interestingly again, in the Draft Guidance on the application of the SCA, the Government has introduced a kind of de facto map of regional spending. According to the Government, relocation would be only allowed taking into account certain specificities of a given area. If the subsidies are granted to move within the same local authority area, they should not be prohibited, as movement within the same area and under the responsibility of the same authority would not cause any distortion or a subsidies race. Conversely, any relocation subsidy where a public authority is moving outside its area and trespasses into another, may trigger the application of the SCA. It remains to be seen how those cases will develop, especially where several authorities - perhaps including a local authority, a devolved administration or the UK Government - may all exercise their responsibilities at the same time and how a local authority may be able 'calculate' exactly the extent and the effect of its granting of a subsidy.[16]

4 A NEW ROLE FOR ALL UK PUBLIC AUTHORITIES?

The application of the 'seven subsidies principles' is delegated entirely to public authorities. Consequently, each and every public body in the UK granting a subsidy will have the power to decide whether that subsidy is consistent with those principles. All public authorities will therefore be in charge of deciding whether or not a certain measure would be considered a subsidy and unlawful.

16. The SCA has also introduced an exception to this rule as it allows the granting of state subsidies if the effect of the subsidy is to 'reduce the social or economic disadvantages of the area that would benefit from the giving of the subsidy' (section 18(5)(7)) allowing a certain degree of positive regional solidarity.

On its face, the SCA seems to attempt to introduce a form of 'localism', a bottom-up model. For those old enough to remember, UK governments have introduced many reforms attempting to decentralize powers. The Localism Act 2011 was, for example, introduced with great fanfare heralding a new era as it was based on a 'general power of competence' idea. Local Councils were given the legal capacity to do anything that an individual can do that is not specifically prohibited. This should have consequently allowed councils additional freedom in promoting the local economy by offering business rate discounts – to help attract firms, investment and jobs and so on. In reality, most of these projects have not been successful and local authorities are still very much under central supervision.[17] Similarly, the SCA, far from being a delocalization reform, could in reality place public authorities under considerable stress. There are legitimate questions as to whether the overwhelming majority of UK public authorities would, in fact, have access to the necessary resources to carry out a subsidy control principles compatibility assessment. In order to fulfil this duty, resources and expertise are a necessity. Compliance with the principles will have to be discharged through a complex legal and economic analysis. Concepts such as market failure or equity rationale are not easy to determine and may require strict counterfactual analysis. Take, for example, the final step of analysis which a public authority needs to undertake when giving the green light to a subsidy: it will be incumbent on the public authority to establish that the benefits of the subsidy that are supposedly linked to a previously identified public policy objective, and that they outweigh the negative effects. Such a delicate balancing exercise would surely require both quantitative and qualitative elements, introducing a discretionary evaluation, as a simple mathematical calculation of costs will not suffice. Furthermore, it may be questionable as to what considerations a public authority should take into account. Take, for instance, the harm side of the balancing scale. It seems plausible that the public authority should look at all the possible negative impacts of granting a subsidy on investment in a particular region, or even on the whole UK, but also – as required by the SCA – the same public authority must evaluate how the disbursement of public funding may impact international trade or investments. This is not easy without relevant expertise. Additionally, the SCA, in line with the TCA provisions, carves out an exception for those subsidies that are granted in order to perform a public service obligation. In the new TCA language, these are defined as Services of Public Economic Interest (SPEI) and the SCA in section 29 requires the public authority to decide whether a service can be classified as such. Again not an easy task as it will require public authorities to: (a) define themselves what an SPEI is; and (b) entrust an undertaking to carry out its assigned tasks, provided the compensation from state resources does not exceed what is necessary for the discharge of those tasks. These principles are borrowed from the EU Commission's practice and case law, where SPEI has developed over 50 years and is one of the most complex areas of EU law.[18] The combination of all these obligations

17. John Stanton, *Rebalancing the Central-Local Relationship: Achieving a Bottom-Up Approach to Localism in England* (2018) Legal Studies 38(3) 429.
18. *See* for instance Commission Decision of 20 December on the application of Article 106(2) of the TFEU to State aid in the form of public service compensation granted to certain undertakings

provides a rather daunting prospect that public authorities will have to deal with mostly on their own. In the old days, the Department for Business, Energy & Industrial Strategy (BEIS) operated as a 'consultant' for any state aid related matters and as a counterpart to the European Commission. Under the SCA, the new considerable burden on public authorities is only partially alleviated for certain kinds of subsidy where it would be possible to seek an opinion from the Competition and Markets Authority (CMA). When granting a subsidy, a public authority would then have the choice as to whether to ask the CMA to prepare a report on the public authority's subsidy control compliance assessment. Only in cases of what the SCA defines as 'a subsidy of particular interest (SOPI)', would a public authority have an obligation to ask the CMA to prepare such a report.[19]

Some relief can come from the application of section 10 of the SCA. The UK Government (but not any other UK public authority) can define 'streamlined subsidy schemes' with a view to allowing 'lower-risk subsidies to be given by public authorities more quickly and easily, without their needing to assess compliance with the principles or other subsidy control requirements.'[20] The scope and extent of these streamlined subsidy schemes has yet to be determined but there are potential negative repercussions to assisting public authorities because a resulting excessive extension of such schemes could be perceived as an attempt to shelter certain economic activities from subsidy control.

There is yet another 'constitutional' issue for all public authorities to reflect upon: in the EU, the balancing test on whether the benefits of an aid outweigh the negative effects is carried out by the European Commission. For good or for bad, the Commission acts as a supranational referee between the different Member States and has gradually developed the 'common European interest' as a benchmark over 60 years of applying state aid law. All UK authorities involved will have to undertake the same process as they would need to gradually identify a UK-wide 'common interest'. Aside from the very real and significant burden imposed on public authorities, it is the very same SCA that reaffirms the centralised character of the UK public law system, because control of distortive and harmful subsidies have actually been made a reserved matter. Consequently, devolved regions and devolved Parliaments are not part of the process in any way. The devolved Parliaments are mentioned in section 6 only as entities that should not be considered public authorities, but nowhere else in the SCA. The UK Government is instead provided with many prerogatives as it may intervene in relation to a proposed subsidy or scheme where the Secretary of State considers that there is a

entrusted with the operation of services of general economic interest [2012] OJ L7/3. In general Daniele Gallo, *Public Services and EU Competition Law* (Springer) 2021, Ch. VI.

19. The Government has proposed that the dividing line between a subsidy of interest and a SOPI should be based mainly on financial thresholds: a general threshold of GBP 10 million for SOPI and of GBP 5 million for subsidies of interest. Subsidies in excess of GBP 10 million would be subject to mandatory referral to the CMA, while subsidies between GBP 5 million and GBP 10 million would be subject to voluntary referral. 'Consultation on subsidies and schemes of interest and of particular interest' at https://assets.publishing.service.gov.uk/government/uploads/system/uploads/attachment_data/file/1063355/ssopi-and-ssoi-consultation.pdf accessed November 2022.
20. Subsidy Control Bill, Explanatory Notes, para. 46.

risk of non-compliance or of 'negative effects' on competition or investment within the UK. The Secretary of State can also require the public authority in question to submit their decision to the CMA.[21] Once again devolved regions are not in any way part of the process.

4.1 The Northern Ireland Question

In relation to devolved regions, at least the SCA may be seen as part of the solution to one of the most controversial and sensitive Brexit related issues: Northern Ireland (NI) and in particular the application of state aid control to Northern Ireland. As is well known, the EU and the UK agreed within the Northern Ireland Protocol Article 10, and Annexes 5 and 6, which provide that state aid provisions continue to apply to the UK 'in respect of measures which affect that trade between Northern Ireland and the Union which is subject to this Protocol'. This provision is there to ensure the integrity of the customs rules applicable to Northern Ireland and to avoid granting aid/subsidies that could advantage goods suppliers in Northern Ireland, who are free to export to the EU without being subject to tariffs. Article 10 and its related Annexes have proven to be extremely controversial and have created sharp disagreements between the UK Government and the European Commission. There has been indeed a general consensus that Article 10 of the Northern Ireland Protocol may have the effect of expanding the application of EU state aid law to virtually any UK Government measure that may affect Northern Ireland, given the low threshold equivalent 'effect on trade' concept which is applied in EU state aid law.[22] Those concerns fail to fully understand how 'effect on trade' operates in EU state aid law. Despite the apparent width of such criteria, the 'effect on trade' is based on a presumption that can, as is the case with any presumption, be rebutted if it is clear that a certain measure does not have actual effects on market actors.[23] It is also well-accepted practice in EU law that if a certain measure has a purely local impact it consequently has no effect on trade between Member States. In those cases the measure would have no more than a marginal effect on the conditions of cross-border investments or establishment.[24] It should also be remembered that effect on trade is just one of the criteria that needs to be satisfied for a measure to be qualified as aid. First, it needs to be shown that a certain measure imposes a financial burden on the state and that it confers a selective advantage for a specific undertaking; a rather arduous test that also excludes horizontal economic policies from the scope of EU State aid law. There will be no advantage and therefore

21. Clauses 55 and 58.
22. *See* George Peretz KC and Alfred Artley, *State Aid in the North Ireland Protocol* (2020) Tax Journal, 11 and George Peretz KC and James Webber, *The UK's Proposed Revisions to Article 10 of the Northern Ireland Protocol: A Sensible Basis for Negotiation*, post at https://uksala.org/the-uks-proposed-revisions-to-article-10-of-the-northern-ireland-protocol-a-sensible-basis-for-negotiation/ (accessed November 2022).
23. Case C-518/13 *Eventech* ECLI:EU:C:2015:9, para. 65.
24. *See* Commission Notice on the notion of State aid as referred to in Article 107(1) TFEU [2016] OJ C262/1, para. 6.3 and See European Commission Decisions Czech Republic – Hradec Králové public hospitals (SA.37432) and Germany – Landgrafen-Klinik (SA.38035).

no aid if the economic benefits are merely indirect or secondary effects of the measure at stake.[25] The European Commission itself explained in clear terms in a Notice to Stakeholders on the application of the Northern Ireland Protocol that 'an effect on trade cannot be merely hypothetical or presumed, but has to be demonstrated.'[26] The possible implications of the application of Article 10 of the Northern Ireland NI Protocol were tested before English courts in *R (British Sugar) v. Secretary of State for International Trade*.[27] The case concerned the imposition of an autonomous tariff quota (ATQ) applicable to imports of raw cane sugar into the UK. The Court found that no violation of Article 10 of the NI Protocol occurred as there was no evidence that the measure was specifically designed so as to apply selectively. Consequently, the measure did not constitute state aid. The court commented on the issue of whether the measure did have an effect on trade. It relied both on the European Commission's practice and especially on the EU Notice where it mentions the need for there to be a 'genuine and direct' link between the measure at issue and an effect on trade in goods between Northern Ireland (NI) and the EU, and interpreted it as a qualification of Article 107(1) Treaty on the Functioning of the European Union. The court then found such a 'genuine and direct' link was not proven as the measure had a very indirect effect, because it involved 'at best very small volumes and is premised on the unproven assertion that the ATQ is liable to lead to the displacement of EU refined sugar from Northern Ireland'.

Recently the UK government has proposed a Bill[28] that would confer the power to the UK to unilaterally amend some of the provisions of the NI Protocol, a move that caused consternation in the EU with the Commission indicating the possibility of bringing infringement proceedings against the UK. In particular, Clause 12 of the Bill removes the effect of Article 10 of the Protocol on state aid, and gives ministers the power to make provision in relation to subsidies in NI going much further than previous proposals made by the UK Government.[29] This approach featured in the Bill, although apparently radical, does not however create a legal vacuum because of the application of the terms of the UK –EU TCA in conjunction with the regime of the SCA due to come into full force in January 2023. There are of course many elements of the

25. Case T-607/17 *Volotea, SA v. European Commission* ECLI:EU:T:2020:180; T-716/17 *Germanwings GmbH v. European Commission* ECLI:EU:T:2020:181; T-8/*18 easyJet Airline Co. Ltd v. European Commission* ECLI:EU:T:2020:182.
26. European Commission, 'Notice to Stakeholders: Withdrawal of the UK and EU rules in the field of state aid' https://ec.europa.eu/info/sites/default/files/notice-stakeholders-brexit-state-aid_en.pdf. Not so differently the UK Government explained that 'in practical terms, subsidies granted in Great Britain are only in scope of Article 10 where there is a clear benefit from and a genuine, direct link between the subsidy and companies in Northern Ireland', at https://www.gov.uk/government/publications/complying-with-the-uks-international-obligations-on-subsidy-control-guidance-for-public-authorities/technical-guidance-on-the-uks-international-subsidy-control-commitments.
27. *R (British Sugar) v. Secretary of State for International Trade* [2022] EWHC 393 (Admin).
28. NI Bill 2022 HL Bill 52 (as brought from the Commons).
29. For instance in the Command Paper of 21 July 2021 it was proposed to promote a (albeit very vague) enhanced form of consultation or referral power in case of subsidies of 'a significant scale relating directly to Northern Ireland as "to enable EU concerns to be properly and swiftly addressed."' (*Northern Ireland Protocol: the way forward*, CP502, 21 July 2021, para. 65).

SCA that could be then used to 'replace' or improve the guarantee of the preservation of a level playing field both within the UK market and also towards the EU. However, the consequences for public authorities and the impact on UK Public Law so far and continuingly as observed in this chapter still stand in the event that the NI Protocol Bill does remove the entirety of Article 10 and its associated annexes.

5 TAX AS AN AFTERTHOUGHT?: PROBLEMS – AND SOLUTIONS – FOR PUBLIC AUTHORITIES

One of the main instruments to promote certain public objectives is taxation. Whilst the UK was usually a very compliant Member State in terms of State aid control, it has often been embroiled in cases dealing with taxation. For instance, the European Commission found that the UK controlled foreign company (CFC) finance company (FinCo) regime constituted illegal state aid as its central objective was to protect the UK tax base by taxing profits arising from UK activities and assets that have been artificially diverted from the UK to a CFC.[30] Brexit has not halted this trend because very recently the Commission has decided, on the basis of the Withdrawal Agreement, to bring the UK before the Court of Justice of the European Union (CJEU) for failing to implement a Commission decision taken before the end of the transition period ordering the recovery of fiscal aid granted by Gibraltar in the form of an exemption for passive interest and royalties.[31]

Within the SCA, there are actually a multitude of opportunities which are available to public authorities to use fiscal measures in a way that grants public resources in a manner that meets the definition of subsidy in section 2. From start-up grants to tax breaks or amnesties, to tax benefits, payment holidays and tax reductions or deductions, the amount of public money at stake is not inconsiderable.[32]

Taxation does not however feature specifically at length in the SCA, but it does feature. However, it is considered almost as an afterthought because unfortunately the SCA appears to equate subsidies in the form of taxation with other subsidies and does not treat taxation sufficiently as a discrete element of the subsidy control regime. As a result, it is not apparently viewed as needing the specific expert advice that is actually required to help support public authorities when undertaking their legal obligations under the SCA. It is instead amalgamated with other areas. This is quite a perplexing choice because the TCA contrastingly provides for detailed regulation when a certain tax, by being specific, violates the provisions on subsidies control. It creates another problem to befall public authorities when taking decisions specifically on tax measures. Whilst turmoil caused by the 2022 'mini-budget' isn't too likely a consequence, at least

30. Decision (EU) 2019/1352 of 2 April 2019 on the State aid SA.44896 implemented by the United Kingdom concerning CFC Group Financing Exemption (OJ 2019 L 216, p. 1) now uphold in Cases T363/19 and T456/19, *UK, ITV and others v. Commission*, ECLI:EU:T:2022:349.
31. https://ec.europa.eu/commission/presscorner/detail/en/ip_21_1266.
32. *See* further Neil Crafts, *Brexit and State Aid*, (2017) 33 Oxford Review of Economic Policy 105 and Kevin Farnsworth, *Public Policies for Private Corporations: The British Corporate Welfare State*, (2013) 21 Renewal, 51.

to that extent, there are possibilities for spillover effects from one public authority decision on tax subsidies to another.

The CMA is the body, which has the remit to consider the application of the SCA. However, this is inappropriate, not because the CMA is not expert, but because it is not expert in taxation. It would instead be rather reasonable to bring in at least an informal dialogue with the true expert that is the Treasury on matters of tax potentially falling within the subsidy control regime. The statutory scheme of the SCA does not prohibit the possibility for informal dialogue with the Treasury. The need for such dialogue is clear and persuasive: to assist public authorities with their task.

There are potential problems which can arise from the current SCA regime, which this proposal for informal dialogue with the Treasury could help to address in the tax context. To name but a few, as discussed above, the role of public authorities in administering the principles contained in the SCA is not an enviable one. This is not alleviated by the subsumation of tax subsidies into general subsidies and therefore specific advice and comment on tax matters, even within the scope of the general control regime, could assist. sections 52 and 53 of the SCA consider mandatory referral to the CMA, and to all intents and purposes this would include referral on tax issues. If so, the CMA will find itself pronouncing on fiscal matters which are not and should not be part of its remit. The potential for a three way dialogue between the relevant public authority, the CMA and Treasury where and to the extent that taxation becomes part of the intended grant of a subsidy could respond to this issue. Furthermore, HM Revenue and Customs (HMRC) would surely be categorised as a public authority under the Act,[33] consequently capable of granting subsidies itself. However, as one of the most significant bodies in the UK for deciding on and administering matters of taxation, including enforcement, it is expert and could therefore be useful to provide guidance to other 'public authorities' when considering the granting or conversely considering avoiding a grant of a subsidy. Effectively, the hybridity of HMRC is not acknowledged let alone addressed in the SCA. This could foreseeably exacerbate the issues already outlined in this chapter regarding the relationship between the levels of devolved government, delocalisation and the paradoxical centralization provisions. Voluntary referrals to the CMA are permitted under section 56 of the SCA in order to obtain a report, although the CMA can refuse to provide a report in response to the request. The report would evaluate the public authority's assessment of the lawfulness of the proposed subsidy, or subsidy scheme, according to section 59 of the SCA. As the evaluation in the referral report must take into account any effects of the proposed subsidy, or subsidy scheme, on investment, under section 59(2), which in relation to a fiscal subsidy, or subsidy scheme would certainly fall within the Treasury's remit, it is hard to see how the CMA can reasonably be asked in isolation to evaluate the lawfulness of a fiscal subsidy on investment without reference to the Treasury's opinion. It is also preferable in those instances where the public authority in question is HMRC, that there is a possibility for informal involvement of the Treasury, because both HMRC and the Treasury will already have a developed relationship in relation to

33. SCA, section 6.

fiscal matters, which it is hardly more efficient to replace with the CMA, whose remit on competition problems and issues does not extend to tax. In fact, it would be rather peculiar to expect HMRC especially, to make a referral to the CMA for an assessment of the lawfulness of a proposed subsidy which may have been prompted by the Treasury's fiscal policy, only for the CMA to assess the lawfulness of the fiscal measure in isolation and outside its competition expertise. Whilst there is opportunity under sections 52 and 56 of the SCA for the referring public authority to provide explanatory information, there is every likelihood that this would not answer all of the CMA's questions because its remit does not include taxation and it would be unreasonable to expect it to make an assessment without reference to details of the greater contextual policy and practice of the Treasury and indeed the Treasury's relationship with HMRC. In addition, the Secretary of State, who is given various powers under the SCA, would not be the Chancellor of the Exchequer but rather the Secretary of State for BEIS. The Secretary of State for BEIS is empowered by the SCA to call-in or make post award referrals[34] to the CMA but this is again not the most appropriate manner in which to treat fiscal subsidies. As the CMA has reporting obligations under section 65 of the SCA, it makes more sense for there to be a facility for informal dialogue and even consultation between the CMA, the relevant public authority and the Treasury, not least because the report is not just to be published, but also under section 65(8) it has to be laid before Parliament. The potential scope and opportunity in the SCA for consultation – which falls short of what is being recommended here but also demonstrates that an informal consultation mechanism would not be prohibited or contradict the SCA – is section 79. This provides the Secretary of State for BEIS with the option to issue guidance on the practical application of specific elements of the subsidy control regime.[35] This option to issue guidance is coupled with a duty under section 79(5) to consult 'such persons as the Secretary of State considers appropriate' and it goes without saying that the Treasury would be unlikely to be inappropriate. Whether HMRC as a public authority itself under the Act would be an appropriate consultee under this section would probably depend on the tax issue upon which the Secretary of State for BEIS was seeking to issue guidance. Interestingly, on timing, section 79(7) permits consultation carried out before the section comes into force to be sufficient to comply with the obligation contained in section 79(5). From the perspective of the public authority, according to section 79(6) they must have regard to guidance issued under section 79 when giving a subsidy or making a subsidy scheme, although the obligation applies 'so far as applicable to the authority and the circumstances of the case'.[36] The opportunities authorised by section 79 do not replace or remove the need for continuing and prospective consultation but they open the door, albeit slightly, for the development of informal dialogue to aid public authority decision making to be in accordance with the spirit of the SCA. Finally, in compliance with Article 373(5) EU-UK TCA, the SCA excludes from the obligation of recovery of unlawful subsidies, Acts of the UK Parliament, therefore conferring to some extent protection for tax schemes

34. For example section 60 SCA.
35. Section 79(10) of the SCA.
36. Section 79(6) of the SCA.

included in UK primary legislation. However, individual tax rulings or tax assessments and specific taxes administered outside of a legislative scheme or under the discretion of a public authority may be considered as individual subsidies and therefore become subject to a recovery action. The breadth of the SCA therefore has the potential to encompass many forms of taxation, including tax rulings, which does not appear to have been given the necessary forethought in the consultation and enforcement mechanisms contained within the SCA. As stated above, HMRC would potentially be categorized as a public authority under the Act,[37] consequently capable of granting subsidies itself. A remarkable feature of the SCA in light of this, which also demonstrates the apparent relegation of taxation to an afterthought, is found in Part 5, which effectively provides for appeals to be reviewed by the Competition Appeal Tribunal (CAT). This is extraordinary because there is nothing in the SCA to potentially stop a tax ruling given by HMRC being reviewed by the CAT as being an unlawful subsidy contrary to the principles of Schedule 1 of the SCA. Furthermore, as it is the Tax Tribunal and not the CAT which is the most appropriate tribunal in the UK (although see the section of this chapter below on judicial review) it is extraordinary to think that a Tribunal which is not the most appropriate should have jurisdiction of assessing the lawfulness of compliance with the regime in a claim for judicial review. Whilst tax rulings have become a prominent feature of the European Commission's state aid enforcement in the EU, the integrity of the UK internal market may mitigate against an identical approach being adopted. This strengthens the need for at least some informal involvement from the Treasury to assist in navigating the issues of tax in the context of subsidies.

6 WHAT KIND OF CONTROL? JUDICIAL REVIEW

If it is a given that the growth of judicial review of government action and public administration has been 'the most notable development of British Law over the past 50 years'[38] well, the SCA certainly seems to confirm that. Actually, Article 372 EU-UK TCA somehow confers a sort of direct effect on the Subsidies Chapter, as it requires the Parties to that agreement to confer on their courts and tribunals the power to review any public authority decisions. Under the SCA interpretation, this would include the public authority in charge of controlling subsidies, being the CMA and then the CAT, and any granting public authority, including their assessments of compliance with the principles in Schedule 1 of the SCA. Courts and tribunals are also given jurisdiction to grant remedies including the suspension, prohibition or requirement of action, the award of damages, and the recovery of a subsidy from its beneficiary. The UK has therefore introduced a private enforcement action whereby interested parties can bring a judicial review claim to challenge the lawfulness of decisions to grant subsidy measures. Such actions will have to be brought before the CAT. As this new action is substantially a judicial review, the CAT will not have to assess whether the decision is

37. SCA, section 6.
38. Birkinshaw, *European Public Law*, cit. above, at p. 363.

correct, but whether it is lawful. The CAT will need to verify whether public authorities have complied with SCA provisions and have respected the subsidy control principles. This may seem like merits review,[39] although limited to lawfulness, and appears inappropriate in the context of taxation, as discussed above. Similarly, remedies would be those available to Claimants in the Administrative Division of the High Court and the Scottish remedies available before the Court of Sessions.[40] However, the CAT will be competent to award an order for recovery, which is not a typical public law remedy. It would arguably be for the CAT to try and imaginatively utilise the usual remedies available in deciding the timeframe for the recovery and also if recovery may apply to some or the entire amount of a subsidy. This is again quite remarkable when considering tax payment holidays or tax rulings. Arguably 'ordinary' public law Judicial Review grounds of illegality, irrationality and procedural impropriety can still presumably be brought before the High Court of England and Wales or the Court of Session in Scotland.[41] As to whether proportionality would apply as a ground for review, as proportionality similar language features in the Schedule 1 principles of the SCA, there is therefore the potential for a proportionality assessment to be undertaken by the CAT also.[42] Finally, a decision of the CAT may be appealed on a point of law, providing for reassessment by the Court of Appeal or the Court of Session on appeal. Two further points are worth noting here. First, the SCA speaks of the right of 'an interested party' to ask the CAT to review the decision to grant a subsidy. An interested party according to section 70(7) would be 'anyone whose interests may be affected by the giving of the subsidy or making of the scheme' therefore including competitors and trade associations but also local authorities and devolved administrations. The Government will also have automatic standing. It would be interesting to monitor how the standing requirements will be dealt with by the CAT, as it may not be automatic that the test will be as generous as the one usually adopted under Judicial Review proceedings. Second, despite the proven efficiency and expertise usually displayed by the CAT, a challenge needs to be brought within a very short deadline, being one month from the 'relevant date' with only very specific exemptions available. This is shorter than the usual challenging three months granted to typical Judicial Review claims.[43] In most cases, the relevant date from which this timescale would be calculated would be the date on which the database entry was made or the date on which, following a written request, the granting public authority provided additional information about the grant of the subsidy or making of a subsidy scheme. Such a very short period of time may be a cause of concern as potentially distortive subsidies may go unchallenged. It is of course too early to assess how the CAT will deal with its new jurisdiction and to what extent in its case law it will adhere to concepts mostly derived

39. *See* Carol Harlow and Richard Rawlings, *Law and Administration* 2nd ed. (CUP, 1997) and 4th ed. (CUP, 2021).
40. William Wade, Christopher Forsyth and Julian Ghosh, *Wade & Forsyth's Administrative Law* 12th ed. (OUP, 2022).
41. *See* Harlow and Rawlings, *Law and Administration* cit. above.
42. *Ibid.*
43. Civil Procedure Rules, Rule 54.5.

from EU law and the case law of the CJEU that have been fully and faithfully applied by the UK in the last 40 years, or whether it will develop a divergent interpretation.

7 CONCLUSION

Public spending comes from many different sources and money is spent for many and varied reasons. The existence of rules on the transparency and accountability of spending decisions has the potential to contribute to ensuring geographic solidarity between the different areas of the UK. Furthermore, a modern economic and industrial model requires not just efficiency and technological advances, but equality and fairness. This chapter has highlighted many issues with the SCA. It is hoped that public authorities find a way of administering the rules in a way, which ensures the fairness and equality expected in public spending in the UK. However, in applying public law concepts in combination with provisions inspired by EU state aid law there is the potential for an interesting future debate which would - we believe - be of interest to Professor Birkinshaw as the original European Public lawyer.

EUROPEAN MONOGRAPH SERIES

1. Lammy Betten (ed.), *The Future of European Social Policy,* 1991 (ISBN 90-654-4585-4).
2. Annemarie Loman, Kamiel Mortelmans, Harry H.G. Post & Stewart Watson, *Culture and Common Law: Before and After Maastricht,* 1992 (ISBN 90-654-4638-9).
3. John A.E. Vervaele, *Fraud against the Community: The Need for European Fraud Legislation,* 1994 (ISBN 90-654-4634-6).
4. Philip Raworth, *The Legislative Process in the European Community,* 1993 (ISBN 90-654-4690-7).
5. Jules Stuyck, *Financial and Monetary Integration in the European Economic Community,* 1993 (ISBN 90-654-4718-0).
6. Jules Stuyck & A.J. Vossestein (eds), *State Entrepreneurship, National Monopolies and European Community Law,* 1993 (ISBN 90-654-4773-3).
7. Jules Stuyck & A. Looijestijn-Clearie (eds), *The European Economic Area EC-EFTA,* 1994 (ISBN 90-654-4815-2).
8. Rosita B. Bouterse, *Competition and Integration: What Goals Count?,* 1995 (ISBN 90-654-4816-0).
9. René Barents, *The Agricultural Law of the EU, 2nd Edition,* 2022 (ISBN 978-94-035-4411-3).
10. Nicholas Emiliou, *Principles of Proportionality in European Law: A Comparative Study,* 1996 (ISBN 90-411-0866-1).
11. Eivind Smith, *National Parliaments as Cornerstones of European Integration,* 1996 (ISBN 90-411-0898-X).
12. Jan H. Jans, *European Environmental Law,* 1996 (ISBN 90-411-0877-7).
13. Síofra O'Leary, *The Evolving Concept of Community Citizenship: From the Free Movement of Persons to Union Citizenship,* 1997 (ISBN 90-411-0878-5).
14. Laurence W. Gormley (ed.), *Current and Future Perspectives on EC Competition Law,* 1983 (ISBN 90-411-0691-X).
15. Simone White, *Protection of the Financial Interests of the European Communities: The Fight against Fraud and Corruption,* 1998 (ISBN 90-411-9647-1).
16. Morten P. Broberg, *Broberg on the European Commission's Jurisdiction to Scrutinise Mergers,* 4th Edition, 2013 (ISBN 978-90-411-3339-7).
17. Doris Hildebrand, *The Role of Economic Analysis in the EC Competition Rules: The European School,* 2nd Edition, 2002 (ISBN 90-411-1706-7).
18. Christof R.A. Swaak, *European Community Law and the Automobile Industry,* 1999 (ISBN 90-411-1140-9).

19. Dorthe Dahlgaard Dingel, *Public Procurement: A Harmonization of the National Judicial Review of the Application of European Community Law,* 1999 (ISBN 90-411-1161-1).
20. John A.E. Vervaele (ed.), *Compliance and Enforcement of European Community Law,* 1999 (ISBN 90-411-1151-4).
21. Martin Trybus, *European Defence Procurement Law: International and National Procurement Systems as Models for a Liberalized Defence Procurement Market in Europe,* 1999 (ISBN 90-411-1167-0).
22. Helen Staples, *The Legal Status of Third Country Nationals Resident in the European Union,* 1999 (ISBN 90-411-1277-4).
23. Damien Geradin (ed.), *The Liberalization of State Monopolies in the European Union and Beyond,* 1999 (ISBN 90-411-1264-2).
24. Katja Heede, *European Ombudsman: Redress and Control at Union Level,* 2000 (ISBN 90-411-1413-0).
25. Ulf Bernitz & Joakim Nergelius (eds), *General Principles of European Community Law,* 2000 (ISBN 90-411-1402-5).
26. Michaela Drahos, *Convergence of Competition Laws and Policies in the European Community,* 2002 (ISBN 90-411-1562-5).
27. Damien Geradin (ed.), *The Liberalization of Electricity and Natural Gas in the European Union,* 2001 (ISBN 90-411-1560-9).
28. Gisella Gori, *Towards an EU Right to Education,* 2001 (ISBN 90-411-1670-2).
29. Brendan P.G. Smith, *Constitution Building in the European Union,* 2001 (ISBN 90-411-1695-8).
30. Friedl Weiss & Frank Wooldridge, *Free Movement of Persons within the European Community,* 2nd Edition, 2007 (ISBN 978-90-411-2545-3).
31. Ingrid Boccardi, *Europe and Refugees: Towards an EU Asylum Policy,* 2002 (ISBN 90-411-1709-1).
32. John A.E. Vervaele & André Klip (eds), *European Cooperation Between Tax, Customs and Judicial Authorities,* 2001 (ISBN 90-411-1747-4).
33. Wouter P.J. Wils, *The Optimal Enforcement of EC Antitrust Law: Essays in Law and Economics,* 2002 (ISBN 90-411-1757-1).
34. Damien Geradin (ed.), *The Liberalization of Postal Services in the European Union,* 2002 (ISBN 90-411-1780-6).
35. Nick Bernard, *Multilevel Governance in the European Union,* 2002 (ISBN 90-411-1812-8).
36. Jill Wakefield, *Judicial Protection through the Use of Article 288(2) EC,* 2002 (ISBN 90-411-1823-3).
37. Sebastiaan Princen, *EU Regulation and Transatlantic Trade,* 2002 (ISBN 90-411-1871-3).
38. Amaryllis Verhoeven, *The European Union in Search of a Democratic and Constitutional Theory,* 2002 (ISBN 90-411-1872-1).
39. Paul L.C. Torremans, *Cross Border Insolvencies in EU, English and Belgian Law,* 2002 (ISBN 90-411-1888-8).

40. Malcolm Anderson & Joanna Apap (eds), *Police and Justice Cooperation and the New European Borders,* 2002 (ISBN 90-411-1893-4).
41. Christin M. Forstinger, *Takeover Law in EU and USA: A Comparative Analysis,* 2002 (ISBN 90-411-1919-1).
42. Antonio Bavasso, *Communications in EU Antitrust Law: Market Power and Public Interest,* 2003 (ISBN 90-411-1974-4).
43. Fiona G. Wishlade, *Regional State Aid and Competition Policy in the European Union,* 2003 (ISBN 90-411-1975-2).
44. Gareth Davies, *Nationality Discrimination in the European Internal Market,* 2003 (ISBN 90-411-1998-1).
45. René Barents, *The Autonomy of Community Law,* 2003 (ISBN 90-411-2251-6).
46. Gerhard Dannecker & Oswald Jansen (eds), *Competition Law Sanctioning in the European Union,* 2004 (ISBN 90-411-2100-5).
47. Nauta Dutilh (ed.), *Dealing with Dominance: The Experience of National Competition Authorities,* 2004 (ISBN 90-411-2211-7).
48. Stefaan van den Bogaert, *Practical Regulation of the Mobility of Sportsmen in the EU Post Bosman,* 2005 (ISBN 90-411-2327-X).
49. Katalin Judit Cseres, *Competition Law and Consumer Protection,* 2005 (ISBN 90-411-2380-6).
50. Philipp Kiiver, *The National Parliaments in the European Union: A Critical View on EU Constitution Building,* 2006 (ISBN 978-90-411-2452-4).
51. Alexander Turk, *The Concept of Legislation in European Community Law,* 2006 (ISBN 978-90-411-2472-2).
52. Dimitrios Sinaniotis, *The Interim Protection of Individuals before the European and National Courts,* 2006 (ISBN 978-90-411-2498-2).
53. M. Holoubek & D. Damjanovic, M. Traimer (eds), *Regulating Content: The European Regulatory Framework for the Media and Related Creative Sectors,* 2006 (ISBN 978-90-411-2597-2).
54. Anneli Albi & Jacques Ziller (eds), *The European Constitution and National Constitutions: Ratification and Beyond,* 2006 (ISBN 978-90-411-2524-8).
55. Gustavo E. Luengo, *Regulation of Subsidies and State Aids in WTO and EC Law: Conflicts in International Trade Law,* 2007 (ISBN 978-90-411-2547-7).
56. Eniko Horvath, *Mandating Identity: Citizenship, Kinship Laws and Plural Nationality in the European Union,* 2007 (ISBN 978-90-411-2662-7).
57. Rass Holdgaard, *External Relations Law of the European Community: Legal Reasoning and Legal Discourses,* 2007 (ISBN 978-90-411-2604-7).
58. Jill Wakefield, *The Right to Good Administration,* 2007 (ISBN 978-90-411-2697-9).
59. Dimitry Kochenov, *EU Enlargement and the Failure of Conditionality: Pre- accession Conditionality in the Fields of Democracy and the Rule of Law,* 2008 (ISBN 978-90-411-2696-2).
60. Despina Mavromati, *The Law of Payment Services in the EU: The EC Directive on Payment Services in the Internal Market,* 2008 (ISBN 978-90-411-2700-6).

61. Anne Meuwese, *Impact Assessment in EU Lawmaking*, 2008 (ISBN 978-90-411-2720-4).
62. Ulf Bernitz, Joakim Nergelius & Cecilia Cardner (eds), *General Principles of EC Law in a Process of Development*, 2008 (ISBN 978-90-411-2705-1).
63. Johan van de Gronden (ed.), *The EU and WTO Law on Services: Limits to the Realisation of General Interest Policies within the Services Markets?*, 2008 (ISBN 978-90-411-2809-6).
64. Alina Tryfonidou, *Reverse Discrimination in EC Law*, 2009 (ISBN 978-90-411-2751-8).
65. Mikael Berglund, *Cross-Border Enforcement of Claims in the EU: History Present Time and Future*, 2014 (ISBN 978-90-411-4564-2).
66. Theodore Konstadinides, *Division of Powers in European Union Law: The Delimitation of Internal Competence between the EU and the Member States*, 2009 (ISBN 978-90-411-2615-3).
67. Mattias Derlén, *Multilingual Interpretation of European Union Law*, 2009 (ISBN 978-90-411-2853-9).
68. René Barents, *Directory of EU Case Law on the Preliminary Ruling Procedure*, 2009 (ISBN 978-90-411-3150-8).
69. Yan Luo, *Anti-dumping in the WTO, the EU and China: The Rise of Legalization in the Trade Regime and Its Consequences*, 2010 (ISBN 978-90-411-3207-9).
70. Patrick Birkinshaw & Mike Varney (eds), *The European Union Legal Order after Lisbon*, 2010 (ISBN 978-90-411-3152-2).
71. Thomas Gr. Papadopoulos, *EU Law and Harmonization of Takeovers in the Internal Market*, 2010 (ISBN 978-90-411-3340-3).
72. Bas van Bockel, *The* Ne Bis In Idem *Principle in EU Law*, 2010 (ISBN 978-90-411-3156-0).
73. Veljko Milutinović, *The 'Right to Damages' under EU Competition Law: From* Courage v. Crehan *to the White Paper and Beyond*, 2010 (ISBN 978-90-411-3235-2).
74. Amandine Garde, *EU Law and Obesity Prevention*, 2010 (ISBN 978-90-411-2706-8).
75. Leonard Besselink, Frans Pennings & Sacha Prechal (eds), *The Eclipse of the Legality Principle in the European Union*, 2011 (ISBN 978-90-411-3262-8).
76. Sacha Garben, *EU Higher Education Law: The Bologna Process and Harmonization by Stealth*, 2011 (ISBN 978-90-411-3365-6).
77. Dimitry Kochenov (ed.), *EU Law of the Overseas: Outermost Regions, Associated Overseas Countries and Territories, Territories Sui Generis*, 2011 (ISBN 978-90-411-3445-5).
78. Pablo Ibáñez Colomo, *European Communications Law and Technological Convergence: Deregulation, Re-regulation and Regulatory Convergence in Television and Telecommunications*, 2012 (ISBN 978-90-411-3829-3).
79. Elise Muir, *EU Regulation of Access to Labour Markets: A Case Study of EU Constraints on Member State Competences*, 2012 (ISBN 978-90-411-3823-1).
80. Tim Corthaut, *EU Ordre Public*, 2012 (ISBN 978-90-411-3232-1).

81. Oana Ştefan, *Soft Law in Court: Competition Law, State Aid and the Court of Justice of the European Union*, 2013 (ISBN 978-90-411-3997-9).
82. Francesco Rossi dal Pozzo, *Citizenship Rights and Freedom of Movement in the European Union*, 2013 (ISBN 978-90-411-4660-1).
83. Jens Hartig Danielsen, *EU Agricultural Law*, 2013 (ISBN 978-90-411-3280-2).
84. Ulf Bernitz, Xavier Groussot & Felix Schulyok (eds), *General Principles of EU Law and European Private Law*, 2013 (ISBN 978-90-411-4683-0).
85. Michelle Everson, Cosimo Monda & Ellen Vos (eds), *European Agencies in between Institutions and Member States*, 2014 (ISBN 978-90-411-2843-0).
86. Stefan Leible & Matthias Lehmann (eds), *European Contract Law and German Law*, 2014 (ISBN 978-90-411-2588-0).
87. Piero Leanza & Ondrej Pridal, *The Right to a Fair Trial: Article 6 of the European Convention on Human Rights*, 2014 (ISBN 978-90-411-4855-1).
88. Patrick J. Birkinshaw, *European Public Law: The Achievement and the Brexit Challenge*, 3rd Edition, 2020 (ISBN 978-90-411-9751-1).
89. George Cumming, *Expert Evidence Deficiencies in the Judgments of the Courts of the European Union and the European Court of Human Rights*, 2014 (ISBN 978-90-411-4123-1).
90. Vesna Rijavec, Tomaž Keresteš & Tjaša Ivanc (eds), *Simplification of Debt Collection in the EU*, 2014 (ISBN 978-90-411-4854-4).
91. Nina Półtorak, *European Union Rights in National Courts*, 2015 (ISBN 978-90-411-5863-5).
92. Kyriaki-Korina Raptopoulou, *EU Law and Healthcare Services: Normative Approaches to Public Health Systems*, 2015 (ISBN 978-90-411-5013-4).
93. Torsten Frank Koschinka & Piero Leanza, *Preliminary Injunctions: Germany, England/Wales, Italy and France*, 2015 (ISBN 978-90-411-5833-8).
94. Vesna Rijavec, Tomaž Keresteš & Tjaša Ivanc (eds), *Dimensions of Evidence in European Civil Procedure*, 2016 (ISBN 978-90-411-6662-3).
95. Stefan Leible (ed.), *General Principles of European Private International Law*, 2016 (ISBN 978-90-411-5955-7).
96. Patrick J. Birkinshaw & Andrea Biondi (eds), *Britain Alone!: The Implications and Consequences of United Kingdom Exit from the EU*, 2016 (ISBN 978-90-411-5832-1).
97. René Barents, *Remedies and Procedures before the EU Courts*, 2nd Edition, 2020 (ISBN 978-94-035-1140-5).
98. Luca Prete, *Infringement Proceedings in EU Law*, 2017 (ISBN 978-90-411-6900-6).
99. Robert van den Hoven van Genderen, *Privacy Limitation Clauses: Trojan Horses under the Disguise of Democracy*, 2017 (ISBN 978-90-411-8599-0).
100. Mariusz Krzysztofek, *Post-Reform Personal Data Protection in the European Union: General Data Protection Regulation (EU) 2016/679*, 2017 (ISBN 978-90-411-6237-3).
101. Gianni Lo Schiavo, *The Role of Financial Stability in EU Law and Policy*, 2017 (ISBN 978-90-411-8230-2).

102. Emmanuel Guinchard & Marie-Pierre Granger (eds), *The New EU Judiciary: An Analysis of Current Judicial Reforms*, 2017 (ISBN 978-90-411-6834-4).
103. Kirsten Henckel, *Cross-Border Transfers of Undertakings: A European Perspective*, 2017 (ISBN 978-90-411-9227-1).
104. Vesna Rijavec, Wendy Kennett, Tomaž Keresteš & Tjaša Ivanc, *Remedies Concerning Enforcement of Foreign Judgements: Brussels I Recast*, 2018 (ISBN 978-90-411-9416-9).
105. Albert Sanchez-Graells & Constant De Koninck, *Shaping EU Public Procurement Law: A Critical Analysis of the CJEU Case Law 2015–2017*, 2018 (ISBN 978-94-035-0160-4).
106. Andrea Biondi, Patrick J. Birkinshaw & Maria Kendrick, *Brexit: The Legal Implications*, 2019 (ISBN 978-90-411-9540-1).
107. Mariusz Krzysztofek, *GDPR: General Data Protection Regulation (EU) 2016/679: Post-Reform Personal Data Protection in the European Union*, 2019 (ISBN 978-94-035-0594-7).
108. Giovanni Bassani, *The Legal Framework Applicable to the Single Supervisory Mechanism: Tapestry or Patchwork?*, 2019 (ISBN 978-94-035-0872-6).
109. Piotr Staszczyk, *A Legal Analysis of NGOs and European Civil Society*, 2019 (ISBN 978-94-035-1251-8).
110. Patrizio Messina, *Finance for SMEs: European Regulation and Capital Markets Union – Focus on Securitization and Alternative Finance Tools*, 2019 (ISBN 978-94-035-0161-1).
111. Jacques H.J. Bourgeois (ed.), *EU Framework for Foreign Direct Investment Control*, 2020 (ISBN 978-94-035-1883-1).
112. Ulf Bernitz, Xavier Groussot, Jaan Paju & Sybe de Vries (eds), *General Principles of EU Law and the EU Digital Order*, 2020 (ISBN 978-94-035-1165-8).
113. Aleksandra Drożdż, *Protection of Natural Persons with Regard to Automated Individual Decision-Making in the GDPR*, 2020 (ISBN 978-94-035-2045-2).
114. Mariusz Krzysztofek, *GDPR: Personal Data Protection in the European Union*, 2021 (ISBN 978-94-035-3270-7).
115. Katarzyna Gromek-Broc (ed.), *Public Law in a Troubled Era: A Tribute to Professor Patrick Birkinshaw*, 2023 (ISBN 978-94-035-3576-0).